Energy Harvesting and Energy Storage Systems, Volume II

Energy Harvesting and Energy Storage Systems, Volume II

Editors

Shailendra Rajput
Moshe Averbukh
Noel Rodriguez

Basel • Beijing • Wuhan • Barcelona • Belgrade • Novi Sad • Cluj • Manchester

Editors

Shailendra Rajput
College of Engineering
Xi'an International University
Xi'an
China

Moshe Averbukh
Electrical and Electronics
Engineering
Ariel University
Ariel
Israel

Noel Rodriguez
Department of Electronics
and Computer Technology
University of Granada
Granada
Spain

Editorial Office
MDPI AG
Grosspeteranlage 5
4052 Basel, Switzerland

This is a reprint of articles from the Special Issue published online in the open access journal *Electronics* (ISSN 2079-9292) (available at: https://www.mdpi.com/journal/electronics/special_issues/Energy_Harvesting_Storage_II).

For citation purposes, cite each article independently as indicated on the article page online and as indicated below:

Lastname, A.A.; Lastname, B.B. Article Title. *Journal Name* **Year**, *Volume Number*, Page Range.

ISBN 978-3-7258-2092-4 (Hbk)
ISBN 978-3-7258-2091-7 (PDF)
doi.org/10.3390/books978-3-7258-2091-7

© 2024 by the authors. Articles in this book are Open Access and distributed under the Creative Commons Attribution (CC BY) license. The book as a whole is distributed by MDPI under the terms and conditions of the Creative Commons Attribution-NonCommercial-NoDerivs (CC BY-NC-ND) license.

Contents

About the Editors vii

Preface ix

Robert Urbina, Luis Baron, Juan-Pablo Carvajal, Manuel Pérez, Carlos-Ivan Paez-Rueda, Arturo Fajardo, et al.
A Bicycle-Embedded Electromagnetic Harvester for Providing Energy to Low-Power Electronic Devices
Reprinted from: *Electronics* **2023**, *12*, 2787, doi:10.3390/electronics12132787 1

José Ángel Fernández-Rubiera, Arsenio Barbón, Luis Bayón and Mokhtar Ghodbane
Sawtooth V-Trough Cavity for Low-Concentration Photovoltaic Systems Based onSmall-Scale Linear Fresnel Reflectors: Optimal Design, Verification, and Construction
Reprinted from: *Electronics* **2023**, *12*, 2770, doi:10.3390/electronics12132770 18

Giovanni Collodi, Monica Righini, Marco Passafiume and Alessandro Cidronali
Energy Efficient Enhancement in a 5.8 GHz Batteryless Node Suitable for Backscattering Communications
Reprinted from: *Electronics* **2023**, *12*, 2256, doi:10.3390/electronics12102256 48

Arsenio Barbón, Javier Aparicio-Bermejo, Luis Bayón and Ramy Georgious
Floating Photovoltaic Systems Coupled with Pumped Hydroplants under Day-AheadElectricity Market Conditions: Parametric Analysis
Reprinted from: *Electronics* **2023**, *12*, 2250, doi:10.3390/electronics12102250 63

Luis Fernando Rico Riveros, César Leonardo Trujillo Rodríguez, Nelson Leonardo Díaz Aldana and Catalina Rus Casas
Modelling of Electric Power Generation Plant Based on Gas Turbines with Agricultural Biomass Fuel
Reprinted from: *Electronics* **2023**, *12*, 1981, doi:10.3390/electronics12091981 88

Mohammad Habibullah, Nadarajah Mithulananthan, Rakibuzzaman Shah, Md Rabiul Islam and S. M. Muyeen
Investigation of Oscillation and Resonance in the Renewable Integrated DC-Microgrid
Reprinted from: *Electronics* **2023**, *12*, 1574, doi:10.3390/electronics12071574 116

Koichi Nono and Toru Tanzawa
One-Dimensional Maximum Power Point Tracking Design of Switched-Capacitor Charge Pumps for Thermoelectric Energy Harvesting
Reprinted from: *Electronics* **2023**, *12*, 1203, doi:10.3390/electronics12051203 140

Mohammad Ashfaq, Neetu Talreja, Neha Singh and Divya Chauhan
2D-Nanolayer (2D-NL)-Based Hybrid Materials: A Next-Generation Material for Dye-Sensitized Solar Cells
Reprinted from: *Electronics* **2023**, *12*, 570, doi:10.3390/electronics12030570 155

B. S. Nalina, M. Chilambarasan, S. Tamilselvi, Ahmad Aziz Al Alahmadi, Mamdooh Alwetaishi, M. A. Mujtaba and M. A. Kalam
Design and Implementation of Embedded Controller-Based Energy Storage and Management System for Remote Telecom
Reprinted from: *Electronics* **2023**, *12*, 341, doi:10.3390/electronics12020341 174

Kaiqi Zhong and Liqun Fu
Throughput Maximization for the Full-Duplex Two-Way Relay System with Energy Harvesting
Reprinted from: *Electronics* **2023**, *12*, 16, doi:10.3390/electronics12010016 192

Kazuma Koketsu and Toru Tanzawa
A Design of a Thermoelectric Energy Harvester for Minimizing Sensor Module Cost
Reprinted from: *Electronics* **2022**, *11*, 3441, doi:10.3390/electronics11213441 208

Orlando David Guerrero-Bermúdez, Sergio Martinez, Eder Molina and John E. Candelo-Becerra
Comparison of Phase-Locked Loops Used for Frequency Measurements in a Low-Inertia Power Grid with Wind Generation
Reprinted from: *Electronics* **2022**, *11*, 3226, doi:10.3390/electronics11193226 221

Tatsuya Nomura and Toru Tanzawa
More Enhanced Swing Colpitts Oscillators: A Circuit Analysis
Reprinted from: *Electronics* **2022**, *11*, 2808, doi:10.3390/electronics11182808 245

Yosuke Demura and Toru Tanzawa
Design of Switched-Capacitor DC-DC Voltage-Down Converters Driven by Highly Resistive Energy Transducer
Reprinted from: *Electronics* **2022**, *11*, 1874, doi:10.3390/electronics11121874 257

Kuei-Hsiang Chao and Jia-Yan Li
Global Maximum Power Point Tracking of Photovoltaic Module Arrays Based on Improved Artificial Bee Colony Algorithm
Reprinted from: *Electronics* **2022**, *11*, 1572, doi:10.3390/electronics11101572 267

Abha Singh, Abhishek Sharma, Shailendra Rajput, Amarnath Bose and Xinghao Hu
An Investigation on Hybrid Particle Swarm Optimization Algorithms for Parameter Optimization of PV Cells
Reprinted from: *Electronics* **2022**, *11*, 909, doi:10.3390/electronics11060909 289

About the Editors

Shailendra Rajput

Dr. Shailendra Rajput is an Associate Professor at Xi'an International University, Xi'an, China. He is also affiliated with the Department of Electrical and Electronic Engineering, Ariel University, Israel, as a Research Fellow. He has been a postdoctoral fellow at Ariel University, Israel (September 2017–April 2021) and Xi'an Jiaotong University, China (May 2015–July 2017). He received B.Sc. and M.Sc. degrees from the Dr. Hari Singh Gour University, Sagar, India, in 2006 and 2008, respectively. He received a Ph.D. degree from the Department of Physics, Birla Institute of Technology, Ranchi, India, in 2014. His main research studies are associated with energy harvesting, solar energy, energy storage, ferroelectricity, piezoelectricity, and the biomedical application of electromagnetic waves.

Moshe Averbukh

Dr. Moshe Averbukh is the Head of Laboratory Electrical Storage Systems at Ariel University. In 1972, he received his B.Sc. and M.Sc. degrees (Summa Cum Laude) from the University of Mining (Moscow) and a Ph.D. degree in 1984 from the Institute of Mining Academy of Science USSR (Moscow). His primary research is focused on energy harvesting, solar energy, energy storage, electrochemical devices, and induction motors.

Noel Rodriguez

Prof. Noel Rodriguez received the Electronics Engineer degree (B.Sc. and M.Eng.) from the University of Granada in 2004, obtaining the first national award of university education. In 2008, he received a double Ph.D. by the University of Granada and the National Polytechnic Institute of Grenoble (France) with the extraordinary award. At the present time, he holds a tenured professor position at the University of Granada, being also head of the Pervasive Electronics Advanced Research Laboratory (PEARL). His research covers the following topics: development of applications based on laser-induced graphene; the development of new transduction platforms for sensors; the investigation of new elemental devices for their application in the neuromorphic field; the development of new memory cells; and the low-power energy conversion.

Preface

Systems for sustainable development are built on three pillars: economic development, environmental stewardship, and social value. One of the core principles of finding harmony between these support points is to restrict the utilization of non-environmentally friendly power sources. The process of extracting energy from the surrounding environment and converting it into electrical power looks like a promising solution to this problem. To make it easier to switch from fossil-fuel energy sources to cleaner, renewable ones, new energy generation technologies like solar, wind, and thermal energy are rapidly being developed. Energy-harvesting systems have emerged as a significant area of research and continue to advance.

Despite the fact that the world has seen critical development in the creation of power from sustainable sources, these sources do not yield a standard stock that is sufficiently versatile for different prerequisites of utilization, so they cannot answer various demands. Thus, the development of this decentralized creation requires a large energy capacity, which is normally made of lead batteries; this is the expected answer to the issue of organizations' load strength. That said, lead batteries cannot store a lot of energy in a small volume or endure high cycling rates. New capacity innovations are therefore being created and trialed. Along these lines, load limits have emerged as an undeniably significant aspect of developing environmentally friendly power; higher limits allow energy to be conveyed to organizations during the busy times at which it is generally required.

This Special Issue reprint consists of sixteen chapters (published papers), covering various aspects of optimization algorithms, evaluations of wind energy turbines, electrostatic vibration energy transducers, battery management systems, thermoelectric generators, distribution networks, issues of renewable energy micro-grid interfacing, fuzzy-logic controller-based direct power controls, parameter estimations of fuel cells, and ultra-low-power supercapacitors.

This reprint is useful for masters and Ph.D. students that pursue studies in engineering sciences. Additionally, this reprint is also very informative for bachelor students who are looking to explore research on energy harvesting and energy storage systems.

We would like to take this opportunity to thank all authors for their outstanding contributions and the reviewers for their fruitful comments and feedback.

Shailendra Rajput, Moshe Averbukh, and Noel Rodriguez
Editors

Article

A Bicycle-Embedded Electromagnetic Harvester for Providing Energy to Low-Power Electronic Devices

Robert Urbina, Luis Baron, Juan-Pablo Carvajal, Manuel Pérez, Carlos-Ivan Paez-Rueda, Arturo Fajardo*, Germán Yamhure and Gabriel Perilla

Department of Electronic Engineering, Pontificia Universidad Javeriana, Bogota 110311, Colombia; gabriel.perilla@javeriana.edu.co (G.P.)
* Correspondence: fajardoa@javeriana.edu.co

Citation: Urbina, R.; Baron, L.; Carvajal, J.-P.; Pérez, M.; Paez-Rueda, C.-I.; Fajardo, A.; Yamhure, G.; Perilla, G. A Bicycle-Embedded Electromagnetic Harvester for Providing Energy to Low-Power Electronic Devices. *Electronics* **2023**, *12*, 2787. https://doi.org/10.3390/electronics12132787

Academic Editors: Noel Rodriguez, Moshe Averbukh and Shailendra Rajput

Received: 20 March 2023
Revised: 22 May 2023
Accepted: 23 May 2023
Published: 24 June 2023

Copyright: © 2023 by the authors. Licensee MDPI, Basel, Switzerland. This article is an open access article distributed under the terms and conditions of the Creative Commons Attribution (CC BY) license (https://creativecommons.org/licenses/by/4.0/).

Abstract: Bicycles are rapidly gaining popularity as a sustainable mode of transportation around the world. Furthermore, the smart bicycle paradigm enables increased use through the Internet of Things applications (e.g., GPS tracking systems). This new paradigm introduces energy autonomy as a new challenge. The energy harvesting technology can capture the energy present in the cycling environment (e.g., kinetic or solar) to give this autonomy. The kinetic energy source is more stable and dense in this environment. There are several wheel kinetic harvesters on the market, ranging from low-complexity dynamos used to power bicycle lights to smart harvester systems that harvest kinetic energy while braking and cycling and store it for when it is needed to power sensors and other electronics loads. Perhaps the hub and the "bottle" dynamos are the most commercially successful systems because of their cost-effective design. Furthermore, the bottle generator is very inexpensive, yet it suffers from significant energy losses and is unreliable in wet weather due to mechanical friction and wheel slippage in the wheel/generator contact. This paper proposes a cost-effective bicycle harvester based on a novel kinetic-electromagnetic transducer. The proposed harvester allows for the generation and storage of harnessed kinetic energy to power low-power electronics loads when the user requires it (e.g., cell phone charging, lighting). The proposed harvester is made up of a power processing unit, a battery, and an optimized transducer based on a Halbach magnet array. An extensive full-wave electromagnetic simulation was used to evaluate the proposed transducer. Circuit simulation was also used to validate the proposed power unit. The proposed harvester generates a simulated output power of 1.17 W with a power processing unit efficiency of 45.6% under a constant bicycle velocity of 30 km/h.

Keywords: electromagnetics; transducers; power conversion; circuit simulation; magnetic circuits; energy harvester

1. Introduction

Megacities around the world are currently grappling with complex issues such as mobility, pollution, and resource sustainability [1]. Urban mobility, in particular, is a major issue that affects almost all of the major cities [2]. Other undesirable effects of inefficient mobility in large cities are related to public health concerns [3]. One of the most promising trends in addressing this issue is the use of alternative transportation methods rather than traditional vehicles, which allows for lower pollution and better air quality in cities [1]. Recently, the use of bikes for short-distance routes has been boosted by city governments building bike paths, lowering taxes, and so on [4]. Despite the availability of appropriate infrastructure, many citizens do not use bicycles as a mode of transportation. In this scenario, the concept of "smart cycling" enables a shift in the perception of bicycles as an important part of the urban technological ecosystem by improving cyclists' experience and safety [5,6]. This paradigm is going to encounter numerous political, economic, and technological challenges. In [1], the authors identify three major research technological trends: smartphone-based cycling (i.e., route planning, delivery services, bike sharing), IoT-bikes (i.e., sustainability and environmental monitoring, promoting health through connected bikes, the Internet of Bikes), and connected e-bikes (i.e., the e-bike market). These applications are supported in a variety of electronic devices (i.e., cell phones, sensors, and lights) that use batteries as an energy source. The widespread use of batteries may harm the environment [7]. The key technology to provide green energy to the low-power electrical components embedded in public transportation is the energy harvesting (EH) technique [8], which can power electrical loads using the energy sources present in the operating environment [9–11]. A generic EH harvester is composed of an environmental energy source, a transducer, and an electrical power processing unit (PPU), as illustrated in Figure 1.

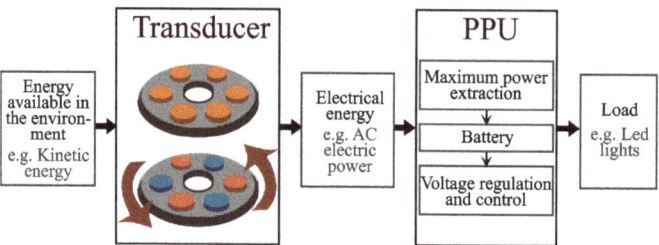

Figure 1. Diagram of an electromagnetic harvester.

The transducer converts environmental energy into electrical energy, which the PPU then conditions and manages for the load. In general, EH systems can be divided into two architectures: those without storage capacity and those with storage capacity [12,13]. In the first approach, the energy is collected by the harvester and immediately supplied to the electric load (e.g., bottle dynamo). In the second, the PPU stores (all or a portion of) the collected energy in order to provide uninterrupted power to its electric load in the future. As a result, under energy neutral operation, the harvester with storage capacity can continuously power the electric device using the environmental energy source. The design goals for achieving this energy autonomy are as follows [9,12,14]: (1) The transducer's energy conversion efficiency must be maximized. (2) The PPU must be able to extract the maximum amount of energy from the harvester. (3) The PPU stores, processes, and delivers electricity to the load without loss. The PPU ensures energy neutral operation, which means that the energy consumed by the payload must always be less than or equal to the ambient energy converted into electrical energy by the harvester.

Mechanical, wind, wave, geothermal, and solar energies are all present in some environments and can be used to generate clean electric energy sources using EH [14]. In the bicycle environment, however, mechanical energy is the source with the highest energy density. The mechanical EH can be separated into three categories: electromagnetic EH, piezoelectric EH, and friction EH [10]. In the piezoelectric EH, the harvester generates electric power from kinetic energy in the environment (e.g., the weaving movement in bicycle riding) using piezoelectric materials. Several authors have researched this EH method in the bicycle context [15–18]. In the friction EH, using a transducer (e.g., a triboelectric generator), the harvester generates electric power from friction between surfaces in the environment, such as the friction produced by the bicycle breaking. This EH approach has been researched recently in the bicycle scenario [19–21]. In the electromagnetic (EM) EH, a harvester produces electric energy from the kinetic energy present in the environment using an EM transducer. The EMEH in the land transportation environment was focused on the harvesting of the kinetic energy present in the movements of the wheels [22]. Furthermore, this kinetic energy source is the one with the highest energy density in the bicycle's environment [23,24]. In addition, to improve the efficiency of the EM harvester, friction, electromagnetic, and electrical losses must be reduced. The friction losses are caused by the contact between the harvester and the wheel, while the electromagnetic losses are caused by the required separation between the stationary and rotational parts of the magnetics device (e.g., the air gap between the stator and rotor of the dynamo). Finally, electrical losses are associated with energy losses caused by heat dissipation of the electric and electronic components involved in power processing. The resulting energy flow is shown in Figure 2a.

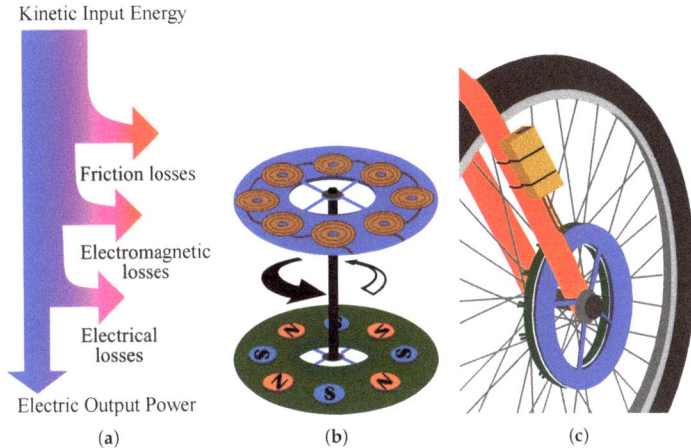

Figure 2. Electromagnetic-hub transduced based on a magnet and coil disks. (**a**) A harvester's generic energy flow based on an electromagnetic transducer. (**b**) Transducer topology detail. (**c**) Standard mounting on a bicycle wheel.

Since the "bottle" dynamo in the 1940s, the concept of EMEH has been popular [25]. During the 1950s, friction-less hub generators at the wheel/generator interface appeared as an improvement, and they were reliable in wet weather [26]. However, it was only in the twenty-first century that it became efficient enough to generate a few watts at a moderate bicycle speed [25,27]. Furthermore, in [26], the author suggests stacking multi-pole dynamos to increase efficiency even further. The concept of an EMEH based on a "bootle" dynamo as a transducer with energy storage capacity was proposed in a pioneering work published in 1991 [28]. Furthermore, this approach has been revisited in some recent works that used hub generators and/or bottle dynamos as transducers [29–31]. These works concentrated on the solution's functionality rather than the harvester optimization (i.e., the transducer or PPU's). The reported generating power was in the units of Watts range at moderate bicycle speeds (between 10 and 30 km per hour). Furthermore, the authors do not analyze the mechanical-electrical efficiency of the harvester, which is a significant drawback. This is because if the efficiency is low, people will experience noticeable resistance when riding bicycle.

In 2009, MIT's Senseable City Lab, in partnership with the city of Copenhagen, developed the Copenhagen Wheel (from harvester to ebike jump). It is based on a brushless motor, advanced sensors, control systems, and a lithium-ion battery, all enclosed within the rear wheel hub [32]. However, it has not achieved commercial success, possibly due to its high cost [32]. Recently, hybrid EH systems have been proposed as a cost-effective alternative to conventional dynamos. These systems generate electricity from multiple EH energy sources [10,23]. In [23], a hybridized nanogenerator based on EM, triboelectric, and thermoelectric generators was presented. Using the generators, the resulting hybrid energy harvester collects all of the energy sources from the relative rotational motions of two disks. The prototyped harvester is a 15 cm diameter disk that can achieve a constant voltage of 5 V and a maximum current peak of 160mA (i.e., 0.8 W) at 3000 rpm (i.e., approximately 80 km/h). In [10], the author proposes a rotational kinetic energy harvester that makes use of a magnet array to deform a piezoelectric sheet and harvest the wheel's kinetic energy. The resulting harvester is a 15 cm diameter disk with a power peak of 10.07 mW at 160 rpm (roughly 5 km/h). The EM harvesters involved in these two works are built on rotating magnet arrays and stationary coils that convert the rotary motion into an induced voltage, as shown in Figure 2. Because this magnetic topology generates flux lines in all directions, it is necessary for at least two windings to capture all of the flux created by the rotating magnet array in order to convert this energy. Consequently, a topology with only a one-sided coil array exhibits low efficiency, which could partially explain the low power contribution of the EM energy source in the proposed hybrid harvesters.

The Halbach array is a type of magnetic array that produces a strong and focused magnetic field on one side while reducing it on the other. Several researchers have investigated its impact on the design of EM energy harvesters in recent years [33–39]. The results of these studies show that energy harvesters using Halbach arrays outperform traditional EM systems in terms of power output and conversion efficiency.

This paper proposes a cost-effective EM harvester that utilizes a non-contact energy harvesting method. It is less affected by weather and ambient temperature and does not require modification of the original bicycle structure for installation. Furthermore, to increase efficiency, reduce mechanical resistance, and enhance the riding experience, various magnet arrays, including Halbach arrays, were systematically tested using full-wave and co-circuit simulations. The electromagnetic simulation was carried out using Ansys Maxwell® software Available online: https://www.ansys.com/products/electronics/ansys-maxwell (accessed on 21 May 2023), based on finite element analysis, and the circuit simulation was performed using Pspice ORCAD® software Available online: https://www.orcad.com/ (accessed on 21 May 2023) . The simulated results demonstrate that under constant speed conditions of 30 km/h (as many city cyclists travel at speeds of up to 50 km/h and rarely slower than 15 km/h [25]), the proposed harvester can generate a constant power of 1.17 W with an PPU efficiency of 45.6 percent. This power output can be utilized to power low-power devices such as WSN network nodes [12]. The rest of this article is organized as follows: Section 2 examines the overall characteristics of the proposed harvester. Section 3 describes the harvester design and validation process. Section 4 discusses the results, while Section 5 summarizes the main conclusions and future work.

2. Proposed Harvester

2.1. Transducer Topology

As shown in Figure 2, the transducer is made up of two disks that seek to be connected between the wheel and the forks of the bicycle frame. The first disk is made up of windings and must be attached to the bicycle's handlebar, while the second disk is made up of magnets and must be attached to the wheel in such a way that the magnet disk spins on the coil disk while the cyclist advances (see Figure 2). Certain harvester dimensions must match those of a standard bicycle with a front brake in order to be easily used and thus reduce the cost involved. Table 1 summarizes the transducer and harvester conditions.

Table 1. Electromagnetic transducer dimensions and external conditions imposed on the harvester design.

Transducer Dimension	Value	Harvester Consideration Parameters	Value
Maximum outer radius	16 cm	Magnet-winding distance separation	5 mm
Minimum inner radius	5 cm	Rim radius	35.35 cm
Maximum height	2 cm	Rotation speed	225 rpm

2.2. Magnets Configuration

The voltage induced on the winding is given in (1) using the Lenz equation. Increasing the magnetic flux (ϕ_B) or increasing the flux variation ($d\phi_B/dt$) increases the voltage induced on a winding (ξ). On one hand, the rotation speed of the magnets can be raised to increase flux variation. However, in this study, this term is linked to the user's pedaling capacity and is treated as a constant parameter. On the other hand, increasing the winding area (A), increasing the magnetic flux density (B), or adjusting the incidence angle (i.e., $\cos(\theta)$) of the fieldlines flowing through the winding region can all enhance the magnetic flux.

$$\zeta = -\frac{d\phi_B}{dt}, \phi_B = B \cdot A \cdot \cos(\theta) \tag{1}$$

The goal of this work is to increase the magnetic flux by using magnet configurations, as shown in Figure 3. The field lines are oriented in a single direction in a unidirectional arrangement (see Figure 3a), resulting in low flow variation. The field lines in a north–south–north (NSN) magnet setup (see Figure 3b) are orientated in the opposite direction, resulting in flux fluctuation but reduced magnetic flux density. In comparison to an NSN array, the Halbach magnet array (HAL) generates a flux fluctuation (see Figure 3c), which causes the magnetic field to be focused (e.g., downwards). As a result, HAL configurations allow an EM induced voltage on the windings to be increased.

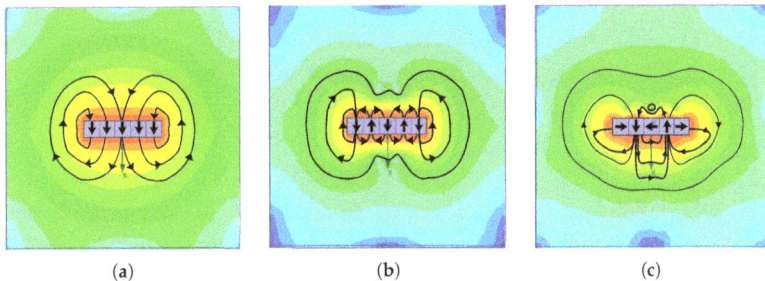

Figure 3. Magnetic field radiated by permanent magnets modified for illustration purposes from a FEM simulation in which the colors correspond to magnetic field magnitude (i.e., red to blue implies higher to lower magnetic field values). (**a**) Unidirectional Arrangement. (**b**) North–south–north arrangement. (**c**) Halbach arrangement.

2.3. Parametric Analysis of Transducer Variables

Figure 4 shows the various degrees of freedom probed in the transducer's parametric design. The coil was divided into an even number of circular planar windings that are connected in opposite phase; the diameter of the windings D_b is chosen so that it occupies the area of two magnets, in order to benefit from the maximum change in magnetic flux produced by the magnets. The following variables were considered in the design (assisted by computer) of the coil disk: the number of turns and size of each planar coil, the gauge of the wire, and the material from which it is made. Following parametric sweeps of the coil disk variables, some insights were: A greater number of turns for each coil increases the flux variation due to an increase in transversal area and, thus, the induced voltage; additionally, increasing the number of turns increases the length of the wire, which affects the resistance of the coil and its quality factor, lowering the current through it. When the wire's gauge is increased, the same effects occur. Finally, magnets with a larger surface area are more effective at increasing power generation than magnets with a higher height. Parameters such as the shape, quantity, orientation, material, and magnetization grade of the magnets were considered when designing the magnet disk.

The parametric simulation results of these variables show that the greater the number of magnets, the greater the amount of electrical energy collected.NdFeB magnets were used for the transducer because of their hardness, high magnetization, and low cost [40,41]. NSN and HAL array orientations were also used. Furthermore, it was found that the voltage induced on a coil decreases as one moves away from the magnets. Furthermore, the generated energy decayed when the angle of incidence of the magnetic field lines was tilted on each flat coil, for which the perpendicular orientation of the field to the windings was maintained in all simulated prototypes. It should be noted that the power delivered by the transducer is directly proportional to the efficiency of the PPU. An equivalent circuit model is extracted from the transducer, allowing the UPP design to be evaluated in order to extract the most power.

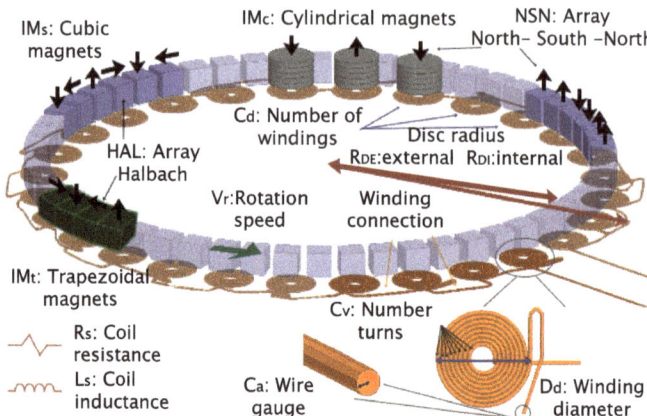

Figure 4. Design parameters of the electromagnetic transducer.

2.4. PPU Design

A full-wave diode bridge, a ripple smoothing filter, and two boost converters constitute the proposed PPU. The transducer output voltage is increased by Boost A to charge the battery (i.e., 3.7 V Li-ion), and Boost B is powered by the battery to drive the 5 V load. This topology is shown in Figure 5. The schematic of the simulated PPU is depicted in Figure6a. As shown in Figure 6b, a full-wave diode bridge and filter were employed to correct the transducer's AC signal and reduce ripple. Due to their low turn-on voltage ($V_{gamma} = 0.3$ V), MBRS410LT3 Schottky type diodes were utilized to rectify the signal [42]. Every inductor and capacitor was modeled using commercial values and their corresponding ESR. Figure 6b also shows the Boost A converter, which was designed to switch at a frequency of 33 kHz, with a SIA414DJ reference mosfet with low on-resistance ($R_{on} = 13$ mΩ). The converter's pulse with modulator circuit is depicted in Figure 6c, and it employs AD8041 reference operational amplifiers because of its rail-to-rail construction and 160 V/µs slew rate characteristics [43]. The converter Boost B design in Figure 6d, was taken from the application note of the TPS61288 fully-integrated synchronous boost converter [44], which already includes a 5 V DC voltage regulator with a typical commutation frequency of 600 kHz. A voltage source, a parasitic resistance (R_{ds}), which represents the cathode conduction losses, and a parallel resistance (R_{ad}), which represents the self-discharge losses made up the battery model that was proposed in the simulation, as illustrated in Figure 6a. Finally, the efficiency of the PPU was improved in this work by designing a Boost A converter with discrete components to research the performance of energy extraction with a control loop that allows the duty cycle of the converter to be varied while maintaining a constant impedance as a load to the transducer (i.e., maximum power point tracking approach).

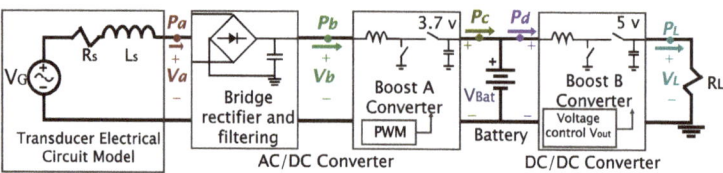

Figure 5. Schematic circuit of the proposed PPU.

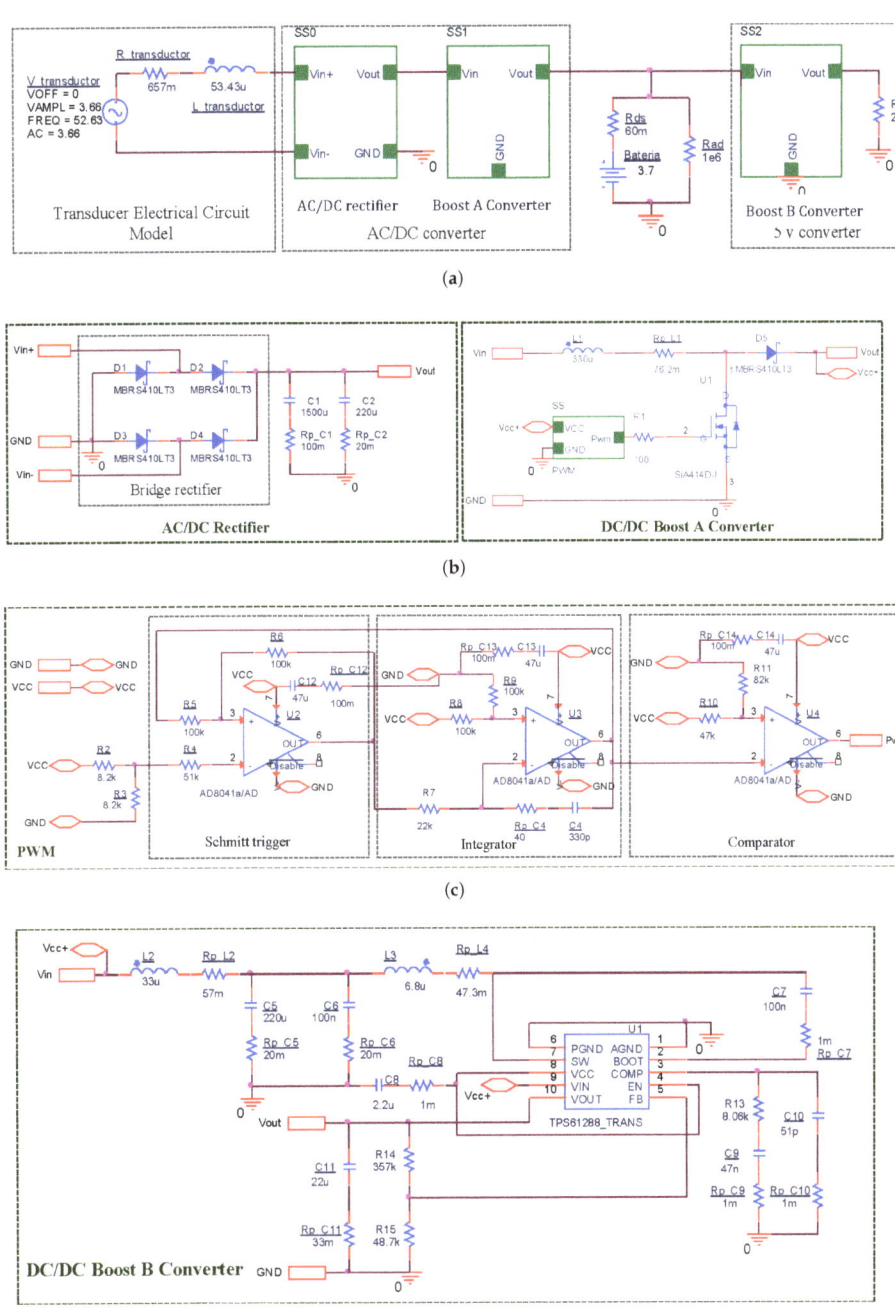

Figure 6. Schematic diagram of the simulated PPU in OrCAD. (**a**) General circuit connection with battery model. (**b**) AC/DC rectifier and Boost A. (**c**) Pulse with modulator used in Boost A. (**d**) Boost B.

3. Design and Validation Methodology

The conditions that the harvester must meet in order to be coupled to a bicycle wheel were first determined for design and validation. To optimize the harvester, full-wave electromagnetic simulation of the transducer based on finite element analysis using the finite element method was carried out using Ansys Maxwell® software. Finally, a lumped circuit was used to model the optimized transducer (see Figure 6a), which was then used to guide the simulation of the proposed PPU and later its validation using Pspice ORCAD® software).

3.1. Transducer Simulation Setup

As shown in Figure 7, the 3D topology was implemented in the Ansys Maxwell® interface, and the EM transducer was simulated using the Magnetic Transient Solver. This solver computes instantaneous magnetic fields at each time step. Each topology's transducer was simulated using 266 ms of simulation time, with time steps of 0.5 ms. As a source, we employ moving permanent magnets. We set the mesh to obtain enough accuracy because this solver does not use adaptive mesh refinement. The equations solved in this approach are [45]:

$$\nabla \times \frac{1}{\sigma} \nabla \times H = -\frac{\partial H}{\partial t}; \nabla \cdot H = 0 \qquad (2)$$

To set up the sources, the magnet's physical properties were set using the parameters listed in Table 2. Furthermore, three-dimensional unit vectors are used to represent the magnetic field's orientation. Knowing that the direction of each magnet on the x-y plane can be denoted by cylindrical parameterization, as expressed in (3).

$$\hat{x} = \pm Cos\left(\frac{2\pi N_i}{N}\right)$$
$$\hat{y} = \pm Sin\left(\frac{2\pi N_i}{N}\right) \qquad (3)$$

where N_i is the magnet's position number and N is the total number of magnets. In the magnetization direction, the sign of sinusoidal operations is chosen for convenience. Depending on the position of the magnet, the $\hat{z}$-direction was assigned as either positive or negative.

Table 2. NdFeB configuration in simulation.

Parameter	Value	Units
Relative Permeability	1.05	
Magnitude	836[a]	kA/m
	796[b]	kA/m
Bulk Conductivity	667	kΩ^{-1}/m
Mass Density	7500	kg/m^3
Core Loss Model	None	w/m^3
Composition	Solid	

[a] For N48 grade magnets. [b] For N52 grade magnets.

An additional geometric structure must be created that completely covers the volume of the magnets without intercepting the coil; this structure is referred to as the movement band with air properties. The magnets' rotation movement is configured on the motion band as shown in Table 3. A simulation region, which is a cube that covers the entire transducer model (see Figure 7), was also created with air properties. A simulation sweep was performed to determine the dimension of the cube, with the length side being varied from a maximum value of 2 m and reduced until convergence with a length of 50 cm.

The simulation model of the coil was built using boolean operations on multiple solids, yielding a 3D solid of a cylinder that starts right at the edge of the simulation region, then curves to generate the respective windings. To assign the two connection ports to the external circuit, the coil must end at the edge of the simulation region. Table 4 displays the common coil parameters set for all topologies. To determine the maximum available power of the transducer, we used co-simulation between the circuit simulator and the FEM simulator. To achieve maximum power, an external circuit was created in Ansys' circuit editor and then imported as a Netlist file into Ansys Maxwell.

Table 3. Motion band setup.

Parameter	Value
Movement	Rotational
Rotation axis	z
Mechanical transient	Deactivated
Initial position angle	0°
Rotation speed	225 rpm

Table 4. Configuration for the coil disk.

Parameter	Value
Material	Copper
Mesh grid	1000
Terminals	CoilTerminals

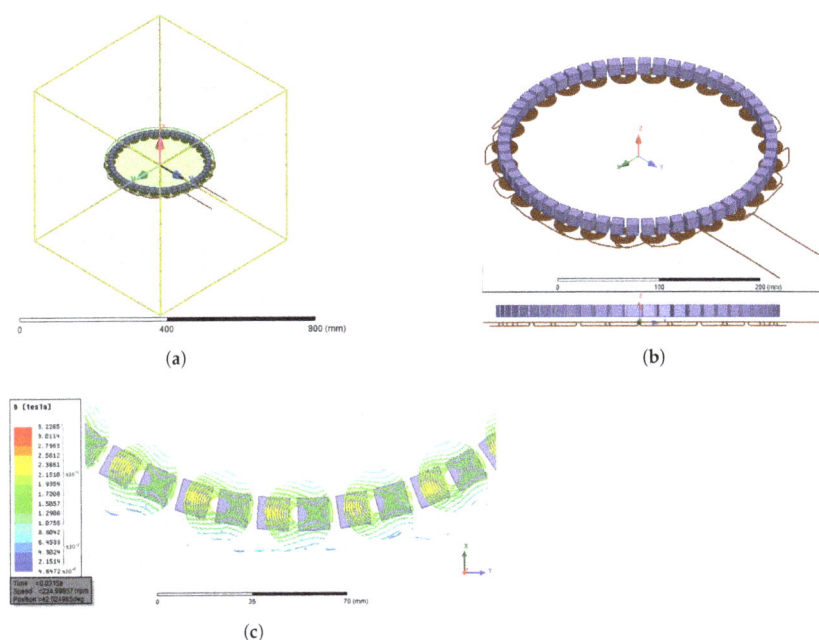

Figure 7. Simulation views. (**a**) Simulation region. (**b**) Top and side view of the transducer. (**c**) Magnetic fields on the coil.

3.2. Transducer Evaluation Methodology

The degrees of freedom to be analyzed in the transducer design were selected, and 9 topologies were defined and simulated. The simulation results and the following figure of merit (FMT) were used to select the best transducer for this application:

$$F_{nMT} = \frac{1}{3}\left(\frac{V_{nGp}}{I_{nGp}max\left(\frac{V_{Gp}}{I_{Gp}}\right)} + \left(1 - \frac{C_{nT}}{max(C_T)}\right) + \frac{P_{nL}}{max(P_L)} \right) \quad (4)$$

where F_{nMT} is the computed figure of merit for transducer n, V_{Gp} is the generated peak voltage, I_{Gp} is the peak current through the circuit at maximum power extraction, C_T is the magnets' total cost, and P_L is the average power provided by the transducer. $max(x)$ denotes the maximum value of a given parameter. This figure of merit permits analyzing the convenience in the design of the PPU through the V_{GP}/I_{GP} ratio, the implementation cost, and the transducer's generated power, all with the same percentage value in the final value.

The transducer was designed using magnetic transient simulations in the FEM software. Considering the degree of magnetization and orientation of neodymium magnets changes depending on the array layout, various set-ups were simulated, as illustrated in Figure 8.

3.2.1. Proposed Topologies

Nine alternative transducer topologies have been simulated. Table 5 presents the geometrical characteristics of each topology (see Figure 4). Figure 8 also displays a 3D representation of the generated topologies.

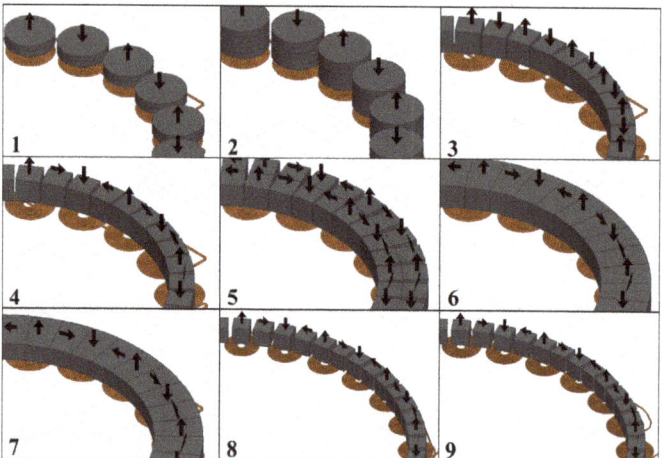

Figure 8. 3D modeling of the different topologies for the transducer. Table 5 summarizes the description of each array.

Table 5. Characteristics of electromagnetic transducers.

ID	R_{DI} [cm]	R_{DE} [cm]	C_d	D_d [cm]	C_a (1)	N_v	Magnets Shape	Grade	Array	Magnets Number
1	6.9	10.3	20	2.7	18	8	Cylindrical magnet[2]	N52	NSN	40
2	6.9	10.3	20	2.7	18	8	Cylindrical magnet	N52	NSN	100
3	6.9	10.3	20	2.7	18	8	Cubical magnet[3]	N48	NSN	40
4	6.9	10.3	20	2.7	18	8	Cubical magnet	N48	HAL	40
5	6.9	10.3	20	2.7	18	8	Cubical magnet	N52	HAL	80
6	6.9	10.3	20	2.7	18	8	Trapezoidal magnet[4]	N52	HAL	40
7	6.9	10.3	20	2.7	18	8	Trapezoidal magnet[5]	N52	HAL	40
8	11.9	15.3	28	2.5	18	8	Cubical magnet	N48	HAL	56
9	11.9	15.3	28	2.7	20	11	Cubical magnet	N48	HAL	56

[1] AWG standard. [2] Cylindrical magnet: Radius 12.5 mm × Heigth 3 mm. [3] Cubical magnet: 12 mm side. [4] Trapezoidal magnet 1: Angle 9° × Radius 25 mm × Heigth 12 mm. [5] Trapezoidal magnet 2: Angle 9° × Radius 25 mm × Heigth 9 mm.

3.2.2. Circuit Model of the Transducer

The initial transducer circuit model is shown in Figure 5, where V_G stands for the induced voltage on the coil, R_s is the coil resistance, L_s is the coil inductance and R_L is the transducer load resistance.

The values of R_s and L_s are initially computed in the static regime (i.e., magnets without movement). For that, the 3D coil model is simulated by connecting the external circuit with an external DC voltage test source. Then from the simulation results R_s y L_s are obtained through the Equation (5).

$$R_s = \frac{V_p}{I_{max}}, L_s = \frac{F_{max}}{I_{max}} \tag{5}$$

where V_p is the DC voltage test source, I_{max} is the flowing current value and F_{max} is the magnetic flux once the transient is finished.

For determining the values of R_s and L_s in the dynamic regime (i.e., magnets in movement), simulations are performed by first, connecting the external circuit to a load resistance of $R_{L1} = 100$ kΩ which allows to estimate voltage V_G in open circuit, which is taken as a null phase shift reference $|\vec{V}|\angle 0$. Then, the circuit is simulated with a resistance load $R_{L2} = R_s$, where R_s is the resistance found in the static regime. Finally, by taken the values of the signal frequency ω, the magnitude and phase shift angle of the current $|\vec{I}|\angle \phi$ obtained from the simulation results, the values of R_s y L_s in the dynamic regime are computed through the Equation (6).

$$R_s = \Re\left\{\frac{|\vec{V}|\angle 0}{|\vec{I}|\angle \phi} - R_{L2}\right\}$$
$$\omega L_s = \Im\left\{\frac{|\vec{V}|\angle 0}{|\vec{I}|\angle \phi} - R_{L2}\right\} \tag{6}$$

Because the values of R_s y L_s in the static and dynamic regimes are so close, only the ones in the dynamic regime are used in the transducer's electric circuit model. Power factor correction was not carried out in the PPU since it had no significant impact on the power extraction of the transducer and was therefore left out of the power management.

3.3. Harvester Simulation Setup in the Circuit Simulator

The circuit model of the chosen transducer was used to simulate the proposed Harvester (transducer and PPU) in Pspice ORCAD® software. We use transient simulation with all of the storage electric element's initial conditions set to zero. This method computes a circuit's response (solves the Kirchhoff laws) over a time interval specified by the user. Internal time steps affect the accuracy of the transient analysis. We use solver 1 with a maximum time step of 1 s and a final simulation time ranging from 40 to 200 ms [46].

4. Analysis Results

This section reports the results of the nine transducer topologies that were examined. Furthermore discussed are the performance indicators and design objectives for choosing the transducer. The outcomes are also shown when the PPU simulation is employed. The performance metrics and the design goals for the transducer selection are also presented. When the PPU simulation is used, the results are also displayed.

4.1. Simulated Results of the Transducer

Table 6 shows the voltage and current simulation results of the different transducer topologies with different circuit values of resistance R_S, inductance L_S, magnets cost and the obtained values of the figure of merit. For the power generated by the transducers, $R_L = R_s$ was chosen as the load resistance because it best approximates maximum power extraction while ignoring the phase shift caused by the inductance.

Table 6. Simulation results of the electromagnetic transducers.

ID	R_s [$m\Omega$]	L_s [μH]	C_T [€] [a]	V_{Gp} [V]	I_{Gp} [A]	f [Hz]	Power [W]	F_{MT}
1	196	20	74	1.13	2.88	37.54	1.04	0.478
2	196	20	170	1.62	4.16	37.54	2.19	0.511
3	196	20	108	1.12	2.85	38.46	0.74	0.416
4	196	20	108	1.26	3.23	38.46	1.04	0.450
5	196	20	176	1.92	4.89	38.46	2.39	0.520
6	196	20	340	2.12	5.42	38.46	2.99	0.434
7	196	20	340	1.72	4.39	37.54	2.65	0.397
8	281	26	134.4	2.35	4.17	52.63	2.54	0.630
9	657	53.4	134.4	3.66	2.81	52.63	2.58	0.830

[a] Taken from [41].

According to the figure of merit results, the transducer of case 9 was the one that best adapted to the previously described criteria, so it was chosen as the final transducer to be circuitly simulated alongside the PPU. Figure 7 shows the 3D model of the final version of the transducer, which met the dimensions specified in Table 1. The proposed design consists of 28 flat coils interconnected in a push-pull pattern with 20 gauge copper wire and N48 grade NdFeB magnets in Halbach configuration. Figure 9 depicts the final transducer signals obtained through simulation. The fast Fourier transform (FFT) of the transducer signal confirms that there is little harmonic interference and that the main frequency is 52.63 Hz. To evaluate the circuit model of the selected transducer, in Figure 10, we compare the current and voltage signals generated by the circuit simulation of the transducer model and the simulation by finite element analysis of the 3D model of the transducer. The resulting mean absolute percentage error between the two models was 3.02%.

4.2. Simulated Results Of the Harvester

The PPU was simulated in OrCAD using the final transducer model obtained from the electromagnetic simulations. The induced voltage signal in the transducer V_G was obtained from the Ansys model's simulation result of the open circuit.

The performance of the Boost A converter with a variable duty cycle was examined, and it was revealed that the control consumed more energy than was gained from the improvement. As a result, the usable cycle of the converter was set at a constant value of 63%. To determine the harvester's efficiency and maximum power generated, the load at the output of the Boost B (see Figure 6d) converter was varied until the lowest load caused zero average power in the voltage source of the battery model. According to the aforementioned, the harvester can power a 21.3 Ω load without using battery power. The voltage signals in different nodes (named in Figure 5) of the PPU are shown in Figure 11. When rectifying the voltage signal, the efficiency of the diode bridge was compromised due to the low magnitude of the induced voltage. Furthermore, because the voltage after the bridge rectifier had a ripple of nearly 1 V, the efficiency of Boost A is affected. The maximum voltage ripple was 100 mV for the battery model and 264 mV for the harvester load. Finally, Figure 12 depicts the efficiency of the power chain at various stages of the PPU, following the notation of Figure 5. The efficiency of the converter between stages was calculated using the steady-state current and voltage signals via Equation (7).

$$\eta_p = \frac{1/T \int_0^T V_{out}(t) \cdot I_{out}(t)\, dt}{1/T \int_0^T V_{in}(t) \cdot I_{in}(t)\, dt} \cdot 100\% \qquad (7)$$

The PPU was able to extract 81.1% of the maximum power that the transducer could produce, according to the efficiency results presented in Figure 12. The rectifier bridge was the stage that lost the most power, while the integrated Boost B converter was the most efficient. The PPU's overall efficiency was 45.6%. The harvester, which was attached to a bicycle wheel moving at 30 km/h, produced 1172 W for the load. In Figure 13, it can be seen that the output voltage is independently regulated if the current is produced by the transducer and/or provided by the battery.

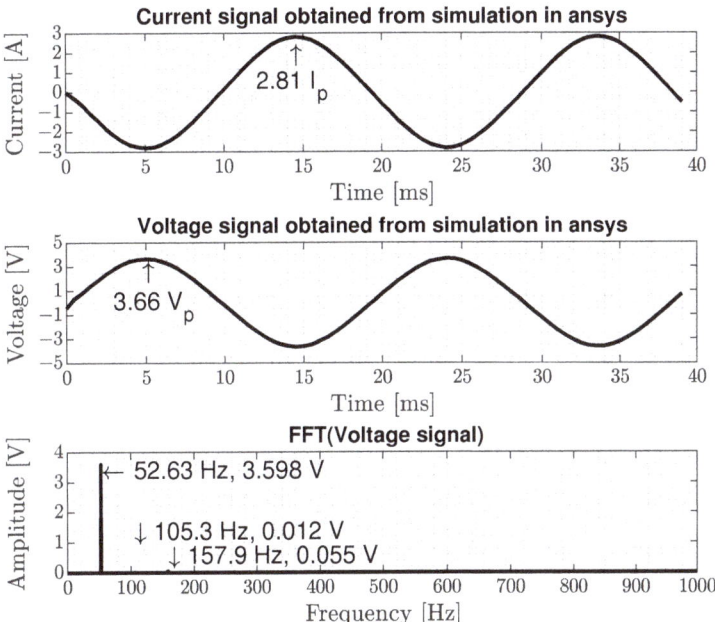

Figure 9. Simulation results for the selected transducer.

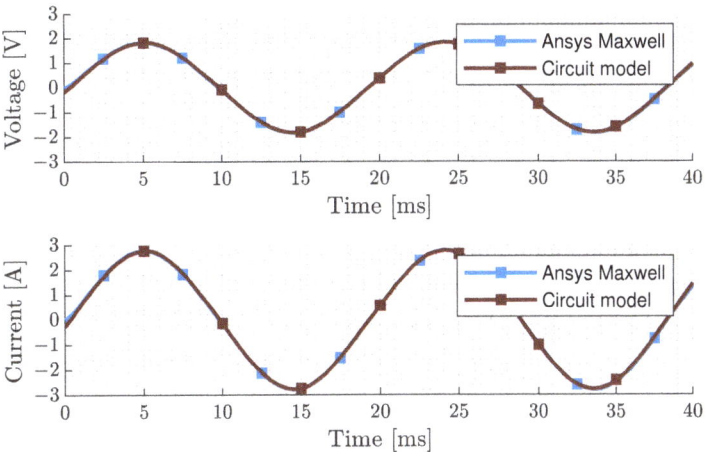

Figure 10. Current voltage signals of the selected transducer with a resistive load $R_L = 657$ mΩ.

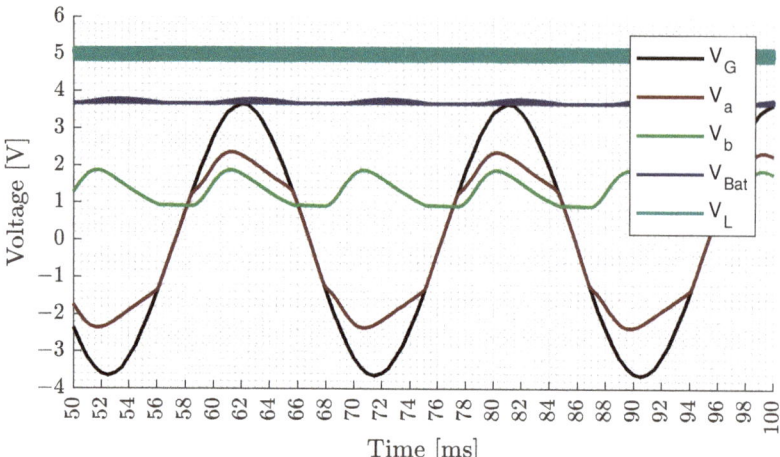

Figure 11. Voltage in the stages of the simulated PPU (see Figure 5).

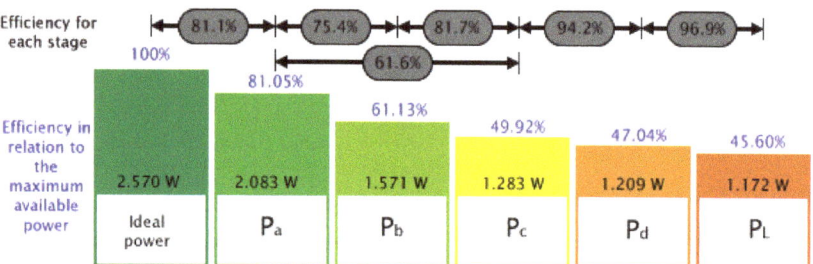

Figure 12. Power flow. P_a, P_b, P_c, P_d, P_L are electric powers that correspond to the notation introduced in Figure 5.

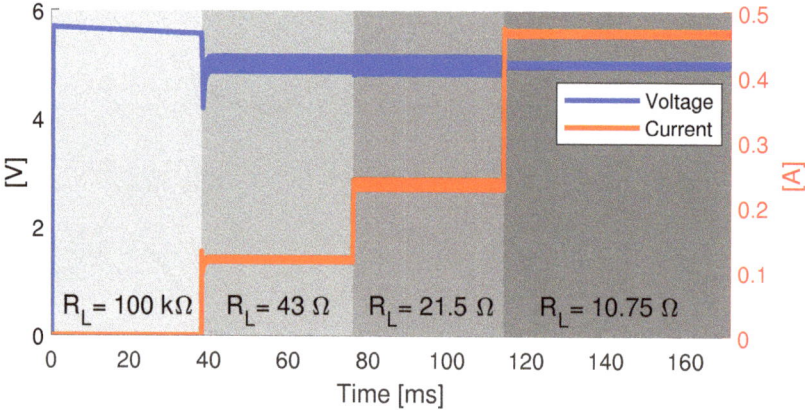

Figure 13. Harvester output voltage and current with different loads.

4.3. Comparison with the State-of-the-Art

The proposed EM harvester is compared to the state of the art in Table 7. As is summarized in the table, there exists a research gap for the development of low-cost EMEH, which could be based on low-cost transceivers (i.e., hub dynamos or two disk generators). Furthermore, the proposed harvester is a cost-effective solution for low-power devices. Another, identified research gap is the lack of standard test conditions, especially in methods related to solving the important question about the mechanical load imposed by the harvester to the bicycle user.

Table 7. Comparison between the proposed EM harvester and the-state-of-the-art.

Harvester	Device	Friction Losses	Electromag. Losses	Electrical Losses	EH Storage Capacity
This Work	Harvester	Low	Low	Medium	Y
Copenhagen Wheel [32]	Byke-Type	N/A***	Medium	Medium	Y
EM Harvester [23]	Transducer	Low	Medium	Medium	N
Hybrid Harvester All [23]	Transducer	Low	Medium	Medium	N
EM Harvester [10]	Transducer	Low	Medium	Medium	N
Hybrid Harvester All [10]	Transducer	Low	Medium	Medium	N
Bottle dynamo [25]	Transducer	High	Low	N/A	N
Hub generator [25]	Transducer	Low	Low	N/A	N

Harvester	Results	Disk Diameter [cm]	Output Generate Power [mW]	Manufacturing Cost [US]
This Work	Sim.*	16	1172 @ 225 rpm	83 [a]–299 [b]
Copenhagen Wheel [32]	Exp.**	N/A	N/A	2313 [c]
EM Harvester [23]	Exp.	15	188 @ 3000 rpm	N/A
Hybrid Harvester All [23]	Exp.	15	800 @ 3000 rpm	N/A
EM Harvester [10]	Exp.	15	5.52 @ 160 rpm	N/A
Hybrid Harvester All [10]	Exp.	15	10.07 @ 160 rpm	N/A
Bottle dynamo [25]	Exp.	700C wheel	1200 @ 30 km/h	47.31 [d]
Hub generator [25]	Exp.	700C wheel	4500–6500 @ 30 km/h	50–210 [c]

[a] Components price for one prototype when is manufactured more than a thousand units without a package. [b] Components price for one prototype without package when is manufactured only one. [c] Comercial price. [d] Comercial price with lamp. * Simulated (Sim.).** Experimental (Exp.). *** N/A (Not Available or Not Apply)

5. Conclusions

Mechanical energy harvesting has gained significant attention as a promising approach for powering various electronic devices in self-sustaining systems. In this paper, we explore the use of Halbach arrays on EMEH coupled to a standard bicycle wheel. To evaluate the impact of Halbach arrays on the proposed energy harvester, we conducted simulations using advanced computational models. The simulations were carried out by considering various parameters, including the geometry of the Halbach array, the rotational speed of the bicycle wheel, and the efficiency of electronic converters. The simulated results indicate a substantial enhancement in the performance of the energy harvester when equipped with Halbach arrays, which was a 41.38% of the increase in harvested energy over the same transducer equipped with a standard north-south magnet array. As a result, the proposed harvester generates a simulated output power of 1.17 W with a power processing unit efficiency of 45.6% under a constant bicycle velocity of 30km/h.

Future research will focus on transducer experimental validation and PPU optimization. We expect to be able to improve performance and lower costs by optimizing the PPU (e.g., commercial systems on chip ADP509 or BQ25504). However, the current prototype cost could be competitive with commercial hub dynamos in the near future when it moves from being a prototype to a commercial product.

Author Contributions: Conceptualization, R.U., L.B., J.-P.C., A.F. and G.P.; methodology, R.U., L.B., G.Y., A.F. and G.P.; software, R.U. and L.B.; validation, R.U., L.B., J.-P.C., G.Y. and A.F.; formal analysis, R.U., L.B., J.-P.C., G.Y. and A.F. ; resources, M.P., C.-I.P.-R., G.Y., A.F. and G.P.; writing—original draft preparation, all authors; writing—review and editing, all authors; visualization, R.U., M.P. and A.F.; supervision, M.P., C.-I.P.-R., G.Y., A.F. and G.P.; funding acquisition, M.P., C.-I.P.-R., A.F. and G.P. All authors have read and agreed to the published version of the manuscript.

Funding: The APC was funded by the Pontificia Universidad Javeriana.

Institutional Review Board Statement: Not applicable.

Informed Consent Statement: Not applicable.

Data Availability Statement: The data presented in this study are available on request from the corresponding author.

Acknowledgments: The APC was funded by the Pontificia Universidad Javeriana too. Additionally, the authors would like to thank the Electronics Department and Electronics Laboratory of the Pontificia Universidad Javeriana, for providing the resources required to conduct this study.

Conflicts of Interest: The authors declare no conflict of interest.

References

1. Oliveira, F.; Nery, D.; Costa, D.G.; Silva, I.; Lima, L. A survey of technologies and recent developments for sustainable smart cycling. *Sustainability* **2021**, *13*, 3422. [CrossRef]
2. Hyder, A.A.; Paichadze, N.; Toroyan, T.; Peden, M.M. Monitoring the decade of action for global road safety 2011–2020: An update. *Glob. Public Health* **2017**, *12*, 1492–1505. [CrossRef] [PubMed]
3. Koszowski, C.; Gerike, R.; Hubrich, S.; Götschi, T.; Pohle, M.; Wittwer, R. Active mobility: Bringing together transport planning, urban planning, and public health. In *Towards User-Centric Transport in Europe: Challenges, Solutions and Collaborations*; Springer: Berlin/Heidelberg, Germany, 2019; pp. 149–171.
4. Kim, J.; Choi, K.; Kim, S.; Fujii, S. How to promote sustainable public bike system from a psychological perspective? *Int. J. Sustain. Transp.* **2017**, *11*, 272–281. [CrossRef]
5. Schwanen, T. Beyond instrument: Smartphone app and sustainable mobility. *Eur. J. Transp. Infrastruct. Res.* **2015**, *15*. [CrossRef]
6. Yang, F.; Ding, F.; Qu, X.; Ran, B. Estimating urban shared-bike trips with location-based social networking data. *Sustainability* **2019**, *11*, 3220. [CrossRef]
7. Chang, Y.N.; Cheng, H.L.; Chan, S.Y.; Huang, L.H. Electromagnetic energy harvester and energy storage system for bike lighting applications. *Sens. Mater.* **2018**, *30*, 1341–1347. [CrossRef]
8. Abu-Rayash, A.; Dincer, I. Development and analysis of an integrated solar energy system for smart cities. *Sustain. Energy Technol. Assess.* **2021**, *46*, 101170. [CrossRef]
9. Jaimes, A.F.; deSousa, F.R. Modeling and design of high-efficiency power amplifiers fed by limited power sources. In Proceedings of the 2016 29th Symposium on Integrated Circuits and Systems Design (SBCCI), Belo Horizonte, Brazil, 29 August–3 September 2016; IEEE: Piscataway, NJ, USA, 2016; pp. 1–6.
10. Dai, X.; Wang, H.; Wu, H.; Pan, Y.; Luo, D.; Ahmed, A.; Zhang, Z. A hybrid energy harvesting system for self-powered applications in shared bicycles. *Sustain. Energy Technol. Assess.* **2022**, *51*, 101891. [CrossRef]
11. Enayati, J.; Asef, P. Review and analysis of magnetic energy harvesters: A case study for vehicular applications. *IEEE Access* **2022**, *10*, 79444–79457. [CrossRef]
12. FajardoJaimes, A. Contributions on the Energy Flow Modeling in a Self-Sustainable Wireless Energy Transfer System Based on Efficient Inductive Links. Ph.D. Thesis, Federal University of Santa Catarina, Florianopolis, Brazil, 2017.
13. Kansal, A.; Hsu, J.; Zahedi, S.; Srivastava, M.B. Power management in energy harvesting sensor networks. *Acm Trans. Embed. Comput. Syst. (Tecs)* **2007**, *6*, 32-es. [CrossRef]
14. Priya, S.; Inman, D.J. *Energy Harvesting Technologies*; Springer: Berlin/Heidelberg, Germany, 2009; Volume 21.
15. Doria, A.; Marconi, E.; Moro, F. Energy harvesting from bicycle vibrations. *IEEE Trans. Ind. Appl.* **2021**, *57*, 6417–6426. [CrossRef]
16. Chen, P.; Yang, Y. Design, Dynamics Modeling, and Experiments of a Vibration Energy Harvester on Bicycle. *IEEE/Asme Trans. Mechatron.* **2023**. [CrossRef]
17. Yang, Y.; Yeo, J.; Priya, S. Harvesting energy from the counterbalancing (weaving) movement in bicycle riding. *Sensors* **2012**, *12*, 10248–10258. [CrossRef] [PubMed]
18. Vasic, D.; Chen, Y.Y.; Costa, F. Self-powered piezoelectric energy harvester for bicycle. *J. Mech. Sci. Technol.* **2014**, *28*, 2501–2510. [CrossRef]
19. Zhou, H.; Liu, G.; Gao, Y.; Wang, Z.; Qin, Y.; Wang, Y.; Lin, Y.; Xie, Y.; Chen, Y.; Zhang, C. Dual mode rotary triboelectric nanogenerator for collecting kinetic energy from bicycle brake. *Adv. Energy Sustain. Res.* **2021**, *2*, 2000113. [CrossRef]
20. Nazar, A.M.; Narazaki, Y.; Rayegani, A.; Sardo, F.R. Recent progress of triboelectric nanogenerators as self-powered sensors in transportation engineering. *Measurement* **2022**, *23*, 112010. [CrossRef]
21. Leng, Q.; Guo, H.; He, X.; Liu, G.; Kang, Y.; Hu, C.; Xi, Y. Flexible interdigital-electrodes-based triboelectric generators for harvesting sliding and rotating mechanical energy. *J. Mater. Chem.* **2014**, *2*, 19427–19434. [CrossRef]
22. Pan, H.; Qi, L.; Zhang, Z.; Yan, J. Kinetic energy harvesting technologies for applications in land transportation: A comprehensive review. *Appl. Energy* **2021**, *286*, 116518. [CrossRef]
23. Wang, X.; Wang, Z.L.; Yang, Y. Hybridized nanogenerator for simultaneously scavenging mechanical and thermal energies by electromagnetic-triboelectric-thermoelectric effects. *Nano Energy* **2016**, *26*, 164–171. [CrossRef]

24. Zhang, C.; Tang, W.; Han, C.; Fan, F.; Wang, Z.L. Theoretical comparison, equivalent transformation, and conjunction operations of electromagnetic induction generator and triboelectric nanogenerator for harvesting mechanical energy. *Adv. Mater.* **2014**, *26*, 3580–3591. [CrossRef]
25. Heine, J.; Oehler, A. Testing the efficiency of generator hubs. *Vintage Bicycl. Q.* **2005**, *3*, 27–30.
26. Kumar, V.; Verma, D.P. Design and fabrication of planetary drive magnet pedal power hub-dynamo. *Adv. Mater. Sci. Eng. Int. J. (MSEJ)* **2015**, *2*, 105–107. [CrossRef]
27. Brito, N.; Ribeiro, L.; Esteves, J.S. Electric power generating bicycle. In Proceedings of the International Conference on Hands on Science, Braga, Portugal, 4–9 September 2006; pp. 1–6, ISBN 989-9509-50-7.
28. Lillington, A. The Rechargalite: A different concept in bicycle illumination. *Electron. Educ.* **1991**, *1991*, 17–18. [CrossRef]
29. Kothari, D.G.; Patel, J.C.; Panchal, B.R.; Goswami, H. Hybrid Bicycle. *IJEDR* **2014**, *2*, 585–588.
30. Suhalka, R.; Khandelwal, M.C.; Sharma, K.K.; Sanghi, A. Generation of electrical power using bicycle pedal. *Int. J. Recent Res. Rev.* **2014**, *7*, 63–67.
31. Jadhav, M.K.; Jadhav, S.A.; Kate, A.A.; Gholap, S.G. Design and analysis of hub dynamo for electric vehicle. In Proceedings of the 2018 International Conference On Advances in Communication and Computing Technology (ICACCT), Sangamner, India, 8–9 February 2018; IEEE: Piscataway, NJ, USA, 2018; pp. 262–264.
32. Superpedestrian Copenhagen Wheel Review. Available online: https://electricbikereview.com/superpedestrian/copenhagen-wheel/ (accessed on 21 May 2023).
33. Salauddin, M.; Rasel, M.; Kim, J.; Park, J.Y. Design and experiment of hybridized electromagnetic-triboelectric energy harvester using Halbach magnet array from handshaking vibration. *Energy Convers. Manag.* **2017**, *153*, 1–11. [CrossRef]
34. Ma, C.; Zhao, W.; Qu, L. Design optimization of a linear generator with dual Halbach array for human motion energy harvesting. In Proceedings of the 2015 IEEE International Electric Machines & Drives Conference (IEMDC), Coeur d'Alene, ID, USA, 10–13 May 2015; IEEE: Piscataway, NJ, USA, 2015; pp. 703–708.
35. Sajwani, H.; AlSuwaidi, N.; Elshikh, M.; AlJaberi, A.; Meribout, M. Hallbach array-based linear generator for human motion energy harvesting. In Proceedings of the 2017 International Conference on Electrical and Computing Technologies and Applications (ICECTA), Ras Al Khaimah, United Arab Emirates, 21–23 November 2017; IEEE: Piscataway, NJ, USA, 2017; pp. 1–6.
36. Li, Z.; Yan, Z.; Luo, J.; Yang, Z. Performance comparison of electromagnetic energy harvesters based on magnet arrays of alternating polarity and configuration. *Energy Convers. Manag.* **2019**, *179*, 132–140. [CrossRef]
37. Liu, X.; Qiu, J.; Chen, H.; Xu, X.; Wen, Y.; Li, P. Design and optimization of an electromagnetic vibration energy harvester using dual Halbach arrays. *IEEE Trans. Magn.* **2015**, *51*, 1–4. [CrossRef]
38. Qiu, J.; Liu, X.; Hu, Z.; Chang, Q.; Gao, Y.; Yang, J.; Wen, J.; Tang, X.; Hu, W. Multi-directional electromagnetic vibration energy harvester using circular Halbach array. *AIP Adv.* **2017**, *7*, 056672. [CrossRef]
39. Kim, J.W.; Salauddin, M.; Cho, H.; Rasel, M.S.; Park, J.Y. Electromagnetic energy harvester based on a finger trigger rotational gear module and an array of disc Halbach magnets. *Appl. Energy* **2019**, *250*, 776–785. [CrossRef]
40. Magnets/Neodymium Iron Boron Magnets Datasheet. Available online: https://www.eclipsemagnetics.com/site/assets/files/19485/ndfeb_neodymium_iron_boron-standard_ndfeb_range_datasheet_rev1.pdf (accessed on 21 May 2023).
41. Superimanes. Available online: https://www.superimanes.com/ (accessed on 21 May 2023).
42. Semiconductor Components Industries LLC. Datasheet MBRS410L Surface Mount Schottky Power Rectifier. Available online: https://www.onsemi.com/pdf/datasheet/mbrs410lt3-d.pdf (accessed on 21 May 2023).
43. Datasheet 160 MHz Rail-to-Rail Amplifier AD8041. Available online: https://www.analog.com/media/en/technical-documentation/data-sheets/AD8041.pdf (accessed on 21 May 2023).
44. Datasheet TPS61288. Available online: https://www.ti.com/product/TPS61288 (accessed on 21 May 2023).
45. PowerPoint Presentation. Available online: https://courses.ansys.com/wp-content/uploads/2021/07/MAXW_GS_2020R2_EN_LE03.pdf (accessed on 21 May 2023).
46. PSpice User Guide—PSpice User Guide. Available online: https://resources.pcb.cadence.com/i/1180526-pspice-user-guide/852? (accessed on 21 May 2023).

Disclaimer/Publisher's Note: The statements, opinions and data contained in all publications are solely those of the individual author(s) and contributor(s) and not of MDPI and/or the editor(s). MDPI and/or the editor(s) disclaim responsibility for any injury to people or property resulting from any ideas, methods, instructions or products referred to in the content.

Article

Sawtooth V-Trough Cavity for Low-Concentration Photovoltaic Systems Based on Small-Scale Linear Fresnel Reflectors: Optimal Design, Verification, and Construction

José Ángel Fernández-Rubiera [1], Arsenio Barbón [1], Luis Bayón [2,*] and Mokhtar Ghodbane [3]

[1] Department of Electrical Engineering, University of Oviedo, 33003 Oviedo, Spain; fernandezrjose@uniovi.es (J.Á.F.-R.); barbon@uniovi.es (A.B.)
[2] Department of Mathematics, University of Oviedo, 33003 Oviedo, Spain
[3] Department of Mechanical Engineering, Saad Dahlab University of Blida, Blida 09000, Algeria; mokhtar.ghod@gmail.com
* Correspondence: bayon@uniovi.es

Citation: Fernández-Rubiera. J.Á.; Barbón, A.; Bayón, L.; Ghodbane, M. Sawtooth V-Trough Cavity for Low-Concentration Photovoltaic Systems Based on Small-Scale Linear Fresnel Reflectors: Optimal Design, Verification, and Construction. *Electronics* **2023**, *12*, 2770. https://doi.org/10.3390/electronics12132770

Academic Editors: Shailendra Rajput, Moshe Averbukh and Noel Rodriguez

Received: 9 May 2023
Revised: 15 June 2023
Accepted: 16 June 2023
Published: 21 June 2023

Copyright: © 2023 by the authors. Licensee MDPI, Basel, Switzerland. This article is an open access article distributed under the terms and conditions of the Creative Commons Attribution (CC BY) license (https:// creativecommons.org/licenses/by/ 4.0/).

Abstract: Ensuring the uniformity of solar irradiance distribution on photovoltaic cells is a major challenge in low-concentrating photovoltaic systems based on a small-scale linear Fresnel reflector. A novel sawtooth V-cavity design method based on an optimization algorithm to achieve uniform irradiance distribution on photovoltaic cells is presented. The reliability of the design was verified using the Monte Carlo ray-tracing method and a laser experiment. A prototype was built using 3D printing technology with a biodegradable green polymer material known as polylactic acid. The new cavity was compared to the standard V-trough cavity, keeping the cavity aperture, reflective surface area, and photovoltaic cell width constant. In addition, the focal height, number of mirrors, mirror width, and mirror spacing were also kept constant; so, the cost of the two configurations was the same from the point of view of the primary reflector system. The new design ensured the uniform distribution of solar irradiation and significantly reduced the height of the cavity. The significant decrease in the height of the proposed cavity has the following advantages: (i) a decrease in the dimensions of the fixed structure of the small-scale linear Fresnel reflector, thus reducing its cost, (ii) a significant decrease in the surface area exposed to wind loads, thus reducing the cost of the fixed structure and secondary system structures, (iii) a reduction in the difficulty of the manufacture, maintenance, and transportation of the cavity's reflecting walls, and (iv) an increase in the cooling surface area, which increases the electrical efficiency of the photovoltaic cells.

Keywords: low-concentration photovoltaic systems; small-scale linear Fresnel reflectors; sawtooth V-trough cavity; uniform distribution

1. Introduction

Solar energy is one of the renewable energy sources that will replace fossil fuels and has received increasing attention due to its properties. The energy produced is clean, free, and unlimited. Moreover, solar photovoltaic (PV) technology is one of the systems that harnesses solar energy and has the potential to generate electricity worldwide.

Concentrated and non-concentrated solar power are two applications of solar PV energy that can produce electricity. A concentrated photovoltaic (CPV) system uses optical devices to concentrate the incident solar irradiance onto a smaller area, thereby increasing the solar energy flux reaching the PV cells. CPV technology can be classified into three categories: low-concentration photovoltaics ($LCPV$), medium-concentration photovoltaics ($MCPV$), and high-concentration photovoltaics ($HCPV$). A concentration from 2 suns to 10 suns is used in $LCPV$, from 10 suns to 100 suns in $MCPV$ and from 100 suns to 1000 suns in $HCPV$ [1].

Some of the characteristics of concentrated and non-concentrated systems are explained below:

(i) The use of non-concentrated solar energy has significantly increased its presence in the electricity sector, mainly due to the lower costs. Based on a recent report from the International Renewable Energy Agency ($IRENA$) [2], the levelized cost of energy ($LCOE$) from non-concentrated photovoltaic (PV) systems is expected to decrease by 0.05 (USD/kWh) by 2050. The lower cost of PV modules is one of the main reasons for this decrease [3]. In this regard, the International Renewable Energy Agency ($IRENA$) presented a report in 2017 predicting a 60% drop in the cost of PV modules over the following 10 years [4]. The spot price of a PV module is currently USD $0.266/Wp$ [5]. Concentrated PV systems replace the large surface area of photovoltaic cells used in non-concentrated photovoltaic systems with cheaper optical materials (e.g., lenses or mirrors), which thus reduces the cost of these systems.

(ii) As with any other technology, non-concentrated solar power ages and degrades over time. Manufacturers of silicon-based PV modules estimate their lifetime to be about 20–25 years. After that, the PV module components need to be dismantled and properly recycled. In 2016, the International Renewable Energy Agency ($IRENA$) and the International Energy Agency Photovoltaic Power Systems (IEA-$PVPS$) [6] presented the first global projections for future PV module waste volumes up to 2050. Annual PV module waste accounted for 250,000 tons in 2016. However, the contribution of global waste from PV modules is expected to considerably increase in the coming years. Waste generation from solar PV modules is estimated to reach 1.7 million tons by 2030 and will continue to increase to around 60 million tons by 2050 [6]. The significant decrease in the large surface area of PV cells used in non-concentrated systems and thus in the resulting waste is one of the main advantages of concentrated PV systems.

(iii) The conversion efficiency of PV cells used in non-concentrated systems is relatively low, typically around 10–20% for commercially available silicon cells [2]. This figure can be up to 39% for more sophisticated multijunction cells used in CPV systems [2]. Hasan et al. [7] demonstrated that a CPV with p-Si solar cells improved the Pmax by 62.5% more than a non-concentrated p-Si solar panel.

(iv) Concentrated systems only use the direct component of solar irradiance and therefore require an accurate solar tracking system [8]. The cost of these systems is not very high when using a small-scale linear Fresnel reflector [9].

(v) The temperature of a cell increases with the increase in solar irradiance concentration, thus leading to a loss in solar cell efficiency. For this reason, concentrated PV systems are equipped with a cooling system. In addition to reducing the cell temperature, cooling systems can also be used to heat water in household applications if a low-concentration photovoltaic system is used. This dual use increases the energy efficiency of the system. Kandilli [10] evaluated the overall efficiency of a CPV system at over 65.1%.

(vi) The available surface area on building roofs is key for the implementation of PV systems in buildings [11]. Low-concentration PV systems require 60% less surface area to produce the same thermal and electrical performance compared to separate PV and thermal modules [12].

(vii) The installation cost of an $LCPV$ system can be more than double (2.3 times) the cost of a non-concentrated PV system [13]. However, under suitable conditions of high direct irradiation (>2.5 (MWh/m^2 year)) and at utility scale, CPV technologies have proven to be competitive with non-concentrated photovoltaic systems [14].

Studies have shown that solar concentrators are suitable for $LCPV$ applications [1]. Therefore, $LCPV$ systems can be based on different solar concentrators: parabolic dishes [15], parabolic concentrators [16], Fresnel lenses [17], and small-scale linear Fresnel reflectors ($SSLFRs$) [18,19].

Low-concentration photovoltaic systems based on small-scale linear Fresnel reflectors are the subject of this study. This solar concentrator uses stretched rows of mirrors to focus direct solar irradiance incident on PV cells running longitudinally above the rows of mirrors over a common focal line across the mirrors [18]. The cavities commonly used in these systems are a standard V-trough cavity [20] and a standard compound parabolic cavity [21]. The standard compound parabolic cavity is difficult to manufacture [22] and therefore comes at a high cost. The standard V-trough cavity has the advantage of being easy to manufacture and low in cost [23]. Ustaoglu et al. [23] presented a comparative study between the standard V-trough cavity and the standard compound parabolic cavity with a constant concentration ratio and the PV cell width. The maximum acceptance angle in the case of the standard V-trough cavity was 32.25% higher. This result was beneficial when using this cavity in an $SSLFR$, as it allowed the use of wider mirrors. The standard V-trough cavity is analyzed to determine whether the cost of $LCPV$ systems may be lowered. A standard V-trough cavity consists of two flat reflectors inclined at an angle (τ) to the aperture of the cavity. The critical parameters governing the ray acceptance in this cavity are the flux concentration ratio (C_{opt}), the trough wall angle (τ), and the height of the cavity (H).

Several authors have studied these types of cavities. Otanicar et al. [24] presented the design of a standard V-trough cavity with a PV cell width of 20 mm, an aperture of 229.60 mm, and a cavity height of 87.93 mm. Al-Shohani et al. [25] presented different standard V-trough cavity designs with varying geometric parameters, geometric concentration ratios, and reflective materials. A standard V-cavity was used in the design of a daylighting system based on optical fiber bundles and a small-scale linear Fresnel reflector [26]. Concentrated photovoltaic systems based on a small-scale Fresnel reflector have also used the standard V-trough cavity [27]. All these studies used a standard V-trough cavity. This paper presents another view of the use of this cavity.

As has already been seen, one of the drawbacks hindering the expansion of $LCPV$ systems is their cost in comparison to non-concentrated PV systems. This means, a lower solar concentrator cost would facilitate the use of these systems. In the case of $SSLFRs$, the parameter that most influences the cost has been proven to be the number of mirrors [28]. Fewer mirrors brings a lower cost. Decreasing the number of mirrors requires increasing the width of the mirrors and thus the aperture of the cavity. This requirement implies that the standard V-trough cavity would need a greater height. Increasing the height of the cavity increases the overall cost of the $SSLFR$. Therefore, there is a need for a new cavity design.

The homogeneous distribution of solar irradiance on the PV cells is the most important design condition in an $LCPV$ system. If this condition is not met, the fill factor and overall electrical efficiency decrease [29], a situation that may even damage the cells [30]. The standard V-trough cavity can fulfill this design condition if the parameters are properly calculated, which is a significant advantage favoring its use [31]. Therefore, this condition was taken into account when designing the new cavity.

The objectives of this study are as follows:

(i) The optimal design of a sawtooth V-trough cavity, which ensures uniform illumination of the photovoltaic cells;
(ii) The verification of the designed sawtooth V-cavity to confirm that the derived equations are correct;
(iii) The manufacture of the designed sawtooth V-cavity, in order to identify any manufacturing difficulties;
(iv) Experimental tests to show that the manufactured sawtooth cavity meets the specifications.

The specific contributions of this study can be summarized in the following proposals:

(i) A methodology for designing a new sawtooth V-cavity;
(ii) A significant reduction in the cavity height of the proposed sawtooth V-trough cavity;
(iii) After (ii), a considerable reduction in the cost of manufacturing an $SSLFR$;

(iv) A comparison between the proposed sawtooth V-cavity and the standard V-cavity, considering that both cavities have the same cavity opening and the same *PV* cell width;
(v) The presentation of a novel graphical system to design the primary reflector system for the *SSLFR*.

The paper is organized as follows: The main parameters of an *SSLFR* used in a low-concentration *PV* system are reviewed in Section 2. Section 3 explains the design idea for the proposed sawtooth V-trough cavity, the optimization algorithm, the verification thereof using a Monte Carlo simulation, the manufacture of the cavity, and a laser beam experiment. Numerical simulations, verifications, and a comparative analysis are described in Section 4, and finally, Section 5 summarizes the main contributions and conclusions of the paper.

2. Overview of an SSLFR

The proposed *LCPV* system is based on an *SSLFR*. The characteristics of this *LCPV* system are described in [18]. The most important features thereof are:

(i) The primary reflector system (see Figure 1).

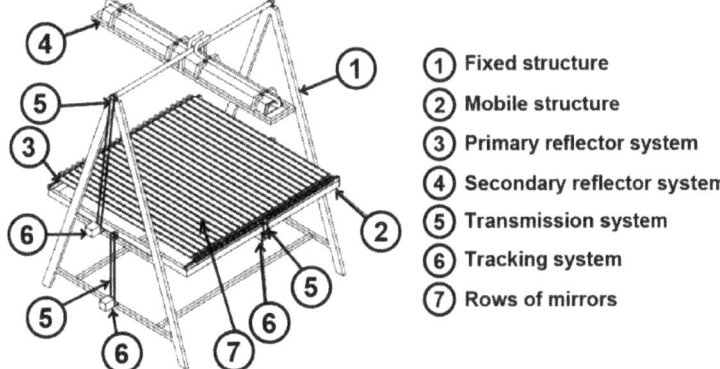

Figure 1. Diagram of an *SSLFR*.

This system is installed on a mobile structure and includes parallel mirror rows and a tracking system [32]. The primary system parameters of interest for this study are shown in Figure 2 and are defined as follows: W_{Mi} is the width of the *i*-th mirror, f is the height to the receiver, d_i is the separation between two consecutive mirrors, L_i is the position of each mirror with respect to the central mirror (in central mirror $i = 0$ and $L_0 = 0$), N is the number of mirrors on each side of the central mirror (the same number of mirrors on each side is assumed; therefore, the total number of mirrors of the *SSLFR* is: $2N + 1$), β_i is the angle that mirror *i* forms with the horizontal line, and θ_i is the angle between the vertical line at the focal point and the line connecting the center point of each mirror to the focal point. For each side of the *SSLFR*, θ_i can be determined as follows [33]:

$$\theta_i = \arctan \frac{L_i}{f}; \ 1 \leq i \leq N. \quad (1)$$

The maximum θ_i on each side (that is, $\theta_{N_r} = \theta_{N_l}$) is the *acceptance angle* of the V-trough cavity:

$$\theta_c = \theta_N. \quad (2)$$

The rows of mirrors synchronously follow the sun's daily movement. The movement of the mirrors is defined by their axis of rotation, the north–south axis, and by the transverse angle θ_t [33]:

$$\theta_t = \arctan\left(\frac{\sin \gamma_S}{\tan \alpha_S}\right), \tag{3}$$

where α_S is the solar altitude (°), and γ_S is the solar azimuth (°), both of which depend on the declination δ, latitude λ, and hour angle ω [34].

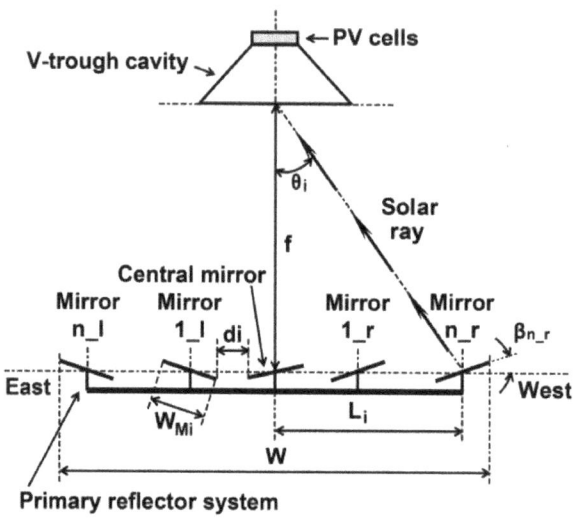

Figure 2. The primary system parameters of interest for this study.

The sun ray is considered to be incident on the midpoint of the mirror i and reflected towards the focal point of the cavity; therefore, the following is fulfilled [33]:

$$\beta_i = \frac{-\theta_t \pm \theta_i}{2}; \ 1 \leq i \leq N, \tag{4}$$

where $\pm$ means: $-$ for mirrors on the left side and $+$ otherwise. By convention, $\beta_i > 0$ when measured counterclockwise above the horizontal line.

Another parameter needed for the uniform distribution of flux on the PV cells is what is known as W_{fi}, which is defined as the width of the PV cells illuminated by the i-th mirror [33]:

$$W_{fi} = W_{Mi} \cdot [\cos \beta_i \pm \sin \beta_i \tan \theta_i]; \ 1 \leq i \leq N. \tag{5}$$

Taking into account that θ_i and β_i depend on W_{Mi}, d_i, N, and f (where the value of f is usually 1.5 m [18,35,36]), these parameters must be optimized (W_{Mi}, d_i, and N) to achieve a uniform flux distribution in the PV cells [18]. The width of the $SSLFR$ (W) can be calculated as [33]:

$$W = 2 \cdot L_n + W_{Mi}. \tag{6}$$

(ii) The secondary system (see Figure 3).

This system is installed on a fixed structure and includes the V-trough cavity, the PV system, the active cooling system, the secondary structure, the isolation material, the protective casing, and the shaft. The PV cells in the PV system are interconnected and encapsulated. Since a large part of the solar irradiance captured by the PV cells is transformed into heat, a cooling system is available to increase the system efficiency. The standard V-trough cavity is symmetrical with respect to the central mirror in the primary system. The standard V-trough cavity parameters of interest for this study are shown in Figure 4 and are defined as follows: W_{PV} is the width of the PV cells, b is the absorber width of the V-trough cavity ($b = W_{PV}$), B is the aperture of the V-trough cavity, H is the height of the V-trough cavity, and τ is the trough wall angle.

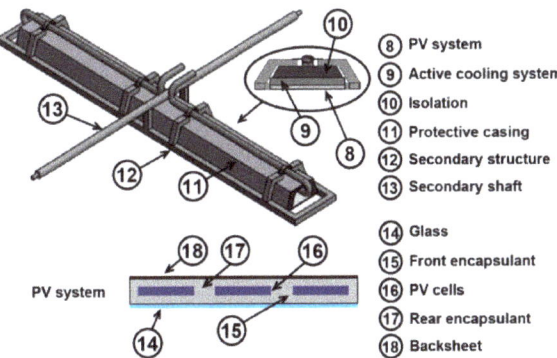

Figure 3. The secondary system.

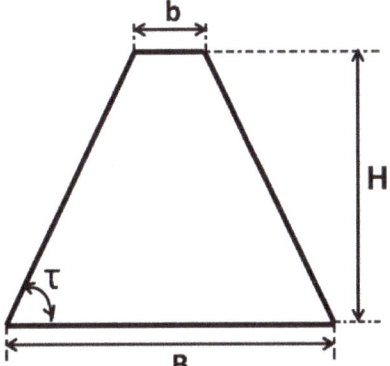

Figure 4. Standard V-trough cavity parameters.

For this paper, the standard V-trough cavity has been replaced with a new sawtooth V-trough cavity that was optimized by utilizing the Mathematica™ Computer Algebra System.

3. Methodology

If the design is not correct, a fraction of the incident solar irradiance will reach the base of the V-trough cavity either directly or through further reflections, and the remaining fraction will eventually escape to the outside of the V-trough cavity after further reflections, when a beam of solar irradiance is incident on the V-trough aperture at the angle provided by one of the mirrors in the primary system. Preventing this fraction of the incident solar irradiance from escaping to the outside of the V-trough cavity is the aim of this research. Another, equally important objective of this design is to achieve the uniform illumination of the photovoltaic cells in order to avoid the detrimental effects of nonuniform illumination.

3.1. The Main Elements of a Concentrator

Shoeibi et al. [37] states that the most common definition of the concentration ratio, area, or geometric concentration ratio is:

$$C_a = \frac{\text{aperture area}}{\text{absorber area}} = \frac{A_a}{A_{abs}}. \tag{7}$$

This ratio has an upper limit. For a two-dimensional (linear) concentrator, such as our V-trough design, and for a given acceptance half angle θ_c, this limit is:

$$C_{ideal}^{2D} = \sin^{-1}\theta_c. \tag{8}$$

Compound parabolic concentrators (*CPC*) are known to actually reach this limit [38]. There are other indices in the literature that measure the goodness of a concentrator. The following notation (also used, for instance, in [25,39,40]) is used for this paper:

$$C_{opt} = \frac{\text{flux at the receiver}}{\text{flux at the absorber}} = C_a \cdot \eta_{ray}, \tag{9}$$

where C_{opt} is the optical concentration ratio, C_a is the area concentration ratio, and η_{ray} is the ray acceptance rate, which provides the fraction of incident light rays reaching the absorber.

Tina and Scandura [39] obtained the following for an ideal concentrator, perfectly aligned with the sun, and with a single reflection:

$$C_a = 1 + 2\cos(2\Phi), \tag{10}$$

where Φ is the trough angle or half angle of the V-shaped cone. Shoeibi et al. [37] studied the use of two angles: the same Φ, and θ_c, the acceptance angle, and then calculated the geometric concentration ratio (see also [41]):

$$C_a = \frac{1}{\sin(\theta_c + \Phi)}. \tag{11}$$

Oprea et al. [42] defined the ray acceptance rate, η_{ray}, which gives the fraction of incident rays reaching the absorber surface. A similar study can be found in Tang [43], where the author considered Φ and C_a as independent parameters determining the geometry of a V-trough cavity and estimated the collectible radiation on its base.

Oprea et al. [42] indicated that the optical efficiency could be estimated by a function of two parameters: the ray acceptance rate and the average number of reflections, n. The role this average n plays when calculating the irradiance losses is briefly recalled: in general [37], the fraction of the radiation incident on the aperture that is transmitted to the absorber needs to be multiplied by ρ_m^n, where ρ_m is the reflectivity of the mirror. Pardellas et al. [27] indicated that slight errors in the calculation of n are almost irrelevant to the final value of ρ_m^n (this is also verified herein).

Finally, one more parameter is needed to conduct a cost analysis: the reflector-to-aperture area ratio (where the height clearly plays a role):

$$R_a = \frac{\text{reflector area}}{\text{aperture area}} = \frac{A_r}{A_a}. \tag{12}$$

The high performance of ideal *CPC* concentrators, for instance, is widely known to have a negative tradeoff: their R_a is rather large.

3.2. The Optimal Design of a Sawtooth V-Trough Cavity

The optimal design of the sawtooth V-trough cavity was developed based on analytical formulas. The sawtooth V-trough cavity presented here was formed by several V-trough cavities. The V-trough cavity parameters used in the design were: the width of the *PV* cells (b), the aperture of the V-trough cavity (B), the height of the cavity (H), the trough wall angle (τ), and the number of V-trough cavities in the sawtooth (m). The cross section of the sawtooth V-trough cavity presented in this paper is shown in Figure 5.

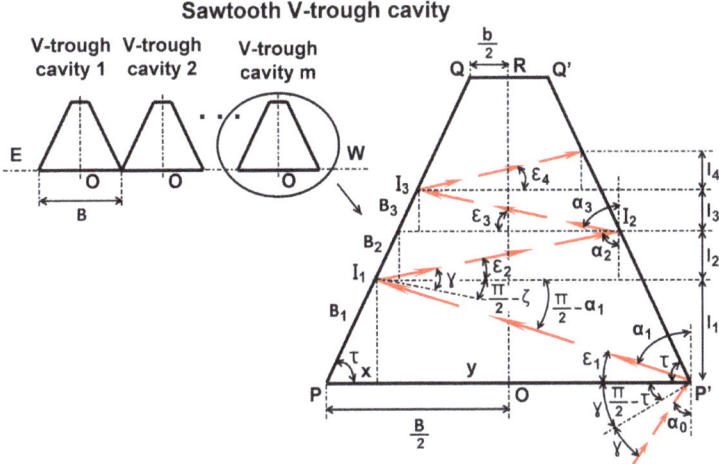

Figure 5. Schematic diagram of a sawtooth V-trough cavity.

A classical V-shaped cavity (V-trough cavity m), as shown in Figure 5, was considered, and the assumptions made in this study were as follows:

(i) The sawtooth V-trough cavity is symmetrical to the central mirror in the primary system.
(ii) The sidewalls (PQ and $P'Q'$) are assumed to be perfectly specular.
(iii) The width of the PV cells, b, is standardized by the PV cell manufacturers.
(iv) The V-trough cavity is east–west aligned.
(v) The trough wall angle (τ) is the complement of Φ [39].
(vi) The trough wall angle (τ) is fixed.
(vii) The OR axis is the reference axis for the angles of the sun's incident rays. θ_i is considered positive for the solar rays coming from the mirrors on the left side and negative for those coming from the mirrors on the right.
(viii) The angle between the solar ray reaching the cavity and OR is denoted as α_0 (i.e., $\alpha_0 = \theta_i$). In addition, each successive reflection of the sun's ray inside the cavity is denoted as α_j, for $j = 1, 2, \ldots$

The sidewalls, PQ and $P'Q'$, concentrate the beam of irradiance incident on the opening of the V-trough cavity (PP') onto the base of the V-trough cavity (QQ'). Four parameters were considered: the inlet beam solar irradiance, the trough wall angle (τ), the aperture of the V-trough cavity (B), and the height of the cavity (H). The width of the PV cells, QQ', is not a free parameter, as it is set by the PV cell manufacturers. As one of the objectives is for 100% of the solar irradiation beam incident on the V-trough aperture to reach the PV cells, the ray acceptance rate η_{ray} must be 1; thus,

$$C_{opt} = C_a; \; |\theta_i| \leq |\theta_c|, \tag{13}$$

where θ_i (°) is the angle of incidence of each ray coming from the different primary mirrors.

Since $\eta_{ray} = 1$, B is maximized to find the maximum C_a under the constraint that all solar rays reaching the cavity opening, PP', reach the photovoltaic cells (the width of which is b and is standardized by the PV cell manufacturers) after a given number of reflections:

$$\max C_a = \max B; \; |\theta_i| \leq |\theta_c|. \tag{14}$$

The worst case scenario occurs when the solar ray coming from the mirrors on the left (right) side is reflected by P' (P) with $\theta_i = \theta_c$. Figure 5 shows this scenario. Using the notation from Figure 5:

$$\theta_i = \alpha_0. \tag{15}$$

The following equality is obtained based on the Law of Reflection:

$$\alpha_n = (\pi - 2\tau) + \alpha_{n-1}, \tag{16}$$

where n is the number of reflections inside the cavity needed to reach the PV cells. Expressing Equation (16) as a function of α_0:

$$\alpha_n = n(\pi - 2\tau) + \alpha_0. \tag{17}$$

The angle between PP' and the i-th reflection, ε_j, can be calculated as:

$$\varepsilon_n = (2\tau - \pi/2) - \alpha_{n-1}. \tag{18}$$

In addition:

$$\varepsilon_n = \frac{\pi}{2} - \alpha_n \Rightarrow \tan\alpha_n = \cot\varepsilon_n. \tag{19}$$

The vertical lengths l_i traveled by the reflected solar ray after each reflection can be calculated by the following equations:

$$l_n = \frac{B - 2\sum_{i=1}^{n-1}(l_i)\cot\tau}{\cot\tau + \tan\alpha_n}. \tag{20}$$

The algorithm can be described, and an optimal design can be implemented with the equations developed above (14).

For the V-trough cavity design, the worst scenario occurs when the vertical component of each wall reflection (if there are any) is larger and touches the width of the PV cells (b) at either Q or Q' [44]. Taking this fact into account, the iterative algorithm can be started by indicating a sequence of different scenarios C_n, for an increasing number of reflections n. The worst case condition is taken into account in each of these scenarios, $\theta_i = \theta_c$. For each scenario C_n, the cavity height H_n, which is a function of B, can be calculated using (20):

$$H_n(B) = \sum_{i=1}^{n} l_i. \tag{21}$$

The value of $H_n(B)$ can be substituted into the equation connecting the cavity parameters b, B, and H to τ:

$$B = b + 2H_n(B)\cot\tau, \tag{22}$$

and solving the above equation for B, after a few simple calculations:

$$(C_n)\ B_n(\tau) = (-1)^n b\cos(\alpha_0 - (2n+1)\tau)\sec(\alpha_0 - \tau). \tag{23}$$

One can see that the functions $B_n(\tau)$ are expressed in terms of b and α_0. The algorithm concludes with the determination of the maximum value of $B_n(\tau)$ used to obtain the optimal angles τ_n^* that maximize B and, hence, C_a.

The algorithm makes it possible to choose the optimal design depending on the number of reflections n. Therefore, from a qualitative perspective, the use of a high number of reflections n, produces an increase in B_n, which means C_a also increases. In fact, C_a asymptotically moves toward the ideal value (8). In each scenario C_n, the number of reflections is n.

Lastly, to calculate the approximate value of n, one can use the property demonstrated by Shoeibi et al. [37]. This property indicates that the average number of reflections in a V-trough cavity is essentially the same as for compound parabolic concentrators ($CPCs$). Therefore, a truncated CPC with the same height as the V-trough cavity can be considered, starting from an integer CPC designed for the specific value of θ_c. Note that the influence of n on the factor ρ_m^n is quite small because ρ_m is always very close to 1.

3.3. Uniform Distribution of Flux on PV Cells

A detailed study of the causes of the nonuniform illumination of PV cells was presented in [18]. The wrong choice of some of the parameters, d_i, N, and W_{Mi}, produces this undesirable effect:

(i) Parameter d_i (small d_i). Shading (one mirror creates a shadow on an adjacent mirror) and blocking (one mirror blocks the reflected rays of an adjacent mirror) obviously depend on the distance between consecutive mirrors (d_i). This distance is not fixed and depends on the width of each mirror.

(ii) Parameter d_i (large d_i). Increasing the value of the parameter d_i prevents the occurrence of the shading and blocking phenomena, but an excessive value of d_i also leads to the nonuniform illumination of the PV cells [18].

(iii) Parameter N. As each mirror has a different W_{Mi}, using a large number of mirrors in the $SSLFR$ design increases the probability of a nonuniform flux distribution in the PV cells [18].

(iv) Parameter W_{Mi}. The ratio between the width of each mirror and the width of the PV cells also influences the uniform illumination of the PV cells [18].

As this research focuses on the design for a sawtooth V-trough cavity of an $SSLFR$, the algorithm proposed in [18] was used to design the primary reflector system. The optimum value of B was obtained once W_{PV} ($b = W_{PV}$) was set by the manufacturer of the PV cells; then, once the number of sawtooth V-trough cavities (m) was set, the design of the primary reflector system could begin.

It is not possible for PV cells to be uniformly illuminated throughout the day. However, it is possible to determine a period of time, called the operation interval (θ_{t_0}), during which the PV cells are uniformly illuminated, without any shading or blocking:

$$\theta_t \in [-\theta_{t_0}, \theta_{t_0}]. \tag{24}$$

The following is fulfilled in the operation interval:

$$W_{fi} = W_{PV}; \ 1 \leq i \leq N, \tag{25}$$

where the width of the PV cells, W_{PV}, is a datum set by the manufacturer.

The operation interval can be determined by an iterative optimization algorithm [18]. A simplified method (graphical method) is proposed in this study based on the research in [18].

As the surface available for the installation of $SSLFRs$ is a key parameter [45], the width of the $SSLFR$ was a good starting point for the design thereof. The relationship between the width of the $SSLFR$ and the operation interval was obtained by applying the iterative optimization algorithm [18] for given values of b and m. Figure 6 shows the curve relating these parameters for: $b = 30$ mm and $\theta_c = 34$ (°) (a plausible value for the typical dimensions of an $SSLFR$ [18]) (therefore, $B = 49.65$ mm), $m = 4$, and various numbers of mirrors (5, 7, 9, and 11 mirrors). This number of mirrors was chosen so that the size of the $SSLFR$ would not be too large and the cost of the $SSLFR$ would not be too high (increasing the number of mirrors increases the cost of the $SSLFR$ [28]). Therefore, the operation interval was obtained once the width of the $SSLFR$ was fixed.

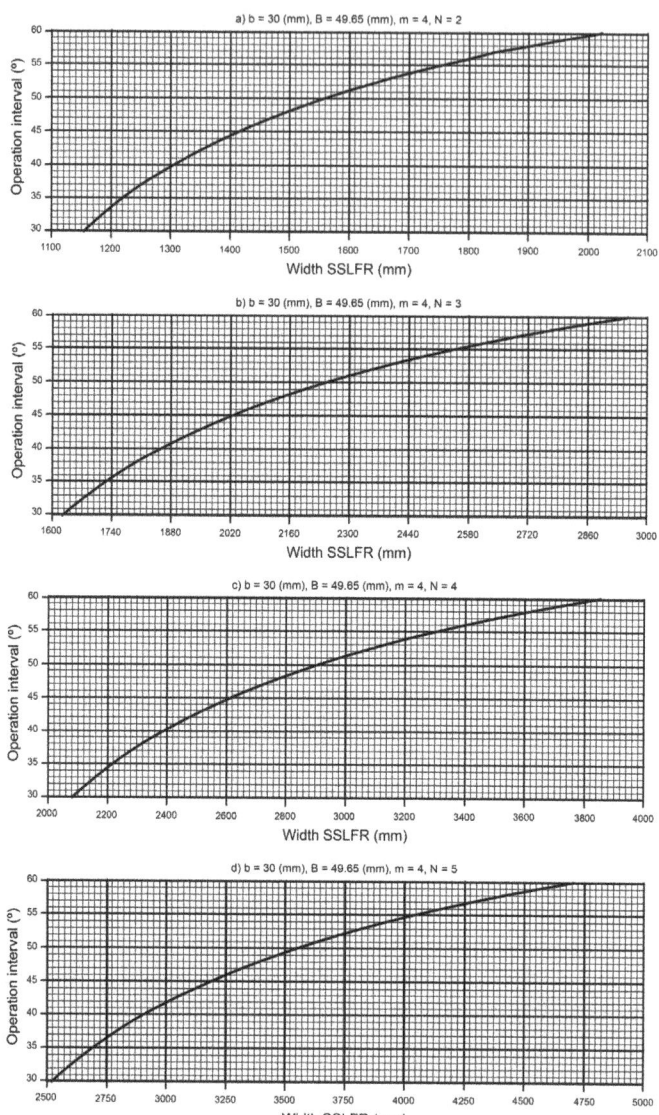

Figure 6. The relationship between the width of the SSLFR and θ_{t_0}.

The position of the mirrors remained to be determined. A graph relating the position of the mirrors and the operation interval obtained by the iterative optimization algorithm proposed in [18] was also obtained. Figure 7 shows the curves relating the operation interval and the position of the mirrors.

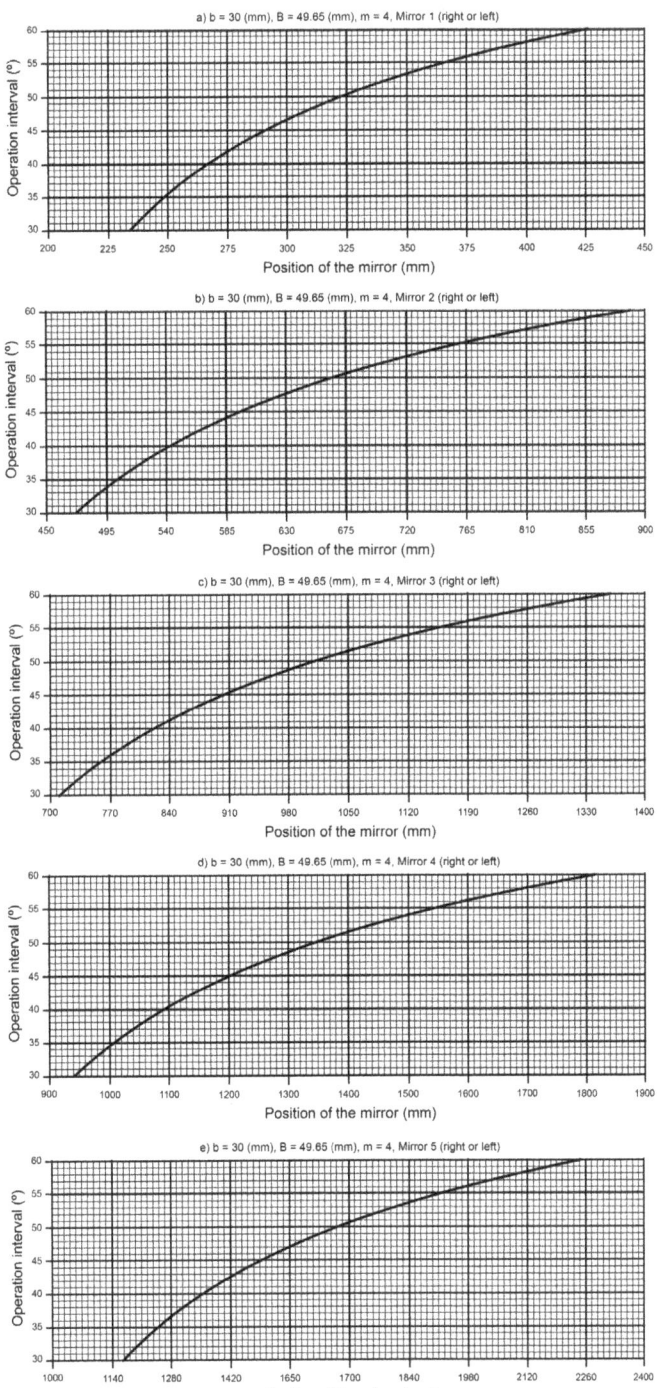

Figure 7. The relationship between the position of the mirrors and θ_{t_0}.

The graph showing the relationship between the mirror width and the operation interval was obtained using the iterative optimization algorithm suggested in [18]. Figure 8 shows the curves relating the operation interval to the width of the mirrors.

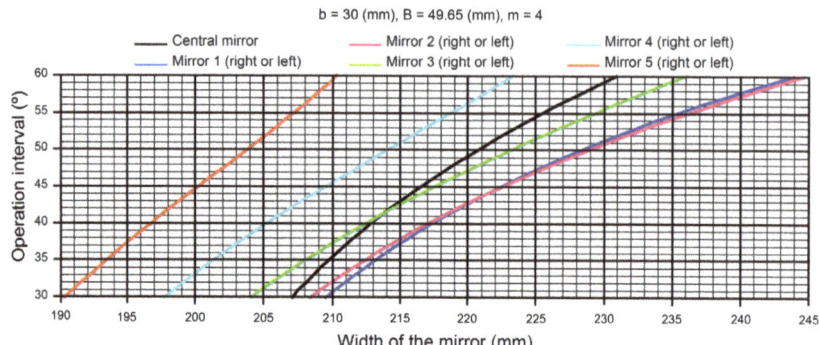

Figure 8. The relationship between the width of the mirrors and θ_{t_0}.

Once θ_{t_0} was determined, it was also possible to determine the number of hours with a guaranteed homogeneous distribution of solar irradiance, without shading or blocking. The length of the operating interval is $I_{N_d} = [h_R(N_d, \theta_{t_0}), h_S(N_d, \theta_{t_0})]$, where N_d is the day of the year. For example, Figure 9 represents the duration of the operating interval for several θ_{t_0} in Almeria (Spain) (latitude 36°50′07″ N, longitude 02°24′08″ W, and elevation 22 m).

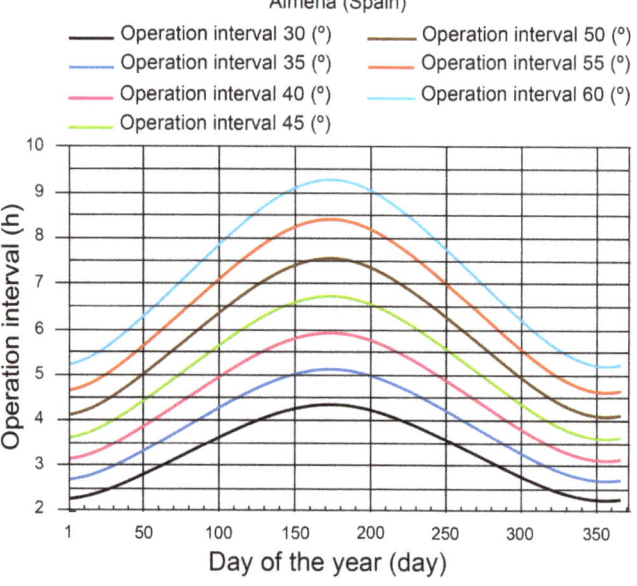

Figure 9. Hours of optimum operation.

The power reaching the PV cells was estimated using the equation proposed by [18], as follows:

$$Q = \sum_{i=1}^{2 \cdot N+1} DNI \cdot \eta_{opt} \cdot L_{PV} \cdot \min\{W_{fi}, W_{PV}\} \cdot F_{bs} \cdot \cos\theta_i \cdot \cos\theta_l, \qquad (26)$$

where DNI is the direct normal irradiance (W/m^2), η_{opt} is the optical efficiency of the $SSLFR$ (this parameter groups together: the mirror reflectivity (ρ), the mirror cleanliness (CI_m), the glass cleanliness (CI_g), and the glass transmissivity (τ_g)), and the effectively illuminated length is L_{PV}. In addition, the full width of the PV cell W_{PV} is illuminated during the optimum operation time I_{N_d}. A shading and blocking factor F_{bs} must be included, the value of which is 1 during the operating interval I_{N_d} (there is none of either). The transverse angle θ_i between the normal to the i-th mirror and the incidence angle of the sun is:

$$\cos \theta_i = \cos(\beta_i \pm \alpha_i), \tag{27}$$

with the configuration chosen in the longitudinal study:

$$\theta_l = \theta_z/2, \tag{28}$$

where θ_l is the longitudinal angle (*rad*), and θ_z is the zenith angle (*rad*).

Therefore, the power of the $SSLFR$ was determined for all hours of the operation interval I_{N_d} and all days of the year N_d as follows:

$$\sum_{N_d=1}^{365} \int_{h_R(N_d,\theta_{t_0})}^{h_S(N_d,\theta_{t_0})} Q \cdot dT. \tag{29}$$

It is pertinent to remember the certainty that in this interval, there is neither shadow nor blockage, and the illumination is uniform.

3.4. Verification

For this paper, the SolTrace software, developed by the National Renewable Energy Laboratory ($NREL$), was used to validate the cavity, since it is currently one of the most widely used and recognized open source programs for the study of solar concentrators [18,46,47]. This software is based on the Monte Carlo ray-tracing methodology. In addition, SolTrace allows the assignment of parameters related to the reflection and refraction at the surface of the material. Another advantage of this software is that the user can specify a certain number of rays to be traced. The rays are generated randomly from the sun to the reflecting elements comprising the system, where the rays intersect. After optimizing the cavity, the determined geometrical parameters of both the cavity and the primary reflector system were entered into SolTrace to establish the geometrical model.

3.5. The Manufacture of the Sawtooth V-Trough Cavity and the Laser Experiment

The designed sawtooth V-trough cavity was manufactured based on 3D printing technology and additive manufacturing [22,48]. Additive manufacturing integrates computer-aided design, material processing, and molding technology [49]. The system used built a solid model of the sawtooth V-trough cavity by stacking special materials, in this case PLA, layer by layer, using software and a numerical control system on the basis of a digital model file [49]. The 3D printer used and a sawtooth V-trough cavity are shown in Figure 10. The cavity walls were covered with reflective mirrors.

A laser experimental platform for the verification of receiver cavities has been widely used [22,48,50]. Therefore, a laser experimental platform was also used for the study presented here.

An experimental test platform was constructed for ray-path control (see Figure 11). This experimental setup was mainly comprised of a level horizontal platform, a laser generator, a digital angle meter, an angle measuring device, and a metal scale. Similar devices were used in references [22,48,50]. The sensitive points of the test were as follows [22,48,50]: (i) to ensure that the equipment used remained perfectly fixed to the level horizontal platform, (ii) to ensure the levelness and stability of the horizontal platform by bubble leveling, (iii) to ensure that the laser generator was rigidly mounted on the rotating arm of the angle measuring device in such a way to maintain the laser generator parallel to the rotating arm,

(iv) to provide a system for sliding the angle-measuring device along the metal scale and securing it to the scale by means of a locking device, and (v) to ensure the distance from the metal scale to the sawtooth V-trough cavity could be adjusted to simulate the position of any mirror in the primary reflector system.

Figure 10. The 3D printer and the sawtooth V-trough cavity under printing.

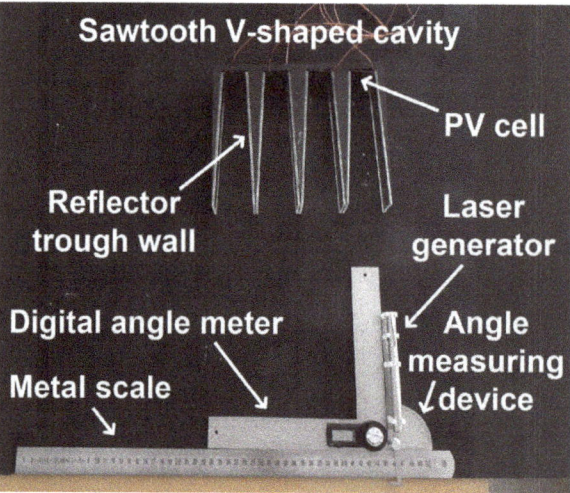

Figure 11. Laser experimental platform.

In the experiment, the laser generator was adjusted to the position of each mirror by the angle of incidence and the position of the angle measuring device on the metal scale. Information on the position of the laser spot that formed when the light hit the reflecting wall of the cavity was recorded, and the position of the successive light reflections was checked.

4. Application of the Methodology and Analysis of the Results

It should be noted that this study is limited to small-scale linear Fresnel reflectors. Their small-scale characteristic is what allows longitudinal movement in the moving structure and the secondary reflector system. This ensures the uniform illumination of the photovoltaic cells from a longitudinal perspective.

The objective of this section is to verify the feasibility of the proposed methodology. The following parameters were used as a starting point in order to apply this methodology:

(i) Available roof surface area. The available roof area was considered to be able to accommodate an $SSLFR$ with the following dimensions: width 2244 mm and length 2000 mm.

(ii) Study location. The rooftop was located in Almería (Spain), for which the geographical data were: latitude 36°50′07″ N, longitude 02°24′08″ W, and altitude 22 m.

(iii) Width of the commercial PV cells ($W_{PV} = b$). A commercial PV cell width of 30 mm was considered. The assumption of this value does not limit the application of the methodology.

(iv) Acceptance angle (θ_c). A $\theta_c = 34$ (°) was considered. It is a plausible value for the typical dimensions of an $SSLFR$ [18].

(v) Number of V-trough cavities in the sawtooth (m). This m was equal to 4 to limit the number of mirrors as well as any increase in the cost of the $SSLFR$ [28]. Any other value of this parameter can be used.

(vi) Height to the receiver (f). Usually, f takes the value of 1500 mm [18,35,36].

(vii) Number of mirrors of the $SSLFR$. The number of mirrors of the $SSLFR$ was considered to be equal to seven so that the cost of the $SSLFR$ was not too high [28]. Therefore, $N = 3$.

(viii) Optical properties. The optical properties of the materials used were as follows [18]: the mirror reflectivity $\rho = 0.94$ [34], the mirror cleanliness $CI_m = 0.96$ [51], the glass cleanliness $CI_g = 0.96$ [51], and the glass transmissivity $\tau_g = 0.92$ [52]. These optical properties were grouped into what is known as total optical yield (η_{opt}).

Mathematica™ Computer Algebra System software was used to implement the optimization algorithm. This software has been widely used in similar studies [8,18]. The amount of direct solar irradiance on the horizontal surface of the site under study must be determined, i.e., the effect of the particular meteorological conditions must be taken into account. For this purpose, the method proposed by [53] was used. This method uses $PVGIS$ [54] data to obtain the monthly average direct solar irradiance.

The new cavity was compared to the standard V-trough cavity, keeping the cavity aperture, reflective surface area, and photovoltaic cell width constant. In addition, the focal height, number of mirrors, mirror width, and mirror spacing were also kept constant, so that the cost of the two configurations was the same from the point of view of the primary reflector system.

Table 1 summarizes the results of the proposed optimization algorithm for the considered parameters.

Table 1. Results of the sawtooth V-trough cavity.

	Parameters	Value
C_a	Area concentration ratio	1.655
τ^*	Trough wall angle	87.00°
B	Aperture of the V-trough cavity	49.65 mm
H	Height of the V-trough cavity	187.47 m

Figure 12a shows the final design of the sawtooth V-trough cavity.

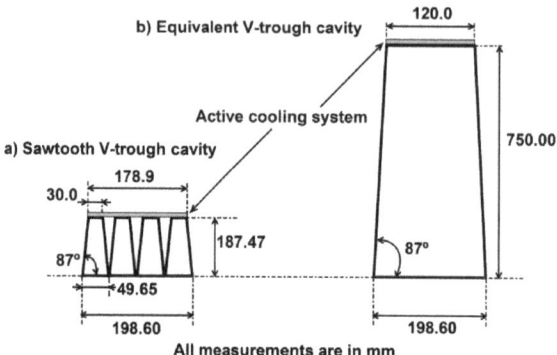

Figure 12. The final design of the sawtooth V-trough cavity and equivalent V-trough cavity.

Using a single equivalent V-trough cavity and considering the same PV cell surface and the same $\theta_c = 34$ (°), the results shown in Table 2 were obtained. Figure 12b shows the final design of the equivalent V-trough cavity.

Table 2. Results of the equivalent V-trough cavity.

	Parameters	Value
C_a	Area concentration ratio	1.655
τ^*	Trough wall angle	87.00 (°)
B	Aperture of the V-trough cavity	198.6 mm
H	Height of the V-trough cavity	750.00 (m)

4.1. Comparison between the Proposed Sawtooth V-Cavity and the Standard V-Cavity

A comparison between the two cavities was made from various aspects, e.g., mechanical and thermal.

4.1.1. Mechanical Aspects

Comparing both designs, the height of the equivalent V-trough cavity was four times greater than the height of the sawtooth V-trough cavity. On the other hand, the refracting surface was the same in both cavities studied, in this case, 3.00 m²; so, they would have the same R_a.

The method for calculating the wind load was defined in code CTE DB-SE-AE [55]. According to this code, the wind load is proportional to the exposure surface. The wind-exposed area of the equivalent V-trough cavity was four times larger than the sawtooth V-trough cavity. Therefore, the fixed structure and the secondary system of the $SSLFR$ would need to be reinforced to withstand four times higher wind loads. This considerably reduces the manufacturing cost of the $SSLFR$, as shown below:

(i) Reduction in the cost of the fixed structure. As the height of the proposed cavity is much lower, the fixed structure of the $SSLFR$ is smaller, which lowers the cost thereof.
(ii) Reduction in the cost of the fixed structure and secondary system structures. By reducing the height of the cavity, the surface area exposed to wind loads is smaller, which lowers the cost of the fixed structure and the secondary system structures.

4.1.2. Thermal Aspects

In the PV cells, the part of the absorbed solar irradiance that is not converted into electricity is completely dissipated into heat, which represents an internal heat source that can be expressed as follows [56]:

$$Q_{th} = I_t \cdot A_{PV} \cdot (1 - \eta_e), \tag{30}$$

where Q_{th} is the internal heat generation in PV cells (W), I_t is the total absorbed solar irradiance for PV cells (W/m²), η_e is the electrical efficiency of the PV system (%), and A_{PV} is the total area of the PV cells (m²). For the two cavities, the internal heat generation in PV cells is the same, because they have the same number of PV cells.

The heat transfer by conduction through the wall of the cooling system is determined by Fourier's law of conduction through a hollow rectangular tube resulting from [57]:

$$Q_{th} = \frac{k \cdot A_{ACS} \cdot (T_{PV} - T_{ACS})}{\delta_{ACS}}, \qquad (31)$$

where k is the thermal conductivity (W/m °C), A_{ACS} is the area of the active cooling system (m²), T_{PV} is the temperature of the PV cells (°C), T_{ACS} is the temperature of the active cooling system PV cells (°C), and δ_{ACS} is the wall thickness of the cooling system (m). As Q_{th}, k, and δ are equal for the two cavities, the area of the cooling system is inversely proportional to the ΔT. The area of the cooling system in the case of the sawtooth V-cavity was $0.1789 \cdot L_{PV}$ (m²), and in the case of the standard V-cavity, it was $0.12 \cdot L_{PV}$ (m²). So, the cooling surface in the case of the sawtooth V-cavity was 1.49 times larger. Therefore, the ΔT in the case of the sawtooth V-cavity was 0.67 times the ΔT in the case of the standard V-cavity. Hence, the temperature of the PV cells with the sawtooth V-cavity is always lower than that of PV cells with the standard V-cavity.

Figure 13 shows the relationship between the number of V-trough cavities of the sawtooth (m) and the width of the cooling system (W_{ACS}), keeping the width of the PV cells constant (W_{PV}). One can see that this relationship was not linear. As m increased, the increase in the W_{ACS} dropped.

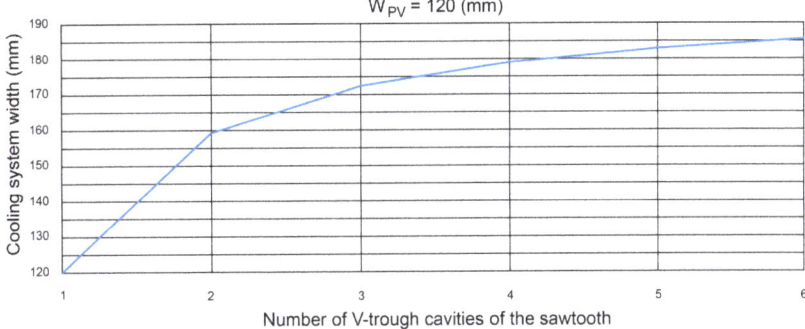

Figure 13. The relationship between the number of V-trough cavities in the sawtooth and the width of the cooling system.

According to Evans [58], the electrical efficiency of a photovoltaic cell depends on the temperature of the PV cell:

$$\eta_e = \eta_{ref} \cdot \left[1 - \beta_{ref} \cdot \left(T_{PV} - T_{ref}\right)\right], \qquad (32)$$

where η_{ref} is the electrical efficiency of the photovoltaic module at a reference temperature (dimensionless), β_{ref} is the temperature coefficient (1/°C), T_{PV} is the PV cell temperature (°C), and T_{ref} is the reference temperature (°C). Among other technical parameters, the manufacturer of the PV module provides the value of η_{ref} and β_{ref}. The η_{ref} value normally refers to a temperature of 25 °C and a solar irradiance of 1000 (W/m²). Therefore, lowering the operating temperature of the PV cells means increasing the electrical efficiency of the PV cells.

4.1.3. Other Beneficial Aspects

Other beneficial aspects of the proposed cavity include:

(i) The same reflective surface for both cavities. The multiple reflective walls of the new cavity, however, are used in combination to replace the two reflective surfaces of the V-trough cavity, which could reduce the difficulty of manufacturing, maintaining, and transporting the large glasses. This would also decrease the total cost of the $SSLFR$.

(ii) The connection of the PV cells. The connection of the photovoltaic cells is facilitated due to the separation between the photovoltaic cells in the new cavity.

4.2. The Application of the Graphic System When Designing the Primary Reflector System

Since the length of the $SSLFR$ was 2000 mm, the length of the mirrors was 2000 mm, and the length of the PV cell system was also 2000 mm. As $N = 3$, the graph shown in Figure 6b was used. On the $SSLFR$ width axis of the graph in Figure 6b, the value of 2244 mm was used, resulting in $\theta_{t_0} = 50°$ on the operation interval axis. Once the operation interval was known, the width of the mirrors was determined using the graph in Figure 7, and the position of the mirrors was determined using the graphs in Figure 8. Table 3 shows the results obtained.

Table 3. Geometric values of the optimal design.

Mirror	L_i (mm)	W_{Mi} (mm)
Central mirror	0	220.6
Mirror 1 (right or left)	323.5	228.3
Mirror 2 (right or left)	664.9	228.8
Mirror 3 (right or left)	1010.2	223.1

Using the $SSLFR$ parameters obtained previously, the annual energy of the sawtooth V-cavity was 2.38266 MWh. The use of the new cavity did not lead to a decrease in the energy obtained.

4.3. Verification through a Monte Carlo Simulation

A sawtooth V-trough cavity was optically modeled in this study. This design was verified using the Monte Carlo ray-tracing method. SolTrace™ is practical software that uses the Monte Carlo ray-tracing method. The application of this software has been used by several references for the optical analysis of solar concentrated systems [18,46,47]. Based on the results obtained previously, a model was implemented in the SolTrace™ software. Certain assumptions, common in this type of study, were made [18]: (i) all the reflective surfaces were flat and perfect; (ii) the errors in tracking the apparent movement of the sun were not considered; and (iii) the $SSLFR$ parameters shown in Tables 1 and 3 were held constant. In total, 10^7 rays were used for the simulations as recommended by other similar studies [18]. The direct normal irradiance for each day of the year was obtained by using the method presented by [53].

To verify the proposed design, the simulation time was during the summer solstice (day 172 of the year) at 9:00 (h) and 7:00 (h). The first simulation time chosen, $T = 9:00$ (h), belonged to the operation interval, where the PV cells were uniformly illuminated. There was also no shading or blocking between adjacent mirrors. In contrast, the second simulation time chosen, $T = 7:00$ (h), did not belong to the operation interval.

The direct normal irradiance for the summer solstice at $T = 9:00$ (h) was 750.19 (W/m^2). Figure 14 shows some simulation results for different surfaces for the simulation time $T = 9:00$ (h). Figure 14a shows the absence of shading and blocking between the adjacent mirrors. This fact can also be seen in Figure 14b–d. Figure 14e–h show the surface of the PV cells in the sawtooth V-trough cavity, where the flux density was completely homogeneous on the PV cells.

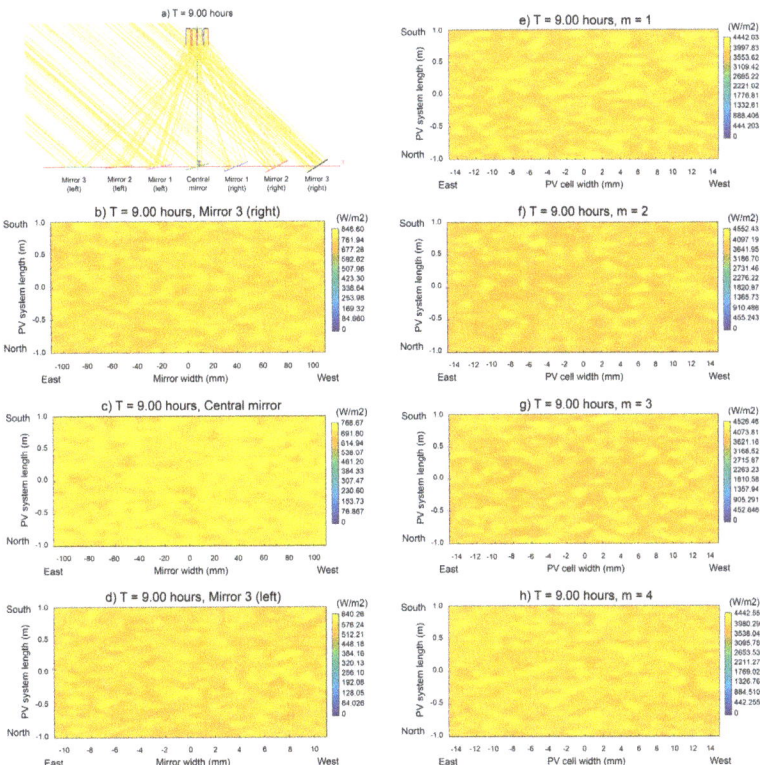

Figure 14. Simulation results for different surfaces, $N_d = 172$, $T = 9{:}00$ (h).

The results of the flux density simulation on all the *SSLFR* surfaces obtained with SolTrace are provided in Table 4. The SolTrace software output parameter called uniformity indicates the homogeneity of the flux density over the studied surface. The lower this parameter, the higher the homogeneity of the flux density. It can be seen that this parameter reflected very low values in the *PV* cells. It is also true that the average value of the flux density over the photovoltaic cells was very similar. It should be noted that the minimum value of the flux density over the mirrors was different from 0, indicating the absence of shading and blocking between mirrors.

Table 4. Results of the flux density simulation at $T = 9{:}00$ (h).

Surface	Max. Irradiance (W/m^2)	Min. Irradiance (W/m^2)	Avg. Irradiance (W/m^2)	Uniformity
Mirror 3 (right)	846.60	668.60	749.17	0.033
Mirror 2 (right)	829.78	647.35	744.11	0.033
Mirror 1 (right)	804.10	651.78	728.44	0.035
Central mirror	768.67	631.41	701.40	0.035
Mirror 1 (left)	741.22	568.53	664.55	0.036
Mirror 2 (left)	693.40	543.74	622.32	0.036
Mirror 3 (left)	640.26	502.12	581.48	0.038
PV cell ($m = 1$)	4442.03	3357.50	3914.13	0.042
PV cell ($m = 2$)	4552.43	3461.41	3957.99	0.041
PV cell ($m = 3$)	4526.46	3402.96	3965.52	0.042
PV cell ($m = 4$)	4422.55	3279.57	3911.85	0.040

The direct normal irradiance for the summer solstice at $T = 7:00$ (h) was 656.53 W/m². Figure 15 shows some simulation results for different surfaces, for the simulation time $T = 7:00$ (h). These surfaces were the same as those studied in Figure 15. Figure 15a shows that mirrors 3 (right), 2 (right), 1 (right), central, and 1 (left) had different degrees of shading. This effect was more pronounced in mirror 3 (right), as the simulation time was before midday. Mirrors 2 (left) and 3 (left) had no shading. This fact can also be seen in Figure 15b–d. Figure 15e shows that the photovoltaic cell surface $m = 1$ had a high degree of inhomogeneity. In contrast, the central PV cells, $m = 2$ and $m = 3$, had a high degree of flux density homogeneity. The flux density homogeneity decreased for the $m = 4$ PV cell.

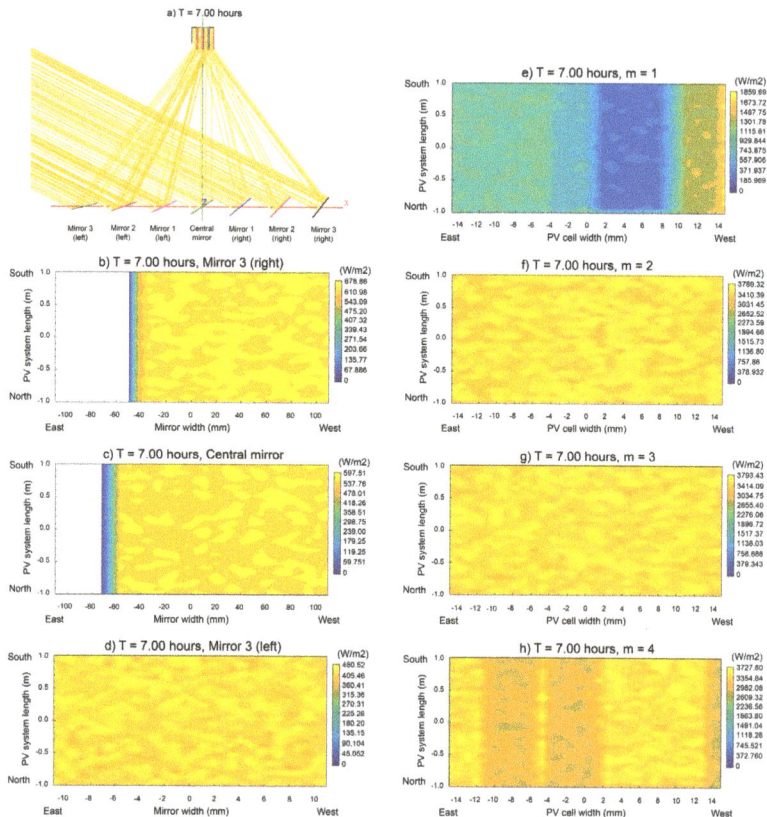

Figure 15. Simulation results for different surfaces, $N_d = 172$, $T = 7:00$ (h).

The results of the flux density simulation on all the $SSLFR$ surfaces obtained with SolTrace are provided in Table 5. The output parameter from the SolTrace software called uniformity reflected high values for the shaded mirrors and the PV cell $m = 1$, which had low flux density homogeneity. The average value of the flux density over the PV cell $m = 1$ was very low, indicating a lack of homogeneity in the flux density. In contrast, for the central PV cells, $m = 2$ and $m = 3$, the average value of the flux density was very similar. The mirrors with a minimum flux density value of 0 had part of their surface shaded by an adjacent mirror.

Table 5. Results of the flux density simulation at $T = 7:00$ (h).

Surface	Max. Irradiance (W/m^2)	Min. Irradiance (W/m^2)	Avg. Irradiance (W/m^2)	Uniformity
Mirror 3 (right)	678.86	0	437.26	0.656
Mirror 2 (right)	681.67	0	440.10	0.615
Mirror 1 (right)	637.91	0	431.45	0.590
Central mirror	597.51	0	427.34	0.520
Mirror 1 (left)	559.36	0	451.93	0.333
Mirror 2 (left)	503.82	407.88	452.41	0.035
Mirror 3 (left)	450.52	362.43	407.87	0.035
PV cell ($m = 1$)	1859.69	238.63	827.51	0.433
PV cell ($m = 2$)	3789.32	2933.53	3409.21	0.037
PV cell ($m = 3$)	3793.43	3044.62	3418.47	0.034
PV cell ($m = 4$)	3727.6	2517.98	3193.99	0.074

To complete the comparative study between the sawtooth V-trough cavity and the equivalent V-trough cavity, Figure 16 shows the simulation time during the summer solstice (day 172 of the year) at 9:00 (h) of the equivalent V-trough cavity. Figure 16a shows the absence of shading and blocking between the adjacent mirrors. Figure 16b shows that the photovoltaic cell surface had a high degree of inhomogeneity. In contrast, for the same hour, the sawtooth V-cavity flux density was completely homogeneous in the PV cells.

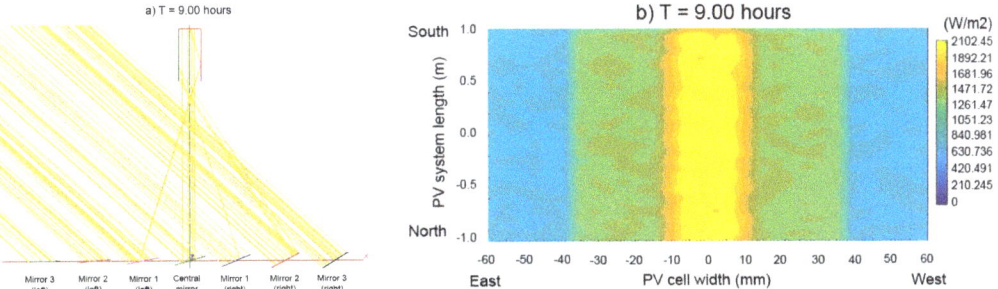

Figure 16. Simulation results of equivalent V-trough cavity, $N_d = 172$, $T = 9:00$ (h).

The results of the flux density simulation on all the $SSLFR$ surfaces obtained with SolTrace are provided in Table 6 for the equivalent V-trough cavity. Comparing Tables 4 and 6, we see there were similar values of incident solar irradiance on the mirrors, and a considerable reduction in the incident solar irradiance on the PV cells in the case of the equivalent V-trough cavity. The high value of the uniformity parameter indicated the non-homogeneity of the photovoltaic cells in the equivalent V-trough cavity. The opposite was the case with the sawtooth V-trough cavity.

Table 6. Results of the flux density simulation at $T = 9:00$ (h) in the equivalent V-trough cavity.

Surface	Max. Irradiance (W/m^2)	Min. Irradiance (W/m^2)	Avg. Irradiance (W/m^2)	Uniformity
Mirror 3 (right)	888.06	623.43	749.38	0.048
Mirror 2 (right)	852.34	659.14	742.37	0.044
Mirror 1 (right)	839.35	625.05	728.45	0.048
Central mirror	808.51	597.45	702.83	0.048
Mirror 1 (left)	806.88	564.98	664.39	0.051
Mirror 2 (left)	738.70	513.03	623.30	0.049
Mirror 3 (left)	660.71	480.56	581.40	0.05
PV cell	2102.45	600.71	1184.97	0.38

4.4. Influence of the Acceptance Angle of the V-Trough Cavity

In the previous sections, a case was presented in which the acceptance angle of the V-trough cavity $\theta_c = 34$ (°) was considered. This value corresponded to an $SSLFR$ with a width of 2244 mm and a number of mirrors equal to seven ($N = 3$). The value of θ_c came from a focal length $f = 1500$ mm and from the center of the mirror 3 (right or left), whose center, as we saw, was at a distance of $L_3 = 1010.2$ mm (see Table 3).

In this section, the influence of the V-trough cavity acceptance angle is analyzed. For this purpose, several simulations were carried out, varying $\theta_c \in [22, 46]$ (°), obtaining the results shown in Figure 17. Figure 17a shows the variation in C_a. Considering the absorber width $b = 30$ mm, the variation in B is shown in Figure 17b, and the variation in H is shown in Figure 17c.

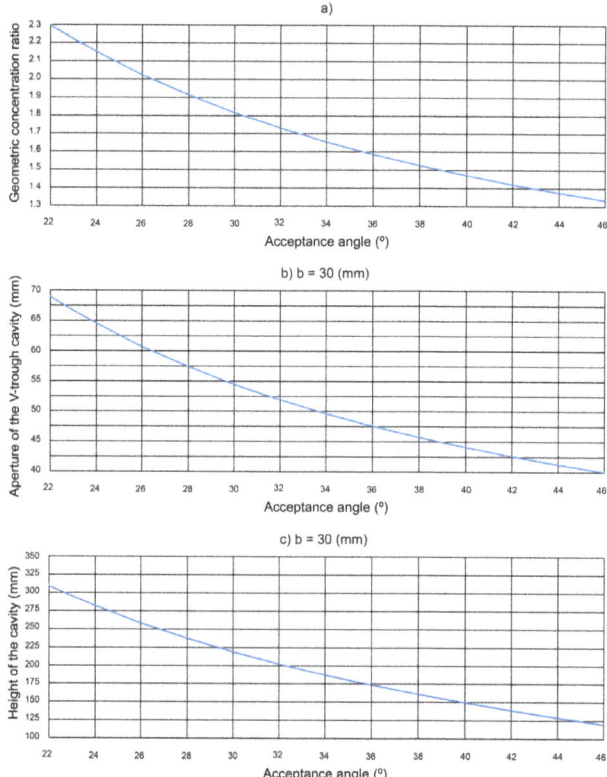

Figure 17. The relationship between the acceptance angle and various cavity parameters.

As shown in Figure 17, as the acceptance angle increased, the geometric concentration ratio decreased nonlinearly. This variation translated almost linearly (obviously) to the value of B and almost linearly also to H. The latter result is due to the fact that the optimal value τ^* of the trough wall angle also showed a linear variation with θ_c, with values ranging from 86.4 to 87.6 (°) for the range of the variation in θ_c.

As discussed below, the variation in the acceptance angle had an influence on the design of the $SSLFR$, as it directly affects the secondary reflector system and, therefore, the primary reflector system.

From the point of view of the secondary reflector, this variation in C_a led to the following situation. Once b was set by the manufacturer of the PV cells, the optimum value of B was obtained. Since the commercial cells used in this work had a fixed value of

$b = 30$ mm, in the base case already analyzed, with $\theta_c = 34°$, and a number of V-trough cavities of the sawtooth $m = 4$, we were guaranteed a swept width of the entire secondary of $4B \simeq 200$ mm. If we then considered a smaller θ_c value, as C_a grew, there came a point where, with a smaller number of V-trough cavities of the sawtooth, in this case, $m = 3$, we achieved the same sweep of the secondary $3B \simeq 200$ mm. This was achieved for $\theta_c = 23°$. Similarly, by increasing θ_c, and decreasing C_a, it was necessary to take $m = 5$, in order to have the same sweep of the secondary $5B \simeq 200$ mm. This situation occurred for $\theta_c = 46°$. Table 7 shows the influence of the variation in the acceptance angle with respect to the parameters of the secondary reflector system.

Table 7. Results of the influence of the acceptance angle on some parameters of the SSLFR.

Secondary Reflector System				Primary Reflector System		
θ_c (°)	C_a	B (mm)	m	N	L_N (mm)	θ_{to} (°)
23	2.22	66.66	3	2	640	49
34	1.66	50	4	3	1010	50
46	1.33	40	5	5	1550	47

The variation in the acceptance angle also influenced the design of the primary reflector system. Considering $f = 1500$ mm, the three cases that were analyzed induced changes in the main parameters of the primary reflector system. Table 7 shows the influence of the variation in the acceptance angle with respect to the parameters of the primary reflector system.

When $\theta_c = 34$ (°), the base case, the optimal design corresponded to $\theta_{to} = 50$ (°), $N = 3$, and $L_N = 1010$ mm.

When the acceptance angle decreased, e.g., $\theta_c = 23°$, to achieve that angle and a very similar operating range of $\theta_{to} = 49°$, the mirror field of the primary had the following parameters: $N = 2$ and $L_N = 640$ mm. In contrast, when the acceptance angle increased, for example, $\theta_c = 46°$ and a very similar operating range $\theta_{to} = 47°$, the mirror field of the primary had the following parameters: $N = 5$ and $L_N = 1550$ mm.

Comparing the three cases, and considering the variation in θ_{to} to be negligible, the case $\theta_c = 46°$ significantly increased the area of the primary field of mirrors; therefore, this case increased the number of PV cells, the solar irradiation received, and the cost of the $SSLFR$. On the other hand, in the case $\theta_c = 23°$, the situation was the opposite: fewer PV cells, a lower solar irradiation received, and a lower cost of the $SSLFR$. Therefore, several factors must be taken into account in the choice of the acceptance angle, such as the economic factor, the energy factor, and the surface area available for the installation of the $SSLFR$.

4.5. The Manufacture of the Sawtooth V-Trough Cavity and the Laser Experiment

The sawtooth V-trough cavity was constructed using a biodegradable green polymer material known as polylactic acid (PLA), with the dimensions shown in Figure 12a. The photograph of the sawtooth V-trough cavity presented in this paper is shown in Figure 18.

As the dimensions of the experimental test platform were smaller than the dimensions of the $SSLFR$, the position of the $SSLFR$ mirrors and the height to the receiver were scaled. The width of the mirrors and the angle of incidence were not affected. Table 8 shows the optimal parameters scaled to the experimental test platform; in this case, $f = 283$ mm. The laser generator was placed in three positions for each mirror tested: an extreme left position, a central position, and an extreme right position.

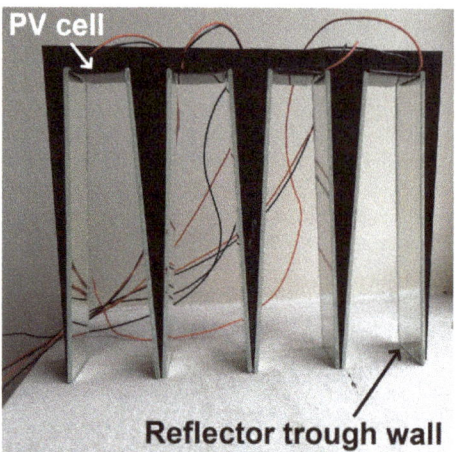

Figure 18. Photograph of the sawtooth V-trough cavity presented in this work.

Table 8. Optimal parameters scaled to the experimental test platform.

Mirror	L_i (mm)	W_{Mi} (mm)	θ_i (°)
Central mirror	0	220.6	0
Mirror 1 (right or left)	61.0	228.3	12.17
Mirror 2 (right or left)	125.4	228.8	23.90
Mirror 3 (right or left)	205.2	223.1	33.95

Figure 19a shows the laser beam emitted by the laser generator, starting from the extreme left position of the mirror 2 (left) with an angle of incidence of 23.90°. As expected, the beam was incident on the cavity $m = 1$. Figure 19b shows the laser beam emitted by the laser generator, starting from the extreme right position of the mirror 2 (left) with an angle of incidence of 23.90° (the maximum acceptance angle that corresponds to that mirror due to the geometry of the $SSLFR$). As expected, the beam was incident on the cavity $m = 4$. These results indicate that the ray acceptance rate is 1. The rest of the tests carried out for the other mirrors also showed that the laser beam hit the PV cell. The experimental results obtained using the cavity designed showed that the constructed cavity met the set conditions.

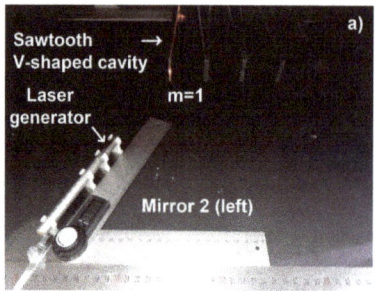 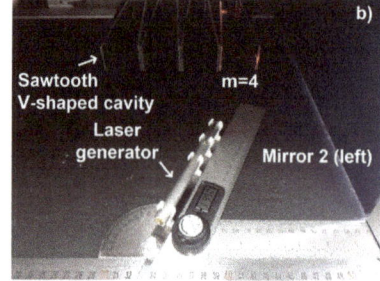

Figure 19. The laser beam emitted by the laser generator located in mirror 2 (left).

The angle measured with the digital angle meter did not match the actual angle of the laser beam when it reached the reflecting surface of the cavity. There are several reasons for this: (i) The laser beam emitted by the laser generator has a certain divergence [50], since the laser is deflected as the optical length increases. (ii) The laser beam emitted by the laser generator is not an absolutely parallel beam [50], which causes the beam spot to reach the surface at a slightly different angle. Therefore, the angle of incidence of the laser beam is affected. In general, these sources of error are considered to have a cumulative effect and do not cancel each other out [50]. However, as the distance from the laser generator to the cavity was 349 mm in the worst case of mirror 3 (left or right), this angle error was considered to be within a reasonable range [48,50].

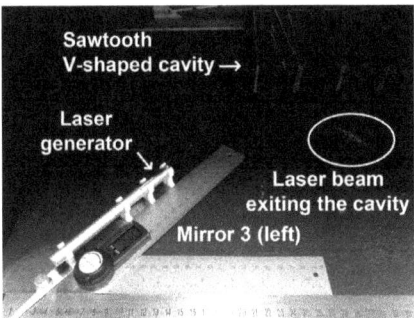

Figure 20. The laser beam emitted by the laser generator located in mirror 3 (left).

Figure 20 shows the laser beam emitted by the laser generator, starting from the extreme left position of the mirror 3 (left) with an angle of incidence of 35.00°. As can be seen in this image, the laser beam exited the cavity.

5. Conclusions

Guaranteeing the uniformity of the solar irradiance distribution in photovoltaic cells is a major issue in concentrating photovoltaic systems based on a small-scale linear Fresnel reflector. For this purpose, a new cavity design for a low-concentration photovoltaic system based on a small-scale linear Fresnel reflector was proposed to decrease the height thereof while maintaining a constant aperture. The design of a sawtooth V-cavity that maintained the ray acceptance rate at 1 and the uniform distribution of the solar irradiance on the photovoltaic cells was calculated analytically using an optimization algorithm. The analytical approach presented provides equations for any number of reflections inside the cavity, which are easily implemented as an iterative algorithm. The proposed design was verified using the Monte Carlo ray-tracing method. SolTrace™ software was used for this purpose. In order to verify the correct sawtooth V-trough cavity design, a prototype was built with a biodegradable green polymer material known as polylactic acid (PLA) using 3D printing technology. An experimental laser platform was built to fix the trajectory of the laser beam to confirm that the ray acceptance rate was 1, i.e., that all the beams entering the cavity reached the photovoltaic cells. The proposed sawtooth V-trough cavity was compared with the standard V-trough cavity, keeping the cavity aperture, reflective surface area, and photovoltaic cell width constant. In addition, the focal height, number of mirrors, mirror width, and mirror spacing were also kept constant, so that the cost of the two configurations was the same from the point of view of the primary reflector system. In the example analyzed, the annual energy of the sawtooth V-trough cavity was 2.38266 MWh. The new design ensured the uniform distribution of the solar irradiation and significantly reduced the height of the cavity. This achievement considerably reduces the manufacturing cost of the small-scale linear Fresnel reflectors, as shown below:

(i) Since the height of the proposed cavity is much lower, in this case four times lower, the fixed structure of the small-scale linear Fresnel reflectors are smaller; therefore, the cost is lower.

(ii) The wind-exposed area of the sawtooth V-trough cavity is four times less than in the case of the standard V-trough cavity, which reduces the cost of the fixed structure and secondary system structures. This is essential considering that the optimal installation location for small-scale linear Fresnel reflectors is on the roofs of buildings.

(iii) The cooling surface in the case of the sawtooth V-cavity is 1.49 times larger, and the ΔT in the case of the sawtooth V-cavity is 0.67 times the ΔT in the case of the standard V-cavity. Hence, the temperature of the PV cells with the sawtooth V-cavity is always lower than that of PV cells with a standard V-cavity, which increases the electrical efficiency.

(iv) Although both cavities have the same reflective surface, the multiple reflective walls of the new cavity are used in combination to replace the two reflective surfaces of the standard V-trough cavity, which could reduce the difficulty in manufacturing, maintaining, and transporting the large glasses. Furthermore, the overall cost of the small-scale linear Fresnel reflector may also decrease.

Other beneficial aspects of the proposed cavity include:

(v) Although the surface area of the photovoltaic cells is the same, the spacing between the photovoltaic cells that characterizes the designed cavity facilitates cooling between the photovoltaic cells and the use of cooling systems with a larger surface area, which improves the efficiency of the cooling system.

(vi) Due to the separation between the photovoltaic cells in the new cavity, the connection between the photovoltaic cells is easier.

Finally, we also presented an innovative graphic system to design the primary reflector system for the small-scale linear Fresnel reflector. All of this makes it possible for users to quickly and easily make the necessary calculations without needing to program formulas.

Author Contributions: Conceptualization, J.Á.F.-R., A.B. and L.B.; Methodology, J.Á.F.-R., A.B., L.B. and M.G.; Software, J.Á.F.-R. and M.G.; Writing—original draft, M.G. All authors have read and agreed to the published version of the manuscript.

Funding: This research received no external funding.

Conflicts of Interest: The authors declare no conflict of interest.

Nomenclature

A_{ACS}	Area of the active cooling system (m^2)
A_{PV}	Total area of the PV cells (m^2)
B	Aperture of the V-trough cavity (m)
b	Absorber width of the V-trough cavity (m)
C_a	Area or geometric concentration ratio (dimensionless)
C_{opt}	Optical concentration ratio (dimensionless)
CL_g	Cleanliness factor of the glass (dimensionless)
CL_m	Cleanliness factor of the mirror (dimensionless)
DNI	Direct normal irradiance (W/m^2)
d_i	Separation between i-th and $i+1$-th mirrors (m)
F_{bs}	Blocking and shading coefficient (dimensionless)
f	Height of the receiver (m)
H	Height of the V-trough cavity (m)
I_{N_d}	Optimum operation time (h)
k	Thermal conductivity (W/m °C)
L_i	Position of i-th mirror (m)
L_{PV}	Effectively illuminated length (m)
l_i	Vertical length (m)
m	Number of V-trough cavities of the sawtooth
N	Number of mirrors on each side of the SSLFR
N_d	Ordinal of the day
n	Number of reflections
Q_{th}	Internal heat generation in PV cells (W)

R_a	Reflector-to-aperture area ratio (dimensionless)
T	Solar time (h)
T_{ACS}	Temperature of the active cooling system (°C)
T_{PV}	Temperature of the PV cells (°C)
T_{ref}	Reference temperature (°C)
W	Width of the $SSLFR$ (m)
W_{ACS}	Width of the active cooling system (m)
W_{PV}	Width of the of the PV cells (m)
W_{fi}	Width of the PV cells illuminated by the i-th mirror (m)
W_{Mi}	Width of the i-th mirror (m)
W_{PV}	Width of the PV cells (m)
α_0	Angle between the solar ray reaching the cavity and OR (°)
α_S	Solar altitude (°)
β_i	Angle that mirror i forms with the horizontal (°)
β_{ref}	Temperature coefficient (1/°C)
γ_S	Solar azimuth (°)
δ	Declination (°)
δ_{ACS}	Wall thickness of the cooling system (m)
ε_j	Angle between PP' and the i-th reflection (°)
η_e	Electrical efficiency of the PV system (dimensionless)
η_{opt}	Optical efficiency (dimensionless)
η_{ray}	Ray acceptance rate (dimensionless)
η_{ref}	Reference electrical efficiency (dimensionless)
θ_c	Acceptance angle of the V-trough cavity (°)
θ_i	Angle between the vertical at the focal point and the line connecting the center point of each mirror to the focal point (°)
θ_l	Longitudinal angle (°)
θ_t	Transversal incidence angle (°)
θ_{t_0}	Operation interval (°)
θ_z	Zenith angle (°)
λ	Latitude (°)
ρ	Reflectivity of the primary mirrors (dimensionless)
ρ_m	Reflectivity of the mirror (dimensionless)
τ	Trough wall angle (°)
τ_g	Transmissivity of glass (dimensionless)
ω	Hour angle (°)

References

1. Yadav, P.; Tripathi, B.; Lokhande, M.; Kumar, M. Estimation of steady state and dynamic parameters of low concentration photovoltaic system. *Sol. Energy Mater. Sol. Cells* **2013**, *112*, 65–72.
2. IRENA. *Future of Solar Photovoltaic: Deployment, Investment, Technology, Grid Integration and Socio-Economic Aspects*; International Renewable Energy Agency: Abu Dhabi, United Arab Emirates, 2019. Available online: https://irena.org/-/media/Files/IRENA/Agency/Publication/2019/Nov/IRENA_Future%_of_Solar_PV_2019.pdf (accessed on 11 June 2023).
3. Barbose, G.; Darghouth, N.; O'Shaughnessy, E.; Forrester, S. *Tracking the Sun: Pricing and Design Trends for Distributed Photovoltaic Systems in the United States*; Lawrence Berkeley National Laboratory: Berkeley, CA, USA, 2021.
4. IRENA. *Solar Costs To Fall Further, Powering Global Demand*; International Renewable Energy Agency: Abu Dhabi, United Arab Emirates, 2017. Available online: https://www.reuters.com/article/singapore-energy-solar-idUSL4N1MY2F8 (accessed on 11 June 2023)
5. Pvinsights. Available online: http://pvinsights.com/ (accessed on 11 June 2023).
6. IRENA; IEA. *End-of-Life Management: Solar Photovoltaic Panels*; International Renewable Energy Agency: Abu Dhabi, United Arab Emirates; International Energy Agency Photovoltaic Power Systems: Paris, France, 2016. Available online: https://www.irena.org/publications/2016/Jun/End-of-life-management-Solar-Photovoltaic-Panels (accessed on 11 June 2023).
7. Hasan, H.A.; Sopian, K.; Jaaz, A.H.; Al-Shamani, A.N. Experimental investigation of jet array nanofluids impingement in photovoltaic/thermal collector. *Sol. Energy* **2017**, *144*, 321–334. [CrossRef]
8. Barbón, A.; Bayón-Cueli, C.; Bayón, L.; Fortuny Ayuso, P. Influence of solar tracking error on the performance of a small-scale linear Fresnel reflector. *Renew. Energy* **2020**, *162*, 43–54. [CrossRef]
9. Barbón, A.; Fernández-Rubiera, J.A.; Martínez-Valledor, L.; Pérez-Fernández, A.; Bayón, L. Design and construction of a solar tracking system for small-scale linear Fresnel reflector with three movements. *Appl. Energy* **2021**, *285*, 116477.

10. Kandilli, C. Performance analysis of a novel concentrating photovoltaic combined system. *Energy Convers. Manag.* **2013**, *67*, 186–196.
11. Barbón, A.; Ghodbane, M.; Bayón, L.; Said, Z. A general algorithm for the optimization of photovoltaic modules layout on irregular rooftop shapes. *J. Clean. Prod.* **2022**, *365*, 132774. [CrossRef]
12. Silva, R.M.; Fernandes, J.L.M. Hybrid photovoltaic/thermal (PV/T) solar systems simulation with Simulink/Matlab. *Sol. Energy* **2010**, *84*, 1985–1996. [CrossRef]
13. Kamath, H.G.; Ekins-Daukes, N.J.; Araki, K.; Ramasesha, S.K. The potential for concentrator photovoltaics: A feasibility study in India. *Prog. Photovoltaics Res. Appl.* **2018**, *27*, 316–327. [CrossRef]
14. Moreno, A.; Chemisana, D.; Fernández, E.F. Hybrid high-concentration photovoltaic-thermal solar systems for building applications. *Appl. Energy* **2021**, *304*, 117647. [CrossRef]
15. Bamroongkhan, P.; Lertsatitthanakorn, C.; Soponronnarit, S. Experimental performance study of a solar parabolic dish photovoltaic-thermoelectric generator. *Energy Procedia* **2019**, *158*, 528–533. [CrossRef]
16. Brahim Kechiche, O.B.H.; Hamza, M. Enhancement of a commercial PV module performance under low concentrated photovoltaic (LCPV) conditions: A numerical study. *Renew. Energy Focus* **2022**, *41*, 258–267.
17. Xu, N.; Ji, J.; Sun, W.; Huang, W.; Li, J.; Jin, Z. Numerical simulation and experimental validation of a high concentration photovoltaic/thermal module based on point-focus Fresnel lens. *Appl. Energy* **2016**, *168*, 269–281.
18. Barbón, A.; Fortuny Ayuso, P.; Bayón, L.; Fernández-Rubiera, J.A. Non-uniform illumination in low concentration photovoltaic systems based on small-scale linear Fresnel reflectors. *Energy* **2022**, *239*, 122217.
19. Wang, G.; Wang, F.; Shen, F.; Jiang, T.; Chen, Z.; Hu, P. Experimental and optical performances of a solar CPV device using a linear Fresnel reflector concentrator. *Renew. Energy* **2020**, *146*, 2351–2361. [CrossRef]
20. Said, Z.; Ghodbane, M.; Kumar Tiwari, A.; Muhammad Ali, H.; Boumeddane, B.; Ali, Z.M. 4E (Energy, Exergy, Economic, and Environment) examination of a small LFR solar water heater: An experimental and numerical study. *Case Stud. Therm. Eng.* **2021**, *27*, 101277.
21. Vihari Parupudi, R.; Singh, H.; Kolokotroni, M. Low Concentrating Photovoltaics (LCPV) for buildings and their performance analyses. *Appl. Energy* **2020**, *279*, 115839.
22. Xu, J.; Chen, F.; Xia, E.; Gao, C.; Deng, C. An optimization design method and optical performance analysis on multi-sectioned compound parabolic concentrator with cylindrical absorber. *Energy* **2020**, *197*, 117212.
23. Ustaoglu, A.; Ozbey, U.; Torlaklı, H. Numerical investigation of concentrating photovoltaic/thermal (CPV/T) system using compound hyperbolic–trumpet, V-trough and compound parabolic concentrators. *Renew. Energy* **2020**, *152*, 1192–1208.
24. Otanicar, T.P.; Wingert, R.; Orosz, M.; McPheeters, C. Concentrating photovoltaic retrofit for existing parabolic trough solar collectors: Design, experiments, and levelized cost of electricity. *Appl. Energy* **2020**, *265*, 11475.
25. Al-Shohani, W.A.M.; Al-Dadah, R.; Mahmoud, S.; Algareu, A. Optimum design of V-trough concentrator for photovoltaic applications. *Sol. Energy* **2016**, *140*, 241–254.
26. Barbón, A.; Sánchez Rodríguez, J.A.; Bayón, L.; Barbón, N. Development of a fiber daylighting system based on a small scale linear Fresnel reflector: Theoretical elements. *Appl. Energy* **2018**, *212*, 733–745. [CrossRef]
27. Pardellas, A.; Fortuny Ayuso, P.; Bayón, L.; Barbón, A. A new two-foci V-trough concentrator for small-scale linear Fresnel reflectors. *Energies* **2023**, *16*, 1597. [CrossRef]
28. Barbón, A.; Sánchez-Rodríguez, J.A.; Bayón, L.; Bayón-Cueli, C. Cost estimation relationships of a small scale linear Fresnel reflector. *Renew. Energy* **2019**, *134*, 1273–1284. [CrossRef]
29. Li, G.; Xuan, Q.; Pei, G.; Su, Y.; Ji, J. Effect of non-uniform illumination and temperature distribution on concentrating solar cell—A review. *Energy* **2018**, *144*, 1119–1136. [CrossRef]
30. Guerriero, P.; Tricoli, P.; Daliento, S. A bypass circuit for avoiding the hot spot in PV modules. *Sol. Energy* **2019**, *181*, 430–438. [CrossRef]
31. Ustaoglu, A.; Kandilli, C.; Cakmak, M.; Torlaklı, H. Experimental and economical performance investigation of V-trough concentrator with different reflectance characteristic in photovoltaic applications. *J. Clean. Prod.* **2020**, *272*, 123072. [CrossRef]
32. Ghodbane, M.; Said, Z.; Amine Hachicha, S.; Boumeddane, B. Performance assessment of linear Fresnel solar reflector using MWCNTs/DW nanofluids. *Renew. Energy* **2020**, *151*, 43–56. [CrossRef]
33. Barbón, A.; Barbón, N.; Bayón, L.; Sánchez-Rodríguez, J.A. Parametric study of the small-scale linear Fresnel reflector. *Renew. Energy* **2018**, *116*, 64–74. [CrossRef]
34. Duffie, J.A.; Beckman, W.A. *Solar Engineering of Thermal Processes*; John Wiley & Sons: Hoboken, NJ, USA, 2013.
35. Zhu, Y.; Shi, J.; Li, Y.; Wang, L.; Huang, Q.; Xu, G. Design and thermal performances of a scalable linear Fresnel reflector solar system. *Energy Convers. Manag.* **2017**, *146*, 174–181. [CrossRef]
36. Zhu, Y.; Shi, J.; Li, Y.; Wang, L.; Huang, Q.; Xu, G. Design and experimental investigation of a stretched parabolic linear Fresnel reflector collecting system. *Energy Convers. Manag.* **2016**, *126*, 89–98. [CrossRef]
37. Shoeibi, H.; Jarrahian, A.; Mehrpooya, M.; Assaerh, E.; Izadi, M.; Pourfayaz, F. Mathematical modeling and simulation of a compound parabolic concentrators collector with an absorber tube. *Energies* **2023**, *16*, 287. [CrossRef]
38. Jaaz, A.H.; Abdulrasool Hasan, H.; Sopian, K.; Haji Ruslan, M.H.B.; Hussain Zaidi, S. Design and development of compound parabolic concentrating for photovoltaic solar collector: Review. *Renew. Sustain. Energy Rev.* **2017**, *76*, 1108–1121. [CrossRef]

39. Tina, G.M.; Scandura, P.F. Case study of a grid connected with a battery photovoltaic system: V-trough concentration vs. single-axis tracking. *Energy Convers. Manag.* **2012**, *64*, 569–578. [CrossRef]
40. Hadavinia, H.; Harjit, S. Modelling and experimental analysis of low concentrating solar panels for use in building integrated and applied photovoltaic (BIPV/BAPV) systems. *Renew. Energy* **2019**, *139*, 815–829. [CrossRef]
41. Madala, S.; Boehm, R.F. A review of nonimaging solar concentrators for stationary and passive tracking applications. *Renew. Sustain. Energy Rev.* **2017**, *71*, 309–322. [CrossRef]
42. Oprea, R.; Istrate, M.; Machidon, D. Analysis of V-trough reflector's geometry influence on low concentration photovoltaic systems. In Proceedings of the 8th International Conference on Modern Power Systems, Cluj-Napoca, Romania, 21–23 May 2019.
43. Tang, R.; Liu, X. Optical performance and design optimization of V-trough concentrators for photovoltaic applications. *Sol. Energy* **2011**, *85*, 2154–2166. [CrossRef]
44. Fernández-Rubiera, J.A.; Barbón, A.; Bayón, L.; Díaz, G.; Bayón-Cueli, C. Low concentration photovoltaic systems based on small-scale linear Fresnel reflectors: Development of a new sawtooth V-trough concentrator. In Proceedings of the IEEE International Conference on Environmental and Electrical Engineering (EEEIC2022), Prague, Czech Republic, 8 June–1 July 2022; pp. 1–6.
45. Barbón, A.; Barbón, N.; Bayón, L.; Sánchez-Rodríguez, J.A. Optimization of the distribution of small scale linear Fresnel reflectors on roofs of urban buildings. *Appl. Math. Model.* **2018**, *59*, 233–250. [CrossRef]
46. Mishra, P.; Pandey, M.; Tamaura, Y.; Tiwari, S. Numerical analysis of cavity receiver with parallel tubes for cross-linear concentrated solar system. *Energy* **2021**, *220*, 119609. [CrossRef]
47. Gong, J.H.; Wang, J.; Lund, P.D.; Zhao, D.D.; Hu, E.Y. Improving the performance of large-aperture parabolic trough solar concentrator using semi-circular absorber tube with external fin and flat-plate radiation shield. *Renew. Energy* **2022**, *159*, 1215–1223. [CrossRef]
48. Xu, J.; Chen, F.; Deng, C. Design and analysis of a novel multi-sectioned compound parabolic concentrator with multi-objective genetic algorithm. *Energy* **2021**, *225*, 120216. [CrossRef]
49. Tan, L.J.; Zhu, W.; Zhou, K. Recent progress on polymer materials for additive manufacturing. *Adv. Funct. Mater.* **2020**, *30*, 2003062. [CrossRef]
50. Chen, F.; Liu, Y. Model construction and performance investigation of multi-section compound parabolic concentrator with solar vacuum tube. *Energy* **2022**, *250*, 123887. [CrossRef]
51. Sharma, V.M.; Nayak, J.K.; Kedare, S.B. Effects of shading and blocking in linear Fresnel reflector field. *Sol. Energy* **2015**, *113*, 114–138. [CrossRef]
52. Theunissen, P.H.; Beckman, W.A. Solar transmittance characteristics of evacuated tubular collectors with diffuse back reflectors. *Sol. Energy* **1985**, *35*, 311–320. [CrossRef]
53. Barbón, A.; Fortuny Ayuso, P.; Bayón, L.; Fernández-Rubiera, J.A. Predicting beam and diffuse horizontal irradiance using Fourier expansions. *Renew. Energy* **2020**, *154*, 46–57. [CrossRef]
54. PVGIS. Joint Research Centre (JRC). Available online: http://re.jrc.ec.europa.eu/pvg_tools/en/tools.html#PVP (accessed on 11 June 2023).
55. ESTIF. *Spanish Technical Building Code Royal Decree 314/2006, 17 March 2006*; European Solar Thermal Industry Federation (ESTIF): Brussels, Belgium, 2006.
56. Aly, S.P.; Ahzi, S.; Barth, N.; Abdallah, A. Using energy balance method to study the thermal behavior of PV panels under time-varying field conditions. *Energy Convers. Manag.* **2018**, *175*, 246–262. [CrossRef]
57. Cengel, Y.A. *Heat Transfer and Mass Transfer: A Practical Approach*, 3rd ed.; McGraw Hill Book Company: New York, NY, USA, 2006.
58. Evans, D.L. Simplified method for predicting photovoltaic array output. *Sol. Energy* **1981**, *27*, 555–560. [CrossRef]

Disclaimer/Publisher's Note: The statements, opinions and data contained in all publications are solely those of the individual author(s) and contributor(s) and not of MDPI and/or the editor(s). MDPI and/or the editor(s) disclaim responsibility for any injury to people or property resulting from any ideas, methods, instructions or products referred to in the content.

Article

Energy Efficient Enhancement in a 5.8 GHz Batteryless Node Suitable for Backscattering Communications

Giovanni Collodi *, Monica Righini, Marco Passafiume and Alessandro Cidronali

Department of Information Engineering, University of Florence, V. S. Marta, 3, 50139 Florence, Italy; monica.righini@unifi.it (M.R.); marco.passafiume@unifi.it (M.P.); alessandro.cidronali@unifi.it (A.C.)
* Correspondence: giovanni.collodi@unifi.it

Abstract: This work presents a compact batteryless node architecture suitable with the backscattering communication (BackCom) approach. The key functional blocks are demonstrated at 5.8 GHz, making use of commercially available components involving a DC/DC step-up converter, a 3.3 V data generator, and an ASK backscattering modulator based on a single GaAs HEMT in a cold-FET configuration. The node integrates a patch antenna exhibiting a non-50 Ω optimal port impedance; the value is defined by means of a source pull-based optimization technique aimed at maximizing the DC/DC input current supplied by the RF to DC converter. This approach maximizes the node compactness, as well as the wireless power conversion efficiency. A prototype was optimized for the −5 dBm power level at the input of the RF to DC converter. Under this measurement condition, the experimental results showed a 63% increase in the harvesting current, rising from 145 to 237 µA, compared to an identical configuration that used a microstrip matching network coupled with a typical 50-Ω patch antenna. In terms of harvested power, the achieved improvement was from −13.2 dBm to −10.9 dBm. The conversion efficiency in an operative condition improved from 15% to more than 25%. In this condition, the node is capable of charging a 100 µF to the operative voltage in about 27 s, and operating the backscattering for 360 ms with a backscattering modulation frequency of about 10 MHz.

Keywords: Internet of Things; backscattering communications; energy harvesting; microwave electronics

Citation: Collodi, G.; Righini, M.; Passafiume, M.; Cidronali, A. Energy Efficient Enhancement in a 5.8 GHz Batteryless Node Suitable for Backscattering Communications. *Electronics* **2023**, *12*, 2256. https://doi.org/10.3390/electronics12102256

Academic Editors: Shailendra Rajput, Moshe Averbukh and Noel Rodriguez

Received: 11 April 2023
Revised: 11 May 2023
Accepted: 13 May 2023
Published: 16 May 2023

Copyright: © 2023 by the authors. Licensee MDPI, Basel, Switzerland. This article is an open access article distributed under the terms and conditions of the Creative Commons Attribution (CC BY) license (https://creativecommons.org/licenses/by/4.0/).

1. Introduction

In recent years, there has been a growing interest in exploiting the Internet of Things (IoT) paradigms in many contexts, such as the control of processes in assisted ambient intelligent [1], industrial environments [2], and environmental quality [3]. A major factor that has fostered the development of IoT on a large scale is the projected growth in distributed communications and computing technologies [4,5]. The application of these technologies has led to IoT technologies fulfilling some key requirements, including low energy consumption [6–8] and, possibly, the development of hardware nodes that feature small batteries (or that even operate without batteries). As a consequence, a number of approaches aimed at overcoming this problem were envisioned in the last few years, including technical solutions such as the concepts of energy harvesting (EH) and wireless power transfer (WPT) [9]. These are complemented by new technical concepts aimed at sustaining the coexistence of a large number of wireless devices for IoT applications (with the drawback of reduced battery life). In order to overcome (or at least minimize) these limitations, one of the most promising solutions is the so-called backscattering communication (BackCom) technique [10–12]. This approach is based on the controlled reflection of the electromagnetic wave that incorporates the data to be forwarded to the receiving node. It can be easily demonstrated that not having any carrier source on board to reflect the IoT node allows for transmitting forward data while minimizing energy consumption. Furthermore, in the BackCom vision, communication is obtained by avoiding the implementation of most of the functional blocks in the transmitting/receiving chain (i.e., oscillators, mixers), reducing device complexity, and decreasing production costs [13,14]. Additionally, such node architectures usually involve EH and/or WPT to fully overcome the energy constraints and extend the battery life, as illustrated in [15–17].

A primitive example of BackCom design principles can be observed in the use of radio-frequency identification (RFID) technology [18] in vehicular communications. Nonetheless, the expected performance associated with a batteryless BackCom-based IoT node requires communication capabilities and ranges that surpass those of a typical RFID device scenario. Following this, the final step in improving the feasibility of IoT paradigms, with respect to power limitations, is the development of fully batteryless BackCom nodes that implement specific solutions supporting both burst and low-rate operations [19].

In this paper, the authors demonstrate the feasibility of a simple yet fully compliant batteryless BackCom node system that is compatible with the implementation of IoT network architectures. The node has been demonstrated at 5.8 GHz, making use of component-off-the-shelf (COTS) devices. The latter includes a harvester block that is based on a rectifier driving a DC/DC boost, as well as a modulator block, which is controlled by a microcontroller included in the node's prototype. Moreover, the proposed BackCom node system integrates a patch antenna, showing a non-50-Ω optimal port impedance. The proposed node system architecture, illustrated in Figure 1, was developed by following an approach that is fully compatible with frequency scalability and with an integrated design based on the standard IC process.

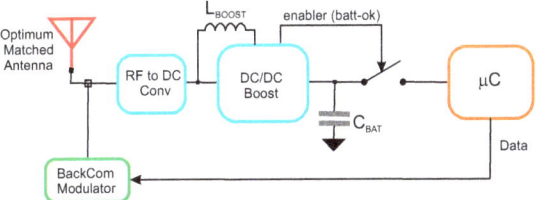

Figure 1. Architecture of the considered IoT BackCom batteryless node. The C_{BAT} capacitor and the inductance L_{BOOST} assume values of 100 µF and 22 nH, respectively.

The paper, in addition to the introduction, is organized into three further sections. The next section is dedicated to the description of the proposed node architecture, including the harvester, the modulator, and the antenna. The third section presents a discussion of the prototype's system-level architecture, while the fourth section describes the performance; the final section presents the conclusive discussion.

2. The BackCom Node Key's Functional Blocks

The batteryless node architecture was designed to be compliant with the operation principle of the BackCom approach, and consists of the following three functional blocks: the harvester, the modulator, and the antenna (Figure 1).

The operational sequence of the proposed node can be summarized as follows:

- Firstly, the base station queries the node and supplies it with a continuous wave RF signal at 5.8 GHz;
- Secondly, the RF to DC converter and the DC/DC boost harvest the received RF energy and charge the C_{BAT};
- Thirdly, when C_{BAT} reaches the desired level, V_{BAT}, the harvester enables the microcontroller, which controls the backscattering modulator through a GPIO pin;
- Finally, under the control of the microcontroller, the modulator backscatters the RF continuous signal by transmitting the data.

A key feature of the proposed architecture consists of the antenna, which exhibits an internal impedance capable of optimizing the RF to DC energy conversion by maximizing the current provided to the DC–DC converter; the impedance of the antenna is estimated using a source pull-based technique. This in turn maximizes the wireless power conversion efficiency of the harvester block [20,21], and permits the inclusion of commercial DC–DC converters.

From an operational point of view, the architecture increases the operational time window suitable for backscattering communication, minimizing the energy harvesting time.

The following subsections illustrate the characteristics of the aforementioned functional blocks.

2.1. RF Energy Harvester

The RF energy harvester block was developed following the approach introduced in [20], and widely discussed and exploited in [21]. The latter makes use of an RF to DC converter based on a voltage multiplier, working on a specific input impedance aimed at maximizing the performance, as well as a commercial nanopower DC/DC boost [22]. Since the harvesting interval sets a lower limit on the querying time, the harvester has to exhibit maximum conversion efficiency during this interval. Based on the previously proposed solution, this objective is obtained by terminating the RF to DC converter with an optimum input impedance. Following [21], the latter consists of the impedance that maximizes the I_{CHG} (Figure 1), with respect to the RF input power at the RF to DC converter. To optimize performance for low impinging power, the RF input reference level at the RF to DC converter was set to -5 dBm. Taking into account this power level, and due to the inherently non-linear behavior of the RF to DC converter, a source pull-based optimization was carried out to identify the optimum impedance that the antenna should exhibit to the RF to DC converter. This was obtained by varying Z_{RF}, which is the impedance shown by the equivalent RF source, V_{RF}, at the RF to DC converter, as illustrated in Figure 2. In this work, the RF to DC converter was implemented by a diode-based voltage tripler configuration.

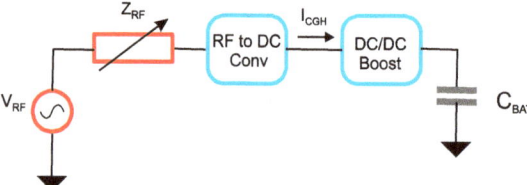

Figure 2. Conceptualization of the source impedance optimization by the source pull-based technique.

Regarding the DC/DC boost, the input port can be described by a behavioral model based on an ideal diode with a threshold voltage V_{TH}. On this basis, the charging current is

$$I_{CHG} = \begin{cases} \dfrac{V_{RFDC} - V_{TH}}{R_{RFDC}} & \text{when } V_{RFDC} > V_{TH} \\ 0 & \text{otherwise} \end{cases} \quad (1)$$

where V_{TH} is 0.34 V, in accordance with the experimental results [20], and on the base of manufacturer specifications [22]. Parameters V_{RFDC} and R_{RFDC} represent, respectively, the output voltage and the output impedance shown by the RF to DC rectifier toward the DC/DC step-up converter.

The value of the optimum impedance Z_{RFopt} is calculated using the previously described approach by using a source pull-based procedure on a commercial CAD for the high-frequency circuit analysis. This technique consists of running a non-linear analysis at 5.8 GHz with a reference input power of -5 dBm, spanning the source impedance across the entire Smith chart; the target is the impedance Z_{RF} that maximizes I_{CHG}. In this work, we adopted the zero bias SMS7630-061 Schottky diode in a voltage tripler configuration on silicon; as a result of the source pull-based procedure, the value $Z_{RF} = Z_{RFopt} = 19.8 - j83.7\,\Omega$ represents the optimum source impedance. As a consequence, Z_{RFopt} is the impedance to which the harvester input should be terminated during the charging interval; this allows for maximizing the performance and minimizing the latency time between the start of the query and the response of the node.

In the present architecture, in order to reduce losses and maximize the compactness of the node, the impedance matching of the voltage tripler is obtained following the approach described in [23]. However, in a BackCom node architecture (Figure 1), the presence of the modulator block cannot be neglected in the harvesting phase (modulator in high impedance state). As a consequence, the identified optimum matching impedance Z_{RFopt} differs from the design impedance that is exhibited by the antenna Z_{RFeff}. The effect of the modulator can be considered by modeling it as a microstrip line with a characteristic impedance Z_T and a length W_T, as illustrated in Figure 3.

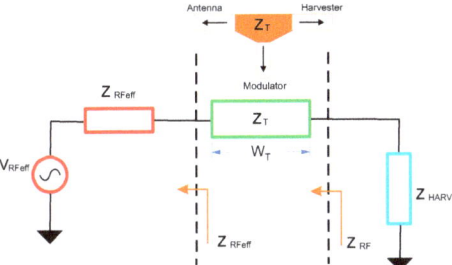

Figure 3. The modeling of a high impedance state modulator for evaluating Z_{RFeff}.

The values of both Z_T and W_T were calculated, starting from the dimensions of the modulator interconnection (the proposed modulator based on a cold-FET configuration, as explained in the specific subsection) between the antenna and the tripler. It is assumed that the modulator exhibits a high impedance at this junction during the harvesting; thus, the Z_{RFeff} can be simply evaluated on the basis of the well-known transmission line equation and the Z_T and W_T values.

$$Z_{RFeff} = \frac{Z_{RFopt} + jZ_T \tan\left(\frac{2\pi}{\lambda_{RF}} W_T\right)}{Z_T + jZ_{RFopt} \tan\left(\frac{2\pi}{\lambda_{RF}} W_T\right)}. \quad (2)$$

2.2. Modulator

The architecture proposed in this paper for implementing the BackCom node utilizes backscattering modulation, which is a well-known approach for low-power communication [24]. Basically, the backscatterer reflects the impinging radio signal while superimposing a modulation; this feature is obtained by varying the reflection coefficient seen by the antenna. In some approaches, the BackCom node may differentiate the energy and communication paths. This technique simplifies the design of the communication chain by implementing one or two antennas or even two different frequencies. On the contrary, the batteryless BackCom node proposed in the present paper follows a single-path approach for both harvesting and communication. As a consequence, the design procedure has to take into account the use of a single antenna for both harvesting and backscattering.

This approach improves the compactness of the system but it introduces some critical issues in the design process. In particular, the modulator stage has to fulfill two different requirements that are not easily achievable simultaneously. Firstly, the modulator has to satisfy the required modulation parameters; in addition, it has to introduce the minimum effects on power delivery during the harvesting phase.

The topology of the implemented modulator is illustrated in Figure 4. It consists of a cold-FET that is driven by the data output of the microcontroller. The microcontroller was chosen to ensure a significant differentiation between the OFF and ON states of the switch at the operative frequency, regardless of other considerations, such as the settling time of the switch. In addition, because the modulator needs to be carefully designed to ensure proper impedance (Z_{MOD} in Figure 5), an accurate model of the device is necessary (which is typically not available at this frequency in other technologies such as CMOS). The cold-FET is connected to the antenna and the harvester by means of a microstrip line, whose length l and width w must be chosen to fulfill the conditions described in (3)

$$|Z_{MOD}| \gg max(|Z_{RF}|, |Z_{HARV}|). \qquad (3)$$

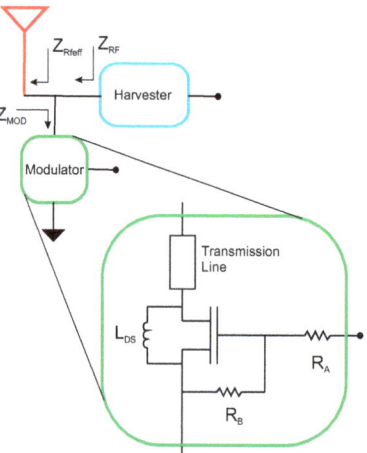

Figure 4. Modulator block for the backscattering mode of the BackCom node.

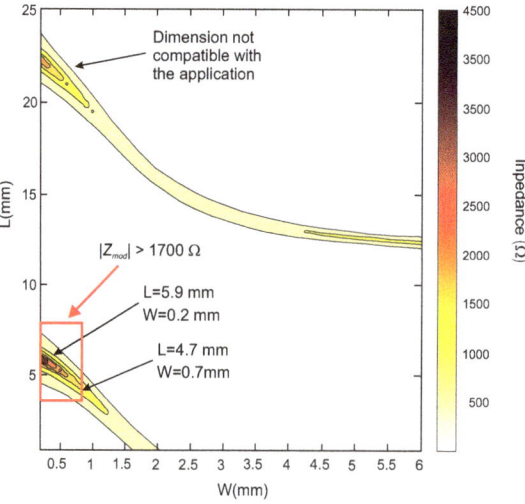

Figure 5. Modulator impedance $|Z_{MOD}|$ with respect to the feeding line dimensions.

In our design, $|Z_{RF}|$ = 1700 Ω, while $|Z_{HARV}|$ = 31.27 Ω. Condition (3) ensures that during the harvesting interval, when the modulator is in a high impedance state, the input power is transferred to the harvester stage, minimizing any losses [21].

The length l and width w of the microstrip feeding line of the backscattering modulator were chosen after simulating modulator impedance in a high impedance state; the results are depicted in Figure 5.

The dimensions of the modulator feeding line fulfill the conditions of the maximum power transfer given by (3) and maximum compactness. Specifically, the resulting optimal values are $l = 4.7$ mm and $w = 0.7$ mm. These values lead to $W_T = 2.15$ mm and $Z_T = 75\ \Omega$; thus, according to (2), the value of the optimum antenna impedance is $Z_{RFeff} = 44.6 - j164.9\ \Omega$.

As detailed in [21], the expected ASK modulation depth for a two-symbol modulation is defined as

$$m_{ASK} = \frac{||A_1| - |A_0||}{\max(|A_1|, |A_0|)} \tag{4}$$

where each A_i is the simulated reflection coefficient at the antenna port related to the i-th symbol state of the modulator. Through simulations, using the optimal dimensioning of the modulator feed line, the reflection coefficient results, respectively, in $mag(A_0) = 0.352$, $phase(A_0) = 213$ degrees for A_0, $mag(A_1) = 0.968$, and $phase(A_1) = 347$ degrees for A_1, as illustrated in Figure 6, where the two symbols are depicted in the Smith chart. Moreover, from Equation (4), the expected value of the modulation depth is $m_{ASK} = 0.60$.

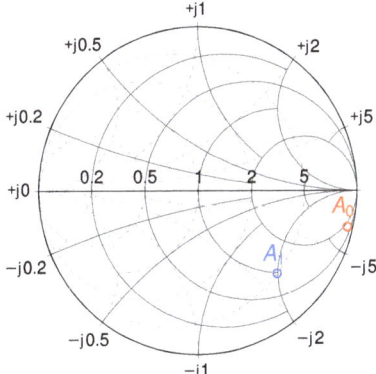

Figure 6. Representation of the A_0 and A_1 symbols on the Smith chart.

2.3. Antenna

The antenna was designed to satisfy the impedance requirements in terms of Z_{RFeff} and it shows a high level of compactness. The antenna topology is based on a single patch antenna printed on the same substrate of the cold-FET backscattering modulator and the three-stage RF–DC converter, namely the Isola FR408 ($\epsilon_r = 3.67$, $\tan \delta = 0.012$). The antenna was designed at 5.8 GHz in order to show an input impedance of $Z_{RFeff} = 44.6 - j164.9\ \Omega$. This non-canonical input impedance value was obtained by using a couple of patches etched on the same plane of the patch itself. Their presence adds an additional degree of freedom in the antenna design, which allows for achieving the desired input impedance. The antenna was simulated with a commercial full-wave electromagnetic simulator. The resulting antenna layout, which is inspired by the one proposed in [25], is shown in Figure 7, where the main dimensional parameters are also illustrated.

The proposed design shows an antenna gain of about 6 dBi as well as an antenna efficiency of about 71.4%. The simulated antenna reflection coefficient is illustrated in Figure 8 in a band of about 1.6 GHz and is centered on 5.8 GHz. The S_{11} parameter is evaluated with respect to the usual normalization impedance $Z_0 = 50\ \Omega$ and the optimum impedance $Z'_0 = 44 - j164.9\ \Omega$. The circle in the graph represents the different normalization impedance values of S_{11} @ 5.8 GHz. The Smith chart confirms that the concept of optimum matching for this application is completely different from the usual matching approach.

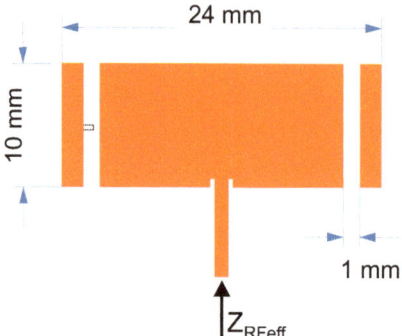

Figure 7. The main dimensions of the antenna for achieving the optimum impedance.

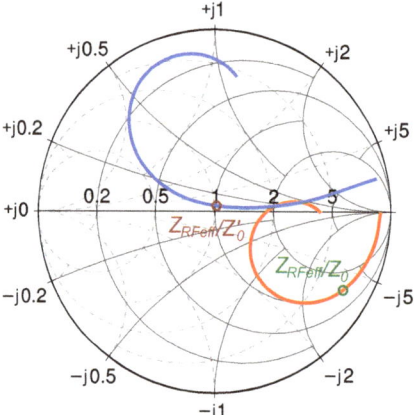

Figure 8. The S_{11} parameter normalized, respectively, to $Z_0 = 50\ \Omega$ (orange) and $Z'_0 = 44 - j164.9\ \Omega$ (blue).

3. The BackCom Node Prototype

The prototype was implemented by making use of two different boards. The first one integrates the optimum matched antenna, the modulator, and the RF to DC converter, while the second board includes the DC–DC boost device, the control electronics, and the data generator. This approach simplifies the development of prototypes as well as the testing phase, allowing for full control over all critical blocks and enabling the measurement of key parameters. The two boards were implemented on the Isola FR408 laminate and the prototypes are illustrated in Figure 9.

The modulator is based on an ATF58143 pseudomorphic HEMT in a cold-FET configuration; the voltage tripler (RF to DC converter) employs three silicon, zero bias SMS7630-061 Schottky detector diodes; the DC–DC boost is based on the commercial BQ25570 [22]. Furthermore, concerning the critical components of the DC/DC converter illustrated in Figure 1, L_{BOOST} and C_{BAT} are the values of 22 µH and 100 µF. The data generator is based on an EEPROM, Atmel AT17LV512A 3.3 V 256 kbit on a PDIP package [26], which emulates the controller block.

Figure 9. BackCom node composed of two boards.

4. The BackCom Node Prototype's Experimental Results

In order to assess the performance of the proposed batteryless BackCom node architecture as a whole, a specific measurement setup was implemented. In particular, it was conceived to investigate the backscattering communication behavior and the performance of the harvester in different conditions.

The measurement setup schematic is illustrated in Figure 10, and consists of a radio link with the node under test from one side and a TX/RX system from the other side. The node, being implemented in the split form illustrated in Section 3, simplifies the testing procedure. Such a configuration allows for accessing the terminal between the RF to DC converter and the DC/DC boost, enabling the measurement of the I_{CHG}, as well as the data line monitoring. On the contrary, the TX/RX system makes use of an RF power generator and a power amplifier in the transmitter path, while the receiver is implemented by means of a spectrum analyzer. The two paths are connected to a single antenna array through a circulator.

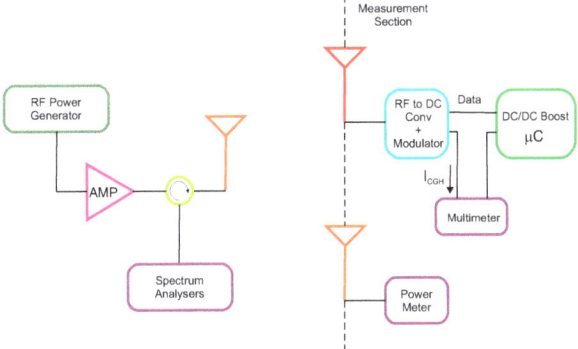

Figure 10. Measurement setup block diagram.

The previously described setup includes a reference antenna on the same BackCom node measurement section. The latter is connected to a power meter in order to evaluate, at the reference section, the effective impinging power. Based on this setup, the BackCom node behavior was characterized. The implemented measurement setup is illustrated in Figure 11

The distance between the reader TX/RX antenna and the node was fixed at 1.8 m in the setup; in addition, the main dimension of such an antenna resulted in 0.25 m, with an EIRP = 37 dB, while the antenna that was integrated in the node showed a gain of about 6 dBi. Therefore, in accordance with the operative data, the limits for the far-field and the near-field are $d > \frac{2D^2}{\lambda} = 2.20$ m (far-field limit) and $d < 0.62\sqrt{\frac{D^3}{\lambda}} = 0.45$ m (near-field limit). Consequently, the system was not tested in either far-field or near-field conditions. The system was characterized in an anechoic setup to take advantage of the absorbing behaviors of the absorbers. Our objective was to obtain reliable data from the characterization by isolating the setup as much as possible from unpredictable environmental contributions, rather than eliminating all of the possible multipath contributions. The data features confirmed the reliability of the measurement setup.

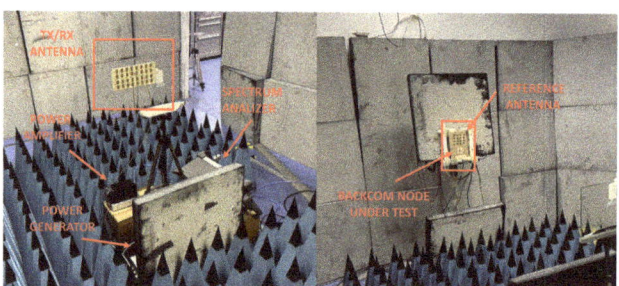

Figure 11. Measurement setup for the characterization of the BackCom node.

The first set of tests was aimed at verifying the effective improvement of the harvesting performance of the node. The results are illustrated in Figures 12 and 13. The measurements confirm that the node was effectively designed to simultaneously follow the approach of the optimum matched antenna and the minimization of the modulator effect during the harvesting phase (3).

Figure 12 compares the I_{CHG} of the proposed architecture with respect to the one exhibited by a standard configuration, using a matching network to implement the optimum impedance. The latter does not include the modulator block. I_{CHG} was evaluated in both configurations, considering the same RF power at the RF to DC converter input by means of the power meter connected to the reference antenna, and taking into account the optimum antenna gain. The architecture proposed in the present paper has demonstrated an overall improvement in I_{CHG} at every input power level. In particular, at the design reference, the RF power is about −5 dBm (at the input of the RF to DC converter section), and the measured current is 237 µA for the node and 145 µA for the standard structure with an improvement of about 92 µA.

Figure 13 illustrates the efficiency of the same two configurations. The measurements confirm that the harvesting efficiency of the BackCom node is improved compared to the standard configuration across the entire range of input power levels. Here, the efficiency is calculated as the ratio of the power supplied to the DC/DC with respect to the impinging power at the input of the RF to DC P_{RFDC} converter, as described in

$$Eff = \frac{I_{CHG} V_{TH}}{P_{RFDC}} \quad (5)$$

Moreover, the above-mentioned figure also shows the incremental efficiency (Δ_{Eff}), which was calculated as the difference between the two cases at each power level.

With reference to (5), at −5 dBm of the RF input power (the design reference level), the node shows an efficiency of about 25.5%, while the standard configuration is at about 16%. This leads to an increased harvester efficiency of about 10.5%, which translates to a reduction of the charging time for a given storage capacitor.

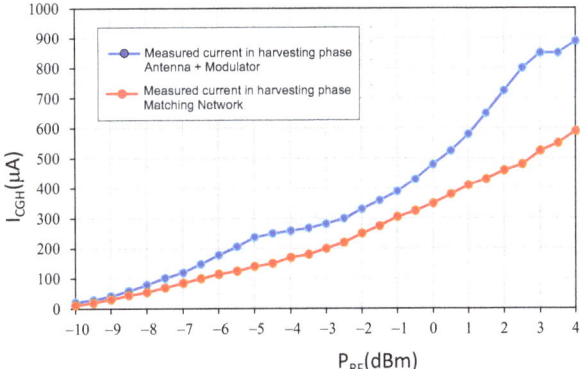

Figure 12. Measured current in harvesting the interval for the actual configuration (without a matching network) and with a matching network.

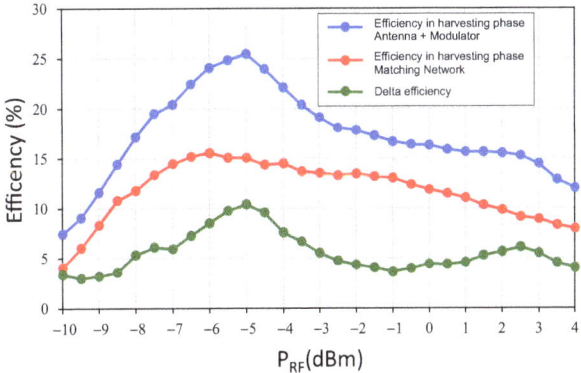

Figure 13. Efficiency in harvesting the interval for the actual configuration (without a matching network) and with a matching network.

The same measurement setup was used to evaluate the harvesting performance of the node during the backscattering condition. Figure 14 illustrates the behavior of the charge current in querying and backscattering state. This result confirms, as expected, the reduced harvesting performance during the communication period. At the input power RF reference level (−5 dBm), I_{CHG} in the backscattering state assumes a value of about 137 µA. This value is 99 µA lower than the harvesting state, which measures 237 µA. These measures show how the node maintains a harvesting performance similar to the one shown by the standard configuration implementing the matching network (during the backscattering communication). The ability of the node to harvest energy during the backscattering state is confirmed by Figure 15, which compares the efficiencies of the two functional states and highlights the delta between them.

Figure 16 confirms that the comparison between I_{CHG} (supplied by the node in the backscattering state) and the corresponding value in the standard configuration (implementing the matching network in the harvesting state) are very similar across all input power levels. This behavior contributes significantly to delaying the discharge of C_{BAT} and, as a consequence, increases the time slot for communication.

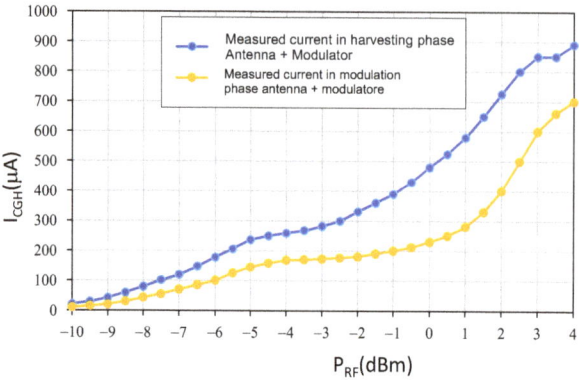

Figure 14. Measured currents in the harvesting state and backscattering state, with a modulating square wave at 10 MHz.

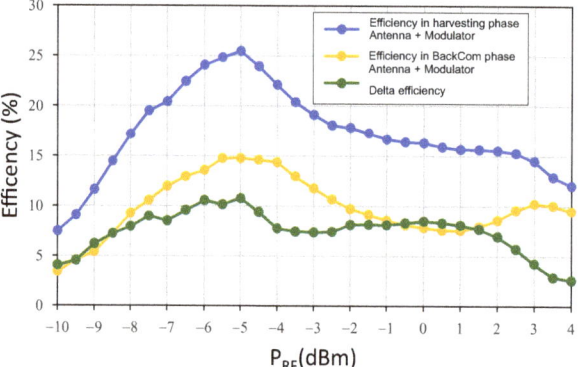

Figure 15. Efficiencies in the harvesting state and backscattering state.

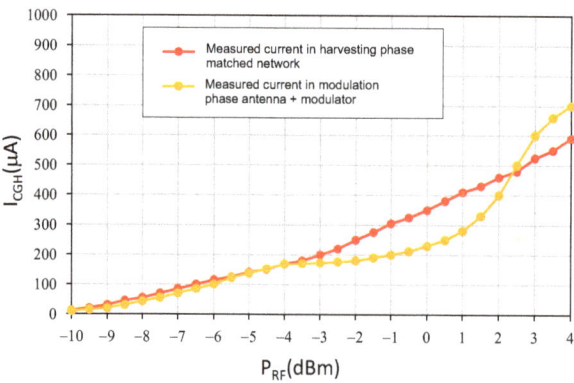

Figure 16. Measured current in the harvesting state with the matched network and in the harvesting state.

A state-of-the-art analysis was carried out in order to compare the harvesting performance shown by the proposed architecture in comparison with other approaches; the results are summarized in Table 1. The harvester performances of the architecture proposed in the present work were evaluated with respect to two solutions proposed by the same authors, operating at 5.8 GHz, as well as four solutions proposed by different authors, three of which work at 5.8 GHz and one at 2.45 GHz. In References [21,27], the performances are evaluated under operating conditions when the system is connected to the BQ25570. The first makes use of a matching network that introduces losses and shows (at −5 dBm) an efficiency of about 16%, while the second adopts a matching network optimized for multi-sine excitation; it shows performance improvements of up to 27% at −5 dBm. The latter shows better performances with respect to the present work but it is not fully compatible with the BackCom approach; it is more oriented to pure harvesting solutions. With respect to the solutions described in [28–30], they operate at 5.8 GHz, while the solution described in [31] operates at 2.45 GHz.

The first shows an efficiency of about 22 % at −5 dBm, the second demonstrates an efficiency of about 15% at −10 dBm, and the third exhibits an efficiency of about 55% at −5 dBm. The fourth, which works at 2.45 GHz, shows an efficiency of about 35% at −10 dBm. Some of these solutions show better efficiencies compared to the present work. The main drawback consists is that they were not evaluated in operational conditions but rather with optimal loads of high value (k Ω order of magnitude). As a consequence, considering the system-level operative conditions, the approach proposed in the present work performed better compared to all other state-of-the-art architectures.

Table 1. Harvesting performance comparison of the system working @ 5.8 GHz.

Reference	Reference Power (dBm)	Eff. (%)	Freq. (GHz)	Load/Condition
[21]	−5	16	5.8	BQ25570 operative condition
[28]	−5	22	5.8	3 kΩ
[31]	−10	35	2.45	5 kΩ
[27]	−5	27	5.8	BQ25570 operative condition
[29]	−10	15	5.8	10 kΩ
[30]	−5	51	5.8	9 kΩ
This work	−5	25.5	5.8	BQ25570 operative condition

The system ability of the proposed architecture to implement an ASK backscattering communication was evaluated by driving the proposed cold-FET modulator by means of a 10 MHz square wave (i.e., a periodic sequence of bit 0 and bit 1), which was generated by the EEPROM, which emulates the controller block. Such a modulating signal provides a reference benchmark for testing the harvesting efficiency in the backscattering phase due to its inherently fixed frequency rate. The setup that was implemented to detect the spectrum of the backscattered signal modulated by the square wave refers to the block diagram, as illustrated in Figure 10.

The results are illustrated in Figure 17, showing the spectrum of the backscattered signal modulated by the square wave. The figure illustrates the signal spectrum across the carrier, where the fundamental, as well as the third harmonic of the modulating signal, are recognizable. The EEPROM, emulating the controller block, is active for the C_{BAT} discharging time interval (i.e., ΔT_{ON}, as stated in [21]) for a maximum of 360 ms, which is independent from the impinging power. On the contrary, the C_{BAT} charge time interval depends directly on the latter. For a power level of about −5 dBm at the input of the RF to DC converter, measurements show a charging time of 27 s. However, the C_{BAT} discharge is a slightly critical phase for the modulation. As a matter of fact, the decrease in V_{BAT} affects the performance of the EEPROM, which in the final part of ΔT_{ON} generates a square wave with a frequency that is below the canonical 10 MHz. As a consequence, both the spectrum of the first and third harmonics show a slight widening.

Based on the previously described backscattering experiment with a modulating square wave signal of 10 MHz, it is possible to argue that this value can be assumed as the maximum data rate. The conversion gain of the node in the backscattering mode was estimated to be 2.7 dB; this enables a typical operative range of 1 m, depending on the reader's EIRP and sensitivity. Regarding power consumption, it is not considered a relevant figure in this context since the component is batteryless.

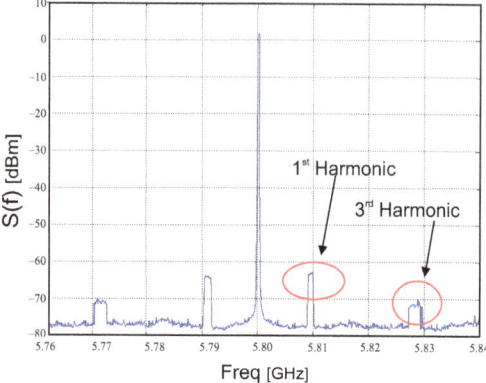

Figure 17. Measured spectrum of the backscattered signal modulated by a 10 MHz square wave.

Consequently, the measured results and analysis conducted in the proposed critical functional block assessment in this paper demonstrate the feasibility of a batteryless BackCom node, as postulated in [32].

5. Conclusions

In this paper, we demonstrated the feature of the key functional blocks for a BackCom node, enabling an integrated architecture for a totally batteryless BackCom node. In particular, the coexistence of a highly efficient harvester configuration, a cold-FET-based modulator, and an antenna designed to exhibit the optimum impedance for maximum charging performances was fully demonstrated. The inclusion of such an antenna leads to an improvement of 63% in the harvesting current, increasing the value from 145 µA to 237 µA, with respect to the identical configuration involving a microstrip-matching network coupled with a typical 50-Ω patch antenna. The conversion efficiency in operative conditions demonstrates an improvement from 15% to 25.5%. Moreover, the effectiveness of the ASK modulation was demonstrated. In summary, the performance comparison of the system proposed in this paper, with respect to comparable technologies, shows that this node system exhibits the best efficiency in operative conditions.

Author Contributions: Conceptualization, A.C. and G.C.; methodology, G.C. and M.P.; data curation, M.R.; validation, G.C.; formal analysis, M.P. and A.C.; investigation, A.C.; resources, G.C. and A.C.; writing—original draft preparation, G.C.; writing—review and editing, A.C.; visualization, G.C. and M.R.; supervision, A.C.; project administration, A.C.; funding acquisition, G.C. All authors have read and agreed to the published version of the manuscript.

Funding: This research received no external funding.

Institutional Review Board Statement: Not applicable.

Informed Consent Statement: Not applicable.

Data Availability Statement: Not applicable.

Conflicts of Interest: The authors declare no conflict of interest.

References

1. Mishu, M.K.; Rokonuzzaman, M.; Pasupuleti, J.; Shakeri, M.; Rahman, K.S.; Hamid, F.A.; Tiong, S.K.; Amin, N. Prospective Efficient Ambient Energy Harvesting Sources for IoT-Equipped Sensor Applications. *Electronics* **2020**, *9*, 1345 [CrossRef]
2. Tubis, A.A.; Rohman, J. Intelligent Warehouse in Industry 4.0—Systematic Literature Review. *Sensors* **2023**, *23*, 4105. [CrossRef]

3. De Capua, C.; Fulco, G.; Lugarà, M.; Ruffa, F. An Improvement Strategy for Indoor Air Quality Monitoring Systems. *Sensors* **2023**, *23*, 3999. [CrossRef]
4. Chen, W.; Zhang, Z.; Hong, Z.; Chen, C.; Wu, J.; Maharjan, S.; Zheng, Z.; Zhang, Y. Cooperative and distributed computation offloading for blockchain-empowered industrial Internet of Things. *IEEE Internet Things J.* **2019**, *6*, 8433–8446. [CrossRef]
5. Bartoli, C.; Bonanni, M.; Chiti, F.; Pierucci, L.; Cidronali, A.; Collodi, G.; Maddio, S. Toward the Web of Industrial Things: A Publish-Subscribe Oriented Architecture for Data and Power Management. *Sensors* **2022**, *22*, 4882. [CrossRef]
6. Liu, W.; Huang, K.; Zhou, X.; Durrani, S. Next generation backscatter communication: Systems, techniques, and applications. *EURASIP J. Wirel. Commun. Netw.* **2019**, *2019*, 69. [CrossRef]
7. Khriji, S.; Chéour, R.; Kanoun, O. Dynamic Voltage and Frequency Scaling and Duty-Cycling for Ultra Low-Power Wireless Sensor Nodes. *Electronics* **2022**, *11*, 4071. [CrossRef]
8. Cidronali, A.; Nair, V.; Collodi, G.; Lewis, J.H.; Camprini, M.; Manes, G.; Goronkin, H. MMIC applications of heterostructure interband tunnel devices. *IEEE Trans. Microw. Theory Tech.* **2003**, *51*, 1351–1367. [CrossRef]
9. Torres, R.; Pereira, F.; Correia, R.; Carvalho, N.B. An All-Digital Ambient Backscatter solution powered by Energy Harvesting. In Proceedings of the 2021 IEEE MTT-S International Microwave and RF Conference (IMARC), Kanpur, India, 17–19 December 2021; pp. 1–3.
10. Rezaei, F.; Galappaththige, D.; Tellambura, C.; Herath, S. Coding Techniques for Backscatter Communications—A Contemporary Survey. *IEEE Commun. Surveys Tutor.* **2023**. [CrossRef]
11. Niu, J.P.; Li, G.Y. An Overview on Backscatter Communications. *J. Commun. Inf. Netw.* **2019**, *4*, 1–14. [CrossRef]
12. Wu, W.; Wang, X.; Hawbani, A.; Yuan, L.; Gong, W. A survey on ambient backscatter communications: Principles, systems, applications, and challenges. *Comput. Netw.* **2022**, *216*, 109235. [CrossRef]
13. Memon, M.L.; Saxena, N.; Roy, A.; Shin, D.R. Backscatter Communications: Inception of the Battery-Free Era—A Comprehensive Survey. *Electronics* **2019**, *8*, 129. [CrossRef]
14. Khan, W.U.; Memon, F.H.; Dev, K.; Javed, M.A.; Do, D.T.; Qureshi, N.M.F. Ambient BackCom in beyond 5G NOMA networks: A multi-cell resource allocation framework. *Digit. Commun. Netw.* **2022**, *8*, 1005–1013. [CrossRef]
15. Correia, R.; Carvalho, N.B.; Kawasaki, S. Continuously Power Delivering for Passive Backscatter Wireless Sensor Networks. *IEEE Trans. Microw. Theory Tech.* **2016**, *64*, 3723–3731. [CrossRef]
16. Belo, D.; Correia, R.; Pinho, P.; Carvalho, N.B. Enabling a constant and efficient flow of wireless energy for IoT sensors. In Proceedings of the IEEE MTT-S International Microwave Symposium (IMS), Honolulu, HI, USA, 4–9 June 2017; pp. 1342–1344.
17. Qaragoez, Y.; Pollin, S.; Schreurs, D. FDD for Low Power Backscattering in Batteryless Sensor Nodes. In Proceedings of the 51st European Microwave Conference (EuMC), London, UK, 4–6 April 2022; pp. 753–756.
18. Cidronali, A.; Maddio, S.; Collodi, G.; Manes, G. Design trade-off for a compact 5.8 GHz DSRC transponder front-end. *Microw. Opt. Technol. Lett.* **2015**, *57*, 1187–1191. [CrossRef]
19. Toro, U.S.; Wu, K.; Leung, V.C.M. Backscatter Wireless Communications and Sensing in Green Internet of Things. *IEEE Trans. Green Commun. Netw.* **2022**, *6*, 37–55. [CrossRef]
20. Passafiume, M.; Collodi, G.; Cidronali, A. Optimum Design of Low Energy Harvesting Detector at 5.8 GHz suitable for COTS devices. In Proceedings of the 2019 IEEE International Conference on RFID Technology and Applications (RFID-TA), Pisa, Italy, 25–27 September 2019; pp. 6–10.
21. Passafiume, M.; Collodi, G.; Cidronali, A. Design Principles of Batteryless Transponder for Vehicular DSRC at 5.8 GHz. *IEEE J. Radio Freq. Identif.* **2020**, *4*, 491–505. [CrossRef]
22. Texas Instruments Incorporated. *BQ25570: Nano Power Boost Charger and Buck Converter for Energy Harvester Powered Applications*; Texas Instruments Incorporated: Dallas, TX, USA, 2019.
23. Collodi, G.; Maddio, S.; Pelosi, G. Design of a compact and highly efficient energy harvester system suitable for battery-less low cost on-board unit applications. *Electronics* **2021**, *10*, 3. [CrossRef]
24. Torres, R.; Correia, R.; Carvalho, N.B.; Daskalakis, S.; Goussetis, G.; Ding, Y.; Georgiadis, A.; Eid, A.; Hester, J.; Tentzeris, M.M. Backscatter communications. *IEEE J. Microwaves* **2021**, *1*, 864–878. [CrossRef]
25. Maddio, S.; Pelosi, G.; Righini, M.; Selleri, S. A slotted patch antenna with enhanced gain pattern for automotive applications. *Prog. Electromagn. Res. Lett.* **2021**, *95*, 135–141. [CrossRef]
26. Atmel Corporation. *AT17LV512A: FPGA Configuration EEPROM Memory 3.3V and 5.0V*; Atmel Corporation: San Jose, CA, USA, 2014.
27. Passafiume, M.; Collodi, G.; Cidronali, A. Improving Wireless Power Transfer Efficiency With DC/DC Boost Charger by Multi-Sine Excitation at 5.8 GHz. *IEEE Microw. Wirel. Components Lett.* **2022**, *32*, 760–763. [CrossRef]
28. Qi, C.; Frederick, Q.; Davis, K.; Lindsay, D.; Cox, J.; Parke, S.; Griffin, J.D.; Durgin, G.D. A 5.8 GHz Energy Harvesting Tag for Sensing Applications in Space. In Proceedings of the 2018 6th IEEE International Conference on Wireless for Space and Extreme Environments (WiSEE), Huntsville, AL, USA, 11–13 December 2018; pp. 218–223.
29. Olule, L.J.A.; Gnanagurunathan, G.; Kumar, N.T.; Kasi, B. Single band RF Energy Harvesting at 5.8 GHz using EBG unit cells. In Proceedings of the 2018 IEEE International RF and Microwave Conference (RFM), Penang, Malaysia, 17–19 December 2018; pp. 352–355.
30. Janhunen, J.; Mikhaylov, K.; Petäjäjärvi, J.; Sonkki, M. Wireless Energy Transfer Powered Wireless Sensor Node for Green IoT: Design, Implementation and Evaluation. *Sensors* **2019**, *19*, 90. [CrossRef]

31. Nguyen, X.V.L.; Gerges, T.; Bevilacqua, P.; Duchamp, J.-M.; Benech, P.; Verdier, J.; Lombard, P.; Linge, P.U.; Mieyeville, F.; Cabrera, M.; et al. Radio-Frequency Energy Harvesting Using Rapid 3D Plastronics Protoyping Approach: A Case Study. *J. Low Power Electron. Appl.* **2023**, *13*, 19. [CrossRef]
32. Han, K.; Huang, K. Wirelessly powered backscatter communication networks: Modeling, coverage, and capacity. *IEEE Trans. Wirel. Commun.* **2017**, *16*, 2548–2561. [CrossRef]

Disclaimer/Publisher's Note: The statements, opinions and data contained in all publications are solely those of the individual author(s) and contributor(s) and not of MDPI and/or the editor(s). MDPI and/or the editor(s) disclaim responsibility for any injury to people or property resulting from any ideas, methods, instructions or products referred to in the content.

Article

Floating Photovoltaic Systems Coupled with Pumped Hydroplants under Day-Ahead Electricity Market Conditions: Parametric Analysis

Arsenio Barbón [1], Javier Aparicio-Bermejo [2], Luis Bayón [3,*] and Ramy Georgious [1]

[1] Department of Electrical Engineering, University of Oviedo, 33003 Oviedo, Spain; barbon@uniovi.es (A.B.); georgiousramy@uniovi.es (R.G.)
[2] Business Development Iberia Northwest Area, Enel Green Power, 28014 Madrid, Spain; javieraparciobermejo@gmail.com
[3] Department of Mathematics, University of Oviedo, 33003 Oviedo, Spain
* Correspondence: bayon@uniovi.es

Citation: Barbón, A.; Aparicio-Bermejo, J.; Bayón, L.; Georgious, R. Floating Photovoltaic Systems Coupled with Pumped Hydroplants under Day-Ahead Electricity Market Conditions: Parametric Analysis. *Electronics* 2023, 12, 2250. https://doi.org/10.3390/electronics12102250

Academic Editors: Noel Rodriguez, Moshe Averbukh and Shailendra Rajput

Received: 28 April 2023
Revised: 11 May 2023
Accepted: 13 May 2023
Published: 15 May 2023

Copyright: © 2023 by the authors. Licensee MDPI, Basel, Switzerland. This article is an open access article distributed under the terms and conditions of the Creative Commons Attribution (CC BY) license (https://creativecommons.org/licenses/by/4.0/).

Abstract: The intermittent nature of the solar resource together with the fluctuating energy demand of the day-ahead electricity market requires the use of efficient long-term energy storage systems. The pumped hydroelectric storage (PHS) power plant has demonstrated its technical and commercial viability as a large-scale energy storage technology. The objective of this paper is to analyse the parameters that influence the mode of operation in conjunction with a floating photovoltaic (FPV) power plant under day-ahead electricity market conditions. This work proposes the analysis of two parameters: the size of the FPV power plant and the total process efficiency of the PHS power plant. Five FPV plant sizes are analysed: 50% ($S1$), 100% ($S2$), 150% ($S3$), 350% ($S4$) and 450% ($S5$) of the PHS plant. The values of the total process efficiency parameter analysed are as follows: 0.77 for old PHS plants, and 0.85 for more modern plants. The number of daily operating hours of the PHS plant is 4 h. These 4 h of operation correspond to the highest prices on the electricity market. The framework of the study is the Iberian electricity market and the Alto Rabagão dam (Portugal). Different operating scenarios are considered to identify the optimal size of the FPV power plant. Based on the measured data on climatic conditions, an algorithm is designed to estimate the energy production for different sizes of FPV plants. If the total process efficiency is 0.85, the joint operation of both plants with FPV plant sizes $S2$ and $S3$ yields a slightly higher economic benefit than the independent mode of operation. If the total process efficiency is 0.77, there is always a higher economic benefit in the independent operation mode, irrespective of the size of the FPV plant. However, the uncertainty of the solar resource estimation can lead to a higher economic benefit in the joint operation mode. Increasing the number of operating hours of the PHS plant above 4 h per day decreases the economic benefit of the joint operation mode, regardless of the total process efficiency parameter and the size of the FPV plant. As the number of operating hours increases, the economic benefit decreases. The results obtained reveal that the coupling of floating photovoltaic systems with pumped hydroelectric storage power plants is a cost-effective and reliable alternative to provide sustainable energy supply security under electricity market conditions. In summary, the purpose of this work is to facilitate decision making on the mode of operation of both power plants under electricity market conditions. The case studies allow to find the optimal answer to the following practical questions: What size does the FPV power plant have to be in order for both plants to be better adapted to the electricity market? What is the appropriate mode of operation of both plants? What is the economic benefit of changing the turbine pump of the PHS power plant? Finally, how does the installation of the FPV power plant affect the water volume of the upper reservoir of the PHS plant? Knowledge of these questions will facilitate the design of FPV power plants and the joint operation of both plants.

Keywords: pumped hydroelectric storage power plant; floating photovoltaic power plant; day-ahead market; economic benefits

1. Introduction

Limiting global average temperature increases to 1.5 (°C) above pre-industrial levels in accordance with the Paris Agreement [1] is a goal for most governments. To achieve this, CO_2 emissions must be reduced to net zero by 2050 as far as possible [2]. In this sense, the European Union (EU) has set decarbonisation strategies for 2030, which can be summarised by means of the objectives set out in the Winter Package [3]: (i) a 40% reduction in greenhouse gas emissions; (ii) 32% renewable energy in the final energy mix; and (iii) 32.5% energy efficiency improvement. The transport, building and industry sectors are currently the main sources of greenhouse gas emissions in the EU [4]. The development of renewable energy technologies to replace fossil fuels in electricity generation has been a focus of research for several decades now. Some of these studies analysed whether renewable energies are ready to support the current and future energy demand.

Solar energy has the potential to play a key role in reducing greenhouse gas emissions because it is abundant, safe, reliable and non-polluting. Solar technologies that can be used to generate electricity include photovoltaic (PV) and concentrated solar power (CSP). PV technology is a growing technology for electricity generation [5] and is the subject of this study. PV power plants have a flexible architecture that allows them to be adapted to different locations [5]. This technology is subject to intermittency and fluctuations in power generation. The intermittent nature of the solar resource refers to the fact that the amount of solar energy that can be captured and converted into electricity using PV systems varies depending on the time of day, season, and weather conditions [6]. These fluctuations in the availability of solar energy can make it challenging to integrate solar PV into the electricity grid and ensure a stable and reliable supply of electricity. To address this issue, several approaches have been developed, including energy storage systems, such as pumped hydroelectric storage power plants. This feature puts PV technology at a disadvantage compared to CSP technology, which allows energy storage. Therefore, overcoming the possible fluctuating operation of a PV plant due to random weather would put this type of technology in a privileged position. However, the joint operation of a PV power plant with a pumped hydroelectric storage power plant can also achieve energy storage. In other words, to achieve a reliable energy source, one can combine sources with strong temporal complementarity, such as photovoltaics, and couple them with some kind of energy storage device, such as a pumped hydroelectric storage power plant.

There are three main types of hydropower plants [7]: impoundment, diversion, and pumped storage. However, it is important to note that impoundment and diversion hydropower plants typically use dams to control the flow of water and create a head of water to drive turbines. Pumped storage hydropower plants also require two reservoirs, with one located at a higher elevation than the other, which can be created by building dams. However, there are also run-of-river hydropower plants that do not require a dam and instead use the natural flow of a river or stream to drive turbines. Tidal and wave energy converters are also considered types of hydropower facilities that do not require dams. In this study, we are interested in hydroelectric power plants with reservoirs, in particular, pumped hydroelectric storage power plant.

A pumped hydroelectric storage (PHS) power plant consists of an upper and a lower reservoir connected to a penstock, and a reversible pump turbine (See Figure 1). When electricity is to be generated (generation mode), water flows through the penstock to drive the hydro turbines. When the hydraulic machine operates as a pump (pumping mode), the water changes direction and is pumped from the lower tank to the upper tank. In pumping mode, energy from an external source (e.g., the grid or a PV plant) powers the pumps. Energy from solar production can be stored under this operating mode.

Some of the operating characteristics of these plants can be summarised as follows: (i) flexibility in start and stop operations, and (ii) a fast response speed so that it can adapt to drastic load changes and, therefore, follow load changes. These operating characteristics enable them to play a balancing role in electrical systems, providing reliability to the system. This advantage is enhanced by the increasing share of intermittent energy sources in the electricity market, such as photovoltaic technologies. Therefore, the flexible characteristics of this type of plant are expected to be used more extensively. In addition to the advantages mentioned above, the integration of FPV and PHS systems has the following advantages for the PHS system:

(i) Water savings. Water savings are due to the reduction in water evaporation due to the partial coverage of the reservoirs in the PHS systems. This value is estimated to depend on climate conditions and the percentage of area covered [8].
(ii) Water quality. In terms of water quality, the lack of light produced by partial water cover creates algae blooms [9].

Over the last three years, the analysis of floating photovoltaic (FPV) systems has been an emerging topic in scientific literature [10]. 89% of the studies conducted on floating PV systems focused on reservoirs for hydroelectric generation [10–13]. Therefore, the study of the joint mode of operation of these power generation systems is an important line of research. Floating PV plants have PV modules and solar inverters similar to ground-mounted PV plants. However, the mounting system of the PV modules is very different. The different components in this type of plant are [8] a main floating body, a connection floating body, and a mooring system. The profits obtained by an FPV system due to its integration in a PHS system are as follows:

(i) No land occupancy. The large land area occupied by ground-mounted PV plants competes with agricultural or green zones [14]. With FPV plants, this disadvantage is resolved.
(ii) Cooling of the PV modules. PV modules profit from the cooling provided by water. This considerably increases the electrical efficiency of the PV modules, resulting in 2.33% [15] to 10% [16] more energy per year.

In the 1990s, the countries of the European Union liberalised their energy systems. The evolution from heavily regulated to liberalised electricity markets was similar in the different countries, as it took place within the framework of common European legislation. The concept of exchange-based zonal markets is the spirit of electricity markets [17]. The electricity supply structure, the price mechanism, the trading mechanism, and the market agents are regulated by the electricity market. The electricity market is responsible for maintaining the balance in the electricity system, as supply (generation) and demand (load) must be continuously balanced in real time to maintain the reliability of the system.

Therefore, there are two systems—FPV and PHS—which have to be adapted to the conditions of the electricity market. Several modes of operation are possible: (i) an independent operation mode, (ii) a joint operation mode, and (iii) an energy storage operation mode. With the first mode, the two plants operate independently by selling electricity. With the second mode, the two plants operate jointly selling electricity, but the energy generated by the FPV plant can be sold as it is generated or it can be used in the pumping process of the PHS plant so that the PHS plant can then sell electricity at the most appropriate times. Finally, with the third mode, the two plants operate jointly storing energy. Choosing the right mode of operation according to electricity market conditions poses a challenge for such systems. Figure 1 shows a diagram reflecting the interaction between the three systems studied.

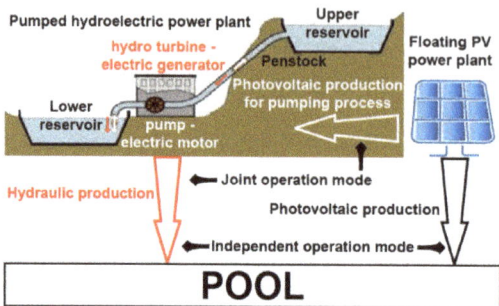

Figure 1. Representation of the three systems under study [18].

The feasibility and cost effectiveness of integrating FPV systems in PHS power plants have been extensively studied in the literature [19–22]. Although this type of configuration was initially used in the electrification of remote areas without access to the public grid, it has nowadays been extended to large PHS power plants.

Rauf et al. [23] evaluated the integration of a 200 (MWp) FPV power plant into an existing conventional 1450 (MW) hydropower plant in Pakistan. The results showed additional energy production of more than 3.5% when the conventional hydropower plant was combined with an FPV system. Kocaman and Modi [24] investigated the cost effectiveness of integrating FPV plants into PHS and conventional hydroelectric systems. The results showed that PHS systems allow a higher solar energy capacity to be installed in an affordable manner than conventional hydropower systems. Therefore, the integration of FPV systems into PHS systems is more cost effective than conventional hydropower systems. These two studies did not take into account electricity market conditions.

Glasnovic and Margeta [25] presented a hybrid system consisting of a PHS plant and an FPV plant to provide a continuous power supply. The energy supplied by the FPV power plant was used for the water pumping process of the PHS power plant. The energy produced by the PHS plant was used to supply electricity to isolated consumers. This paper only considered one of the possible modes of operation of the proposed system. In addition, the electricity market conditions are not taken into account.

Due to climate change, decreasing rainfall causes water shortages in some hydroelectric power plant reservoirs. As a result, some hydroelectric power plants remain out of service for a few months of the year. Bhattacharjee and Nayak [26] analysed the impact of an FPV power plant on restoring the constant annual output of a PHS power plant. The results corroborate that this hybrid system is a viable option for restoring the constant annual yield from a PHS power plant.

In addition to the references provided above, Jurasz et al. [19] presented a detailed literature review on the joint operation of FPV and PHS systems. These authors stated that there are a limited number of papers directly dedicated to the joint operation of an FPV and a PHS plant operating in a day-ahead market. The following are some of the few papers that address this issue. Jurasz et al. [19] presented an efficient trading strategy for FPV and PHS systems operating in a day-ahead market. The presented model takes into account several uncertainties, such as inflow and solar irradiance in a simplified approach. Study [18] presented analyses of different scenarios of joint operation of FPV and PHS plants as well as the optimal operating strategy for the day-ahead Iberian electricity market, depending on the accuracy of the forecasts.

Considering that the inclusion of electricity market conditions has been barely discussed in the scientific literature, the main objective of this paper is to analyse how certain parameters of the two electricity generation systems affect their mode of operation in the Iberian electricity market. For this purpose, we analyse two parameters of a system consisting of an existing PHS power plant and an FPV power plant to be integrated, taking into account the conditions of the Iberian electricity market. These parameters are the size of the FPV power plant and the efficiency of the pumping process of the PHS power plant. The indicators used to evaluate the study are the water volume gain and the economic benefit. This study will be carried out at one of the hydroelectric reservoirs in Portugal, i.e., the Alto Rabagão hydroelectric power plant, to assess the influence of the three parameters on the feasibility of installing a large-scale PV system.

The main contributions of this work are as follows:

(i) Analysing the size of a floating PV power plant under Iberian electricity market conditions. To do so, the available reservoir area, terrain elevations, and existing electrical infrastructure at the pumped-storage hydroelectric power plant must be estimated.
(ii) Analysing how the efficiency of the pumping process of the hydroelectric power plant affects the mode of operation of both plants under Iberian electricity market conditions.
(iii) Analysing the energy storage possibilities of a floating PV power plant when both plants are operated under Iberian electricity market conditions.
(iv) Analysing the optimal mode of operation of an integrated floating PV-hydroelectric power plant in order to obtain the maximum economic benefit.

In summary, the purpose of this work is to facilitate decision making in the mode of operation of both power plants under electricity market conditions. The case studies make it possible to determinate the optimal answer to the following practical questions: What size does the FPV power plant have to be in order for both plants to be better adapted to the electricity market? What is the appropriate mode of operation of both plants? What is the economic benefit from changing the turbine-pump of the PHS power plant? Finally, how does the installation of an FPV power plant affect the water volume of the upper reservoir of a PHS plant? Establishing the answers to these questions would facilitate the design of FPV power plants and the joint operation of both plants.

This paper is structured as follows: Section 2 provides the context for the case study location. Section 3 describes the methodological approach to the operation of a floating PV power plant integrated with a pumped hydro power plant in the day-ahead market. The results are presented in Section 4. Finally, Section 5 summarises the main contributions and conclusions of the paper.

2. Context for the Case Study Location

The Iberian Peninsula, comprising Spain and Portugal, is a typical case of an area of high solar potential and growing energy demand. Renewable energies have been widely accepted by the population of the Iberian Peninsula; there were 15.4 (GWp) installed photovoltaic systems in operation at the end of 2021 [4]. The installed capacity of hydroelectric power plants was around 23.5 (GW) at the end of 2021 [4].

Most electricity is sold in EU member states through day-ahead markets [27]. In these markets, the hourly price of electricity depends on supply (amount and sources of energy available) and demand.

Portugal and Spain operate the same electricity market (Iberian Electricity Market, $MIBEL$ by its acronym in Spanish). This market was created in 2004. $MIBEL$ includes two main markets, where most transactions are carried out: the day-ahead market and the intra-day market. However, energy is mainly traded on the day-ahead market. In addition, it has the technical restrictions market and the complementary services market, where the number of transactions is lower. In this type of market, there are two main agents called the market operator and the system operator. The market operator is the market manager of the day-ahead and intra-day market. In $MIBEL$, it is called $OMIE$, for its Spanish acronym. The system operator is the market manager of the technical restrictions market and complementary services market. The system operator in Portugal is called REN, and in Spain, it is called REE.

$OMIE$ uses the marginalist model for its transactions. In this model, electricity producers make their bids based on the marginal cost of production. This model includes all costs, such as the cost of emissions, the cost of fuel, the variable cost of operation and maintenance. It also includes taxes.

2.1. Description of the Day-Ahead Market

The operating principle of the day-ahead market is that of an auction. As in any auction, there are two types of agents: selling agents and buying agents. The generating plants and energy importers are the selling agents. The traders who resell their energy on the retail market or export it and the end consumers who use the wholesale market are the buying agents.

The mechanism of operation of the day-ahead market is as follows: (i) On day $D-1$, at 12:00, selling agents submit the electricity bid for each hour of day D. (ii) On day $D-1$, at 12:00, buying agents submit the purchase offer for each hour of day D. (iii) On day $D-1$, $OMIE$ builds the supply and demand curves according to the criteria shown in Figure 2.

The intersection of the supply and demand curves determines the market price for each hour of day D. Therefore, all matched sell (buy) bids are charged (paid) at the same price. Figure 2 shows an example of this procedure.

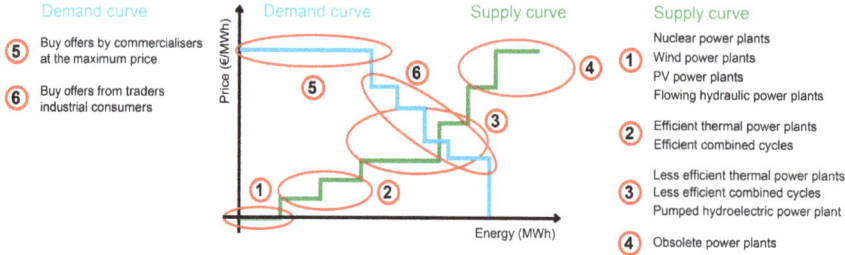

Figure 2. Supply and demand curve.

The supply and/or demand for each hour of day D may vary, resulting in an imbalance. Several reasons can cause such an imbalance: (i) generation failures, (ii) transmission failures, and (iii) variations in expected weather conditions. An imbalance in the system is called a deviation. Therefore, the deviation is the difference between the predicted power and the actual power available. Deviations can be classified according to their direction: upward deviation and downward deviations.

From a power plant perspective, there is an upward deviation when there is overproduction and a downward deviation when there is underproduction. By contrast, on the demand side, there is an upward deviation when there is a shortfall in consumption, and a downward deviation when there is overconsumption. When a deviation occurs, a payment obligation may occur, depending on the market's needs.

Market needs in the Iberian Electricity System are determined by the concept known as the net system balancing need ($NNBS$, by its acronym in Spanish). This indicator examines whether the total production is higher or lower than the scheduled production. Therefore, the $NNBS$ determines whether the production deviation is favourable or detrimental to the electricity system. Two situations can occur:

(i) If $NNBS > 0$, the net production of the electricity system is lower than scheduled in the market and thus more energy is required.
(ii) If $NNBS < 0$, the net production of the electricity system is greater than scheduled in the market and thus less energy is required.

According to the $NNBS$ indicator, deviations can be classified according to whether they are in favour or against the market:

(i) Deviation in favour. This is a deviation that occurs in the same direction as the market need. For example, the power plant produces less energy than scheduled and the

$NNBS < 0$, or when the power plant produces more energy than scheduled and the $NNBS > 0$.

(ii) Against deviation. This is a deviation that occurs in the opposite direction to the market need. For example, the power plant produces less energy than scheduled and the $NNBS > 0$, or when the power plant produces more energy than scheduled and the $NNBS < 0$.

Deviations have an economic impact, which are either positive or negative. Therefore, deviations in favour are associated with a price (PUD/PDD) and deviations against are associated with a cost (CUD/CDD). $OMIE$ sets the PUD and the PDD. The cost of deviation CUD (CDD) is the difference between the absolute value of the marginal market price and the PUD (PDD).

2.2. Case under Study

The Alto Rabagão pumped hydroelectric storage power plant is located in the district of Vila Real in Northern Portugal (latitude 41°44′16″ N, longitude 7°51′14″ W, and altitude of 880 (m)) [28]. The project is led by the Portuguese energy company EDP. The upper reservoir of the Alto Rabagão has already been built. The surface area is 2200 (ha), and it has a volume of 569 (hm^3), and a maximum water level of 185 (m) [28]. The River Rabagão feeds this reservoir. In order to guarantee the environmental flow of the lower part of the river, the power plant always discharges a part of the flow without generating electricity. In this case, the reserved volume is 11 (hm^3). Figure 3 shows a Google Earth image of the Alto Rabagão pumped hydroelectric storage power plant.

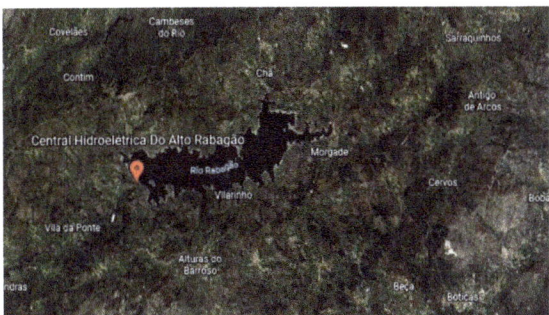

Figure 3. Google Earth map of the Alto Rabagão PHS power plant.

This hydroelectric power plant was commissioned with a total output of 67 (MW) in the year 1964 [28]. This plant uses 2 binary groups (hydro turbine-pump) [28]. The total power in pumping mode is 62 (MW) [28]. Obviously, the total maximum flow rate is not the same in generation mode as in pumping mode. These values are 46.5 (m^3/s) and 33 (m^3/s), respectively [28].

3. Methodology

When the objective of the FPV–PHS system is to maximise economic benefits by offering energy in the day-ahead market, the aim is to sell the available energy during the times when market prices are the highest. Under these conditions, the uncertainty provided by the FPV system is a major drawback. Therefore, analysing the size of the FPV plant can help make the right decision.

In order to achieve the objectives sought with this study, the following methodology is proposed:

(i) Deducing possible modes of operation.
(ii) Parametric analysis.
(iii) Meteorological data selection.

(iv) FPV power plant design.
(v) FPV power plant size

The first step is to define the possible modes of operation of both plants under the Iberian electricity market conditions. In the second step, the parameters of the power plants that make up the system will be identified and those that may influence the mode of operation of both power plants under electricity market conditions will be analysed. The third step is the selection of meteorological data. The step before calculating the photovoltaic energy is to select the meteorological data from the location of the pumped-storage hydroelectric power plant. Obtaining the energy generated by the floating PV plant per square metre of PV field is the fourth step of this methodology. Finally, step 5 defines the indicator used to evaluate the operating model for both plants.

3.1. Deducing Possible Modes of Operation

The size of a floating PV plant determines the mode of operation of both plants in the electricity market. In addition, the efficiency of the pumping process is also a factor conditioning the mode of operation of both power plants. Therefore, the possible modes of operation of both plants under electricity market conditions must be determined.

The possible modes of operation, regardless of market conditions, are as follows:

(i) Continuous operation of the hydropower plant, i.e., 24 h a day, is a mode of operation that would deplete the available water in the upper reservoir, meaning there would not be a sufficient annual flow to maintain the required average flow at full power. Therefore, the mode of operation of a hydroelectric power plant is intermittent. Forecasting the times with the highest energy prices determines the operating times of the hydropower plants. The water stored in the upper reservoir is conserved for use during the times that provide the greatest economic benefit. The rest of the time, it can operate in pumping mode. Due to the mode of operation of these plants, the transmission lines to the grid also operate intermittently. Therefore, they can be used by a floating PV plant.
(ii) Selling electricity as it is generated would be the operation mode of a floating PV power plant without the possibility of storing energy (Mode A). If the floating PV power plant has a storage system, as in this case, another mode of operation is to store electricity, in the form of stored water, as it is generated (Mode B). To do this, water would be pumped from the lower reservoir to the upper reservoir. In this way, a greater economic benefit could be obtained by turbining this water at times of high prices. Considering Modes A and B, it is also possible to sell and store electricity simultaneously as it is generated (Mode C).

The decision to use one mode of operation or another is determined by the electricity market conditions. Five cases are possible:

(i) Case 1: No deviation. This would be the ideal case (a highly unlikely situation). The energy bid on day $D-1$ coincides with the energy available on day D. This case is characterised by the absence of a penalty, as there are no deviations. The marginal market price would be the selling price. The floating PV plant operates in Mode A (selling electricity as it is generated). The two power plants operate independently.
(ii) Case 2: An upward deviation (energy bid on day $D-1$ is less than the energy available on day D) and $NNBS > 0$. As the deviation is in favour of the system, there is no penalty, and a collection right is generated. The marginal market price would be the selling price. The floating PV plant operates in Mode A (selling electricity as it is generated). The two plants operate independently of each other.
(iii) Case 3: An upward deviation (energy bid on day $D-1$ is less than the energy available on day D) and $NNBS < 0$. As the deviation goes against the system, the right to be charged for the surplus energy will be lower than the marginal market price. Therefore, the floating PV plant may store the surplus energy in order to sell it on another day at the marginal market price. The floating PV plant operates in Mode C. The joint

operation of the two plants may be the best option. In this case, the size of the floating PV plant will be a determining factor in the choice of its mode of operation. The efficiency of the pumping process also influences the choice.

(iv) Case 4: An downward deviation (the energy bid on day $D-1$ is greater than the energy available on day D) and $NNBS > 0$. As the deviation is against the system, a payment obligation is generated. This price is higher than the market price. Therefore, it is the worst situation for the floating PV plant as the plant loses money. The floating PV plant operates in Mode A (selling electricity as it is generated). The mode of operation will be joint, as the pumped hydroelectric power plant helps to cover the energy imbalance of the floating PV power plant.

(v) Case 5: An downward deviation (the energy bid on day $D-1$ is greater than the energy available on day D) and $NNBS < 0$. As the deviation is in favour of the system, there is no penalty. The marginal market price would be the selling price. The floating PV plant operates in Mode A (selling electricity as it is generated). The two plants operate independently of each other.

3.2. Parametric Analysis of a Pumped Hydroelectric Storage Power Plant

A pumped hydroelectric storage power plant has a configuration of two water reservoirs (upper and lower reservoirs) at different heights, connected by penstocks. In generation mode, power is generated as water flows down the penstock from one reservoir to the other, passing through a turbine that is coupled to an electric generator. Once the water has been turbined, it is stored in the lower reservoir. Therefore, this system acts similarly to a battery, as it can store energy and release it when needed. In pumping mode, the system absorbs electrical energy as it pumps water back to the upper reservoir. In this mode of operation, the electric generator functions as a motor and the hydraulic turbine as a pump. This system generally uses a single penstock, which is used in both modes of operation.

The power flow is bidirectional depending on the operation mode. Therefore, each mode of operation, generation mode and pumping mode, will have certain parameters.

3.2.1. Generation Mode

The parameters involved in the generation mode are the available head (h_a), the turbined flow rate (q_t), the density of water (ρ), the acceleration due to gravity (g), the electric generator efficiency (η_g), and the hydro turbine efficiency (η_t). Therefore, the hydroelectric power can be calculated using Equation (1) [26]:

$$P_g = P_t \cdot \eta_g = \eta_t \cdot \rho \cdot g \cdot h_a \cdot q_t \cdot \eta_g \quad (1)$$

As the hydroelectric power plant is built, the parameter h_a can be considered to remain constant, as replacing the penstocks or modifying h_a would not be a cost that can be assumed. The replacement of the turbine and the electric generator, although costly, could be feasible.

Another aspect to be taken into account is the variation of the water level in the upper reservoir. When the upper reservoir has a large capacity, several studies have considered this parameter to be constant over the operation interval [26,29].

3.2.2. Pumping Mode

The parameters involved in the pumping mode are the elevating head (h_e), the pumped flow rate (q_p), the density of water (ρ), the acceleration due to gravity (g), the electric motor efficiency (η_m), and the pump efficiency (η_p). Therefore, the electrical power absorbed in the pumping process can be calculated using Equation (2) [26]:

$$P_a = \frac{\rho \cdot g \cdot h_e \cdot q_p}{\eta_m \cdot \eta_p} \quad (2)$$

Following the same reasoning as above, it can be considered that the parameter h_e remains constant, and that the substitution of the pump and the electric motor is admissible.

Next, the two modes of operation are related. For this purpose, the following parameters are defined: the turbine generating coefficient (k_t), the water pumping coefficient of the pumping process (k_p), and the total process efficiency (μ). The following are the equations:

$$k_t = \eta_g \cdot \eta_t \cdot \rho \cdot g \cdot h_a \tag{3}$$

$$k_p = \frac{\rho \cdot g \cdot h_e}{\eta_m \cdot \eta_p} \tag{4}$$

$$\mu = \frac{k_t}{k_p} = \eta_g \cdot \eta_t \cdot \eta_m \cdot \eta_p \tag{5}$$

For water pumped and then used for generation, all efficiency factors are applied in both pumping and production modes. The following is therefore fulfilled:

$$P_g = k_t \cdot q_t \tag{6}$$

$$P_a = k_p \cdot q_p = \frac{k_t}{\mu} \cdot q_p \tag{7}$$

The typical μ of this type of hydroelectric plant ranges from 65% to 80%, depending on the technical characteristics of the equipment [30]. Obviously, the lower value corresponds to older plants. Other studies estimate that a maximum of 70% to 85% of the electrical energy absorbed from the grid can be recovered for the pumping process [29]. Technological advances over the last 25 years have resulted in modern systems with μ of up to 87% [21].

The Alto Rabagão pumped-storage hydropower plant has a turbine generation coefficient (k_t) of 1.44086 (MWs/m^3), and the total efficiency of the pumping process (μ) is 0.77 [28].

Taking into account the volume of water available, the Alto Rabagão pumped-storage hydroelectric power station operates at full power for 4 h a day [28]. Therefore, the energy generated each day is 268 (MWh).

There are several parameters that can be used to evaluate and analyse PHS power plants, such as (i) capacity, (ii) total process efficiency, (iii) energy yield, (iv) power output, (v) cost, (vi) environmental impact, (vii) cycle time, (viii) maintenance requirements, and (ix) lifetime. As the PHS plant is already built and the impact of the implementation of an FPV plant in its upper reservoir is analysed, parameter (ii) is considered to be appropriate. The influence of the parameter μ on the joint operation of both plants is analysed in this paper. The parameter μ is 0.77 in old plants. In contrast, this parameter is usually 0.85 in modern plants.

3.3. Parametric Analysis of a Floating PV Power Plant

The main component of a floating PV plant is the PV modules; therefore, the parameters of this type of plant are related to this element. These parameters are the technology used to manufacture of the PV module (solar transmittance of glazing (τ), and solar absorptance of PV layer (α)), the number of PV modules (N_{PV}), the module dimensions (module width (W_{PV}), module length (L_{PV}) and module surface (A_{PV})), the efficiency electrical of the PV module (η_e), the available solar resource, the tilt angle of the PV module (β), and the orientation of the PV module (γ). The last three parameters are included in the incident solar irradiance parameter (I_t). Therefore, the power generated by a floating PV power plant can be calculated using Equation (8) [31]:

$$P_{PV} = N_{PV} \cdot A_{PV} \cdot (\tau \cdot \alpha) \cdot I_t \cdot \eta_e \tag{8}$$

3.3.1. Technology Used to Manufacture of the PV Module

Currently, there are three PV module technologies: monocrystalline, polycrystalline and thin film (CdTe). These three technologies have different electrical efficiencies. However, in this section, we are interested in the transmittance–absorption product. The commonly used value of the transmittance–absorption product ($\tau \cdot \alpha$) is 0.9 [32,33].

3.3.2. Electrical Efficiency

Electrical efficiency is defined as the efficiency of the module to convert incident solar irradiance into electrical energy. This efficiency depends on the type of manufacturing technology used for the PV module. The manufacturer of the PV module provides the electrical efficiency (η_{ref}) at the reference temperature (T_{ref}) of 25 (°C) and a solar irradiance of 1000 (W/m^2). To obtain the electrical efficiency (η_e) under other conditions of temperature (T_c) and solar irradiance (I_t), the equation provided by Evans [34] is often used [35,36]. This equation is as follows [34]:

$$\eta_e = \eta_{ref} \cdot \left[1 - \beta_{ref} \cdot \left(T_c - T_{ref}\right)\right] \quad (9)$$

where β_{ref} is the temperature coefficient; (1/°C) is normally provided by the PV module manufacturer.

According to the literature, if the operating temperature of the PV modules exceeds 25 (°C), the electrical efficiency decreases [36,37]. The effects of the ambient temperature, the incident solar irradiance and the wind speed must be considered. The number of models for predicting the operating temperature of a PV module is high [38]. Dutra et al. [37] show 20 models in their work. One such model is presented by Mattei et al. [39], which offers satisfactory results. This model uses the normal operating cell temperature (NOCT). This parameter is provided by the PV module manufacturer. This model uses the ambient temperature (T_a), the solar irradiance (I_t) and the NOCT (determined under the following conditions: 800 (W/m^2) of solar irradiance, 20 (°C) of ambient temperature and 1 (m/s) of wind speed at the height of the PV module). The proposed equation is as follows:

$$T_c = T_a + (NOCT - 20) \cdot \frac{I_t}{800} \quad (10)$$

The electrical efficiency of FPV plants is higher than that of ground-mounted PV plants. This increase depends on the environmental conditions at the installation site: (i) For Choi [40], efficiency increases up to 11%. (ii) For Liu et al. [16], the efficiency increases up to 10%. (iii) For Oliveira-Pinto and Stokkermans [41], the efficiency ranges from 0.31% to 2.59%. (iv) For El Hammoumi et al. [15], the efficiency increases up to 2.33%.

3.3.3. Incident Solar Irradiance

The equation proposed by Duffie and Beckman [42] is usually used to determine the total solar irradiance $I_t(n, T, \beta)$ on tilted surfaces:

$$I_t(n, T, \beta) = I_{bh}(n, T) \cdot \frac{\cos \theta_i}{\cos \theta_z} + I_{dh}(n, T) \cdot \left(\frac{1 + \cos \beta}{2}\right) + \\ + (I_{bh}(n, T) + I_{dh}(n, T)) \cdot \rho_g \cdot \left(\frac{1 - \cos \beta}{2}\right) \quad (11)$$

where I_{bh} is the beam irradiance on the horizontal plane, I_{dh} is the diffuse irradiance on the horizontal plane, θ_z is the zenith angle of the sun, θ_i is the incident angle calculated using the equation proposed by Duffie and Beckman [42], β is the tilt angle, and ρ_g is the ground reflectance.

According to the above, the energy supply must be hourly. For this purpose, Equation (11) is integrated from sunrise (T_R) to sunset (T_S) in one-hour intervals:

$$H_t(n, \beta) = \int_{T_R(n)}^{T_S(n)} I_t(n, T, \beta) dT \qquad (12)$$

where H_t is the total solar irradiation, n is the day of the year, and T is the solar time.

3.3.4. Number and Dimensions of PV Modules

Once the location of the PHS power plant, the tilt angle, the orientation, the PV module technology, and the model of the PV module used have been defined, the only parameter that will influence the size of the floating PV power plant is N_{PV}. This value is determined in the section on the optimisation of the floating PV power plant.

There are several parameters that can be used to evaluate and analyse FPV power plants: (i) capacity, (ii) efficiency, (iii) energy yield, (iv) cost, (v) environmental impact, (vi) maintenance requirements, and (vii) durability. Although all parameters are important, parameters (i), (ii) and (iii) are adapted to the subject matter of this work, as the size of the FPV power plant encompasses these parameters.

3.4. Meteorological Data Selection

The third step is the selection of meteorological data. The previous step in the calculation of the photovoltaic energy is to select the meteorological data from the location of the PHS power plant.

Precise knowledge of the amount of incident solar irradiance on a horizontal surface is essential to optimising the FPV plant. However, it is unlikely that a weather station is available at the dam to record global and diffuse solar irradiance over the horizontal surface. For this reason, using a proven solar model, such as the one proposed in [43], is necessary. This model has been validated with real data from weather stations [44], and has been used in similar studies, as it more accurately predicts solar irradiance under different climate conditions [18,45,46]. In addition, meteorological data must be expressed in hours, as this is the time interval used in the Iberian electricity market. The method presented by [43] meets these specifications, as it determines the hourly beam and diffuse solar irradiance on a horizontal surface under the meteorological conditions of a specific location and for each day of the year. This method follows three steps: (i) Hottel's clear-day model [47] to estimate the solar irradiance transmitted through a clear atmosphere; (ii) Liu and Jordan's clear-day model [48] to determine the diffuse solar irradiance for clear skies; and (iii) Fourier series approximation to adapt the clear-sky models to the meteorological conditions of the reservoir. Therefore, the I_{bh} and I_{dh} values of Equation (11) are determined by the method proposed in [43].

Monthly beam and diffuse solar irradiation on horizontal surfaces are necessary to apply the method [43]. The data should cover at least 10 years of meteorological measurements to build a good picture of the local climate, thus reducing the uncertainty that could be caused by using meteorological data from a specific year. Although there are several sources of meteorological data available, this method uses the $PVGIS$ tool [49], an EU project which provides freely accessible solar radiation databases. Specifically, the $PVGIS$-$SARAH$2 database, with data which are satellite based and a time period from 2011 to 2020, was used.

Figure 4 shows the monthly beam and diffuse solar irradiation on horizontal surfaces at the Alto Rabagão dam obtained using the $PVGIS$ tool [49]. Figure 5 shows the results obtained using the method proposed in [43] for beam and diffuse solar irradiation on a horizontal surface under the meteorological conditions at the Alto Rabagão dam.

The monthly mean daytime and nighttime temperatures are presented in Figure 4. The average monthly maximum daytime temperature is 27.7 ($°$C), and the average monthly maximum night-time temperature is 14.9 ($°$C).

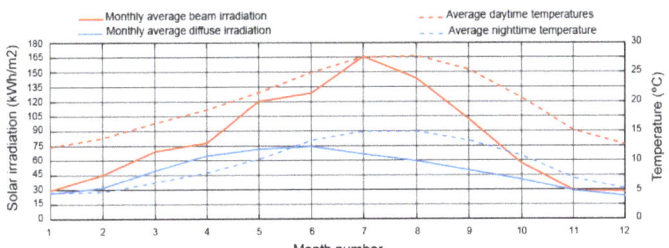

Figure 4. Environmental conditions.

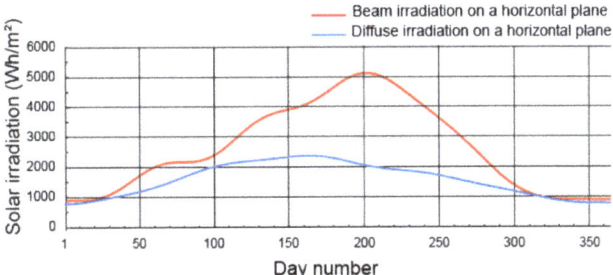

Figure 5. Beam and diffuse solar irradiation on a horizontal surface.

3.5. The FPV Power Plant Design

The design of a ground-mounted photovoltaic plant has been studied by several authors [31,46]. In contrast, there are few studies on FPV power plants from this point of view [50].

The following considerations have been taken into account in this study:

(i) The shape of the available area. In ground-mounted PV power plants, the irregular shape of the ground greatly influences the design [46]. In the case of FPV power plants, complex irregular shapes are not possible due to the nature of the floating platform. Therefore, the design of FPV power plants is more similar to designs with regular shapes [51]. The dimensions of the main floating body component chosen defines the shape of the FPV power plant. The system chosen for mounting the PV modules uses two main floating bodies. Each of them has the following dimensions: $1160 \times 935 \times 370$ (mm) [52]. The usual shape of FPV power plants is rectangular, or they can be decomposed into this type of shape [53,54].

(ii) The tilt angle. Another aspect is the tilt angle of the PV modules. In ground-mounted photovoltaic plants, the tilt angle is chosen to maximise the incident solar irradiance on the PV modules. This tilt angle is related to the latitude at the site. In FPV power plants, on the other hand, the tilt angle is chosen to ensure the stability of the PV modules. Therefore, tilt angles are chosen that are not related to the latitude at the site. With FPV systems, the tilt angle is chosen in accordance with the stability of the floating platform. The tilt angle of a PV module must avoid the detrimental effects of wind loads, waves and water currents. Therefore, floating platforms limit the tilt angle of PV modules. Specifically, there are three standard values for tilt angles: 5 (°) [52,55], 12 (°) [56]. In [18], the FPV power plants using each of these tilt angles are summarised.

Floating platforms with a tilt angle of 5 (°) [52,55] are chosen. They can withstand wind loads of 180 (km/h).

(iii) The orientation. As is the case with ground-mounted photovoltaic plants, the use of an optimal orientation is not a problem. Therefore, the optimum orientation is 0 (°) in the northern hemisphere and 180 (°) in the southern hemisphere [42]. As the chosen *PHS* power plant is in the northern hemisphere, an orientation of 0 (°) will be used.

(iv) The shading effect between modules. Due to the connecting floating body component, which connects the main floating bodies to each other, and the low tilt angle of the modules, the shading between *PV* modules will be quite low. However, the algorithm will take this into account.

(v) The albedo. Typical albedo values for different ground surfaces were calculated by [57–59]. Where no information is available, a value of 0.2 is often used [60]. In contrast, the albedo of water bodies ranges between 0.05 [16,41,50] and 0.07 [16]. Therefore, an albedo of 0.05 was used.

(vi) Only one commercial *PV* module model will be used. The model chosen is the JAM72S30 525-550/MR, which is manufactured by JASolar. The characteristics of the module are as follows: power, 550 (Wp); dimensions, 2279 × 1134 (mm); and surface area, 2.58 (m^2). The algorithm works for any *PV* module.

(vii) *FPV* power plant configuration. In ground-mounted photovoltaic plants, several rack configurations can be used [46]: $1V \times N_{PV}$, $2V \times N_{PV}$, $3V \times N_{PV}$, $2H \times N_{PV}$, $3H \times N_{PV}$, etc. In *FPV* systems, by contrast, the $1H \times N_{PV}$ configuration is typically used to minimise wind loads on the *PV* modules.

(viii) The transversal and longitudinal installation distance. The system chosen for mounting the *PV* modules uses two main floating bodies [52]. Each of them has the following dimensions: 1160 × 935 × 370 (mm) [52]. The transverse maintenance distance is $e_t = 25$ (mm), and the longitudinal maintenance distance is $e_l = 378$ (mm) [52].

(ix) The number of *PV* modules. According to the dimensions of the *PV* modules and the main floating bodies, the basic configuration will be 10×20 *PV* modules. An almost square shape measuring 23.62 × 31.09 (m) ($A_T = 734.19$ (m^2)), and a power of 0.11 (MWp) is obtained with these configurations. This basic unit is surrounded by floating connecting bodies. The connection floating body acts as a foothold during the construction and maintenance of the *FPV* system. The dimensions of the connection floating bodies vary depending on the manufacturer. In this study, they have the following dimensions: 1097 × 575 × 240 (mm) [52].

The algorithm used to determine the total energy is based on 3 steps: (i) the determination of total solar irradiance; (ii) the determination of the total surface area of the *PV* modules; and (iii) the determination of the total energy. These steps are explained in more detail below:

(i) The determination of total solar irradiance (H_t). This can be calculated using Equation (12) and the restrictions indicated above.

(ii) The determination of the total surface area of the *PV* modules (A_T). The total surface area of the *PV* modules (A_T) can be found with

$$A_T = \sum_{i=1}^{N_{PV}} W_{PV} \cdot L_{PV} \quad (13)$$

where N_{PV} is the number of *PV* modules, W_{PV} is the module width, and L_{PV} is the module length. The shadows that each row casts on the adjacent row in the longitudinal direction is an aspect taken into account by the algorithm designed.

(iii) The determination of the total energy. The total energy can be determined by the following equation:

$$E_{PV} = H_t \cdot A_T \quad (14)$$

3.6. The FPV Power Plant Size

The size of the *FPV* power plant can be chosen according to several criteria:

(i) The power of the *PHS* power plant. The power of the *PHS* power plant is 67 (MW) and its capacity is 973 (GWh).

(ii) The area available for deployment of *FPV* plant. The available area is 2200 (ha).

(iii) The volume of water in the upper reservoir. The size of the FPV power plant to supply the electrical energy required to raise the water level of the upper reservoir by a certain level by means of the pumping mode of operation of the PHS plant.
(iv) The pumping mode. The size of the FPV plant to supply the electrical energy required for the pumping mode of operation of the PHS plant.
(v) The number of operating hours of the PHS plant. The size of the FPV power plant to supply the electrical energy necessary to increase the number of operating hours of the PHS plant.

Each of these criteria is discussed in the Results section.

4. Results and Discussion

In this paper, the year 2022 was selected to frame the study presented. The daily hourly marginal market price (MMP), the price of upward deviations (PUD) and the price of downward deviations (PDD) can be found in [61]. Figure 6 shows the daily hourly marginal Iberian market price for the year 2022.

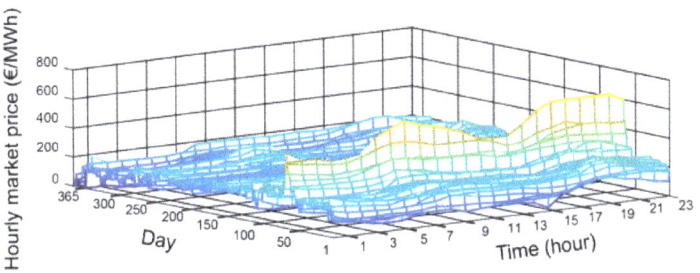

Figure 6. Daily hourly marginal Iberian market price for the year 2022.

Figure 7 shows the annual average hourly marginal Iberian market price for the year 2022. As can be seen in Figures 6 and 7, the four hours with the highest prices are 19:00, 20:00, 21:00 and 22:00. Therefore, these will be the hours of the PHS plant operation. The FPV plant will obviously not generate power during these hours.

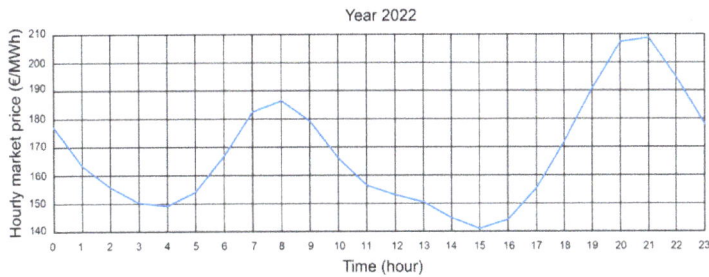

Figure 7. Annual average hourly marginal Iberian market price for the year 2022.

As the power of the PHS power plant is 67 (MW), the following power ratings for the FPV power plant are chosen as a starting point for the study: 33.55 (MWp) (50% PHS), 67.1 (MWp) (100% PHS), 100.65 (MWp) (150% PHS), 201.30 (MWp) (300% PHS), and 301.95 (MWp) (450% PHS).

Table 1 summarises the parameters of the FPV plant sizes studied based on the proposed methodology.

Table 1. Parameters of the FPV plant sizes studied.

Parameter			Size		
Designation	S1	S2	S3	S4	S5
Power (MWp)	33.50	67.10	100.65	201.30	301.95
Occupied area (hm^2)	22.39	44.78	67.18	134.35	201.53
Occupied area (%)	1.018	2.04	3.05	6.12	9.16
Number of total PV modules	61,000	122,000	183,000	366,000	549,000
Annual energy (GWh)	49.82	99.65	149.47	298.94	448.41

The capacity of all the plant sizes studied does not exceed the plant capacity of 973 (GWh).

Two values for the parameter μ are analysed in this paper. They are 0.77 for old *PHS* plants and 0.85 for modern *PHS* plants.

4.1. The Area Available for Deployment of an FPV Plant

In this case, an area of 2200 (ha) is available. According to Table 1, the surface area is not a limiting factor. The size of the plant could be further increased in accordance with the available area, but other aspects limiting the size of the *FPV* plant have to be analysed.

4.2. The Volume of Water in the Upper Reservoir

Water scarcity has become a topical issue. Water resources are necessary for human consumption and agriculture. The shortage of rainfall means that the upper reservoirs of the *PHS* power plants are not at their maximum capacity. For example, Figure 8 shows the water volume of the upper reservoir of the Alto Rabagão during the year 2022 [62]. The year 2022 was particularly dry. As a result, the upper reservoir level was approximately 20% for almost all the months of the year. The increase in volume in the last few months of the year is due to the *PHS* power plant operating in pumping mode, with the resulting loss in economic benefit.

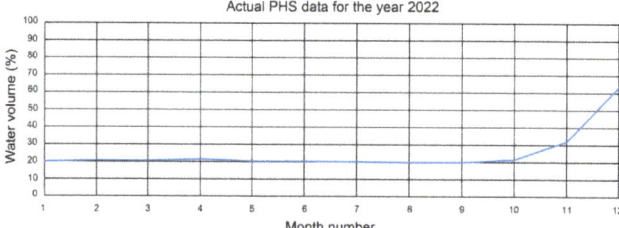

Figure 8. Volume of water in the upper reservoir in 2022.

Figure 9 shows the estimated water volume of the upper reservoir of the Alto Rabagão for different sizes of *FPV* plants if all the energy generated were to be used to pump water.

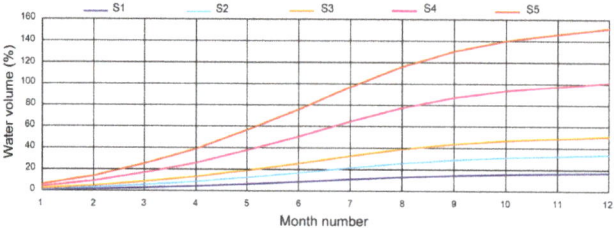

Figure 9. Volume of water in the upper reservoir.

The sizes of the analysed *FPV* plants occupy a very small water body compared to the total surface of the upper reservoir and reach remarkable upper reservoir levels. For example, size S1 occupies 1.018% of the upper reservoir and manages to pump a volume of water representing 16.85% of the upper reservoir. For size S2, these values would be 2.04% and 33.71%, respectively. For size S3, these values would be 3.05% and 50.56%, respectively. For size S4, these values would be 6.12% and 101.13%, respectively. For size S5, these values would be 9.16% and 151.69%, respectively.

As can be seen in Figure 9, the S5 size of the *FPV* plant obtains a water volume of more than 100%, so this power is not suitable. Similarly, larger sized *FPV* plants are not suitable.

The S4 sized *FPV* plant achieves 100% of the capacity of the upper reservoir. This is the limiting size for an *FPV* plant. All other sizes of *FPV* plants studied are suitable.

Therefore, sufficient energy can be stored for load management in the electricity grid with the *FPV* plant sizes studied (S1, S2, S3 and S4).

4.3. Usual Operation of the PHS Plant

The number of daily *PHS* plant operating hours is four. These four hours of operation correspond to the highest prices on the electricity market. In addition, the *PHS* plant operates under the conditions of Case 1: No deviation.

Figure 10 shows the daily energy generated with 4 daily hours of *PHS* plant operation during the year 2022. According to Figure 10, the number of *PHS* plant operating days is 71 days (20% of the days). The purpose of installing an *FPV* plant in the upper reservoir is for the *PHS* plant to operate 365 days a year.

The annual energy generated was 18.60 (GWh). This falls far short of its capacity, which is 973 (GWh). From an economic point of view, this earned EUR 4956259.88 from the sale of the energy generated.

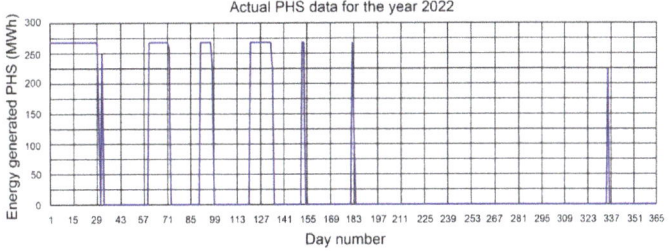

Figure 10. Daily energy generated by the PHS plant during the year 2022.

Figure 11 shows the daily energy absorbed during the pumping mode of the *PHS* plant in the year 2022. The correspondence between these two figures can be seen when comparing Figures 8 and 11.

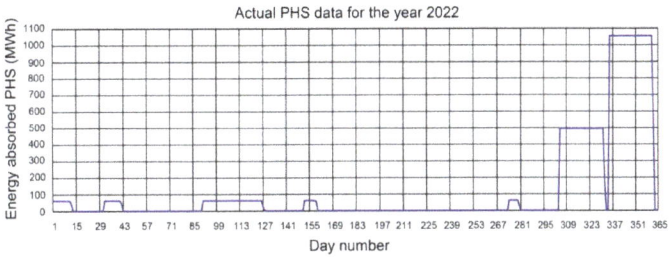

Figure 11. Daily energy absorbed by the PHS plant during the year 2022.

The annual energy absorbed in pumping mode was 47.09 (GWh). Therefore, in 2022, this plant absorbed more energy than it generated: specifically, 28.49 (GWh).

From an economic point of view, the cost of this absorbed energy was EUR 5,047,474.74. It can be concluded that this PHS plant operated under economic losses during the year 2022.

4.4. Operation of the PHS Plant Together with the FPV Plant

Figure 12 shows the energy generated by the analysed FPV plants. Figure 12a shows the hourly distribution of the energy generated by the FPV plant size $S2$ on 21 June (Summer Solstice). Figure 12b shows the daily distribution of the energy generated by each FPV plant size.

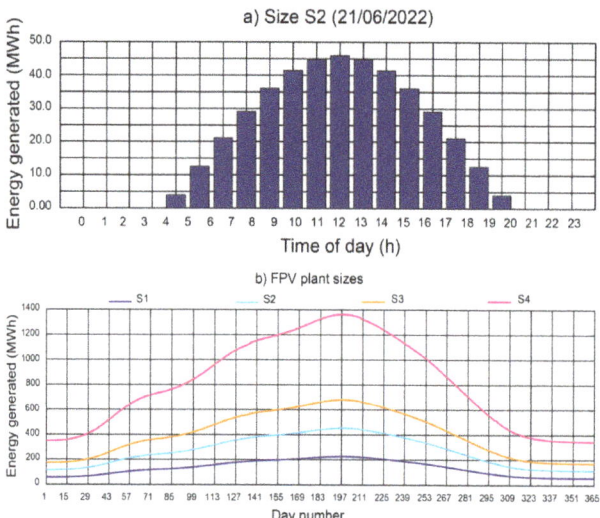

Figure 12. Energy generated by the sizes of FPV plants analysed.

4.4.1. 4 h of Daily PHS Plant Operation

Figure 13 shows the daily energy generated with 4 h daily PHS plant operation during the year 2022, using the water pumped with the energy generated by each size of the FPV plant, i.e., joint operation mode of both plants. With the FPV plant size $S1$, the PHS plant is not operational every day of the year. In contrast, the PHS plant is operational every day of the year with the other sizes. In addition, water storage is achieved in the upper reservoir, namely 12.28% and 51.21%, respectively, with the FPV plant sizes $S3$ and $S4$. The PHS plant operates under Case 1 conditions: No deviation. In addition, it operates during the 4 h of highest electricity market prices.

Figure 14 shows the economic benefit from the independent and joint operation modes of both plants, for the sizes $S1$ and $S2$ and pumping process efficiency of 0.77 and 0.85.

The joint operation mode is characterised by 4 h of PHS plant operation per day during the year 2022, using the water pumped with the energy generated by the FPV plant sizes $S1$ and $S2$.

The independent operation mode is characterised by 4 h of daily PHS plant operation during the year 2022 depending on the available water and FPV plant sizes selling the energy as it is generated. The FPV plant operates under Case 1 conditions: No deviation.

For $\mu = 0.77$, the economic benefit is always higher in the independent mode of operation. This is true even if there are deviations of 10%, in Cases 3 and 4.

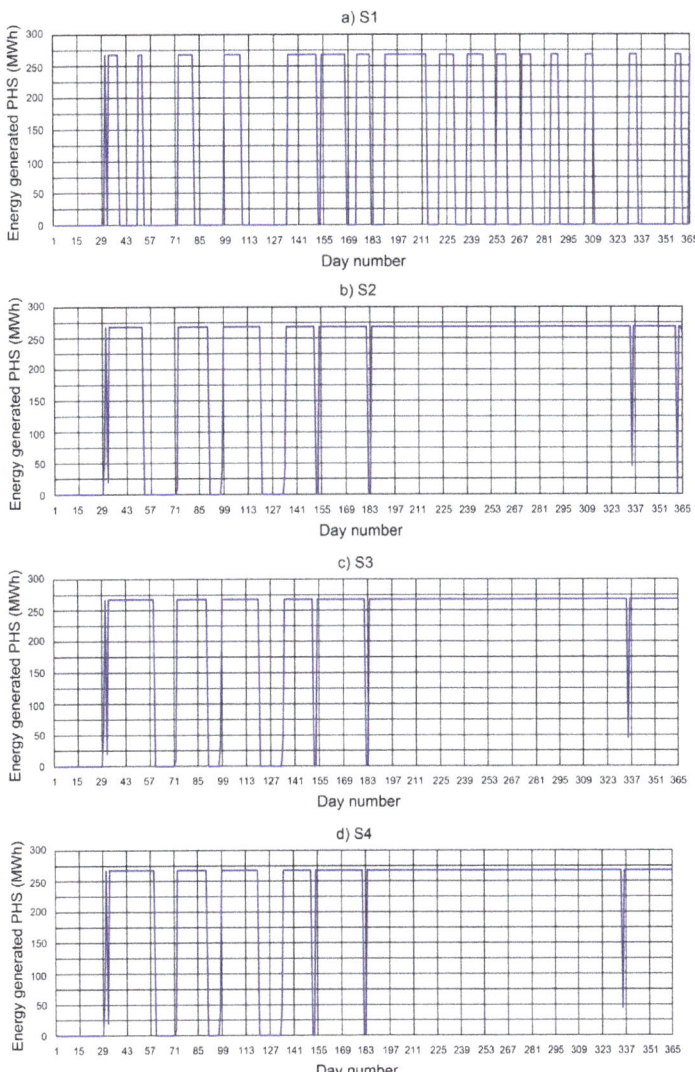

Figure 13. Daily energy generated by the PHS plant during the year 2022.

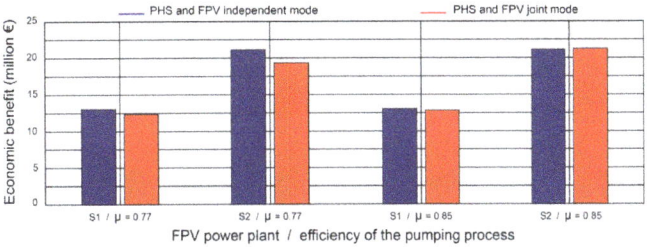

Figure 14. Economic benefit from the independent and joint operation modes with S1 and S2.

For $\mu = 0.85$, the economic benefit is slightly higher in the joint operation mode of FPV plant size $S2$. If the FPV plant size is $S1$, the economic benefit is slightly higher in the independent operation mode. However, if deviations of 10% occur in Cases 3 and 4, the economic benefit is slightly higher in the joint operation mode.

Figure 15 shows the economic benefit from the independent and joint operation modes of both plants, for the sizes $S3$ and $S4$ and the pumping process efficiency of 0.77 and 0.85.

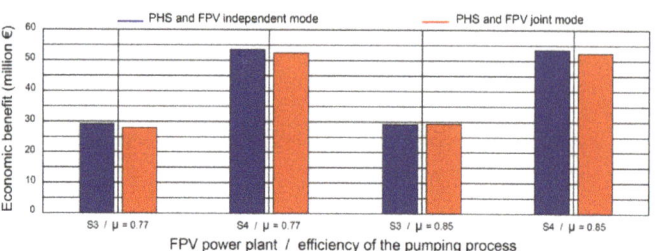

Figure 15. Economic benefit of the independent and joint operation modes with $S3$ y $S4$.

The joint operation mode is characterised by 4 h of daily PHS plant operation during the year 2022, using the water pumped with the energy generated by the FPV plant sizes $S3$ and $S4$. The surplus energy from the FPV plant is sold as it is generated. The FPV plant operates under Case 1 conditions: No deviation.

The independent operation mode is characterised by 4 h daily PHS plant operation during the year 2022 depending on the available water and FPV plant sizes selling the energy as it is generated. The FPV plant operates under Case 1 conditions: No deviation.

For $\mu = 0.77$, the economic benefit is always higher in the independent mode of operation. This is true even if there are deviations of 10%, in Cases 3 and 4.

For $\mu = 0.85$, the economic benefit is slightly higher in the joint operation mode of the FPV plant size $S3$. If the FPV plant size is $S4$, the economic benefit is slightly higher in the independent operation mode. This is true even if there are deviations of 10%, in Cases 3 and 4.

The more important renewable energies become in the electricity market, the greater the need for an energy storage system. Therefore, as the results obtained here are very similar in the joint and independent operation mode of both plants, it can be assumed that the economic benefit from the joint operation mode of both plants will increase as the need for energy storage increases. Several studies confirm that the joint operation mode of both plants can play an important role in balancing systems with a high penetration of variable renewables [26].

4.4.2. 5 or More Daily Hours of PHS Plant Operation

Figure 16 shows the economic benefit from the independent and joint operation modes of both plants for the size $S4$ with the pumping process efficiencies of 0.77 and 0.85, and 5 daily hours of PHS plant operation.

The joint operation mode is characterised by 5 h per day of PHS plant operation during the year 2022, using the water pumped with the energy generated by the FPV plant size $S4$ and when the surplus energy from the FPV plant is sold as it is generated. The FPV plant operates under Case 1 conditions: No deviation.

The independent operation mode is characterised by 4 h of daily PHS plant operation during the year 2022 depending on the available water and FPV plant selling the energy as it is generated. The FPV plant operates under Case 1 conditions: No deviation.

For $\mu = 0.77$ and $\mu = 0.85$, the economic benefit is always higher in the independent mode of operation. This is true even if there are deviations of 10% in Cases 3 and 4.

For all other plant sizes, the economic benefit is always higher in the independent mode of operation. This profit increases as the power of the FPV plant decreases.

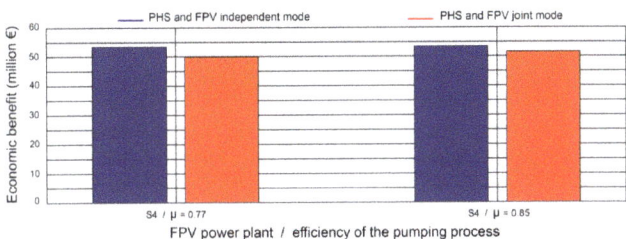

Figure 16. Economic benefit from the independent and joint operation modes with S4.

5. Conclusions

This paper examines the sizing of a floating photovoltaic (FPV) power plant for integration into an existing pumped hydroelectric storage (PHS) power plant in order to improve the performance thereof. In addition, the parameter known PHS plant total process efficiency is also used to evaluate the plant. The Alto Rabagão pumped hydroelectric storage power plant in Northern Portugal was the subject of the study. The following power outputs were analysed for the FPV plant: 33.55 (MWp) (50% PHS), 67.1 (MWp) (100% PHS), 100.65 (MWp) (150% PHS), 201.30 (MWp) (300% PHS), and 301.95 (MWp) (450% PHS). These FPV plant sizes are referred to as S1, S2, S3, S4 and S5, respectively. The values of the total process efficiency parameter analysed are 0.77 for old PHS plants, and 0.85 for more modern plants. The results obtained confirm which scenarios earn economic benefits from a PHS plant and an FPV plant operating together or independently.

The study shows the following conclusions regarding the volume of water in the upper reservoir:

(i) The actual data showed that the volume of water available in the upper reservoir is a critical parameter that determines the PHS plant operating days. The PHS plant only operated 20% of the days in 2022. In addition, more energy is absorbed in the pumping process than the energy generated by the PHS plant. Therefore, the economic benefit was negative.

(ii) The sizes of the FPV plants analysed occupy a very small body of water compared to the total surface area of the upper reservoir, specifically, 1.018% for S1, 2.04% for S2, 3.05% for S3, 6.12% for S4, and 9.16% for S5.

(iii) The FPV plant sizes analysed have the capacity to reach significant higher reservoir levels (if all the energy generated by the FPV plant sizes was used to pump water), specifically, 16.85% for S1, 33.71% for S2, 50.56% for S3, 101.13% for S4 and 151.69% for S5.

(iv) In total, 100% of the water volume of the upper reservoir is obtained with an occupied water body surface of 6.12%.

From an economic benefit point of view and taking into account 4 h of PHS plant operation per day during the year 2022 (the 4 h of highest electricity market prices and the PHS plant always operating under the conditions of Case 1: No deviation), the study shows the following conclusions:

(i) During joint operation of both plants, the S1 size FPV plant is not able to operate the PHS plant every day of the year. In addition, the economic benefit is slightly higher with the independent operation mode (Case 1: No deviations), regardless of the value of the total process efficiency parameter analysed. However, if deviations of 10% occur in Cases 3 and 4, the economic benefit is slightly higher in the joint operation mode.

(ii) During the joint operation of both plants, the S2 size of the FPV plant is able to operate the PHS plant every day of the year. If the total process efficiency is 0.85, this mode of operation earns a slightly higher economic benefit than the independent operation of both plants (Case 1: No deviations).

(iii) During joint operation of both plants, the FPV plant sizes $S3$ and $S4$ are able to operate the PHS plant every day of the year and, in addition, obtain a surplus water volume of 12.28% and 51.21%, respectively, of the capacity of the upper reservoir.

(iv) During joint operation of both plants, the $S3$ size of FPV plant is able to operate the PHS plant every day of the year and sell the surplus energy directly as it is generated (in this case, no water is stored). If the total process efficiency is 0.85, this mode of operation earns a slightly higher economic benefit than the independent operation mode of both plants (Case 1: No deviations).

(v) In the joint operation of both plants, the FPV plant size $S4$ is able to operate the PHS plant every day of the year and sell the surplus energy directly as it is generated (in this case, no water is stored). The economic benefit is slightly higher with the independent operation mode (Case 1: No deviations), regardless of the value of the total process efficiency parameter analysed.

In summary, if the total process efficiency is 0.85, the joint operation of both plants with FPV plant sizes $S2$ and $S3$ yields a slightly higher economic benefit than the independent mode of operation. If the total process efficiency is 0.77, there is always a higher economic benefit in the independent operation mode, irrespective of the size of the FPV plant. However, the uncertainty of the solar resource estimation can lead to a higher economic benefit in the joint operation mode.

Increasing the number of PHS plant operating hours above 4 h per day decreases the economic benefit from the joint operation mode, regardless of the total process efficiency parameter and the size of the FPV plant. The economic benefit decreases as the number of operating hours increases.

Author Contributions: Conceptualization, A.B. and L.B.; methodology, A.B. and L.B.; software, J.A.-B.; validation, R.G.; writing—original draft preparation, R.G. and J.A.-B.; visualization, R.G.; supervision, A.B. and L.B. All authors have read and agreed to the published version of the manuscript.

Funding: This research received no external funding.

Data Availability Statement: Not applicable.

Acknowledgments: We wish to thank EDP [28] for its contribution to this paper.

Conflicts of Interest: The authors declare no conflict of interest.

Nomenclature

A_T	Total surface area of the PV modules (m^2)
E_{PV}	Total energy (Wh)
g	Acceleration due to gravity (m/s^2)
H_t	Total irradiation on a tilted surface (Wh/m^2)
h_a	Available head (m)
h_e	Elevating head (m)
I_{bh}	Beam irradiance on a horizontal surface (W/m^2)
I_{dh}	Diffuse irradiance on a horizontal surface (W/m^2)
I_t	Total irradiance on a tilted surface (W/m^2)
k_p	Water pumping coefficient (W· s/m^3)
k_t	Turbine generating coefficient (W· s/m^3)
L_{PV}	Module PV length (m)
$NOCT$	Normal operating cell temperature (°)
n	Ordinal of the day (day)
P_a	Power input of the electric motor (W)
P_g	Power output of the electric generator (W)
P_{PV}	Power output of the PV module (W/m^2)
P_t	Power output of the hydro turbine (W)
q_t	Turbined flow rate (m^3/s)
q_p	Pumped flow rate (m^3/s)

T	Solar time (h)
T_a	Ambient temperature (°)
T_c	PV cell temperature (°C)
T_{ref}	Reference temperature (°C)
T_R	Sunrise solar time (h)
T_S	Sunset solar time (h)
W_{PV}	Module PV width (m)
α	Solar absorptance of PV layer (dimensionless)
β	Tilt angle of photovoltaic module (°)
β_{ref}	Temperature coefficient (1/°C)
γ	Azimuth angle of photovoltaic module (°)
δ	Solar declination (°)
η_e	PV module efficiency (%)
η_g	Electric generator efficiency (%)
η_m	Motor generator efficiency (%)
η_p	Pump efficiency (%)
η_{ref}	PV module efficiency at the reference temperature (%)
η_t	Hydro turbine efficiency (%)
θ_i	Incidence angle (°)
θ_z	Zenith angle of the Sun (°)
λ	Latitude angle (°)
μ	Total pumping process efficiency (%)
ρ	Density of water (kg/m^3)
ρ_g	Ground reflectance (dimensionless)
τ	Solar transmittance of glazing (dimensionless)
ω	Hour angle (°)

References

1. The Paris Agreement. Paris Agreement. In Proceedings of the Conference of the Parties to the United Nations Framework Convention on Climate Change (21st Session), Paris, France, 30 November–13 December 2015.
2. Bouckaert, S.; Pales, A.F.; McGlade, C.; Remme, U.; Wanner, B.; Varro, L.; D'Ambrosio, D.; Spencer, T.; Abergel, T.; Arsalane, Y.; et al. Net Zero by 2050: A Roadmap for the Global Energy Sector. International Energy Agency (IEA). 2021. Available online: https://www.iea.org/reports/net-zero-by-2050 (accessed on 10 April 2023).
3. BPIE. 9 Ways to Make the Energy Performance of Buildings Directive More Effective. 2016. Available online: http://bpie.eu/wp-content/uploads/2016/08/EPBD-paper_Eng.pdf (accessed on 27 January 2023).
4. BP Statistical Review of World Energy. 2021. Available online: https://www.bp.com/content/dam/bp/business-sites/en/global/corporate/pdfs/energy-economics/statistical-review/bp-stats-review-2021-full-report.pdf (accessed on 27 January 2023).
5. Barbón, A.; Fortuny Ayuso, P.; Bayón, L.; Silva, C.A. A comparative study between racking systems for photovoltaic power systems. *Renew. Energy* **2021**, *180*, 424–437. [CrossRef]
6. Lin, F.; Zhang, Y.; Wang, J. Recent advances in intra-hour solar forecasting: A review of ground-based sky image methods. *Int. Forecast.* **2023**, *39*, 244–265. [CrossRef]
7. U.S. Department of Energy, Energy Efficiency and Renewable Energy. Types of Hydropower Plants. 2023. Available online: https://www.energy.gov/eere/water/types-hydropower-plants (accessed on 10 April 2023).
8. Agrawal, K.K.; Jha, S.K.; Mittal, R.K.; Vashishtha, S. Assessment of floating solar PV (FSPV) potential and water conservation: Case study on Rajghat Dam in Uttar Pradesh, India. *Energy Sustain. Dev.* **2022**, *66*, 287–295. [CrossRef]
9. Sanseverino, I.; Conduto, D.; Pozzoli, L.; Dobricic, S., Lettieri, T. Algal Bloom and Its Economic Impact, European Commission, Joint Research Centre. 2016. Available online: https://op.europa.eu/en/publication-detail/-/publication/4d384d1b-1804-11e6-ba9a-01aa75ed71a1/language-en (accessed on 10 April 2023).
10. Muñoz-Cerón, E.; Osorio-Aravena, J.C.; Rodríguez-Segura, F.J.; Frolova, M.; Ruano-Quesada, A. Floating photovoltaics systems on water irrigation ponds: Technical potential and multi-benefits analysis. *Energy* **2023**, *271*, 127039. [CrossRef]
11. Nguyen, N.H.; Le, B.C.; Nguyen, L.N.; Bui, T.T. Technical analysis of the large capacity grid-connected floating photovoltaic system on the hydropower reservoir. *Energies* **2023**, *16*, 3780. [CrossRef]
12. Al-Widyan, M.; Khasawneh, M.; Abu-Dalo, M. Potential of floating photovoltaic technology and their effects on energy output, water quality and supply in Jordan. *Energies* **2021**, *14*, 8417. [CrossRef]
13. Padilha Campos Lopes, M.; Nogueira, T.; Leandro Santos, A.J.; Castelo Branco, D.; Pouran, H. Technical potential of floating photovoltaic systems on artificial water bodies in Brazil. *Renew. Energy* **2022**, *181*, 1023–1033. [CrossRef]
14. Martín-Chivelet, N. Photovoltaic potential and land-use estimation methodology. *Energy* **2016**, *94*, 233–242. [CrossRef]
15. El Hammoumi, A.; Chalh, V.; Allouhi, A.; Motahhir, S.; El Ghzizal, A.; Derouich, A. Design and construction of a test bench to investigate the potential of floating PV systems. *J. Clean. Prod.* **2021**, *278*, 123917. [CrossRef]

16. Liu, H.; Krishna, V.; Lun Leung, J.; Reindl, T.; Zhao, L. Field experience and performance analysis of floating PV technologies in the tropics. *Prog. Photovolta. Res. Appl.* **2018**, *26*, 957–967. [CrossRef]
17. Cramton, P. Electricity market design. *Oxf. Rev. Econ. Policy* **2017**, *33*, 589–612. [CrossRef]
18. Barbón, A.; Gutiérrez, A.; Bayón, L.; Bayón-Cueli, C.; Aparicio-Bermejo, J. Economic analysis of a pumped hydroelectric storage-integrated floating PV system in the day-ahead Iberian electricity market. *Energies* **2023**, *16*, 1705. [CrossRef]
19. Jurasz, J.; Canales, F.A.; Kies, A.; Guezgouz, M.; Beluco, A. A review on the complementarity of renewable energy sources: concept, metrics, application and future research directions. *Sol. Energy* **2020**, *195*, 703–724. [CrossRef]
20. Kougias, I.; Szabó, S. Pumped hydroelectric storage utilization assessment: Forerunner of renewable energy integration or Trojan horse? *Energy* **2017**, *140*, 318–329. [CrossRef]
21. Rehman, S.; Al-Hadhrami, L.M.; Alam, M.M. Pumped hydro energy storage system: A technological review. *Renew. Sustain. Rev.* **2015**, *44*, 586–598. [CrossRef]
22. Margeta, J.; Glasnovic, Z. Theoretical settings of photovoltaic-hydro energy system for sustainable energy production. *Solar Energy* **2012**, *86*, 972–982. [CrossRef]
23. Rauf, H.; Gull, M.S.; Arshad, N. Complementing hydroelectric power with floating solar PV for daytime peak electricity demand. *Renew. Energy* **2020**, *162*, 1227–1242. [CrossRef]
24. Kocaman, A.S.; Modi, V. Value of pumped hydro storage in a hybrid energy generation and allocation system. *Appl. Energy* **2017**, *205*, 1202–1215. [CrossRef]
25. Glasnovic, Z.; Margeta, J. The features of sustainable solar hydroelectric power plant. *Renew. Energy* **2009**, *34*, 1742–1751. [CrossRef]
26. Bhattacharjee, S.; NayakP.K. PV-pumped energy storage option for convalescing performance of hydroelectric station under declining precipitation trend. *Renew. Energy* **2019**, *135*, 288–302. [CrossRef]
27. Ciucci, M. Internal Energy Market, Fact Sheets on the European Union. 2022. Available online: https://www.europarl.europa.eu/factsheets/en/sheet/45/internal-energy-market (accessed on 27 January 2023).
28. EDP. Available online: https://portugal.edp.com/en/alto-rabagao-hydro-power-plant (accessed on 27 December 2022).
29. Bayón, L.; Grau, J.M.; Ruiz, M.M.; Suárez, P.M. Mathematical modelling of the combined optimization of a pumped-storage hydro-plant and a wind park. *Math. Comput. Model.* **2013**, *57*, 2024–2028. [CrossRef]
30. Ibrahim, H.; Ilinca, A.; Perron, J. Energy storage systems–characteristics and comparisons. *Renew. Sustain. Energy Rev.* **2008**, *12*, 1221–1250. [CrossRef]
31. Khalil Zidane, T.E.; Bin Adzman, M.R.; Naim Tajuddin, M.F.; Mat Zali, S.; Durusu, A. Optimal configuration of photovoltaic power plant using grey wolf optimizer: A comparative analysis considering CdTe and c-Si PV modules. *Sol. Energy* **2019**, *188*, 247–257. [CrossRef]
32. Kalogirou, S.A.; Agathokleous, R.; Panayiotou, G. On-site PV characterization and effect of soiling on their performance. *Energy* **2013**, *51*, 439–446. [CrossRef]
33. Skoplaki, E.; Palyvos, J.A. On the temperature dependence of photovoltaic module electrical performance: A review of efficiency/power correlations. *Sol. Energy* **2009**, *83*, 614–624. [CrossRef]
34. Evans, D.L. Simplified method for predicting photovoltaic array output. *Sol. Energy* **1981**, *27*, 555–560. [CrossRef]
35. Kichou, S.; Skandalos, N.; Wolf, P. Floating photovoltaics performance simulation approach. *Heliyon* **2022**, *8*, 11896. [CrossRef] [PubMed]
36. Lawrence Kamuyu, W.C.; Rok Lim, J.; Sub Won, C.; Keun Ahn, H. Prediction model of photovoltaic module temperature for power performance of floating PVs. *Energies* **2018**, *11*, 447. [CrossRef]
37. Dutra Silva, D.; Marson, V.; Rodrigues de Souza, R.; Diehl de Oliveira, J.; Campos Silva, J.B.; Cardoso, E.M. A new predictive model for a photovoltaic module's surface temperature. *Energy Rep.* **2022**, *8*, 15206–15220. [CrossRef]
38. Skoplaki, E.; Palyvos, J.A. Operating temperature of photovoltaic modules: A survey of pertinent correlations. *Renew. Energy* **2009**, *34*, 23–29. [CrossRef]
39. Mattei, M.; Notton, G.; Cristofari, C.; Muselli, M.; Poggi, P. Calculation of the polycrystalline PV module temperature using a simple method of energy balance. *Renew. Energy* **2006**, *31*, 553–567. [CrossRef]
40. Choi, Y.K. A study on power generation analysis of floating PV system considering environmental impact. *Int. J. Softw. Eng. Appl.* **2014**, *8*, 75–84. [CrossRef]
41. Oliveira-Pinto, S.; Stokkermans, J. Assessment of the potential of different floating solar technologies–Overview and analysis of different case studies. *Energy Convers. Manag.* **2020**, *211*, 112747. [CrossRef]
42. Duffie, J.A.; Beckman, W.A. *Solar Engineering of Thermal Processes*, 4th ed.; John Wiley & Sons: New York, NY, USA, 2013.
43. Barbón, A.; Fortuny Ayuso, P.; Bayón, L.; Fernández-Rubiera, J.A. Predicting beam and diffuse horizontal irradiance using Fourier expansions. *Renew. Energy* **2020**, *154*, 46–57. [CrossRef]
44. WRDC. World Radiation Data Centre. 2022. Available online: http://wrdc.mgo.rssi.ru/ (accessed on 27 January 2023).
45. Bhavani, S.; Chithambaram, V.; Muthucumaraswamy, R.; Shanmugan, S.; Essa, F.A.; Elsheikh, A.H.; Selvaraju, P.; Janarthanan, B. Laplacian tactic for the prediction of the temperature components of solar cooker with logical prediction by fuzzy rules. *Sol. Energy* **2022**, *236*, 369–382. [CrossRef]
46. Barbón, A.; Bayón-Cueli, C.; Bayón, L.; Carreira-Fontao, V. A methodology for an optimal design of ground-mounted photovoltaic power plants. *Appl. Energy* **2022**, *314*, 118881. [CrossRef]

47. Hottel, H.C. A simple model for estimating the transmittance of direct solar radiation through clear atmosphere. *Sol. Energy* **1976**, *18*, 129–134. [CrossRef]
48. Liu, B.Y.H.; Jordan, R.C. The interrelationship and characteristic distribution of direct, diffuse and total solar radiation. *Sol. Energy* **1960**, *4*, 1–19. [CrossRef]
49. PVGIS, Joint Research Centre (JRC). 2022. Available online: http://re.jrc.ec.europa.eu/pvg_tools/en/tools.html#PVP (accessed on 27 January 2023).
50. Ghigo, A.; Faraggiana, E.; Sirigu, M.; Mattiazzo, G.; Bracco, G. Design and analysis of a floating photovoltaic system for offshore installation: The case study of Lampedusa. *Energies* **2022**, *15*, 8804. [CrossRef]
51. Bayón-Cueli, C.; Barbón, A.; Fernández-Conde, A.; Bayón, L. Optimal distribution of PV modules on roofs with limited space. In Proceedings of the 2021 IEEE International Conference on Environmental and Electrical Engineering (EEEIC2021), Bari, Italy, 7–10 September 2021; pp. 50–55.
52. Isifloating. Available online: https://www.isifloating.com/en/solar-flotante-isifloating-by-isigenere-english/ (accessed on 27 January 2023).
53. Osborne, M. Sungrow Targets Teading Role in Supply of Floating Solar Systems to Booming Market. Available online: https://www.pv-tech.org/sungrow-targets-leading-role-in-supply-of-floating-solar-systems-to-booming/ (accessed on 10 April 2023).
54. Sahu, A.; Yadav, N.; Sudhakar, K. Floating photovoltaic power plant: A review. *Renew. Sustain. Energy Rev.* **2016**, *66*, 815–824. [CrossRef]
55. Ciel. Available online: https://ciel-et-terre.net/solutions/products/ (accessed on 27 January 2023).
56. Intech. Available online: https://intechcleanenergy.com/floating-panels.php (accessed on 27 January 2023).
57. Muneer, T. *Solar Radiation and Day Light Models*, 1st ed.; Elsevier: Oxford, UK, 2004.
58. Dobos, E. Albedo. *Encycl. Soil Sci.* **2006**, *2*, 24–25.
59. Weihs, P.; Mursch-Radlgruber, E.; Hasel, S.; Gützer, C.; Brandmaier, M.; Plaikner, M. Investigation of the effect of sealed surfaces on local climate and thermal stress. In *EGU General Assembly Conference Abstracts*; Copernicus GmbH: Göttingen, Germany, 2015; p. 12616.
60. Pérez-Gallardo, J.R.; Azzaro-Pantel, C.; Astier, S.; Domenech, S.; Aguilar-Lasserre, A. Ecodesign of photovoltaic grid-connected systems. *Renew. Energy* **2014**, *64*, 82–97. [CrossRef]
61. ESIOS, 2023; Iberian Market Operator, Market Results. Available online: https://www.esios.ree.es/es/mercados-y-precios (accessed on 27 January 2023).
62. SNIRH. 2023. Available online: https://snirh.apambiente.pt/index.php?idMain=1&idItem=1.3&sbaciaid=&szonas=&salbufeirasimbolo=03J/03A&n_mesBOLETIM=01&n_anoH= (accessed on 27 January 2023).

Disclaimer/Publisher's Note: The statements, opinions and data contained in all publications are solely those of the individual author(s) and contributor(s) and not of MDPI and/or the editor(s). MDPI and/or the editor(s) disclaim responsibility for any injury to people or property resulting from any ideas, methods, instructions or products referred to in the content.

Article

Modelling of Electric Power Generation Plant Based on Gas Turbines with Agricultural Biomass Fuel

Luis Fernando Rico-Riveros [1], César Leonardo Trujillo-Rodríguez [2], Nelson Leonardo Díaz-Aldana [2] and Catalina Rus-Casas [3,4,*]

[1] Department of Electronic Engineering, Faculty of Engineering, Universidad ECCI, Bogotá 111311, Colombia; direccion.electronica@ecci.edu.co
[2] Facultad de Ingeniería, Universidad Distrital Francisco José de Caldas, Bogotá 110231, Colombia; cltrujillo@udistrital.edu.co (C.L.T.-R.); nldiaza@udistrital.edu.co (N.L.D.-A.)
[3] Department of Electronic and Automatic Engineering, University of Jaén, 23071 Jaén, Spain
[4] Center for Advanced Studies on Earth Sciences, Energy and Environment CEACTEMA, Campus Las Lagunillas, University of Jaén, 23071 Jaén, Spain
* Correspondence: crus@ujaen.es

Abstract: To ensure the survival of society, an enormous amount of energy is required to sustain the economic and social development of communities. In addition, there is a pressing need to achieve significant reductions in climate change and the associated costs of implementing systems based on traditional energy sources, as well as addressing the issue of providing electricity to isolated areas. In rural environments, there is an alternative energy source with enormous potential, agricultural biomass, which can produce electrical and thermal energy and can progressively help to reduce dependence on fossil fuels. The purpose of this work is to present a dynamic simulation model of a power generation plant that uses the Joule Brayton thermodynamic cycle, based on a gas turbine which is fueled by residual agricultural biomass; the cycle converts mechanical energy to electrical energy. The problem is approached through the characterization of the biomass, mathematical models of the plant components, and simulation of the system behavior in different scenarios. The simulations are processed in Matlab/Simulink, which allows the model to be verified, validating the equilibrium relationship between generation and load demand.

Keywords: integrated models; simulation; biomass plant; gas turbine; mechanical to electrical energy conversion

1. Introduction

Biomass power generation has been identified as an alternative for meeting future energy demand. As part of promoting the development of biomass technology, it is essential to understand the advantages and disadvantages of biomass technology, as well as the technological implementation of biomass plants and their start, operation and shutdown characteristics [1].

Over the last few decades, there has been a significant growth in biomass research, conversion technologies, and the end use of the products obtained. Within this growth is further progress in gasification, given the number of advantages it presents. Simultaneously to its development, this work has been carried out on different models that allow for better understanding, optimization, and management of this type of processes [2].

Mathematical modeling of a gasification process has proven to be a relatively fast and inexpensive solution compared to the direct construction of pilot units. Mathematical models, based on theoretical, experimental, and practical operational work, aim to analyze the thermochemical processes involved in biomass gasification and to evaluate the influence of the main input variables on the properties of the gaseous products (e.g., gas composition and calorific value). Different types of models have been developed for gasification systems, including Computational Fluid Dynamics (CFD), Artificial Neural Networks (ANN), and thermodynamic equilibrium and kinetic models [3].

There is a large amount of work in the literature on gas turbine modeling [4]. The complexity of the model varies according to the intended application [5]. These models describe the spatially distributed nature of gas flow dynamics by dividing the gas turbine into several sections [6,7]. Mathematically, the complete description of the partial differential equation model boils down to a set of ordinary differential equations that facilitate application in a computer simulation program [4,8]. The simplest models for simpler applications, such as microgeneration, divide the gas turbine into only three sections corresponding to the main components of the turbine, i.e., compressor, combustion, and turbine [8].

Based on the referenced literature review and classification of studies presented, and focusing on energy generation through biomass plants and gasification processes with gas turbines, this work aims to develop a comprehensive model of an energy generation plant based on a gas turbine using agricultural biomass waste as fuel in a methodical manner. The model is simulated using the specialized software Matlab/Simulink.

The scope of this work is to verify the mathematical model through simulation, which will allow for continuity in subsequent developments towards the small-scale application of integrating a hybrid microgrid in a local environment in the department of Cundinamarca, Colombia. Therefore, the model must be comprehensive enough to represent the primary steady-state and transient characteristics of the plant, yet simple enough computationally to avoid complex implementation or long processing times during verification [4].

In this work, we implement models oriented towards the application of gas turbine-based microgeneration and highlight the relative simplicity of these models, which we verify mathematically and under simulation. The goals of this paper include: achieving control to stabilize variables at desired values, ensuring the necessary dynamic behavior when changing from one operating point to another, controlling fuel flow to achieve a desired load, controlling fuel/air ratio to provide the correct outlet gas temperature, and controlling injected water flow to prevent NOx emissions, as well as flow and temperature control.

The article is organized as follows. The materials and methods section presents a characterization of fuel based on agricultural biomass, references to studies based on models, a description of the used mathematical models, and a description of the control system and simulation model in Matlab/Simulink of the whole system.

Likewise, in the results discussion section, an analysis of the simulations carried out for various system test scenarios with variation in the load and fuel is presented. These variations are regulated by a classic PID control system, obtaining a satisfactory response for the biomass plant, generator, and control. The small-scale application of the mathematical models, plant modules, and control modules are verified, allowing the application to be oriented towards a projected integration of energy resources in a local microgrid in a non-interconnected area.

2. Materials and Methods

The following sections are presented in an orderly and consistent manner according to the development of consultation and application:

A. Characterization of fuel based on agricultural biomass;
B. References to model-based studies: thermodynamic, techno-economic, simulation, and mathematical;
C. Description of mathematical models;
D. Control system description;
E. Matlab/Simulink simulation model of the whole system.

A. Characterization of Biomass as fuel

Biomass means biological mass and corresponds to the amount of living matter produced on a given area of the earth's surface by organisms of a specific type [9]. The importance of biomass lies in the fact it can be transformed into energy, either electrical or as a source of heat, given that organic substances are produced from plant matter, and when burned they produce energy and some other compounds such as CO_2 and water (H_2O). Biomass is classified into several types, depending on how it is constituted and its production sector. The types found are agricultural biomass, forestry biomass, livestock biomass, and Organic Urban Solid Waste (OUSW) biomass [10]. The use of agricultural biomass as fuel in a gas turbine plant has some important advantages, but also presents significant challenges that must be carefully considered; Table 1 summarizes some advantages and disadvantages presented by the use of agricultural biomass as fuel.

Table 1. Advantages and disadvantages of the use of agricultural biomass as fuel.

Source	Advantages	Disadvantages
[11]	Renewable energy source	May require processing
[12]	Reduction of greenhouse gas emissions	Combustion generates ash and tar
[13]	Waste reduction	Limited availability
[14]	Contribution to rural development	Requires space and resources
[15]	Local production	Can compete with food production

Source: Own.

Table 1 presents some characteristics of the advantages and disadvantages of the use of agricultural biomass residues as fuel. It can be seen that the advantages are that it is greater in terms of mitigating the environmental impact, the contribution of local economic developments in agricultural regions where there is a large amount of waste that can be processed and used, and using energy content as a renewable and sustainable resource.

The energy content of biomass is usually measured in terms of the calorific value of the resource. The calorific value of a fuel refers to the number of calories it is capable of producing by the combustion of a unit mass of each element. Not only biomass, but each fuel has an associated value against which it can be compared with others of similar characteristics [16].

The units are determined based on the state of the fuel, whether it is solid, such as firewood and agro-industrial waste, liquid, such as diesel, or gaseous [17,18]. The agricultural sector produces a significant amount of biomass [6]. In this sector, the by-products generated during the collection process are referred to as agricultural crop residues. For energy crops, plants that have fast growth and do not require much supervision for cultivation are usually used. Some crops, such as aquatic plants, soybeans, and peanuts, are used to produce biodiesel, while others, such as corn, cassava, wheat, and sugar cane, are used to produce bioethanol.

Table 2 shows the source of biomasses, the type of waste and their energy potential as a result of a characterization that was carried out in the Department of Cundinamarca in Colombia.

Table 2. Calorific value according to the crop.

Type of Crop	Type of Waste	LCV (kcal/kg)	Energy Potential (TJ/Year)	Energy Potential (GWh/Year)
Oil Palm	Fart	3.988	239.29	66.471
	Fibre	4.274	618.24	171.733
	Palm rachis	4.021	601.11	166.974
Panelera Cane	Bagasse	4.456	9524.84	2645.791
	Leaves—Bud	4.007	2866.22	796.173
Coffee	Pulp	4.259	217.76	60.489
	Cisco	4.430	100.73	27.981
	Stems	4.384	1165.21	323.67

Table 2. Cont.

Type of Crop	Type of Waste	LCV (kcal/kg)	Energy Potential (TJ/Year)	Energy Potential (GWh/Year)
Corn	Stubble	3.429	318.01	88.336
	Tusa	3.390	97.27	27.019
	Doormat	3.815	110.88	30.8
Rice	Tamo	3.113	143.98	39.995
	Husk	3.603	49.63	13.787
Banana	Banana rachis	1.809	12.05	3.347
	Banana stem	2.032	79.15	21.986
	Rejected banana	2.488	7.4	2.056
Plantain	Plantain rachis	1.808	10.03	2.786
	Plantain stem	2.032	65.88	18.3
	Rejected plantain	2.480	6.16	1.711

Source: [18].

Table 2 presents characterized values of the energy potential of crop and residue types, which depend on the climatic conditions of the agricultural area in which they are developed. This is an important criterion to consider when determining the availability of the residue with the highest energy potential that can be used. For example, in the study area of the department of Cundinamarca, Colombia, the most common crops are coffee, banana, and plantain. Table 2 shows that coffee stems have the highest energy potential. These models can be represented as mathematical functions that relate the different variables involved in the process, as shown in Table 3.

Table 3. The mathematical model for biomass characterization.

Equation	Parameter	Description	Value	Unit
$PE = M_{rs} * E$	PE	Energy Potential		[TJ/year]
	M_{rs}	Mass of dry residue		[t/year]
	E	Energy of the residue per unit mass		[TJ/t]
$M_{rs} = A * R_C * M_{rg} * Y_{rs}$	A	Cultivated area		[ha/year]
	R_C	Crop yield		[t main product/ha planted]
	M_{rg}	Mass of residue generated from the cultivation		[t of waste/t of main product]
	Y_{rs}	Dry residue fraction		[t dry residue/t wet residue]
$M_{RS} = \alpha * A * R_C * \sum_{i=1}^{n}\sum_{k=1}^{m} M_{rgki} * Y_{rski}$	"k" "i"	Biomass classification Types of waste biomass		[t/year]
	α	Unit conversion constant	1×10^{-6}	
$PE_{BRA} = \alpha * A * R_C * \sum_{i=1}^{n}\sum_{k=1}^{m} M_{rgki} * Y_{rski} * PCI_{ki}$	PE_{BRA}	The overall energy potential of agricultural waste biomass		
	PCI	Lower Caloric Value of the residue		[TJ/t]

Source: Own.

The mathematical models for assessing the energy potential of biomass are based on the fact that the energy contained in its matter is proportional to its dry mass.

The Lower Calorific Value (LCV) is defined as the amount of energy given off in the combustion of a unit of mass of a combustible material in which water is released as vapor. If this water condenses, it gives off heat, and the Higher Calorific Value (HCV) would then be obtained, adding this given-off heat to the LCV. Therefore, the LCV is lower than the HCV, and the higher the moisture content of the fuel, the greater this difference will be. Therefore, the energy content of biomass is measured by the calorific value of the resource. It is necessary to clarify that the calorific value of resources, in the case of biomass, varies according to the level of humidity at which it is found. In particular, the higher the humidity, the lower the calorific value. In the case of biomass, it is necessary that the moisture content is less than 30% [19].

In many cases, the waste has a high moisture content, which requires conditioning, which is why the resources are usually subjected to prior drying processes, either naturally or induced, to make the raw material as suitable as possible for energy transformation processes [12].

The most suitable method to realize the energy utilization of agricultural biomass is through thermochemical processes. In the case of the agricultural sector, it must be taken into account that biomass residues contain a portion of the main product of the crop, and this fraction is usually larger than the unit [20].

Taking the LCV for different types of waste from different crops as a reference, the amount of biomass required to produce a certain amount of electricity can be dimensioned, for which calculations are presented in Table 4, taking generation as an example:

- Power required: 1 kW
- 1 kW = 860 kcal/h, equivalence
- PCI: 4.384 (kcal/kg). Average value of the PCI of the coffee stem taken from Table 2
- 1 cal = 4.1855 kJ, equivalence

Table 4. Calculation of the biomass required to produce electrical energy.

Equation	Parameter	Description	Value	Unit
	Biomass	Biomass quantity		$\left[\frac{kg}{h}\right]$
$\text{Biomass}\left[\frac{kg}{h}\right] = \frac{\text{Power required}[kW]}{\text{PCI}[kcal/kg]}$	Power	Power required		[kW]
	PCI	Lower Calorific Value		$\left[\frac{kcal}{kg}\right]$
$\text{PCI}\left[\frac{kcal}{Kg}\right] = 4.384\left[\frac{kcal}{Kg}\right] \times 4.1855[kJ]$ $= 18.349232\left[\frac{kJ}{kg}\right]$	PCI	Lower Calorific Value	4.384	$\left[\frac{kcal}{kg}\right]$
	cal	1 calorie	4.1855	kJ
	PCI ∗ cal	Product	18.349232	$\left[\frac{kJ}{kg}\right]$
$= 1[kW] \times 860\left[\frac{kcal}{h}\right] \times 4.1855[kJ] = 3599.53\left[\frac{kJ}{h}\right]$		Power required	3599.53	$\left[\frac{kJ}{h}\right]$
$\text{Biomass}\left[\frac{kg}{h}\right] = \left[\frac{3599.53\left[\frac{kJ}{h}\right]}{18.3492\left[\frac{kJ}{kg}\right]}\right] = 0.215\left[\frac{kg}{h}\right]$	Biomasa	Quantity of biomass required to produce 1 kW	0.215	$\left[\frac{kg}{h}\right]$

Source: Own.

With ideal efficiency values of the generation system of 100%, 0.215 kg/h would be required, but under an estimated lower performance, e.g., 90%, the following is obtained:

$$\text{Biomass}\left[\frac{kg}{h}\right] = \left[\frac{0.215\left[\frac{kg}{h}\right]}{0.9}\right] = 0.238\left[\frac{kg}{h}\right]$$

To produce 1 kW of power, 0.238 kg/h of agricultural biomass would be required, with an estimated efficiency of 90%.

B. References of studies based on different methods

The studies and references consulted based on different models, for a greater understanding of this work, are classified as follows: thermodynamic studies, techno-economic studies, studies based on simulation platforms, and studies of mathematical models. For the first three, a brief reference is made, and for the last, which is the mathematical classification, a greater depth is presented, since the main objective of this work is to develop a complete mathematical model of a power generation plant based on a gas turbine whose fuel is agricultural biomass residue. Some references for each study are presented below.

References from thermodynamic studies. Table 5 presents some references based on the biomass gasification process, and energy, mass, exergy, chemical, and thermodynamic analyses.

Table 5. References of thermodynamic studies.

Source	Description	Process	Contribution
[2]	The complete evaluation of the thermodynamic performance of an integrated biomass-supported combined plant is investigated. For thermodynamic investigation, the mass, energy, entropy, and exergy balance relationships of the modelled plant and sub-plants are applied.	Biomass gasification	It performs a comprehensive thermodynamic calculation of the combined cycle supported by biomass gasification to produce electric heat, fresh water, and hydrogen.
[21]	Gasification modelling procedures fall into two main categories: equilibrium and kinetic models.	Biomass gasification	Develop a code using MATLAB software to apply the GA procedure for the purpose of system optimization from thermodynamic and economic perspectives.
[22]	It presents the simulation of a real mCHP plant, based on a biomass gasifier coupled to an internal combustion engine (ICE), in the Aspen Plus environment to predict the system behavior.	Biomass gasification	The model reproduces the operation of the syngas cleaning unit, the ICE, and the thermal recovery system. In particular, the thermal recovery system has been reproduced by implementing the detailed geometrical characteristics of the actual heat exchangers of the mCHP with Aspen EDR environment.
[23]	They propose computational fluid dynamics (CFD) simulation validated against experiments.	Biomass gasification	The results showed that all models can represent biomass combustion in a reasonable way. Biomass gasification is completed at a temperature of 1050 °K.
[3]	They develop and implement a zero-dimensional model for downdraft biomass gasification in fixed-bed or slow-bed gasifiers.	Biomass gasification	The proposed model considers the main gasification sub-processes (drying, pyrolysis, gasification) and their products. The model successfully predicts the conversion behaviors of different types of biomasses during a gasification process in terms of yield and product composition.

Source: Own.

References of techno-economic studies. Table 6 presents some references of studies, analyses, and case studies on the technological, economic, and environmental components aimed at energy sustainability using biomass gasification resources.

References of studies based on simulation platforms. Table 7 lists some references based on the use of specialized simulation software, and some other case studies oriented toward the knowledge and implementation of strategies and computational tools for optimization and modern control in biomass gasification processes are presented.

Table 6. References techno-economic studies.

Source	Description	Process	Contribution
[24]	The study shows that various techno-economic parameters have significant effects on the reduction of the normalized cost of electricity—LCOE in different power plant configurations.	CSP-biomass-TES hybrid power plant.	In the paper, they model and simulate three power plant configurations to calculate the cost of electricity for each.
[25]	They propose a novel concept of BECCS (Bioenergy with carbon capture and storage) for energy production.	Downdraft gasifier	The innovative energy system presented is defined based on the integration of a downdraft gasifier, an external combustion gas turbine, an MCFC section, an organic Rankine cycle and a cryogenic CO_2 capture. The proposed system is modelled and analyzed on the basis of exergy and exergy-economic analysis.
[26]	They evaluate the performance of an advanced biomass-fueled hybrid power generation system and model a modern biomass-based electrochemical power generation system.	Biomass gasifier, SOFC, Direct Combustion GT and ORC.	They present a detailed parametric study of the system to exhibit thermo-economic and environmental behaviors.
[27]	They present the latest statistical data on energy generation from bioenergy resources using available sources.	Biomass gasification	They include descriptions of gasification conversion routes, with their sustainability conditions, as well as the government policies necessary for their implementation in the Indian context.
[28]	A review of the sustainability aspects of biomass gasification and the use of biomass synthesis gas for small-scale power generation is presented, taking the UN Sustainable Development Goals (ODS) as a frame of reference.	Synthesis gas from biomass	The sustainability framework provided by the ODS, together with the concepts of energy transition and the energy trilemma, give bioenergy great importance in what should be its participation in an energy matrix geared towards distributed energy systems.
[29]	It assesses the feasibility of new renewable energy systems, and analyses the sustainability impact of these technologies along the entire supply chain in the environmental, social, and economic pillars.	Systems of Renewable energy	They consider not only the cost of energy but also the environmental and socio-economic impacts involved throughout the life cycle of the technology.
[30]	They present an analysis to achieve the EU's goals of a climate-neutral economy by 2050, highlighting that an adjustment of the current economy to one based on renewable raw materials (bioeconomic) must take place.	Bioeconomic	They stress that renewable solutions should be introduced into our existing production chain and should be conceived not as immediate solutions, but as long-term solutions, to be used as early as possible and improved over time.
[31]	They present an analysis of micro-scale biomass-fueled applications, with wood, straw, energy crop plants, and agricultural products being the most used fuels.	Applications Microscale	They study various types of boilers for each type of biomass, resulting from different fuel properties and investors' expectations (e.g., in relation to price and operational parameters such as the convenience of use).

Source: Own.

Table 7. References simulation platforms studies.

Source	Description	Process	Contribution
[32]	They point out that there are very few published studies on the modelling of biomass gasification based on the ANN method and even fewer in the field of fixed-bed downdraft gasifiers.	Biomass gasification based on the ANN method	They develop an integrated ANN model with a thermodynamic equilibrium approach for the downstream biomass gasification integrated power generation unit, which aims to predict the net power output of systems derived from various types of biomass feedstocks under atmospheric pressure and various operating conditions.
[33]	It presents an Artificial Neural Network (ANN) based model hybridized with a Particle Swarm Optimization (PSO) algorithm for a Biomass Gasification Plant (BGP) to estimate the amount of biomass needed to produce the syngas required to satisfy the energy demand.	Biomass gasification plant	The proposed model is compared with two traditional ANN models: Backward Feedback Propagation (FF-BP) and Forward Cascade Propagation (CF-P). ANNs are trained in MATLAB software using a real historical data set from a BGP located in the Distributed Energy Resources Laboratory of the Universitat Politècnica de València in Spain.
[34]	They researched about the possibility of using NARX ANN in a fixed-bed downdraft gasifier to predict syngas composition for lower data logging frequency.	Biomass downdraft fixed-bed downdraft gasifier	They obtain results from an open-loop network consisting of input and output layers connected with a hidden layer of 5 neurons. The application of the network allows online prediction and control of the gasification process.
[35]	They present two case studies that combining PV, biomass gasifier and batteries; one in Honduras and the other in Zambia.	Biomass gasification	The simulation resulting from the research allowed to review the performance of a gasifier in two HRES case studies that combine PV, biomass gasifier and batteries; one in Honduras and the other in Zambia.

Source: Own.

Mathematical modelling studies. Table 8 presents some references that are oriented toward mathematical modelling, simulation, and control, where the majority are based on the same models, but with different scopes of application in biomass gasification.

As has been mentioned, the main objective of this article is to develop the mathematical models of each component that is part of a gas turbine-based power generation plant. Although the other models which were consulted and referenced are important, it is considered that mathematical models are the basis for sizing. Simulating and evidencing behaviors of the components of the plant, and managing to establish a stable, reliable, and reproducible plant model, are the basis to determine and apply the other models. The referenced mathematical models are comprehensive enough to represent the primary steady-state and transient characteristics of the plant, yet simple enough computationally to avoid complex implementation or long processing times during verification.

The following section presents a detailed description of the mathematical models of each subsystem of the biomass-fueled gas turbine power plant.

C. Description of the Mathematical Models

Gas turbines have played an important role in recent decades, due to their low initial investment cost and operational versatility. They can be used efficiently not only for emergency services to cover peak daily demand if required, but also as microgrid-based generation systems, which integrate energy resources into a comprehensive, manageable, and coordinated hybrid system.

Plants that use gas turbines to operate mechanical power, which is converted to electrical power by a generator, can operate either in closed or open loops. Figure 1 shows a schematic of an open loop gas turbine power plant.

Table 8. References mathematical models.

Source	Description	Process	Contribution
[4]	The book presents comprehensive information on CC combined cycle and CHP combined heat and power cycle systems.	Biomass gasification	It presents in detail the mathematical, control, and simulation models of gas turbine, steam turbine, and combined gas turbine-based power plants. From the book the following references are highlighted [8,28,36–40], being the basis for the development and application of gas turbines.
[6]	The book presents comprehensive information on distributed generation using gas microturbines, apart from mathematical models, it highlights control models and microgrid applications.	Distributed electricity generation with gas microturbine	Control models and micro-grid oriented applications are highlighted.
[7]	In the Thesis, it is applied the dynamic models described in the book [27] by generating simulations of gas, steam, and combined cycle turbine plants, which validate the models for his own application.	Modeling and dynamic simulation of cogeneration schemes	It presents simulations of gas, steam, and combined cycle turbine plants, which validate the models for their own application.
[41]	It presents an application of mathematical models oriented to simulation and control based on neuro-fuzzy controllers, controlling several scenarios of variation of power, torque, active, and reactive load.	Neuro-fuzzy Control	Neuro-fuzzy controller applied to various scenarios of variation of power, torque, active, and reactive load.
[42–49]	They are based on the same mathematical and control models	Gas turbine	There is no great detail of the mathematical models, calculations, or parameters of each subsystem, each study focuses its development on specific applications.

Source: Own.

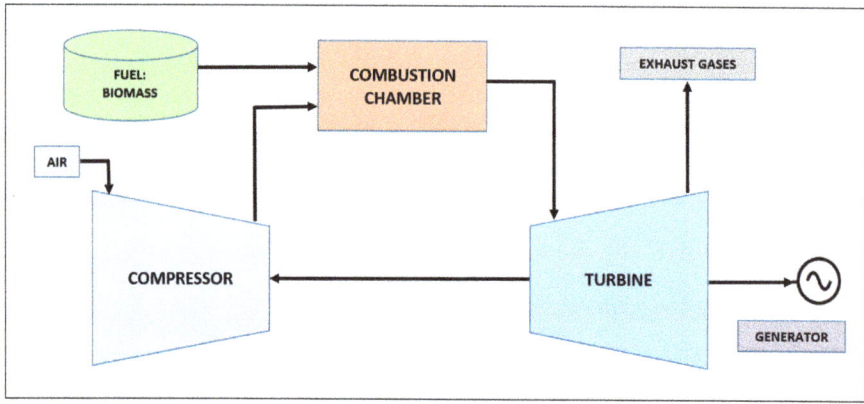

Figure 1. Open circuit gas turbine power plant. Source: [7].

In this configuration, fuel and air enter the combustion chamber and, after the chemical reaction is generated, the gas exits to the turbine producing mechanical power; the gases leaving the turbine are not recycled. This type of "open loop" plant does not constitute a thermodynamic cycle. However, its performance is often evaluated as if it were operating as a "closed loop" plant, Figure 2a illustrates this type of plant.

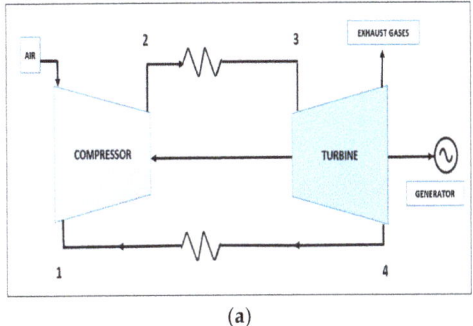
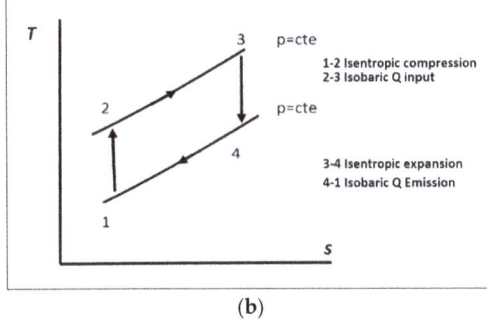

Figure 2. (**a**) Closed-loop diagram; (**b**) Temperature – Entropy (T – S) diagram of the thermal cycle of mechanical power generation with a gas turbine. Source: [7].

Power plants that utilize gas turbines are based on the constant pressure Joule Brayton cycle [28]. In this cycle, a constant flow of air or gas is compressed, heated, and expanded through the turbine, and then cooled in a heat exchanger, in the case of a closed thermal cycle. The turbine provides mechanical power to both the compressor and the generator.

In Figure 2, it can be seen that the main components of power plants using gas turbines are: the compressor, the combustion chamber, and the turbine. The way in which these plants operate is: at point 1, the air is taken from the atmosphere and enters the compressor to achieve the most favorable conditions for combustion. Then, at point 2, the air is mixed with fuel in gas form in the combustion chamber for combustion to take place, and then, at point 3, the hot gases that leave the chamber go to the turbine to produce mechanical power. In terms of energy conversion, the chemical energy that is released due to combustion is transferred to the gas flow. This energy, which is measured in terms of the enthalpy of the gases, is converted into mechanical power by the gas flow that turns the turbine. It must be considered that, in this process, part of the mechanical power which is handled goes to the compressor and the rest to the desired application.

In the T-s diagram of Figure 2b, the area under each of the process curves represents the heat transferred by that process; therefore, the area under the curve joining point 2 to 3 represents the heat transferred by the combustion taking part in the combustion chamber, as shown in Equation (1):

$$q_{ent} = \int_{s_2}^{s_3} T(s)_{2,3} ds \qquad (1)$$

Equation (1) is valid for all processes, the limits of integration should be adjusted to the limits in which the process is carried out, and also the temperature as a function of entropy for that process. Then, the heat given off in the Joule Brayton thermal cycle is given by the area under the curve from 1 to 4, as shown in Equation (2):

$$q_{sal} = \int_{s_1}^{s_4} T(s)_{1,4} ds \qquad (2)$$

Finally, by the first law of thermodynamics, the difference between the areas 2 and 3 and from 1 to 4 represents the net work produced in the thermal cycle, as shown in Equation (3):

$$W_{neto} = q_{ent} - q_{sal} \tag{3}$$

It is evident that the higher the temperatures handled in the 2 to 3 process and the lower the temperatures handled in the 4 to 1 process, the higher the efficiency of the thermal cycle.

In order to model the various components of gas turbine power plants, the following considerations are usually made [36,46]:

- Air and the products of combustion are considered ideal gases;
- The specific heats are considered constant for the products of combustion, air, and injected steam;
- The flow through the nozzles (compressor) is described as a polytropic, one-dimensional, and uniform adiabatic process;
- The energy storage and transport delay in the compressor, turbine, and combustion chamber are relatively small, which is why steady state equations are applied;
- The kinetic energy at the inlet of the gas flow in the compressor and turbine is considered negligible;
- The mass flow of air through the compressor is controllable by means of the blades at the inlet.

Taking into account the previous equations and considerations, more detailed information on the mathematical models resulting from analyzing the gas turbine as a process of compression and expansion of combustion gases (behavior of a nozzle) is presented below, for which the system is decomposed into four main subsystems. These are illustrated in Figure 3, where input, process, and output variables are highlighted.

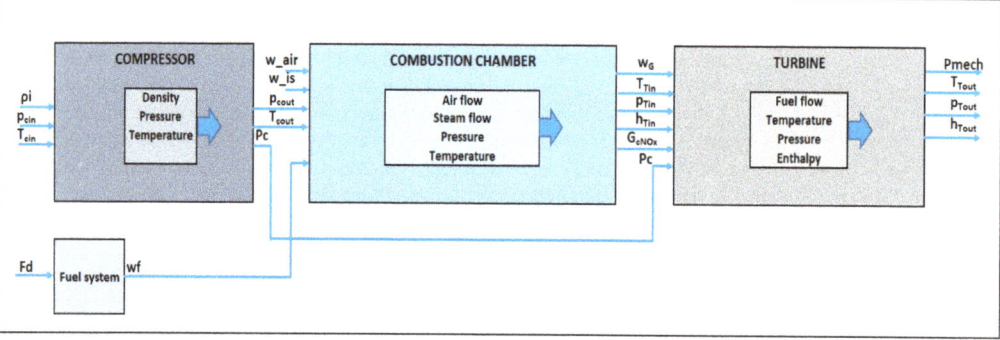

Figure 3. Gas Turbine Subsystems. Source: Own.

For the application and projected environments, a very high load requirement is not required, and all mathematical, simulation, and control models are dimensioned for the operation of a 5 kW power plant at a frequency of 60 Hz.

The mathematical models for the four (4) subsystems that make up the gas turbine-based power generation plant, as well as the electrical generator subsystem as a transducer of mechanical power to electrical power, are described below:

1. Fuel system (valve with actuator)
2. Compressor
3. Combustion chamber
4. Turbine
5. Electric generator

1. Fuel System

This system provides the fuel necessary for combustion to take place. In other words, from a fuel demand signal, this system operates by increasing the flow or decreasing the flow as required. The fuel flowing from the fuel system is the result of the inertia of the actuator and valve positioner, which are controlled by the PID controller's designer for this purpose. The equations in the Laplace domain, describing the dynamics of the system, are presented in Table 9, which shows: the equations, parameters, description, value, units, and procedure, as well as whether the value obtained arises from applying a calculation process, from a parameter, or from a constant.

Table 9. The mathematical model of the Fuel System.

Equation	Parameter	Description	Value	Unit	Procedure
$w_f = \frac{k_{ff}}{\tau_f S + 1} e_1$	W_f	Fuel mass flow.	2.889×10^{-4}	kg/s	Calculation
	k_{ff}	System Gain.	1	No Unit	Parameter
	τ_f	System time constant.	0.01	s	Parameter
	e_1	Valve positioner.	dynamic	No Unit	Calculation
$e_1 = \frac{a}{bS+c} e_2$	a, b, c	Valve parameters.	10, 1, 0	No Unit	Parameter
	e_2	Internal positioning signal.	dynamic	No Unit	Calculation
$e_2 = MF + F_d \omega_T e^{-S\tau} - w_f k_f$	MF	Minimum fuel signal.	0.8	p.u.	Calculation
	k_f	Feedback coefficient.	1	No Unit	Parameter
	F_d	Fuel demand signal.	1	p.u.	Calculation
	ω_T	Turbine speed.	188.45	rad/s	Calculation
	τ	System time delay.	0.01	s	Parameter

Source: Own.

2. Compressor

Compressors are positive displacement machines that maintain a constant volume in their chamber and a range of pressures at the outlet; the pressures depend proportionally on the inlet pressure to the compressor and are inversely proportional to the ratio of inlet-outlet densities. That is, the gas density at the compressor outlet is greater than the inlet density. The compressor is modelled as an equivalent nozzle in which an isentropic compression of the air is carried out, and the turbine as an equivalent nozzle in which an isentropic expansion of the gases leaving the combustion chamber is carried out, because this simplifies the models and, even with these simplifications, the relevant physics of the process, such as the change in temperature, pressure, and enthalpy, are still represented. Table 10 presents the mathematical model of the compressor.

The dynamics of the compressor are developed using the mathematical model outlined in Table 10. The following aspects can be observed: equations, parameters, descriptions, values, units, and procedures. The value obtained can arise from a calculation process, a parameter, or a constant. This model describes stable one-dimensional flow through the nozzle for uniform polytropic compression.

3. Combustion chamber

In this subsystem, combustion takes place where the hot gases, as a product of combustion, are directed to the gas turbine. The mathematical model of the combustor is presented in Table 11. The combustion of the gas turbine is modelled using the steady-state energy balance for combustion at the reference temperature.

4. Turbine

The turbine subsystem is where the gases leaving the combustion chamber expand. As the gases expand against the turbine blades, the turbine acquires kinetic energy, thus delivering mechanical power to the electrical generator.

Table 12 presents the mathematical model of the turbine, which is modelled using standard one-dimensional steady state gas flow equations.

Table 10. The mathematical model of the Compressor.

Equation	Parameter	Description	Value	Unit	Procedure
$w_a = A_0 \left\{ \frac{2m_a}{\eta_{\infty c}(m_a-1)} (p_{cin}\rho_i) \left[(r_c)^{\frac{2}{m_a}} - (r_c)^{\frac{(m_a+1)}{m_a}} \right] \right\}^{0.5}$	w_a	Air mass flow inside the compressor.	5.767×10^{-1}	kg/s	Calculation
	A_0	Compressor outlet area.	1.2×10^{-2}	m²	Parameter
	$\eta_{\infty c}$	Polytropic compressor efficiency.	0.9	No Unit	Parameter
	ρ_i	Inlet air density.	1.21	kg/m³	Parameter
	p_{cin}	Inlet air pressure.	15.62	Pa	Parameter
	m_a	Polytropic index.	1.417	No Unit	Calculation
	r_c	Pressure ratio (p_{out}/p_{in}).	10	No Unit	Calculation
$m_a = \left\{ \frac{\gamma_a}{\gamma_a - \frac{(\gamma_a-1)}{\eta_{\infty c}}} \right\}$	γ_a	(c_{pa}/c_{va}) Specific heat ratio for air (constant).	1.411	No Unit	Calculation
	c_{pa}	Specific heat of air at constant pressure.	1.012	J/(kg °K)	Parameter
	c_{va}	Specific heat of air at constant volume.	0.717	J/(kg °K)	Parameter
$\left(\frac{p}{p_0}\right) = r_c = \left[\frac{2}{(m_a+1)}\right]^{\frac{(m_a)}{(m_a-1)}}$	r_c	Pressure ratio (p_{out}/p_{in}).	10	No Unit	Calculation
$p_{cout} = p_{cin} r_c$	p_{cout}	Outlet air pressure	156	Pa	Calculation
$\frac{T_{cout}}{T_{cin}} = (r_c)^{\frac{(\gamma_a-1)}{\gamma_a \eta_{\infty c}}}$	T_{cout}	Outlet air temperature	547	°K	Calculation
	T_{cin}	Inlet air temperature.	288	°K	Parameter
$P_c = \frac{w_{ain} \Delta h_I}{\eta_c \eta_{trani}}$	P_c	Compressor power consumption	1820	W	Calculation
	Δh_I	isoentropic enthalpy change. Corresponding to the compression of P_{cin} with respect to P_{cout}	2.698×10^5	J/kg	Calculation
	η_c	Total compressor efficiency.	0.863	No Unit	Calculation
	η_{trans}	Transmission efficiency from turbine to compressor.	0.99	No Unit	Parameter
$\eta_c = \left\{ \frac{1-(r_c)^{\frac{(\gamma_a-1)}{\gamma_a}}}{1-(r_c)^{\frac{(\gamma_a-1)}{\gamma_a \eta_{\infty c}}}} \right\}$	η_c	Total compressor efficiency.	0.863	No Unit	Calculation
$\Delta h_I = c_{pair} T_{cin} \left((r_c)^{\frac{R_{air}}{c_{pair}}} - 1 \right)$	c_{pair}	Specific heat of air at constant pressure.	1005	J/(kg °K)	Parameter
	R_{air}	Ideal gas constant for air.	287	J/(kg °K)	Parameter

Source: Own.

Table 11. Mathematical model of Combustion Chamber.

Equation	Parameter	Description	Value	Unit	Procedure
$w_G = w_a + w_f + w_{is}$	w_G	Outlet gas mass flow.	5.77×10^{-1}	kg/s	Calculation
	w_{is}	Steam mass flow injection.	2.9×10^{-5}	kg/s	Calculation
	w_f	Fuel mass flow to the turbine.	2.88×10^{-4}	kg/s	Calculation
$w_G c_{pg}(T_{Tin} - 298) + w_a c_{pa}(298 - T_{cout}) + w_f \Delta h_{25} + w_{is} c_{ps}(298 - T_{is}) = 0$		Equation for the energy of combustion at temperature 25 °C, is cleared for T_{Tin}.			

Table 11. Cont.

Equation	Parameter	Description	Value	Unit	Procedure
$w_G c_{pg}(T_{Tin} - 298) + w_a c_{pa}(298 - T_{cout}) + w_f \Delta h_{25} + w_{is} c_{ps}(298 - T_{is}) = 0$	c_{pg}	Specific heat of flue gases	1144	J/(kg °K)	Parameter
	c_{ps}	Specific heat of steam.	2005	J/(kg °K)	Parameter
	c_{pa}	Specific heat of air.	1005	J/(kg °K)	Parameter
	T_{Tin}	Turbine inlet gas temperature.	1420	°K	Calculation
	Δh_{25}	Specific enthalpy of reaction at the reference temperature, (25 °C).	(-4.0×10^7)	J/(kg)	Parameter
	T_{is}	Steam temperature.	601	°K	Parameter
$p_{Tin} = p_{cout} - \Delta p$	p_{Tin}	Loss of combustion chamber pressure.	159	Pa	Calculation
$\Delta p = \left[\left(k_1 + k_2\left(\frac{T_{Tin}}{T_{cout}} - 1\right)\right)\frac{R}{2}\left(\frac{w_G}{A_m p_{cout}}\right)^2 T_{cout}\right]$	Δp	Loss of pressure in the combustion chamber.	2.698	Pa	Calculation
	k_1, k_2	Pressure loss coefficients	1	No Unit	Parameter
	R	Universal gas constant for flue gases	287	J/(kg °K)	Constante
	A_m	Cross-sectional area of the combustion chamber.	1	m^2	Parameter
	T_{ref}	Reference combustion temperature.	1000	°K	Parameter
	h_{ref}	Reference flue gas enthalpy.	1.2×10^6	J/kg	Parameter
	h_{Tin}	Turbine inlet gas enthalpy.	1.685×10^6	J/kg	Calculation

Source: Own.

Table 12. The mathematical model of the Turbine.

Equation	Parameter	Description	Value	Unit	Procedure
$\frac{T_{Tout}}{T_{Tin}} = (r)_T^{\eta_{\infty T}\left(\frac{\gamma_{cg}-1}{\gamma_{cg}}\right)}$	T_{tout}	Gas temperature at the turbine outlet.	763	°K	Calculation
	r_T	p_{Tout}/p_{Tin} Turbine pressure ratio.	6.29×10^{-2}	No Unit	Calculation
	p_{Tout}	Turbine outlet air pressure.	9.4	Pa	Calculation
	$\eta_{\infty T}$	Polytropic turbine efficiency	0.9	No Unit	Parameter
	γ_{cg}	c_{pg}/c_{vg}, Specific heat ratio for flue gases.	1.33	No Unit	Calculation
$w_G = A_{T0}\left\{\frac{2m_{cg}}{\eta_{\infty T}(m_{cg}-1)}(p_{Tin}\rho_{Ti})\left[(r_T)^{\frac{2}{m_{cg}}} - \left(\frac{p}{p_0}\right)^{\frac{(m_{cg}+1)}{m_{cg}}}\right]\right\}^{0.5}$	w_G	Turbine gas mass flow	5.77×10^{-1}	kg/s	Calculation
	A_{To}	Turbine outlet area	0.14	m^2	Parameter
	$\eta_{\infty T}$	Polytropic turbine efficiency	0.9	No Unit	Parameter
	ρ_{Tin}	Inlet gas density	3.778×10^{-4}	kg/m^3	Calculation
	p_{Tin}	Turbine inlet air pressure.	159	Pa	Calculation
	m_{cg}	Polytropic flue gas index.	1.384	No Unit	Calculation
$\rho_{Tin} = \frac{p_{Tin}}{R_{cg} T_{Tin}}$	ρ_{Tin}	Inlet gas density	3.778×10^{-4}	kg/m^3	Calculation
$m_{cg} = \left\{\frac{\gamma_{cg}}{\gamma_a - \frac{(\gamma_{cg}-1)}{\eta_{\infty T}}}\right\}$	m_{cg}	Polytropic flue gas index.	1.384	No Unit	Calculation
$\left(\frac{p}{p_0}\right) = r_T = \left[\frac{2}{(m_{cg}+1)}\right]^{\frac{(m_{cg})}{(m_{cg}-1)}}$	r_T	p_{Tout}/p_{Tin} Turbine pressure ratio.	6.29×10^{-2}	No Unit	Calculation
$\eta_T = \left\{\frac{1-(r_T)^{\frac{(\gamma_{cg}-1)}{\gamma_{cg}}}}{1-(r_T)^{\frac{(\gamma_{cg}-1)}{\gamma_{cg}\eta_{\infty T}}}}\right\}$	η_T	Overall turbine efficiency.	0.931	No Unit	Calculation

Table 12. Cont.

Equation	Parameter	Description	Value	Unit	Procedure
$\Delta h_I = c_{pg} T_{Tin}\left((r_T)^{\frac{R_{cg}}{c_{pg}}} - 1\right)$	Δh_I c_{pg} R_{cg}	Isentropic enthalpy change. Specific heat of flue gas. Ideal gas constant for gas.	1.27×10^4 1144 287	J/(kg °K) J/(kg °K) J/(kg °K)	Calculation Parameter Parameter
$h_{Tout} = h_{Tin} - \eta_T \Delta hI$	h_{Tout}	Enthalpy of the turbine exhaust gases.	1.697×10^6	J/kg	Calculation
$P_T = \eta_T W_G \Delta hI$	P_T	Mechanical power delivered by the turbine.	6820	W	Calculation
$P_{mech} = P_T - P_c$	P_c	Power required by the compressor.	1820	W	Calculation
	P_{mech}	Net mechanical power available in the turbine.	5000	W	Calculation

Source: Own.

In addition to the description of the four subsystems of the plant, the mathematical model of the electric generator is presented.

5. Electric Generator

In order to convert the mechanical energy from the PGT into electrical energy, it is necessary to use an electric generator. Table 13 highlights some comparative advantages and disadvantages between synchronous and asynchronous generators [50]. This comparison allows for the establishment of a series of technical criteria in order to select the most suitable generator for the present application [51].

Table 13. Advantages and disadvantages of synchronous and asynchronous generators.

Advantages	Disadvantages
Synchronous Generator	
Greater efficiency	Greater complexity
Increased stability	Requires an excitation source
Lower long-term cost	Higher initial cost
Reactive power	Increased maintenance
Good power quality	Accurate grid synchronization
Low noise	Increased inertia
Greater responsiveness to load variations	Increased sensitivity to network disturbances
Accuracy in frequency control	
Asynchronous generator	
Simplicity	Lower efficiency
Does not require an excitation source	Lower power quality
Lower initial cost	Slower response time
No regular maintenance required	No regular maintenance required
Increased capacity to withstand network disturbances	

Source: [50,52].

Based on Table 13, and taking into account aspects such as efficiency, stability, power quality, greater responsiveness to load variations—which allows for greater precision in frequency control, and the parameter that relates to load requirements and fuel system control, it has been determined that the generator to be used in the simulation of the PGT plant is a synchronous generator whose equivalent in Matlab/Simulink is the Simplified

Synchronous Machine. Table 14 presents the mathematical model of the selected generator.

Table 14. The mathematical model of the Electric Generator.

Equation	Parameter	Description	Value	Unit	Procedure
	$\Delta\omega(t)$	Deviation from nominal operating speed	dynamic	rad/s	Calculation
$\Delta\omega(t) = \frac{1}{2H}\int_0^t (T_m - T_e)dt - Kd\Delta\omega(t)$ $\omega(t) = \Delta\omega(t) + \omega_0$	H	Inertia constant	3	s	Parameter
	T_m	Mechanical torque		N/m	Parameter
	T_e	Electromagnetic torque		N/m	Parameter
	kd	Damping factor	64.3	pu	Calculation
	$\omega(t)$	Mechanical rotor speed	188.45	rad/s	Parameter
	ω_0	Nominal operating rotor speed	188.45	rad/s	Calculation

Source: Own.

D. Description of the control system

The gas turbine controller regulates both the gas turbine and the electric generator. One of the most popular designs is the SpeedTronic MarK IV system [39] developed for General Electric gas turbines. For the purpose of this article only, the control of the mechanical side of the gas turbine is the main focus; therefore, the model is significantly simplified.

The simplified model of the gas turbine controller is realized with a classic PID controller (supervisory), consisting of four inputs and three outputs. The inputs to the controller, which are outputs of the gas turbine model, are:

- Delivered mechanical power: Pmech, in W;
- Rotational speed (related to electrical frequency): ω in rad/s;
- Exhaust gas temperature: T_{Tout} in °K;
- Exhaust gas composition (NOx and CO content): g_{cNOx} in p.p.m.

The controller outputs that are inputs to the gas turbine model are:

- Fuel flow: conversion of fuel quantity Fd to p.u.;
- Air flow (inlet guide vane position): w_{air} in kg/s;
- Steam (or water) injection flow into the combustion chamber: w_{is} in kg/s.

Figure 4 shows the blocks of the control system, which consists of: PI controller for the electrical power signal Pe, PD controller for the rotational speed ω, P controller for the temperature signal T_{Tout}, PI controller of NOx gas emissions, and the LVF and MVF blocks which complement the system.

Each block of the control system is described below, and Table 15 presents the internal diagrams of each control block, as well as the parameters, description, value, and unit of each element that is part of each block.

- Power control Pe: this is implemented with the electrical power signal Pe coming from the generator GTP (Gas Turbine Plant); this in turn receives the mechanical power signal Pmech coming from all of the dynamics of the GTP. This signal is subtracted from the reference signal Pe_ref, and the result of the subtraction is integrated in the PI controller generating the required dynamic power signal according to the requirements of the load and the dynamic behavior of the other signals;
- Speed control: similar to power control, the rotor speed signal ω comes from the GTP generator and performs a similar procedure; it is subtracted from a reference value ω_ref, and the result of the subtraction is derived in the PD controller generating the required dynamic speed signal according to the requirements of the load and the dynamic behavior of the other signals. This control must be considered in safety conditions so that the turbine does not lose balance and overspeed;
- Temperature Control T_{Tout}: the temperature signal comes from the Turbine block, and the temperature value is the highest of the compression and expansion process that

occurs inside the plant; this parameter is important to control so that the temperature level does not exceed the upper temperature limit that the plant can withstand;
- Control of Outlet gases NOx: although a more robust and complex control of this block is not carried out, as it requires a deeper and more detailed development, it is important to take into account what it produces as a result in the outlet gases and pollutant components, as well as with the working temperatures; the behavior is reviewed as its process results in the steam flow of gases w_{is} are the steam mass flow injection;
- LVF Block (Minimum Value Selector): this allows discrimination of the lowest value signal coming from the power, speed, and temperature controls, with the power signal predominating, without disregarding the other signals that are considered more for plant safety procedures, in terms of speed overflow and temperature level overshoot;
- MVF Block (Maximum Value Selector): this also complements the system, as it allows the higher signal of the two incoming signals to pass, which are the ones coming from the LVF block and Fd_Mín; this last block is very important as it provides the minimum flow signal that must be injected to the plant so that it does not shut down and maintains the flame of the combustion system.

E. Matlab/Simulink simulation model of the whole system.

By interconnecting all the subsystems developed up to this point, we have an equivalent that involves the fuel flow input, which will come from a controller and the mechanical power as output; this concept is illustrated in Figure 5. All the subsystems obtained can be part of an equivalent system, in which only the fuel flow is required as input and the mechanical power and the gas temperature parameters at the turbine outlet as output. Through the mechanical power, the generator system based on a simplified synchronous machine is connected.

Table 15. Gas Turbine—Generator PID Control Model.

Control	Parameter	Description	Value	Units
Electrical Power: Pe	Pe_pu	Signal power generator	1	p.u.
	Pe_set_pu	Reference signal generator power		
	PI_Pe	Proportional—Integral		
	P	Proportional		
	I	Integral		
Rotor Speed: ω	ω_pu	Rotor speed of operation		p.u.
	ω_set_pu	Reference rotor speed of operation		p.u.
	PID_ω	Proportional—Integral—Derivative		
	P	Proportional		
	I	Integral		
	D	Derivative		
Temperature: T_{Tout}	T_Tout_pu	Turbine outlet temperature		
	Función CR	Radiation field		
	T_Tout_set_pu	Outlet reference temperature Turbine		
	FunciónT	Termocouple		
	P_T_Tout	Proportional_T_Tout		
	P	Proportional		
	PI_w_air	Proportional—Integral airflow		
	P	Proportional		
	I	Integral		

Table 15. Cont.

Control	Parameter	Description	Value	Units
Gases NOx: g_{cNOx}	g_{cNOx}	Mass flow of NOx		
	w_{is}	Steam mass flow inyection.	2.9×10^{-5}	kg/s
	w_f	Fuel mass flow to the turbine.	2.88×10^{-4}	kg/s
	f_{GT2}	Experimental curve: NOx steam mass flow to fuel ratio		
	g_{cNOx_set}	Reference mass flow of NOx		
		Delay	0.001	
		Dead Zone	−0.1–0.1	
	PI_w_is	Proportional—Integral mass flow of steam		
	P	Proportional	0.0002	
	I	Integral	0.001	

Source: Own.

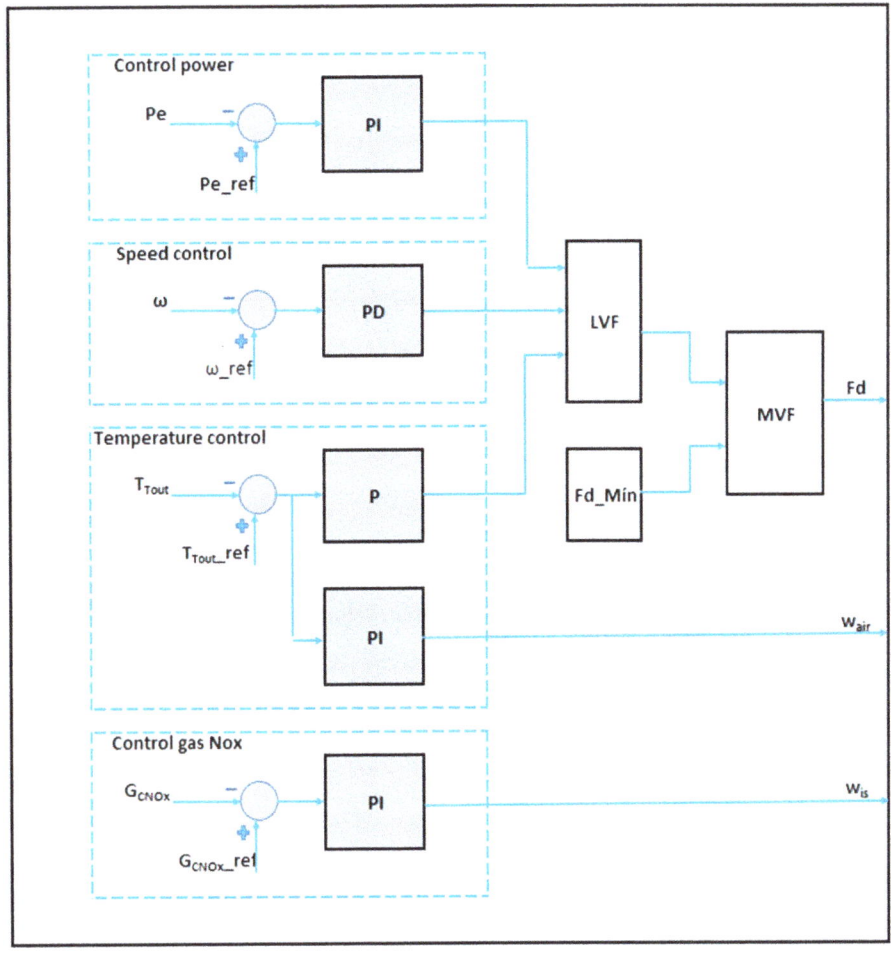

Figure 4. Control system blocks. Source: Own.

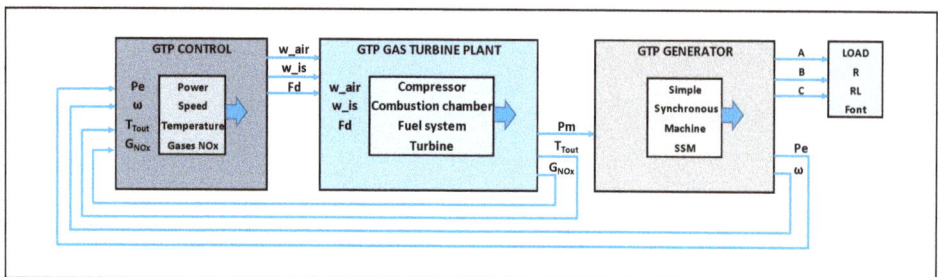

Figure 5. Blocks of the whole system: GTP control, GTP Plant, GTP generator and load. Source: Own.

As a result of the procedure described above, in terms of the implementation of all the models, in the first instance, all the mathematical models were transferred to Excel for monitoring, verification, and interaction of each equation for each component that is part of each subsystem. The appropriate dimensioning and parameterization were carried out on a small scale for the application of a 5 kW full-scale generation plant. From the monitoring and verification in Excel, all the models were implemented in Matlab/Simulink. Figure 6 shows the implementation in blocks of each component of the GTP system with fuel characterized as agricultural biomass residue.

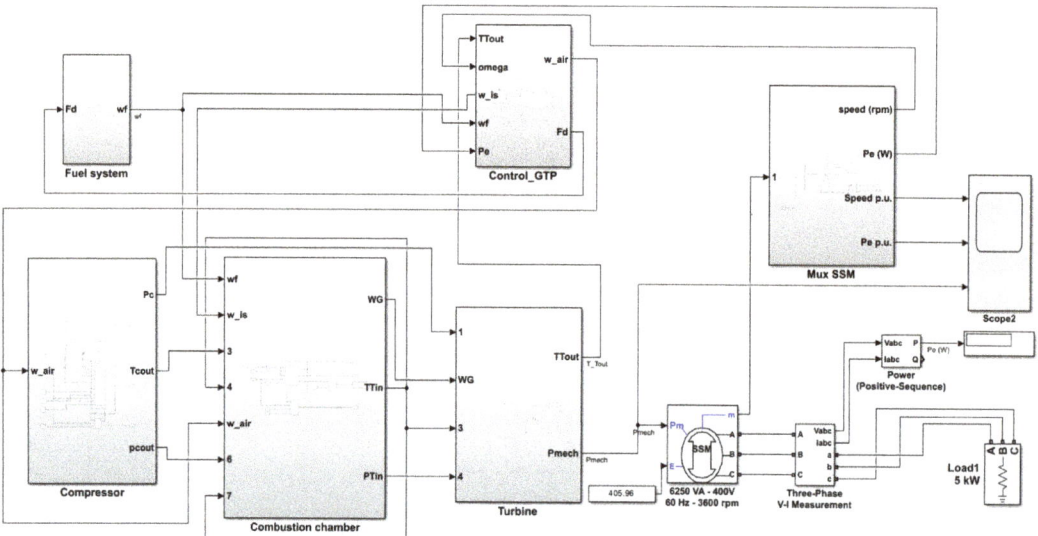

Figure 6. Matlab/Simulink model: GTP control, GTP plant, GTP generator and load. Source: Own.

The sub-systems are listed below:
1. GTP Control (Gas Turbine Plant);
2. Fuel System;
3. Compressor;
4. Combustion Chamber;
5. Gas Turbine;
6. Simple Synchronous Machine (SSM);
7. Simple Synchronous Machine (SSM) output multiplexer: speed in rpm, electrical power Pe (W);
8. Three-phase outputs;

9. Three-phase resistive load.

3. Discussion of Results

According to the entire procedure developed for the implementation and verification of the mathematical models of each of the subsystems described and which constitute the GTP-based generation plant, two generalized scenarios are presented for the verification of the results, which are aimed at operating with resistive load for basic consumption in a rural domestic environment. The scenarios are described below:

1. Checking of nominal values:

In this scenario, there is variation in the load requirement, which leads to fuel variation. Figure 7 shows the load variations of a 1 kW and 5 kW requirement. For simplification of the calculations and presentation of the data, the parameterization and conversion of the SI international average system to parts per unit p.u. is used, corresponding to the parameterization of 5 kW to 1 p.u., 4 kW to 0.8 p.u., and so on until a value of 1 kW corresponding to 0.2 p.u. is obtained.

As an example of checking the low nominal value, Figure 7a shows the variation in the load requirement of 1 kW. The red graph illustrates the mechanical power output of the GTP, denoted as Pmech, with the conversion of units for a 1 kW variation of 0.2 p.u. being obtained. Similarly, the blue graph represents the output of the Simple Synchronous Machine, also demonstrating a variation of 0.2 p.u.

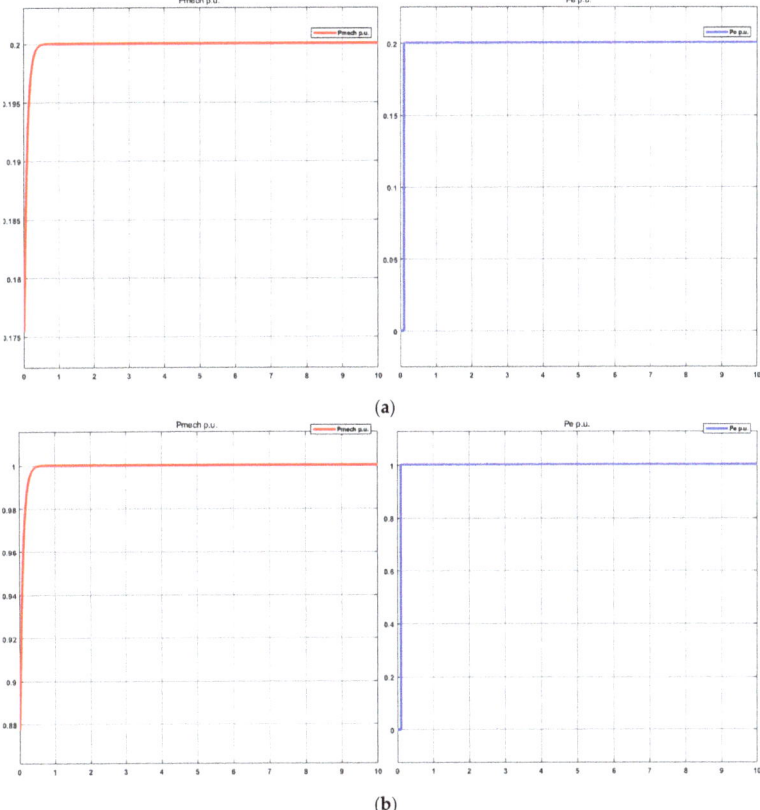

Figure 7. 1 kW and 5 kW load requirement with varying Pmech and Pe. (**a**) 1 kW load requirement, (**b**) 5 kW load requirement. Source: Own.

For the case of variation in the highest nominal value, Figure 7b represents the variation in the load requirement of 5 kW, the red graph illustrates the mechanical power Pmech being the output of the GTP, with the conversion of units for a 5 kW variation of 1.0 p.u. being obtained. Likewise, the graph in blue represents the output of the Simple Synchronous Machine, also representing a variation of 1.0 p.u.

For the two example cases, when there is variation in the load requirement, there is a correspondence in output variation in both the GTP and the Simple Synchronous Machine. The operation of the integration and interaction of the generation plant based on a gas turbine and electric generator is checked for the nominal values of 1 kW and 5 kW.

From Figure 7, it can be seen that, in general the operation of the GTP can be checked and verified, given the load requirement. In the plant, a dynamic occurs in the subsystems and in the control system when there is a load requirement. When the load requirement occurs, it generates an electrical power requirement and rotor speed variation requirement, which is detected by the control system of each of these variables, as presented in the previous section; in the dynamics of the PID controller the amount of fuel flow required for each case is determined.

2. Dynamic load requirement variation:

The dynamic response of the modelled and implemented system with dynamic behavior is tested in the transitions of load variation in an upward and downward manner. Figure 8 shows the variations every 10 s, from 1 kW to 5 kW upwards and load variation from 5 kW to 1 kW downwards. Every 10 s there is a load change transition of 1 kW; the scenario starts at 0 and, after 10 s, the load varies for a consumption of 1 kW, then, after another 10 s, the load requires a consumption of 2 kW. This variation continues until 50 s, when it reaches full load with a consumption of 5 kW.

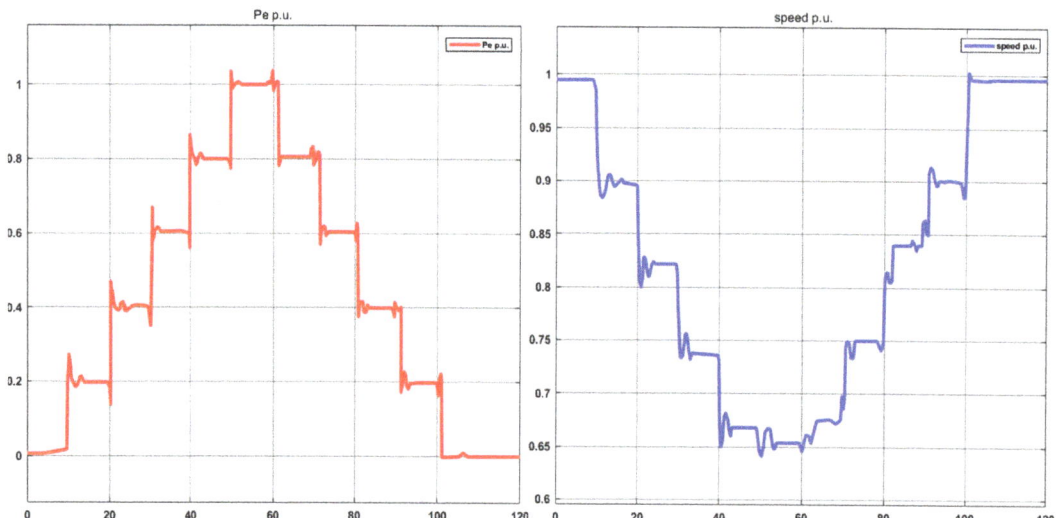

Figure 8. Variation in load requirement—variation in rotor speed. Source: Own.

Likewise, the dynamic response of the system in a downward manner is checked in the transitions of load variation from 5 kW to 1 kW, where every 10 s a transition of 1 kW load change is made. The scenario is reversed after 60 s when switching to a load for a consumption of 4 kW, then, after another 10 s the load requires a consumption of 3 kW, and this variation continues until 100 s when it is allowed to have no load.

Figure 8 shows the dynamic behavior with the transitions described above for the variation in electrical power Pe (p.u.) in the red color and speed variation (p.u.) in the blue color. When carrying out these variations, the measurements on the y-axis are made in p.u. and the x-axis is the time variation. Each variation in the load requirements corresponds to a variation of 0.2 p.u., corresponding 1 p.u. to the load requirement of 5 kW and so on for the other transitions until 0.2 is obtained, which corresponds to a load requirement of 1 kW. The integration and interaction of the generation plant based on a gas turbine and electric generator is tested for the nominal values of 1 kW, 2 kW, 3 kW, 4 kW, and 5 kW.

Table 16 presents information for all nominal test values, where the operation of the whole system is characterized, taking the values of: load variation (power, W), transition time between ascending states (seconds, s), transition time between descending states (seconds, s), fuel flow variation (wf, kg/s), air flow variation (wa, kg/s), and steam mass flow variation (w_{is}, kg/s), with these flow variables being the ones that provide the dynamic behavior of the whole system.

Table 16. System characterization with load variation, response times, and flows.

Load (W)	Upward Transition Time (s)	Downward Transition Time (s)	wf (kg/s) Fuel Flow	w_a (kg/s) Airflow	w_{is} (kg/s) Steam Mass Flow
1000	3.5	1.4	5.77938×10^{-5}	0.115351848	5.80188×10^{-6}
2000	5.2	3.7	0.000115588	0.230703695	1.16038×10^{-5}
3000	3	2.5	0.000173381	0.346055543	1.74056×10^{-5}
4000	4	3.5	0.000231175	0.46140739	2.32075×10^{-5}
5000	3.1	3.5	0.000288969	0.576759238	2.90094×10^{-5}

Source: Own.

From the graphs in Figure 8 and the data obtained in the simulations presented in Table 16, it can be determined that:

- The average settling times for state transitions resulting from variations in the load requirement of a 1 kW are: 3.76 s for up states and 2.92 s for the down states, with the times being slightly lower for down states;
- Although the dynamic behavior of the flows referenced in Table 16 shows a certain regularity and proportionality oriented towards a linear behavior, these behaviors are not reflected in the establishment times; because a more stable system is not available for these variations, work continues on the regularization of the control strategies used;
- There is a logical behavior in the fuel flow consumption, which is reflected in the variation in the air flow and mass flow, as more fuel flow is required when there is a higher load requirement, and with the opposite behavior being observed when there is a lower load requirement, requiring less fuel flow, air flow, and mass flow of steam;
- The rotor speed variation in the simple synchronous machine presents more irregularities due to the behavior of the non-linear parameters of the mathematical model, which are translated in the simulation into more abrupt changes due to the transitions in the load requirement states. The control strategies must be able to linearize the damping factor and the deviation from the nominal operating speed.

3. Contrast variation in consumption profile and plant model

For the presentation of this scenario, indicators of official demand forecasts are taken as a reference on the website of the company xm [53], and they can be consulted and downloaded to find the information regarding the monthly balance of the indicators of the official forecast of the demand of the NES (National Electric System) according to regulations of the National Council of Operations through Agreement NCO 1303 [54]. The NES and NCO are governmental organizations of Colombia, and in the consulted files, information can be found on the consumption provided by the company Codensa S.A.

ESP (Company of distribution and commercialization of electric energy, provider of public services especially in the regions of Bogotá and Cundinamarca in Colombia) [55].

To meet the load requirement of the GTP in this scenario, the consumption variation from the reference file was adjusted to match the plant's load variation, allowing for a realistic simulation of the load profile behavior. Simulations were carried out for all seven days of each week in February 2023. As an example, Figure 9 shows an Excel graph representing the consumption variation in kW for Wednesdays, while Figure 10 presents the simulation results using Matlab/Simulink for the same day. The consumption variation is presented in p.u. and the simulation duration was 240 s.

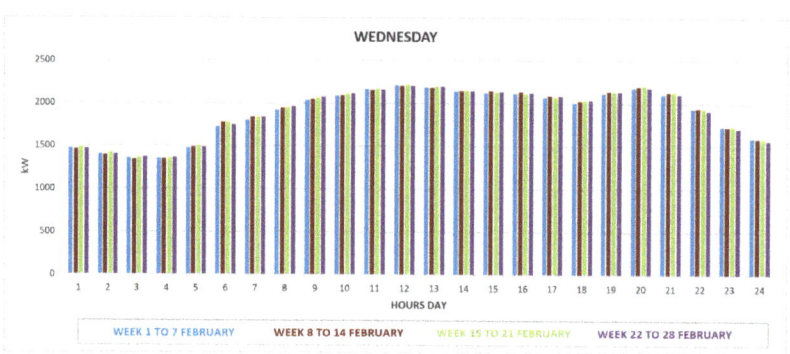

Figure 9. Variation in consumption reference file—Codensa for Wednesdays of the month of February 2023.

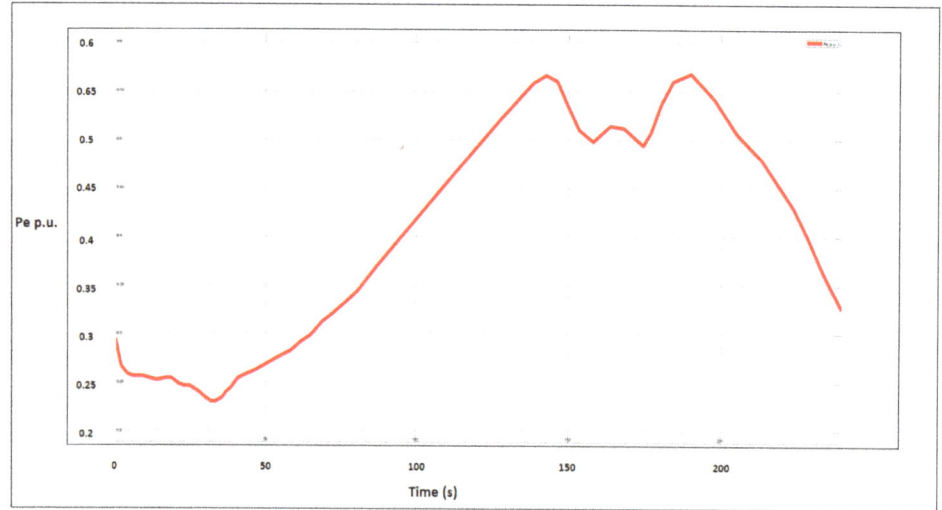

Figure 10. Simulation of consumption variation based on reference file—Codensa. Source: own.

Table 17 presents information on the variation in the consumption profile of the file taken as a reference. The values of load variation in W are presented, as well as the values of load variation in the simulation. These values are shown in their equivalent in p.u. and, according to the load variation, the variations of fuel flow (w_f, kg/s) are presented alongside variation in air flow (w_a, kg/s) and variation in steam mass flow (w_{IS}, kg/s). These flow variables are those that provide the dynamic behavior of the entire system.

After reviewing and monitoring the variation in consumption in the behavior generated in Figures 9 and 10 and Table 17, the following changes in consumption are observed from the actual load profile of the simulation taken from the reference file:

- There is a drop in load from hours 1 to 4, which is observed in the simulation between 0 and 40 s;
- From hour 5 to hour 12 in the Excel graph and from 50 to 150 s in the simulation, there is a higher demand for load;
- From 13 to 18 h, there is a decrease in the demand for load, which is also observed in the simulation between 130 and 180 s;
- There is an increase in consumption again between 18 and 20 h, which is observed in the simulation between 180 and 190 s;
- Finally, from hour 21 to 24 and from 190 to 240 s in the simulation, there is a drop in the demand for load.

Table 17. Example consumption profile variation applied to simulation.

Hour Day	Load Variation in W Reference File Figure 9 (W)	Load Variation in p.u. of the Simulation in Figure 10 (p.u.)	w_f (kg/s) Fuel Flow	w_a (kg/s) Airflow	w_{is} (kg/s) Steam Mass Flow
1–4	1486	0.3	0.0000858815868	0.1714128455336	0.00000862159368
	1360	0.26	0.000078599568	0.156878512736	0.0000078905568
5–12	1499	0.3	0.000078599568	0.1729124195524	0.00000869701812
	2201	0.55	0.0001272041538	0.2538894165676	0.2538894165676
13–18	2194	0.57	0.0001272041538	0.2530819536344	0.2530819536344
	2034	0.48	0.0001175525892	0.2346256580184	0.2346256580184
18–20	2034	0.48	0.0001175525892	0.2346256580184	0.2346256580184
	2202	0.56	0.0001272619476	0.2540047684152	0.2540047684152
21–24	2127	0.45	0.0001272619476	0.2453533798452	0.2453533798452
	1587	0.38	0.0000917187606	0.1830633821412	0.00000920758356

Source: own.

It should be noted that the consumption variations presented in the reference file are taken and followed by the plant simulation.

Comparing the graphs in Figures 9 and 10, although there are some peak values that deviate slightly in the simulation, it can be determined that the plant model generally produces variations in the simulation that correspond with those presented in the reference Excel file values.

The behavior of the variables is verified according to the plant models in tracking the variation in consumption per hour on Wednesdays, which are taken as reference values.

Of the results obtained in terms of the verification of the models in the scenarios in the simulations, the applied methodology is highlighted, of which the following stand out:

1. A classification of the studies consulted is proposed and generated, whether they are thermodynamic, techno-economic, based on simulation with specialized software, and mathematical, which is the main object of this work. The proposal is made in this way because, in all of the reference consultations, no differentiation is made, which generates confusion and mixture between models, which does not indicate that the models discard each other;
2. Mathematical verification of each equation implemented in each subsystem of the plant, initially in Excel and later in Matlab/Simulink in the simulations which were carried out.
3. Detailed presentation of all mathematical models, with equations, parameters, and values obtained if they are calculations, constants, and units. In most references which were consulted, especially articles, no further details of the models can be found;

4. Results were obtained for a proposal for small-scale generation, facilitating sizing, where the gas turbine model is the most suitable plant option for these applications, as it provides fewer complex calculations, dynamics, and control. The mathematical model was mostly linear with the application of algebraic equations, and the most dynamic sequences are found in the fuel and control systems;
5. The load requirements determine the fuel flow requirements, which affects the air and steam mass flows; consequently, it also affects the mechanical power, electrical power, rotor speed, and transition times both up and down, affecting the stability and reliability of the system. To improve this behavior, the responses of the control strategies must be further adjusted and sensitized;
6. For an integration application in a hybrid microgrid where more energy resources are involved, control strategies more akin to a management system must be considered and developed.

4. Conclusions

In the GTP modeled and simulated under several test scenarios, the electric power generation system was able to prioritize the balance relationship between generator and load, controlling the flow of fuel in all of the situations which were experienced.

It was found that the variation in the fuel flow is determined by the variation of the load, influencing the variation in rotor speed and variation in electrical power, which are both variables that were controlled, generating stability, repeatability, and reliability in the tests and experimental results.

From the results of the simulation, it is obtained that, in the plant, the variation in rotor speed is constantly corrected; when presenting an increase or decrease in this speed, the control system that relates the power and demand are balanced, correcting the situation when the power is above the demand, or otherwise when the power production is not sufficient for the demand. Consequently, in the results of the simulations, it was possible to stabilize the speed, with that being one of the main tasks of the plant control system.

As a control strategy, classical P, PI, and PD controllers were implemented. For the application of this article, they were adopted and adapted through adjustments to the small-scale requirements that were carried out. In the results which were obtained, these controllers provided safe and fast operation. However, it is appreciated that, for the requirements of plants with greater complexity, the performance of other more robust control techniques can be explored.

The objective of verifying the mathematical models of the plant in their implementation and testing through the scenarios proposed in the simulations has been achieved, but we are aware that adjustments must be made in the dynamic response, especially in the control system.

In order to continue with this work, the focus should be on integrating the plant into hybrid microgrid applications. This evolution is aimed at generating synergy with other energy resources such as photovoltaic solar panels and backup batteries. The objective in the continuation of this work is to carry out the integration in an energy management model.

Author Contributions: Conceptualization, L.F.R.-R., C.L.T.-R., N.L.D.-A. and C.R.-C.; formal analysis, L.F.R.-R.; investigation, L.F.R.-R., C.L.T.-R. and N.L.D.-A.; methodology, L.F.R.-R., C.L.T.-R., N.L.D.-A. and C.R.-C.; resources, L.F.R.-R., C.L.T.-R., N.L.D.-A. and C.R.-C.; supervision and validation, L.F.R.-R., C.L.T.-R., N.L.D.-A. and C.R.-C.; writing—original draft preparation L.F.R.-R., C.L.T.-R. and N.L.D.-A.; writing—review and editing, C.L.T.-R., N.L.D.-A. and C.R.-C. All authors have read and agreed to the published version of the manuscript.

Funding: This research was supported in part by the University of Jaén (Programa Operativo Proyectos de I+D+i en el marco del Programa Operativo FEDER Andalucía 2014/2020. Project Contribución al abastecimiento de energía eléctrica en pequeñas y medianas empresas de Andalucía. AcoGED_PYMES. Ref: 1380927 and CEACTEMA).

Institutional Review Board Statement: Not applicable.

Informed Consent Statement: Not applicable.

Data Availability Statement: Not applicable.

Conflicts of Interest: The authors declare no conflict of interest.

References

1. Herbert, G.M.J.; Krishnan, A.U. Quantifying Environmental Performance of Biomass Energy. *Renew. Sustain. Energy Rev.* **2016**, *59*, 292–308. [CrossRef]
2. Yilmaz, F.; Ozturk, M.; Selbas, R. Design and Thermodynamic Assessment of a Biomass Gasification Plant Integrated with Brayton Cycle and Solid Oxide Steam Electrolyzer for Compressed Hydrogen Production. *Hydrog. Energy* **2020**, *45*, 34620–34636. [CrossRef]
3. Trninić, M.; Stojiljković, D.; Manić, N.; Skreiberg, Ø.; Wang, L.; Jovović, A. A Mathematical Model of Biomass Downdraft Gasification with an Integrated Pyrolysis Model. *Fuel* **2020**, *265*, 116867. [CrossRef]
4. Ordys, A.W.; Pike, A.W.; Johnson, M.A.; Katebi, R.M.; Grimble, M.J. Process Models. In *Modelling and Simulation of Power Generation Plants*; Springer: Berlin/Heidelberg, Germany, 2000; Chapter 4; pp. 144–208.
5. Saravanamuttoo, H.I.H.; Cohen, H.; Rogers, G.F.C. Introduction. In *Gas Turbine Theory*, 5th ed.; Pearson: London, UK, 2013; Chapter 1; pp. 38–44.
6. Jurado, M.F.; Cano, O.A. Capítulo 5 Microturbina de Gas. In *Generación Eléctrica Distribuida Con Microturbina de Gas*; Koobeht International, European Union: Jaén, Spain, 2005; pp. 187–205.
7. Ortega, V.M. Modelado y Simulación Dinámica de Esquemas de Cogeneración. Doctorado Thesis, Universidad Autónoma de Nuevo León, Monterrey, Mexico, 2001.
8. Hussain, A.; Seifi, H. Dynamic Modeling of a Single Shaft Gas Turbine. *IFAC Control. Power Plants Power Syst.* **1992**, *25*, 43–48. [CrossRef]
9. Serrato Monroy, C.C.; Lesmes Cepeda, V. *Metodología Para El Cálculo de Energía Extraída a Partir de La Biomasa En El Departamento de Cundinamarca, Ingeniería*; Universidad Distrital: Bogotá, Colombia, 2016; p. 79.
10. Ramirez Balaguera, L.F.; Barrera Ojeda, D.F. *Potencial Energético de La Biomasa Residual Pecuaria Del Departamento de Cundinamarca–Colombia, Ingeniería*; Universidad Distrital: Bogotá, Colombia, 2017; p. 147.
11. Pozzobon, V.; Salvador, S.; Bézian, J. Biomass Gasification under High Solar Heat Flux_Advanced Modelling_Elsevier Enhanced Reader. *Fuel* **2018**, *214*, 300–313. [CrossRef]
12. Toklu, E. Biomass Energy Potential and Utilization in Turkey. *Renew. Energy* **2017**, *107*, 235–244. [CrossRef]
13. Nunes, L.J.R.; Matias, J.C.O.; Catalão, J.P.S. Biomass in the Generation of Electricity in Portugal: A Review. In *Renewable and Sustainable Energy Reviews*; Elsevier Ltd.: Amsterdam, The Netherlands, 2017; pp. 373–378. [CrossRef]
14. Caliano, M.; Bianco, N.; Graditi, G.; Mongibello, L. Analysis of a Biomass-Fired CCHP System Considering Different Design Configurations. *Energy Procedia* **2017**, *105*, 1683–1691. [CrossRef]
15. Ashok, S.; Balamurugan, P. Biomass Gasifier Based Hybrid Energy System for Rural Areas. In Proceedings of the 2007 IEEE Canada Electrical Power Conference, EPC, Montreal, QC, Canada, 25–26 October 2007; pp. 371–375. [CrossRef]
16. Gómez, B.S. *Diseño e Implementación de Un Sistema de Aprovechamiento de Residuos Orgánicos y Generación de Energía Renovable, Ingeniería*; Universidad ECCI: Bogotá, Colombia, 2017; p. 89.
17. CIGEPI. *Eficiencia de Calderas Para El Uso de Biomasa*; Superintendencia de Industria y Comercio: Antioquia, Colombia, 2017; p. 68.
18. UPME; IDEAM; COLCIENCIAS; UIS. Anexo B Muestreo y Caracterización de La Biomasa Residual En Colombia. In *Atlas del Potencial Energético de la Biomasa Residual en Colombia*; República de Colombia ministerio de Minas y Energía: Bogotá, Colombia, 2013; pp. 131–142.
19. Jiang, R.; Tong Wang, T.; Shao, J.; Guo, S.; Zhu, W.; Jun Yu, Y.; Lin Chen, S.; Hatano, R. Modeling the Biomass of Energy Crops: Descriptions, Strengths and Prospective. *J. Integr. Agric.* **2017**, *16*, 1197–1210. [CrossRef]
20. UPME; Aene. Potencialidades de Los Cultivos Energéticos y Residuos Agrícolas en Colombia. In *Resumen Ejecutivo*; República de Colombia ministerio de Minas y Energía: Bogotá, Colombia, 2003; D.#ANC-631-03,REVISON 1; pp. 98–129.
21. Cao, Y.; Mihardjo, L.W.W.; Dahari, M.; Tlili, I. Waste Heat from a Biomass Fueled Gas Turbine for Power Generation via an ORC or Compressor Inlet Cooling via an Absorption Refrigeration Cycle: A Thermoeconomic Comparison. *Appl. Therm. Eng.* **2021**, *182*, 116117. [CrossRef]
22. Cirillo, D.; Di Palma, M.; La Villetta, M.; Macaluso, A.; Mauro, A.; Vanoli, L. A Novel Biomass Gasification Micro-Cogeneration Plant: Experimental and Numerical Analysis. *Energy Convers. Manag.* **2021**, *243*, 114349. [CrossRef]
23. Elfasakhany Ashraf. Investigation of Biomass Powder as a Direct Solid Biofuel in Combustion. *Ain Shams Eng. J.* **2021**, *12*, 2991–2998. [CrossRef]
24. Hussain, C.M.I.; Norton, B.; Duffy, A. Comparison of Hybridizing Options for Solar Heat, Biomass and Heat Storage for Electricity Generation in Spain. *Energy Convers. Manag.* **2020**, *222*, 113231. [CrossRef]

25. Akrami, E.; Ameri, M.; Rocco, M.V. Developing an Innovative Biomass-Based Power Plant for Low-Carbon Power Production: Exergy and Exergoeconomic Analyses. *Therm. Sci. Eng. Prog.* **2020**, *19*, 100662. [CrossRef]
26. Roy, D.; Samanta, S.; Ghosh, S. Performance Assessment of a Biomass Fuelled Advanced Hybrid Power Generation System. *Renew. Energy* **2020**, *162*, 639–661. [CrossRef]
27. Bisht, A.S.; Thakur, N.S. Small Scale Biomass Gasification Plants for Electricity Generation in India: Resources, Installation, Technical Aspects, Sustainability Criteria & Policy. *Renew. Energy Focus* **2019**, *28*, 112–126. [CrossRef]
28. Sandoval, L.P.; Díaz, C.A. Sustainability Aspects of Biomass Gasification Systems for Small Power Generation. *Renew. Sustain. Energy Rev.* **2020**, *134*, 110180.
29. Herrera, I.; Rodríguez-Serrano, I.; Lechón, Y.; Oliveira, A.; Krüger, D.; Bouden, C. Sustainability Assessment of a Hybrid CSP/Biomass. Results of a Prototype Plant in Tunisia. *Sustain. Energy Technol. Assess.* **2020**, *42*, 100862. [CrossRef]
30. Rey, J.R.C.; Pio, D.T.; Tarelho, L.A.C. Biomass Direct Gasification for Electricity Generation and Natural Gas Replacement in the Lime Kilns of the Pulp and Paper Industry: A Techno-Economic Analysis. *Energy* **2021**, *237*, 321–330. [CrossRef]
31. Krzysztof, S.; Maciej, Z.; Wojciech, G.; Rafal, F. The Operation of a Micro-Scale Cogeneration System Prototype–A comprehensive experimental and numerical analysis. *Fuel* **2021**, *295*, 1–18.
32. Safarian, S.; Ebrahimi Saryazdi, S.M.; Unnthorsson, R.; Richter, C. Artificial Neural Network Integrated with Thermodynamic Equilibrium Modeling of Downdraft Biomass Gasification-Power Production Plant. *Energy* **2020**, *213*, 491–512. [CrossRef]
33. Chiñas-Palacios, C.; Vargas-Salgado, C.; Aguila-Leon, J.; Hurtado-Pérez, E. A Cascade Hybrid PSO Feed-Forward Neural Network Model of a Biomass Gasification Plant for Covering the Energy Demand in an AC Microgrid. *Energy Convers. Manag.* **2021**, *232*, 113896. [CrossRef]
34. Cerinski, D.; Baleta, J.; Mikulčić, H.; Mikulandrić, R.; Wang, J. Dynamic Modelling of the Biomass Gasification Process in a Fixed Bed Reactor by Using the Artificial Neural Network. *Clean Eng. Technol.* **2020**, *1*, 100029. [CrossRef]
35. Ribó-Pérez, D.; Herraiz-Cañete, Á.; Alfonso-Solar, D.; Vargas-Salgado, C.; Gómez-Navarro, T. Modelling Biomass Gasifiers in Hybrid Renewable Energy Microgrids; a Complete Procedure for Enabling Gasifiers Simulation in HOMER. *Renew. Energy* **2021**, *174*, 501–512. [CrossRef]
36. Ahluwalia, K.S.; Domenichini, R. Dynamic Modelling of a Combined Cycle Plant. *ASME* **1989**, *79160*, V004T09A009.
37. Hung, W.W. Dynamic Simulation of Gas-Turbine Generating Unit. *IEE Proc.* **1991**, *138*, 342–350. [CrossRef]
38. Rowen, W.I. Simplified Mathematical Representations of Heavy Duty Gas Turbines. *ASME* **1983**, *105*, 865–869. [CrossRef]
39. Barker, W.; Cronin, M. *Speedtronic Mark IV Control System, Alsthom Gas Turbine Reference Library*. 2000, Volume 4193A. Available online: https://vdocuments.mx/ger-4193a-speedtronic-mark-vi-turbine-control-system-2021-4-6-speedtronica.html?page=1 (accessed on 20 April 2023).
40. Yacobucci, R.B. A Control System Retrofit for a GE Frame 5 Turbine Generator Unit. *IEEE Trans. Energy Convers.* **1991**, *6*, 225–230. [CrossRef]
41. Jurado, F.; Ortega, M.; Cano, A. Neuro-Fuzzy Controller for Gas Turbine in Biomass-Based Electric Power Plant. *Electr. Power Syst. Res.* **2002**, *60*, 123–135. [CrossRef]
42. Zhu, Z.; Wang, X.; Xie, D.; Gu, C. Control Strategy for MGT Generation System. *Energies* **2019**, *12*, 3101. [CrossRef]
43. Jonathan, A.E.; Olubiwe, M.; Okozi, S.O.; Agubor, C.K. Exhaust Temperature Control of Heavy Duty Gas Turbine Due to Incremental Load Demand. *Int. J. Eng. Res. Technol.* **2018**, *7*, 420–426. [CrossRef]
44. Shankar, G.; Mukherjee, V. Load-Following Performance Analysis of a Microturbine for Islanded and Grid Connected Operation. *Int. J. Electr. Power Energy Syst.* **2014**, *55*, 704–713. [CrossRef]
45. El-Sharif, I.A.; El-Fandi, M.M. Micro Gas Turbine Simulation and Control. In Proceedings of the Conference for Engineering Sciences and Technology (CEST), Castelverde, Libya, 25–27 September 2018; pp. 1–10.
46. Shakur, S.A.; Jain, S.K. Micro-Turbine Generation Using Simulink. *Int. J. Electr. Eng.* **2012**, *5*, 95–110.
47. Guda, S.R.; Wang, C.; Nehrir, M.H. Modeling of Microturbine Power Generation. *Electr. Power Compon. Syst.* **2006**, *34*, 1027–1041. [CrossRef]
48. Singh, N.K.; Tiwari, P.; Srivastava, J. Simulation Of Microturbine Generation System For Unbalance Grid Power. *Int. J. Eng. Res. Technol.* **2013**, *2*, 967–974.
49. Abdollahi, S.E.; Vahedi, A. Dynamic Modelling of Micro-Turbine Generation Systems Using Matlab/Simulink. *Renew. Energy Power Qual. J.* **2005**, *1*, 146–152. [CrossRef]
50. Herrador, C.M. *Modelado En Matlab-Simulink de Generadores Eléctricos Conectados a La Red*; Universidad de Sevilla: Sevilla, Spain, 2016.
51. Chiguano, B.A. Estimación de Parámetros Eléctricos de La Máquina Sincrónica Utilizando Matlab-Simulink. Bachelor's Thesis, Escuela Politecnica Nacional, Quito, Ecuador, 2018.
52. Sistemas de Generación. Generadores Síncronos y Asíncronos. Available online: https://biblus.us.es/bibing/proyectos/abreproy/4991/fichero/4+Sistemas+de+generaci%C3%B3n.pdf (accessed on 4 April 2023).
53. Sistema Interconectado Nacional. Indicadores de Pronósticos Oficiales de Demanda. Available online: https://www.xm.com.co/consumo/informes-demanda/indicadores-de-pronosticos-oficiales-de-demanda (accessed on 2 April 2023).

54. Consejo Nacional de Operaciones-CNO. Acuerdo 1303 Por el Cual se Actualizan los Procedimientos Para la Gestión Integral de la Demanda. Available online: https://www.cno.org.co/content/acuerdo-1303-por-el-cual-se-actualizan-los-procedimientos-para-la-gestion-integral-de-la (accessed on 2 April 2023).
55. Enel-Codensa. Innovación y Sostenibilidad. Available online: https://www.enel.com.co/es/medio-ambiente-desarrollo-sostenible.html (accessed on 2 April 2023).

Disclaimer/Publisher's Note: The statements, opinions and data contained in all publications are solely those of the individual author(s) and contributor(s) and not of MDPI and/or the editor(s). MDPI and/or the editor(s) disclaim responsibility for any injury to people or property resulting from any ideas, methods, instructions or products referred to in the content.

Article

Investigation of Oscillation and Resonance in the Renewable Integrated DC-Microgrid

Mohammad Habibullah [1], Nadarajah Mithulananthan [1], Rakibuzzaman Shah [1,2,*], Md Rabiul Islam [3,*] and S. M. Muyeen [4]

[1] School of Information Technology and Electrical Engineering, University of Queensland, Saint Lucia, QLD 4072, Australia
[2] Centre for New Energy Transition Research (CfNETR), Federation University Australia, Mt. Helen, VIC 3353, Australia
[3] School of Electrical, Computer, and Telecommunications, University of Wollongong, Wollongong, NSW 2522, Australia
[4] Department of Electrical Engineering, College of Engineering, Qatar University, Doha 2713, Qatar
* Correspondence: m.shah@federation.edu.au (R.S.); mrislam@uow.edu.au (M.R.I.)

Abstract: This paper assessed the small-signal stability performance of a multi-converter-based direct current microgrid (DCMG). The oscillation and potential interactions between critical modes are evaluated. First, the complete analytical model of the DCMG is developed with the converter and associated controllers. Three methodologies, impedance scanning, eigenvalue analysis, and time-domain simulation, along with the fast Fourier transform (FFT) analysis, have been used to comprehensively investigate the oscillations and interactions. The simulation results show inherent weak modes, with a wide range of oscillations in the studied DCMG, which may destabilize the system under disturbances. Based on the sensitivity analysis, controller gains and DC-link capacitance are identified as the most critical parameters and substantially influence the weak modes leading to oscillations, interactions, and resonance. Finally, the performance of the various control synthesis methods is compared. This examination would help the researchers, planning, and design engineers to design and stably operate a multi converter-based DC microgrid.

Keywords: direct current microgrid; DC-link capacitance; fast Fourier transform (FFT); oscillations; resonance; sensitivity analysis; time-domain simulation

1. Introduction

DCMGs or DC distribution systems are emerging as the future electricity delivery systems that could enable the extensive integration of renewable energy sources (RESs) into the power grid without multiple conversions. A DCMG consists of several DC–DC converters (e.g., buck and boost converters), inverters that are usually connected through a cable to a common DC bus [1–5]. Several key technical challenges associated with DCMGs have received moderate attention in the literature. For example, the identification of oscillations and resonance sources in DCMGs and their mitigation are always considered challenging tasks. Furthermore, these issues so far have limited coverage and understanding and are yet to be comprehensively investigated [6–10].

Power oscillations in the DCMG can originate from poorly tuned controllers, line switching, sudden changes in demand or generator outputs, and others [9–11]. In the DCMG, generated power primarily comes from distributed and intermittent energy resources, e.g., photovoltaic (PV)/wind/energy storage. For example, the sudden change in power output at the sources may reduce the DC bus voltage, or DC voltage fluctuation may be observed at the DC bus. Therefore, the scale of disturbances in the DC system may vary from small to severe. Furthermore, these disturbances may lead to power and voltage oscillations in the DC bus, with drastic consequences. Therefore, the security of the system would be compromised [12,13]. The consequence of security and the nature of instability depends on the types of the DCMG grid.

Additionally, several power electronic converters are connected through the common DC bus in industrial DCMGs. This DC bus acts as a resonant or tuned circuit with a finite inductor and capacitor. In contrast, each DC–DC converter has its capacitor bank. Therefore, when several PWM DC–DC converters simultaneously act together, converters' frequencies could coincide with the DC-link bus frequency [12]. Therefore, the system could face severe disturbances, such as power oscillations, overshoot, or undershoot in the DC bus voltage. In the worst case, this may lead to the blackout of the system [10–12]. Therefore, it is essential to understand the root cause and impact of disturbances in power oscillations in DC grids and develop innovative solutions to avoid the possibilities of such consequences.

In this respect, a few excellent research works have been conducted to investigate the small-signal stability in the DC microgrid [1–3]. Furthermore, constant power loads and disturbances have introduced power oscillations in resonance for the DC bus, as reported in [4,5]. However, this investigation has been conducted for a small-scale DC microgrid (only two units of converters). The work in [13] focused on modelling the buck converter to supply the constant impedance, current, and power load. In addition, the Kharitonov theory has been applied for a robustness assessment with several controls (i.e., P, PI, and PID). The large-signal stability of a DC microgrid using the Lyapunov method is proposed in this work [14]. Furthermore, the load limit under the stability and voltage violation restriction is presented. However, a simple system is used without any details about the control. The effect of the cascaded converter on the stability of the DC system is proposed in [15]. Individual stable converters are used to create the multiple stage cascaded converter without informing the types of load and controls. The work in [16] compared the droop control and virtual inertia control of the DC microgrid using the eigenvalue method. The research work in [17] developed a reduced-order impedance model starting from the DC-side load converter for stability analysis in a three-terminal DC distribution system. The local sensitivity index has been used to identify the direction of stability enhancement.

Furthermore, the DC microgrid is expected to experience increasing uncertainty in parameters due to the distinct stochastic nature of RESs and the proliferation of new types of loads. However, only some of these uncertainties are critical for system operation and control. Therefore, estimating the essential parameters under various operating conditions would enable secure and reliable operation with targeted control action and monitoring requirements. Several sensitivity analysis (SA) methods are applied in the literature for AC power system application, i.e., load classification, ranking of the generator, and ranking the critical load in terms of the voltage and frequency stability [18,19]. However, no reported work has considered the SA method for critical parameter identification in the DC system. With the increasing number of uncertain parameters and their coupling, a cost-efficient technique to identify the most critical parameters of the DC microgrid in terms of low frequency and resonance is required.

Furthermore, few works have proposed controller design/retuning for DC microgrid stability enhancement [20]. For example, the LQR-based control is proposed in [21] to enhance the DC microgrid's low frequency and resonance performance. However, the LQR controller needs to be more robust, with a complex and high-order model, which is challenging to implement. Furthermore, several works have proposed the PI controller without assessing the limits of the controllers. Therefore, a comprehensive assessment of various control methods for the DC microgrid and their impact on stability is sought.

The summary of the key review is given in Table 1. It is noticed in Table 1 that work in the literature has yet to comprehensively assess the key parameters affecting the stability of the DC grid under various operating conditions. Furthermore, most of the research works focused on various stability assessment methods with different complexities and less on mitigation and the control design.

Table 1. Summary of the critical review.

Reference	Detailed Load Model	Sensitivity Analysis	Key Parameter Identification	Control Method
[13]	✓	✓	✗	✓
[14]	✓	✓	✗	✗
[15]	✗	✓	✗	✗
[16]	✗	✓	✗	✗
[17]	✓	✓	✗	✗
[20]	✗	✓	✗	✗
[21]	✗	✗	✗	✓
This work	✓	✓	✓	✓

Therefore, the HF oscillation assessment of the DC system has been conducted in this study using both the impedance and eigenvalue methods. The numerical studies have been conducted using MATLAB Simulink, with a detailed state-space model of the DCMG and considering the dynamics of the power electronic converters. The main contributions of the paper can be listed as follows:

1. A comprehensive analytical model for investigating high-frequency oscillations and resonance has been developed. The impedance analysis and eigenvalue-based method are used simultaneously to identify the source of oscillation/instability in the DC microgrid.
2. Most of the prior studies have considered a constant power load for the high-frequency and resonance assessment of DC microgrids. This work has considered the various types of loads in the DC microgrid and their impact on the overall high-frequency oscillations and resonance.
3. A semi-global sensitivity analysis technique has been used to rank the most critical parameters of the DC microgrid, considering the cross-coupling of various parameters and uncertainties.
4. Three control synthesis methods are described and compared in their suitability to the conventional PI controller in terms of high-frequency oscillations and resonance.

The rest of the paper is organized as follows. Section 2 provides a brief synopsis of the state-of-the-art oscillation challenges of DCMGs. Section 3 presents the modelling of DCMGs for small-signal stability studies. Section 4 illustrates the key results and discussions, including the sensitivity studies and control comparisons. The conclusions, contributions, and future directions of this research are highlighted in Section 5.

2. Oscillation Challenges in DCMG

The DCMG facilitates the integration of RESs better and has many advantages compared to an ACMG. However, the DCMG has some technical challenges. Recently, several studies have focused on the technical challenges of DCMGs and the application of power electronic devices in the DC network. These can be divided into five general categories, which are the protection, standardization of voltage, power quality, voltage stability, and overall security of the system, as described in [6–9]. The challenges associated with the oscillation phenomena of DCMGs are given next.

Power oscillation is a severe issue in DC or AC microgrids. In the present literature, the extensive analysis and investigation of power oscillations in AC microgrids are reported. It is identified that numerous types of power oscillations can be observed in AC power systems, including intra-plant mode oscillations, local plant mode oscillations, inter-area mode oscillations, and control mode oscillations [22,23]. On the other hand, in the DC grid, two types of oscillations are found in the contemporary literature: HF oscillations and LF oscillations [24,25]. In addition, distributed energy resources such as PV and wind sources have significant effects on the damping performance and generation of HF oscillation, as reported in [24,25]. However, the effect of sub-synchronous oscillations and the mitigation of power oscillations in the DC system is overlooked and has not been extensively investigated in the literature.

Another possibility for power oscillations in the sub-synchronous range could be in the form of resonance. A dynamic system can lose its equilibrium state temporarily due to disturbances. A sub-synchronous frequency of oscillation could occur when two dynamic systems are bilaterally coupled. One can affect others and may lead to instability. The sub-synchronous frequency of oscillation poses a significant threat to system stability, as reported in [26–28]. It can be significantly amplified with time, causing system instability. Furthermore, if the disturbing force frequency is near or equal to one of the natural frequencies of the system, resonance may potentially occur in the system. Sub-synchronous resonances could lead to voltage fluctuation and light flickering, and an abnormal vibration of the control. In the previously mentioned literature, the effect of sub-synchronous oscillations and the mitigation of power oscillations in the DC bus is yet to be extensively investigated.

Recently, significant research has been conducted to find a suitable methodology to investigate the various aspects of stability, particularly the oscillatory type of instability problems, in DC grids. For instance, the authors in [2] have investigated two methods: impedance and eigenvalue analyses in the HVDC system. The impedance analysis is useful for local stability, while the eigenvalue analysis is suitable for global stability [29]. Both assessment methods were recommended for the accuracy of the analysis in [29]. However, a comprehensive SSS analysis of HF oscillation and a detailed state-space model of a DC microgrid with the dynamics of power electronic converters are yet to be covered in the present literature.

Typically, power system engineers use stabilizers with synchronous machines to provide damping to obstruct HF and LF oscillations in the AC system. However, the same approach may not be appropriate for dealing with these types of oscillations in the DCMG [30]. Some researchers suggested optimal capacitor banks for the DC distribution networks. The negative aspect known as resonance could be reduced by adding a filter in the capacitor bank. However, the effects of the DC link and its control were ignored in this study. The resonance can be generated from either capacitors or impedances or from both in DC grids, as reported in [9]. If the driving system frequency coincides with the driven subsystem frequency, then the system could face catastrophic consequences and a high possibility of a blackout via the resonance path. In addition, the power electronic converters have EMI filters, which may cause inrush currents and might lead to voltage oscillations in the DC bus.

Therefore, finding the source of the power oscillation and how to maintain the stability of a DC distribution network under such oscillatory conditions require further exploration. Therefore, these are the critical interests of this work. The flowchart of the complete work is given in Figure 1.

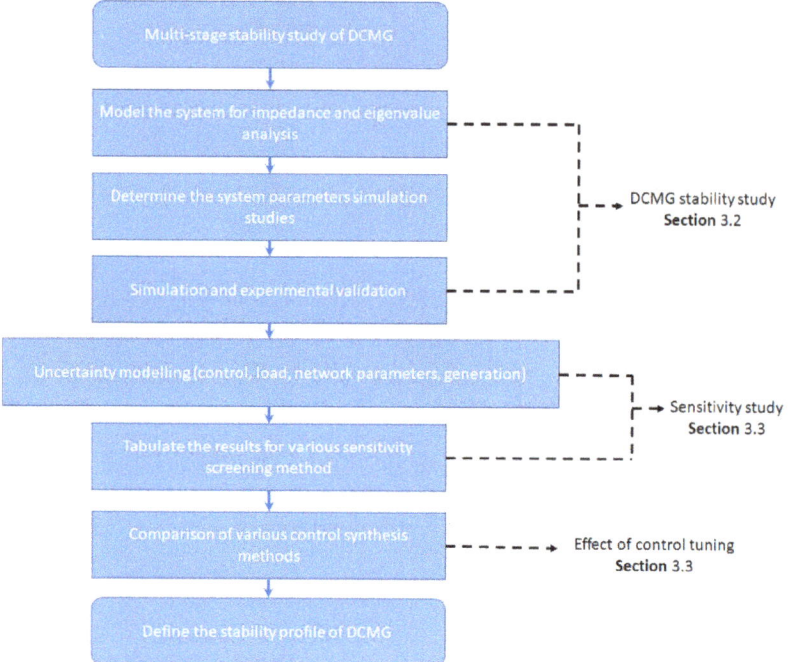

Figure 1. Flowchart of the study.

3. Methodology and Modelling

A multi-converter-based DC microgrid is composed of highly nonlinear components and often operated in a constantly changing environment. Hence, the stability of the system should be ensured for the wide operating ranges to avoid any adverse consequences. A multi-converter-based DC microgrid of a 1-MW capacity has been designed at the University of Queensland, Australia, as shown in Figure 2a. The details of the microgrid parameters are presented in Table 2.

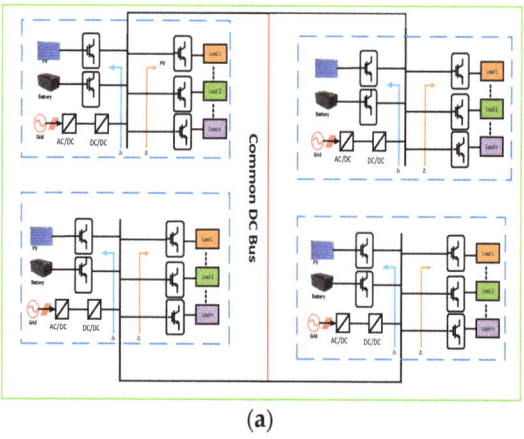

(a)

Figure 2. *Cont.*

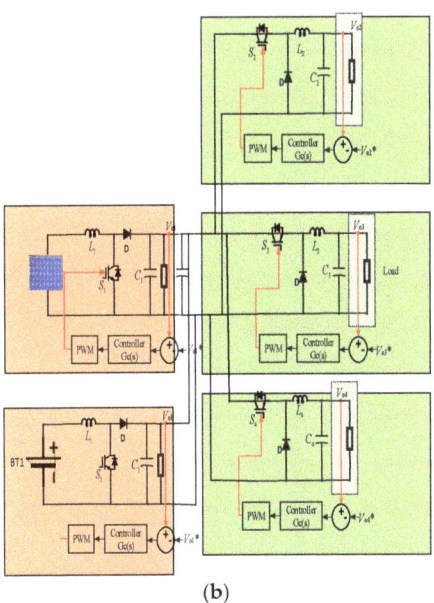

(b)

Figure 2. System topology; (**a**) typical DCMG; (**b**) topology of DC microgrid using in this work.

Table 2. Parameters of the DC microgrid used in this work.

Parameter	Symbol	Value
Rated power of the simulated system	P_o	20 kW
Rated power of boost converter 1	$P_{o-boost1}$	12 kW
Rated power of boost converter 2	$P_{0-boost2}$	8 kW
Rated power of buck converter 1	$P_{o-bucik1}$	10 kW
Rated power of buck converter 2	$P_{o-bucik2}$	5 kW
Rated power of buck converter 3	$P_{o-bucik3}$	1 kW
Boost converter source voltage	V_{s1}	375 V
Boost converter output voltage	V_{o1}	750 V
DC link voltage	V_{dc}	750 V
Switching frequency of boost converters	$f_{sw-boost}$	20 kHz
Switching frequency of buck converter	$f_{sw-buck1}$	10 kHz
	$f_{sw-buck2}$	20 kHz
	$f_{sw-buck3}$	20 kHz
Input voltage of buck converter	V_{in}	750 V
Buck converter output voltage	V_{02}	400 V

The campus microgrid includes a large-scale solar PV, EV bidirectional DC fast charging station with a rooftop solar PV system, BESS, and interfaces with the existing conventional AC grid. Additionally, various types of loads, i.e., a DC load and AC load, are interfaced with the power electronic converters in the DC microgrid. In this investigation, the main focus is the stability of the DC bus voltage. Two units of the converter on the generation side and three units of the converter at the load sides are considered. The topology of the DC microgrid with five converters is given in Figure 2b.

3.1. State Space Modelling

A detailed small-signal state-space mathematical model is necessary to conduct the eigenvalue (participation factor assessment) and sensitivity analysis. A proportional and integral (PI) controller has been used to regulate the output voltage of the boost and buck converters. The state-space model of a boost converter along with a PI controller can be expressed, as given in (1).

$$\begin{bmatrix} \frac{di_l}{dt} \\ \frac{dv_0}{dt} \\ \frac{d\beta}{dt} \end{bmatrix} = \begin{bmatrix} 0 & \frac{1}{L_1}\left(-1 + K_p V_{ref} - 2V_0 K_p + K_i \beta\right) & \frac{K_i V_0}{L_1} \\ \left(\frac{1}{C_1+C_2}\right)\left(1 - K_p V_{ref} + K_p V_0 - K_i \beta\right) & \left(\frac{1}{C_1+C_2}\right)\left(K_p I_l - \frac{1}{R_1}\right) & \left(\frac{K_i I_l}{C_1+C_2}\right) \\ 0 & -1 & 0 \end{bmatrix} \begin{bmatrix} i_l \\ v_0 \\ \beta \end{bmatrix} \quad (1)$$

In (1), C_1, L_1, and R_1 represent the capacitor, inductor, and resistor of the boost converter. Additionally, i_l is the inductor current in the boost converter, V_0 and V_g are the capacitor and input voltages of the boost converter, and d is the duty cycle. In (1), K_P is the proportional gain and K_i is the integral gain of the PI controller. The parameter β is introduced to represent the state vector of the integrator. The small-signal state-space model of a buck converter with a PI controller can be expressed as in (2).

$$\begin{bmatrix} \frac{di_l}{dt} \\ \frac{dv_0}{dt} \\ \frac{d\beta}{dt} \end{bmatrix} = \begin{bmatrix} 0 & \frac{1}{L_2}(-1 - V_{in} K_p) & \frac{K_i V_{in}}{L_2} \\ \frac{1}{C_3} & -\frac{1}{R_2 C_3} & 0 \\ 0 & -1 & 0 \end{bmatrix} \begin{bmatrix} i_l \\ v_0 \\ \beta \end{bmatrix} \quad (2)$$

In (2), C_2, L_2, and R_2 are the capacitor, inductor, and resistor in the buck converter, K_P is the proportional gain, and K_i is the integral gain of the given PI controller. The parameter β is introduced to represent the state vector of the integrator. The overall system state matrix is essential to conduct a sensitivity analysis on weak modes with respect to parameter variations. The complete state-space model can be obtained by using the individual subsystem, given in (1) and (2).

3.2. Analytical Expression for Impedance Scanning

A detailed analytical impedance model is required to conduct impedance scanning. The closed-loop output impedance of the boost converter can be expressed as in (3).

$$Z_{ocl}(s) = \frac{Z_o(s)}{1 + T(s)} \quad (3)$$

where $Z_0(s)$ is the open-loop output impedance of the boost converter and $T(s)$ is the loop gain. Open-loop output impedance and loop gain can be expressed as given in (4) and (5), respectively.

$$Z_0(s) = \frac{s^2 + s(C_1 \times R_1(1 + D^2) + L_1 + (R_1 \times D^2))}{L_1 \times C_1 \times R_1} \quad (4)$$

$$T(s) = \left(K_p + \frac{K_i}{s}\right) \times \frac{\left(\frac{V_{in}}{(1-D)^2}\right) \times \left(1 - s\frac{L_1}{(1-D)^2 \times R_1}\right)}{\left(\frac{L_1 \times C_1}{(1-D)^2}\right)\left(s^2 + s\left(\frac{1}{C_1 \times R_1} + \frac{(1-D)^2}{L_1}\right)\right) + \frac{(1-D)^2}{L_1 \times C_1}} \quad (5)$$

here, two individual converters with power ratings of 12 kW and 8 kW have been used at the source side. Since the converters have been connected in parallel, the total output impedance can be written as (6).

$$Z_{ts} = \frac{Z_{ocl1} \times Z_{ocl2}}{Z_{ocl1} + Z_{ocl2}} \quad (6)$$

Three individual converters with power ratings of 1 kW, 5 kW, and 10 kW, respectively, have been used at the load side of the system, and the input impedance of the closed-loop buck converter can be estimated as in (7).

$$Zicl(s) = \frac{Z_i(s) \times R_2 \times (1 + T(s))}{R_2 + Z_i(s) - D^2 \times T(s)} \quad (7)$$

where $Z_i(s)$ and $T(s)$ are the open-loop input impedance and loop gain, respectively. These can be expressed in (8) and (9).

$$T(s) = \left(K_p + \frac{K_i}{s}\right) \times \left[\left(\frac{V_{in}}{L_2 \times C_2}\right) \times \frac{(1 + s \times C_2)}{s^2 + s\left(\frac{1}{C_2 \times R_2} + \frac{1}{L_2}\right) + \frac{1}{L_2 \times C_2}}\right] \quad (8)$$

$$Z_i(s) = \frac{(s^2 LC) + R}{D^2 \times (1 + sRC)} \quad (9)$$

The open-loop input impedance of the individual unit can be expressed as (10)–(12).

$$Z_{i3}(s) = \frac{(s^2 L_3 C_3) + R_3}{D^2 \times (1 + sR_3 C_3)} \quad (10)$$

$$Z_{i4}(s) = \frac{(s^2 L_4 C_4) + R_4}{D^2 \times (1 + sR_4 C_4)} \quad (11)$$

$$Z_{i5}(s) = \frac{(s^2 L_5 C_5) + R_5}{D^2 \times (1 + sR_5 C_5)} \quad (12)$$

where Z_{i3}, Z_{i4}, and Z_{i5} are the open-loop input impedances of the load side buck converters. Since all converters have been connected in parallel, the total impedance can be expressed using (13).

$$Z_{tin} = \frac{Z_1 \times Z_2 \times Z_3}{(Z_1 \times Z_2) + (Z_2 \times Z_3) + (Z_1 \times Z_3)} \quad (13)$$

In (13), Z_{tin} is the total input impedance from the load side. Eventually, the DC bus impedance can be expressed as given in (14).

$$Z_{bus} = \frac{Z_{ts} \times Z_{tin}}{Z_{ts} + Z_{tin}} \quad (14)$$

3.3. Sensitivity Analysis

The most critical input to the system's output can be numerically identified using the sensitivity analysis method. Three methods are available for sensitivity analysis: local, semi-global, and global. The local method, or the one-at-a-time (OAT) method, considers the slight variation in the input around its nominal value and ignores the coupled relationship among different parameters, whilst the global sensitivity method considers the influence of a given parameter across the full parametric range with cross dependencies. However, it requires a high simulation and computational time, deemed infeasible for a system with large variables. Therefore, a semi-global sensitivity analysis, known as the Morris method, has been used in this work.

The semi-global Morris method generates a multi-dimensional trajectory in search space [18,19]. To generate the search space, the base value (initial) is randomly selected for each uncertainty (Δ to $1 - \Delta$). The step is bounded in such a way that the search space boundary is not violated. In the Morris method, one variable is changed at a time by the magnitude of Δ, whilst other variables remain fixed. This process runs until the n steps are completed for each variable. From this point, the method selects another variable and changes the value by Δ in the multi-dimensioned space. This is effectively a random walk in the search space where the dimension of work depends on the number of uncertainties and is limited by the steps. The elementary effect of a Δ change can be defined as in (15) [19].

$$E_t^i(x) = \frac{[Y(x_1, x_2 \ldots \ldots x_{i-1}, x_i + \Delta, x_{i+1} \ldots \ldots, x_t) - Y(x)]}{\Delta} \quad (15)$$

In this work, the mean (μ) given in (16) would be used as the index of the Morris method. This mean expresses the sensitivity strength between the tth input and the Y output.

$$\mu = \frac{1}{n} \sum_{i=1}^{n} \left| EE_t^i \right| \quad (16)$$

The higher value of μ indicates the higher contribution of the input to the output variables. This method requires $nt + 1$ simulations, where t indicates the variables and n is the step size (ranges between 4 to 10). In this work, the n value of 5 has been considered.

3.4. Overview of Control Tuning

In this work, the suitability and the performance of three control design methods are illustrated. At first, the LQR control proposed in [20,21] has been developed in this work. For the sake of brevity and to avoid repetition, the details about the LQR control implementation are not illustrated here. It should be worth noting that the structure of the LQR control is different from the structure of the conventional PI control.

Recently, a PI+clegg integrator has been reported in the literature with the capability of enhancing the control performance by resetting the part of the controller. This can be easily implemented in the standard PI control structure without changing the structure. Therefore, a PI+clegg integrator is considered in this work. The reset-based control has been reported in [31] to enrich the performance of the integrator. In this control strategy, the controller state is reset to zero under certain conditions. As a result, the phase lag could be reduced. The transfer function of the PI+clegg control can be expressed as [31].

$$G = K_p \left(1 + \frac{1}{sT_i} + \frac{j4^{P_r}/\pi}{sT_i} \right) \quad (17)$$

where P_r is the parameter reset rate, and $0 \leq P_r \leq 1$ [32]. The control structure forms into the PI structure when $P_r = 0$, and with the PI+clegg structure when $P_r = 1$.

Several works have reported the suitability of the IP control over the PI control. The IP controller may overcome the inherent lacking in the K_P gain of the PI controller. It has already been implemented in [33] for the tuning of the current controller in VSC-HVDC under a weak grid condition. In this work, the IP controller has been used in the converter control of the DC microgrid.

4. Numerical Analysis and Discussion

4.1. Impedance Analysis

This subsection presents an impedance-based assessment to investigate the small-signal stability of DCMG. Two groups of converters have been considered for this research work. The boost converter has been considered on the source side, whereas the buck converter has been placed on the load side. To construct a prototype of the DC microgrid, the converters are first designed individually in the MATLAB Simulink platform. Then, a proportional and integral controller is designed based on the PM, step response, and GM requirements. The values of the proportional (P) and integral (I) gains (i.e., **K_p** = 0.00005 pu and **K_i** = 0.003 pu) are selected, based on the PM = 95 degrees and GM = 15 dB for the source-side converters. Following the same procedure, a conventional PI controller is designed for the load-side buck converters. An optimal proportional and integral gain (i.e., **K_p** = 0.9 pu and **K_i** = 0.005 pu) is considered, with a PM and GM of 90 degrees and 16 dB, respectively. Lastly, the multiple-converter-based DC microgrid is formed by combining these converters with their controllers. The parameters of the individual converters are given in Tables 3 and 4, respectively.

Then, an impedance analysis has been conducted in the MATLAB Simulink platform for the given system. Figure 3a presents the output and input impedances, whereas Figure 3b presents the total impedance seen from the DC link. From Figure 3a, it is evident that the output impedance is far away from the input impedance except for three resonance peaks, which are 230 Hz, 2280 Hz, and 2790 Hz, respectively. Figure 3b presents the total input impedance seen from the DC link, whereas only 230 Hz of the potential oscillatory mode is observed.

Table 3. Parameters of the DC–DC boost converters.

Boost Converter 1		Boost Converter 2	
V_s = 375 V	L = 157 µH	V_s = 400 V	L = 147 µH
V_0 = 750 V	R = 47 Ω	V_0 = 750 V	R = 70 Ω
D = 0.5 (no unit)	C = 1000 µF	D = 0.5 (no unit)	C = 1000 µF
K_p = 0.005 pu	K_i = 0.003 pu	K_p = 0.005 pu	K_i = 0.003 pu

Table 4. Parameters of the DC–DC buck converters.

Parameters	Converter 1	Converter 2	Converter 3
Input voltage (V)	750	750	750
Output voltage (V)	400	400	400
Inductance (H)	0.00428	0.0044	0.0033
Resistance (ohm)	16	145	147
Duty cycle	0.5	0.5	0.5
Proportional gain (pu)	0.9	0.9	0.9
Integral gain (pu)	0.005	0.005	0.005

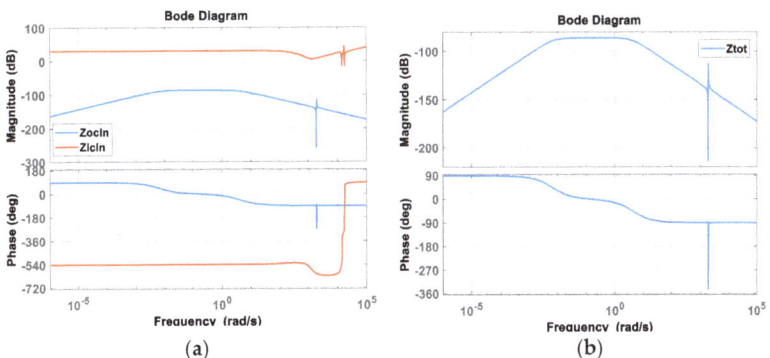

Figure 3. Frequency response of the system: (**a**) Output and input impedance; (**b**) total impedance seen from DC link.

From the impedance analysis, three sensitive modes have been identified, and they are 230 Hz, 2280 Hz, and 2790 Hz. However, the source of the problem and the critical mode that contributes to oscillation could not be identified via impedance scanning. For this reason, the eigenvalue and participation factor analyses are recommended. To find out the sensitivity of the modes, an eigenvalue analysis has been conducted in the following subsection.

4.2. Eigenvalue Analysis

This section presents the eigenvalue-based approach to identify the critical modes and the associated modal characteristics in the DC microgrid. To find out the source of the problem, interaction among controllers and devices as well as the detailed investigation produced by the eigenvalue analysis has been conducted with cross participation factor. Table 5 shows the frequency of oscillations and damping ratios of oscillatory modes in the DCMG. The HF oscillation of the weakest mode (λ_1) was found with 153 Hz and a damping ratio of 0.09, as shown in Figure 4. Hence, it is assumed that the critical mode might move further right in the s-plane and reduce the stability margin of the system with the variation in the system parameters. Subsequently, a participation factor analysis has been conducted to see the modes and associated devices that contribute to the modes, as presented in Table 5.

Table 5. Eigenvalue for the complete system.

Critical Mode	Damping (%)	f (Hz)	Associated Mode	Remarks
$-0.83 \pm j953$	0.09	151	Controller	Boost converter
$-7.91 \pm j1443$	0.55	230	Controller	Boost converter
$-7.33 \pm j18,080$	0.04	2878	Controller	Buck converter
$-66.48 \pm j57,931$	0.11	9224	Controller	Buck converter
$-17.36 \pm j14,184$	0.12	2258	Controller	Buck converter

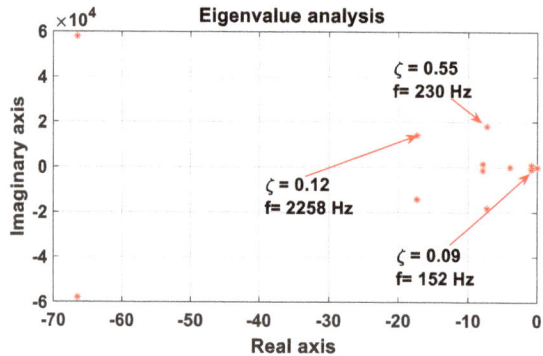

Figure 4. Eigenvalue analysis result—stable operation in DC grid.

From the participation factor analysis, it is found that the 152 Hz and 230 Hz modes are contributed by the two boost converters. The HF modes (e.g., 2878 Hz, 9224 Hz, and 2258 Hz) are contributed by the three buck converters. Consequently, to see the system sensitivity against small changes in the parameters, a detailed sensitivity analysis has been conducted in the following subsections.

4.2.1. Case Study 1 (Parameter Variation in 12-kW Boost Converter)

In this case study, a small variation in the control parameters is made to the source-side boost converters. The trajectories of the sensitive modes are recorded and presented in Figure 5a–d. Figure 5a,b illustrate the root locus of the critical modes under the variation in the proportional gain of the 12-kW and 8-kW boost converters, respectively. As the parameter of the gain decreased, modes 1 and 2 moved to the right half-plane, which indicates the degradation of the dynamic response of the system stability. Trajectories of sensitive modes under the variation in the integral controller are presented in Figure 5c,d. In Figure 5c, mode 1 shifts to the right half-plane with the decrease in the integral gain. However, in Figure 5d, an interesting phenomenon has been observed. Increasing the value of the boost converter integral gain considerably influenced the eigenvalue movements. The imaginary parts of modes 1 and 2 become equal when boost converters are tuned at 0.003 pu and 0.0012 pu, respectively. The 230-Hz oscillation frequency has been observed during the interaction point. Hence, the interaction between these modes occurred. The interaction event might lead to the system being in an unstable situation. It is an indication of resonance conditions, which may deteriorate the stability margin of the system. From the results, it is evident that the system is very sensitive to the parameters of the PI controllers. Furthermore, it is evident that the proportional and integral parameters of the boost converter should be tuned between 0.00005 to 0.005 pu and 0.003 to 0.03 pu, respectively. It is also observed that the system stability margin deteriorates with the larger value of the proportional and integral gains.

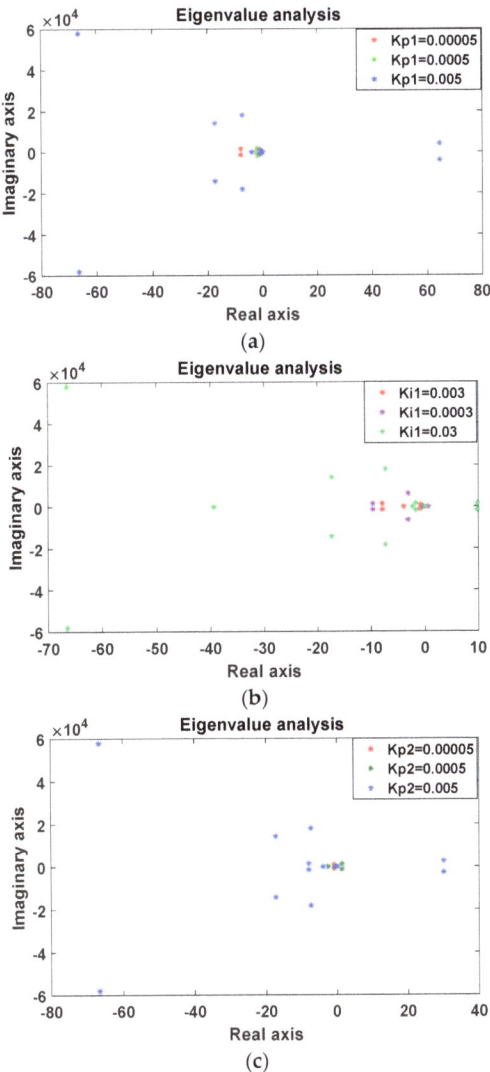

Figure 5. *Cont.*

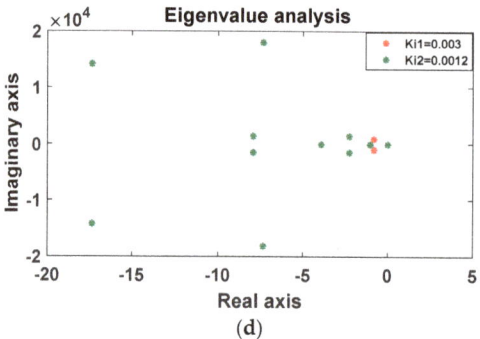

(d)

Figure 5. Impact of variation in relation to control parameters (boost converter). (**a**) Variation in K_p in 12-kW boost converter; (**b**) variation in K_i in 8-kW boost converter; (**c**) variation in K_p in 8-kW boost converter on DC grid; (**d**) variation in K_i in 8-kW boost converter on DC grid.

4.2.2. Case Study 2 (Parameter Variation in Buck Converter)

This case study investigates the sensitivity of the individual and multiple units of buck converter gains on the stability of the overall DC microgrid. A small variation in the PI gain has been considered for this case study. Figure 6a–c present the root loci due to the variation in the proportional and integral gain separately and concurrently. Under the variation in the proportional and integral gains of the buck converter, the eigenvalues are found in the stable region. However, the incremental value of the proportional gain of multiple units of converters considerably influenced the movements of the eigenvalues, as given in Figure 6d. The imaginary parts of modes 1 and 3 become equal when the proportional gain of the buck converter is tuned at 0.0044 pu. An oscillation at a frequency of 230 Hz has been observed around the interaction point, as marked by the rectangular box. Hence, the interaction between these modes potentially occurs in the system.

Furthermore, as a result of the arbitrary selection of the control parameters, (K_{i2} = 0.0012; K_{p4} = 0.0044; K_{p5} = 0.0079), an interesting scenario can be observed, which is depicted in Figure 6e. Changes in the controller gain notably influenced the eigenvalues movements. It is also noted that the imaginary parts of modes 1, 2, 4, and 5 become equal when the converters' integral gains are tuned at 0.0012 pu, 0.0044 pu, and 0.0079 pu, respectively. A 230-Hz oscillation frequency has been observed during the interaction point, as marked by a rectangular box plot. Hence, the interaction between these modes occurs in the system. The interaction event might lead to the system developing into an unstable situation. This is an indication of resonance, which can lead to the deterioration of the system stability. As can be observed, with the change in the PI controller parameters, the overall system becomes very sensitive, and the system becomes unstable as the eigenvalues move to the right-half plane.

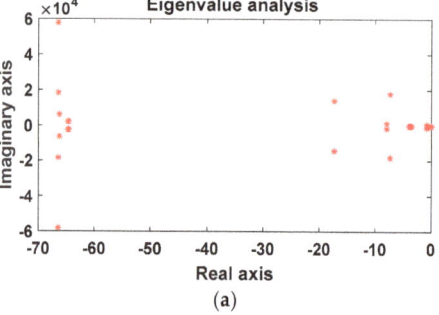

(a)

Figure 6. *Cont.*

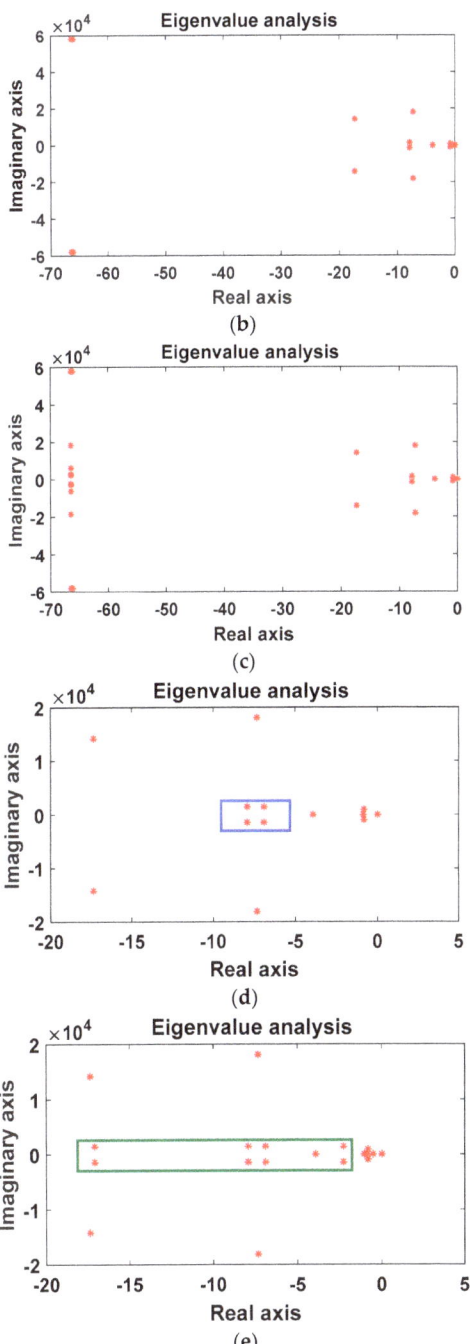

Figure 6. Impact of variation in relation to control parameters (buck converter). (**a**) Variation in K_p in 10-kW buck converter; (**b**) variation in K_i in 10-kW buck converter; (**c**) variation in both K_p and K_i in 10-kW buck converters; (**d**) incremental K_p value for multiple units of converters; (**e**) arbitrarily selected controller parameter.

4.2.3. Case Study 3 (Variation in DC-Link Capacitance)

The DC-link capacitor is a crucial part in connecting the PV/BESS systems as it acts as an electrostatic energy-storing device to release the energy at the time of the disturbances. The third case study is dedicated to investigating the sensitivity of the systems with respect to the variation in the DC-link capacitance. Figure 7 presents the stability margin of the system with respect to changes in the DC-link capacitance between 400 µF to 2700 µF. As can be seen, the eigenvalue with the 153-Hz mode slowly moves to the adjacent imaginary axis with the DC-link capacitance. The eigenvalue of the system moves to the right-hand side, and the system becomes unstable after 2400 µF. This study shows that in a converter-connected power system, an appropriate calculation of the DC-link capacitance by considering the stability analysis is very crucial. This investigation clearly shows the significance of the stability analysis before adding the converters and capacitor bank. Hence, it has been strongly proposed for its utility in industry to conduct a comprehensive stability analysis before adding any capacitor bank and power electronic devices into renewable energy-integrated DCMGs.

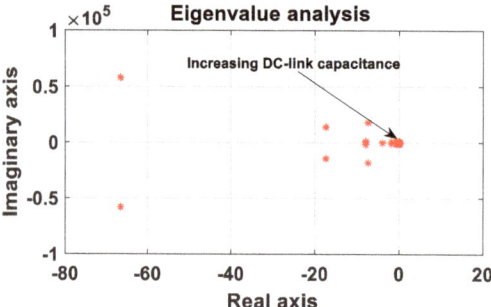

Figure 7. Impact of the DC-link capacitance on the DC grid.

4.2.4. Case Study 4 (Variation in Load Power)

The fourth case study presents the stability of the overall system with respect to load changes. The ZIP load has been considered for the analysis. The assessment results are given in Figure 8. The load is varied with 5-kW steps. From Figure 8, it is observed that the eigenvalues gradually move to the left half-plane with the gradual decrease in the load. On the other hand, the eigenvalues slowly move adjacent to the imaginary axis with the increase in the load, but still stay within the complex of the left half-plane. Therefore, the system remains stable. Table 6 shows the load compositions and their impact on the overall stability margin. Based on the results discussed in this section, it can be concluded that changing the load compositions and parameters has little impact on the system stability.

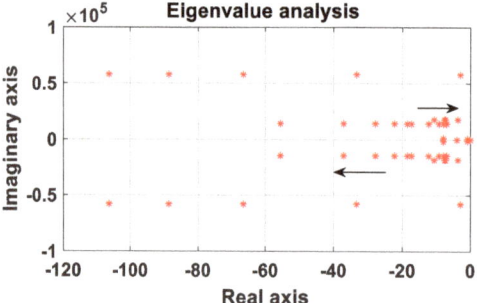

Figure 8. Impact of the variation in load power on the DC grid.

Table 6. Damping performance of complete system under different loads.

Load Type	Damping of Mode 1	Damping of Mode 2	Damping of Mode 3	Damping of Mode 4	Damping of Mode 5
Constant P	0.091	0.56	0.041	0.112	0.121
Constant I	0.092	0.55	0.038	0.111	0.122
Constant Z	0.093	0.55	0.039	0.113	0.122
ZIP	0.091	0.54	0.041	0.114	0.121

4.2.5. Case Study 5 (Variation in Inductance Parameter)

The fifth case study is dedicated to investigate the sensitivity of the systems with the variation in the converter inductance between 1 mH to 4 mH. The eigenvalue does not move to the right half-plane with the variation in the inductance (see Figure 9). Overall, two sensitive modes to inductance change have been identified. One is 230 Hz, and the other one is 153 Hz. It has been noted that both the eigenvalue and impedance analyses detect 230 Hz and 2880 Hz of oscillation. However, in the impedance analysis, a high frequency, such as a reading of 9224 Hz, was not picked up. Some of the key results are validated in the time-domain simulation in the following section.

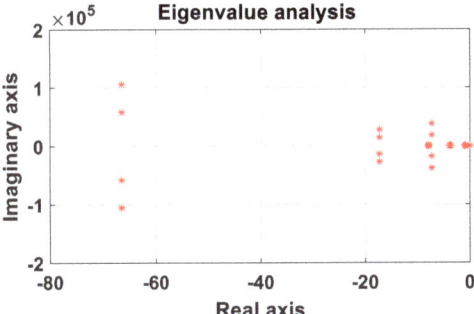

Figure 9. Impact of the variation in inductance on the DC grid.

4.3. Time-Domain Simulations and Experimental Studies

The effect of the controller dynamics on a DC microgrid is visualized in a time-domain simulation, as given in Figure 10a–d. These results corroborated the previous steady-state analysis obtained using the eigenvalue analysis, as given in Figures 5 and 6. Figure 10a presents the impact of the integral controller dynamics on the DC bus of the DCMG. It is observed that at an appropriate gain setting and an oscillation-free and stable DC bus voltage can be obtained, since, in this gain setting, the two sensitive modes and their oscillation frequency were far away from the imaginary axis. Hence, an oscillation-free DC bus voltage is observed. When the integral control gain is tuned at 0.5 pu, a continuous voltage oscillation has been found in the DC bus. At this gain setting, the eigenvalue moves towards the right half-plane. Therefore, the significant deterioration of the DC bus voltage is observed. Furthermore, an FFT analysis is conducted on the DC bus. A 240-Hz oscillation has been observed, as shown in Figure 10b. Likewise, a very similar scenario has been observed when the parameters of the buck converters are changed, as depicted in Figure 10c. In contrast, a different scenario has been observed when the proportional gain of the boost converter is tuned to 0.5 pu. In this setting, a continuous voltage oscillation is observed from the beginning of the simulation period, as presented in Figure 10d. Furthermore, to see the worst-case scenario, simultaneous disturbances have been applied both on the source side and load side. The recorded results are depicted in Figure 10e,f. Results show that with respect to the disturbances, a large overshoot along with a power oscillation is observed in the DC bus.

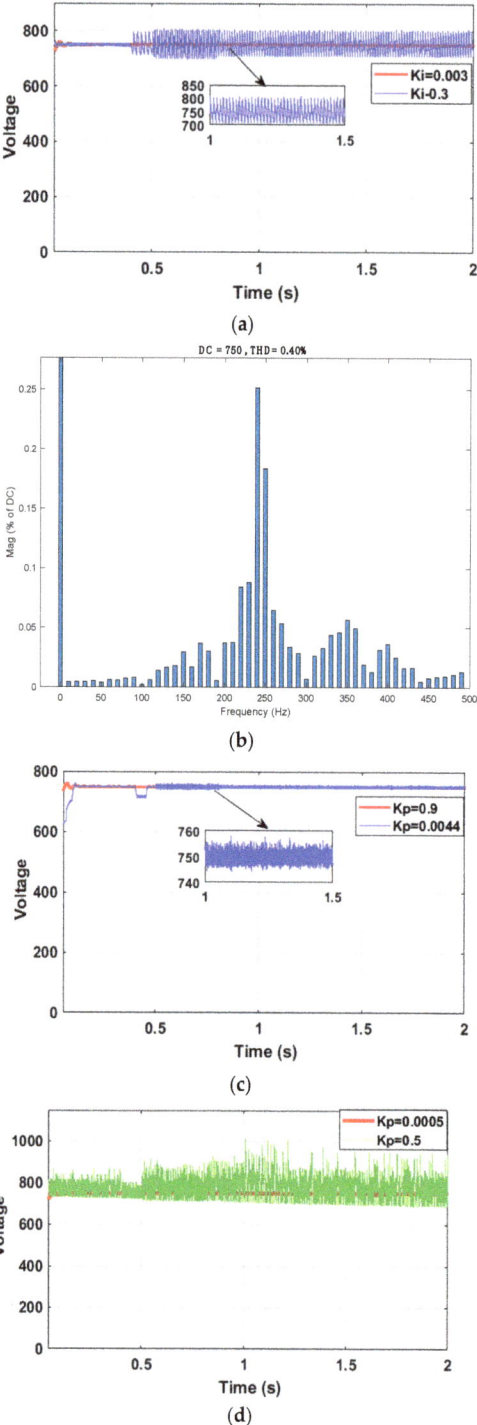

Figure 10. Cont.

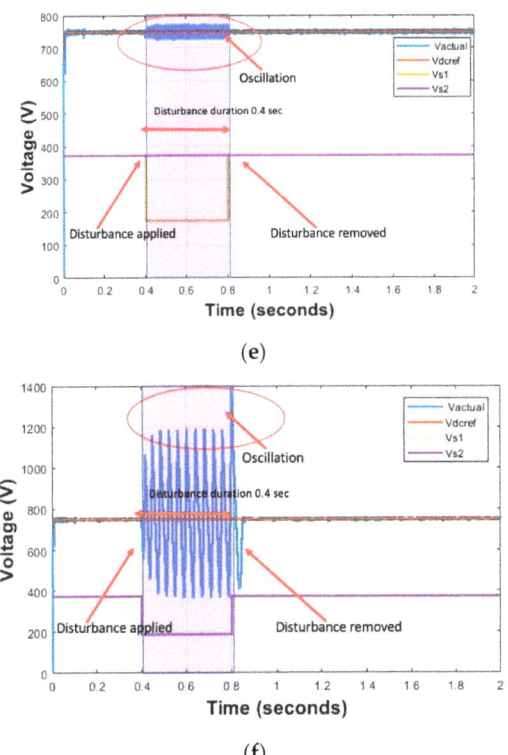

Figure 10. Impact of the controller and DC link dynamics on DC bus. (**a**) DC bus voltage influenced by integral controller dynamics; (**b**) FFT analysis on DC bus; (**c**) parameter variations of the controller (buck converters); (**d**) DC bus voltage influenced by the proportional controller dynamics; (**e**) impact of simultaneous disturbances (50% voltage disturbances in source 1 and 50% load disturbances); (**f**) impact of simultaneous disturbances (50% voltage disturbances in source 1 and source 2, and 50% load disturbances).

From the results given in Figure 10, it is observed that the DC bus voltage at the DC microgrid is very sensitive and becomes unstable due to small variations in the controller parameters and DC-link capacitance, which are similar to the eigenvalue results that are presented in Figures 5–9. The impacts of the various parameters on the stability of the DC grid are investigated in the prior sections. However, from these analyses, it is difficult to identify the most critical parameters via cross-coupling various parameters and uncertainties. Therefore, a comparative ranking of the uncertain parameters has been investigated in the next section.

To understand the stability behavior in DCMG, a mathematical modelling, time-domain simulation, and hardware implementation are inevitable. However, capturing all the dynamics and interactions in a mathematical model is hard. Hence, a real-time simulation is essential. In the simulation, by looking at the overshoot, mode of oscillation, and damping ratio, the stability-related problem in the power system can be identified. However, no industry standard exists in terms of a weak mode related to DCMGs. Hence, experimental validation is inevitable to understand the stability behavior of DCMGs. To further verify the theoretical analysis, an experimental setup (a prototype of DCMG) has been built in the University of Queensland (UQ) power engineering lab. The detailed system parameters for the experimental study are given in the Appendix. The experiment platform mainly consisted of a boost converter, a buck converter, a DC link capacitance, and a resistor. In this investigation, for the converter, SEMIKRON-SKM75 is used as the IGBT switch, SKYPER 32 R is used as the IGBT driver, and the dSPACE controller board is used as an interface between the hardware and MATLAB simulation. In addition, the LEM current and voltage transducers have been used as measurement units, and current and voltage probes are used for control and measurement purposes. The experimental setup has been built in two steps. Firstly, by creating a DC–DC converter separately/individually, then running a hardware loop and checking the output voltage. Secondly, by connecting them to form a small/lab-scale DCMG. After running the hardware loop, the output voltage of the boost and buck converter has been documented separately, which is shown in Figure 11b,c.

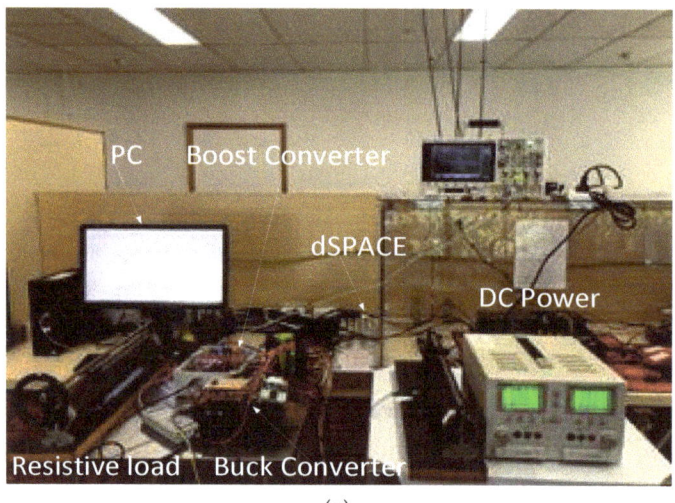

(a)

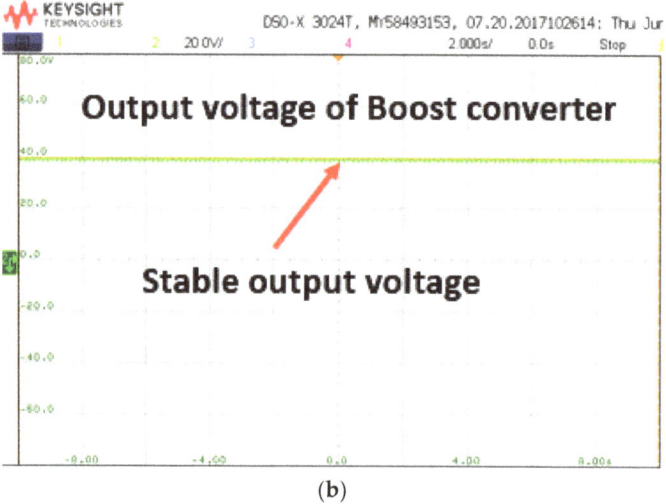

(b)

Figure 11. *Cont.*

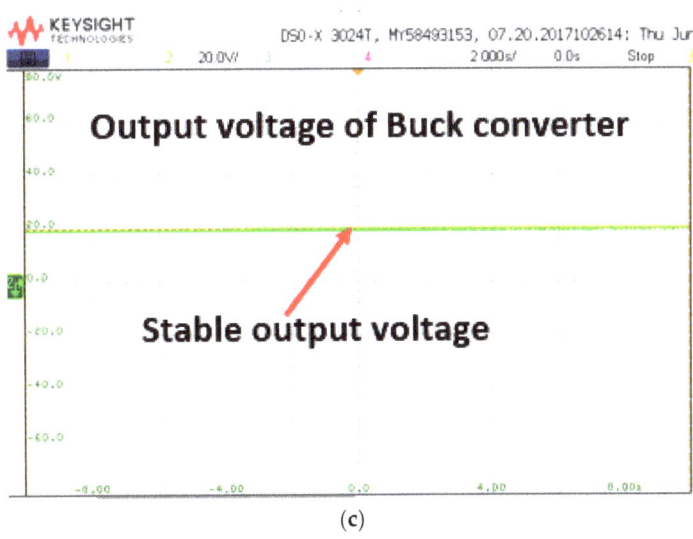

(c)

Figure 11. Experimental investigation. (a) A prototype of DC microgrid setup; (b) output voltage of boost converter; (c) output voltage of buck converter.

4.4. Critical Parameter Ranking

This section illustrates the critical parameter ranking for low frequencies and resonance. For the sensitivity study, the probabilistic system variables are considered. There are a total of ten uncertainties considered with respect to the converters. Three uncertainties are considered and related to the load and DC link. Furthermore, two uncertainties are considered in the network parameters. The probabilistic modelling of the input parameters and sensitivity is conducted in MATLAB. The stability studies for the DCMG are done by using MATLAB Simulink. Figure 12 shows the heatmap for ranking the critical parameters affecting the low-frequency oscillation of the DC grid under different loading conditions. The results in Figure 13 show that the proportional and integral gains of boost converter 1 are the most critical parameters. Figure 11 shows the heatmap for ranking critical parameters affecting the resonance of the DC grid. From the figure, it is evident that the DC-link capacitance is the most critical parameter affecting the performance of the resonance. Table 7 illustrates the performance of different sensitivity methods applied for the DC microgrid. The one-at-a-time (OAT) method, Morris screening, and Pearson method are compared. From the table, it is evident that all methods have good agreement in terms of ranking the most influential parameters, since the top three are the same for all methods (with position differences). The ranking performance of the Morris screening is between the OAT and Pearson methods. The OAT, Morris screening, and Pearson simulation times are 17 s, 120 s, and 19 m, respectively.

Figure 12. Heatmap of ranking critical parameter for oscillatory stability.

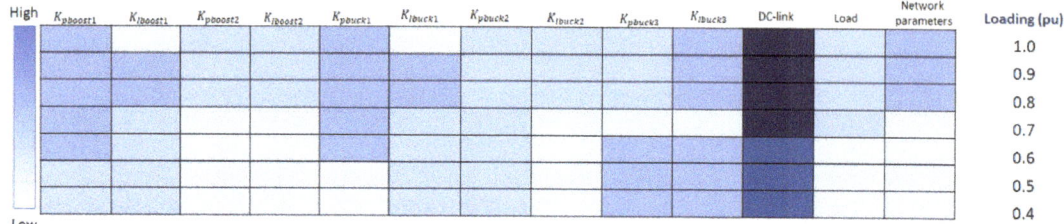

Figure 13. Heatmap for ranking critical parameter for resonance.

Table 7. Influential parameters identified using the different sensitivity method (oscillation stability).

Ranking	OAT	Morris	Pearson
1	$k_{iboost\ 1}$	$k_{pboost\ 1}$	$k_{pboost\ 1}$
2	$k_{pboost\ 1}$	$k_{iboost\ 1}$	$k_{iboost\ 1}$
3	$k_{pboost\ 2}$	$k_{pboost\ 2}$	$k_{pboost\ 2}$
4	DC-link	$k_{iboost\ 2}$	$k_{pbuck\ 2}$

4.5. Control Performance Assessment

Table 8 shows the effect of different control tunings on the damping performance of the critical modes. Four different controller tuning methods are compared here. From the given results in Table 8, it is evident that the PI+clegg provides better damping performance, followed by IP control tuning. The control parameters are given in the Appendix of the paper.

Table 8. Damping performance of complete system under different controls.

Mode	Damping with PI	Damping with PI+clegg	Damping with IP	Damping with LQR
1	0.091	0.122	0.105	0.11
2	0.551	0.593	0.573	0.57
3	0.041	0.071	0.055	0.054
4	0.112	0.134	0.123	0.115
5	0.122	0.151	0.134	0.125

5. Conclusions

This paper presents a complete analytical model of DCMGs to analyze the small-signal stability performance. Then, the semi-global sensitivity analysis is presented to rank the most critical parameter in terms of high-frequency oscillation and resonance. The ranking of the critical parameter is different for high-frequency oscillations and resonance. It is found that control dynamics can significantly contribute to voltage oscillations in DC buses. In the worst case, it can destabilize the DC bus voltage. It is also observed that the DC link capacitance is the key contributor to the resonance in the DC bus. Furthermore, this paper reviews and compares the dynamic characteristics (i.e., high-frequency oscillation and resonance) of the DC microgrid, considering different controllers such as LQR, PI+clegg, and IP instead of the conventional PI controller. From the results, it is evident that the PI+clegg provides a better dynamic performance, followed by the IP, LQR, and conventional PI with retuning. Due to the worldwide interest in DC microgrids with a high penetration of renewable resources, it appears more important to pay attention to the modelling and development of a normalized control method for DC microgrids. Furthermore, a framework to distinguish between the modelling and solver issues needs to be established for practitioners dealing with power system modelling as well as for and software and hardware implementation.

Author Contributions: Conceptualization, M.H. and R.S.; methodology, M.H.; software, M.H.; validation, R.S., M.H. and N.M.; formal analysis, M.H.; investigation, M.H. and R.S.; resources, M.H.; data curation, M.H.; writing—original draft preparation, R.S.; writing—review and editing, N.M., M.R.I. and S.M.M.; visualization, M.R.I. All authors have read and agreed to the published version of the manuscript.

Funding: This research received no external funding.

Data Availability Statement: Not applicable.

Conflicts of Interest: The authors declare no conflict of interest.

Nomenclature

Variables

BESS	Battery energy storage system
DCMG	DC microgrid
EMI	Electromagnetic interference
EV	Electric vehicle
GM	Gain margin
HF	High frequency
HVDC	High-voltage DC
LF	Low frequency
LQR	Linear Quadratic Regulator
MVDC	Medium voltage DC
PI	Proportional integral
PID	Proportional integral derivative
PM	Phase margin
PV	Photovoltaic
PWM	Pulse-width modulated
RESs	Renewable energy sources
SSS	Small-signal stability

Appendix A

Table A1 shows the parameters used for the experimental studies.

Table A1. The parameters used for the experimental studies.

Parameter	Symbol	Value
Boost converter source voltage	V_s	20 V
Boost converter inductor and capacitor	$L_1\ C_1$	$147e-6H$ & $470e-6\mu F$
Parasitic inductor resistor	r_{L1}	$70e-3\ \Omega$
Boost converter output voltage	V_{o1}	40 V
DC link voltage	V_{dc}	40 V
Switching frequency	f_{sw}	20 KHz
Proportional and integral gain of PI controller in boost converter	$K_{p1}\ K_{i1}$	0.0011262 0.05
Input voltage of buck converter	V_{in}	40 V
Buck converter output voltage	V_{o2}	20 V
Boost converter inductor and capacitor	$L_2\ C_2$	$1.5e-3H$ $470e-6\mu F$
Proportional and integral gain of PI controller in buck converter	$K_{p2}\ K_{i2}$	0.9 0.5
Switching frequency	f_{sw}	20 KHz
Load	R	75 Ω
Rated output power	P_o	500 W

Table A2 shows the control parameters used in this work.

Table A2. Controller parameters.

Converter	PI	LQR	IP	PI+clegg
1	Proportional: 0.9 Integral: 0.005	Proportional: 0.0011 Integral: 1.73	Proportional: 0.0013 Integral: 0.707	Proportional: 0.0015 Integral: 1.25
2	Proportional: 0.9 Integral: 0.005	Proportional: 0.0011 Integral: 1.73	Proportional: 0.0012 Integral: 0.707	Proportional: 0.0012 Integral: 1.23
3	Proportional: 0.9 Integral: 0.005	Proportional: 0.0011 Integral: 1.73	Proportional: 0.0011 Integral: 0.707	Proportional: 0.0012 Integral: 1.22

References

1. Amin, M.; Molinas, M. Non-parametric impedance based stability and controller bandwidth extraction from impedance measurements of HVDC-connected wind farms. *arXiv* **2017**, arXiv:1704.04800.
2. Amin, M.; Molinas, M. Small-signal stability assessment of power electronics based power systems: A discussion of impedance- and eigenvalue-based methods. *IEEE Trans. Ind. Appl.* **2017**, *53*, 5014–5030. [CrossRef]
3. Hamzeh, M.; Ghazanfari, A.; Mohamed, Y.A.-R.I.; Karimi, Y. Modeling and design of an oscillatory current-sharing control strategy in DC microgrids. *IEEE Trans. Ind. Electron.* **2015**, *62*, 6647–6657. [CrossRef]
4. Habibullah, M.; Mithulananthan, N.; Zare, F.; Alkaran, D.S. Investigation of power oscillation at common DC bus in DC grid. In Proceedings of the IEEE International Conference on Industrial Technology (ICIT), Melbourne, VIC, Australia, 13–15 February 2019; pp. 1695–1700.
5. Habibullah, M.; Mithulananthan, N.; Zare, F.; Sharma, R. Impact of control systems on power quality at common DC bus in DC grid. In Proceedings of the IEEE PES GTD Grand International Conference and Exposition Asia (GTD Asia), Bangkok, Thailand, 19–23 March 2019; pp. 411–416.
6. Augustine, S.; Quiroz, J.E.; Reno, M.J.; Brahma, S. *DC Microgrid Protection: Review and Challenges*; Sandia National Lab. (SNL-NM): Albuquerque, NM, USA, 2018.
7. Planas, E.; Andreu, J.; Gárate, J.I.; De Alegría, I.M.; Ibarra, E. AC and DC technology in microgrids: A review. *Renew. Sustain. Energy Rev.* **2015**, *43*, 726–749. [CrossRef]
8. Whaite, S.; Grainger, B.; Kwasinski, A. Power quality in DC power distribution systems and microgrids. *Energies* **2015**, *8*, 4378–4399. [CrossRef]
9. Kumar, D.; Zare, F.; Ghosh, A. DC microgrid technology: System architectures, AC grid interfaces, grounding schemes, power quality, communication networks, applications, and standardizations aspects. *IEEE Access* **2017**, *5*, 12230–12256. [CrossRef]
10. Beheshtaein, S.; Cuzner, R.M.; Forouzesh, M.; Savaghebi, M.; Guerrero, J.M. DC microgrid protection: A comprehensive review. *IEEE J. Emerg. Sel. Top. Power Electron.* **2019**. [CrossRef]
11. Augustine, S.; Reno, M.J.; Brahma, S.M.; Lavrova, O. Fault current control and protection in a standalone DC microgrid using adaptive droop and current derivative. *IEEE J. Emerg. Sel. Top. Power Electron.* **2020**, *9*, 2529–2539. [CrossRef]
12. Bayati, N.; Hajizadeh, A.; Soltani, M. Impact of faults and protection methods on DC microgrids operation. In Proceedings of the IEEE International Conference on Environment and Electrical Engineering and IEEE Industrial and Commercial Power Systems Europe (EEEIC/I & CPS Europe), Palermo, Italy, 12–15 June 2018; pp. 1–6.
13. Pourmohammd, M.; Toulabi, M.; Rayati, M.; Khajehoddin, S.A. Load type impacts on the stability and robustness of DC microgrids. *Int. J. Electr. Power Energy Syst.* **2022**, *140*, 108036. [CrossRef]
14. Zhang, Z.; Yang, X.; Zhao, S.; Wu, D.; Cao, J.; Gao, M.; Zheng, G.; Wang, Z. Large signal stability of islanded DC microgrids with multiple types of loads. *Int. J. Electr. Power Energy Syst.* **2022**, *143*, 108450. [CrossRef]
15. He, B.; Chen, W.; Hu, H.; Zhan, D.; Zhang, C. Small signal stability analysis and criterion of triple stage cascaded DC system. *IEEE J. Emerg. Sel. Top. Power Electron.* **2022**, *10*, 2576–2586. [CrossRef]
16. Lin, G.; Li, W.Z.Y.; Liu, J.; Wang, S.; Wang, P. Comparative analysis on the stability mechanism of droop control and VID control in DC microgrid. *Chin. J. Electr. Eng.* **2021**, *7*, 37–46. [CrossRef]
17. Chen, P.; Zhao, W.; Chen, X.; Zhao, W.; Chen, X.; Jiang, J. An impedance based parameter design method for active damping of load converter station in MTDC distribution. *J. Mod. Power Syst. Clean Energy* **2022**, *10*, 1423–1435. [CrossRef]
18. Hasan, K.; Preece, R.; Milanovic, J. Priority ranking of critical uncertainties affecting small-signal stability using sensitivity analysis techniques. *IEEE Trans. Power Syst.* **2017**, *32*, 2629–2639. [CrossRef]
19. Fatah, R.; Hasan, K.; Preece, R. Comparative ranking of critical uncertainties affecting the stability of mixed AC/DC system. In Proceedings of the Power System Computational Conference (PSCC), Dublin, Ireland, 11–15 June 2018; pp. 1–6.
20. Habibullah, M.; Mithulananthan, N.; Bhumkittipich, K.; Amin, M. A comprehensive investigation on high-frequency oscillation in DC microgrid. *IEEE Access* **2021**, *9*, 54850–54861. [CrossRef]
21. Habibullah, M.; Bhumkittipich, K.; Mithulananthan, N.; Sharma, R.; Zare, F. Damping oscillation and removing resonance in a RE based DC microgrids. *IEEE Access* **2021**, *9*, 163516–163525. [CrossRef]
22. Vijayakumari, A. Design of Microgrids. In *Smart Microgrids*; CRC Press: Boca Raton, FL, USA, 2020; pp. 13–117.

23. Farrokhabadi, M.; Cañizares, C.A.; Simpson-Porco, J.W.; Nasr, E.; Fan, L.; Mendoza-Araya, P.A.; Tonkoski, R.; Tamrakar, U.; Hatziargyriou, N.; Lagos, D.; et al. Microgrid stability definitions, analysis, and examples. *IEEE Trans. Power Systems* **2019**, *35*, 13–29. [CrossRef]
24. Carpintero-Rentería, M.; Santos-Martín, D.; Guerrero, J.M. Microgrids literature review through a layer's structure. *Energies* **2019**, *12*, 4381. [CrossRef]
25. Laaksonen, H. Technical Solutions for Low-Voltage Microgrid Concept. PhD Dissertation, The University of Vaasa, Vaasa, Finland, 2011.
26. Abdelgawad, H.; Sood, V.K. A comprehensive review on microgrid architectures for distributed generation. In Proceedings of the 2019 IEEE Electrical Power and Energy Conference (EPEC), Montreal, QC, Canada, 16–18 October 2019; pp. 1–8.
27. Anderson, P.M.; Agrawal, B.L.; Van Ness, J.E. *Subsynchronous Resonance in Power Systems*; John Wiley & Sons: Hoboken, NJ, USA, 1999.
28. Padiyar, K. *Analysis of Subsynchronous Resonance in Power Systems*; Springer Science & Business Media: Berlin/Heidelberg, Germany, 2012.
29. Egwebe, A.M.; Fazeli, M.; Igic, P.; Holland, P.M. Implementation and stability study of dynamic droop in islanded microgrids. *IEEE Trans. Energy Convers.* **2016**, *31*, 821–832. [CrossRef]
30. Setiadi, H.; Krismanto, A.U.; Mithulananthan, N.; Hossain, M. Modal interaction of power systems with high penetration of renewable energy and BES systems. *Int. J. Electr. Power Energy Syst.* **2018**, *97*, 385–395. [CrossRef]
31. Wu, G.; Sun, H.; Zhao, B.; Xu, S.; Zhang, X.; Egea-Alvarez, A.; Wang, S.; Li, G.; Li, Y.; Zhou, X. A low-frequency converter-driven oscillations in weak grids: Explanation and damping improvement. *IEEE Trans. Power Syst.* **2021**, *36*, 5944–5947. [CrossRef]
32. Banos, A.; Barreiro, A. *Reset Control Systems*; Springer Science and Business Media: Berlin, Germany, 2011.
33. Li, C.; Wang, S.; Colas, F.; Liang, J. Dominant instability mechanism of VSI connecting to a very weak grid. *IEEE Trans. Power Syst.* **2022**, *37*, 828–831. [CrossRef]

Disclaimer/Publisher's Note: The statements, opinions and data contained in all publications are solely those of the individual author(s) and contributor(s) and not of MDPI and/or the editor(s). MDPI and/or the editor(s) disclaim responsibility for any injury to people or property resulting from any ideas, methods, instructions or products referred to in the content.

Article

One-Dimensional Maximum Power Point Tracking Design of Switched-Capacitor Charge Pumps for Thermoelectric Energy Harvesting

Koichi Nono and Toru Tanzawa *

Graduate School of Integrated Science and Technology, Shizuoka University, Hamamatsu 432-8561, Japan
* Correspondence: toru.tanzawa@shizuoka.ac.jp

Abstract: This paper proposes a one-dimensional (1D) maximum power point tracking (MPPT) design which only requires measurement of one parameter (the input voltage of a switched-capacitor charge pump) for calibrating a power converter including the charge pump and thermoelectric generator. The frequency of the clock to drive the charge pump is designed to minimize the circuit area of the entire charge pump circuit for generating a target output current at a specific output voltage. The ratio of the capacitance value of each boosting capacitor (C) to the size of the switching MOSFET can be determined to maximize the transferring current at the same time. When a thermoelectric generator (TEG) is given, its output impedance is determined. Its open-circuit voltage varies with the temperature difference between two plates of the TEG. MPPT maximizes the output power of the charge pump even when the temperature difference varies. It was indicated that the number of stages of charge pump (N) needs to increase when the temperature difference lowers, whereas C needs to decrease inversely proportional to N, meaning that the C–N product should be kept unchanged for MPPT. Demonstration of the circuit design was conducted in 65 nm CMOS, and the measured results validated the concept of the 1D MPPT.

Keywords: one-dimensional; maximum power point tracking; charge pump; thermoelectric generator; energy harvesting

Citation: Nono, K.; Tanzawa, T. One-Dimensional Maximum Power Point Tracking Design of Switched-Capacitor Charge Pumps for Thermoelectric Energy Harvesting. *Electronics* **2023**, *12*, 1203. https://doi.org/10.3390/electronics12051203

Academic Editors: Shailendra Rajput, Moshe Averbukh and Noel Rodriguez

Received: 15 February 2023
Revised: 24 February 2023
Accepted: 1 March 2023
Published: 2 March 2023

Copyright: © 2023 by the authors. Licensee MDPI, Basel, Switzerland. This article is an open access article distributed under the terms and conditions of the Creative Commons Attribution (CC BY) license (https://creativecommons.org/licenses/by/4.0/).

1. Introduction

More and more Internet of things (IoT) devices are being connected to each other around the globe for a safer society and highly efficient healthcare, agriculture, and industries [1,2]. IoT devices to be placed somewhere with no alternating current (AC) main need to have batteries for powering. Rapid increases in the cost for replacing wasted batteries and in the amount of waste are becoming problematic. Energy-harvesting technology is expected to solve such an economic and environmental challenge by powering IoT devices with environmental energy sources such as lights, vibration, and heat flow [3,4]. Thermoelectric generators (TEGs) generate electric power with heat flow or a temperature gradient [5–7]. Powering sensors with heat flow from heat pipes to air to monitor surrounding temperature and other physical properties is used in chemical plants and fabs [8]. Wearable electronic devices can also work with TEG from body temperature without batteries [9].

Because the nominal open-circuit voltage of TEG (V_{OC}) is below 1 V, boost converters are needed to drive sensor integrated circuits (ICs). Switched capacitor charge pumps (CPs) [10] are used, especially in applications which require a small form factor and low power. The design challenge is how high power conversion efficiency can be maintained, namely, maximum power point tracking (MPPT), over wide variations in temperature difference between the two plates of TEG (ΔT) or, in other words, over wide variations in V_{OC} because V_{OC} is proportional to ΔT. Figure 1 illustrates a general power supply system composed of TEG and CP for sensor ICs, as shown in [11,12]. The design parameters of CP are the stage capacitance C, the number of stages N, the size of charge transfer switches W, and the clock frequency f. Those parameters are determined by a given condition for the input voltage V_S, output voltage V_{PP}, and current I_{PP}. When V_S varies according to V_{OC}, one or more design parameters need to be varied for the CP to operate at or around the maximum power point. In previous designs [13–15], multidimensional MPPT was proposed and evaluated. However, a greater circuit area was needed to have largely flexible input impedance of CP.

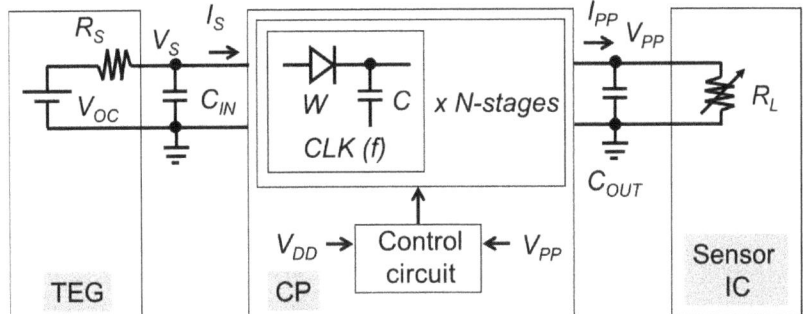

Figure 1. Circuit diagram of CP with TEG as a power source and sensor IC as a load.

This paper is aimed at proposing and validating a one-dimensional MPPT to minimize the area overhead of CP even with MPPT capability by applying reconfigurability for CP. This paper is organized as follows: Section 2 reviews previous studies on CP with MPPT and reconfigurable CP in detail. The concept of a reconfigurable charge pump toward maximum output power density is proposed in Section 3. The circuit design is demonstrated in Section 4. Section 5 compares the proposed 1D MPPT design with the previous 2D or 3D ones.

2. Previous Work on TEG-CP System with MPPT and Reconfigurable CP

2.1. 2D (N, f) MPPT [13]

Figure 2 illustrates a 2D MPPT algorism [13]. The steps to determine the optimum N are as follows:

1. (Step 1) N is set to be the maximum assuming V_{OC} is at the minimum (otherwise, the output voltage cannot reach the target output voltage V_{PP_TGT}). f is set to be the minimum for having room to increase the input power to the CP with faster f during the following searching procedure.
2. (Step 2) CP runs in a predetermined period T_P. The peak output voltage is measured as V_{PP_past}.
3. (Step 3) CP runs in T_P with a decreased N. The peak output voltage is measured as V_{PP_now}.
4. (Step 4) V_{PP_now} is compared with V_{PP_past}. If $V_{PP\_now} > V_{PP\_past}$, then Step 3 is done. Otherwise, the procedure moves on to Step 5.
5. (Step 5) N is considered optimum at the current V_{OC}, which makes the CP to output the maximum I_{PP}.

Then, the steps to determine the optimum f are as follows:

6. (Step 6) CP runs in T_P with an increased f. The peak output voltage is measured as V_{PP_now}.
7. (Step 7) V_{PP_now} is compared with V_{PP_past}. If $V_{PP\_now} > V_{PP\_past}$, then Step 6 is done. Otherwise, the procedure stops.

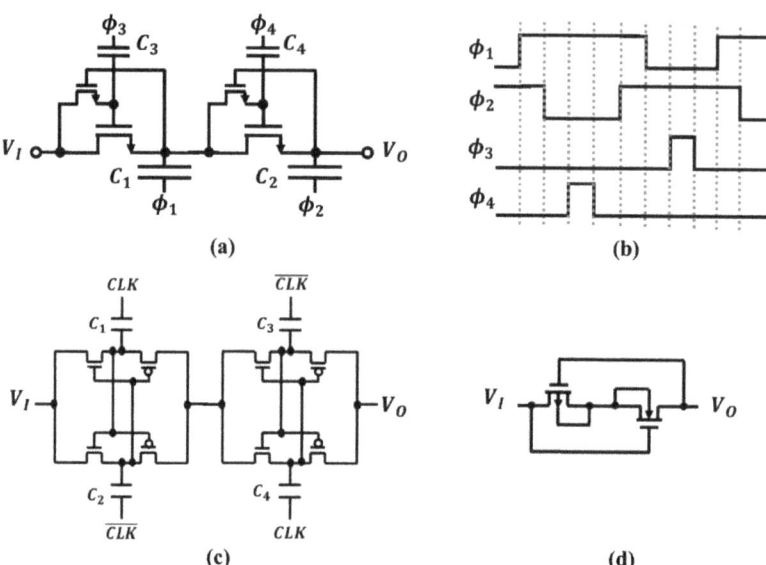

Figure 2. Charge transfer switches (CTSs) with local gate boosters (**a**), four-phase clock (**b**), CMOS latch or cross-coupled CSTs (**c**), and ULPD (**d**).

The value of N right after Step 5 can be optimum as long as V_S stays at the value at Step 5. However, V_S decreases as f increases because an increased input current decreases V_S from an IR drop in the output impedance of TEG (R_S). Therefore, the optimum N needs to depend on f. In order for the procedure to run the CP at the MPP regardless of V_{OC}, a fully 2D MPPT would be needed to scan (N, f) points on the N–f plane. When the numbers of possible N and f are N_N and N_f, respectively, one needs to run the CP with different combinations of $N_N \times N_f$ in the worst case, which can take significant time to determine the MPP.

2.2. 2D (N, f) MPPT Algorism for CP System with a Supercapacitor and a Linear Regulator [14]

In [14], another 2D MPPT was proposed for the CP system with a supercapacitor and a linear regulator. MPPT is performed only during ramping up the output voltage of CP (V_{PP}). While V_{PP} is ramping up, the clock frequency f and the number of stages N are controlled independently. f is controlled in such a way that the input voltage of CP (V_S) is around a target voltage (V_{MPPT}) for MPPT. For example, when the energy transducer is TEG, V_{MPPT} is $V_S/2$. As f increases, the input impedance of CP decreases; therefore, V_S decreases, or vice versa. N is controlled in such a way that V_{PP} reaches a target voltage V_{PP_TGT}. CP can generate V_{PP_TGT} even with a low V_S when N is sufficiently large. In other words, at the beginning of ramping up, N is controlled to be sufficiently large. As V_{PP} is approaching V_{PP_TGT}, N is decreased to the number of stages, which is barely sufficient under a given condition of V_{OC}. Thus, MPPT is realized at the interface between TEG and CP rather than that between CP and the load.

2.3. 3D (C, N, f) MPPT Algorism [15]

In [15], a 3D MPPT was proposed with three design parameters f, C, and N controlled. In the first MPPT step, f is set at the maximum of 4.25 MHz. N is initially set to be the minimum value. Under a certain load condition, CP is run. Because the input impedance is minimum with the smallest N and the largest C, the input voltage of CP (V_S) is expected to be lower than the target voltage of $V_{OC}/2$ in case of TEG. V_S is monitored to see if $V_S > V_{OC}/2$. Until $V_S > V_{OC}/2$, N is increased and C is decreased. Note that the input impedance can vary when a load varies over time; therefore, the CP configuration in terms of N and C may not depend only on V_{OC}. Once N and C are determined as an MPPT configuration, f is controlled in such a way that V_{PP} stays at a target voltage V_{PP_TGT} under the given load condition. As a result, even with 3D MPPT, the final combination of C, N, and f may not achieve MPPT at the CP output.

2.4. Reconfigurable CP

Various charge transfer switches (CTSs) have been proposed to reduce the effective threshold voltage (V_{TH}) per CTS. Umezawa et al. proposed effectively zero V_{TH} CTS by using a four-phase clock [16], as shown in Figure 2a,b. C_1 and C_2 are the stage capacitors which mainly determine the circuit area. The other capacitors can be small, which aim at boosting the gate of CTSs. After the gate node is left floating, the small gate-boosting capacitors C_3, C_4 allow the transfer transistors to operate in triode region, resulting in effectively zero V_{TH}. Gariboldi et al. proposed CTS with a CMOS latch or cross-coupled CMOS with two-phase clock [17], as shown in Figure 2c. A stage capacitor is halved for each of the two capacitors C_1, C_2 to remain the same stage capacitance in total. Charges can be fully transferred from C_1 to C_3 with CLK high and /CLK low in the first half period. Charges can be fully transferred from C_2 to C_4 with CLK low and /CLK high in the second half period. As a result, the same amount of charge can be transferred from one stage to the next in one clock cycle. Levacq et al. proposed an ultralow-power diode (ULPD) [18], as shown in Figure 2d. In a forward biasing condition, either the NMOSFET or the PMOSFET with a lower threshold voltage determines the forward bias current. In a reverse biasing condition, a significant reduction in off-leak current is expected.

To improve the power conversion efficiency of the RF-DC converter for RF energy harvesting over a wide input power range, a reconfigurable CTS was proposed in [19], as shown in Figure 3. Selectors can connect the gates of PMOSFETs with those of NMOS to be configured as a CMOS latch, as shown in Figure 3a, in a relatively low-input-power condition where the forward bias current is prioritized rather than low reverse leakage. CTS can be reconfigurable as a hybrid topology, as shown in Figure 3b, in a relatively high input power condition where low reverse leakage is prioritized rather than the forward bias current.

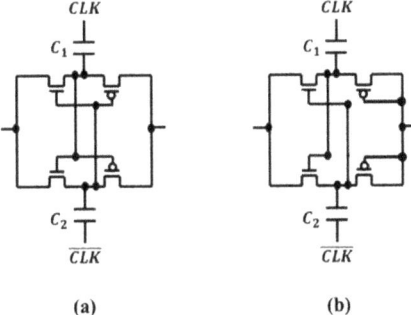

Figure 3. Reconfigurable CP with variable topology of CTSs; CMOS latch CTS in a low input power range (**a**) and a hybrid CTS n a high input power range (**b**).

Figure 4a shows the schematic diagram of two-stage unit based on the structure of Figure 2a. Control signals *ENP1*, *ENP2*, and *ENS* determine the charge transfer path among IN-to-OUT_S, IN-to-OUT_P, IN_S-to-OUT_S, and IN_S-to-OUT_P. Figure 4b illustrates a symbol of the two-stage unit.

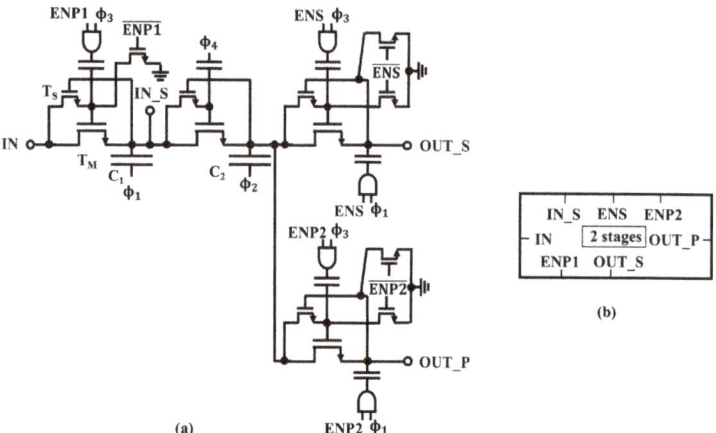

Figure 4. (a) Two-stage unit; (b) symbols of the two-stage unit.

Using this structure, one can configure two two-stage units (see Figure 5a) connected in series as shown in Figure 5b or in parallel as shown in Figure 5c [20,21]. When two two-stage units are connected in series, CP has a single array of four stages. When two two-stage units are connected in parallel, CP has two stages with twofold larger stage capacitance. As a result, the former configuration has higher maximum attainable output voltage and higher output resistance than the latter. Thus, the rise time of the output voltage can be reduced when the latter configuration is set to increase the output current while the output voltage is low, and the former configuration is set to increase the output voltage while the output voltage is high [20]. Another use case of this reconfiguration is that the load is varied such that a high output current at a low output voltage is required in the first operation and a low output current at a high output voltage is required in the second operation [21].

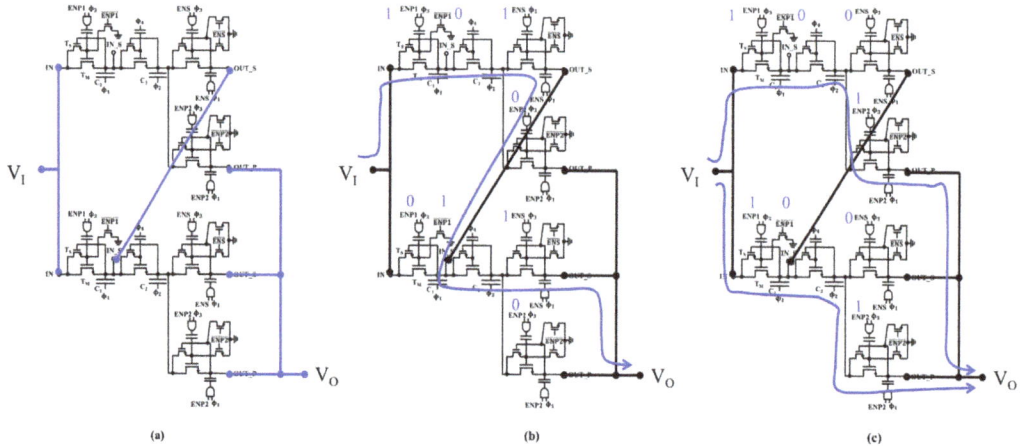

Figure 5. (a) Reconfigurable CP with two two-stage units; (b) operation of the CP with two two-stage units connected in series; (c) operation of the CP with two two-stage units connected in parallel.

3. Concept of 1D MPPT

In this paper, MPPT at the CP output is the focus. In [22], a circuit model for TEG-driven CP is developed to determine C and N to maximize the output current I_{PP} at

V_{PP} with a predetermined f. The model equation is expressed below, while the circuit parameters are defined in Table 1. A flexible type of TEG [23] is proposed in this work, which has a relatively high R_S.

$$I_{PP} = \frac{(N+1)(V_{OC} - V_{TH}) - V_{PP} - \delta V}{(N+1)^2 R_S + \frac{N}{fC} + \delta R}. \quad (1)$$

Table 1. Definition of circuit parameters.

	Parameter	Definition	Default Value
TEG	V_{OC}	Open-circuit voltage as a function of temperature gradient	0.5, 0.7, 1.0, 1.5, 2.0 V
	R_S	Output resistance	600 Ω
CP	C	Stage capacitance	TBD
	N	Number of stage capacitors	TBD
	f	Clock frequency	10 MHz
	V_{PP}	Target output voltage	3.0 V
	V_T	Effective thermal voltage of charge transfer switches (CTS)	26 mV
	I_{SAT}	Saturation current of CTS	40 nA
	α_T	Ratio of top plate capacitance to C	0.05
	α_B	Ratio of bottom plate capacitance to C	0.1

An effective threshold voltage of charge transfer switches (CTS) V_{TH}, a loss in the voltage gain due to the parasitic capacitance δV, and an additional output resistance due to the parasitic capacitance δR are given by Equations (2)–(4), respectively.

$$V_{TH} = V_T \ln\left(4^{\frac{1}{N+1}} \frac{(1+\alpha_T)fCV_T}{I_{SAT}}\right). \quad (2)$$

$$\delta V = (V_{PP} + (N+1)V_{TH})\{NfCR_S(\alpha_T + \alpha_B + \alpha_T\alpha_B) + \alpha_T\} - \alpha_T V_{OC}. \quad (3)$$

$$\delta R = (\alpha_T + \alpha_B N^2) R_S. \quad (4)$$

Determination of the optimum combination of C and N for a given V_{OC} was demonstrated in [22]. f is set at the predetermined value which maximizes I_{PP} at V_{PP_TGT} [24]. In other words, the predetermined value of f can minimize the CP area to output a target I_{PP} at V_{PP_TGT}. To determine f, I_{PP} at V_{PP_TGT} of 3.0 V was measured as a function of f with SPICE. Four CP configurations, as discussed below in detail, were tested in the case of (N, C) of (2, 160 pF), (4, 80 pF), (8, 40 pF), and (16, 20 pF), namely, 8-2, 4-4, 2-8, and 1-16 modes at V_{OC} of 2.0 V, 1.5 V, 1.0 V, and 0.5 V, respectively, as shown in Figure 6a. Figure 6b shows I_{PP} normalized by the maximum value in each configuration. Regardless of configuration, f of 8–10 MHz gave the maximum output current. Thus, f of 10 MHz was selected in this work.

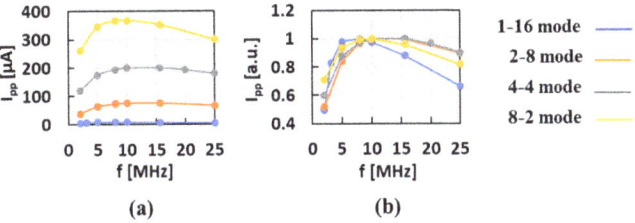

Figure 6. Clock frequency vs. output current at V_{PP} of 3.0V. (**a**) absolute value; (**b**) arbitrary unit.

Unlike a given V_{OC} in [22], how the optimum combinations of C and N vary with V_{OC} was the concern in this paper. Figure 7 shows the contour plots of the output power P_{OUT} over the C–N plane in the case of V_{OC} = 0.5 V (a), 0.7 V (b), 1.0 V (c), 1.5 V (d), and

2.0 V (e) [25]. Points in red indicates the optimum combinations of C and N, namely, C_{OPT} and N_{OPT}, respectively, which enable CP to generate the largest P_{OUT}.

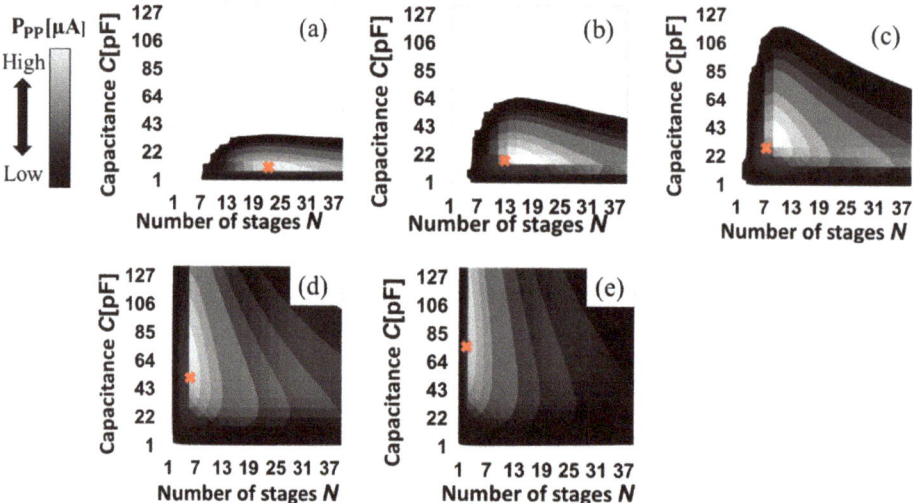

Figure 7. Contour plots of P_{OUT} in case of V_{OC} of 0.5 V (**a**), 0.7 V (**b**), 1.0 V (**c**), 1.5 V (**d**), and 2.0 V (**e**). "x" in each figure indicates the maximum power point.

Figure 8 shows how C_{OPT} and N_{OPT} vary with V_{OC}. The slope of the approximate line is −1, which suggests that their product, i.e., the CP area, should be constant. Intuitively, as V_{OC} decreases, N needs to increase to remain the voltage gain from the input to the output. If C is unchanged, the input current should increase with larger N. This means that the input impedance would decrease. To keep the impedance matching at the interface between TEG and CP, C needs to decrease as N increases. Conversely, as V_{OC} increases, N must decrease whereas C must increase to keep the voltage gain and the input impedance at the same time. To operate CP in MPPT at the CP output, one needs to design CP so that N can vary while C can vary inversely proportional to N when V_{OC} varies. As a result, the following functionalities are needed: (1) periodical detection of V_{OC}, (2) determination of C–N combination for the present value of V_{OC}, and (3) reconfiguration of CP to have C_{OPT} and N_{OPT} for the present value of V_{OC}. In Section 4, the design is demonstrated. This procedure can be called a one-dimensional MPPT because one only needs to determine the combination of C_{OPT} and N_{OPT} for the present value of V_{OC}.

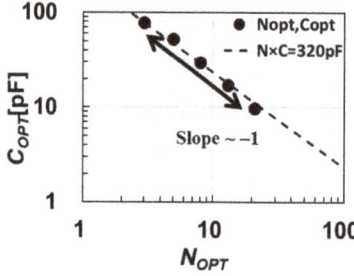

Figure 8. Relationship between C_{OPT} and N_{OPT} for TEG with R_S = 600 Ω and V_{OC} = 0.5–2.0 V.

4. Circuit Design

4.1. Reconfigurable CP

In [15], a reconfigurable CP with fine-tuning capability to allow N of 1, 2, 3, 4, or 5 was proposed. As a result, 12 capacitors and 88 switches are needed for the five-stage CP. Many switches increase parasitic capacitance to the stage capacitors, which can affect voltage gain and power efficiency. Instead, another reconfiguration approach [21,22] was used to minimize the area overhead in this paper. Sixteen switches are added to the original 16-stage CP to allow CP to have two, four, eight, and 16 stages depending on the measured value of V_{OC}, as shown in Figure 8. Figure 9 shows a reconfigurable CP with eight two-stage units. With the signals in red are high and those in black are low, it can be reconfigured as a single-array 16-stage mode (1-16 mode), two-array eight-stage mode (2-8 mode), four array four-stage mode (4-4 mode), or eight-array two-stage mode (8-2 mode), as shown in Figure 9b–e. The lines in red show the conduction paths.

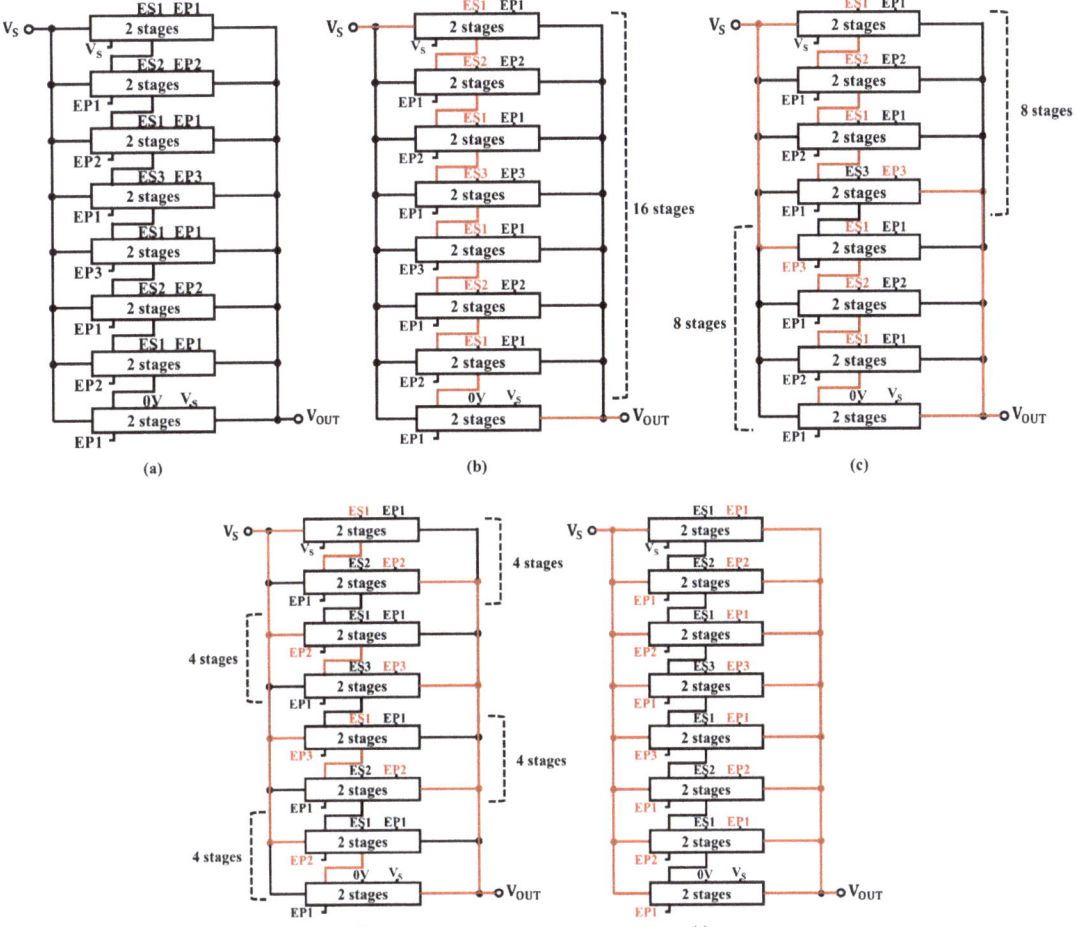

Figure 9. (**a**) Reconfigurable CP, (**b**) single-array 16-stage mode, (**c**) two-array eight-stage mode, (**d**) four array four-stage mode, (**e**) eight-array two-stage mode.

Figure 10a–e show P_{OUT}, V_S, P_S, η_{CP}, and η_{CP_MPPT} as a function of V_{OC}, respectively, in different modes. The aim of this work was to achieve MPPT at the CP output. According to Figure 10a, the boundaries in V_{OC} between 1-16 and 2-8 modes, between 2-8 and 4-4 modes, and between 4-4 and 8-2 modes are 0.55 V, 1.05 V, and 1.80 V, respectively. When the CP operates with 1-16, 2-8, 4-4, and 8-2 modes in $V_{OC} < 0.55$ V, 0.55 V $< V_{OC} < 1.05$ V, 1.05 V $< V_{OC} < 1.80$ V, and 1.80 V $< V_{OC}$, respectively, one can maximize P_{OUT} regardless of V_{OC}. Figure 10b shows V_S under the CP operation in MPPT. As suggested in [22], V_S in cases where CP operates in MPPT for the output (V_{MPPT_OUT}) is basically larger than that in cases where CP operates in MPPT for the input (V_{MPPT_IN}), even though there are tiny ranges in V_{OC} where $V_{MPPT\_OUT} < V_{MPPT\_IN}$. Figure 10c indicates that the input power to the CP converges as V_{OC} increases. As a result, power efficiency η_{CP} or η_{CP_MPPT} is maximized, as shown in Figure 10d or Figure 10e, where η_{CP} and η_{CP_MPPT} are defined by Equations (5) and (6), respectively [15].

$$\eta_{CP} = \frac{P_{OUT}}{P_S}. \qquad (5)$$

$$\eta_{CP\_MPPT} = \frac{P_{OUT}}{P_{AV}}. \qquad (6)$$

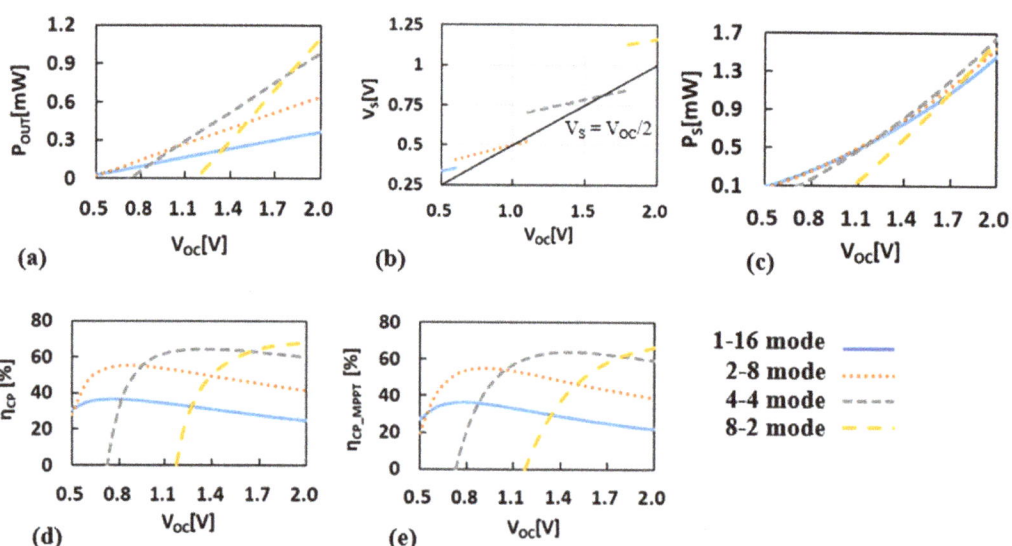

Figure 10. P_{OUT} (a), V_S (b), P_S (c), η_{CP} (d), and η_{CP_MPPT} (e) as a function of V_{OC} in different modes.

P_{AV} is the maximum attainable power of TEG when the impedance at the interface between TEG and CP is matched, as defined by Equation (7).

$$P_{AV} = \frac{V_{OC}^2}{4R_S}. \qquad (7)$$

Figure 11a–d show P_{OUT}, η_{CP}, η_{TEG}, and η_{CP_MPPT} as a function of V_{OC}, respectively, in MPPT and fixed 1-16 modes. η_{TEG} is defined by Equation (8) showing how much power is actually input to the CP normalized by P_{AV}.

$$\eta_{TEG} = \frac{P_S}{P_{AV}}. \qquad (8)$$

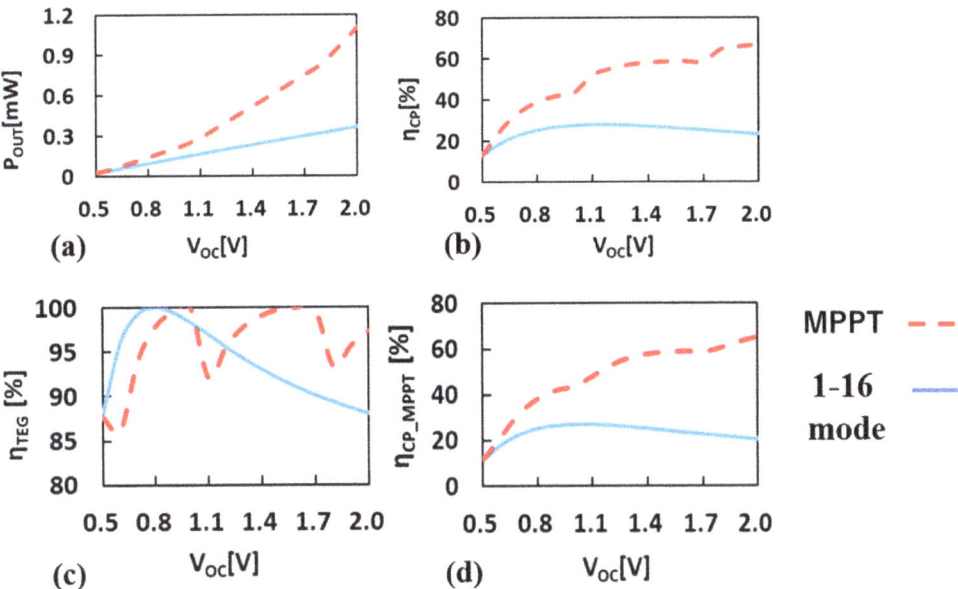

Figure 11. P_{OUT} (**a**), η_{CP} (**b**), η_{TEG} (**c**), and η_{CP_MPPT} (**d**) as a function of V_{OC} in MPPT and a fixed 1-16 modes.

The monotonic increase in η_{CP_MPPT} with MPPT indicates that this simple circuit structure with binary steps in N can be sufficient with respect to system power efficiency. As a result, the average CP output power increases by a factor of 2.3 with the proposed MPPT when V_{OC} varies in a rage of 0.5 V and 2.0 V randomly.

4.2. System Design

Figure 12a,b show the CP system and V_{PP} waveform in ramping up, calibration, and user modes, respectively [26]. V_{OC} can be measured when V_{PP} stays high. Because the A/D converter (ADC) and bandgap reference (BGR) are powered by V_{PP}, one cannot know a value of V_{OC} until V_{PP} goes high. As a result, CP is set to the 1-16 mode initially, which can be boosted up to a target V_{PP} of 3 V even with low V_{OC}. In the above demonstration, N_0 and C_0 are 16 and 20 pF, respectively. Once V_{PP} reaches a target of 3 V, a calibration mode starts. The oscillator to drive CP is disabled to increase the input impedance of CP sufficiently high. After the input voltage V_S is saturated to be close to V_{OC}, ADC measures the V_{OC} value for C/N selector to determine the logic values for the CP control signals such as *ES1* and *EP1*. CP is reconfigured to the optimum one for the current value of V_{OC}. Even without no CP operation in calibration mode, a voltage droop in V_{PP} can be sufficiently small with low power ADC and BGR and large C_{OUT}. In the following user mode, CP operates in the current configuration. For a given application, the temperature gradient of TEG drifts in a specific time. The next calibration should start earlier than that specific time, but it is often not necessary.

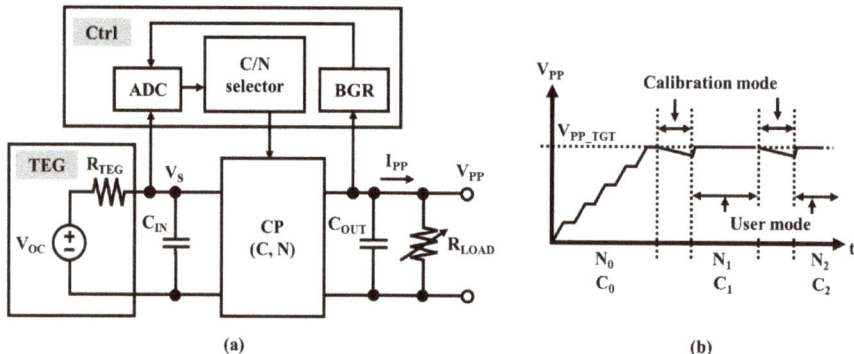

Figure 12. CP system (**a**), V_{PP} waveform in ramping-up, calibration, and user modes (**b**).

To validate the design, V_{OC} shown in Figure 13a was input. V_{OC} was varied from 0.5 V to 0.7 V and to 1.2 V. To save the simulation time, a step response in V_{OC} was used. V_{PP} was regulated at 3 V in 1-16 mode. After CP entered in steady state, a calibration signal was input with high in 100 ns. CP was reconfigured to 2-8 mode. Figure 13c shows 16 capacitor voltages in T_{M1}. Only eight signals are visible because the same stage voltages of two arrays of the eight-stage CP were overlaid. Similarly, Figure 13d shows 16 capacitor voltages in 4-4 modes. Only four signals are visible because the same stage voltages of four arrays of the four-stage CP were overlaid. The ripple in V_{PP} increased from T_{ST} to T_{M2} with I_{PP}, which means that output power increased with V_{OC}.

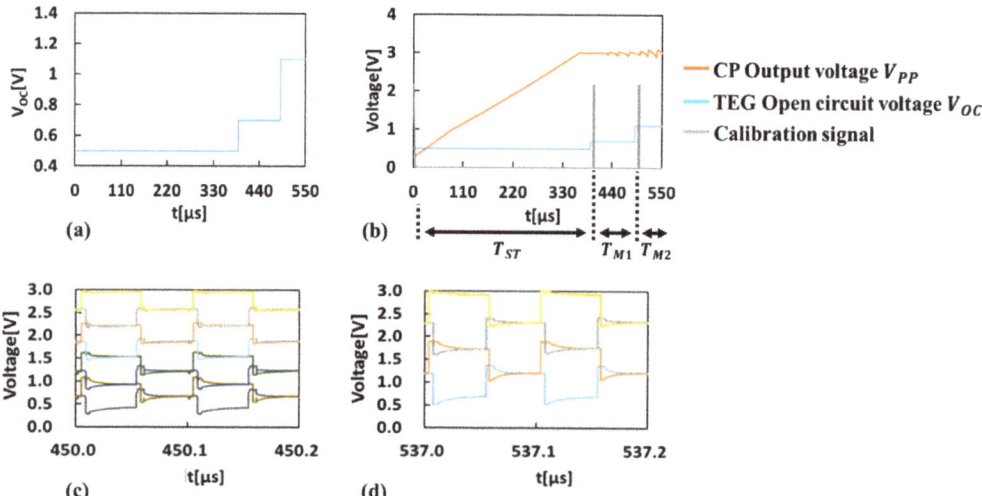

Figure 13. Input voltage V_{OC} (**a**), V_{PP}, V_{OC}, and calibration signal (**b**), 16 capacitor voltages in T_{M1} (**c**), and 16 capacitor voltages in T_{M2} (**d**).

In the CP system shown in Figure 8, another feedback loop to disable CP when the input voltage V_S lowers below a critical point where the output current becomes zero, as proposed in [11,12], was omitted for simplicity. Such a feedback loop is needed in a practical design.

5. Experiment

A part of the CP system was implemented in 65 nm CMOS to validate the design, as shown in Figure 14. Eight two-stage units were placed in order horizontally. CTS and small gate boosting capacitors were placed in the center. Clock and control signals were routed over the CTS region. Thus, additional circuit elements for CP to run with MPPT were minimal. The on-chip oscillator generated four clocks at 10 MHz. In this design, two-bit signals were input to select one among four configuration modes externally, instead of using ADC.

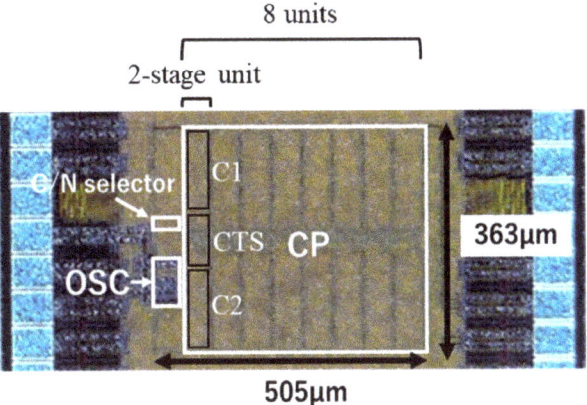

Figure 14. Die photo.

Figure 15 shows the measured V_{OUT}–I_{OUT} at V_S of 0.6V. C_{IN} and C_{OUT} of 1 nF were connected to the circuit. The slope in each mode was proportional to fC/N. The expected ratios between 1-16 and 2-8 modes, between 2-8 and 4-4 modes, and between 4-4 and 8-2 modes were as large as a theoretical value of 4 (a factor of 2 from C and another factor of 2 from N). According to the measured maximum attainable output voltage, the effective threshold voltage was estimated to be 50 mV. Thus, V_{OUT}–I_{OUT} curves in different modes were verified. Unfortunately, further measurement was not possible because all three fabricated dies were broken by accident.

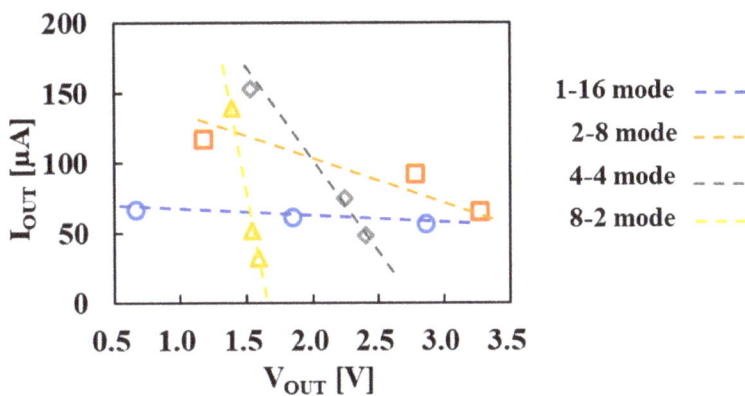

Figure 15. Measured V_{OUT}–I_{OUT} at V_S of 0.6 V in four CP modes.

6. Comparison with Previous Work

Table 2 compares this study with previous work [13–15]. In these previous studies, f was used as a control circuit parameter to adjust the CP operation to MPPT. When one has room to decrease f, such a design needs larger C than that of the CP, which is designed with an optimum f for the minimum circuit area. As a result, the CP needs to prepare more area than the minimum. In this work, f was fixed at 10 MHz regardless of V_{OC}. Therefore, the ratio of the size of CTS to C, whose optimum value was a function of f [18], was designed to be a single value. Thus, the two-stage unit can be commonly used for any configuration mode. Additional switches to change the connection state from serial to parallel or vice versa can be simple and implemented in the CTS region with a small area overhead. As a result, the output power density could be reduced in this study.

Table 2. Comparison with previous work.

		Liu, 2015 [13]	Bautista, 2016 [14]		Yoon, 2018 [15]	This Work
	Technology [nm]	180	180		130	65
	Energy transducer	TEG/PV (*1)	TEG/PV/MFC (*1)		TEG	TEG
	Operation range of V_S [V]	1.28~3.0	0.25~1.1		0.27~1.0	0.34~1.2 (V_{OC} = 0.5~2.0 V)
	Target output voltage V_{PP_TGT} [V]	3.3	1.8		1.0	3.0
MPPT	Procedure	Two steps in order	Two steps in parallel		Two steps in order	Single step
	Parameters to be measured	ΔV_{PP}, i.e., I_{PP}	V_S~V_{MPPT}	V_{PP}~V_{PP_TGT}	(1) V_S~V_{MPPT}, (2) V_{PP}~V_{PP_TGT}	V_{OC}
	Parameters to be updated	(1) N, (2) f	f	N	(1) Combination of C, N, (2) f	Combination of C, N
	Parameter to be maximized	P_{OUT}	P_{IN}		P_{IN}	P_{OUT}
	Area [mm^2]	1.03	2.82		0.835	0.302 (*2)
	Maximum power efficiency of CP η_{CP_MAX} [%]	79 (TEG) 89 (PV)	57		64	67
	Maximum output power P_{OUT_MAX} [mW]	0.04	1.62		0.40	1.11
	P_{OUT_MAX}/Area [mW/mm^2]	0.04	0.57		0.48	3.66 (*2)

(*1) PV: photovoltaic, MFC: microbial fuel cell; (*2) ADC to measure V_{OC} is not included.

7. Summary

One-dimensional maximum power tracking was proposed to achieve both increased extracted power to the load and squeezed circuit area at the same time. A key finding in this paper is that MPPT at the output of CP was realized with the C–N product, i.e., CP area, constant even at different open-circuit voltages of TEG. In calibration mode, V_{OC} was measured with ADC while CP was disabled to determine an optimum CP configuration at the current V_{OC}. In the following user mode, CP was run with the updated reconfigured mode. By repeating this procedure periodically, CP can always stay under the MPPT condition. In the future, it will be verified whether the proposed MPPT method is applicable to other DC energy transducers such as photovoltaic and microbial fuel cells.

Author Contributions: Conceptualization, T.T.; methodology, K.N. and T.T.; software, K.N.; validation, K.N. and T.T.; formal analysis, K.N. and T.T.; investigation, K.N. and T.T.; writing—original draft preparation, K.N.; writing—review and editing, T.T.; funding acquisition, T.T. All authors have read and agreed to the published version of the manuscript.

Funding: This research was partially funded by Zeon Corp.

Institutional Review Board Statement: Not applicable.

Informed Consent Statement: Not applicable.

Data Availability Statement: Not applicable.

Conflicts of Interest: The authors declare no conflict of interest.

References

1. Zanella, A.; Bui, N.; Castellani, A.; Vangelista, L.; Zorzi, M. Internet of Things for Smart Cities. *IEEE Internet Things J.* **2014**, *1*, 22–32. [CrossRef]
2. Al-Fuqaha, A.; Guizani, M.; Mohammadi, M.; Aledhari, M.; Ayyash, M. Internet of Things: A Survey on Enabling Technologies, Protocols, and Applications. *IEEE Commun. Surv. Tutorials* **2015**, *17*, 2347–2376. [CrossRef]
3. Mitcheson, P.D.; Yeatman, E.M.; Rao, G.K.; Holmes, A.S.; Green, T.C. Energy Harvesting from Human and Machine Motion for Wireless Electronic Devices. *Proc. IEEE* **2008**, *96*, 1457–1486. [CrossRef]
4. Sudevalayam, S.; Kulkarni, P. Energy Harvesting Sensor Nodes: Survey and Implications. *IEEE Commun. Surv. Tutorials* **2010**, *13*, 443–461. [CrossRef]
5. Huesgen, T.; Woias, P.; Kockmann, N. Design and fabrication of MEMS thermoelectric generators with high temperature efficiency. *Sens. Actuators A Phys.* **2008**, *145*, 423–429. [CrossRef]
6. Date Sheet of TGP-651, Micropelt. Available online: http://www.micropelt.com/ (accessed on 15 February 2023).
7. Du, Y.; Xu, J.; Paul, B.; Eklund, P. Flexible thermoelectric materials and devices. *Appl. Mater. Today* **2018**, *12*, 366–388. [CrossRef]
8. Garofalo, E.; Bevione, M.; Cecchini, L.; Mattiussi, F.; Chiolerio, A. Waste heat to power: Technologies, current applications, and future potential. *Energy Technol.* **2020**, *8*, 2000413. [CrossRef]
9. Nozariasbmarz, A.; Collins, H.; Dsouza, K.; Polash, M.H.; Hosseini, M.; Hyland, M.; Liu, J.; Malhotra, A.; Ortiz, F.M.; Mohaddes, F.; et al. Review of wearable thermoelectric energy harvesting: From body temperature to electronic systems. *Appl. Energy* **2020**, *258*, 114069. [CrossRef]
10. Dickson, J.F. On-Chip High-Voltage Generation in MNOS Integrated Circuits Using an Improved Multiplier Technique. *IEEE J. Solid-State Circuits* **1976**, *11*, 374–378. [CrossRef]
11. Koketsu, K.; Tanzawa, T. A Design of Cold Start Charge Pump for Flexible Thermoelectric Generator with High Output Impedance. In Proceedings of the 2020 27th IEEE International Conference on Electronics, Circuits and Systems, Glasgow, UK, 23–25 November 2020. [CrossRef]
12. Koketsu, K.; Tanzawa, T. Design of a charge pump circuit and system with input impedance modulation for a flexible-type thermoelectric generator with high-output impedance. *Electronics* **2021**, *10*, 1212. [CrossRef]
13. Xiaosen, L.; Sanchez-Sinencio, E. A 0.45-to-3V reconfigurable charge-pump energy harvester with two-dimensional MPPT for Internet of Things. In Proceedings of the 2015 IEEE International Solid-State Circuits Conference-(ISSCC) Digest of Technical Papers, San Francisco, CA, USA, 22–26 February 2015; pp. 1–3.
14. Carreon-Bautista, S.; Huang, L.; Sanchez-Sinencio, E. An autonomous energy harvesting power management unit with digital regulation for IoT applications. *IEEE J. Solid-State Circuits* **2016**, *51*, 1457–1474. [CrossRef]
15. Yoon, S.; Carreon-Bautista, S.; Sánchez-Sinencio, E. An Area Efficient Thermal Energy Harvester with Reconfigurable Capacitor Charge Pump for IoT Applications. *IEEE Trans. Circuits Syst.—II Express Briefs* **2018**, *65*, 1974–1978. [CrossRef]
16. Umezawa, A.; Atsumi, S.; Kuriyama, M.; Banba, H.; Imamiya, K.; Naruke, K.; Yamada, S.; Obi, E.; Oshikiri, M.; Suzuki, T.; et al. A 5-V-only operation 0.6- mu m flash EEPROM with row decoder scheme in triple-well structure. *IEEE J. Solid-State Circuits* **1992**, *27*, 1540–1546. [CrossRef]
17. Gariboldi, R.; Pulvirenti, F. A 70 mΩ Intelligent High Side Switch with Full Diagnostics. *IEEE J. Solid-State Circuits* **1996**, *31*, 915–923. [CrossRef]
18. Levacq, D.; Liber, C.; Dessard, V.; Flandre, D. Composite ULP diode fabrication, modelling and applications in multi-Vth FD SOI CMOS technology. *Solid-State Electron.* **2004**, *48*, 1017–1025. [CrossRef]
19. Lian, W.X.; Yong, J.K.; Chong, G.; Churchill, K.K.P.; Ramiah, H.; Chen, Y.; Mak, P.-I.; Martins, R.P. A Reconfigurable Hybrid RF Front-End Rectifier for Dynamic PCE Enhancement of Ambient RF Energy Harvesting Systems. *Electronics* **2023**, *12*, 175. [CrossRef]
20. Tanzawa, T.; Tanaka, Y.; Tanaka, T.; Nakamura, H.; Oodaira, H.; Sakui, K.; Momodomi, M.; Shiratake, S.; Nakano, H.; Oowaki, Y.; et al. A quick boosting charge pump circuit for high density and low voltage flash memories. In Proceedings of the 1994 IEEE Symposium on VLSI Circuits, San Diego, CA, USA, 9–11 June 1994; pp. 65–66.
21. Tanzawa, T.; Tanaka, T.; Takeuchi, K.; Nakamura, H. Circuit Techniques for a 1.8-V-Only NAND Flash Memory. *IEEE J. Solid-State Circuits* **2002**, *37*, 84–89. [CrossRef]
22. Tanzawa, T. Design of DC-DC Switched-Capacitor Voltage Multiplier driven by DC Energy Transducer. In Proceedings of the IEEE International Conference on Electronics, Circuits and Systems, Marseille, France, 7–10 December 2014; pp. 327–330.
23. Suemori, K.; Hoshino, S.; Kamata, T. Flexible and lightweight thermoelectric generators composed of carbon nanotube–polystyrene composites printed on film substrate. *Appl. Phys. Lett.* **2013**, *103*, 153902. [CrossRef]
24. Tanzawa, T. A Switch-Resistance-Aware Dickson Charge Pump Model for Optimizing Clock Frequency. *IEEE Trans. Circuits Syst. II Express Briefs* **2011**, *58*, 336–340. [CrossRef]

25. Nono, K.; Tanzawa, T. A Design of Adaptive Charge Pumps with Minimum Circuit Area for Thermoelectric Energy Harvesting under Temperature Variations. IEICE General Conference, C-12-27, March 2021. Available online: http://hdl.handle.net/10297/00027950 (accessed on 15 February 2023).
26. Nono, K.; Tanzawa, T. A Design of Charge Pump System with Maximum Power Point Tracking for Low Cost Thermoelectric Energy Harvesting, IEICE Society Conference, C-12-3, September 2021. Available online: http://hdl.handle.net/10297/00028355 (accessed on 15 February 2023).

Disclaimer/Publisher's Note: The statements, opinions and data contained in all publications are solely those of the individual author(s) and contributor(s) and not of MDPI and/or the editor(s). MDPI and/or the editor(s) disclaim responsibility for any injury to people or property resulting from any ideas, methods, instructions or products referred to in the content.

Review

2D-Nanolayer (2D-NL)-Based Hybrid Materials: A Next-Generation Material for Dye-Sensitized Solar Cells

Mohammad Ashfaq [1,*], Neetu Talreja [2,*], Neha Singh [3] and Divya Chauhan [4,*]

1. Department of Biotechnology & University Centre for Research & Development (UCRD), Chandigarh University, Gharaun, Mohali 140413, Punjab, India
2. Faculty of Science and Technology, Department of Science, Alliance University, Bengaluru 562106, Karnataka, India
3. Centre for Environmental Science and Engineering, Indian Institute of Technology Kanpur, Kanpur 208016, Uttar Pradesh, India
4. Department of Drinking Water and Sanitation, Ministry of Jal Shakti, 1208-A, Pandit Deendayal Antyodaya Bhawan, CGO Complex, Lodhi Road, New Delhi 110003, Delhi, India
* Correspondence: mohdashfaqbiotech@gmail.com (M.A.); neetutalreja99@gmail.com (N.T.); deep2424@gmail.com (D.C.)

Abstract: Two-dimensional (2D) materials, an electrifying family of innovative materials, have recently attracted wide attention due to their remarkable characteristics, primarily their high optical transparency, exceptional metallic conductivity, high mechanical strength, carrier mobility, tunable band gap values, and optimum work function. Interestingly, 2D-nanosheets/nanolayers (2D-NLs) might be synthesized into single/multi-layers using simple processes such as chemical vapor deposition (CVD), chemical bath deposition (CBD), and mechanical and liquid-phase exfoliation processes that simply enhance optoelectronic properties. However, the stability of 2D-NLs is one of the most significant challenges that limits their commercialization. Researchers have been focusing on the stability of 2D-NLs with the aim of developing next-generation solar cells. Easily tunable distinctive 2D-NLs that are based on the synthesis process, surface functional groups, and modification with other materials/hybrid materials thereby improve the stability of the 2D-NLs and their applicability to the hole transport layer (HTL) and the electron transport layer (ETL) in solar cells. Moreover, metal/non-metal-based dopants significantly enhance band gap ability and subsequently improve the efficacy of dye-sensitized solar cells (DSSCs). In this context, research has focused on 2D-NL-based photoanodes and working electrodes that improve the photoconversion efficiency (PCE) and stability of DSSCs. Herein, we mainly focus on synthesizing 2D-NLs, challenges during synthesis, stability, and high-performing DSSCs.

Keywords: two-dimensional materials; nanosheets; solar cells; optoelectronic devices; energy harvesting

1. Introduction

Presently, energy demand has been increasing with the growing population; globally, that inevitably decreases the amount of fossil fuels (oil, coal, and gases) and affects the environment. It is estimated that around 15 terawatts (TW) is consumed every year, which will increase to 30 TW by 2050. Approximately 80% of daily energy requirements are fulfilled by fossil fuels, whereas ~20% are fulfilled by renewable energy sources. The unremitting decrease in fossil fuels alongside increased energy consumption and environmental pollution as they burn increases the cost of raw materials/manufacturing. Usually, fossil fuel use, or the burning of fossil fuels, is a contributing factor to the production of greenhouse gases and, subsequently, global warming. Moreover, these fossil fuels are inadequate for the long term in terms of consumption rate [1–4]. Therefore, there is a need for renewable sources of energy that fulfil the energy demand without affecting the environment.

Researchers have continuously focused on fulfilling energy requirements by using renewable energy resources, especially sunlight, to produce electricity without impacting the environment. Solar power is an eco-friendly, simple, cost-effective route that converts photon energy into electricity. However, low solar conversion efficiency, non-ecofriendly materials/devices, complex fabrication processes, and the photovoltaic device's stability remain a concern [5–8]. In this aspect, researchers have continued to devote their efforts toward the design of semiconductor materials/photovoltaic devices with higher solar conversion efficiency, a simple fabrication process, and cost-effectiveness to resolve issues related to energy industries.

Several materials have been used so far for solar cell applications, including both metals (Zn, Fe, Ni, Ce, Cu, Cd, Pb, and TiO_2) and non-metals (fullerenes, carbon nanotubes (CNTs), carbon nanofibers (CNFs), graphene, graphene oxide (GO), and graphite). However, the relatively low conversion efficiency, toxicity, and stability of these metal/nonmetal-based solar cells is ongoing challenges nowadays [9–14]. Therefore, the requirement for newer materials/modifying existing semiconductor materials is to improve conversion efficiency, reduce toxicity, and enhance the stability of solar cells. In this aspect, two-dimensional nanolayers (2D-NLs) can improve solar conversion efficiency with high stability.

Recently, 2D-NLs have aroused widespread interest in their potential application in batteries, supercapacitors, environmental remediation, photocatalytic solar cells, antibiotic materials, wound dressing materials, and sensors. The 2D-NLs are in demand because of their incomparable characteristics, such as their charge carrying ability, tunable band gaps, high mechanical strength, high surface-to-volume ratios, and exceptional conductivity. Several 2D-NLs have been discovered (e.g., graphene, GO, TMDs (WS_2, MoS_2, TeS_2, etc.), black phosphorous, blue phosphorous, C_3N_4, MXene, boron nitride, and borophene) and effectively applied in numerous applications, such as agriculture, photocatalysis, the development of antibiotic materials, and the production of solar cells, mainly due to their nano-size thickness [15–28]. However, maintaining efficiency with such nano-metric thicknesses is one of the major concerns when fabricating solar cells. The thickness of 2D-NLs in a photovoltaic device is related to the stability of solar cells and can be controlled by changing their synthesis processes through methods such as liquid-phase exfoliation, chemical vapor deposition (CVD), chemical bath deposition (CBD), and hydrothermal synthesis, etc. Moreover, some methods are specific to synthesized single-layered structures with a thickness of 1 to 10 nm. CVD is one of the most popular methods for controlling thickness. The synthesized 2D-NLs can be used to design high-performance photovoltaic devices/solar cells.

Numerous types of solar cells/devices can be designed using 2D-NLs (either electron-transport layers (ETLs) or hole-transport layers (HTLs)), such as dye-sensitized solar cells (DSSCs), organic–inorganic solar cells, and perovskite solar cells (PSCs), etc. However, achieving high photo conversion efficiency (PCE) and stability is still a concern, as the stability of 2D-NLs is one of the greatest challenges when designing solar cells. Therefore, research is still required to enhance the stability of 2D-NLs for solar cell application. In this aspect, several methods have been adopted to alter the electronic structure of 2D-NLs, including metal or non-metal doping and surface functionalization using organic and inorganic moieties. Tuning the electronic properties might impact the band gap structure, and lowering the conduction band up to the desired value directly impacts the efficiency of solar cells as photoelectrons might be easily captured by photoactive material and thus take part in the final reaction. Another important property that needs to be considered is the solar cell's flexibility. Polymeric, paper, and fabric-based substrates have recently been used to achieve portability and flexibility in 2D-NLs. As these substrates can perform a dual role, (1) these substrates can provide mechanical strength to the 2D-NLs and (2) they can help enhance their surface area. This review focuses mainly on the current status of solar cells, different 2D-NL-based DSSCs, and their conversion efficiency. We also discuss the stability and performance prospects of the 2D-NL–hybrid material-based DSSCs, such as how to improve the stability of the 2D-NL hybrid materials used in high-performance

DSSCs. This review might provide newer insight into the generation of next-generation solar cell devices.

2. Solar Cells and Their Current Status

The incessant growth of the market for solar cells/panels since 1980 is due to their ability to operate as multi-megawatt power plants. The current scenario of the solar cells/panels market is growth of around 30–40%; this became possible mainly due to reduced costs, better reliability, and the economic development of solar cell supply. DSSCs are feasible and appropriate replacements for conventional energy sources such as solar power. They have emerged as one of the substitutes for extensively used silicon-based photovoltaic devices that convert solar energy to electrical energy.

In contrast, modern solar cells are primarily based on the creation of electron holes composed mainly of two layers (p- and n-type semiconductor materials). Usually, in solar irradiation imposed on the p- and n-type materials, it is the electron that has been ejected that moves from one layer to another layer. It creates an electron and a hole, thus producing energy [6,8,29–31]. Solar cells can be categorized based on semiconductor materials, including the following: (1) Crystalline silicon (c-Si) solar cells. c-Si solar cells utilize crystalline silicon and mainly single or multi-crystalline junction types. They are normally brittle and rigid. However, they still preferred due to their cost effectiveness. (2) Thin film-based solar cells. These second-generation solar cells are fabricated using thin films to decrease the cost of manufacture, with the trade-off being lower effectiveness compared to single crystal cells (except expensive gallium arsenide (GaAs) cells). (3) Hybrid solar cells. The third-generation of solar cell technologies which mainly consists of multi-junction cells, organic photovoltaic (OPV) cells, and hybrid solar cells. Hybrid solar cells employ inorganic and organic semiconductor material combinations, which can be seen DSSCs and perovskite solar cells. Moreover, hybrid solar cells are yet to make a noteworthy entry into large-scale commercial applications [32–38]. Usually, materials with high power generation efficiency enable the development of smaller and more cost-effective solar cells. The highest PCE, ~25.6%, was achieved for single junction-based solar cells (monocrystalline solar cells). Moreover, monocrystalline solar cells are one of the pillars of the market. However, high production cost, a sophisticated fabrication process, and energy payback time (EPBT) remain a concern. In this aspect, researchers have focused on decreasing production costs, simplifying the fabrication process, and tuning EPBT. With the help of relatively inexpensive vapor deposition processes/equipment, researchers have successfully reduced the cost of solar cells and simplified fabrication by reducing the utilization of semiconductor materials. Vapor deposition techniques contribute considerably to the simplified fabrication of thin film-based solar cells. The highest associated PCE of ~21.5% was achieved with CdTe-solar cells, which was lower than single junction-based solar cells [39,40]. In recent years, organic and hybrid material-based solar cells have shown great potential in terms of accomplishing solar conversion efficiency and stability improvements, especially for flexible solar cell devices.

3. 2D-NL-Based Solar Active Materials

2D-NL-based materials (graphene, graphene oxide, WS_2, MOS_2, MXene, TiO_2, and ZnO) are a newer class of materials with different characteristics, such as surface phenomena and interface chemistry with their bulk materials. Furthermore, symmetrical lowering at the interface prevents newer environments from being manageable in the bulk equivalent. Consequently, the physicochemical characteristics, such as photon involvement in redox reactions, an acid base, and catalytic reactivity, are different and maybe dissuade the design of newer materials. Therefore, 2D-NLs are considered revolutionary due to their potential to fulfil the demand for next-generation solar cells with high power conversion efficiency (PCE). In this aspect, researchers have continued to focus on developing 2D-NL-based solar cells. Usually, incorporating 2D-NLs within the solar cells might enhance charge transport and the absorption of light while suppressing the carrier recombination that leads to an enhancement in PCE with the increased fill factor (FF) and short-circuit current density (Jsc) of OSCs. Moreover, appropriate 2D-NLs might be replaced with an unstable layer of solar cells, which is one of the possible strategies for improving next-generation highly stable solar cells. With this approach, the PCE of DSSCs, organic solar cells, and organic perovskite solar cells significantly improved by more than ~12%, 18%, and 25%, respectively [41–46]. Researchers are currently focusing on newer semiconductor materials, the combination of two or three materials, or hybrid material-based solar cells that might improve PCE and stability.

4. Strategies to Improve Stability

Global energy demand and rapid population growth necessitate the high performance and stability of next-generation DSSCs. The high PCE and stability of DSSCs supports their increased share in the market. However, the stability and PCE of the DSSCs remains a concern for commercialization. Moreover, long-term uses in real-time operation remain a concern for commercialization. Numerous strategies have been applied to augment the stability and PCE of DSSCs, such as the incorporation of metals, the use of polymers or carbon, surface functionalization, the design of heterojunctions, the application of 2D-NLs, and control of the thickness of 2D-NLs. Incorporating these materials might improve dye adsorption ability and mesoporosity, help tune the band gap, and increase conductivity, thereby improving the PCE and stability of DSSCs [47–51].

Usually, a dopant is an impurity that is incorporated into a bulk matrix to tune/adjust semiconductor properties. With the help of dopant materials, structural and electronic properties can be easily tuned, which might be advantageous for crystallinity, band gap value, and the relocation of electrons to the conduction band. Usually, two types of dopant materials can tune the band gap value: (1) organic dopants and (2) inorganic dopants. Organic dopants such as metals can change the electronic structure of the materials and subsequently, their band gap value. Band gap tuning facilitates the movement of electrons to the next energy level so that photon energy can be easily captured. The captivated energy helps the electron eject from the valence band. Numerous studies have suggested that the metals and their oxides that efficiently decrease/increase band gap values subsequently improve the performance of the semiconductor materials [52–57]. Inorganic dopants are a class of dopants that includes carbon-based nanomaterials (CB-NMs) such as carbon nanotubes (CNTs), carbon nanofibers (CNFs), graphene, GO, and rGO. CB-NMs exhibit high tensile strength, a large surface area, and large pore size distribution and can therefore be effectively used in numerous applications, including DSSCs. Interestingly, carbon-based 2D-NLs such as graphene, GO, and rGO have gained considerable attention, particularly in terms of application in electronics and solar cells. This is largely due to their unique characteristics, such as high surface area, high conductivity, and flexibility. The conductivity of the graphene, GO, and rGO mainly depends on the number of layers that directly affect electronic properties, thus affecting the PCE of solar cells [58–64].

Usually, 2D-NL-based doping within the other 2D-NL materials attracts interest due to their excellent electronic, optical, and mechanical characteristics. The single/multi-layer of these dopant (2D-NLs) materials provides exceptional surface area, large pore volume, and beneficial charge transport ability, making them a favorable candidate for solar cell application as an absorbing layer, HTL, or ETL with the aim of amplifying the performance and stability of solar cells, including DSSCs. Moreover, achieving high PCE and stability with DSSCs is one of the greatest challenges for commercialization. With the incorporation of 2D-NLs, we can easily enhance the PCE and stability of the solar cells, including DSSCs. It is important to mention here that excess incorporation of dopants might decrease PCE; therefore, the optimum amount of dopants should be determined for high PCE-based DSSCs.

5. 2D-NL-Based DSSCs

DSSCs, a type of third-generation solar cell, have advanced significantly since their invention in 1991 by Brian O'Regan and Michael Grätzel. Numerous advantages make these cells exceptional solar devices, mainly recyclability, environmental friendliness, chemical stability, high energy conversion efficiency, and high artificial light performance. Moreover, roll-to-roll production and high energy efficiency are not the only advantages of using DSSCs. Since their productivity does not decline with increasing temperatures, this extends the efficiency of harvesting energy from sunlight [65–70]. DSSCs have five essential components: (1) transparent conducting oxide (TCO), i.e., glass substrate, (2) a photoanode (a coating of direct bandgap semiconductor materials on TCO), (3) a photosensitizer, (4) a cathode (carbon–platinum layer on TCO), and (5) an electrolyte [71–73]. When solar irradiation strikes the photoanode surface, the adsorbed dye molecules are photo-stimulated, producing excited electrons. The excited electrons move through the TCO and jump into the conduction band, producing an electric current. It is important to mention that degradation of DSSC preformation is one of the greatest challenges nowadays at multiple levels, including the molecular, module or panel, cell, and system levels. Usually, a DSSC's complex system, either the photoanode, dye, or electrolyte on their own, does not generate electricity, but when these elements come together with an accurate balance in all aspects (mainly diffusion that effectively controls the components of solar cells) they produce solar cells with high stability [74–77]. Figure 1 shows a schematic illustration of the different components of DSSCs. In general, the PCE and stability of the DSSCs depends on each component; therefore, it is necessary to improve each component to enhance the PCE and stability of these cells. In this regard, researchers have continued looking towards newer materials with high stability and PCE for the production of next-generation solar cells.

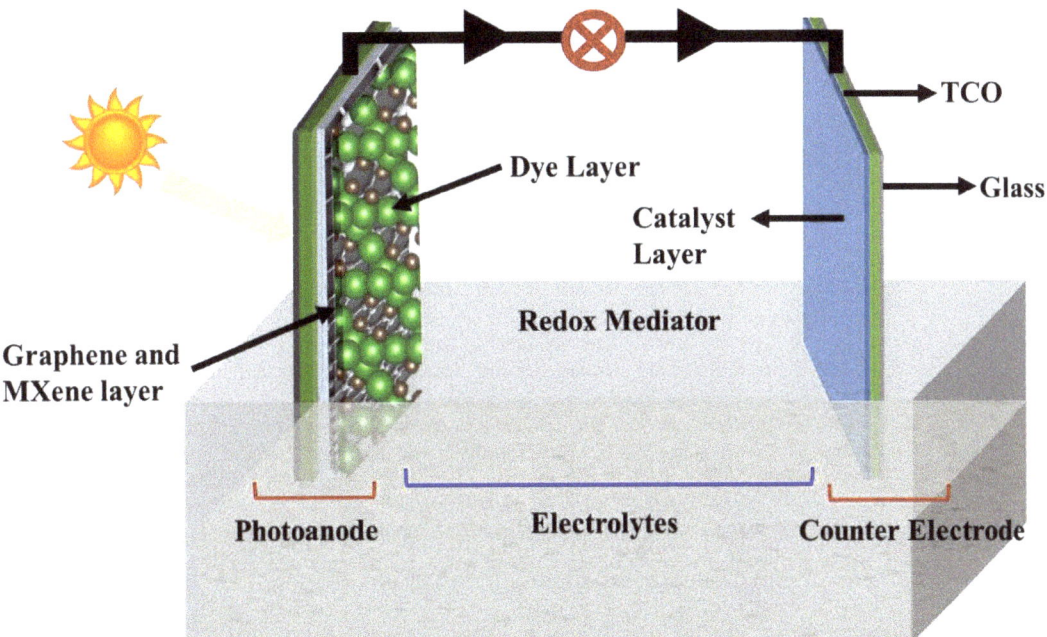

Figure 1. Schematic illustration of the different components of DSSCs.

5.1. Graphene and Its Derivative-Based DSSCs

Graphene, the first synthesized 2D-NL, has gained a remarkable amount of attention from researchers due to its unique characteristics, mainly its exceptional carrier mobility. Another class of graphene-like oxygen-containing derivatives of graphene or graphene oxide (GO) and reduced graphene oxide (rGO) has also been comprehensively applied in numerous applications (including environmental remediation, photocatalysis, energy, the dressing of materials, and solar cells) because of their high carrier mobility, great conductivity, high dispersion ability, and high biocompatibility [78–80]. Numerous methods and precursors have been used to synthesize graphene in order to increase the PCE of solar cells. Organic and inorganic functional groups have been incorporated within the graphene skeleton through simple covalent interaction between the GO and other functional groups, thus providing stability and PCE. Incorporating these functional moieties facilitated unceasing diffusion paths between the donor and acceptor interfaces that led to the conquest/suppression of exciton recombination and the promotion of charge transport. Graphene can be decorated with metal nanoparticles that tune intrinsic properties for photovoltaic applications. Moreover, a derivative of graphene (rGO) has good conductivity compared to GO. Furthermore, stacking interaction and poor dispersion ability make individual rGO sheets inaccessible in terms of modification or functionalization. However, research into preventing aggregation and achieving high PCE with rGO and other graphene-based composites continues. Several studies have reported about the application of graphene and graphene-based derivatives in high-performance DSSCs. For instance, Ju et al. synthesized N-doped graphene (N-graphene) using a two-step reaction sequence, which was further deposited over fluorine-doped SnO_2 (FTO)/glass substrates using an electrospray technique. The synthesized N-graphene showed a PCE of 9.05% with a fill factor of 74.2% [81]. Using hydrothermal synthesis, Yu et al. synthesized dual atom (nitrogen and sulfur)-doped graphene (N-S-graphene). Nitrogen and sulfur co-doped graphene was used as a metal-free counter electrode (CE) in DSSCs. Due to the synergistic effect of dual atoms in graphene, it shows high catalytic activity towards I_3^- reduction. The large surface area and interconnectivity of pores facilitate mass transfer, which exhibits a PCE of 9.40% [82]. Paranthaman et al. synthesized rGO through the thermal reduction of GO and applied it as a CE in DSSCs. The surface area and pore size distribution of synthesized rGO were 110.16 $m^2\,g^{-1}$ and 0.5182 $cm^3\,g^{-1}$, respectively, thus supporting electrolyte migration and a higher PCE of 5.8% [83]. Casaluci et al. synthesized graphene using a liquid-phase exfoliation process and applied it as a CE for DSSCs. The data suggested that graphene-based CEs could be used effectively in DSSCs (PCE of 3.5%) [84]. Zhang et al. synthesized graphene using an exfoliation process and dispersed it onto FTO glass. The prepared graphene-based CE was annealed to create a 3D structure that improved PCE (6.81%) [85]. Prasad et al. synthesized rGO-Cu_2S-based composite materials and deposited them on onto FTO glass using an electrochemical method to fabricate quantum dot-based DSSCs. Figure 2 includes SEM images of the Cu_2S and rGO-Cu_2S at lower and higher magnification levels. The images indicate the uniform wrapping of rGO within the Cu_2S. The synthesized rGO-Cu_2S nanocomposites demonstrated a PCE of 4.26% using organic electrolytes, with short-circuit current density (Jsc), open circuit voltage (Voc), and fill factor of 17.2 mA cm^{-2}, 0.57 V, and 44%, respectively [86].

Jiang et al. synthesized Co_3S_4-NS-rGO-based composites using a hydrothermal process and applied them as CEs for DSSCs. The synthesized Co_3S_4-NS-rGO-based nanocomposite showed a PCE of 8.08%. Interestingly, Co_3S_4-NS shows excellent reduction skills for I^{3-} compared to the bulk and more active sites for the catalytic reaction [87]. Ngidi et al. synthesized dual atom (pyridinic and pyrrolic N)-doped rGO (N-N-rGO) using the hydrothermal method. Synthesized dual atom-doped rGO exhibited a large surface area of 161.51 $m^2\,g^{-1}$ and enhanced electrical conductivity of 22.07 S cm^{-1}. The presence of dual atoms enhanced iodide reduction and subsequently led to higher PCE (4.13%) compared to pristine rGO [88]. Salleh et al. synthesized nickel sulfide-doped rGO (Ni-S-rGO) to fabricate DSSCs. The prepared Ni-S-rGO-based DSSCs showed PCE of 1.42% due to the incorporation of thiourea that improved the reduction current [89]. Khoa et al. thermally synthesized rGO and synthesized a platinum (rGO-Pt)-based nanocomposite using a spray technique to apply them as CEs in DSSCs. The data suggested that rGO-Pt improved electron transport in the photoanode, thereby leading to high PCE (5.78%). The hybrid rGO-Pt composite reduced recombination by providing electrons to the I^-/I_3^- electrolyte, which significantly increased the PCE of DSSCs [90]. Khan et al. synthesized polypyrrole–graphene (P-graphene)-based Pt-free DSSCs. The data suggested that the P-graphene could be used effectively in DSSCs with PCE of 3.06% with 4% graphene content within the composite [91]. Oh et al. synthesized graphene-$Cu_2ZnNiSe_4$-WO_3 (GCZNSW) using a hydrothermal process and applied it as a CE for DSSCs. The data indicate that the prepared GCZNSW-based hybrid composite achieved 12.16% PCE, which is greater than the Pt electrode and suggests that the prepared GCZNSW-based hybrid composite has the potential ability to replace it [92]. The aforementioned studies and Table 1 (a summary of graphene and composite DSSCs) suggests that graphene and graphene composite materials can be used efficiently as photoanode and CE materials in DSSCs due to superior performance stemming from their exceptional surface area, wide-range absorption spectrum, high conductivity, improved photon absorption, and excellent electron transport. The doping of metals/polymers within the graphene significantly affects the PCE of the DSSCs. Moreover, the environmental friendliness and high stability of graphene and its composite materials make them promising candidates for future DSSCs.

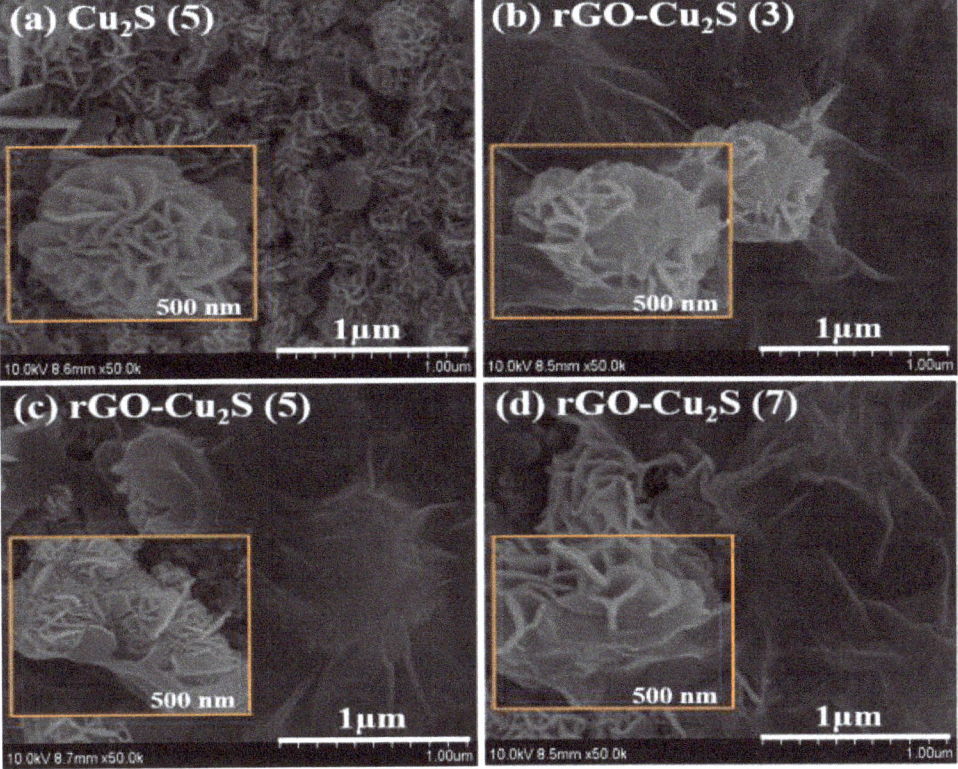

Figure 2. SEM images of (**a**) Cu_2S and (**b–d**) rGO-Cu_2S. The images have been reproduced with permission [86].

Table 1. Graphene and graphene composite-based DSSCs.

S. No.	Graphene and Graphene Composites	Synthesis Process	PCE (%)	Remarks	References
1.	N-graphene	E-spray deposition	9.05	A thin film of N-graphene-based CEs shows high PCE.	[81]
2.	N-S-graphene	Hummer's method	9.40	The dual atom (N-S) doping of graphene improved PCE.	[82]
3.	rGO	Thermal process	5.8	rGO facilitates electrolyte migration and, subsequently, higher PCE.	[83]
4.	Graphene	Liquid-phase exfoliation	3.5	Large surface area and high transparency might replace Pt.	[84]
5.	Graphene	Liquid-phase exfoliation	6.81	Graphene-based CE annealing creates a 3D network that improves PCE.	[85]
6.	rGO-Cu_2S	Electrochemical deposition	4.26	The uniform wrapping of rGO within Cu_2S improved PCE.	[86]
7.	Co_3S_4-NS-rGO	Hydrothermal	8.08	Co_3S_4-NS improved reduction ability for I_3^- more than bulk and created more active sites for catalytic reaction, thereby leading to higher PCE.	[87]
8.	N-N-rGO	Hydrothermal	4.13	The dual atom-doped rGO improved the tri-iodic reduction reaction, thereby leading to higher PCE.	[88]
9.	Ni-S-rGO	Hummer's method and spin coating	1.42	The sulfur content improved PCE while also exhibiting a high reduction current.	[89]
10.	rGO-Pt	Hummer's method and a thermal process	5.78	rGO-Pt improved electron transport in the photoanode.	[90]
11.	P-graphene	Polymerization	3.06	Graphene content affected PCE.	[91]
12.	GCZNSW	Hydrothermal	12.16	The graphene-based hybrid electrode showed higher PCE than Pt.	[92]

5.2. TiO_2-Based DSSCs

TiO_2 is the most chosen semiconductor material due to its inexpensive cost, high adsorption ability, and non-toxicity. Moreover, TiO_2 is a frequently utilized semiconductor due to its excellent dispersion and degree of crystallinity. The 2D-NLs, especially those with mesoporous structure, play a crucial role in DSSCs because of their high surface area, larger pore volume, and tunable nanostructure, which results in high adsorption ability toward dye molecules and a high ability to receive electrons from an excited dye. The dye injects an electron into the conduction band of the 2D-NLs during photoexcitation, which is then followed by transmission to the reference/CE (counter) that completes the cycle. Several studies have suggested the effective use of TiO_2 in DSSCs. For example, Yu et al. synthesized TiO_2 nanosheets (TiO_2-NS) using a hydrothermal process and HF acid was used as a shape-controlling agent for the fabrication of DSSCs. Figure 3 shows the SEM, TEM, and HR-TEM images of TiO_2-NS that confirm the formation of 2D-NL-based TiO_2. The high crystallinity, pore volume, and exceptional light scattering ability of TiO_2-NS enable higher PCE (4.56%) compared to other types of TiO_2, such as TiO_2 nanoparticles (4.24%) and commercial grade T25 TiO_2 nanoparticles (3.64%). The data suggest that 2D-NLs might improve the PCE of DSSCs [93]. Wu et al. synthesized TiO_2-NS using a simple hydrothermal process and fabricated DSSCs where TiO_2-NS was used as a scattering layer. TiO_2-NS improves PCE (7.54%) compared to the use of TiO_2 nanoparticles. Exceptional light scattering offers rapid charge transfer, the least resistance, and high charge collection [94]. Peng et al. synthesized TiO_2-NS with a highly exposed facet (001) using a hydrothermal process and fabricated DSSCs. TiO_2-NS achieved PCE of 8.77%, which was higher than commercial grade T25 TiO_2 nanoparticles (6.92%) due to higher photocurrent density [95]. Laskova et al. synthesized crystal faces of (001) and (101) with TiO_2-NS and tested them against DSSCs. The data indicate that the different crystal face of TiO_2-NS shows different PCE, and the highest PCE (4.7%) was ultimately observed with TiO_2-NS (101) [96].

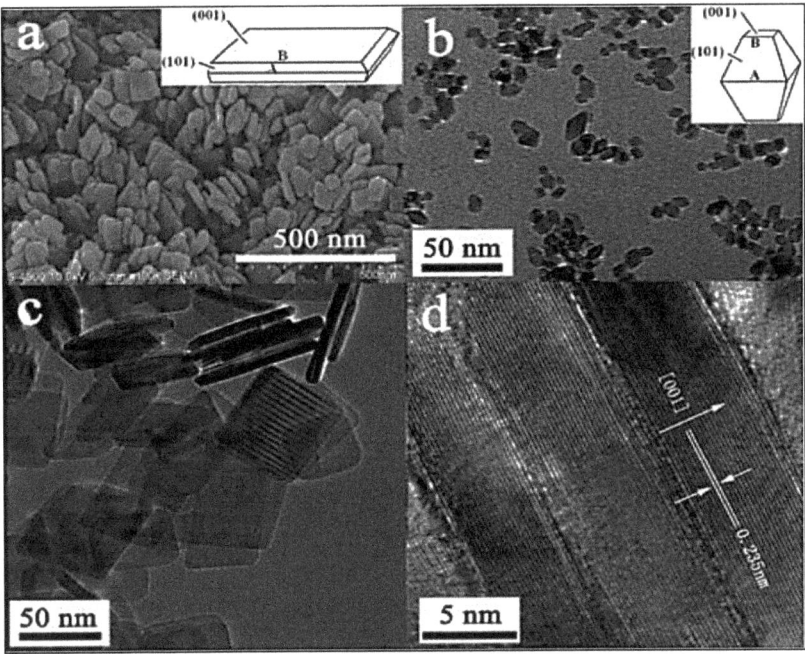

Figure 3. (a) SEM, (b,c) TEM, and (d) HR-TEM images of TiO$_2$-NS. The images have been reproduced with permission [93].

Numerous modifications have been made to semiconductors with the aim of improving the photovoltaic effects of DSSCs, including the doping of transition metals and polymers. For example, Miles et al. synthesized TiO$_2$-NS onto ZnO nanowires (TiO$_2$-NS-ZNW) and fabricated DSSCs. Figure 4 shows the SEM and TEM images of ZnO nanowires and TiO$_2$-NS-ZNW. The images show a uniform coating of TiO$_2$-NS on the ZnO nanowires. The prepared TiO$_2$-NS-ZNW-based DSSCs show 7.5% PCE, which is around 30% more than that of TiO$_2$. The significant improvement in PCE is mainly due to the improved surface area, electron transport, and light scattering ability. Moreover, bare ZnO nanowire-based DSSCs decrease PCE and stability, whereas the smaller quantity of TiO$_2$-NS drastically improves the performance of DSSCs [97]. Jiang et al. synthesized Niobium-doped TiO$_2$-NS (Nb-TiO$_2$-NS) and used it as a photoelectrode for DSSCs. The theoretical study suggested that Nb-TiO$_2$-NS might achieve 10% PCE, which is around 22% higher than without the use of doped TiO$_2$-based DSSCs [98]. Xu et al. synthesized g-C$_3$N$_4$-incorporated TiO$_2$-NS using a simple heating process and applied it in DSSCs. The data suggested that g-C$_3$N$_4$-TiO$_2$-NS is effectively used in DSSCs with a PCE of 7.34%, largely due to the additional electron in the photoanode. Moreover, incorporating urea and g-C$_3$N$_4$ within g-C$_3$N$_4$-TiO$_2$-NS increases PCE [99]. Lin et al. synthesized ZnO-NS using the chemical bath deposition (CBD) technique and incorporated it with TiO$_2$ (ZnO-NS/TiO$_2$). The data indicate that the ZnO-NS-based DSSCs show PCE of 6.6%, whereas incorporating TiO$_2$ significantly improved PCE to 7.07%, which was attributed to TiO$_2$ increasing dye loading ability [100]. Kim et al. synthesized ZnO-NS using an electrochemical process and incorporated it with CdSe and TiO$_2$ to produce CdSe-ZnO-NS and TiO$_2$-ZnO-NS and applied it for the fabrication of DSSCs. The data suggested that, upon the incorporation of CdSe and TiO$_2$ within ZnO-NS, PCE increased compared to the use of bare ZnO-NS. Moreover, CdSe-ZnO-NS-based DSSCs show the highest PCE (1.30%), whereas TiO$_2$-ZnO-NS shows PCE of around 0.70%. The improvement in PCE is due to the inhibited recombination of electron hole pairs at the interface of CdSe and TiO$_2$ [101]. The aforementioned studies and Table 2 suggest that TiO_2-NS is the most commonly used 2D-NL in DSSCs due to its high adsorption ability, cost-effectiveness, mesoporous texture, ability to receive electrons from dye, and high crystallinity. Moreover, TiO_2-NS shows higher PCE than other forms of TiO_2, such as nanoparticles and commercially available TiO_2, because the 2D-NL form of TiO_2 increases surface area and thereby leads to higher adsorption ability toward dye molecules. Interestingly, the doping of transition metals and polymers within TiO_2-NS considerably improved the PCE of DSSCs. Therefore, TiO_2-NS-based hybrid materials might become next-generation materials for DSSCs with high PCE and stability.

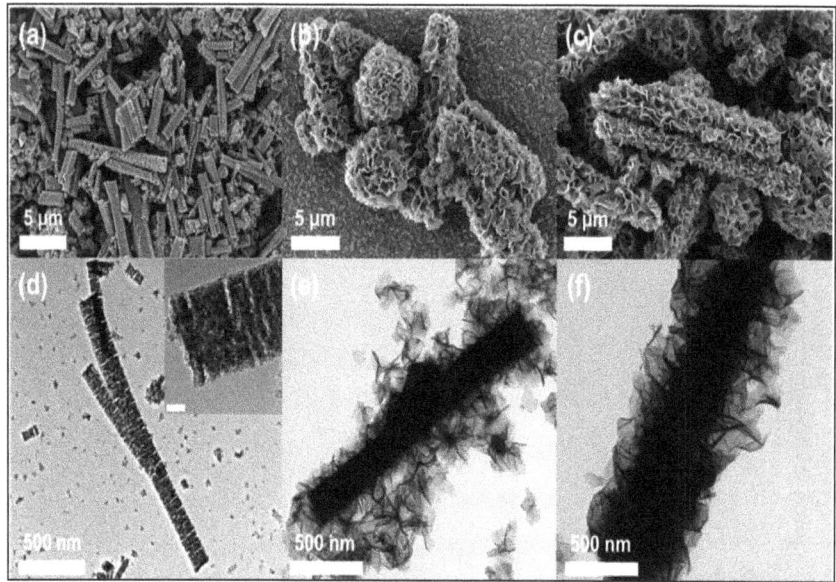

Figure 4. SEM images of (**a**) ZnO nanowires and (**b**,**c**) TiO_2-NS-ZNW and TEM images of (**d**) ZnO nanowires and (**e**,**f**) TiO_2-NS-ZNW. The images have been reproduced with permission [97].

Table 2. TiO_2-NS and TiO_2-NS composite materials for DSSCs.

S. No.	TiO_2-NS and TiO_2-NS Composites	Synthesis Process	PCE (%)	Remarks	References
1.	TiO_2-NS	Hydrothermal	4.56	TiO_2-NS shows high PCE compared to TiO_2 nanoparticles.	[93]
2.	TiO_2-NS	Hydrothermal	7.54	TiO_2-NS improves charge transfer and has the least resistance.	[94]
3.	TiO_2-NS	Hydrothermal	8.77	TiO_2-NS shows higher photocurrent density than TiO_2 nanoparticles.	[95]
4.	TiO_2-NS	Hydrothermal	4.7	Different crystal faces of TiO_2-NS show different PCE.	[96]
5.	TiO_2-NS-ZNW	Hydrothermal	7.5	The incorporation of TiO_2-NS significantly improved the performance of solar cells.	[97]
6.	Nb-TiO_2-NS	–	10	Incorporation of Nb within Nb-TiO_2-NS significantly improves PCE.	[98]
7.	g-C_3N_4-TiO_2-NS	Heating process	7.34	The incorporation of g-C_3N_4 within TiO_2-NS significantly improves PCE.	[99]
8.	ZnO-NS/TiO_2	CBD	7.07	The incorporation of TiO_2 within ZnO-NS significantly improved dye loading and PCE.	[100]
9.	CdSe-ZnO-NS and TiO_2-ZnO-NS	Electrochemical deposition	1.30 and 0.70	The incorporation of CdSe and TiO_2 within ZnO-NS significantly improved PCE.	[101]

5.3. MXene-Based DSSCs

MXenes are a newer class of transition metal carbides and/or nitrides that were discovered by Gogotsi and W. Barsoum in 2011. MXene, a newer class of ceramic material, has been attracting attention due to its high conductivity (10^5 S cm^{-1}) that stems from high mechanical strength and flexibility. This high conductivity is applied in the hole transport layer, electron transport layer, and protective layer of advanced solar cells. However, synthesis complications limit their application. In particular, acid-based exfoliation requires modification in terms of synthesis, as green synthesis is preferred over the use of acids. The excessive use of strong acid (especially HF acid) for the exfoliation of MXene layers from the MAX phase requires further consideration in terms of large-scale applications. However, high tensile strength, high conductivity, and a tunable band gap prove applicability to photovoltaics.

MXene-based materials have very low band gaps, which promote recombination. The higher the recombination rate, the lower the electric properties of the NLs. To use these materials for solar cell devices, there must be a minimal band gap so that the flow of electrons from the valence band to the conduction band can be maintained. Doping and functionalization can tune the band gap of MXene-based materials [102–104]. MXene has gained continuous interest and is extensively used in numerous applications, including environmental remediation, photocatalysis, energy storage, solar cell, biocidal agent, and biomedical applications [20,105–109]. Recently, a few studies have suggested that MXene and its hybrid materials can be used effectively for the development of high-performance DSSCs. For example, Dall'Agnese et al. synthesized MXene and TiO$_2$ (MXene-TiO$_2$)-based photoanodes and oxidized them at a different temperature to improve the performance of DSSCs. The data suggested that upon increasing the oxidizing temperature, PCE continuously increased up to 450 °C (2.66%). However, a temperature of more than 450 °C decreased the DSSC performance, mainly due to the smaller surface area [110]. Chen et al. synthesized MXene-CoS using an etching process and a hydrothermal process. Initially, MXene was synthesized by a simple etching process that involved HF acid. Next, the heterostructure composite was synthesized using a hydrothermal process. Figure 5 shows the SEM and TEM images and elemental mapping of MXene and the MXene-CoS-based composite. The SEM images indicate that the separated MXene sheets and CoS nanoparticles attached to MXene sheets. Moreover, no changes in the layer were observed after incorporating the CoS nanoparticles into the MXene, which makes it a suitable candidate for DSSCs. The data suggest that the prepared MXene-CoS-based composite shows high electrochemical performance (8.09% PCE). The high PCE of the MXene-CoS-based composite, mainly due to MXene-NS and the incorporation of CoS nanoparticles, creates more catalytic sites that improve permeability and charge transfer; therefore, MXene might become a next-generation material that could be used in the production of solar cells [111].

Another study focused on the use of Poly (3,4-ethylene dioxythiophene) (PEDOT)-decorated MXene (PEDOT-MXene) in DSSCs. Figure 6 shows a schematic representation of the PEDOT-MXene. The PEDOT-MXene-based DSSCs showed high electrochemical activity and mass transport ability, with PCE of 7.12%. Moreover, the prepared PEDOT-MXene-based DSSCs were stable for up to 15 days and an increase in PCE of around 40% was observed, which suggests that PEDOT-MXene-based DSSCs having the potential ability to replace Pt-based DSSCs [112]. Wen et al. synthesized a MXene-reduced graphene oxide (rGO)-polyethylene oxide/poly(vinylidene fluoride-co-hexafluoropropylene) (MXene-rGO-P)-based composite for use as a printable electrolyte. The data suggested that rGO and polymer incorporation within the MXene improves PCE. The maximum PCE observed was 8.255% [113]. Ahmad et al. synthesized MXene to replace the Pt and transparent conducting oxide (TCO) layer used in DSSCs. The data suggested that TCO- and Pt-free MXene were effective when used in DSSCs, as shown by 8.68% PCE. Moreover, PCE mainly depends on the thickness of MXene. PCE increased with the increasing thickness of MXene (up to 8 μm thickness) [114]. The literature suggests that MXene can potentially be applied to the development of solar cells, especially DSSCs with high PCE, thus replacing TCO and Pt within DSSCs. Moreover, incorporating other 2D-NLs, polymers, and nanoparticles within the MXene significantly improved PCE due to enhanced surface area, conductivity, adsorption of dye/loading of dye, and permeability. Moreover, the thickness of the MXene layer is an important factor that directly affects the PCE of DSSCs.

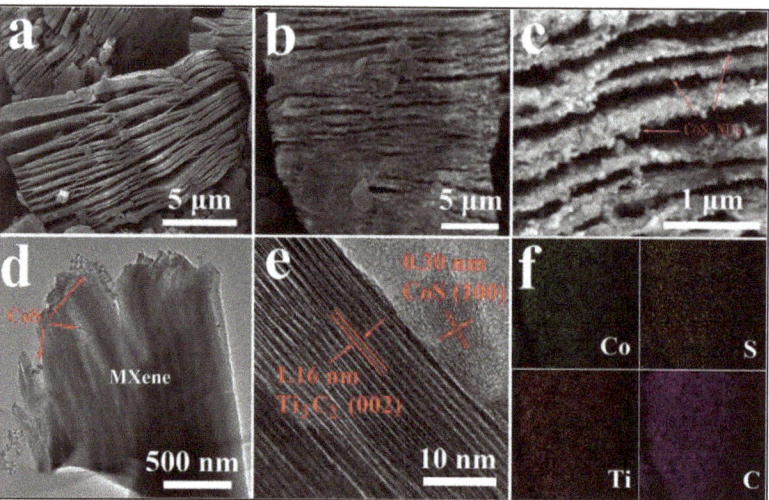

Figure 5. SEM images of (**a**) MXene and (**b**,**c**) MXene-CoS, TEM images of (**d**,**e**) MXene-CoS, and (**f**) an elemental mapping of MXene-CoS. The images have been reproduced with permission [111].

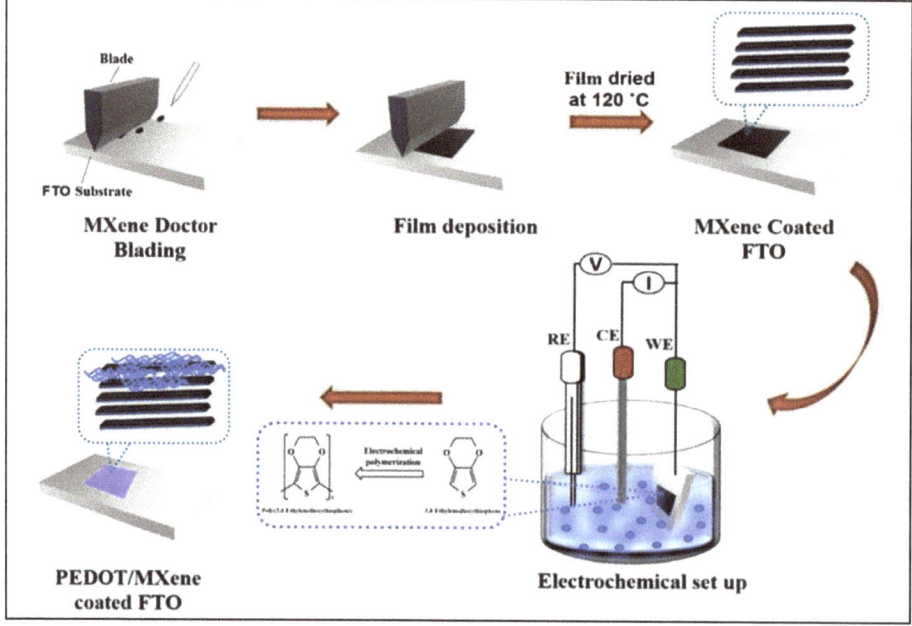

Figure 6. A schematic illustration of a PEDOT-MXene-based DSSC. The images have been reproduced with permission [112].

5.4. Black Phosphorus (BP)-Based DSSCs

BP is a novel class of 2D-NL that is highly reactive under normal conditions and therefore unstable. BP was synthesized using a liquid-phase exfoliation process and demonstrated exceptional performance, mainly in terms of energy, biomedical, electronic, sensor, and solar cell applications. The high applicability of BP is mainly due to the tunable band gap value and high carrier mobility, which makes BP a promising candidate for solar cell applications. However, poor stability and high-density charge transfer limit the applicability of BP in solar cells [115–119]. So far, few studies have been conducted concerning the fabrication of high-performance solar cells, especially DSSCs with high stability. For instance, Xu et al. synthesized a BP-TiO_2-based photoanode that was used in DSSCs. The prepared BP-TiO_2-based DSSCs showed 9.73% PCE, which is higher than TiO_2-based DSSCs (6.98%). Moreover, the high PCE of the BP-TiO_2-based DSSCs is due to charge separation and transfer [120]. Song et al. synthesized BP-TiO_2-based electrodes for the fabrication of DSSCs. The photon adsorption ability of BP-TiO_2 depends on the number of layers. The BP-TiO_2-based DSSCs showed high PCE that represented an improvement of ~38% compared to TiO_2 [121]. For future research, surface-modified BP incorporating metals, polymers, and other 2D-NLs might provide better PCE and easily replace Pt electrodes.

5.5. Other 2D-NL-Based DSSCs

Another interesting group of 2D-NLs that has been efficiently used for solar cell applications is TMDs (MoS_2, $MoSe_2$, WS_2, WSe_2, TiS_2, $TiSe_2$, TeS_2, VSe_2, $NbSe_2$, etc.). Usually, TMDs are mainly composed of MX_2 (M (transition metal) and X (chalcogen)), where M is a sandwich between two X layers using covalent bonds and Vander Waal forces. MoS_2- and WS_2-NLs have been effectively used in various types of applications (including the areas of antibiotic materials, energy, the environment, and solar cells) due to their extraordinary characteristics, such as high surface area, transparency, high conductivity, a tunable band gap, and high biocompatibility [22,122–125]. The tunable band gap's ability to change its thickness is one of the fascinating characteristics of TMDs that might be beneficial for solar cell applications [126]. Numerous TMD-based 2D-NLs have been effectively used to fabricate solar cells such as DSSCs. For instance, Gurulakshmi et al. synthesized MoS_2-based CEs for DSSCs using an electrodeposition process. The data suggested that the MoS_2-based CEs were effective when used in DSSCs, as shown by 4.21% PCE [127]. Vijaya et al. synthesized MoS_2 and graphene-MoS_2 using a hydrothermal process and fabricated CEs for DSSCs. The data suggested that graphene-MoS_2 shows higher PCE (8.1%) than MoS_2 (6.6%) [128]. Krishnamoorthy et al. synthesized MoS_2 and a graphene-MoS_2-based photoanode for DSSCs. Interestingly, the incorporation of graphene within MoS_2 reduced the band gap value and reduced the recombination of electron photogeneration, thus subsequently improving PCE to 8.92%, which is higher than bare MoS_2 (3.36% PCE) [129]. Menon et al. synthesized TiO_2-incorporated MoS_2 (TiO_2-MoS_2)-based photoanodes for DSSCs. The data indicate that the TiO_2-MoS_2-based DSSCs show a high PCE of 6.0% compared to the bare TiO_2-based DSSCs (4.7% PCE), mainly due to high photoadsorption. Moreover, more than 0.1% MoS_2 decreases the PCE of the DSSCs [130]. Xu et al. synthesized PEDOT-MoS_2-based CEs for DSSCs. The data suggested that incorporating MoS2 within PEDOT effectively improved PCE to 7.0% [131]. Li et al. synthesized WS_2-based CEs for DSSCs using the doctor blade method. Incorporation of TiO_2 and carbon particles within the WS_2 film improved conductivity and adhesion, thus significantly improving the PCE of the DSSCs. The fabricated DSSCs with the prepared TiO_2/carbon particles/WS_2-based counter showed 4.56% PCE [132]. Krishnamoorthy et al. synthesized graphene-incorporated WS_2 (graphene-WS_2)-based photoanodes for the fabrication of DSSCs. Incorporating graphene within WS_2 improved the adsorption ability of the dye, which significantly improved PCE. The prepared graphene-WS_2-based DSSCs showed 9.6% PCE. The high PCE is mainly due to the large surface area and mesoporous property of graphene-WS_2-based photoanodes [133]. Huang et al. synthesized CoS_2-N-C-Co-WS_2-based CEs for the fabrication of DSSCs. The prepared CoS_2-N-C-Co-

WS$_2$-based composite had a large surface area and yolk–shell structure that improved PCE. The prepared CoS$_2$-N-C-Co-WS$_2$ based DSSCs showed a high PCE of 9.21%, which is comparatively higher than Pt [134]. Hussain et al. synthesized CuS-WS$_2$- and CuS-MoS$_2$-based CEs to fabricate DSSCs. The sulfur-based heterostructure improved electrocatalytic activity and decreased charge transfer resistance, thus improving PCE. The prepared CuS-WS$_2$- and CuS-MoS$_2$-based DSSCs showed 8.21% and 7.12% PCE, which is comparable to Pt-based electrodes [135]. The aforementioned studies and Table 3 summarize the different 2D-NLs, including TMDs that are effectively used as photoanodes and CEs in the fabrication of DSSCs. Moreover, incorporating metal, carbon, and polymers significantly improved the PCE of DSSCs. Additionally, TMDs, mainly WS$_2$ and MoS$_2$, showed high or comparable PCE compared to the Pt-based DSSCs, suggesting that expensive Pt can be easily replaced with TMDs.

Table 3. Different 2D-NLs, their hybrid material-based DSSCs, and PCE.

S. No.	2D-NLs	Synthesis Process	PCE (%)	Remarks	References
1.	MXene-TiO$_2$	Deposition	2.66	Increasing the oxidizing temperature improved PCE.	[110]
2.	MXene-CoS	Etching and hydrothermal	8.09	The incorporation of CoS nanoparticles within MXene improves permeability and PCE.	[111]
3.	PEDOT-MXene	Deposition	7.12	Incorporation of PEDOT within MXene improves PCE.	[112]
4.	MXene-rGO-P	Printing	8.255	The incorporation of rGO and co-polymer improves PCE.	[113]
5.	MXene	Etching	8.68	TCO- and Pt-free DSSCs show high PCE.	[114]
6.	MoS$_2$	Electrodeposition	4.21	Surface modification of the electrode improves current density and PCE.	[127]
7.	MoS$_2$ and graphene-MoS$_2$	Hydrothermal	6.6 and 8.1	Graphene-incorporated MoS$_2$ shows high PCE.	[128]
8.	Graphene-MoS$_2$	Hydrothermal	8.92	Incorporation of graphene effectively reduces the band gap value and lowers photoelectron recombination.	[129]
9.	TiO$_2$-MoS$_2$	Deposition	6.0	The incorporation of MoS$_2$ within TiO$_2$ increases PCE.	[130]
10.	PEDOT-MoS$_2$	Hydrothermal	7.0	Incorporation of MoS$_2$ within PEDOT significantly improves PCE.	[131]
11.	TiO$_2$/carbon particles/WS$_2$	Deposition	4.56	TiO$_2$ and carbon particles incorporated within WS$_2$ improve the film's bonding and conductivity.	[132]
12.	Graphene-WS$_2$	Hydrothermal	9.6	The incorporation of graphene within WS$_2$ improves adsorption ability, thereby leading to higher PCE.	[133]
13.	CoS$_2$-N-C-Co-WS$_2$	Sol–gel	9.21	The yolk–shell structure and high surface area improve PCE.	[134]
14.	CuS-WS$_2$ and CuS-MoS$_2$	CVD	8.21 and 7.12	High electrocatalytic activity and low charge transfer resistance improve PCE.	[135]

6. Conclusions

Researchers have continued to focus on the fabrication of DSSCs with different 2D-NLs (photoanode and CE) with the aim of enhancing the performance and stability of DSSCs in order to achieve higher or comparable PCE compared to commercially available solar cells. Moreover, researchers are also looking towards replacing the Pt-based electrode to reduce the cost of solar cells. Researchers and scientists in the solar cell industry are unremittingly working to develop a newer class of materials, including 2D-NL-based photoanodes and CEs that can considerably improve the PCE and stability of DSSCs. This review article focused on how 2D-NLs and their hybrid materials have been used as photoanode and CE materials in the fabrication of DSSCs. Previous studies have clearly shown that 2D-NLs significantly improve crystallinity, surface area, tuned band gap values, the adsorption of dye molecules, the migration of electrons, mass transfer, mesoporous properties, conductivity, flexibility, and electron transport while also facilitating light scattering, thereby improving the PCE of DSSCs. Moreover, incorporating dopants (metal, polymers, carbon particles, and other 2D-NLs) improved the PCE and stability of the DSSCs. It is important to mention here that the commercialization of DSSCs requires a simple process, cost-effectiveness, high PCE, and longer stability. With the help of 2D-NLs and their hybrid materials, we can easily resolve such issues and fulfil the requirements associated with the commercialization of DSSCs. Graphene-, MXene-, MoS$_2$-, and WS$_2$-based 2D-NLs have more active sites that facilitate the adsorption of dye molecules, thereby easily achieving high PCE and stability while also demonstrating the potential to replace Pt-based electrode materials in DSSCs. Moreover, further research on developing newer 2D-NLs and hybrid materials is still required to improve the PCE and stability of DSSCs.

Author Contributions: M.A., N.T. and D.C., conceptualized, writing, figures, and revised the manuscript. N.S. writing the manuscript. All authors have read and agreed to the published version of the manuscript.

Funding: This research received no external funding.

Conflicts of Interest: The authors declare no conflict of interest.

References

1. Kannan, N.; Vakeesan, D. Solar energy for future world: A review. *Renew. Sustain. Energy Rev.* **2016**, *62*, 1092–1105. [CrossRef]
2. Mekhilef, S.; Saidur, R.; Safari, A. A review on solar energy use in industries. *Renew. Sustain. Energy Rev.* **2011**, *15*, 1777–1790. [CrossRef]
3. Shafiee, S.; Topal, E. When will fossil fuel reserves be diminished? *Energy Policy* **2009**, *37*, 181–189. [CrossRef]
4. Asafu-Adjaye, J. The relationship between energy consumption, energy prices and economic growth: Time series evidence from Asian developing countries. *Energy Econ.* **2000**, *22*, 615–625. [CrossRef]
5. Kumar, J.C.R.; Majid, M.A. Renewable energy for sustainable development in India: Current status, future prospects, challenges, employment, and investment opportunities. *Energy Sustain. Soc.* **2020**, *10*, 2. [CrossRef]
6. Nayak, P.K.; Mahesh, S.; Snaith, H.J.; Cahen, D. Photovoltaic solar cell technologies: Analysing the state of the art. *Nat. Rev. Mater.* **2019**, *4*, 269–285. [CrossRef]
7. Kirchartz, T.; Rau, U. What Makes a Good Solar Cell? *Adv. Energy Mater.* **2018**, *8*, 1703385. [CrossRef]
8. Rathore, N.; Panwar, N.L.; Yettou, F.; Gama, A. A comprehensive review of different types of solar photovoltaic cells and their applications. *Int. J. Ambient Energy* **2021**, *42*, 1200–1217. [CrossRef]
9. Zhu, H.; Wei, J.; Wang, K.; Wu, D. Applications of carbon materials in photovoltaic solar cells. *Sol. Energy Mater. Sol. Cells* **2009**, *93*, 1461–1470. [CrossRef]
10. Deshmukh, M.A.; Park, S.-J.; Hedau, B.S.; Ha, T.-J. Recent progress in solar cells based on carbon nanomaterials. *Sol. Energy* **2021**, *220*, 953–990. [CrossRef]
11. Fei Guo, C.; Sun, T.; Cao, F.; Liu, Q.; Ren, Z. Metallic nanostructures for light trapping in energy-harvesting devices. *Light: Sci. Appl.* **2014**, *3*, e161. [CrossRef]
12. Sebastián, D.; Baglio, V.; Girolamo, M.; Moliner, R.; Lázaro, M.J.; Aricò, A.S. Carbon nanofiber-based counter electrodes for low cost dye-sensitized solar cells. *J. Power Sources* **2014**, *250*, 242–249. [CrossRef]
13. Batmunkh, M.; Biggs, M.J.; Shapter, J.G. Carbon Nanotubes for Dye-Sensitized Solar Cells. *Small* **2015**, *11*, 2963–2989. [CrossRef] [PubMed]
14. Muchuweni, E.; Martincigh, B.S.; Nyamori, V.O. Recent advances in graphene-based materials for dye-sensitized solar cell fabrication. *RSC Adv.* **2020**, *10*, 44453–44469. [CrossRef]
15. Sun, Z.; Talreja, N.; Tao, H.; Texter, J.; Muhler, M.; Strunk, J.; Chen, J. Catalysis of Carbon Dioxide Photoreduction on Nanosheets: Fundamentals and Challenges. *Angew. Chem. Int. Ed.* **2018**, *57*, 7610–7627. [CrossRef] [PubMed]
16. Tao, H.; Gao, Y.; Talreja, N.; Guo, F.; Texter, J.; Yan, C.; Sun, Z. Two-dimensional nanosheets for electrocatalysis in energy generation and conversion. *J. Mater. Chem. A* **2017**, *5*, 7257–7284. [CrossRef]
17. Gasso, S.; Mahajan, A. MXene based 2D-2D heterostructures for Counter Electrode in third generation Dye Sensitized Solar Cells. *Chem. Phys. Lett.* **2022**, *808*, 140144. [CrossRef]
18. Hussain, S.; Shaikh, S.F.; Vikraman, D.; Mane, R.S.; Joo, O.-S.; Naushad, M.; Jung, J. Sputtering and sulfurization-combined synthesis of a transparent WS2 counter electrode and its application to dye-sensitized solar cells. *RSC Adv.* **2015**, *5*, 103567–103572. [CrossRef]
19. Talreja, N.; Chauhan, D.; Mangalaraja, R.V. Two-dimensional nanolayers for wearable supercapacitors. In *Nanostructured Materials for Sustainable Energy and Environmental Remediation*; IOP Publishing: Bristol, UK, 2022; pp. 3-1–3-20.
20. Talreja, N.; Ashfaq, M.; Chauhan, D.; Mangalaraja, R.V. Cu-MXene: A potential biocide for the next-generation biomedical application. *Mater. Chem. Phys.* **2023**, *294*, 127029. [CrossRef]
21. Chauhan, D.; Ashfaq, M.; Mangalaraja, R.V.; Talreja, N. 2D-Nanosheets Based Hybrid Nanomaterials Interaction with Plants. In *Nanomaterial Interactions with Plant Cellular Mechanisms and Macromolecules and Agricultural Implications*; Al-Khayri, J.M., Alnaddaf, L.M., Jain, S.M., Eds.; Springer International Publishing: Cham, Switzerland, 2023; pp. 299–316.
22. Ashfaq, M.; Talreja, N.; Chauhan, D.; Viswanathan, M.R. Synthesis of Cu-doped 2D-WS2 nanosheet-based nano-antibiotic materials for inhibiting E. Coli and S. aureus bacterial strains. *New J. Chem.* **2022**, *46*, 5581–5587. [CrossRef]
23. Tomy, M.; Ambika Rajappan, A.; Vm, V.; Thankappan Suryabai, X. Emergence of Novel 2D Materials for High-Performance Supercapacitor Electrode Applications: A Brief Review. *Energy Fuels* **2021**, *35*, 19881–19900. [CrossRef]
24. Qin, Z.; Chen, Y.; Zhu, K.; Zhao, Y. Two-Dimensional Materials for Perovskite Solar Cells with Enhanced Efficiency and Stability. *ACS Mater. Lett.* **2021**, *3*, 1402–1416. [CrossRef]
25. Lin, Q.-L.; Liang, H.; Zhou, C.-Q.; Qian, Z.-F.; Sun, Y.-L.; Wang, X.-Y.; Wang, R.-H. Defect-induced magnetism in χ3 borophene. *Rare Met.* **2022**, *41*, 3486–3494. [CrossRef]
26. Lin, Q.-L.; Qian, Z.-F.; Dai, X.-Y.; Sun, Y.-L.; Wang, R.-H. Regulation of electronic structure of monolayer MoS$_2$ by pressure. *Rare Met.* **2022**, *41*, 1761–1770. [CrossRef]

27. Lin, Q.; Miao, L.; Qian, Z.; Sun, Y.; Wang, R. First-Principles Calculations on Magnetism Induced by Vacancies in β12-Borophene Nanosheets: Implications for Property Modulation. *ACS Appl. Nano Mater.* **2022**, *5*, 113–119. [CrossRef]
28. Wang, R.; Dai, X.; Qian, Z.; Zhong, S.; Chen, S.; Fan, S.; Zhang, H.; Wu, F. Boosting Lithium Storage in Free-Standing Black Phosphorus Anode via Multifunction of Nanocellulose. *ACS Appl. Mater. Interfaces* **2020**, *12*, 31628–31636. [CrossRef]
29. Al-Ezzi, A.S.; Ansari, M.N.M. Photovoltaic Solar Cells: A Review. *Appl. Syst. Innov.* **2022**, *5*, 67. [CrossRef]
30. Dambhare, M.V.; Butey, B.; Moharil, S.V. Solar photovoltaic technology: A review of different types of solar cells and its future trends. *J. Phys. Conf. Ser.* **2021**, *1913*, 012053. [CrossRef]
31. Li, J.; Aierken, A.; Liu, Y.; Zhuang, Y.; Yang, X.; Mo, J.H.; Fan, R.K.; Chen, Q.Y.; Zhang, S.Y.; Huang, Y.M.; et al. A Brief Review of High Efficiency III-V Solar Cells for Space Application. *Front. Phys.* **2021**, *8*, 631925. [CrossRef]
32. Ushasree, P.M.; Bora, B. Chapter 1 Silicon Solar Cells. In *Solar Energy Capture Materials*; The Royal Society of Chemistry: London, UK, 2019; pp. 1–55.
33. Satharasinghe, A.; Hughes-Riley, T. A Review of Solar Energy Harvesting Electronic Textiles. *Sensors* **2020**, *20*, 5938. [CrossRef]
34. Katagiri, H.; Jimbo, K.; Maw, W.S.; Oishi, K.; Yamazaki, M.; Araki, H.; Takeuchi, A. Development of CZTS-based thin film solar cells. *Thin Solid Films* **2009**, *517*, 2455–2460. [CrossRef]
35. Asim, N.; Mohammad, M.; Badiei, M. Chapter 8—Novel Nanomaterials for Solar Cell Devices. In *Nanomaterials for Green Energy*; Bhanvase, B.A., Pawade, V.B., Dhoble, S.J., Sonawane, S.H., Ashokkumar, M., Eds.; Elsevier: Amsterdam, The Netherlands, 2018; pp. 227–277.
36. Müller-Buschbaum, P.; Thelakkat, M.; Fässler, T.F.; Stutzmann, M. Hybrid Photovoltaics—From Fundamentals towards Application. *Adv. Energy Mater.* **2017**, *7*, 1700248. [CrossRef]
37. Michaels, H.; Benesperi, I.; Freitag, M. Challenges and prospects of ambient hybrid solar cell applications. *Chem. Sci.* **2021**, *12*, 5002–5015. [CrossRef] [PubMed]
38. Lu, Z.; Hou, G.; Zhu, Y.; Chen, J.; Xu, J.; Chen, K. High efficiency organic–Si hybrid solar cells with a one-dimensional CdS interlayer. *Nanoscale* **2021**, *13*, 4206–4212. [CrossRef] [PubMed]
39. Lin, S.; Peng, X. Current Status and Challenges of Solar Cells Based on Semiconductor Nanocrystals. *Energy Fuels* **2021**, *35*, 18928–18941. [CrossRef]
40. Kim, M.R.; Ma, D. Quantum-Dot-Based Solar Cells: Recent Advances, Strategies, and Challenges. *J. Phys. Chem. Lett.* **2015**, *6*, 85–99. [CrossRef]
41. Sengupta, D.; Das, P.; Mondal, B.; Mukherjee, K. Effects of doping, morphology and film-thickness of photo-anode materials for dye sensitized solar cell application—A review. *Renew. Sustain. Energy Rev.* **2016**, *60*, 356–376. [CrossRef]
42. Devadiga, D.; Selvakumar, M.; Shetty, P.; Santosh, M.S. Recent progress in dye sensitized solar cell materials and photo-supercapacitors: A review. *J. Power Sources* **2021**, *493*, 229698. [CrossRef]
43. Castillo-Robles, J.A.; Rocha-Rangel, E.; Ramírez-de-León, J.A.; Caballero-Rico, F.C.; Armendáriz-Mireles, E.N. Advances on Dye-Sensitized Solar Cells (DSSCs) Nanostructures and Natural Colorants: A Review. *J. Compos. Sci.* **2021**, *5*, 288. [CrossRef]
44. Bera, S.; Sengupta, D.; Roy, S.; Mukherjee, K. Research into dye-sensitized solar cells: A review highlighting progress in India. *J. Phys. Energy* **2021**, *3*, 032013. [CrossRef]
45. Lee, C.-P.; Li, C.-T.; Ho, K.-C. Use of organic materials in dye-sensitized solar cells. *Mater. Today* **2017**, *20*, 267–283. [CrossRef]
46. Tontapha, S.; Uppachai, P.; Amornkitbamrung, V. Fabrication of Functional Materials for Dye-sensitized Solar Cells. *Front. Energy Res.* **2021**, *9*, 641983. [CrossRef]
47. Zhou, Q.; Duan, J.; Duan, Y.; Tang, Q. Review on engineering two-dimensional nanomaterials for promoting efficiency and stability of perovskite solar cells. *J. Energy Chem.* **2022**, *68*, 154–175. [CrossRef]
48. Chiu, W.-H.; Lee, K.-M.; Suryanarayanan, V.; Hsu, J.-F.; Wu, M.-C. Controlled Photoanode Properties for Large-Area Efficient and Stable Dye-Sensitized Photovoltaic Modules. *Nanomaterials* **2021**, *11*, 2125. [CrossRef]
49. Cheng, C.-K.; Lin, C.-H.; Wu, H.-C.; Ma, C.-C.M.; Yeh, T.-K.; Chou, H.-Y.; Tsai, C.-H.; Hsieh, C.-K. The Two-Dimensional Nanocomposite of Molybdenum Disulfide and Nitrogen-Doped Graphene Oxide for Efficient Counter Electrode of Dye-Sensitized Solar Cells. *Nanoscale Res. Lett.* **2016**, *11*, 117. [CrossRef] [PubMed]
50. Hsieh, C.-T.; Yang, B.-H.; Lin, J.-Y. One- and two-dimensional carbon nanomaterials as counter electrodes for dye-sensitized solar cells. *Carbon* **2011**, *49*, 3092–3097. [CrossRef]
51. Ghartavol, H.M.; Mohammadi, M.R.; Afshar, A.; Li, Y. On the assessment of incorporation of CNT–TiO_2 core–shell structures into nanoparticle TiO_2 photoanodes in dye-sensitized solar cells. *Photochem. Photobiol. Sci.* **2019**, *18*, 1840–1850. [CrossRef]
52. Roy-Mayhew, J.D.; Aksay, I.A. Graphene Materials and Their Use in Dye-Sensitized Solar Cells. *Chem. Rev.* **2014**, *114*, 6323–6348. [CrossRef]
53. Kim, S.-B.; Park, J.-Y.; Kim, C.-S.; Okuyama, K.; Lee, S.-E.; Jang, H.-D.; Kim, T.-O. Effects of Graphene in Dye-Sensitized Solar Cells Based on Nitrogen-Doped TiO_2 Composite. *J. Phys. Chem. C* **2015**, *119*, 16552–16559. [CrossRef]
54. Kundu, A.; Shit, A.; Nandi, S. Carbon Dot Assisted Synthesis of Nanostructured Polyaniline for Dye Sensitized Solar Cells. *Energy Fuels* **2017**, *31*, 7364–7371. [CrossRef]
55. Talreja, N.; Ashfaq, M.; Chauhan, D.; Mera, A.C.; Rodríguez, C.A. Strategic Doping Approach of the Fe–BiOI Microstructure: An Improved Photodegradation Efficiency of Tetracycline. *ACS Omega* **2021**, *6*, 1575–1583. [CrossRef] [PubMed]
56. Ünlü, B.; Çakar, S.; Özacar, M. The effects of metal doped TiO_2 and dithizone-metal complexes on DSSCs performance. *Sol. Energy* **2018**, *166*, 441–449. [CrossRef]

57. Kausar, A.; Sattar, A.; Xu, C.; Zhang, S.; Kang, Z.; Zhang, Y. Advent of alkali metal doping: A roadmap for the evolution of perovskite solar cells. *Chem. Soc. Rev.* **2021**, *50*, 2696–2736. [CrossRef] [PubMed]
58. Subalakshmi, K.; Chung, W.; Lee, S. Synergistically improved photovoltaic performances of dye-sensitized solar cells with metal-free organic cosensitizer and hybrid rGO-TiO$_2$ photoanode. *Dye. Pigment.* **2023**, *209*, 110892. [CrossRef]
59. Wu, Q.; Chen, R.; Su, P.; Shi, D.; Zhang, Y.; Chen, K.; Li, H. Co$_9$S$_8$/NC@FeCoS$_2$/NC composites with hollow yolk shell structure as the counter electrode for Pt-free dye-sensitized solar cells. *Electrochim. Acta* **2023**, *438*, 141587. [CrossRef]
60. Van Cuong, L.; Lam Tuan Cuong, D.; Tran Trung Nghia, L.; Khac Hung, L.; Thai Hoang, N.; Tan Nhiem, L.; Trong Liem Chau, P.; Thanh Phong, M.; Huu Hieu, N. Effect of reducing agents on co-precipitation synthesis of titanium dioxide/reduced graphene oxide composite materials for upgrading the performance of dye-sensitized solar cells. *Chem. Eng. Sci.* **2022**, *264*, 118145. [CrossRef]
61. Gupta, R.; Kumar, R.; Sharma, A.; Verma, N. Novel Cu–carbon nanofiber composites for the counter electrodes of dye-sensitized solar cells. *Int. J. Energy Res.* **2015**, *39*, 668–680. [CrossRef]
62. Ashfaq, M.; Chauhan, D.; Mangalaraja, R.V. Micro-mesoporous carbon-based nanostructured materials for flexible supercapacitors. In *Nanostructured Materials for Sustainable Energy and Environmental Remediation*; IOP Publishing: Bristol, UK, 2022; pp. 4-1–4-19.
63. Miao, X.; Tongay, S.; Petterson, M.K.; Berke, K.; Rinzler, A.G.; Appleton, B.R.; Hebard, A.F. High Efficiency Graphene Solar Cells by Chemical Doping. *Nano Lett.* **2012**, *12*, 2745–2750. [CrossRef]
64. Kadam, K.D.; Rehman, M.A.; Kim, H.; Rehman, S.; Khan, M.A.; Patil, H.; Aziz, J.; Park, S.; Abdul Basit, M.; Khan, K.; et al. Enhanced and Passivated Co-doping Effect of Organic Molecule and Bromine on Graphene/HfO$_2$/Silicon Metal–Insulator–Semiconductor (MIS) Schottky Junction Solar Cells. *ACS Appl. Energy Mater.* **2022**, *5*, 10509–10517. [CrossRef]
65. Hagfeldt, A.; Boschloo, G.; Sun, L.; Kloo, L.; Pettersson, H. Dye-Sensitized Solar Cells. *Chem. Rev.* **2010**, *110*, 6595–6663. [CrossRef]
66. Lin, L.-Y.; Ho, K.-C. Dye-Sensitized Solar Cells. In *Encyclopedia of Modern Optics*, 2nd ed.; Guenther, B.D., Steel, D.G., Eds.; Elsevier: Oxford, UK, 2018; pp. 270–281.
67. Sharma, K.; Sharma, V.; Sharma, S.S. Dye-Sensitized Solar Cells: Fundamentals and Current Status. *Nanoscale Res. Lett.* **2018**, *13*, 381. [CrossRef]
68. Ito, S.; Murakami, T.N.; Comte, P.; Liska, P.; Grätzel, C.; Nazeeruddin, M.K.; Grätzel, M. Fabrication of thin film dye sensitized solar cells with solar to electric power conversion efficiency over 10%. *Thin Solid Films* **2008**, *516*, 4613–4619. [CrossRef]
69. James, E.M.; Barr, T.J.; Meyer, G.J. Evidence for an Electronic State at the Interface between the SnO$_2$ Core and the TiO$_2$ Shell in Mesoporous SnO$_2$/TiO$_2$ Thin Films. *ACS Appl. Energy Mater.* **2018**, *1*, 859–867. [CrossRef]
70. Mathew, S.; Yella, A.; Gao, P.; Humphry-Baker, R.; Curchod, B.F.E.; Ashari-Astani, N.; Tavernelli, I.; Rothlisberger, U.; Nazeeruddin, M.K.; Grätzel, M. Dye-sensitized solar cells with 13% efficiency achieved through the molecular engineering of porphyrin sensitizers. *Nat. Chem.* **2014**, *6*, 242–247. [CrossRef]
71. Deepak, T.G.; Anjusree, G.S.; Thomas, S.; Arun, T.A.; Nair, S.V.; Sreekumaran Nair, A. A review on materials for light scattering in dye-sensitized solar cells. *RSC Adv.* **2014**, *4*, 17615–17638. [CrossRef]
72. Chen, H.; Liu, T.; Wang, B.; Liu, Z.; Li, Y.; Zhao, Q.; Wang, N.; He, H.; Liu, H.; Guo, Z. Highly efficient charge collection in dye-sensitized solar cells based on nanocomposite photoanode filled with indium-tin oxide interlayer. *Adv. Compos. Hybrid Mater.* **2018**, *1*, 356–363. [CrossRef]
73. Snaith, H.J.; Schmidt-Mende, L. Advances in Liquid-Electrolyte and Solid-State Dye-Sensitized Solar Cells. *Adv. Mater.* **2007**, *19*, 3187–3200. [CrossRef]
74. Iftikhar, H.; Sonai, G.G.; Hashmi, S.G.; Nogueira, A.F.; Lund, P.D. Progress on Electrolytes Development in Dye-Sensitized Solar Cells. *Materials* **2019**, *12*, 1998. [CrossRef]
75. Cavallo, C.; Di Pascasio, F.; Latini, A.; Bonomo, M.; Dini, D. Nanostructured Semiconductor Materials for Dye-Sensitized Solar Cells. *J. Nanomater.* **2017**, *2017*, 5323164. [CrossRef]
76. Asim, N.; Ahmadi, S.; Alghoul, M.A.; Hammadi, F.Y.; Saeedfar, K.; Sopian, K. Research and Development Aspects on Chemical Preparation Techniques of Photoanodes for Dye Sensitized Solar Cells. *Int. J. Photoenergy* **2014**, *2014*, 518156. [CrossRef]
77. Kharkwal, D.; Sharma, N.; Kumar Gupta, S.; Mohan Singh Negi, C. Enhanced performance of dye-sensitized solar cells by co-sensitization of metal-complex and organic dye. *Sol. Energy* **2021**, *230*, 1133–1140. [CrossRef]
78. Sasidharan, V.; Sachan, D.; Chauhan, D.; Talreja, N.; Ashfaq, M. Three-dimensional (3D) polymer—Metal–carbon framework for efficient removal of chemical and biological contaminants. *Sci. Rep.* **2021**, *11*, 7708. [CrossRef]
79. Ashfaq, M.; Talreja, N.; Chauhan, D.; Rodríguez, C.A.; Mera, A.C.; Ramalinga Viswanathan, M. Synthesis of reduced graphene oxide incorporated bimetallic (Cu/Bi) nanorods based photocatalyst materials for the degradation of gallic acid and bacteria. *J. Ind. Eng. Chem.* **2022**, *110*, 447–455. [CrossRef]
80. Ashfaq, M.; Wongpakham, T.; Talreja, N.; Chauhan, D.; Tharasanit, T.; Srituravanich, W. Synthesis of polymeric composite grafted with mineral particles/graphene oxide-based biomaterial: A promising robust hemostatic bandage. *Mater. Today Commun.* **2022**, *33*, 104786. [CrossRef]
81. Ju, M.J.; Kim, J.C.; Choi, H.-J.; Choi, I.T.; Kim, S.G.; Lim, K.; Ko, J.; Lee, J.-J.; Jeon, I.-Y.; Baek, J.-B.; et al. N-Doped Graphene Nanoplatelets as Superior Metal-Free Counter Electrodes for Organic Dye-Sensitized Solar Cells. *ACS Nano* **2013**, *7*, 5243–5250. [CrossRef] [PubMed]
82. Yu, Z.; Bai, Y.; Wang, Y.; Liu, Y.; Zhao, Y.; Liu, Y.; Sun, K. One-step synthesis of three-dimensional nitrogen and sulfur co-doped graphene networks as low cost metal-free counter electrodes for dye-sensitized solar cells. *Chem. Eng. J.* **2017**, *311*, 302–309. [CrossRef]

83. Paranthaman, V.; Sundaramoorthy, K.; Chandra, B.; Muthu, S.P.; Alagarsamy, P.; Perumalsamy, R. Investigation on the Performance of Reduced Graphene Oxide as Counter Electrode in Dye Sensitized Solar Cell Applications. *physica status solidi a* **2018**, *215*, 1800298. [CrossRef]
84. Casaluci, S.; Gemmi, M.; Pellegrini, V.; Di Carlo, A.; Bonaccorso, F. Graphene-based large area dye-sensitized solar cell modules. *Nanoscale* **2016**, *8*, 5368–5378. [CrossRef]
85. Zhang, D.W.; Li, X.D.; Li, H.B.; Chen, S.; Sun, Z.; Yin, X.J.; Huang, S.M. Graphene-based counter electrode for dye-sensitized solar cells. *Carbon* **2011**, *49*, 5382–5388. [CrossRef]
86. Krishna Prasad, A.; Jo, I.-R.; Kang, S.-H.; Ahn, K.-S. Novel method for synthesis of reduced graphene oxide–Cu2S and its application as a counter electrode in quantum-dot-sensitized solar cells. *Appl. Surf. Sci.* **2021**, *564*, 150393. [CrossRef]
87. Jiang, T.; Yang, S.; Dai, P.; Yu, X.; Bai, Z.; Wu, M.; Li, G.; Tu, C. Economic synthesis of Co3S4 ultrathin nanosheet/reduced graphene oxide composites and their application as an efficient counter electrode for dye-sensitized solar cells. *Electrochim. Acta* **2018**, *261*, 143–150. [CrossRef]
88. Ngidi, N.P.D.; Muchuweni, E.; Nyamori, V.O. Dual heteroatom-doped reduced graphene oxide and its application in dye-sensitized solar cells. *Opt. Mater.* **2021**, *122*, 111689. [CrossRef]
89. Salleh, S.A.; Rahman, M.Y.A.; Aziz, T.H.T. Dye-sensitized solar cell using nickel sulfide-reduced graphene oxide counter electrode: Effect of sulphur content. *Inorg. Chem. Commun.* **2022**, *135*, 109086. [CrossRef]
90. Khoa, N.T.; Thuan, D.V.; Kim, S.W.; Park, S.; Tam, T.V.; Choi, W.M.; Cho, S.; Kim, E.J.; Hahn, S.H. Facile fabrication of thermally reduced graphene oxide–platinum nanohybrids and their application in catalytic reduction and dye-sensitized solar cells. *RSC Adv.* **2016**, *6*, 1535–1541. [CrossRef]
91. Mahmood Khan, I.; Nazar, R.; Mehmood, U. Development of polypyrrole/graphene (PPY/graphene) based electrocatalyst for platinum free dye-sensitized solar cells (DSSCs). *Mater. Lett.* **2022**, *320*, 132331. [CrossRef]
92. Oh, W.C.; Cho, K.Y.; Jung, C.H.; Areerob, Y. Hybrid of Graphene based on quaternary $Cu_2ZnNiSe_4$ –WO_3 Nanorods for Counter Electrode in Dye-sensitized Solar Cell Application. *Sci. Rep.* **2020**, *10*, 4738. [CrossRef]
93. Yu, J.; Fan, J.; Lv, K. Anatase TiO_2 nanosheets with exposed (001) facets: Improved photoelectric conversion efficiency in dye-sensitized solar cells. *Nanoscale* **2010**, *2*, 2144–2149. [CrossRef] [PubMed]
94. Wu, C.; Qi, L.; Chen, Y.; Ouyang, Q.; Li, C. Dye-sensitized solar cells based on two-dimensional TiO_2 nanosheets as the scattering layers. *Res. Chem. Intermed.* **2016**, *42*, 5653–5664. [CrossRef]
95. Peng, J.-D.; Shih, P.-C.; Lin, H.-H.; Tseng, C.-M.; Vittal, R.; Suryanarayanan, V.; Ho, K.-C. TiO_2 nanosheets with highly exposed (001)-facets for enhanced photovoltaic performance of dye-sensitized solar cells. *Nano Energy* **2014**, *10*, 212–221. [CrossRef]
96. Laskova, B.; Zukalova, M.; Kavan, L.; Chou, A.; Liska, P.; Wei, Z.; Bin, L.; Kubat, P.; Ghadiri, E.; Moser, J.E.; et al. Voltage enhancement in dye-sensitized solar cell using (001)-oriented anatase TiO_2 nanosheets. *J. Solid State Electrochem.* **2012**, *16*, 2993–3001. [CrossRef]
97. Miles, D.O.; Lee, C.S.; Cameron, P.J.; Mattia, D.; Kim, J.H. Hierarchical growth of TiO_2 nanosheets on anodic ZnO nanowires for high efficiency dye-sensitized solar cells. *J. Power Sources* **2016**, *325*, 365–374. [CrossRef]
98. Jiang, L.; Sun, L.; Yang, D.; Zhang, J.; Li, Y.-J.; Deng, W.-Q. Niobium-Doped (001)-Dominated Anatase TiO_2 Nanosheets as Photoelectrode for Efficient Dye-Sensitized Solar Cells. *ACS Appl. Mater. Interfaces* **2017**, *9*, 9576–9583. [CrossRef] [PubMed]
99. Xu, J.; Wang, G.; Fan, J.; Liu, B.; Cao, S.; Yu, J. g-C_3N_4 modified TiO_2 nanosheets with enhanced photoelectric conversion efficiency in dye-sensitized solar cells. *J. Power Sources* **2015**, *274*, 77–84. [CrossRef]
100. Lin, C.-Y.; Lai, Y.-H.; Chen, H.-W.; Chen, J.-G.; Kung, C.-W.; Vittal, R.; Ho, K.-C. Highly efficient dye-sensitized solar cell with a ZnO nanosheet-based photoanode. *Energy Environ. Sci.* **2011**, *4*, 3448–3455. [CrossRef]
101. Kim, Y.T.; Park, M.Y.; Choi, K.H.; Tai, W.S.; Shim, W.H.; Park, S.Y.; Kang, J.W.; Lee, K.H.; Jeong, Y.; Kim, Y.D.; et al. ZnO nanosheets decorated with CdSe and TiO_2 for the architecture of dye-sensitized solar cells. *J. Nanosci. Nanotechnol.* **2011**, *11*, 2263–2268. [CrossRef] [PubMed]
102. Saeed, M.A.; Shahzad, A.; Rasool, K.; Mateen, F.; Oh, J.-M.; Shim, J.W. 2D MXene: A Potential Candidate for Photovoltaic Cells? A Critical Review. *Adv. Sci.* **2022**, *9*, 2104743. [CrossRef] [PubMed]
103. Yin, L.; Li, Y.; Yao, X.; Wang, Y.; Jia, L.; Liu, Q.; Li, J.; Li, Y.; He, D. MXenes for Solar Cells. *Nano-Micro Lett.* **2021**, *13*, 78. [CrossRef]
104. Shi, Z.; Khaledialidusti, R.; Malaki, M.; Zhang, H. MXene-Based Materials for Solar Cell Applications. *Nanomaterials* **2021**, *11*, 3170. [CrossRef]
105. Wang, Y.; Guo, T.; Tian, Z.; Bibi, K.; Zhang, Y.-Z.; Alshareef, H.N. MXenes for Energy Harvesting. *Adv. Mater.* **2022**, *34*, 2108560. [CrossRef]
106. Sun, Y.; Li, Y. Potential environmental applications of MXenes: A critical review. *Chemosphere* **2021**, *271*, 129578. [CrossRef]
107. Agresti, A.; Pazniak, A.; Pescetelli, S.; Di Vito, A.; Rossi, D.; Pecchia, A.; Auf der Maur, M.; Liedl, A.; Larciprete, R.; Kuznetsov, D.V.; et al. Titanium-carbide MXenes for work function and interface engineering in perovskite solar cells. *Nat. Mater.* **2019**, *18*, 1228–1234. [CrossRef] [PubMed]
108. Li, X.; Bai, Y.; Shi, X.; Su, N.; Nie, G.; Zhang, R.; Nie, H.; Ye, L. Applications of MXene (Ti_3C_2Tx) in photocatalysis: A review. *Mater. Adv.* **2021**, *2*, 1570–1594. [CrossRef]
109. Ramezani Farani, M.; Nourmohammadi Khiarak, B.; Tao, R.; Wang, Z.; Ahmadi, S.; Hassanpour, M.; Rabiee, M.; Saeb, M.R.; Lima, E.C.; Rabiee, N. 2D MXene nanocomposites: Electrochemical and biomedical applications. *Environ. Sci. Nano* **2022**, *9*, 4038–4068. [CrossRef]

110. Dall'Agnese, C.; Dall'Agnese, Y.; Anasori, B.; Sugimoto, W.; Mori, S. Oxidized Ti_3C_2 MXene nanosheets for dye-sensitized solar cells. *New J. Chem.* **2018**, *42*, 16446–16450. [CrossRef]
111. Chen, X.; Zhuang, Y.; Shen, Q.; Cao, X.; Yang, W.; Yang, P. In situ synthesis of Ti_3C_2Tx MXene/CoS nanocomposite as high performance counter electrode materials for quantum dot-sensitized solar cells. *Sol. Energy* **2021**, *226*, 236–244. [CrossRef]
112. Priya Nagalingam, S.; Grace, A.N. Poly(3,4-ethylenedioxythiophene) decorated MXene as an alternative counter electrode for dye-sensitized solar cells. *Mater. Today Chem.* **2022**, *26*, 101113. [CrossRef]
113. Wen, J.; Sun, Z.; Qiao, Y.; Zhou, Y.; Liu, Y.; Zhang, Q.; Liu, Y.; Jiao, S. Ti_3C_2 MXene-Reduced Graphene Oxide Composite Polymer-Based Printable Electrolyte for Quasi-Solid-State Dye-Sensitized Solar Cells. *ACS Appl. Energy Mater.* **2022**, *5*, 3329–3338. [CrossRef]
114. Ahmad, M.S.; Pandey, A.K.; Abd Rahim, N.; Aslfattahi, N.; Mishra, Y.K.; Rashid, B.; Saidur, R. 2-D Mxene flakes as potential replacement for both TCO and Pt layers for Dye-Sensitized Solar cell. *Ceram. Int.* **2021**, *47*, 27942–27947. [CrossRef]
115. Yang, Y.; Gao, J.; Zhang, Z.; Xiao, S.; Xie, H.-H.; Sun, Z.-B.; Wang, J.-H.; Zhou, C.-H.; Wang, Y.-W.; Guo, X.-Y.; et al. Black Phosphorus Based Photocathodes in Wideband Bifacial Dye-Sensitized Solar Cells. *Adv. Mater.* **2016**, *28*, 8937–8944. [CrossRef]
116. Xue, Y.; Min, S.; Wang, F. Dye-sensitized black phosphorus nanosheets decorated with Pt cocatalyst for highly efficient photocatalytic hydrogen evolution under visible light. *Int. J. Hydrog. Energy* **2019**, *44*, 21873–21881. [CrossRef]
117. Lin, S.; Li, Y.; Qian, J.; Lau, S.P. Emerging opportunities for black phosphorus in energy applications. *Mater. Today Energy* **2019**, *12*, 1–25. [CrossRef]
118. Chen, W.; Ouyang, J.; Liu, H.; Chen, M.; Zeng, K.; Sheng, J.; Liu, Z.; Han, Y.; Wang, L.; Li, J.; et al. Black Phosphorus Nanosheet-Based Drug Delivery System for Synergistic Photodynamic/Photothermal/Chemotherapy of Cancer. *Adv. Mater.* **2017**, *29*, 1603864. [CrossRef] [PubMed]
119. Wang, X.; Xiang, Y.; Zhou, B.; Zhang, Y.; Wu, J.; Hu, R.; Liu, L.; Song, J.; Qu, J. Enhanced photocatalytic performance of Ag/TiO_2 nanohybrid sensitized by black phosphorus nanosheets in visible and near-infrared light. *J. Colloid Interface Sci.* **2019**, *534*, 1–11. [CrossRef] [PubMed]
120. Xu, Y.; Wang, X.; Jin, M.; Zhou, G.; Shui, L. Enhanced performance of dye-sensitized solar cells anodes modified with black phosphorus nanosheets. *J. Mater. Sci.* **2020**, *55*, 5499–5509. [CrossRef]
121. Song, J.; Wang, J.; Lin, X.; He, J.; Liu, H.; Lei, Y.; Chu, Z. Black Phosphorus/TiO_2 Composite Photoanode with Enhanced Photoelectrical Performance. *ChemElectroChem* **2017**, *4*, 2373–2377. [CrossRef]
122. Yin, X.; Tang, C.S.; Zheng, Y.; Gao, J.; Wu, J.; Zhang, H.; Chhowalla, M.; Chen, W.; Wee, A.T.S. Recent developments in 2D transition metal dichalcogenides: Phase transition and applications of the (quasi-)metallic phases. *Chem. Soc. Rev.* **2021**, *50*, 10087–10115. [CrossRef] [PubMed]
123. Chhowalla, M.; Liu, Z.; Zhang, H. Two-dimensional transition metal dichalcogenide (TMD) nanosheets. *Chem. Soc. Rev.* **2015**, *44*, 2584–2586. [CrossRef]
124. Choi, W.; Choudhary, N.; Han, G.H.; Park, J.; Akinwande, D.; Lee, Y.H. Recent development of two-dimensional transition metal dichalcogenides and their applications. *Mater. Today* **2017**, *20*, 116–130. [CrossRef]
125. Ali, M.; Afzal, A.M.; Iqbal, M.W.; Mumtaz, S.; Imran, M.; Ashraf, F.; Ur Rehman, A.; Muhammad, F. 2D-TMDs based electrode material for supercapacitor applications. *Int. J. Energy Res.* **2022**, *46*, 22336–22364. [CrossRef]
126. Rashidi, S.; Rashidi, S.; Heydari, R.K.; Esmaeili, S.; Tran, N.; Thangi, D.; Wei, W. WS2 and MoS2 counter electrode materials for dye-sensitized solar cells. *Prog. Photovolt. Res. Appl.* **2021**, *29*, 238–261. [CrossRef]
127. Gurulakshmi, M.; Meenakshamma, A.; Siddeswaramma, G.; Susmitha, K.; Venkata Subbaiah, Y.P.; Narayana, T.; Raghavender, M. Electrodeposited MoS_2 counter electrode for flexible dye sensitized solar cell module with ionic liquid assisted photoelectrode. *Sol. Energy* **2020**, *199*, 447–452. [CrossRef]
128. Vijaya, S.; Landi, G.; Wu, J.J.; Anandan, S. MoS2 nanosheets based counter electrodes: An alternative for Pt-free dye-sensitized solar cells. *Electrochim. Acta* **2019**, *294*, 134–141. [CrossRef]
129. Krishnamoorthy, D.; Prakasam, A. Preparation of MoS2/graphene nanocomposite-based photoanode for dye-sensitized solar cells (DSSCs). *Inorg. Chem. Commun.* **2020**, *118*, 108016. [CrossRef]
130. Menon, H.; Gopakumar, G.; Sankaranarayanan Nair, V.; Nair, S.V.; Shanmugam, M. 2D-Layered MoS2-Incorporated TiO_2-Nanofiber- Based Dye-Sensitized Solar Cells. *ChemistrySelect* **2018**, *3*, 5801–5807. [CrossRef]
131. Xu, T.; Kong, D.; Tang, H.; Qin, X.; Li, X.; Gurung, A.; Kou, K.; Chen, L.; Qiao, Q.; Huang, W. Transparent MoS_2/PEDOT Composite Counter Electrodes for Bifacial Dye-Sensitized Solar Cells. *ACS Omega* **2020**, *5*, 8687–8696. [CrossRef]
132. Li, S.; Chen, Z.; Zhang, W. Dye-sensitized solar cells based on WS2 counter electrodes. *Mater. Lett.* **2012**, *72*, 22–24. [CrossRef]
133. Krishnamoorthy, D.; Prakasam, A. Graphene Hybridized with Tungsten disulfide (WS2) Based Heterojunctions Photoanode Materials for High Performance Dye Sensitized Solar Cell Device (DSSCs) Applications. *J. Clust. Sci.* **2021**, *32*, 621–630. [CrossRef]
134. Huang, J.; Qian, X.; Yang, J.; Niu, Y.; Xu, C.; Hou, L. Construction of Pt-free electrocatalysts based on hierarchical CoS2/N-doped C@Co-WS2 yolk-shell nano-polyhedrons for dye-sensitized solar cells. *Electrochim. Acta* **2020**, *340*, 135949. [CrossRef]
135. Hussain, S.; Patil, S.A.; Memon, A.A.; Vikraman, D.; Naqvi, B.A.; Jeong, S.H.; Kim, H.-S.; Kim, H.-S.; Jung, J. CuS/WS2 and CuS/MoS2 heterostructures for high performance counter electrodes in dye-sensitized solar cells. *Sol. Energy* **2018**, *171*, 122–129. [CrossRef]

Disclaimer/Publisher's Note: The statements, opinions and data contained in all publications are solely those of the individual author(s) and contributor(s) and not of MDPI and/or the editor(s). MDPI and/or the editor(s) disclaim responsibility for any injury to people or property resulting from any ideas, methods, instructions or products referred to in the content.

Article

Design and Implementation of Embedded Controller-Based Energy Storage and Management System for Remote Telecom

B. S. Nalina [1], M. Chilambarasan [1], S. Tamilselvi [2], Ahmad Aziz Al Alahmadi [3], Mamdooh Alwetaishi [4], M. A. Mujtaba [5] and M. A. Kalam [6],*

[1] Electronics Engineer, Senior Associate Technical Support Engineer, Valeo India Pvt Ltd., Skill Lync, Tamil Nadu 600097, India
[2] Department of Electrical Engineering, Sri Sivasubramaniya Nadar College of Engineering, Tamil Nadu 603110, India
[3] Department of Electrical Engineering, College of Engineering, Taif University, P.O. Box 11099, Taif 21944, Saudi Arabia
[4] Department of Civil Engineering, College of Engineering, Taif University, P.O. Box 11099, Taif 21944, Saudi Arabia
[5] Department of Mechanical Engineering, Faculty of Engineering, University of Malaya, Kuala Lumpur 50603, Malaysia
[6] School of Civil and Environmental Engineering, FEIT, University of Technology Sydney, Sydney, NSW 2007, Australia
* Correspondence: mdabul.kalam@uts.edu.au

Abstract: The source of energy extracted in renewable form has turned out to be a primary mainstream energy source, especially in the telecom sectors. Rapid growth of renewable sources has led to telecom operators concentrating more on designing the system with appropriate energy storage elements, providing control facilities, improving system efficiency and verifying uninterrupted power supplies. Therefore, this paper gives a novel approach of utilizing embedded control in energy generation consisting of a solar-wind hybrid energy system placed in isolated areas. For the purpose of integration of wind, together with the solar energy sources, into an increasingly efficient system, a single Cuk-Luo integrated DC-DC converter has been put forward. The proposed system has been modeled using MATLAB/Simulink and verified under various combinations of solar-wind energy sources without compromising the required power. In order to verify the proposed Cuk-Luo integrated converter with the energy management controller system, a prototype hardware is implemented and tested.

Keywords: embedded controller; energy management system; Cuk-Luo integrated DC-DC converter; telecom

1. Introduction

Mobile networks have gained more interest in modern communications [1,2]. According to Bhattacharya et al. [3] and Kumar et al., [4], the use of mobile networks raises a crucial concern regarding their energy consumption, environmental protection and carbon footprint. The nature-friendly energy sources, coupled with suitable energy storage elements, could turn out to be the major source in the reduction of discharge through greenhouse gases. However, renewable energy relies on wind speed or solar radiation to a large extent. In order to offer a continuous supply by taking the advantages of the complementary nature of both of the energy sources, the solution is to hybridize the two types of sources in the form of the microgrid. A study performed by Bhattacharya et al. [5], Joga Rao et al. [6] and Pandiyan et al. [7] demonstrated that a hybrid solar-wind power system can offer a cost effective and environmentally protected solution. On the other hand, the intermittent nature of Renewable Energy Sources (RES) means proper energy management is required in order to improve the performance and increase the lifespan of the microgrid components to a large extent [8]. Therefore, sufficient management of the energy flow through the hybrid RES and the establishment of a supervisory system are highly in demand. Energy storage systems are required to balance transient stability during the rapid change of solar and wind systems and load variations.

The literature reveals that new energy management techniques for PV/wind/grid RES have been carried out and several energy management systems have been evaluated to find the most effective one. In addition, there are works showing a dynamic energy management model and the development of a coordinated control strategy for a hybrid system maintaining around 75% battery state and DG power above 40% of its nominal value [9].

From their analysis, it has been proved that a continuous and constant power is provided at two points, namely the load, together with the Point of Intersection with Common Coupling (PCC) [10]. Numerous variations of DC-DC-based converter topologies have been explored and compared in this paper. Initially, the authors Rashid [11] and Mengi et al. [12] discussed different DC-DC converters which are placed across each source of energy in parallel. Various independent converters are attached at an intersection point with common coupling, which ultimately is joined with a controller, purely independently. Major drawbacks of having such a type of system may arise due to problems such as being bulky, less efficient, having a large cumulative count of components, higher fare and complexity because of several stages involved in the converter [13,14]. Additionally, a requirement for individual controllers with a DC bus, common to all the controllers in every stage of conversion, leads to a system being disordered and having an increased cumulative weight. Shrivastava et al. [15] and Ayang et al. [16] have preferred mainly multi-input DC-DC converters to interface the number of storage devices and additional input sources of energy with the use of a primary power conversion arena with minimal part count and easier control.

A Non-isolated Three-Port DC–DC Converter with continuous input and output currents is based on Cuk topology, accommodating a PV cell and Fuel Cell [17]. A wind-electric system with a permanent magnet alternator, DC-DC buck-Boost or Cuk converter, diode rectifier, and a three-phase five-level inverter has appeared for a combined harmonic reduction and DC voltage regulation [18]. A substitute for the energy source that has made a lot of progress is the fuel cell. A proton exchange membrane fuel cell needs a DC-DC boost converter as an interface between the fuel cell and the load to give large-gain regulated voltage [19]. A new hybrid flyback-Cuk converter with a single switch, a single isolated input and dual output based on flyback and Cuk topologies has been discussed in [20] for reduced switching losses. An isolated power-factor-corrected Cuk converter for brushless DC ceiling fan applications is proposed in [21]. The Cuk converter operates in continuous conduction mode, wherein the current multiplier control loop ensures a near-unity power factor and a low total harmonic distortion in the current. The current loop also provides over-current protection, enhancing the reliability of the system [21]. Neeraj et al. have evaluated the performance of solar-PV-based switched-capacitor high-step-up and non-isolated switched-inductor Cuk converters. [22]. The topologies implemented in this work have improved boosting ability compared to conventional Cuk and boost converters with lower voltage stress of the main switch. High conversion gain is needed for the grid integration of RES, like PV, fuel cells and wind. The combination of Cuk converters and voltage-multiplier units is provided and the converter utilizes a boost converter to give input to the Cuk converter, resulting in a rise in the gain value [23].

The whale optimization algorithm is applied for the tuned Interleaved Luo Converter for the PV-array-fed BLDC motor driving centrifugal pumps. This is carried out when retrieving the generated power from the PV array using a positive interleaved Luo converter that boosts the output with low switching losses. [24]. The algorithm tunes the parameters of the PI controller to maintain the steady-state voltage at the output of the Luo converter. Chincholkar et al. have designed and analyzed a voltage mode non-linear control of a non-minimum-phase positive output elementary Luo converter. [25]. Gholizadeh et al.

implemented single-switch step-up DC-DC converters based on cascaded boost and Luo converters [26].

As per the report of the author [27], a brief estimation of different components involved between conventional separate SEPIC, Cuk and Cuk-SEPIC fused converter has been presented. The efficiency obtained of conventional and proposed converters were 80% and 96%, respectively. The efficiency obtained of improved Cuk-buck and Cuk-buck converters [28] were 92.69% and 83.38%, respectively. However, buck and SEPIC converters have a pulsating output current which needs a current handling capability. To reduce ripple voltage and current, Luo-type converters are usually employed [29,30].

In this paper, a primary dual input Cuk-Luo integrated-type converter employing an efficient solar-wind-battery system has been proposed, with the aim of addressing the performance gap faced in the Cuk converter and Luo converter individually. The converter presented here makes it feasible to employ dual-input solar-wind sources for sending power towards the load simultaneously or individually for making the conversion of energy with an increased performance.

For any renewable type of energy system with a hybrid mode, it is recommended to employ a sharp power management controller for the integration of cumulative elements of storage and sources of energy [31]. This literature focuses on a dedicated controller in order to manage the various inputs for consumption and investigate the power flow in the direction towards the load from the source [32,33].

The remaining portions of the paper are culminated as follows. Firstly, the primary structure of the converter system is presented, followed by descriptions of each block, namely, the various sources, operating modes and the controller in itself for energy management in the proposed system. These details are put forward in the second and third parts. The next section discusses the various results obtained from the simulation of the designed topology. The brief descriptions of the hardware are presented in fifth section, following which, the observations and findings of the investigations will be highlighted in the conclusion section.

2. Block Diagram

As described in the previous section, we begin with the proposition of a block diagram for the proposed solar-wind energy sources powered primarily by a Cuk-Luo integrated DC-DC converter having an inbuilt embedded controller used for applications such as powering telecom load, as presented in Figure 1.

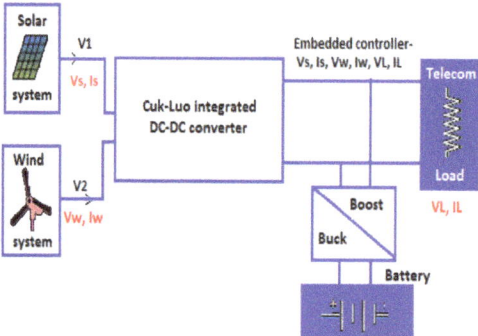

Figure 1. Overview and Block diagram of the proposed system.

The above-stated system is physically composed with solar-wind hybrid energy sources [34], Cuk-Luo integrated type converters and energy management and storage systems for controlling the duty cycle, as seen from the various input sources. These solar-wind-type energy sources are attached together in a parallel configuration by means of Cuk-Luo integrated into a converter for multiple purposes, namely, to power the battery in case of excess energy being generated and to power the load. Luo and Cuk converters are joined together in order to produce an efficient integrated converter.

The common components of Luo- and Cuk-based converters are joined among them. In case of any viability of wind and solar energy sources being available, energy is given to the load individually or altogether. Once the inability to meet the power expectation is found on the sources, the battery makes up for it as a compensation. Moreover, the selection of the battery is involved if it is able power the load by itself, lasting at least a day. Energy management using an embedded-based controller is achieved through regulating current together with the voltage, with the help of sources back to the load [35,36].

3. System Blueprint

3.1. Wind and Solar System

The sizes of Cuk-Luo segregated converters together with the solar-wind energy system have to determined based on mean day-to-day energy utilization by the BTS load. For the present situation, a solar panel comprising of a 53 V /22 A /1125 W rating is used.

Table 1 comprises various electrical parameters whose considerations are necessary for developing the solar storage source having an insolation of 1000 W/m^2 and a temperature around 29 °C. The cumulative equation describing the I-V characteristics comprising of a single solar cell is shown below:

$$I = I_{pv} - I_o \left[\exp\left(\frac{q.V}{n.k.T}\right) - 1 \right], \quad (1)$$

where

q—Charge of the electron (1.602×10^{-19} C)
k—Boltzman constant (1.3806×10^{-23} J/K)
T—Temperature present in p-n junction
n—Constant for Diode ideality
I_{PV}—Incident sunlight current
I_0—Shockley diode equation.

Table 1. Major electrical constraints of the solar system.

S.No	Solar Constraints	Gain
1	Voltage present at highest power	53 V
2	Current present at highest power	22 A
3	Reference temperature	60 °C
4	Voc, open circuit voltage	52.8 V
5	Isc, short circuit current	21 A

Among the different systems, wind-type storage has values of 323 V /3 A /1260 W. Table 2 corresponds to the electrical constraints that make up a wind system with the speed of 12 m/s. A primitive system comprises of a permanent magnet synchronous generator (PMSG), which is coupled to a wind turbine of a suitable head, together with a rectification staged circuit. Cumulative wind power (Pm), which is derived from the head of the turbine, can be obtained from the formula [2],

$$P_m = \frac{1}{2}.C_p.(\lambda,\beta).\rho.A.w^3, \quad (2)$$

where

Cp—Turbine's coefficient of performance
P—Density of air(kg/m^3)
A—Coverage of turbine blades (m^3)

w—Velocity of the wind (m/s)
λ—Ratio of tip speed on the rotor blade tip
β—Blade pitch angle (deg).

Table 2. Electrical parameters of the wind system.

S.No	Solar Parameters	Values
1	Wind speed	12 m/s
2	Voltage present at highest power	323 V
3	Current present at highest power	3 A
4	Type of DC Machine	PMSM
5	Maximum power	1260 W

Based on Equations (1) and (2), Simulink modelling of solar cell and wind system was carried out and Figure 2a,b show the solar power, voltage and current, and the wind power, voltage, and current, respectively [37,38].

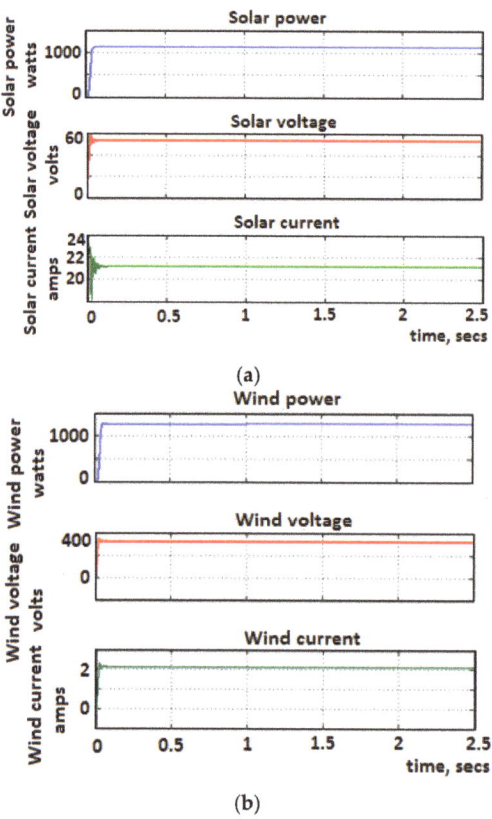

Figure 2. (a) Solar power, voltage and current. (b) Wind power, voltage and current.

3.2. Cuk-Luo Integrated Converter

The Cuk-Luo integrated converter circuit used in the application of telecom-load powering with the help of the solar-wind system is presented in Figure 3. As shown, it utilizes both Luo and Cuk converters. The Cuk converter has a regulation method for stepping down, making it feasible in minimal-voltage-rating systems such as BTS.

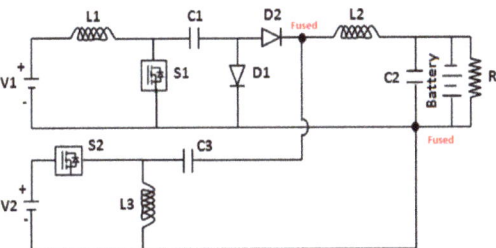

Figure 3. Circuit topology with the Cuk-Luo integrated converter.

The current, together with voltage, of different functional modes of given Cuk-Luo converters is presented in Figure 4. The relationship existing among voltages, the output and the input for the proposed Cuk-Luo-integrated-based converter can be obtained with the notion of utilizing volt-second balance on the coils L_1, L_2 and L_3. Coil L_1 shows that

$$V_1 - (1-d_1).(V_{C_1}) = 0, \qquad (3)$$

when applied to coil L_3,

$$-d_1.(1-d_2).V_{C_1} + (1-d_2).(V_{C_1}) + d_2.V_2 = 0, \qquad (4)$$

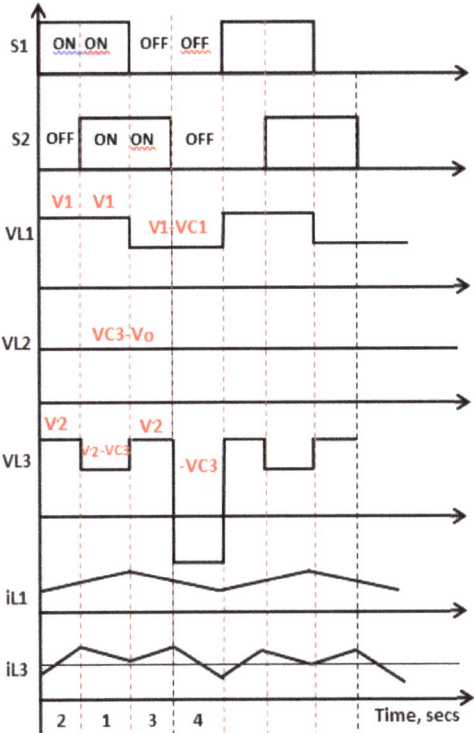

Figure 4. Various functional modes.

On inductor L_2,
$$-V_{C_2} + V_{C_1} = 0. \quad (5)$$

By shuffling the various Formulas (3)–(5), the equation is obtained for the output voltage,

$$V_0 = V_{C_1} = \left(\left(\frac{d_1}{1-d_1}\right).V_1\right) - \left(\left(\frac{d_2}{1-d_2}\right).V_2\right), \quad (6)$$

where

V_1—Solar system voltage
V_2—Wind system voltage
d_1—Duty cycle 1 (switch S_1)
d_2—Duty cycle 2 (switch S_2).

Figures 5a,b and 6a,b and Table 3 show real-time working demonstrations of different Cuk-Luo converter modes with energy sources of solar-wind systems [39,40].

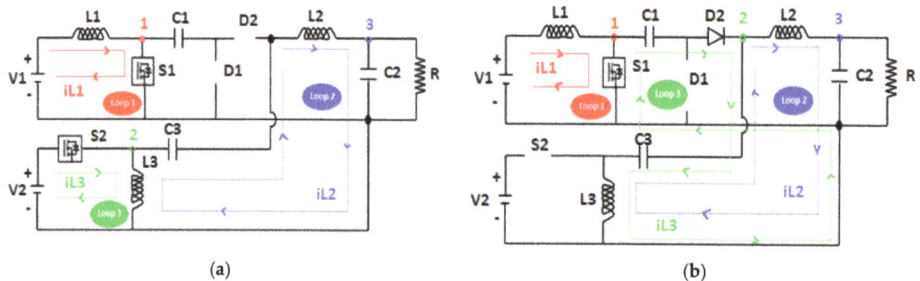

Figure 5. (a) S1, S2-ON; (b) S1-ON, S2- OFF.

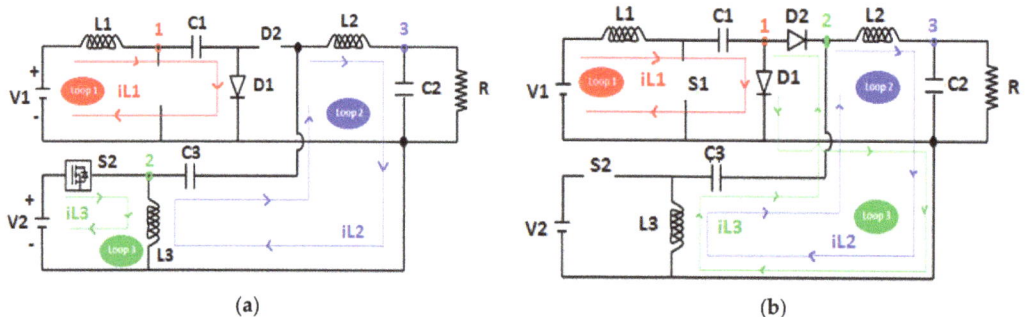

Figure 6. (a) S_1-OFF, S_2- ON; (b) S_1, S_2- OFF.

Table 3. Demonstration of different modes.

Modes	Switch		V_{L1}	V_{L2}	V_{L3}
	Sw_1	Sw_2			
1	ON	ON	V_1	V_{C3}-V_o	V_2
2	ON	OFF	V_1	V_{C3}-V_o	V_2-V_{C3}
3	OFF	ON	V_1-V_{C1}	V_{C3}-V_o	V_2
4	OFF	OFF	V_1-V_{C1}	V_{C3}-V_o	-V_{C3}

Figure 5a shows the equivalent circuit of (Sw_1-ON, Sw_2-ON). In this mode, solar power (V_1) generates the necessary charge on coil L_1, together with the wind voltage (V_2), which in turn charges coil L_3. As soon as both the switches reach conduction mode, rectifiers D_1, D_2 should be in reverse conduction mode. Stored charge in the coil L_3 is brought back to the load by the battery and charge capacitor C_2.

Figure 5b corresponds to the cumulative circuit with Sw_1- ON, Sw_2-OFF. By the medium of the above image, it can be comprehended that the rectifier D_2 is in forward conduction, whereas D_1 is in reverse conduction. Primary solar source (V_1) powers the coil L_1 and the stored energy at capacitor C_1; coils L_3 and L_2 are transferred to the battery and charge capacitor C_2, which in turn feeds the telecom load.

Figure 6a corresponds to the cumulative circuit with Sw_1- OFF, and Sw_2-ON. By the medium of the above image, it can be comprehended that the rectifier D_1 is in forward conduction, whereas D_2 is in reverse conduction. In addition to this, the energy in coil L_1 powers the capacitor C_1. The other system, namely the wind, powers coil L_3. The energy stored in L_2 in turn powers the charge capacitor C_2, thereby feeding the load by means of a battery.

The equivalent circuit of Sw_1, Sw_2-OFF is represented in Figure 6b. As both the switches are in the OFF position, the diodes D_1, and D_2 are in forward conduction mode. For this mode, the energy stored in coil L_1 can be utilized for charging C_1. Energy stored in coils L_3 and L_2 in turn power the battery and the charge capacitor C_2 directed to feed the load.

The power dissipation of the proposed Cuk-Luo converter is 1164 watts and the power obtained is 1200 watts. Therefore, the efficiency is calculated as 97%. The efficiency of conventional Cuk and SEPIC separate converters and the proposed Cuk-SEPIC fused converter are 80% and 96%, respectively [16]. The efficiency of Cuk-buck and improved Cuk-buck converters [17] are 83.38% and 92.69%, respectively. Thus, it can be concluded that the Cuk-Luo fused converter is more efficient.

3.3. Embedded Controller Design Procedure for the Cuk-Luo Integrated Converter

The detailed logic flow chart is shown in Figure 7.

Figure 7. Detailed logic of proposed embedded-based controller.

For the present system, the smart controller with power management gathers the instantaneous current (battery current I_B, state of charge SOC, I_S, I_W), together with the voltage (V_W, battery voltage V_B, V_S) of numerous sources of inputs. According to the gathered data, controller signals choose the duty cycle width gate pulses (d_S, d_W), discharging and charging battery duty cycles (dbc, dbd). It is utilized for developing intersections with voltages at a common coupling $V_{PCC} = -48V$, as per Equations (7) and (8) for wind and solar energy sources,

$$d_{Sref} = \frac{V_{PCC} - V_S}{V_{PCC}} \qquad (7)$$

and

$$d_{Wref} = \frac{V_{PCC} - V_W}{V_{PCC}} \qquad (8)$$

where

V_{PCC}—Common coupling voltage

V_S—Cuk converter input voltage when connected to the solar system

V_W—Luo converter input voltage when connected to the wind system.

For any deviation in the V_{pcc} from -48 V, the input sources connected to the converter are aligned through the correction of duty cycles. As soon as V_{pcc} is assigned with -48 V, the controller estimates the load current with the directed wind and solar input currents. If the input current is lower than the load current, the I_{bcref} becomes congruent with the excess power available at V_{pcc} and it is estimated as follows.

$$(I_{Sref} + I_{wref}) - I_L = I_{Bcref}, \qquad (9)$$

where

I_{Sref}—Reference solar current

I_{Wref}—Reference wind current

I_L—Load voltage

I_{BCref}—Reference battery charging current.

Once we reach the BC phase, the energy needed for the load becomes lesser than the extracted energy, which in turn leads to power delivery at the receiving end of VO up to VH. Post reaching VH, excess extracted residual energy can be used to power the battery by means of an integral-based charging method, which powers the battery until the current in the coil is exhausted.

As soon as the generated power becomes insufficient enough to direct it to the receiving end, the battery drains with its duty cycle of d_{bd}. The design of the controller makes its discharge possible only if the SOC (state of charge) is found to be above 40%. The calculation for the discharging reference current is

$$I_L - (I_{Sref} + I_{Wref}) = I_{Bdref}, \qquad (10)$$

where:

I_{Bcref}—Reference battery discharging current.

Even after this demand at the receiving end is large, the load should be taken off from the supply.

3.3.1. Battery Specifications

The SOC (state of charge) with a 24 V charging and discharging battery method is found from the battery current and voltage (battery hand book).

Table 4a,b show the voltage present at the end of different discharging and charging currents for a lead acid battery with a terminal voltage of 24 V. The SOC is estimated using the formula

$$SOC = \left(\frac{(B-A).(V-V_1)}{(V_2 - V_1)} + C \right), \qquad (11)$$

where

V—Voltage of the battery

C—Capacity of the battery

V_1—Values of voltage being lesser than the terminal or end voltage for each column with a current value

V_2—Values of voltage being higher than the terminal or end voltage for each column with a current value

A—V_1 row SOC reference

B—V_2 row SOC reference.

In addition, the determination of the state of charge while discharging can be estimated from the discharge data using the above-mentioned procedure.

Table 4. (**a**) Battery charging currents; (**b**) battery discharging currents.

(a)				
	At Charging			
SOC	Voltage at (C/15)	Voltage at (C/30)	Voltage at (C/50)	Voltage at (C/75)
10	22.5	22	21.4	21
20	22.32	22.21	22.1	22
30	22.63	22.4	22.3	22.2
40	22.92	22.5	22.45	22.42
50	23.98	23.25	23.2	23.1
60	23.52	23.5	23.4	23.3
70	23.74	23.63	23.61	23.5
80	24	23.9	23.7	23.6
90	24.24	24.13	24.12	24.24
100	24.46	24.2	24.15	24.1

(b)					
	At discharging				
SOC	Voltage at (C/15)	Voltage at (C/30)	Voltage at (C/50)	Voltage at (C/75)	Voltage at (C/150)
10	24	22.6	21.23	21.22	21.2
20	23.2	22.82	22.8	22.7	22
30	23.3	23.2	23	22.9	22.4
40	23.6	23.4	23.3	23.2	22.6
50	23.7	23.5	23.4	23.3	22.8
60	24.2	23.9	23.6	23.5	22.9
70	24.4	24.4	24.2	23.9	23
80	24.8	24.45	24.3	24.2	23.2
90	25	24.6	24.4	24.3	23.3
100	25.2	24.8	24.5	23.4	23.6

3.3.2. Battery Operation

The modes of operation for any devices utilized as a storage medium (battery) is discussed as follows. The net energy of the proposed system is the difference among load demand in any instant of time and the net output energy.

$$E_{net}(t) = E_g(t) - E_L(t), \qquad (12)$$

where

$E_{net}(t)$—Net energy generated
$E_g(t)$—Energy generated through renewable energy sources
$E_L(t)$—Estimated load demand.

Mode 1

In this mode, the energy level of the battery bank is equal to its previous hour energy level as the net energy developed from wind-solar hybrid medium can be estimated to be zero.

The estimated load can be supplied by the previous hour energy stored in the battery.

$$E_{\text{supplied Load}}(t) = E_{disch}(t), \qquad (13)$$

where

$E_{\text{Load supplied}}(t)$—Load supplied
$E_{disch}(t)$—Battery discharging energy.

Mode 2

For this mode, the cumulative input energy extracted from the wind-solar hybrid system can be found to be greater than the total power demand. The excess energy $E_{ch}(t)$ generated to power the battery through buck converter (Figure 1) is.

$$E_{ch}(t) = E_g(t) - E_L(t), \qquad (14)$$

where

$E_{ch}(t)$—Battery charging energy.

Mode 3

If the energy generated by the wind-solar hybrid medium exceeds the load demand and the largest battery storage, this leads to a greater energy being disposed through the dump load.

Mode 4

In this mode, the output energy extracted from solar-wind hybrid medium can be insufficient in order to feed the required demand of load; then the battery power is compensated for supplying power through the boost converter (Figure 1). It is written as

$$E_{ch}(t) = E_L(t) - E_g(t). \qquad (15)$$

Mode 5

For this mode, the output energy extracted from hybrid solar-wind systems is lesser than the battery energy level and the load demand is at the lowest level; then the load is disconnected.

4. Simulation Results and Discussion

Analysis for the designated integrated Cuk-Luo-based converter is analyzed using simulation from MATLAB.

MATLAB simulation for the proposed circuit is carried out using the constraints L_1 of 158 µH, L_2 of 1808 µH, L_3 of 158 µH, C_1 of 1389 µF, C_2 of 1545 µF, C_3 of 407 µF, R=1.32 Ω and a switching frequency of 20 kHz to analyze the system. The generated power was obtained from the regulation parameters of 48 V/23 A/1.2 kW. Figure 8 shows the output current and voltage from the waveforms of the Cuk-Luo DC-DC converter powering the telecom load.

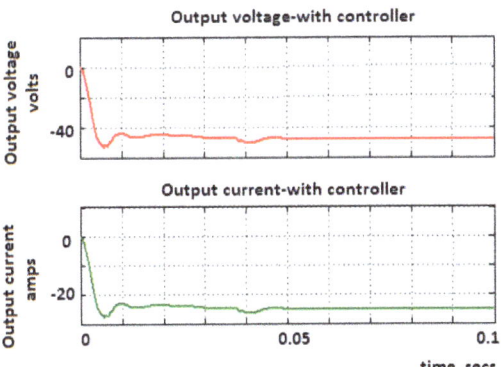

Figure 8. Final output voltage and current.

Figure 9 depicts the highest current and voltage from the S_1 and S_2 switching device. Conduction losses and switching losses from switches Sw_1 and Sw_2 are estimated from 100 W and 1.48 W, and 30 W and 0.007 W, respectively. The copper losses of the coils L_1, L_2 and L_3 and storage capacitors C_1, C_2 and C_3 are found as 5.52 W, 4.69 W, 0.24 W and 123 W, 26.8 W, 26.85 W, respectively.

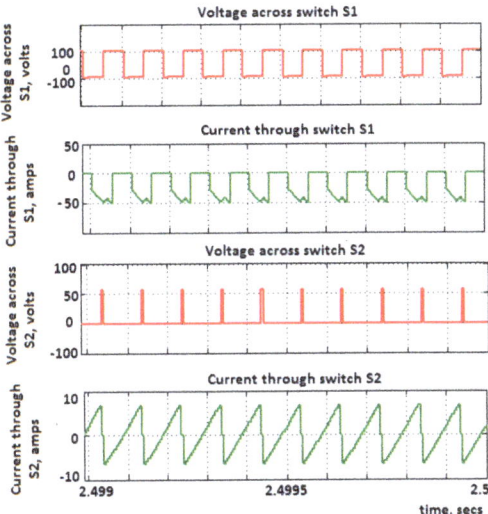

Figure 9. Final switch voltages and currents of S_1 and S_2.

Figure 10a,b give the voltage across the capacitors C_1 and C_3 and coils L_1, L_2 and L_3. The performance of the Cuk-Luo-based converter can be estimated to be 91%. Thus, the integrated converter implemented from wind-solar mediums have a higher level of performance. The SOC estimation, battery current and voltage can be measured from the embedded-based controller.

Figure 11a depicts the estimated waveforms obtained from the designed controller. Using the current from the battery, the excess power obtained can be reverted back to the battery from the opposite direction. For duty cycles d_S, d_W, dbc and dbd, the controller performances are shown in Figure 11b.

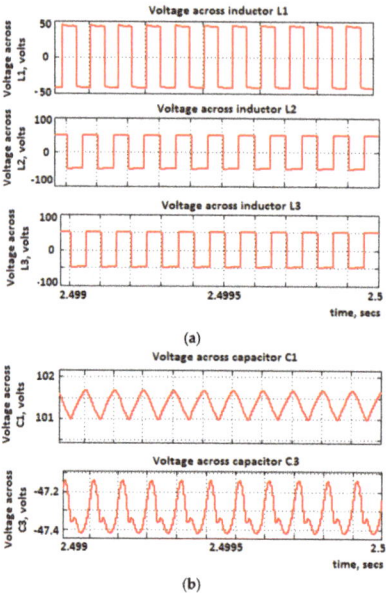

Figure 10. (a) Voltage across inductors L_1, L_2 and L_3; (b) voltage across capacitors C_1 and C_3.

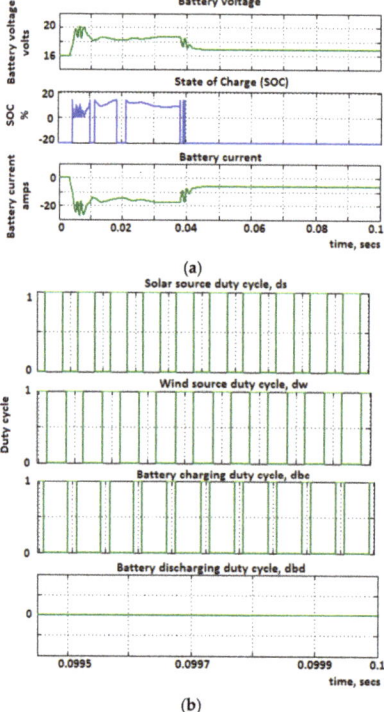

Figure 11. (a) Battery voltage, final SOC and battery current; (b) final duty cycles.

5. Prototype Implementation

The prototype model for the given integrated Cuk-Luo-based converter has been designed utilizing a FPGA controller with a couple of DC sources. Table 5 depicts the numerical values utilized for the implementation process for Cuk-Luo topology. The low-key pulses manifested through the FPGA controller can be utilized as a trigger for MOSFET-type switches. Figure 12 depicts the prototype design for the Cuk-Luo integrated strategy utilizing a FPGA controller.

Table 5. Hardware component values.

Elements Involved in Hardware		
Coil (Inductor)	L_1	140 µH
	L_2	420 µH
	L_3	480 µH
Charging Capacitors	C_1	300 µf
	C_2	330 µf
	C_3	330 µf
Load	DC	100 watts
Input DC sources	V_1	54 V
	V_2	55 V
Frequency		20 kHz

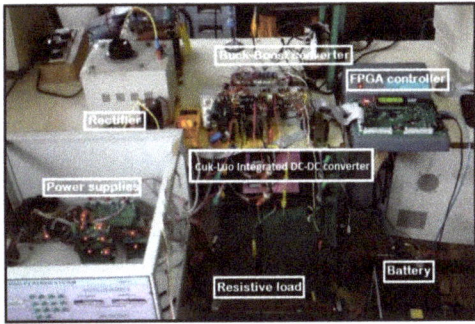

Figure 12. Demonstration of the hardware setup of the Cuk-Luo converter having variable DC input sources.

Field Programmable Gate Arrays (FPGA) and Cyclone-IV EEP4CE0F484 were known to be reprogrammable logic devices and majorly flexible. As demonstrations of peripherals and processors, Xilinx FPGAs suggests they are completely user-programmable.

The proposed embedded controller for the Cuk-Luo converter is implemented utilizing a ML605 controller board along with a XC6VLX240T-1FFG1156 array. It gives the gate arrays with an option of being linked with the Simulink mode. Hardware demonstration is developed to approve the overall structure on the ML605 controller with the XC6VLX240T-1FFG1156 array. Running the board onto the PC will close the loop. The Xilinx ISE application gives the file in bit format which can be loaded to the required array by means of connection using JTAG.

In the present literature, pulses from the gate are obtained from the FPGA-based controller array. It has an undue advantage of a higher efficiency at a reasonable rate of economy. The input voltages are maintained at V_1 = 54 V and V_2 = 55 V. Figure 13a depicts the hardware results of the output voltage and current. The measured voltage and current from the hardware are 48 V and 2.18 A, respectively. Figure 13b presents the switching pulses of Sw_1 and Sw_2. Figure 14 depicts the battery current and voltage. It can be noted that the obtained battery voltage and current is 22.9 V and 4.68 A, respectively.

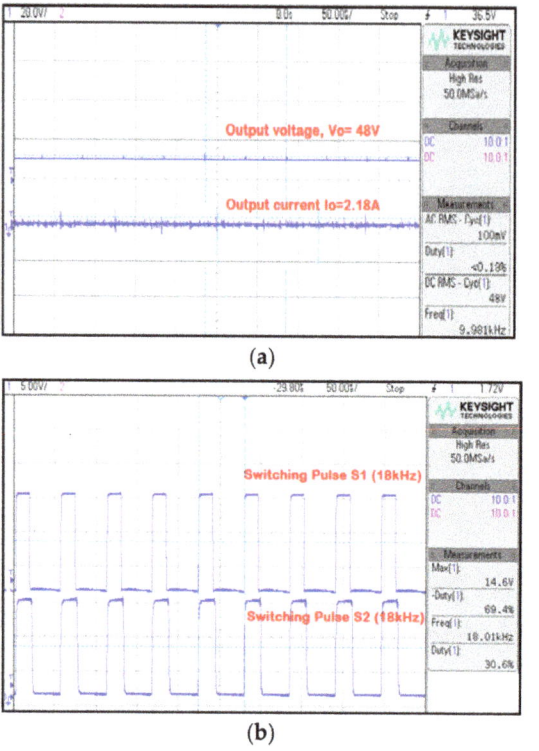

Figure 13. (a) Output voltage and output current; (b) switching pulses.

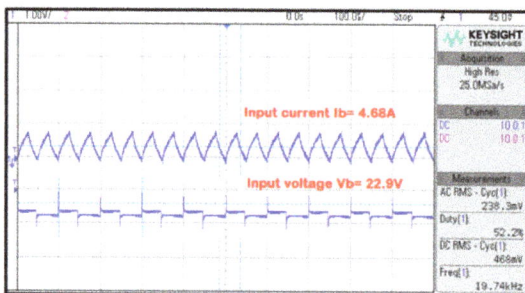

Figure 14. Battery current and voltage.

From Figure 15, it is clear that the input currents are 2.65 A and 4.17 A and the output current is 4.17 A. Therefore, the cumulative remaining current can be employed for powering the battery, which gives a current of 2.07 A.

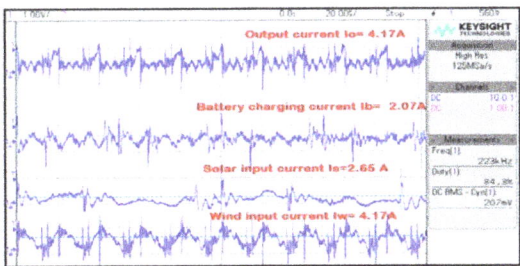

Figure 15. Battery charging current.

6. Conclusions

An integrated Cuk-Luo DC-DC-based converter network having hybrid solar-wind energy system for applications of telecom network powering is verified and proposed in the present literature. It should be able to supply the load independently or simultaneously, based on the presence of any input energy sources. Resulting circuits offer a comparatively lower cost since it gives increased performance at reduced component parts. The management of energy has been programmed using the algorithm in order to consistently make the power at equal levels from the PCC point, which in turn leads to making the reference currents regulate, depending upon the instantaneous power which can be supplied by load and source requirements. Any storage device such as a battery can be used as a backup for the present work. Instantaneous determination of the state of charge, discharging and charging of batteries directed to a known sink or source of the power input, which can be based on the load demand, is presented.

Author Contributions: Conceptualization, B.S.N. and M.C.; methodology, B.S.N.; software, M.C.; validation, S.T., A.A.A.A. and B.S.N.; formal analysis, S.T. and M.A.; investigation, A.A.A.A., and M.A.; resources, M.A.M.; data curation, S.T.; writing—original draft preparation, B.S.N.; writing—review and editing, M.C.; visualization, M.A.M.; supervision, M.A.K.; project administration, M.A.K.; funding acquisition, A.A.A.A. and M.A. All authors have read and agreed to the published version of the manuscript.

Funding: Taif University Researchers Supporting Project number (TURSP-2020/121), Taif University.

Data Availability Statement: Not applicable.

Acknowledgments: The authors would like to acknowledge the support received by Taif University Researchers Supporting Project number (TURSP-2020/121), Taif University, Taif, Saudi Arabia.

Conflicts of Interest: The authors declare no conflict of interest.

References

1. Naziruddin, N.; Abdurahman, F.; Radhiah, R.; Maimun, M.; Bakar, S.A. Design and Implementation of Substitution Power Supply at Base Transceiver Station (BTS) Using Hybrid Distributed Generator Wind Turbine and Solar Cell Powers. *Sci. J. PPI-UKM* **2017**, *4*, 70–75.
2. Ahmed, F.; Naeem, M.; Ejaz, W.; Iqbal, M.; Anpalagan, A.; Kim, H.S. Renewable Energy Assisted Traffic Aware Cellular Base Station Energy Cooperation. *Energies* **2018**, *11*, 99. [CrossRef]
3. Bhattacharya, D.; Kumar, T. Modeling and Control of a Solar/Wind Hybrid Energy System for BTS. *Int. J. Appl. Eng. Res.* **2014**, *9*, 11621–11630.
4. Kumar, K.S.; Bhaskar, G.; Raghaveder, C. Power Management of Cell Sites. *Int. Refereed J. Eng. Sci. (IRJES)* **2013**, *2*, 41–45.
5. Hossam, K.; Mikhail, A.R.; Hafez, I.M.; Anis, W.R. Optimum Design of PV Systems for BTS in Remote and Urban Areas. *Int. J. Sci. Technol. Res.* **2016**, *5*, 1–9.
6. Joga Rao, G.; Shrivastava, S.K.; Ranjith, V.L. Analysis and simulation of hybrid solar- wind renewable energy systems. *Int. J. Innov. Res. Electr. Electron. Instrum. Control Eng.* **2016**, *4*, 33–38.
7. Pandiyan, P.; Sitharthan, R.; Saravanan, S.; Prabaharan, N.; Ramji Tiwari, M.; Chinnadurai, T.; Yuvaraj, T.; Devabalaji, K.R. A comprehensive review of the prospects for rural electrification using stand-alone and hybrid energy technologies. *Sustain. Energy Technol. Assess.* **2022**, *52*, 102155. [CrossRef]

8. Manikandan, A.; Vadivel, N. Design and implementation of luo converter for electric vehicle applications. *Int. J. Eng. Trends Technol. (IJETT)* **2013**, *4*, 4437–4441.
9. Taylor, P.; Aravind, C.K.; Ilango, G.S.; Nagamani, C.; Jaya Bharata Reddy, M. A control strategy for hybrid autonomous power system with a battery management scheme. *Electr. Power Compon. Syst.* **2015**, *43*, 37–41.
10. He, Y.; Luo, F.L. Analysis of Luo converters with voltage-lift circuit. *IEEE Proc. -Electr. Power Appl.* **2005**, *152*, 1239–1252. [CrossRef]
11. Rashid, M.H. *Power Electronics Handbook*; Butterworth-Heinemann: Oxford, UK, 2017.
12. Mengi, O.O.; Altas, I.H. A New energy management technique for PV/wind/grid renewable energy system. *Int. J. Photo Energy Hindawi Publ. Corp.* **2015**, *2015*, 1–20. [CrossRef]
13. Almi, M.F.; Arrouf, M.; Belmili, H.; Boulouma, S.; Bendib, B. Energy management of wind/PV and battery hybrid system. *Int. J. New Comput. Archit. Appl. (IJNCAA)* **2014**, *4*, 30–38. [CrossRef]
14. Zarrad, O.; Hajjaji, M.A.; Jemaa, A.; Mansouri, M.N. Sizing Control and Hardware Implementation of a Hybrid Wind-Solar Power System, Based on an ANN Approach, for Pumping Water. *Int. J. Photo Energy Hindawi Publ. Corp.* **2019**, *2019*, 1–15. [CrossRef]
15. Shrivastava, A.; Calhoun, B.H. Modelling DC-DC converter efficiency and power management in ultralow power systems. In Proceedings of the IEEE Subthreshold Microelectronics Conference (SubVT), Waltham, MA, USA, 9–10 October 2012; pp. 1–3.
16. Ayang, A.; Ngohe-Ekam, P.S.; Videme, B.; Temga, J. Power consumption: Base stations of telecommunication in sahel zone of cameroon: Typology based on the power consumption—Model and energy savings. *J. Energy Hindawi Publ. Corp.* **2016**, *2016*, 3161060. [CrossRef]
17. Chandrasekar, B.; Nallaperumal, C.; Dash, S.S. A nonisolated three-port DC–DC converter with continuous input and output currents based on Cuk topology for PV/fuel cell applications. *Electronics* **2019**, *8*, 214. [CrossRef]
18. Thayumanavan, P.; Kaliyaperumal, D.; Subramaniam, U.; Bhaskar, M.S.; Padmanaban, S.; Leonowicz, Z.; Mitolo, M. Combined Harmonic Reduction and DC Voltage Regulation of A Single DC Source Five-Level Multilevel Inverter for Wind Electric System. *Electronics* **2020**, *9*, 979. [CrossRef]
19. Alavi, O.; Rajabloo, T.; De Ceuninck, W.; Daenen, M. Non-Isolated DC-DC Converters in Fuel Cell Applications: Thermal Analysis and Reliability Comparison. *Appl. Sci.* **2022**, *12*, 5026. [CrossRef]
20. Mahafzah, K.A.; Obeidat, M.A.; Al-Shetwi, A.Q.; Ustun, T.S. A Novel Synchronized Multiple Output DC-DC Converter Based on Hybrid Flyback-Cuk Topologies. *Batteries* **2022**, *8*, 93. [CrossRef]
21. Khan, H.R.; Kazmi, M.; Ashraf, H.B.; Hashir Bin Khalid, M.; Hasan, A.; Qazi, S.A. An Isolated Power Factor Corrected Cuk Converter with Integrated Magnetics for Brushless DC Ceiling Fan Applications. *Electronics* **2021**, *10*, 1720. [CrossRef]
22. Priyadarshi, N.; Bhaskar, M.S.; Azam, F.; Singh, M.; Dhaked, D.K.; Taha, I.B.; Hussien, M.G. Performance Evaluation of Solar-PV-Based Non-Isolated Switched-Inductor and Switched-Capacitor High-Step-Up Cuk Converter. *Electronics* **2022**, *11*, 1381. [CrossRef]
23. Haider, Z.; Ulasyar, A.; Khattak, A.; Zad, H.S.; Mohammad, A.; Alahmadi, A.A.; Ullah, N. Development and Analysis of a Novel High-Gain CUK Converter Using Voltage-Multiplier Units. *Electronics* **2022**, *11*, 2766. [CrossRef]
24. Jegha, A.; Darcy, G.M.S.P.; Nallapaneni, M.K.S.; Ghosh, A. Optimally tuned interleaved Luo converter for PV array fed BLDC motor driven centrifugal pumps using whale optimization algorithm—A resilient solution for powering agricultural loads. *Electronics* **2020**, *9*, 1445. [CrossRef]
25. Chincholkar, S.H.; Malge, S.V.; Patil, S.L. Design and analysis of a voltage-mode non-linear control of a non-minimum-phase positive output elementary Luo converter. *Electronics* **2022**, *11*, 207. [CrossRef]
26. Gholizadeh, H.; Shahrivar, R.S.; Hashemi, M.R.; Afjei, E.; Gorji, S.A. Design and implementation a single-switch step-up DC-DC converter based on cascaded boost and luo converters. *Energies* **2021**, *14*, 3584. [CrossRef]
27. Margaret Amutha, W.; Harshini, H.; Rajini, V. A new green energy interface for telecommunications. *Int. J. Electron.* **2018**, *105*, 1831–1854. [CrossRef]
28. Amutha, W.; Margaret, V.R.; Rajini, V. A novel parallel power conversion technique for efficiency improvement in hybrid DC/DC converter based rural telephony. In Proceedings of the 2013 International Conference on Renewable Energy and Sustainable Energy (ICRESE), Coimbatore, India, 5–6 December 2013; IEEE: Piscataway, NJ, USA, 2013; pp. 64–69.
29. Roumila, Z.; Rekioua, D.; Rekioua, T. Energy management based fuzzy logic controller of hybrid system wind/photovoltaic/diesel with storage battery. *Int. J. Hydrog. Energy* **2017**, *42*, 19525–19535. [CrossRef]
30. Bendary, A.F.; Ismail, M.M. M. Battery Charge Management for Hybrid PV/Wind/Fuel Cell with Storage Battery. *Energy Procedia* **2019**, *162*, 107–116. [CrossRef]
31. Schimpe, M.; Becker, N.; Lahlou, T.; Holger, C.; Hesse, A.J. Energy efficiency evaluation of grid connection scenarios for stationary battery energy storage systems. *Energy Procedia* **2018**, *155*, 77–101. [CrossRef]
32. Ibrahim, H.; Anani, N. Variations of PV module parameters with irradiance and temperature. *Energy Procedia* **2017**, *134*, 276–285. [CrossRef]
33. Chong, L.W.; Wong, Y.W.; Rajkumar, R.K.; Isa, D. Modelling and Simulation of Standalone PV Systems with Battery super capacitor Hybrid Energy Storage System for a Rural Household. *Energy Procedia* **2016**, *107*, 232–236. [CrossRef]
34. Barta, G.; Pasztor, B.; Prava, V. Optimized Charge Controller Schedule in Hybrid Solar-Battery Farms for Peak Load Reduction. *Energies* **2021**, *14*, 7794. [CrossRef]

35. Munzke, N.; Schwarz, B.; Hiller, M. Intelligent control of household Li-ion battery storage systems. *Energy Procedia* **2018**, *155*, 17–31. [CrossRef]
36. Gajewski, P.; Pieńkowski, K. Control of the Hybrid Renewable Energy System with Wind Turbine, Photovoltaic Panels and Battery Energy Storage. *Energies* **2021**, *14*, 1595. [CrossRef]
37. Znaczko, P.; Szczepanski, E.; Kaminski, K.; Chamier-Gliszczynski, N.; Kukulski, J. Experimental diagnosis of the heat pipe solar collector malfunction. A case study. *Energies* **2021**, *14*, 3050. [CrossRef]
38. Tasmin, N.; Farjana, S.H.; Hossain, M.R.; Golder, S.; Parvez Mahmud, M.A. Integration of Solar Process Heat in Industries: A Review. *Clean Technol.* **2022**, *4*, 97–131. [CrossRef]
39. Uzhytchak, M.; Smolková, B.; Lunova, M.; Jirsa, M.; Frtús, A.; Kubinová, Š.; Dejneka, A.; Lunov, O. Iron oxide nanoparticle-induced autophagic flux Is regulated by interplay between p53-mTOR axis and Bcl-2 signaling in hepatic cells. *Cells* **2020**, *9*, 1015. [CrossRef]
40. Jafari, S.; Sohani, A.; Hoseinzadeh, S.; Pourfayaz, F. The 3E Optimal Location Assessment of Flat-Plate Solar Collectors for Domestic Applications in Iran. *Energies* **2022**, *15*, 3589. [CrossRef]

Disclaimer/Publisher's Note: The statements, opinions and data contained in all publications are solely those of the individual author(s) and contributor(s) and not of MDPI and/or the editor(s). MDPI and/or the editor(s) disclaim responsibility for any injury to people or property resulting from any ideas, methods, instructions or products referred to in the content.

Article

Throughput Maximization for the Full-Duplex Two-Way Relay System with Energy Harvesting

Kaiqi Zhong and Liqun Fu *

School of Informatics, Xiamen University, Xiamen 361005, China
* Correspondence: liqun@xmu.edu.cn

Abstract: The full-duplex technique can improve the transmission capacity of the communication systems, and energy harvesting (EH) is a promising operation to prolong the lifespan of a wireless node by utilizing the radio-frequency signals. In this paper, the throughput performance of a full-duplex two-way energy EH capable relay system is investigated. In particular, a practical EH protocol, named the time-switching-based relaying (TSR) protocol, is used for EH and the decode-and-forward (DF) policy for information transmission. The outage probability is successfully obtained, and the corresponding system throughput for TSR protocol can be derived by it. The derived throughput is a function of different system parameters, including the time-switching (TS) ratio, power allocation ratio, and the length of the communication time slot. Meanwhile, the throughput is used to characterize a joint time and power allocation scheme for the system, and we aim to find the optimal time and power allocation to achieve the optimal throughput. Due to the existence of three variables and the integral form of throughput expression, an optimization for the throughput is difficult. However, a modified simulated annealing-based search (SABS) algorithm can be used to optimize the throughput. The modified SABS algorithm overcomes being highly impacted by the initial point, and derives the optimal solution fast. Simulation results show that the analytical throughput expression is related with the TS ratio, power allocation ratio, and the length of the communication time slot. The analytical curve of the throughput matches with the simulated one well, which shows that the obtained analytical system throughput for the TSR protocol is valid. Meanwhile, the proposed modified SABS algorithm could be used to derive accurate throughput when SNR is higher than 10 dB.

Keywords: full-duplex; energy harvesting; throughput; SABS algorithm

---

Citation: Zhong, K.; Fu, L. Throughput Maximization for the Full-Duplex Two-Way Relay System with Energy Harvesting. *Electronics* **2023**, *12*, 16. https://doi.org/10.3390/electronics12010016

Academic Editor: M. Tariq Iqbal

Received: 2 November 2022
Revised: 18 November 2022
Accepted: 24 November 2022
Published: 21 December 2022

Copyright: © 2022 by the authors. Licensee MDPI, Basel, Switzerland. This article is an open access article distributed under the terms and conditions of the Creative Commons Attribution (CC BY) license (https://creativecommons.org/licenses/by/4.0/).

1. Introduction

Energy harvesting (EH), which enables network nodes to obtain energy from the controllable radio-frequency (RF) signal, is a promising technology that could significantly extend the lifespans of wireless networks [1]. Considering EH, although it has been shown that simultaneous energy and information transmission is optimal for using the RF energy in wireless systems [2], it is difficult to be implemented due to the limitation of current circuits. Therefore, a practical receiver protocol, named the time switching-based relaying (TSR) protocol is introduced [3–6]. The TSR protocol allows the relay node to switch either the information processing or the EH for the received RF signals at a time, which can be implemented easier [4].

On the other hand, the full-duplex technique could improve the throughput of communication systems by simultaneously transmitting and receiving signals in the same frequency band [7]. In the two-way relay system, the relay node is key to receive and forward the signal to the destination. If the relay node operates with a full-duplex, the system throughput will be enhanced [8,9]. Therefore, it is of great significance to investigate the full-duplex two-way relay system, where the relay node can perform both EH and full-duplex transmissions.

In this paper, we are interested in the throughput performance of the full-duplex (FD) two-way relay system, where the relay node can use RF signals to harvest energy. The relay node needs to simultaneously perform both full-duplex operation and energy harvesting, and it adopts the TSR protocol and the decode-and-forward (DF) policy for EH and full-duplex transmissions, respectively [10].

2. Related Works

There are a number of works that have considered the relay system and its performance analysis. In [11], though the relay node worked with a half-duplex, the authors presented a generalized approach to the performance analysis of relay-aided communication systems, and an expression of the outage probability that is valid for all fading scenarios. In fact, the outage probability is key to derive the system throughput [3,4,12]. Furthermore, a number of works have considered the full-duplex relay system design without energy harvesting [13,14]. In [13], the outage performance of the full-duplex relay system was investigated. In [14], the full-duplex cooperative cognitive radio network with multiple full-duplex secondary users was analyzed, and the optimal system throughput was derived. Since the EH technique was not used in these works, the system does not need to consider time or power allocation.

With energy harvesting, Refs. [15–17] further investigated the full-duplex relay system with the TSR protocol (TS-FDR-I protocol). In these papers, the system adopted the TSR protocol (TS-FDR-I protocol) so that it could optimize the time allocation to improve its own performance [15–17], and the system also optimized the power allocation for improving system performance [15,17]. In particular, with the TS-FDR-I protocol, the authors in [15] derived the optimal ergodic outage probability by considering different TS ratio, and the authors in [16] derived the optimal system throughput by optimizing the TS ratio. On the other hand, Refs. [15,17] considered the effect of power allocation, and the optimal ergodic outage probability was derived by optimizing the power allocation ratio.

2.1. Motivation

The aforementioned literature focused on the one-way relaying system, and only considered time allocation or power allocation. Compared with the FD one-way relay system, the outage probability and throughput calculation of the FD two-way relay system is more complicated, as we need to consider both destination nodes simultaneously [18,19]. In [18], the authors showed that the outage probability of FD two-way relay system consists of two complicated integral analytic expressions. Furthermore, a joint optimal transmission and power allocation scheme was proposed to improve the throughput of the relay networks [20], but it is difficult to be applied to the FD two-way relay system. Similarly, the authors in [21] used an alternating optimization method to optimize the outage and throughput performance of the full-duplex cooperative relaying system with EH. Its joint time and power allocation scheme is also difficult to be applied to our system. To the best of our knowledge, for the FD two-way relay system, Ref. [22] considered the system average rate analysis with power allocation, and Ref. [23] considered a joint transmit power and relay two-way beamforming optimization method to derive the system sum rate. Therefore, the throughput performance of the FD two-way EH capable relay system with joint time allocation and power allocation scheme is still to be solved, and we aim to propose a useful method to optimize the system throughput.

2.2. Contributions

In this paper, we give a comprehensive study on the throughput performance of the two-way energy harvesting relay system with full-duplex operation. In particular, we consider the joint time allocation and power allocation to maximize the network throughput of the two-way energy harvesting relay system. A new analytical method to obtain the outage probability is adopted, then the corresponding achievable system throughput is derived to characterize the joint time and power allocation scheme for the system. Based on the analytical expression, it is difficult to determine the optimal power allocation ratio and time allocation ratio because the complicated analytical expression contains three variables (TS ratio, power allocation ratio, and the length of communication time slot) and is in the integral form. For multiple variables optimization, the traditional exhaustive search method has high time complexity. To optimize the system throughput more efficiently, we further propose a simulated annealing based search (SABS) algorithm, and show that the close-to-optimal time and power allocation ratio that controls the trade-off between the energy and the information transmission can be efficiently obtained. The main contributions of this paper are summarized as follows:

- Using the DF policy, the signal-to-interference-plus-noise ratio (SINR) of the two-way system is derived. Therefore, the non-outage probability of the system can be calculated by these SINRs with a new analytical method.
- Using the derived non-outage probability, the system throughput expression is derived, which is further formulated as an optimization problem with three variables.
- A modified SABS algorithm is used to solve the throughput optimization problem. The algorithm is not dependent on the selection of the initial point.
- Simulation results show that the analytical throughput matches well with the simulated throughput, and the biggest gap between the analytical throughput with the simulated throughput is 0.8%. Furthermore, the results derived by the modified SABS algorithm is accurate when the SNR varies from 10 dB to 40 dB.

The remainder of this paper is organized as follows: Section 2 introduces the full-duplex system model. Section 3 presents the system throughput and proposes the modified simulated annealing based search algorithm. In Section 4, we present the simulation results. Finally, Section 5 concludes the paper.

3. System Model

A full-duplex two-way EH relaying system is considered, which consists of two terminal nodes S and D, and one relay node R, as shown in Figure 1. The direct path between S and D is ignored. Thus, S and D exchange information with the help of the relay node, which is energy-constrained. The relay node R adopts decode and forward (DF) in the full-duplex transmission. With the energy harvesting technique, node R can harvest energy by the RF signals transmitted from S and D for forwarding information. We assume that the information processing energy consumed by R is negligible, compared with the transmit energy. With the FD technique, the information exchange between S and D can be completed in two time slots.

Let h_1, h_2, g_1, g_2 denote the channel gains of the links in the FD two-way relay system, and f_1, f_2 denote the channel gains of the self-interference link. A reasonable assumption is that all the channel gains do not change during the transmission block time T, which are independent and identically distributed from one block to the next. Furthermore, we assume that h_1, h_2, g_1, g_2 follow Rayleigh distribution and f_1, f_2 follow Gaussian distribution.

In this paper, we focus on the TS-FDR-I protocol [17], which can be implemented easily in practice. In the TS-FDR-I protocol, the information exchange is completed with two phases. In the first phase, S and D transmit to R for energy harvesting. In the second phase, it is further divided into two slots for information transmission of S-D and D-S, respectively. Let α and θ denote the time allocation factor for energy harvesting and the time allocation factor between the two link information transmission, respectively. Thus, the time allocation of TS-FDR-I protocol is given as follows:

$$T \begin{cases} \alpha T & \text{EH from D and S.} \\ (1-\alpha)T & \begin{cases} \theta(1-\alpha)T, & S \to R \to D, \\ (1-\theta)(1-\alpha)T, & D \to R \to S, \end{cases} \end{cases}$$

where S → R → D and D → R → S denote the two full-duplex information transmission processes. For finding notations of this paper more conveniently, the key notations are listed in Table 1.

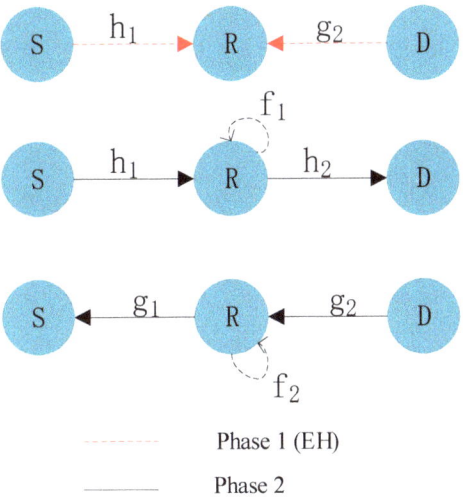

Figure 1. Full-duplex two-way relay system.

Table 1. Notation setting.

Notation	Physical Meaning
h_1, h_2, g_1, g_2	channel gains of the two-way links (Rayleigh distribution)
f_1, f_2	channel gains of the self-interference channel (Gaussian distribution)
$\hat{f}_1, \hat{f}_2$	the residual loop-back interference channel coefficient
α	time-switching ratio
β	power allocation ratio
θ	deciding the length of communication time slot for per phase
T	the total communication time
$x_1(t), x_2(t)$	normalized signals transmitted by S and D
P_1, P_2	transmission power of S and D
η	the energy conversion efficiency
$r_1(t), r_2(t)$	signals transmitted by R
$P_{r_{21}}, P_{r_{22}}$	transmission power of R in phase 1 and phase 2
$n_\bullet$	noise symbol
$\sigma_\bullet^2$	noise power
$\gamma_\bullet$	the derived SINR
γ_0	the required SINR threshold
U	signal transmission rate
$p(\cdot)$	the non-outage probability
p_{out}	the outage probability of the system
τ	the achievable system throughput
$\lambda_{h_1}, \lambda_{h_2}, \lambda_{g_1}, \lambda_{g_2}$	mean values of the exponential random variables

3.1. Phase 1 (Energy Harvesting)

In the first phase, S and D transmit normalized signals $x_1(t)$ and $x_2(t)$ to R with powers P_1 and P_2, respectively. Without loss of generality, suppose that $E\{|x_1(t)|^2\} = E\{|x_2(t)|^2\} = 1$. The received signal at R is

$$y_r(t) = \sqrt{P_1}h_1x_1(t) + \sqrt{P_2}g_2x_2(t) + \tilde{n}_{r_{1,a}}(t), \quad (1)$$

where $\tilde{n}_{r_{1,a}}(t)$ is the additive Gaussian noise at the relay node. In Phase 1, the time duration for EH is αT. Thus, the harvested energy at node R is given by

$$E_h = \eta \left(P_1|h_1|^2 + P_2|g_2|^2 \right) \alpha T, \quad (2)$$

where η is the energy conversion efficiency, which depends on the EH technology. Figure 2 shows a intuitive energy-harvesting process.

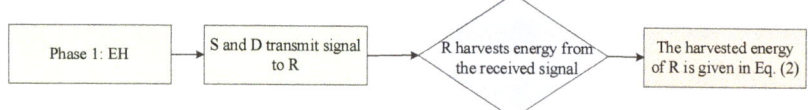

Figure 2. The flow chart of EH.

3.2. Phase 2 (Information Processing)

In this phase, S and D exchange their own information by R. Therefore, relay node R allocates a part of its harvested energy (in phase 1) to help S transmit the signal to D, and the remaining harvested energy of R is used to finish transmitting the signal from D to S. The intuitive information process is showed in Figure 3.

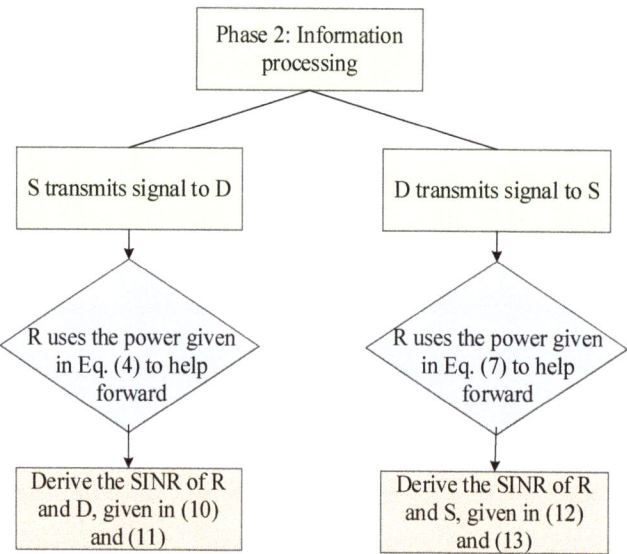

Figure 3. The flow chart of information processing.

3.2.1. S Transmits Signal to D

In the second phase, S first continues to transmit signal $x_1(t)$, and R transmits to D with the harvested energy in the previous phase. Notice that the received signal at R not only includes the signal from S, but also includes the self-interference by R. Thus, the received signal at R is given by

$$y_{r_{21}}(t) = \sqrt{P_1}h_1 x_1(t) + f_1 r_1(t) + \tilde{n}_{r_{21,a}}(t), \quad (3)$$

where $\tilde{n}_{r_{12,a}}(t)$ is the additive Gaussian noise, and $r_1(t)$ is the relay transmit signal satisfying $E\{|r_1(t)|^2\} = P_{r_{21}}$. Since the time duration for information transmission from R to D is $(1-\alpha)\theta T$, if part of the harvested energy is allocated to this link (the allocated factor is β), the transmission power of R can be computed as follows [15]:

$$P_{r_{21}} = \frac{\beta E_h}{(1-\alpha)\theta T} = \frac{\beta \alpha \eta \left(P_1|h_1|^2 + P_2|g_2|^2\right)}{(1-\alpha)\theta}. \quad (4)$$

In the full-duplex relaying system, the relay node usually applies the self-interference cancellation technology to reduce the loop-back interference [24,25]. Therefore, after the interference cancellation and sampling, the post-cancellation sampled signal $y_{r_{21}}(k)$ is given by

$$\begin{aligned} y_{r_{21}}(k) &= \sqrt{P_1}h_1 x_1(k) + \hat{f}_1 r_1(k) + n_{r_{21,a}}(k) + n_{r_{21,c}}(k) \\ &= \sqrt{P_1}h_1 x_1(k) + \hat{f}_1 x_1(k-\mu) + n_{r_{21,a}}(k) + n_{r_{21,c}}(k), \end{aligned} \quad (5)$$

where $\hat{f}_1$ is the residual loop-back interference channel coefficient caused by imperfect cancellation. Because the relay node uses the DF policy for information transmission, it will first decode the original source signal and then regenerate the signal. Hence, the relay transmit signal can be expressed as $r_1(k) = x_1(k-\mu)$, where μ is the processing delay at the relay [26]. Furthermore, let $n_{r_{21}}(k)$ denote $n_{r_{21,a}}(k) + n_{r_{21,c}}(k)$ with a noise power of $\sigma^2_{n_{r_{21}}(k)}$.

The final received signal at D is

$$y_d(k) = \sqrt{P_{r_{21}}} h_2 x_1(k-\mu) + n_d(k), \quad (6)$$

where $n_d(k) \triangleq n_{d,a}(k) + n_{d,c}(k)$ is the noise introduced at D. The power of noise $n_d(k)$ is denoted by $\sigma^2_{n_d(k)}$.

3.2.2. D Transmits Signal to S

Since the time duration for D to S link is $(1-\theta)(1-\alpha)T$ and all the remaining harvested energy is used by R, the transmission power of R is given by

$$P_{r_{22}} = \frac{(1-\beta)E_h}{(1-\alpha)(1-\theta)T} = \frac{(1-\beta)\alpha\eta\left(P_1|h_1|^2 + P_2|g_2|^2\right)}{(1-\alpha)(1-\theta)}. \quad (7)$$

Following a similar analysis of $x_1(t)$, we can show that the received signal at R is given by

$$\begin{aligned} y_{r_{22}}(k) &= \sqrt{P_2}g_2 x_2(k) + \hat{f}_2 r_2(k) + n_{r_{22,a}}(k) + n_{r_{22,c}}(k) \\ &= \sqrt{P_2}g_2 x_2(k) + \hat{f}_2 x_2(k-\mu) + n_{r_{22,a}}(k) + n_{r_{22,c}}(k), \end{aligned} \quad (8)$$

where $\hat{f}_2$ is the residual loop-back interference channel coefficient, and $r_2(k) = x_2(k-\mu)$ ($E\{|r_2(k)|^2\} = P_{r_{22}}$) is the relay transmit signal. In particular, $n_{r_{22}}(k) \triangleq n_{r_{22,a}}(k) + n_{r_{22,c}}(k)$ with a noise power of $\sigma^2_{n_{r_{22}}(k)}$.

After information processing, R forwards the signal to S and the final received signal at S is

$$y_s(k) = \sqrt{P_{r_{22}}} g_1 x_2(k-\mu) + n_s(k), \quad (9)$$

where $n_s(k) \triangleq n_{s,a}(k) + n_{s,c}(k)$ is the noise introduced at S. The power of noise $n_s(k)$ is denoted by $\sigma^2_{n_s(k)}$.

We assume that $\sigma^2_{n_{r_{21}}(k)} = \sigma^2_{n_{r_{22}}(k)} = \sigma^2_{n_s(k)} = \sigma^2_{n_d(k)} = \sigma^2$. Therefore, the signal-to-interference-plus-noise ratio (SINR) at S, R and D is given by

$$\gamma_{r_{21}} = \frac{P_1|h_1|^2}{|\hat{f}_1|^2 P_{r_{21}} + \sigma^2}, \quad (10)$$

$$\gamma_d = \frac{P_{r_{21}}|h_2|^2}{\sigma^2} = \frac{\beta\alpha\eta\left(P_1|h_1|^2 + P_2|g_2|^2\right)|h_2|^2}{(1-\alpha)\theta\sigma^2}, \quad (11)$$

$$\gamma_{r_{22}} = \frac{P_2|g_2|^2}{|\hat{f}_2|^2 P_{r_{22}} + \sigma^2}, \quad (12)$$

$$\gamma_s = \frac{P_{r_{22}}|g_1|^2}{\sigma^2} = \frac{\beta\alpha\eta\left(P_1|h_1|^2 + P_2|g_2|^2\right)|g_1|^2}{(1-\alpha)(1-\theta)\sigma^2}. \quad (13)$$

4. Throughput Analysis

In this section, we derive the analytical achievable throughput of the FD two-way system with EH. For the full-duplex system with the DF policy, we first need to derive the expression of outage probability, and then compute the achievable throughput.

4.1. Achievable Throughput

Let γ_0 denote the required SINR threshold for correct reception with transmission rate U, i.e., $\gamma_0 = 2^U - 1$. Since the relay uses the DF relaying policy, the outage probability is given by

$$p_{out} = 1 - p(\gamma_{r_{21}} \geq \gamma_0)p(\gamma_s \geq \gamma_0)p(\gamma_{r_{22}} \geq \gamma_0)p(\gamma_d \geq \gamma_0). \quad (14)$$

The above equation shows that the outage probability of the full-duplex system in the DF relaying scheme consists of four components. Next, we will show how to compute each component in (14).

The non-outage probability $p(\gamma_{r_{21}} \geq \gamma_0)$ is given by

$$\begin{aligned} p(\gamma_{r_{21}} \geq \gamma_0) &= p\left(\frac{P_1|h_1|^2}{|\hat{f}_1|^2 P_{r_{21}} + \sigma^2} \geq \gamma_0\right) = p\left(\frac{P_1|h_1|^2}{|\hat{f}_1|^2 \left(\frac{\beta\alpha\eta(P_1|h_1|^2 + P_2|h_2|^2)}{(1-\alpha)\theta}\right) + \sigma^2} \geq \gamma_0\right) \\ &= p\left(\frac{(1-\alpha)\theta P_1|h_1|^2}{|\hat{f}_1|^2 \beta\alpha\eta\left(P_1|h_1|^2 + P_2|g_2|^2\right) + (1-\alpha)\theta\sigma^2} \geq \gamma_0\right) \\ &= p\left(|h_1|^2 \geq \frac{\gamma_0|\hat{f}_1|^2 \beta\alpha\eta P_2|g_2|^2 + \gamma_0(1-\alpha)\theta\sigma^2}{(1-\alpha)\theta P_1 - \gamma_0|\hat{f}_1|^2 \beta\alpha\eta P_1}\right). \end{aligned} \quad (15)$$

Since h_1 and g_2 follow Rayleigh distribution, $|h_1|^2$ and $|g_2|^2$ are exponential random variables with mean values of λ_{h_1} and λ_{g_2}, respectively. Thus, we have

$$\begin{aligned} &p(\gamma_{r_{21}} \geq \gamma_0) \\ &= p\left(|h_1|^2 \geq \frac{\gamma_0|\hat{f}_1|^2 \beta\alpha\eta P_2|g_2|^2 + \gamma_0(1-\alpha)\theta\sigma^2}{(1-\alpha)\theta P_1 - \gamma_0|\hat{f}_1|^2 \beta\alpha\eta P_1}\right) \\ &= \int_{z=0}^{\infty} f_{|g_2|^2}(z) p\left(|h_1|^2 \geq \frac{\gamma_0|\hat{f}_1|^2 \beta\alpha\eta P_2 z + \gamma_0(1-\alpha)\theta\sigma^2}{(1-\alpha)\theta P_1 - \gamma_0|\hat{f}_1|^2 \beta\alpha\eta P_1}\right) \end{aligned}$$

$$= \frac{1}{\lambda_{g_2}} \exp\Big(-\frac{\gamma_0(1-\alpha)\theta\sigma^2}{\lambda_{h_1}(1-\alpha)\theta P_1 - \gamma_0|\hat{f}_1|^2\beta\alpha\eta P_1\lambda_{h_1}}\Big) *$$
$$\Big(\frac{\lambda_{g_2}\big(\lambda_{h_1}(1-\alpha)\theta P_1 - \gamma_0|\hat{f}_1|^2\beta\alpha\eta P_1\lambda_{h_1}\big)}{\lambda_{h_1}(1-\alpha)\theta P_1 - \gamma_0|\hat{f}_1|^2\beta\alpha\eta P_1\lambda_{h_1} + \lambda_{g_2}\gamma_0|\hat{f}_1|^2\beta\alpha\eta P_2}\Big). \tag{16}$$

Furthermore, the non-outage probability $p(\gamma_{r_{21}} \geq \gamma_0)$ can also derive some insights form the work [4,12].

Similarly, the non-outage probability $p(\gamma_{r_{22}} \geq \gamma_0)$ is given by

$$\begin{aligned}
&p(\gamma_{r_{22}} \geq \gamma_0) \\
&= p\Big(\frac{P_2|g_2|^2}{|\hat{f}_2|^2 P_{r_{22}} + \sigma^2} \geq \gamma_0\Big) \\
&= p\Big(\frac{P_2|g_2|^2}{|\hat{f}_2|^2\big(\frac{(1-\beta)\alpha\eta(P_1|h_1|^2+P_2|g_2|^2)}{(1-\alpha)(1-\theta)}\big) + \sigma^2} \geq \gamma_0\Big) \\
&= p\Big(|g_2|^2 \geq \frac{\gamma_0|\hat{f}_2|^2(1-\beta)\alpha\eta P_1|h_1|^2 + \gamma_0(1-\alpha)(1-\theta)\sigma^2}{(1-\alpha)(1-\theta)P_2 - \gamma_0|\hat{f}_2|^2(1-\beta)\alpha\eta P_2}\Big) \\
&= \frac{1}{\lambda_{h_1}} \exp\Big(-\frac{\gamma_0(1-\alpha)(1-\theta)\sigma^2}{\lambda_{g_2}(1-\alpha)(1-\theta)P_2 - \gamma_0|\hat{f}_2|^2(1-\beta)\alpha\eta P_1\lambda_{g_2}}\Big) * \\
&\Big(\frac{\lambda_{h_1}\big(\lambda_{g_2}(1-\alpha)(1-\theta)P_2 - \gamma_0|\hat{f}_2|^2(1-\beta)\alpha\eta P_2\lambda_{g_2}\big)}{\lambda_{g_2}(1-\alpha)(1-\theta)P_2 - \gamma_0|\hat{f}_2|^2(1-\beta)\alpha\eta P_2\lambda_{g_2} + \lambda_{h_1}\gamma_0|\hat{f}_2|^2(1-\beta)\alpha\eta P_2}\Big).
\end{aligned} \tag{17}$$

When R forwards signal to D, the non-outage probability at D is given by

$$p(\gamma_d \geq \gamma_0) = p\Big(\frac{\beta\alpha\eta\big(P_1|h_1|^2 + P_2|g_2|^2\big)|h_2|^2}{(1-\alpha)\theta\sigma^2} \geq \gamma_0\Big), \tag{18}$$

and its analytical expression could be derived by the following proposition.

Proposition 1. (1) *If* $P_1\lambda_{h_1} \neq P_2\lambda_{g_2}$, *the non-outage probability* $p(\gamma_d \geq \gamma_0)$, *defined in* (18), *is given by*

$$\begin{aligned}
p(\gamma_d \geq \gamma_0) = \\
\frac{1}{P_1\lambda_{h_1} - P_2\lambda_{g_2}} \sqrt{\frac{4\gamma_0(1-\alpha)\theta\sigma^2 P_1\lambda_{h_1}}{\lambda_{h_2}\beta\alpha\eta}} K_1\Big(\sqrt{\frac{4\gamma_0(1-\alpha)\theta\sigma^2}{\lambda_{h_2}\beta\alpha\eta P_1\lambda_{h_1}}}\Big) \\
- \frac{1}{P_1\lambda_{h_1} - P_2\lambda_{g_2}} \sqrt{\frac{4\gamma_0(1-\alpha)\theta\sigma^2 P_2\lambda_{g_2}}{\lambda_{h_2}\beta\alpha\eta}} K_1\Big(\sqrt{\frac{4\gamma_0(1-\alpha)\theta\sigma^2}{\lambda_{h_2}\beta\alpha\eta P_2\lambda_{g_2}}}\Big),
\end{aligned} \tag{19}$$

where the notation $K_n(x)$ *denotes the nth order modified Bessel function of the second kind.*

(2) *If* $P_1\lambda_{h_1} = P_2\lambda_{g_2}$, *the non-outage probability at D is given by*

$$p(\gamma_d \geq \gamma_0) = \frac{2\gamma_0(1-\alpha)\theta\sigma^2}{\lambda_{h_2}\beta\alpha\eta P_1\lambda_{h_1}} K_2\Big(2\sqrt{\frac{\gamma_0(1-\alpha)\theta\sigma^2}{\lambda_{h_2}\beta\alpha\eta P_1\lambda_{h_1}}}\Big). \tag{20}$$

Proof. See Appendix A. □

Similarly, the expression of the non-outage probability at S is shown as follows: (1) If $P_1 \lambda_{h_1} \neq P_2 \lambda_{g_2}$,

$$p(\gamma_s \geq \gamma_0) = p\left(\frac{(1-\beta)\alpha\eta\left(P_1|h_1|^2 + P_2|h_2|^2\right)|g_1|^2}{(1-\alpha)(1-\theta)\sigma^2} \geq \gamma_0\right)$$

$$= \frac{1}{P_1 \lambda_{h_1} - P_2 \lambda_{g_2}} \left(\sqrt{\frac{4\gamma_0(1-\alpha)(1-\theta)\sigma^2 P_1 \lambda_{h_1}}{\lambda_{g_1}(1-\beta)\alpha\eta}} K_1\left(\sqrt{\frac{4\gamma_0(1-\alpha)(1-\theta)\sigma^2}{\lambda_{g_1}(1-\beta)\alpha\eta P_1 \lambda_{h_1}}}\right) \right. \quad (21)$$

$$\left. - \sqrt{\frac{4\gamma_0(1-\alpha)(1-\theta)\sigma^2 P_2 \lambda_{g_2}}{\lambda_{g_1}(1-\beta)\alpha\eta}} K_1\left(\sqrt{\frac{4\gamma_0(1-\alpha)(1-\theta)\sigma^2}{\lambda_{g_1}(1-\beta)\alpha\eta P_2 \lambda_{g_2}}}\right)\right).$$

(2) If $P_1 \lambda_{h_1} = P_2 \lambda_{g_2}$,

$$p(\gamma_d \geq \gamma_0) = \frac{2\gamma_0(1-\alpha)(1-\theta)\sigma^2}{\lambda_{g_1}(1-\beta)\alpha\eta P_1 \lambda_{h_1}} K_2\left(2\sqrt{\frac{\gamma_0(1-\alpha)(1-\theta)\sigma^2}{\lambda_{g_1}(1-\beta)\alpha\eta P_1 \lambda_{h_1}}}\right). \quad (22)$$

Finally, the achievable system throughput is given by

$$\tau = (1 - p_{out})2U \times (1-\alpha)\min(\theta, 1-\theta). \quad (23)$$

4.2. System Throughput Optimization

In the energy harvesting FD two-way relay system, we aim to optimize the time and power allocation to maximize the system throughput. In particular, it can be formulated as the following optimization problem:

$$\begin{aligned} \max \quad & \tau(\alpha, \beta, \theta) = (1 - p_{out})2U \times (1-\alpha)\min(\theta, 1-\theta). \\ \text{s.t.} \quad & 0 \leq \alpha \leq 1, 0 \leq \beta \leq 1, 0 \leq \theta \leq 1. \end{aligned} \quad (24)$$

However, problem (24) contains three variables and p_{out} is in the integral form which make problem (24) difficult to solve. The exhaustive search method for all three variables has high time complexity, and this motivates us to propose a simulated annealing based search (SABS) algorithm to obtain the optimal system configuration parameters that maximize system throughput. Note that the SABS algorithm is very dependent on the selection of the initial point. To overcome this problem, we improve its performance using the principle of alternating optimization, i.e, deriving α and (β, θ) by exhaustive search and SABS, respectively.

Solving problem (24) by the modified SABS algorithm, we first set initial value of β and θ randomly, and obtain the optimal value of $\alpha^{(j)}$ by exhaustive search (see the step 1 of Algorithm 1). Then we construct the vector solution $x = (\alpha^{(j)}, \beta, \theta) \in \Omega$, where Ω is the solution space consisting of $\alpha^{(j)}, \beta$ and θ. In step 3 of Algorithm 1, we design an accept probability which could help select the alternative point $z^{(k)}$ as the next iteration point. The accepted probability is given by

$$p(k, \tau(z^{(k)}), \tau(x^{(k)})) = \min\{1, \exp\left(\frac{-(\tau(z^{(k)}) - \tau(x^{(k)}))}{T_k}\right)\}, \quad (25)$$

where T_k is a sequence of positive numbers, i.e., T_k is cooling schedule [27]. From the accepted probability, we could observe that if $\tau(z^{(k)}) \leq \tau(x^{(k)})$, the value of $p(k, \tau(z^{(k)}), \tau(x^{(k)}))$ is equal to 1, which means $x^{(k+1)} = z^{(k)}$. Furthermore, although $\tau(z^{(k)}) > \tau(x^{(k)})$, the probability that $x^{(k+1)} = z^{(k)}$ is $\exp\left(\frac{-(\tau(z^{(k)}) - \tau(x^{(k)}))}{T_k}\right)$. Generally, cooling schedule T_k monotonically decreases to 0, and this denotes the cooling process. In Algorithm 1, T_k is given by

$$T_k = 0.95^k T_0 \ (T_0 = 100), \quad (26)$$

where T_0 denotes the initial temperature.

Algorithm 1 The modified simulated annealing based search algorithm
---
Input: $\beta, \theta, j = 0, k = 0, \delta, J$ and K
Output: the optimal $\alpha^*, \beta^*, \theta^*$
1 Derive the value of $\alpha^{(j)}$ by exhaustive search with β and θ;
2 Initialize value $x = x^{(0)}$ ($x^{(0)} \in \Omega$);
3 Select an alternative point $z^{(k)}$ at random from Ω;
4 Design a random event, and the probability of the event happening is $p(k, \tau(z^{(k)}), \tau(x^{(k)}))$;
5 Perform the event. If the event occurred, let $x^{(k+1)} = z^{(k)}$; Otherwise, let $x^{(k+1)} = x^{(k)}$;
6 If $\tau(x^{(k+1)}) - \tau(x^{(k)}) < \delta$ and $k \geq K$, $j = j+1$;
7 Let $k = k+1$ and return to step 3;
8 If $j \leq J$, return to step 1; otherwise, the algorithm terminates;

In Algorithm 1, it is worth noting that the larger the gap between $\tau(z^{(k)})$ and $\tau(x^{(k)})$, the more impossible $z^{(k)}$ is selected as the next iteration point. Similarly, the smaller T_k is, the less likely $z^{(k)}$ is to be selected as an iteration point. In other words, Algorithm 1 first searches the optimal solution from the overall solution space Ω. As k increases, the search scope will concentrate to the vicinity of the global optimal point. Meanwhile, the computational complexity of the Algorithm 1 in terms of the number of variables and the loops is $O(N)$. Deriving the β and θ, Algorithm 1 returns to step 1 and repeats the above process. Compared with the exhaustive search and the classical SABS algorithm, Algorithm 1 not only improves the search efficiency significantly, but also no longer depends on the selection of the initial point.

5. Numerical Results and Simulation

In this section, the throughput of this system is investigated. Furthermore, we compare the analytical results with simulated results for proving the analytical framework. Unless otherwise specified, the parameters in the simulation are set as follows: $P_1 = P_2 = 1$ W, $U = 3$ bits/s/Hz, $\eta = 1$, $\lambda_{h_1} = \lambda_{h_2} = \lambda_{g_1} = \lambda_{g_2} = 1$ [12], $|\hat{f}_1|^2 = |\hat{f}_2|^2 = 0.001$, $\sigma^2 = 0.001$ W.

5.1. Model Validation

Figure 4 shows the analytical throughput and the simulated throughput of the full-duplex system. We find that the analytical throughput matches well with the simulated throughput. Furthermore, we can find that the system throughput varies with different parameters, including α, β and θ.

5.1.1. The Effect of α

Figure 4a shows the system throughput as a function of α when the other two parameters are set as $\beta = 0.5$ and $\theta = 0.5$. For the analytical results of $P_1 \lambda_{h_1} \neq P_2 \lambda_{g_2}$, we set $P_1 = 1$ W, $P_2 = 2$ W. We can observe that the biggest gap between the analytical throughput and the simulated throughput is 0.5% when $\alpha = 0.08$. For the analytical results of $P_1 \lambda_{h_1} = P_2 \lambda_{g_2}$, we set $P_1 = P_2 = 1$ W. The biggest gap between the analytical throughput and the simulated throughput is 0.8% when $\alpha = 0.1$. These results show that the analytical throughput reflects the practical throughput well. On the other hand, the system throughput first increases and then decreases as α increases. This is because that when α is too small, the harvested energy at R is not enough, so the transmitted energy for R is also not enough. When α is close to 1, the harvested energy at R is large. However, the time for information transmission is reduced, which leads to a decrease in the system throughput, too.

5.1.2. The Effect of β

Figure 4b shows the system throughput as a function of β when the other two parameters are set as $\alpha = 0.5$ and $\theta = 0.5$. The analytical results are also close to the simulated throughput. When β is very small, the energy for the link S-D is small, and this will make the transmission from S to D fail, and thus, the throughput will become small; otherwise, when β is very large, the energy for the link D-S is small, and this will make the transmission from D to S fail. Thus, the throughput will also become small.

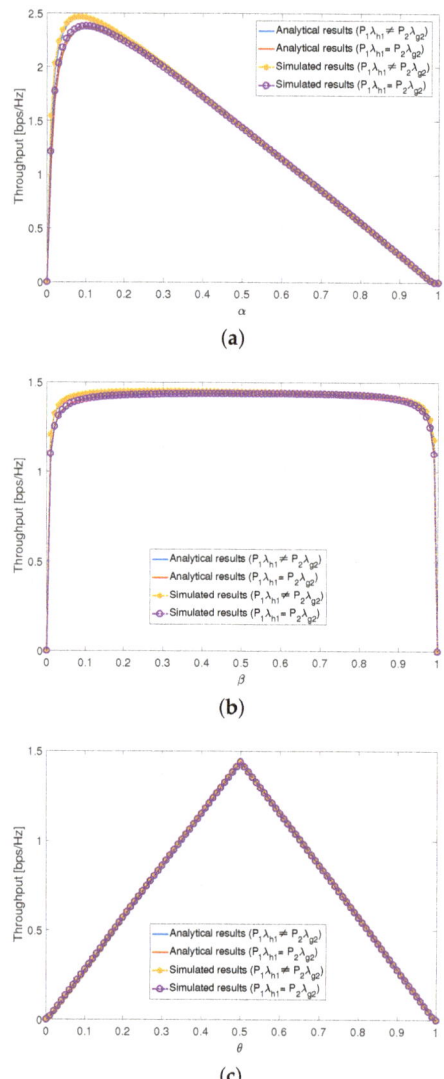

Figure 4. The system throughput as a function of α, β, and θ. Other parameter $\sigma^2 = 0.001$ W. (**a**) Throughput as a function of α. (**b**) Throughput as a function of β. (**c**) Throughput as a function of θ.

5.1.3. The Effect of θ

Figure 4c shows the system throughput as a function of θ when the other two parameters are set as $\alpha = 0.5$ and $\beta = 0.5$. We could observe that the system throughput first increases with θ rapidly, and then decreases with θ rapidly. This is because from (23), θ mainly works in $\min(\theta, 1 - \theta)$, which makes the curve very steep.

5.2. The Non-Outage Probability

In fact, the non-outage probability is the key to obtain the system throughput. Figure 5 shows that the non-outage probability is related with SNR, and its value ranges from 0 to 1. The effect of noise power variation is equivalent to the effect of the transmission power variation, and it could be observed that the non-outage probability increases with the increases in SNR, i.e., the larger transmission power brings a larger non-outage probability. Meanwhile, Figure 5 shows that there is little gap between optimal non-outage probability and non-outage probability with fixed system parameters. Thus, we cannot optimize the non-outage probability alone, but should further consider optimizing the system throughput.

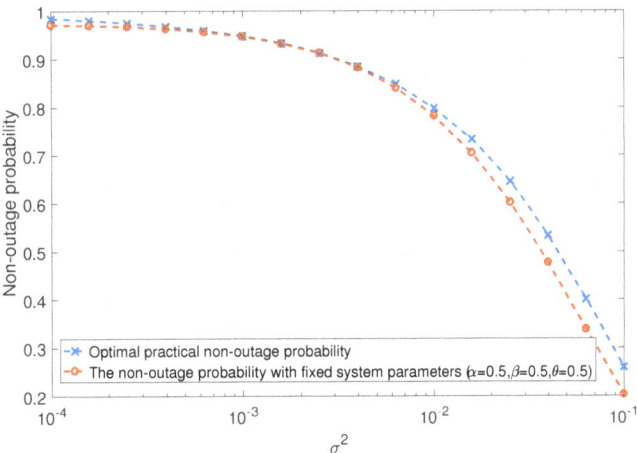

Figure 5. The non-outage probability as a function of noise power.

5.3. The Optimal Throughput

We further investigate the optimal throughput of the full-duplex system. From Figure 6a, we find that the system throughput of fixed parameters is smaller than the practical optimal throughput. In Figure 6b, we give the comparison of practical throughput with the throughput derived by different methods, and we set the search step length $\epsilon = 0.02$ for the exhaustive search method. We can observe that the throughput of these two methods is relatively accurate when SNR varies from 10 dB to 40 dB. The throughput derived by the exhaustive search method or Algorithm 1 has the biggest gap between the practical throughput when SNR is 10 dB.

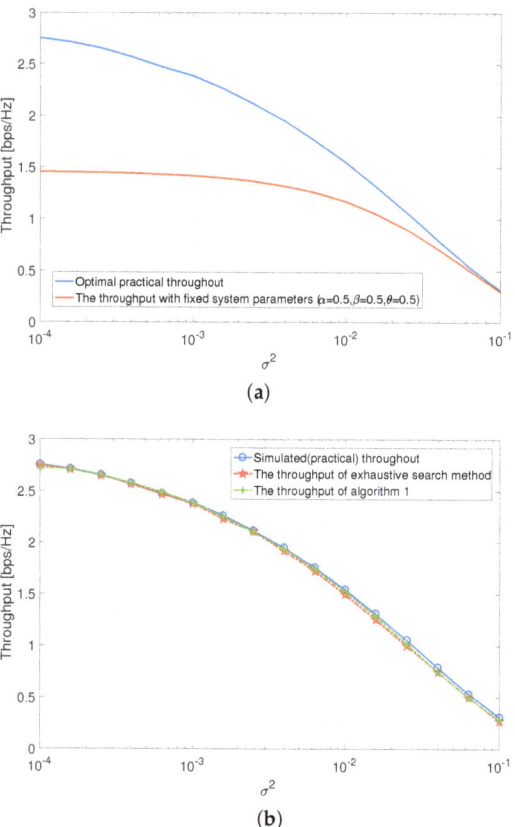

Figure 6. Optimal throughput as a function of noise power. (**a**) Optimal throughput vs. throughput with fixed system parameters. (**b**) The throughput obtained by different methods.

6. Conclusions

In this paper, a joint time and power allocation scheme for the FD two-way EH-capable relay system from the perspective of system throughput is investigated. Considering the system using DF policy to transmit information, the SINRs at S, R and D are first derived. Thus, the non-outage probability of the system can be obtained by these SINRs. Furthermore, a new analytical method is used to obtain the non-outage probability so that the corresponding system throughput can be derived. We find that the system throughput contained three variables, i.e., time switching ratio, power allocation ratio, and the length of communication time slot, and is in the integral form. To achieve the optimal system throughput, these three variables need to be optimized simultaneously. Since the traditional exhaustive search method has high time complexity for solving the problem with multiple variables, we propose a modified SABS algorithm that could efficiently find the close-to-optimal time and power allocation to maximize throughput. Numerical results are provided to demonstrate the accuracy and the effectiveness of our new analytical framework, and they show that the SABS algorithm can derive accurate throughput results.

Author Contributions: Writing—original draft preparation, K.Z.; writing—review, L.F. All authors have read and agreed to the published version of the manuscript.

Funding: This research received no external funding.

Data Availability Statement: The raw data supporting the conclusion of this article will be made available by the authors without undue reservation.

Conflicts of Interest: The authors declare no conflict of interest.

Appendix A

Proof of Proposition 1. (1) $P_1\lambda_{h_1} \neq P_2\lambda_{g_2}$. Let $Z = P_1|h_1|^2 + P_2|g_2|^2$, and we can derive the probability distribution function (PDF) of Z:

$$f_Z(z) = \begin{cases} \left(\frac{1}{P_1\lambda_{h_1} - P_2\lambda_{g_2}}\right)\left(e^{-\frac{z}{P_1\lambda_{h_1}}} - e^{-\frac{z}{P_2\lambda_{g_2}}}\right), & z \geq 0, \\ 0, & \text{otherwise.} \end{cases}$$

Thus, the non-outage probability at D is given by

$$\begin{aligned} p(\gamma_d \geq \gamma_0) &= p\left(\frac{\beta\alpha\eta\left(P_1|h_1|^2 + P_2|g_2|^2\right)|h_2|^2}{(1-\alpha)\theta\sigma^2} \geq \gamma_0\right) \\ &= p\left(\frac{\beta\alpha\eta|h_2|^2 Z}{(1-\alpha)\theta\sigma^2} \geq \gamma_0\right) = p\left(|h_2|^2 \geq \frac{\gamma_0(1-\alpha)\theta\sigma^2}{\beta\alpha\eta Z}\right) \\ &= \int_{z=0}^{\infty} f_Z(z) p\left(|h_2|^2 \geq \frac{\gamma_0(1-\alpha)\theta\sigma^2}{\beta\alpha\eta z}\right) dz \\ &= \int_{z=0}^{\infty} \frac{1}{P_1\lambda_{h_1} - P_2\lambda_{g_2}} \left(e^{-\frac{z}{P_1\lambda_{h_1}}} - e^{-\frac{z}{P_2\lambda_{g_2}}}\right) \exp\left(-\frac{\gamma_0(1-\alpha)\theta\sigma^2}{\lambda_{h_2}\beta\alpha\eta z}\right) dz \\ &= \frac{1}{P_1\lambda_{h_1} - P_2\lambda_{g_2}} \int_{z=0}^{\infty} \exp\left(-\frac{z}{P_1\lambda_{h_1}}\right) \exp\left(-\frac{\gamma_0(1-\alpha)\theta\sigma^2}{\lambda_{h_2}\beta\alpha\eta z}\right) dz \\ &\quad - \frac{1}{P_1\lambda_{h_1} - P_2\lambda_{g_2}} \int_{z=0}^{\infty} \exp\left(-\frac{z}{P_2\lambda_{g_2}}\right) \exp\left(-\frac{\gamma_0(1-\alpha)\theta\sigma^2}{\lambda_{h_2}\beta\alpha\eta z}\right) dz \\ &= \frac{1}{P_1\lambda_{h_1} - P_2\lambda_{g_2}} \sqrt{\frac{4\gamma_0(1-\alpha)\theta\sigma^2 P_1\lambda_{h_1}}{\lambda_{h_2}\beta\alpha\eta}} K_1\left(\sqrt{\frac{4\gamma_0(1-\alpha)\theta\sigma^2}{\lambda_{h_2}\beta\alpha\eta P_1\lambda_{h_1}}}\right) \\ &\quad - \frac{1}{P_1\lambda_{h_1} - P_2\lambda_{g_2}} \sqrt{\frac{4\gamma_0(1-\alpha)\theta\sigma^2 P_2\lambda_{g_2}}{\lambda_{h_2}\beta\alpha\eta}} K_1\left(\sqrt{\frac{4\gamma_0(1-\alpha)\theta\sigma^2}{\lambda_{h_2}\beta\alpha\eta P_2\lambda_{g_2}}}\right), \end{aligned} \quad (A1)$$

where $K_n(x)$ denotes the nth order modified Bessel function of the second kind. Meanwhile, equation $\int_{x=0}^{\infty} \exp\left(-\frac{\beta}{4x} - \gamma x\right) dx = \sqrt{\frac{\beta}{\gamma}} K_1(\sqrt{\beta\gamma})$ is used.

(2) $P_1\lambda_{h_1} = P_2\lambda_{h_2}$. Let $Z = P_1|h_1|^2 + P_2|g_2|^2$, and the PDF of Z could be given by

$$f_Z(z) = \begin{cases} \frac{1}{(P_1\lambda_{h_1})^2} z e^{-\frac{z}{P_1\lambda_{h_1}}}, & z \geq 0, \\ 0, & \text{otherwise.} \end{cases}$$

Thus, the non-outage probability at node D is given by

$$\begin{aligned} p(\gamma_d \geq \gamma_0) &= p\left(\frac{\beta\alpha\eta\left(P_1|h_1|^2 + P_2|h_2|^2\right)|h_2|^2}{(1-\alpha)\theta\sigma^2} \geq \gamma_0\right) \\ &= p\left(\frac{\beta\alpha\eta|h_2|^2 Z}{(1-\alpha)\theta\sigma^2} \geq \gamma_0\right) = p\left(|h_2|^2 \geq \frac{\gamma_0(1-\alpha)\theta\sigma^2}{\beta\alpha\eta Z}\right) \\ &= \int_{z=0}^{\infty} f_Z(z) p\left(|h_2|^2 \geq \frac{\gamma_0(1-\alpha)\theta\sigma^2}{\beta\alpha\eta z}\right) dz \end{aligned}$$

$$
\begin{aligned}
&= \int_{z=0}^{\infty} \frac{1}{(P_1 \lambda_{h_1})^2} z e^{-\frac{z}{P_1 \lambda_{h_1}}} p\left(|h_2|^2 \geq \frac{\gamma_0(1-\alpha)\theta\sigma^2}{\beta\alpha\eta z}\right) dz \\
&= \int_{z=0}^{\infty} \frac{1}{(P_1 \lambda_{h_1})^2} z e^{-\frac{z}{P_1 \lambda_{h_1}}} \exp\left(-\frac{\gamma_0(1-\alpha)\theta\sigma^2}{\lambda_{h_2}\beta\alpha\eta z}\right) dz \\
&= \frac{1}{(P_1 \lambda_{h_1})^2} \int_{z=0}^{\infty} z \exp\left(-\frac{z}{P_1 \lambda_{h_1}} - \frac{\gamma_0(1-\alpha)\theta\sigma^2}{\lambda_{h_2}\beta\alpha\eta z}\right) dz \\
&= \frac{2\gamma_0(1-\alpha)\theta\sigma^2}{\lambda_{h_2}\beta\alpha\eta P_1\lambda_{h_1}} K_2\left(2\sqrt{\frac{\gamma_0(1-\alpha)\theta\sigma^2}{\lambda_{h_2}\beta\alpha\eta P_1\lambda_{h_1}}}\right),
\end{aligned}
\tag{A2}
$$

where the equation $\int_{x=0}^{\infty} x \exp(-\beta x - \frac{\gamma}{x}) dx = \frac{2\gamma}{\beta} K_2(2\sqrt{\beta\gamma})$ is used. □

References

1. Hu, S.; Chen, X.; Ni, W.; Wang, X.; Hossain, E. Modeling and analysis of energy harvesting and smart grid-powered wireless communication networks: A contemporary survey. *IEEE Trans. Green Commun. Netw.* **2020**, *4*, 461–496. [CrossRef]
2. Zhong, C.; Suraweera, H.A.; Zheng, G.; Krikidis, I.; Zhang, Z. Improving the throughput of wireless powered dual-hop systems with Full Duplex relaying. In Proceedings of the 2015 IEEE International Conference on Communications (ICC), London, UK, 8–12 June 2015.
3. Atapattu, S.; Evans, J. Optimal energy harvesting protocols for wireless relay networks. *IEEE Trans. Wirel. Commun.* **2016**, *15*, 5789–5803. [CrossRef]
4. Nasir, A.A.; Zhou, X.; Durrani, S.; Kennedy, R.A. Relaying protocols for wireless energy harvesting and information processing. *IEEE Trans. Wirel. Commun.* **2013**, *12*, 3622–3636. [CrossRef]
5. Xun, Z.; Rui, Z.; Ho, C.K. Wireless information and power transfer: Architecture design and rate-energy tradeoff. *IEEE Trans. Commun.* **2013**, *61*, 4754–4767.
6. Singh, D.; Ouamri, M.A.; Alzaidi, M.S.; Alharbi, T.E.A.; Ghoneim, S.S.M. Performance analysis of wireless power transfer enabled dual hop relay system under generalised fading scenarios. *IEEE Access* **2022**, *10*, 114364–114373. [CrossRef]
7. Kolodziej, K.E.; Perry, B.T.; Herd, J.S. In-band full-duplex technology: Techniques and systems survey. *IEEE Trans. Microw. Theory Tech.* **2020**, *67*, 3025–3041. [CrossRef]
8. Wang, D.; Zhang, R.; Cheng, X.; Yang, L.; Chen, C. Relay selection in full-duplex energy-harvesting two-way relay networks. *IEEE Trans. Green Commun. Netw.* **2017**, *1*, 182–191. [CrossRef]
9. Nguyen, B.C.; Tran, X.N.; Tran, D.T. Performance analysis of full-duplex decode-and-forward two-way relay networks with transceiver impairments. *Ann. Telecommun.* **2022**, *77*, 187–200. [CrossRef]
10. Gu, Y.; Aïssa, S. RF-based energy harvesting in Decode-and-Forward relaying systems: Ergodic and outage capacities. *IEEE Trans. Wirel. Commun.* **2018**, *14*, 6425–6434. [CrossRef]
11. Singh, D.; Ouamri, M.A.; Muthanna, M.S.A.; Adam, A.B.M.; Muthanna, A.; Koucheryavy, A.; El-Latif, A.A.A. A generalized approach on outage performance analysis of dual-hop decode and forward relaying for 5G and beyond scenarios. *Sustainability* **2022**, *14*, 12870. [CrossRef]
12. Cao, H.; Fu, L.; Dai, H. Throughput analysis of the two-way relay system with network coding and energy harvesting. In Proceedings of the 2017 IEEE International Conference on Communications (ICC), Paris, France, 21–25 May 2017.
13. Khafagy, M.; Ismail, A.; Aissa, S. On the outage performance of full-duplex selective decode-and-forward relaying. *IEEE Commun. Lett.* **2013**, *17*, 1180–1183. [CrossRef]
14. Ozfatura, M.E.; Elazzouni, S.; Ercetin, O.; Elbatt, T. Optimal throughput performance in full-duplex relay assisted cognitive networks. *Wirel. Netw.* **2018**, *25*, 1931–1947. [CrossRef]
15. Rabie, K.M.; Adebisi, B.; Alouini, M.S. Half-Duplex and Full-Duplex AF and DF relaying with Energy-Harvesting in Log-Normal fading. *IEEE Trans. Green Commun. Netw.* **2017**, *1*, 468–480. [CrossRef]
16. Zhong, K.; Fu, L. Optimal throughput of the full-duplex two-way relay system with energy harvesting. In Proceedings of the 2021 IEEE 94th Vehicular Technology Conference (VTC2021-Fall), Norman, OK, USA, 27–30 September 2021.
17. Wang, D.; Zhang, R.; Xiang, C.; Yang, L. Capacity-enhancing Full-Duplex relay networks based on power splitting (PS-)SWIPT. *IEEE Trans. Veh. Technol.* **2017**, *66*, 5445–5450. [CrossRef]
18. Hu, R.; Hu, C.; Jiang, J.; Xie, X.; Song, L. Full-Duplex mode in Amplify-and-Forward relay channels: Outage probability and ergodic capacity. *Int. J. Antennas Propag.* **2014**, *2014*, 347540. [CrossRef]
19. Zhang, Z.; Ma, Z.; Ding, Z.; Xiao, M.; Karagiannidis, G.K. Full-duplex two-way and one-way relaying: Average rate, outage probability, and tradeoffs. *IEEE Trans. Wirel. Commun.* **2016**, *15*, 3920–3933. [CrossRef]
20. Lin, J.-Y.; Chang, R.Y.; Tsao, H.-W.; Su, H.-J. Energy harvesting-enabled full-duplex DF relay systems with improper gaussian signaling. In Proceedings of the 2020 IEEE Wireless Communications and Networking Conference (WCNC), Seoul, Republic of Korea, 25–28 May 2020.

21. Aswathi, V.; Babu, A.V. Outage and throughput analysis of full-duplex cooperative NOMA system with energy harvesting. *IEEE Trans. Veh. Technol.* **2021**, *70*, 11648–11664. [CrossRef]
22. Cheng, X.; Yu, B.; Cheng, X.; Yang, L. Two-Way Full-Duplex Amplify-and-Forward relaying. In Proceedings of the MILCOM 2013–2013 IEEE Military Communications Conference, San Diego, CA, USA, 18–20 November 2013.
23. Okandeji, A.; Khandaker, M.; Wong, K.-K.; Zheng, Z. Joint transmit power and relay two-way beamforming optimization for energy-harvesting full-duplex communications. In Proceedings of the 2016 IEEE Globecom Workshops (GC Wkshps), Washington, DC, USA, 4–8 December 2016.
24. Bharadia, D.; Mcmilin, E.; Katti, S. Full Duplex radios. In Proceedings of the ACM SIGCOMM 2013 Conference, Hong Kong, China, 12–16 August 2013.
25. He, Y.; Zhao, H.; Guo, W.; Shao, S.; Tang, Y. Frequency-domain successive cancellation of nonlinear self-interference with reduced complexity for full-duplex radios. *IEEE Trans. Commun.* **2022**, *70*, 2678–2690. [CrossRef]
26. Liu, H.; Kim, K.J.; Kwak, K.S.; Vincent Poor, H. Power splitting-based SWIPT with Decode-and-Forward Full-Duplex relaying. *IEEE Trans. Wirel. Commun.* **2016**, *15*, 7561–7577. [CrossRef]
27. Hajek, B. Cooling schedules for optimal annealing. *Math. Oper. Res.* **1987**, *13*, 311–329. [CrossRef]

Disclaimer/Publisher's Note: The statements, opinions and data contained in all publications are solely those of the individual author(s) and contributor(s) and not of MDPI and/or the editor(s). MDPI and/or the editor(s) disclaim responsibility for any injury to people or property resulting from any ideas, methods, instructions or products referred to in the content.

Article

A Design of a Thermoelectric Energy Harvester for Minimizing Sensor Module Cost

Kazuma Koketsu and Toru Tanzawa *

Graduate School of Integrated Science and Technology, Shizuoka University, Hamamatsu 432-8561, Japan
* Correspondence: toru.tanzawa@shizuoka.ac.jp

Abstract: This paper discusses a relationship between thermoelectric generator (TEG) electrical parameters, power efficiency of converters, and power consumption of loads in autonomous sensor modules. Based on the method discussed, one can determine the total number of TEG units together with the number of TEG arrays and the number of TEG units connected in series per array when the characteristics of TEG unit, the minimum temperature difference in operation, the power conversion efficiency of the converter and the load condition are given. A practical design flow to minimize TEG cost is proposed and demonstrated, taking the maximum open circuit voltage of TEG and the dependence of the power conversion efficiency of the converter on the input voltage of the converter into consideration. The entire system including TEG and a Dickson charge pump converter, which were designed through the proposed flow, was validated with SPICE.

Keywords: thermoelectric generator; converter; load; equivalent circuit model; maximum power point; sensor

1. Introduction

A thermoelectric generator (TEG) is a device generating electric power based on temperature differences, which is known as the Seebeck effect [1–3]. A TEG is a key device for energy harvesting among many alternatives such as photovoltaic generators and electrostatic, electromagnetic, magnetostrictive or piezoelectric vibration devices [4]. Given that a nominal TEG can only generate an output voltage on an order of 10–100 mV with a few K temperature difference, a power converter is needed to operate integrated circuits (ICs) including sensor and RF at a higher voltages such as 3 V in autonomous sensor modules [5–9], as shown in Figure 1, where V_{OC} (R_{TEG}) is the open circuit voltage (output resistance) of TEG, η is the power conversion efficiency of the converter, and V_{PP} (I_{PP}, P_{OUT}) is the output voltage (average output current, average output power) of the converter to drive sensor and RF blocks.

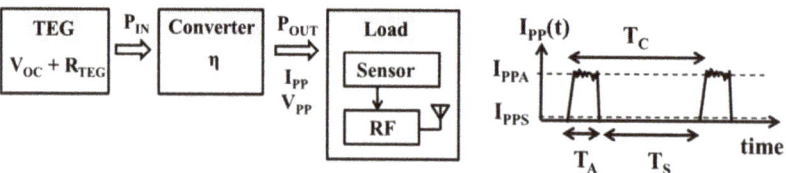

Figure 1. Block diagram of an energy harvesting system with TEG, converter, sensor and RF.

Characteristics of the output current (I_{OP}) and voltage (V_{OP}) of TEGs are described in Figure 2a with an equivalent circuit with V_{OC} and R_{TEG} as shown in Figure 2b, where I_{SC} is the short circuit current of the TEG and P_{IN} is the output power of the TEG or the input power of the converter.

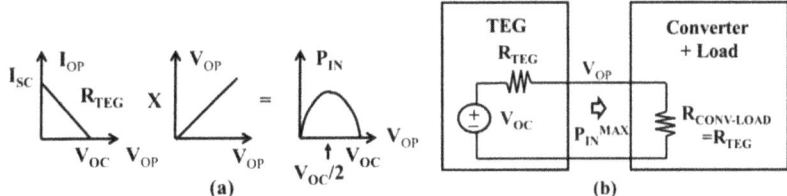

Figure 2. (a) I_{OP} and P_{IN} of TEG as a function of V_{OP} and (b) equivalent circuit under a maximum-output-power condition with impedance matching.

As a result, P_{IN} is described by a parabola where the peak power is given at the interface voltage $V_{OP} = V_{OC}/2$. Based on the equivalent circuit of a TEG system as shown in Figure 2b, the converter is designed to operate TEG at the maximum power point with a given I_{OP}-V_{OP} characteristic of TEG [10,11]. When TEG cannot operate at the maximum power point due to low input voltage, the converter needs to control the input voltage as well as the output voltage [12]. Once the application is determined, the required output current of the converter (I_{PP}) can be estimated by using (1),

$$I_{PP} = (I_{PPA} T_A + I_{PPS} T_S)/T_C \tag{1}$$

where I_{PPA}, T_A, I_{PPS}, T_S, and T_C are an average current in operation, an operation period per sense and data transmission, an average stand-by current, a stand-by period, and a cycle time per operation, respectively, as shown in Figure 1. Note that a rechargeable battery or a large capacitor is usually connected at the input terminal of the loading device to stabilize the input voltage of the sensor/RF IC against large I_{PPA}. Figure 3 shows the average power as a function of T_C in case of V_{PP} of 3 V, I_{PPS} of 1 µA, I_{PPA} of 10 mA, a bit rate of 1 Mbps, and 1 k-bytes/packet with Bluetooth low energy [13]. At a duty of 10^{-4} or lower, I_{PP} can be as low as 10 µW. Thus, the requirement for the output power of the converter is determined. From a system viewpoint, one may want to design a TEG structure in such a way that the output power of the converter is maximized under a given load condition.

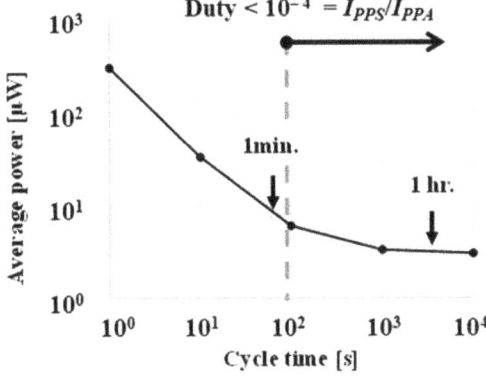

Figure 3. Average power of a sensor module as a function of the cycle time.

Table 1 illustrates a TEG composed of multiple pairs of n- and p-type thermocouples (TC). N_S (N_P) is the number of TCs connected in series (parallel). In this example, 8 TCs are connected in series (a) or arranged with two arrays of 4 TCs serially connected (b). The former configuration has higher V_{OC} and larger R_{TEG} than the latter does, as shown by (a) and (b) of Figure 4.

Table 1. Electrical parameters depending on TEG array structure.

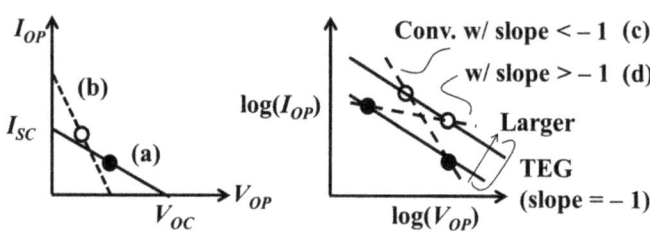

	$N_S \times N_P$	TEG Array Structure	V_{OC}	R_{TEG}	I_{SC}
(a)	8×1		8	8	1
(b)	4×2		4	2	2

Figure 4. $V_{OP} - I_{OP}$ curves of the TEGs (a) and (b) shown in Table 1 and those of the converters whose slope are smaller (c) or larger (d) than -1.

Thus, even though the area is given, one has a degree of freedom in a combination of N_S and N_P while the multiple of them is constant. In [14], a design technique was proposed to extract the maximum power over a wide V_{OC} range in case of a lack of converter by varying a combination of N_S and N_P. However, to the author's knowledge, there have been no design considerations for TEG with converters under given load conditions in the literature to answer the question of how one can determine N_S and N_P under given system conditions. For example, as shown in Figure 4, the operating point given by the cross point of the $V_{OP} - I_{OP}$ curves for the TEG and the converter depends on the slope of the $V_{OP} - I_{OP}$ curve for the converter of smaller (c) or larger (d) than -1. Since TEG is one of the most significant devices in terms of sensor module cost, its size or area must be minimized to enable massively distributed sensor modules.

This paper discusses a relationship between TEG electrical parameters, power efficiency of the converter, and power of the load toward minimizing TEG cost. How V_{OC} or R_{TEG} should be determined is shown. In addition, a design flow is proposed to minimize TEG area when the load condition is given, a Dickson charge pump (CP) [15] as converter is used to be integrated in the sensor, with an RF chip as a cost-effective solution.

2. Equations between TEG, Converter, and Load

By definition, as described in Figure 1,

$$P_{OUT} = \eta \, P_{IN} \tag{2}$$

To extract power from TEG as much as possible, the converter needs to be operated to match the input impedance of the converter with the output impedance of TEG for impedance matching, as illustrated in Figure 2b. Under the maximum-output-power condition, P_{IN} is given by (3).

$$P_{IN} = (V_{OC}/2)^2 / R_{TEG} \tag{3}$$

From (2) and (3), TEG device parameters and circuit parameters are related by (4).

$$V_{OC}^2 / R_{TEG} = 4 \, V_{PP} \, I_{PP} / \eta \tag{4}$$

V_{OC} is proportional to ΔT [2]. V_{OC} and R_{TEG} can be varied proportionally by changing TEG structure as described in Table 1. As a result, when specific TCs are characterized, V_{OC} and R_{TEG} are related as in (5).

$$V_{OC} = N_S V_{TC}, R_{TEG} = N_S/N_P R_{TC} \tag{5}$$

where V_{TC} and R_{TC} are an open circuit voltage and an output impedance of a TC, respectively. The area of TEG can be estimated by the area of TC (A_{TC}) from (5),

$$A_{TEG} = N_S N_P A_{TC} = (V_{OC}^2/R_{TEG})/(V_{TC}^2/R_{TC}) A_{TC} \tag{6}$$

V_{OC} can be also shown with R_{TEG}, instead of N_S from (5), as below.

$$V_{OC} = (V_{TC}/R_{TC}) N_P R_{TEG} \tag{7}$$

Finally, TEG with minimum area and the maximum operating point are determined by the filled circle rather than the blank one on the curve (c) or (d) in Figure 4, depending on the converter characteristic with a slope of <-1 or >-1. A trajectory of the maximum power point of TEG with a given area on $\log(I_{OP}) - \log(V_{OP})$ plane has a slope of -1. The trajectory of smaller TEG becomes closer to the origin. When the converter has a slope of <-1 as described by the curve (c) in Figure 4, the maximum power point is located at a relatively higher V_{OP} and a relatively lower I_{OP} than the case of using a converter whose slope is greater than -1.

Several conditions for TEG design are studied as follows. When the TEG area and structure are given, V_{OC} can be varied only by increasing ΔT. The minimum ΔT is determined by (4). V_{OC} depends on the square root of V_{PP}, I_{PP}, R_{TEG}, and η. Among them, V_{PP} and η are expected to not change significantly, at least in a short term. Figure 5 shows V_{OC} vs. η with $I_{PP} = 30$ μA or 3 μA and $R_{TEG} = 300$ Ω or 1 kΩ at $V_{PP} = 3$ V based on (4). When η is nominally 50%, an improvement in η by 10% only gives 10% reduction in V_{OC}. Similar goes to V_{PP}. As a result, it is considered that V_{PP} and η are not effective design parameters to mitigate the requirement for reducing V_{OC}.

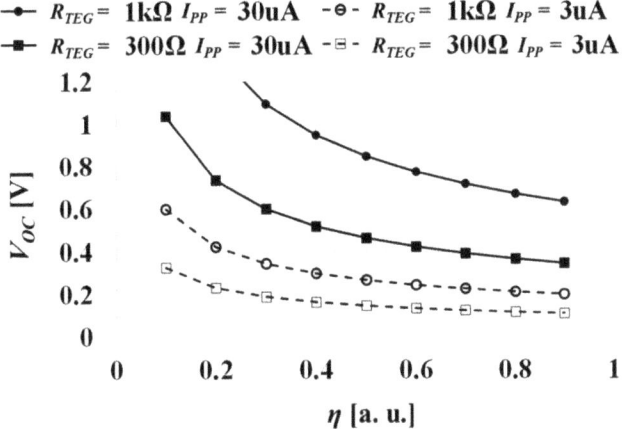

Figure 5. V_{OC} vs. η with $I_{PP} = 30$ μA or 3 μA and $R_{TEG} = 300$ Ω or 1 kΩ at $V_{PP} = 3$ V.

On the other hand, when applications allow 10X longer cycle time as shown in Figure 3, the required V_{OC} can be significantly reduced, resulting in reduction in TEG cost with reduced N_S. Next, let's look at the relationship between V_{OC} and R_{TEG} when η and the load condition are assumed. Figure 6 shows V_{OC} vs. R_{TEG} with different I_{PP}, $\eta = 0.5$, $V_{PP} = 3$ V, based on (4). If R_{TEG} needs to increase for small form factor by a factor of 10, V_{OC} has to increase by a factor of 3.2. Alternately, if T_C can be relaxed by a factor of 10 by reducing the frequency of sense and data transmission to $1/10$ in a certain application, I_{PP} can decrease by a factor of 10, which allows the system to work with V_{OC} unchanged.

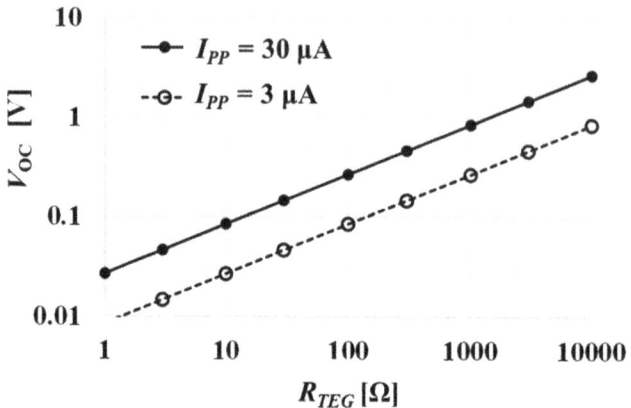

Figure 6. V_{OC} vs. R_{TEG} with different I_{PP}, $\eta = 0.5$, $V_{PP} = 3$ V.

How can one determine R_{TEG} when V_{OC} is limited by the minimum operation voltage of the converter $V_{DD}{}^{MIN}$? Figure 7 shows R_{TEG} vs. I_{PP} with $V_{OC} = 0.4$ V or 0.8 V, $\eta = 0.5$, $V_{PP} = 3$ V. Even if $V_{DD}{}^{MIN}$ of the converter can be reduced from $V_{OP} = V_{OC}/2 = 0.4$ V in case of $V_{OC} = 0.8$ V to $V_{OP} = 0.2$ V with converter designers' effort, R_{TEG} also has to be reduced by a factor of 4 with the same ΔT and I_{PP}, or I_{PP} also has to be reduced by a factor of 4 with the same ΔT and R_{TEG}, instead. Thus, the effort of improving the converter with respect to reduction in $V_{DD}{}^{MIN}$ requires more effort of reducing R_{TEG} for TEG designers or of reducing I_{PP} for system designers.

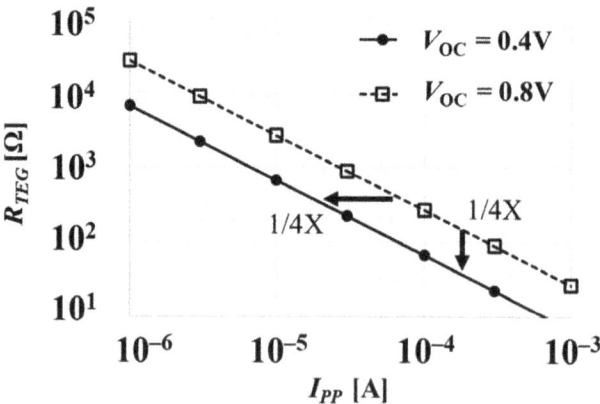

Figure 7. R_{TEG} vs. I_{PP} with $V_{OC} = 0.4$ V, 0.8 V, $\eta = 0.5$, $V_{PP} = 3$ V.

Figure 8 shows a relationship between (4) and (7). The cross points of them express the values of R_{TEG} and V_{OC} for a given condition of $V_{TC}/R_{TC} = 0.45$ mA, $I_{PP} = 30$ μA, $\eta = 0.5$, $V_{PP} = 3$ V. Given that η is assumed to be constant over V_{OP} for simplicity in this section, one cannot determine N_S and N_P to minimize TEG area. Therefore, in order to design TEG with minimum cost, a converter needs to be optimally designed by V_{OP} precisely.

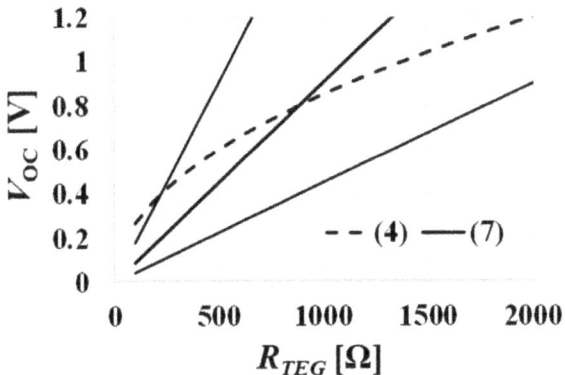

Figure 8. V_{OC}-R_{TEG} curves for TEG/converter power condition (4) and TEG characteristics (7) when V_{TC}/R_{TC} = 0.45 mA, I_{PP} = 30 μA, η = 0.5, V_{PP} = 3 V.

3. Design Flow of TEG with Minimum Area

In the above section II, η was assumed to be constant to overview the relationship between TEG electrical characteristics, converter power efficiency, and the load condition of the sensor module. In this section, a more practical design flow is proposed to determine both N_S and N_P of TEG and the design parameters of CP whose η can vary as V_{OP} at the same time.

(Assumption) The following parameters are given: V_{TC}, R_{TC}, and the target I_{PP_TGT} at V_{PP}.

(Parameters to be determined) N_S, N_P, in such a way that TEG area, i.e., the product $N_S N_P$, is minimum, as well as the number of stage N_{CP}, capacitance per stage C_{CP} and clock frequency f_{CP} to design CP.

(Step 1) Design CP with the maximum power conversion efficiency for each V_{OP} when the target I_{PP} is given at a specific V_{PP}, based on [16] as below.

It is assumed that (1) CP to be designed is a Dickson type [15], (2) it operates in slow switching limit (SSL) where the clock frequency is low enough to transfer the charges from one stage to the next one through a switching MOSFET in the subthreshold region or namely a switching diode, a unit of the diode has a voltage(V_D)–current(I_D) relationship specified by (8), and the oscillator cell consumes much lower power than the CP. Design flow in fast switching limit is open for the future work.

$$I_D = I_S e^{V_D/V_T} \tag{8}$$

The output voltage(V_{OUT})–current(I_{OUT}) relationship of the CP is given by (9) where the output impedance R_{PMP} and the maximum attainable voltage V_{MAX} are given by (10) and (11), respectively. The top plate parasitic capacitance α_T is assumed to be given by (12), where N_D, A_D, and C_J are the number of unit diodes, the junction area of a unit diode, and the junction capacitance of a unit diode. V_{TH}^{EFF} is an effective threshold voltage given by (13) [17], which is defined by the voltage difference between the adjacent capacitors at the negative clock edge, indicating the voltage loss per stage.

$$I_{OUT} = (V_{MAX} - V_{OUT})/R_{PMP} \tag{9}$$

$$R_{PMP} = \frac{N_{CP}}{f_{CP} C_{CP}(1 + \alpha_T)} \tag{10}$$

$$V_{MAX} = \left(\frac{N_{CP}}{1 + \alpha_T} + 1\right) V_{OP} - (N_{CP} + 1) V_{TH}^{EFF} \tag{11}$$

$$\alpha_T = N_D A_D C_J / C_{CP} \tag{12}$$

$$V_{TH}{}^{EFF} = V_T \ln(4^{\frac{1}{N_{CP}+1}} \frac{(1+\alpha_T)f_{CP}C_{CP}V_T}{N_D A_D I_S}) + \frac{N_{D A_D} I_S}{2 f_{CP} C_{CP}(1+\alpha_T)} \tag{13}$$

The input current I_{OP} of the CP is given by (14) as a function of the output current I_{PP} and the input voltage V_{OP}. The last term comes from the reverse leakage of switching diodes.

$$I_{OP} = \left(\frac{N_{CP}}{1+\alpha_T}+1\right)I_{PP} + \left(\frac{\alpha_T}{1+\alpha_T}+\alpha_B\right)N_{CP}f_{CP}C_{CP}V_{OP} + \frac{N_{CP}N_{D A_D} I_S}{2} \tag{14}$$

The power conversion efficiency is defined by (15).

$$\eta = \frac{V_{PP} I_{PP}}{V_{OP} I_{OP}} \tag{15}$$

The optimum number of stages N_{OPT} to maximize the power efficiency is estimated by (16) using the minimum number of stages to output V_{PP} with zero output current given by (17) [18,19], where [X] indicates a rounded integer number of X.

$$N_{OPT} = [1.4 N_{MIN}] \tag{16}$$

$$N_{MIN} = \frac{V_{PP} - V_{OP} + V_{TH}{}^{EFF}}{V_{OP}/(1+\alpha_T) - V_{TH}{}^{EFF}} \tag{17}$$

CP design flow starts with an initial condition on the target I_{PP_TGT} at V_{PP}, V_{OP}, CP area $A_{CP}{}^{INIT}$. I_{PP} and V_{PP} are specified by the loading devices such as sensor and RF ICs. The goal is determining the TEG configuration and the circuit parameters of the CP such that TEG and CP areas are minimized.

Consequently, N_D and $V_{TH}{}^{EFF}$ are treated as variables. One can calculate the flowing parameters step by step: N_{MIN} by (17), N_{OPT} by (16), C_{CP} by (18), and α_T by (12). It is assumed in (18) that the CP area is occupied by the capacitors and switching diodes, where C_{OX} is the capacitance density of each capacitor.

$$C_{CP} = \left(A_{CP}{}^{INIT}/N_{OPT} - (1+1/N_{OPT})N_D A_D\right)C_{OX} \tag{18}$$

One can numerically solve (13) for f_{CP} because the remaining parameters are determined. From (10) and (11), R_{PMP} and V_{MAX} are calculated. Then, I_{PP} is determined by (19).

$$I_{PP} = (V_{MAX} - V_{PP})/R_{PMP} \tag{19}$$

When I_{PP} is not equal to I_{PP_TGT}, C_{CP} and N_D need to be scaled up or down by the scaling factor S_F given by (20). When both C_{CP} and N_D are scaled proportionally, the optimum f_{CP} can stay the same value because (13) has C_{CP} and N_D only as their ratio. Thus, the required CP area to output I_{PP_TGT} at V_{PP} is determined by (21).

$$S_F = I_{PP\_TGT}/I_{PP} \tag{20}$$

$$A_{CP} = S_F A_{CP}{}^{INIT} \tag{21}$$

This flow can be done with various combinations of $V_{TH}{}^{EFF}$ and N_D. One can determine the best combination of all the CP parameters such as $V_{TH}{}^{EFF}$, N_D, N_{CP}, C_{CP}, and f_{CP} to have the maximum η for a given V_{OP}. One then needs to repeat the above procedure for various V_{OP}. The resultant $V_{OP} - I_{OP}$ and $V_{OP} - A_{CP}$ curves will be used together with those for TEG to determine the target configurations of TEG and CP with minimum areas as presented below.

(Step 2)
2-1: When $V_{OP} < V_{OC\_MAX}/2$ where V_{OC_MAX} is V_{OC} with $N_P = 1$, find the operating point (V_{OP}, I_{OP}) in such a way that $V_{OC} = 2\ V_{OP}$ and $R_{TEG} = V_{OP}/(2\ I_{OP})$ which meets the maximum power condition (3), as shown by the line (a) in Figure 9.

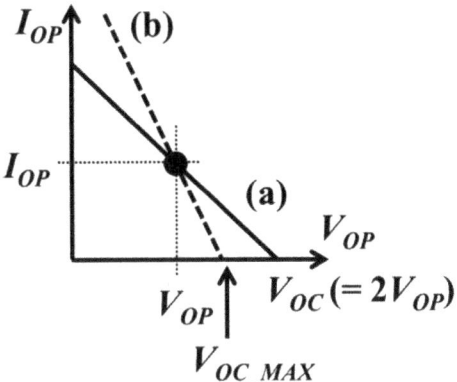

Figure 9. Operating point of TEG/Conv. vs. V_{OC} depending on V_{OC_MAX}.

Hence, one can determine

$$N_S = 2\ V_{OP}/V_{TC},\ N_P = 4\ R_{TC}I_{OP}/V_{TC} \qquad (22)$$

Then, A_{TEG} is estimated by (23), based on (6).

$$A_{TEG} = (8\ V_{OP}I_{OP})/(V_{TC}^2/R_{TC})\ A_{TC} \qquad (23)$$

2-2: When $V_{OP} > V_{OC\_MAX}/2$, one cannot design TEG to run at the maximum operating point even with $N_P = 1$, as shown by the line (b) in Figure 9. Instead, TEG needs to have the following parameters:

$$V_{OC} = V_{OC\_MAX} = N_S\ V_{TC},\ R_{TEG} = (V_{OC\_MAX} - V_{OP})/I_{OP} \qquad (24)$$

Then, A_{TEG} is estimated by (25), based on (6).

$$A_{TEG} = (V_{OC\_MAX}/V_{TC})\ A_{TC} \qquad (25)$$

where N_S and N_P are given by (26).

$$N_S = 2\ V_{OP}/V_{TC},\ N_P = 1 \qquad (26)$$

(Step 3) Find V_{OP} to minimize A_{TEG} among the values found in Step 2 in the V_{OP} range. One can also determine the design parameters of CP such as N_{CP}, C_{CP}, and f_{CP} at the same time.

Let's see how the above flow works using the parameters in Table 2, which were presented in [16], for demonstration.

Figure 10a–e show η vs. CP area when V_{TH}^{EFF} is varied between 0.02 V and 0.15 V and N_D is varied among 10, 30, 100, 300, 1000 at V_{OP} of 1.25 V in (a) through 0.25 V in (e), respectively. In this work, η is the highest priority, but a very strict constraint could need too large a CP area. Considering a trade-off between η and CP area, the best combination of the CP design parameters is determined, in order to have 2% lower η than its peak value, which is shown by an arrow in each figure. There were two groups in Figure 10b. One has $\eta > 0.55$ and the other has $\eta < 0.5$. The former has N_{CP} of three whereas the latter has N_{CP}

of four. As V_{OP} decreases, the number of groups with different numbers of N_{CP} increases. Smooth variations on η—CP area curves come from variations in V_{TH}^{EFF} or N_D while N_{CP} is unchanged.

Table 2. Design and device parameters for demonstration.

Parameter	Symbol	Value
Output voltage of CP	V_{PP} [V]	3.0
Output target current of CP	I_{PP_TGT} [μA]	30
Thermal voltage of switching diodes	V_T [mV]	25
Saturation current density of the diodes	I_S [nA/μm^2]	0.1
Junction capacitance density of the diodes	C_J [fF/μm^2]	3.5
Capacitance density of CP capacitors	C_{OX} [fF/μm^2]	10
Junction area of a unit diode	A_D [μm^2]	10
Bottom plate parasitic cap ratio to the CP cap	α_B [a.u.]	0.1

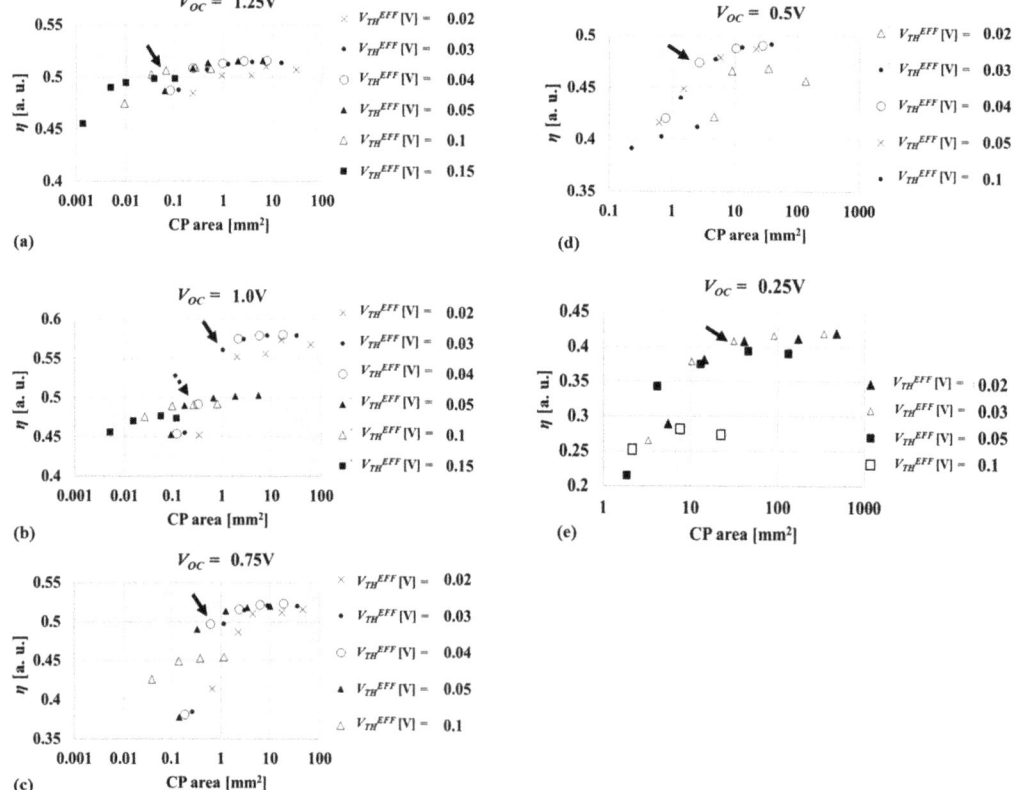

Figure 10. η vs. CP area at V_{OP} at 1.25 V (**a**), 1.0 V (**b**), 0.75 V (**c**), 0.5 V (**d**), and 0.25 V (**e**). V_{TH}^{EFF} is varied between 0.02 V and 0.15 V and N_D is varied among 10, 30, 100, 300, 1000.

Figure 11 show how smooth the functions of η, f_{CP}, CP area over N_D and V_{TH}^{EFF} are when V_{OP} is 0.25 V. V_{TH}^{EFF} is 0.03 V in Figure 11a–c. N_D is 30 in Figure 11d–f. The arrows in Figure 11a,c indicate the optimum design plotted in Figure 10e. As N_D increases, CP can run faster to keep V_{TH}^{EFF}, as shown in Figure 11b. To obtain a target output current at a target output voltage, capacitors can be scaled with f_{CP} in SSL, resulting in scaled CP area with larger N_D, as shown in Figure 11c. Faster operation increases the current for top and bottom parasitic capacitances, resulting in less power efficiency, as shown in Figure 11a. Similar tendencies are valid for the sensitivities of η, f_{CP}, CP area on V_{TH}^{EFF}. To reduce the voltage difference between the next neighbor stages at the falling edge, f_{CP} needs to be lower, as shown in Figure 11e. As a result, η and CP area decreases as V_{TH}^{EFF} increases, as shown in Figure 11d,f, respectively.

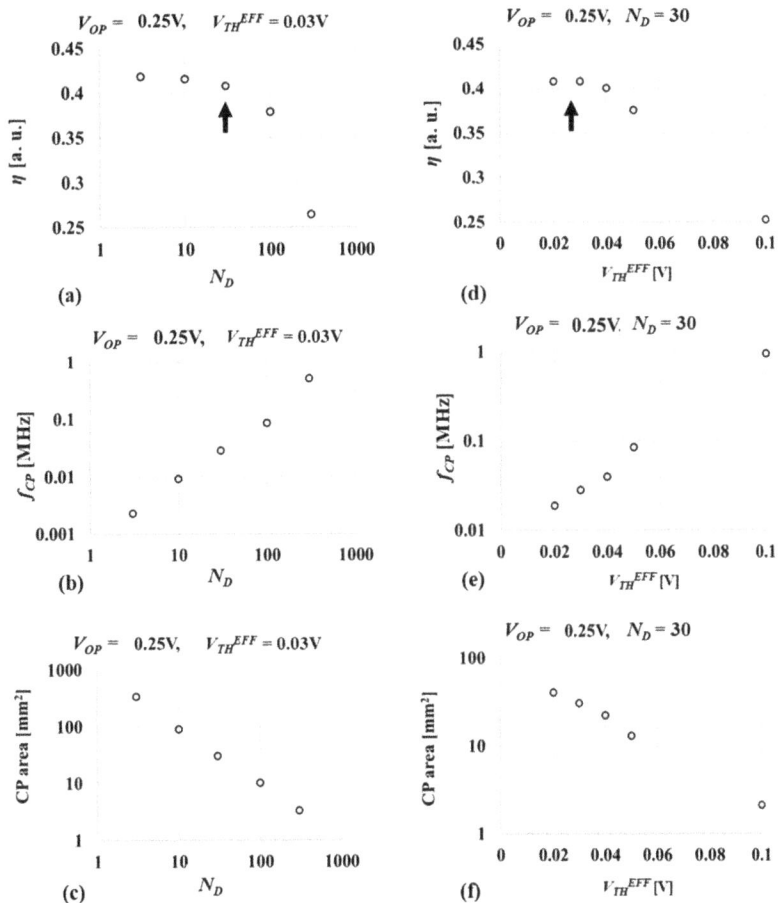

Figure 11. (a) η, (b) f_{CP}, (c) CP area vs. N_D and (d) η, (e) f_{CP}, (f) CP area vs. V_{TH}^{EFF}.

Figure 12a shows the relative design parameter values normalized by the values at V_{op} = 0.75 V, which are N_D = 300, N_{CP} = 5, C_{CP} = 1.1 nF, f_{CP} = 113 kHz, α_T = 2.9 %, V_{TH}^{EFF} = 40 mV, A_{CP} = 0.62 mm², I_{OP} = 240 µA, η = 0.50. Capacitance per stage and CP area have strong V_{op} dependence except for the glitches at V_{op} = 1.0 V, as explained above on Figure 10b. Higher V_{op} is generally required to have small CP for cost reduction. Figure 12b shows the input current of CP, I_{OP}, when the CP is designed to run at the input voltage of V_{OP} to output I_{PP} at V_{PP} with the high η. The slope was about -1.16 like the curve (c) of Figure 4, which indicates that a higher V_{OP} basically allows a smaller TEG.

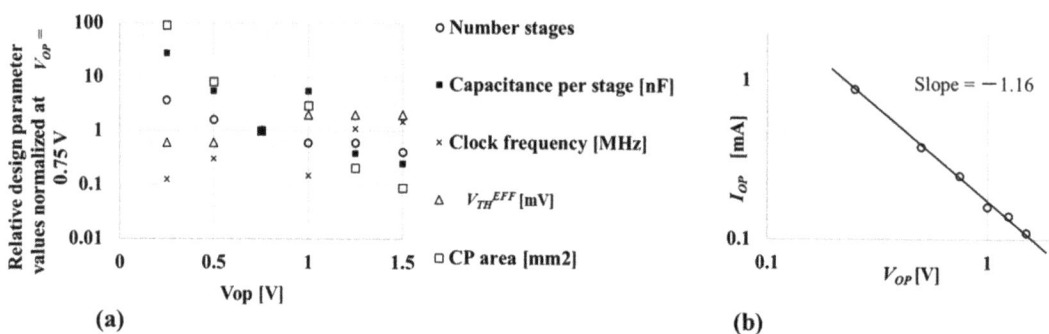

Figure 12. Trend of optimum design parameters (**a**) and I_{OP} (**b**) across V_{OP}.

Figure 13a shows η of CP vs. V_{OP}. CP1's were the optimized designs as shown by the bold arrows in Figure 10a–e. CP2 indicates another design with 6% lower η and 90% smaller area at $V_{OP} = 1$ V shown by the broken arrow in Figure 10b. η tends to increase as V_{OP}. Figure 13b shows TEG area as a function of V_{OP} by using (9) or (11) for the CPs depending on whether a variable V_{OC} range is unlimited or limited. Equation (9) is valid across the entire V_{OP} range in case of $V_{OC\_MAX} \geq 3$ V whereas (11) is used when $V_{OP} \geq 0.8$ V in case of $V_{OC\_MAX} = 1.6$ V. TEG can be minimized at a higher V_{OP} when $V_{OC\_MAX} \geq 3$ V because CP nominally has a higher η at a higher V_{OP}. On the other hand, when V_{OC_MAX} is limited, V_{OP} around $V_{OC\_MAX}/2$ provides the minimum area for TEG. In this demonstration, V_{OP} to have TEG area as small as minimum is 1.0 V with CP1 or between 0.5 V and 0.75 V with CP1 or 1.0 V with CP2. Figure 13c shows CP area as a function of V_{OP}. Basically, CP area exponentially increases as V_{OP} decreases. When V_{OC_MAX} is limited at 1.6 V, the minimum TEG cost is realized with CP1 operated at 1.0 V. CP1 area is about 1.0 mm^2. If 10% larger TEG cost is acceptable, CP2 with 0.1 mm^2 would be another option. Thus, once the actual operating point V_{OP} and I_{OP} are determined based on such graphs as Figure 13b,c, one can design TEG based on (22) or (26) under the condition that R_{TC} and the minimum V_{TC} of a unit TEG are given, depending on the V_{OC_MAX} condition as discussed above.

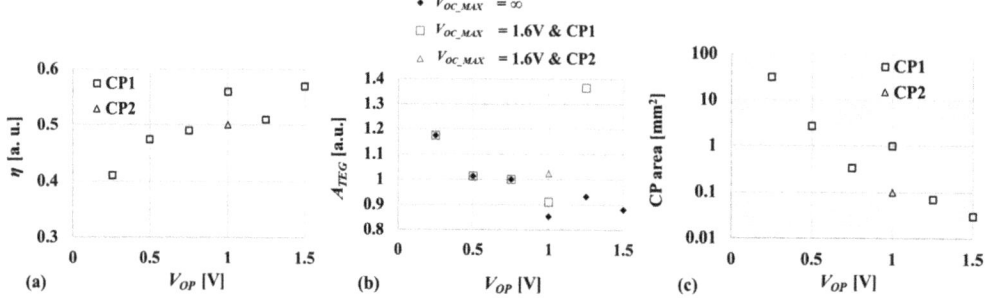

Figure 13. η of CP (**a**), A_{TEG} (**b**) and CP area (**c**) vs. V_{OP}.

In summary, CP design flow is as follows:

(1) The minimum required output current I_{PP_TGT} at the target output voltage V_{PP} are specified by the load.
(2) The optimum CP is designed to have the minimum input power as a function of the input voltage V_{OP} based on equations (9) through (21).
(3) The results provide the required TEG output current I_{OP} at every V_{OP}.

TEG design flow is then as follows:

(4) The minimum temperature difference in operation is specified, which determines the output impedance RTC and open circuit voltage VTC of a TEG unit.

(5) The number of TEG arrays NP and the number of TEG units connected in series per array NS are determined to minimize the TEG area, i.e., the TEG cost, based on equations (22) through (26).

To see if the CP design flow using Table I is sufficiently valid, the gate-level CP2 circuit to operate at V_{OP} of 1.0 V was designed in 65 nm CMOS. Ultra-low-power diodes [20] were used for switching diodes. The CP was simulated together with TEG whose V_{OC} and R_{TEG} were 1.6 V and 2.5 kΩ, respectively. The V_{PP}–I_{PP} curve of the model was in good agreement with SPICE simulation as shown in Figure 14.

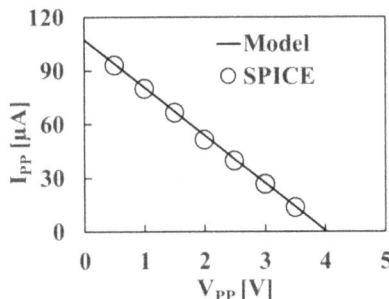

Figure 14. V_{PP}–I_{PP} of CP2 operating with TEG whose V_{OC} and R_{TEG} are 1.6 V and 2.5 kΩ.

When the parasitic resistance of the interconnection to connect multiple TEG units is not negligibly small or the oscillator cell consumes substantial power, proper corrections would need to be done to accurately design the TEG–CP system with minimum cost.

4. Conclusions

A practical design flow for minimizing TEG energy harvester was proposed and demonstrated taking interaction between the TEG electrical parameters such as the open circuit voltage and output resistance of TEG and the load conditions such as the input voltage and current of sensor/RF chip and the power conversion efficiency of the Dickson charge pump converter in autonomous sensor modules into consideration. By using the proposed design flow, one can determine the total number of TEG units together with the number of TEG arrays and the number of TEG units connected in series per array for minimum TEG cost.

Author Contributions: Conceptualization, T.T.; methodology, K.K. and T.T.; software, K.K.; validation, K.K. and T.T.; formal analysis, K.K. and T.T.; investigation, K.K. and T.T.; writing—original draft preparation, K.K.; writing—review and editing, T.T.; funding acquisition, T.T. All authors have read and agreed to the published version of the manuscript.

Funding: This research was funded by Zeon Corp.

Data Availability Statement: Not applicable.

Conflicts of Interest: The authors declare no conflict of interest.

References

1. Riffat, S.B.; Ma, X. Thermoelectrics: A review of present and potential applications. *Appl. Therm. Eng.* **2003**, *23*, 913–935. [CrossRef]
2. Venkatasubramanian, R.; Watkins, C.; Stokes, D.; Posthill, J.; Caylor, C. Energy harvesting for electronics with thermoelectric devices using nanoscale materials. In Proceedings of the 2007 IEEE International Electron Devices Meeting, Washington, DC, USA, 10–12 December 2007; IEEE: New York, NY, USA, 2007; pp. 367–370. [CrossRef]
3. Li, Y.; Buddharaju, K.; Singh, N.; Lo, G.Q.; Lee, S.J. Chip-level thermoelectric power generators based on high-density silicon nanowire array prepared with top-down CMOS technology. *IEEE Electron Device Lett.* **2011**, *32*, 674–676. [CrossRef]

4. Manoli, Y. Energy harvesting—From devices to systems. In Proceedings of the IEEE ESSCIRC Digest of Technical Paper, Seville, Spain, 14–16 September 2010; IEEE: New York, NY, USA, 2010; pp. 27–36. [CrossRef]
5. Doms, I.; Merken, P.; Van Hoof, C.; Mertens, R.P. Capacitive power management circuit for micropower thermoelectric generators with a 1.4 µA controller. *IEEE J. Solid-State Circuits* **2009**, *44*, 2824–2833. [CrossRef]
6. Weng, P.; Tang, H.; Ku, P.; Lu, L. 50 mV-input batteryless boost converter for thermal energy harvesting. *IEEE J. Solid-State Circuits* **2013**, *48*, 1031–1041. [CrossRef]
7. Ballo, A.; Grasso, A.D.; Palumbo, G. A Subthreshold cross-coupled hybrid charge pump for 50-mV cold-start. *IEEE Access* **2020**, *8*, 188959–188969. [CrossRef]
8. Bose, S.; Anand, T.; Johnston, M.L. Integrated cold start of a boost converter at 57 mV using cross-coupled complementary charge pumps and ultra-low-voltage ring oscillator. *IEEE J. Solid-State Circuits* **2019**, *54*, 2867–2878. [CrossRef] [PubMed]
9. Dezyani, M.; Ghafoorifard, H.; Sheikhaei, S.; Serdijn, W.A. A 60 mV input voltage, process tolerant start-up system for thermoelectric energy harvesting. *IEEE Trans. Circuits Syst. I Regul. Pap.* **2018**, *65*, 3568–3577. [CrossRef]
10. Lu, C.; Park, S.P.; Raghunathan, V.; Roy, K. Analysis and design of ultra low power thermoelectric energy harvesting systems. In Proceedings of the 16th ACM/IEEE International Symposium on Low Power Electronics and Design, Austin, TX, USA, 18–20 August 2010; pp. 183–188. [CrossRef]
11. Tanzawa, T. Design of DC–DC switched-capacitor voltage multiplier driven by DC energy transducer. In Proceedings of the 2014 21st IEEE International Conference on Electronics, Circuits and Systems (ICECS), Marseille, France, 7–10 December 2014; IEEE: New York, NY, USA, 2014; pp. 327–330. [CrossRef]
12. Koketsu, K.; Tanzawa, T. Design of a charge pump circuit and system with input impedance modulation for a flexible-type thermoelectric generator with high-output impedance. *Electronics* **2021**, *10*, 1212. [CrossRef]
13. Tosi, J.; Taffoni, F.; Santacatterina, M.; Sannino, R.; Formica, D. Performance evaluation of bluetooth low energy: A systematic review. *Sensors* **2017**, *17*, 2898. [CrossRef] [PubMed]
14. Wan, Q.; Teh, Y.-K.; Gao, Y.; Mok, P.K.T. Analysis and design of a thermoelectric energy harvesting system with reconfigurable array of thermoelectric generators for IoT applications. *IEEE Trans. Circuits Syst. I Regul. Pap.* **2017**, *64*, 2346–2358. [CrossRef]
15. Dickson, J.F. On-chip high-voltage generation in MNOS integrated circuits using an improved voltage multiplier technique. *IEEE J. Solid-State Circuits* **1976**, *11*, 374–378. [CrossRef]
16. Tokuda, S.; Tanzawa, T. Toward a minimum-operating-voltage design of DC-DC charge pump circuits for energy harvesting. In Proceedings of the IEEE International Symposium on Circuits and Systems (ISCAS), Sapporo, Japan, 26–29 May 2019; IEEE: New York, NY, USA, 2019. [CrossRef]
17. Tanzawa, T. An analytical model of charge pump DC-DC voltage multiplier using diodes. *IEICE Trans. Fundam. Electron. Commun. Comput. Sci.* **2017**, *100*, 1137–1144. [CrossRef]
18. Palumbo, G.; Pappalardo, D.; Gaibotti, M. Charge-pump circuits: Power-consumption optimization. *IEEE Trans. Circuits Syst. I Fundam. Theory Appl.* **2002**, *49*, 1535–1542. [CrossRef]
19. Tanzawa, T. An optimum design for integrated switched-capacitor Dickson charge pump multipliers with area power balance. *IEEE Trans. Power Electron.* **2014**, *29*, 534–538. [CrossRef]
20. Levacq, D.; Liber, C.; Dessard, V.; Flandre, D. Composite ULP diode fabrication, modelling and applications in multi-Vth FD SOI CMOS technology. *Solid-State Electron.* **2004**, *48*, 1017–1025. [CrossRef]

Article

Comparison of Phase-Locked Loops Used for Frequency Measurements in a Low-Inertia Power Grid with Wind Generation

Orlando David Guerrero-Bermúdez [1], Sergio Martinez [1,*], Eder Molina [2] and John E. Candelo-Becerra [3]

1. Escuela Técnica Superior de Ingenieros Industriales, Universidad Politécnica de Madrid, 28040 Madrid, Spain
2. Centro de Investigación Audacia, Universidad Simón Bolívar, Barranquilla 080002, Colombia
3. Facultad de Minas, Departamento de Energía Eléctrica y Automática, Universidad Nacional de Colombia-Sede Medellín, Carrera 80 No. 65-223, Robledo, Medellín 050041, Colombia
* Correspondence: sergio.martinez@upm.es

Abstract: The need for more precise frequency measurements in electric power systems is increasing because of the growing penetration of renewable energy and the subsequent reduction in inertia, which gives rise to more intense frequency fluctuations. Phase-locked loops (PLLs) are now more accurate and present faster dynamic responses, helping to implement primary frequency controllers for renewable generators connected to the grid through power electronics. However, there are differences among PLL implementations that affect their behavior when estimating frequency, depending on factors as location, voltage level, or penetration of renewable energy, among other things. How this affects the ability of PLL-based frequency controllers to adequately estimate the instantaneous mismatch between generation and demand, especially in low-inertia power systems, is still unclear, and constitutes an open research topic. This paper contributes to this research effort by presenting a comparative study of different PLL configurations in order to gain insight into their performance in different scenarios in a low-inertia power system with a high share of wind energy. Constant and variable wind speed scenarios are considered, and PLL behavior is assessed in terms of the absolute mean value and the root-mean-square value of the frequency error, and the absolute value of the frequency derivative error. The results show that the PLL behavior depends on the voltage level and the location, and it was found that the further away the PLL is from the source that controls the frequency, the more noise is produced, which impacts the quality of the frequency measurement.

Keywords: frequency; wind generator; synchronous machine; phase-locked loop; low-inertia power grid

1. Introduction

The current trend in electric power systems of displacing conventional power plants by renewable energy ones has unquestionable environmental and economic benefits, but it also poses new challenges. Apart from the evident intermittent character of renewable resources, photovoltaic solar and wind energies also cause some stability, power quality, and reliability issues [1,2]. In contrast to conventional synchronous generators, which are directly connected to the grid, renewable generators are mainly connected through electronic converters [3]. This decoupling reduces the synchronous equivalent inertia of the power system [4] and impacts its dynamic behavior in the case of disturbances of different natures [5].

In alternating current power systems, the rotational speed of online synchronous generators determines the frequency of current and voltage waveforms. Under steady-state conditions, all synchronous generators in the power system rotate at the same electrical speed, which is proportional to the unique system frequency. The frequency deviation from its rated value (50 or 60 Hz) is closely related to the transient differences between the mechanical power input to synchronous generators and the electrical power demand. These mismatches are assumed by the kinetic energy stored in rotating masses, impacting the rotational speed of the generators and, consequently, the system's frequency. This natural inertial response of conventional generators to mismatches in the demand–generation balance is not present in renewable generators connected to the grid through electronic converters. To include the power response of these generators to frequency variations, their controllers must include accurate frequency measurements at the connection point.

A phase-locked loop (PLL) is the most common technology for performing frequency measurements in a power system, helping to synchronize the power converters with the grid. In addition, it is now widely used because its indirect measurement system detects deviations quickly, contributing to the frequency, voltage, and power control of the network, which are required to maintain power system stability.

There are various PLL technologies applied in power converters, some of them used for different applications and studies, including the synchronous reference frame PLL (SRF–PLL) [6], Lag PLL (LAG-PLL) [7], Low-Pass Filter PLL (LPF-PLL) [8], Enhanced PLL (E-PLL) [9], Moving Average Filter PLL (MAF-PLL) [10], second-order generalized integrator–frequency-locked loop (SOGI-FLL) [11], second-order generalized integrator PLL (SOGI-PLL) [12], and double second-order generalized integrator PLL (DSOGI-PLL) [13]. As the commercial PLLs consider a wide variety of devices that comply with the measurement function using different methods, it is interesting to evaluate the behavior of each one under different signal variations, for example, due to wind speed variations.

Some authors have compared the use of PLLs for power system applications. For example, the authors of [14] performed experimental tests of PLLs implemented on a digital signal processor (DSP), comparing the filtering capacities of SRF-PLL, E-PLL, QPLL, and DSOGI-PLL. They considered internal and external filtering harmonics in the voltage to identify the behaviors and solutions provided by each PLL implementation. However, other PLLs were not included, and the frequency response on different locations in a power system was not considered. In [15], the authors performed simulations and experiments to compare SRF-PLL algorithms under distorted utility conditions to perform a performance evaluation. However, not all PLLs were evaluated in this research.

In [8], the authors evaluated different PLLs to develop improved noise filtering and reduce numerical spikes after sudden variations of the voltage at the AC bus of the converter. The paper compared the dynamic behavior of SRF-PLL, Lag-PLL, LPF-PLL, E-PLL, and SOGI-FLL, considering both contingencies and noise [8]. However, these PLLs were not tested to evaluate the frequency behavior in different buses and consider wind speed variations. In [16], the authors compared SRF-PLL, LAG-PLL, LPF-PLL, E-PLL, and SOGI-FLL to estimate frequency deviations. They used the IEEE nine-bus test power system, and the evaluation focuses on accuracy and sensitivity to noise. However, they evaluated the system at one bus, and no wind speed scenarios were considered. In [17], a comparison of the performance of SRF-PLL, DSRF-PLL, and DSOGI-PLL was presented in response to the grid voltage magnitude changes with symmetrical and asymmetrical changes similar to those found in rural networks with renewable energies. In this last paper, the authors used a general power system model and focused on balanced and unbalanced grid voltage scenarios. In [18], a comparison of the SOGI-FLL and the SOGI-PLL for single-phase grid-connected inverters was presented. The authors considered frequency and voltage magnitude changes of a single-phase power input.

In [19], the authors conducted a comparison of SFR-PLL, DSOGI-PLL, enhanced synchronous reference frame PLL (ESRF-PLL), and Decoupled Double Synchronous Reference Frame PLL (DDSRF-PLL) to estimate the system frequency under unbalances, harmonics, and frequency variations. However, they evaluated the performance of PLLs in a numerical case study and did not consider a system with renewable energy sources. In [20], the authors compared the PLL and SRF controllers for six-pulse D-STATCOM to compensate voltage flicker due to electric arc furnace load in the IEEE 13 distribution bus test system. They only considered the main energy source and a medium-sized industrial plant, and did not compare other PLLs. In [21], the authors validated the performance of different PLLs under voltage-sag, varying grid frequency, phase jump, and dc-offset disturbances on the basis of simulation and experimental results. They modeled the SOGI-PLL, cascaded SOGI-PLL (CSOGI-PLL), second-order SOGI-PLL (SO-SOGI-PLL), modified SOGI-PLL (MSOGI-PLL), and mixed second- and third-order generalized integrator PLL (MSTOGI-PLL). They performed simulation and experimental tests to evaluate power quality by changing the parameters of the source and without considering other types of sources.

In [22], the authors evaluated the SRF-PLL, MAF-PLL, and cascaded delayed signal cancellation PLL (CDSC-PLL) for grid voltages contaminated with interharmonics in the presence of different grid disturbances, such as frequency jump, phase angle jump, and dc offset. They performed the test by changing the grid parameters to evaluate the performance of the PLLs, but they did not use a power system with different voltages and renewable sources. In [23], the authors compared the behavior of abc reference frame PLL (abc-PLL), stationary reference frame PLL ($\alpha\beta$-PLL), synchronous reference frame PLL (dq-PLL), voltage reforming synchronous reference frame PLL (VRSR-PLL), and decoupled double synchronous reference frame PLL (DDSRF-LL) under balanced and unbalanced voltages. They changed the grid voltage parameters to perform the test, and no detailed power system models were included to represent wind energies.

To the best of our knowledge, the literature review shows that PLLs are widely used, and have been compared for different applications in order to evaluate their measurement capacities. However, some authors compare few PLLs [17], do not perform an evaluation on different voltage levels in the power network [18], or do not consider wind speed scenarios [8]. In addition, other papers have compared PLLs in other applications [22,24–26]. In summary, there are differences among PLL implementations that affect their behavior when estimating frequency, depending on factors such as location, voltage level or penetration of renewable energy, among others. How this affects the ability of PLL-based frequency controllers to adequately estimate the instantaneous mismatch between generation and demand, especially in low-inertia power systems, is still unclear and constitutes an open research topic.

The aim of the work presented in this paper is to contribute towards this research effort by presenting a comparative study of different PLL configurations to gain insight on their performance in different scenarios of a low-inertia power system with high share of wind energy. This study is conducted on the basis of simulations on a test power system with a synchronous generator, a wind farm, and a constant impedance load, and it is structured as follows: (1) Different PLLs (SRF-PLL, LAG-PLL, SOGI-PLL, DSOGI-PLL, and MAF-PLL) are located at different buses in the power system and their performance on dynamic frequency measurement is compared. (2) The simulations are carried out in two operation scenarios for the wind generators: with constant wind speed (steady-state operation) and with variable wind speed (small signal disturbances). (3) The work analyzes the measurement error of the PLLs with typical deviation indexes compared to the rotation speed of the synchronous generator, used as reference. (4) The research concludes by identifying the configurations that best suit the needs at different operation points of the power system.

In summary, constant and variable wind speed scenarios are considered, and the PLL behavior is assessed in terms of the absolute mean value and the root-mean-square value of the frequency error, and the absolute value of the frequency derivative error. The results show that the PLL behavior depends on the voltage level and the location, indicating that the further away the PLL is from the source that controls the frequency, the more noise is produced, which impacts the quality of the frequency measurement.

The remainder of the paper is structured as three more sections. Section 2 outlines the materials and methods, where the general concepts, diagrams, and mathematical models of the PLLs are presented. In addition, this section includes the power system models and parameters and defines the scenarios chosen to perform the tests. Section 3 presents the frequency measurement results and the errors from each PLL implementation at different buses in the test power system, including a summary of the advantages and drawbacks of the different alternatives. Finally, Section 4 summarizes the conclusions and suggests future work.

2. Materials and Methods

This section introduces the theoretical foundation of PLLs, the general description of each PLL, the scenarios used to perform the comparison, and the power system used to evaluate the methods.

2.1. Phase-Locked Loop

A PLL is a power electronic application that indirectly measures frequency, voltage magnitude, and voltage angle. These variables are essential to identifying the operating state of a power system. All signals are monitored to guarantee the power system stability according to the applicable standards.

Figure 1 presents a basic diagram of a PLL, comprising a phase detector (PD), a loop filter (LF), and a voltage-controlled oscillator (VCO).

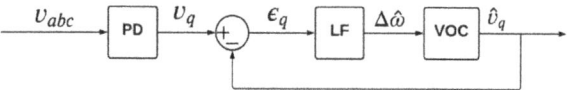

Figure 1. Basic diagram of a phase-locked loop (PLL).

The PLL works by receiving a single-phase or three-phase voltage signal and returning signals through algorithms with fast and precise detection, such as the network frequency.

2.1.1. Phase Detector (PD)

The PD uses a three-phase voltage vector at the desired measurement point, $v_{abc}(t)$, as shown in Figure 2a. This voltage is converted using spatial vectors from an *abc* representation (see Figure 2a) to an $\alpha\beta$ representation (see Figure 2b).

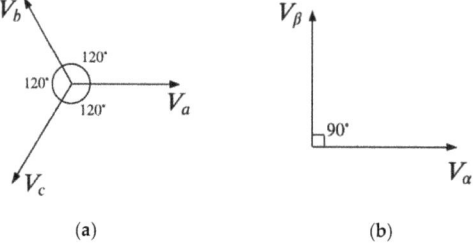

(a)   (b)

Figure 2. Clarke transformation [27]: (**a**) *abc* representation and (**b**) $\alpha\beta$ representation.

The three-phase voltages of a balanced network are given by Equation (1):

$$V_{abc} = \begin{bmatrix} v_a \\ v_b \\ v_c \end{bmatrix} = V_m \begin{bmatrix} \cos(wt + \theta_a) \\ \cos(wt + \theta_a - 2\pi/3) \\ \cos(wt + \theta_a + 2\pi/3) \end{bmatrix}, \tag{1}$$

where v_a, v_b, and v_c, are the instantaneous phase voltages, V_m is the voltage amplitude, θ_a is the v_a initial phase angle, and w is the angular frequency.

The Clarke transformation is given by Equation (2):

$$\begin{bmatrix} V_\alpha \\ V_\beta \end{bmatrix} = \frac{2}{3} \begin{bmatrix} 1 & -1/2 & -1/2 \\ 0 & \sqrt{3}/2 & -\sqrt{3}/2 \end{bmatrix} \begin{bmatrix} v_a \\ v_b \\ v_c \end{bmatrix}. \tag{2}$$

This can be written in a more compact way as Equation (3):

$$V_{\alpha\beta} = [T_{\alpha\beta}] \, V_{abc}. \tag{3}$$

The $\alpha\beta$ representation can be simplified as shown in Equation (4), where θ is the instantaneous angle of the angular frequency w ($\theta = wt + \theta_a$):

$$\begin{bmatrix} V_\alpha \\ V_\beta \end{bmatrix} = V_m \begin{bmatrix} \cos\theta \\ \sin\theta \end{bmatrix}. \tag{4}$$

The phase angle θ can be tracked by synchronizing the voltage vector along the direct axis (d). The $\alpha\beta$ stationary reference frame is transformed into a rotating reference frame (dq) using the Park transform, as shown in Figure 3.

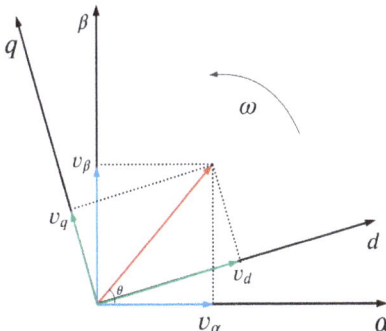

Figure 3. Park and Clarke transformations [28].

Equation (5) presents the Park transform, where θ' is the instantaneous angle of the rotating reference frame. Equation (5) can be written in a more compact way as Equation (6).

$$\begin{bmatrix} V_d \\ V_q \end{bmatrix} = \begin{bmatrix} \cos(\theta') & \sin(\theta') \\ -\sin(\theta') & \cos(\theta') \end{bmatrix} \begin{bmatrix} V_\alpha \\ V_\beta \end{bmatrix} \tag{5}$$

$$V_{dq} = [T_{dq}] \, V_{\alpha\beta} \tag{6}$$

Equation (7) displays the dq transform, as a combination of Park and Clarke transformations.

$$\begin{bmatrix} V_d \\ V_q \end{bmatrix} = [T_{dq}] \, [T_{\alpha\beta}] \, V_{abc} = V_m \begin{bmatrix} \cos(\theta - \theta') \\ \sin(\theta - \theta') \end{bmatrix}. \tag{7}$$

2.1.2. Loop Filter (LF)

After transforming the voltage signal from abc to dq, the loop filter (LF) compares the error $\varepsilon_q(t)$ between the voltage measurement on the q axis and the value estimated by the PLL. Several methods are used in PLLs to perform filtering, including stages such as attenuation, low-pass filtering, or high-pass filtering.

2.1.3. Voltage-Controlled Oscillator (VCO)

After the signal is filtered, it enters the voltage-controlled oscillator (VCO), which takes the frequency deviation and provides the estimation of the q-axis component to obtain the error $\varepsilon_q(t)$. The VCO generally consists of a pure integrator to avoid steady-state signal noise.

2.2. Phase-Locked Loop Configurations

Different PLLs on the market can measure frequency. Some of these configurations are reviewed to identify their characteristics and compare their functioning.

2.2.1. Synchronous Reference Frame PLL (SRF-PLL)

Synchronous reference frame PLL (SRF-PLL) is one of the most used types today, and is one of the simplest to implement. This PLL considers a PD modeled as a pure delay, the LF is implemented with a PI controller, and the VCO is an integrator [14,29], as displayed in Figure 4.

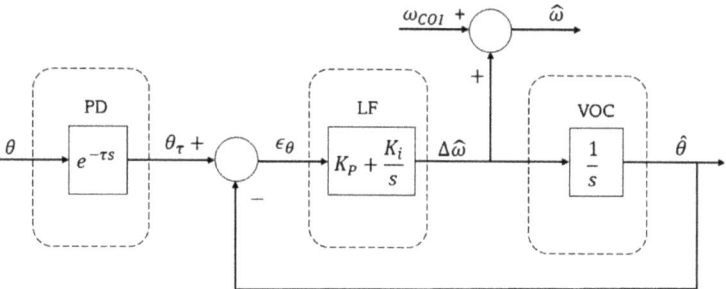

Figure 4. Diagram of the synchronous reference frame (SRF)-PLL.

2.2.2. Lag-PLL

Lag-PLL is an SRF-PLL with a low-pass filter before the PI on the LF, as indicated in Figure 5. A low-pass filter after the T_{dq} transform reduces the sensitivity of the PLL to harmonics (or noise), preventing numerical errors in the frequency measurement [15].

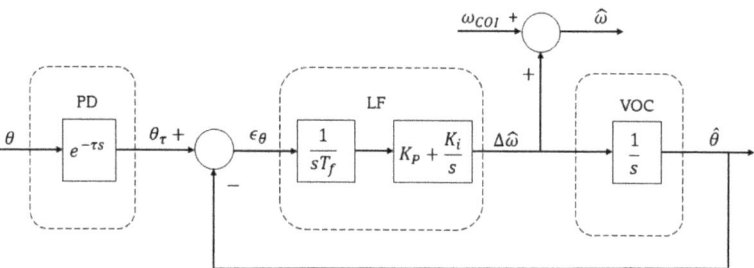

Figure 5. Diagram of the Lag-PLL.

2.2.3. Second-Order Generalized Integrator PLL (SOGI PLL)

This PLL is typically used in single-phase systems and works under the concept of the second-order generalized integrator (SOGI) for sinusoidal signals [30], as presented in Figure 6. As stated in [31], this integrator is derived from the principle whereby the time domain convolution product of a sinusoidal function gives the original function multiplied by the time variable. Therefore, a processing block, whose transfer function matches the Laplace transform of a sinusoidal function, will act as an amplitude integrator for a sinusoidal signal applied to its input. Furthermore, the quadrature combination of the sine and cosine transfer functions gives rise to an ideal integrator independent of the phase angle of the sinusoidal input signal.

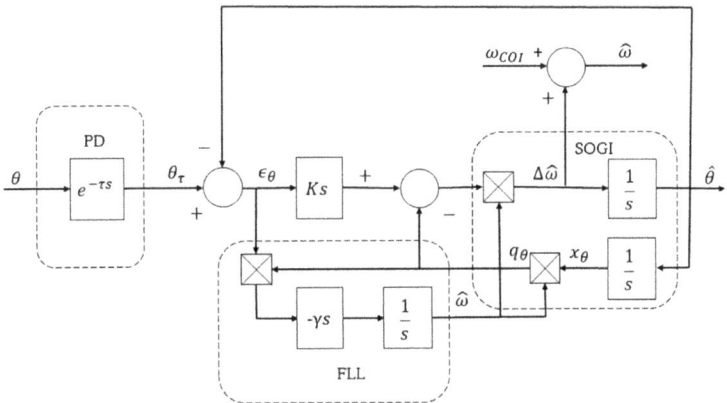

Figure 6. Diagram of the SOGI-PLL.

Figure 7 presents the low-pass filter stage of the SOGI-PLL.

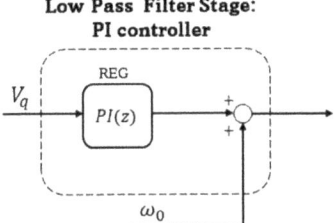

Figure 7. Low-pass filter of the SOGI-PLL.

2.2.4. Dual Second-Order Generalized Integrator PLL (DSOGI-PLL)

For three-phase systems, it is common to use two SOGIs in parallel, as specified in Figure 8. The signal then enters an SRF-PLL to take advantage of its filtering characteristics. This provides excellent protection against voltage unbalances in the network. This technique has demonstrated fast, accurate, and adaptive frequency response to grid fault conditions [32].

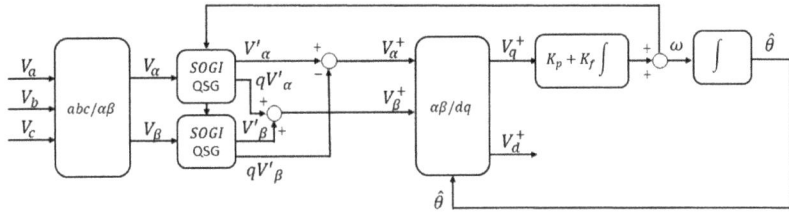

Figure 8. Diagram of the DSOGI-PLL.

2.2.5. Moving Average Filter PLL (MAF-PLL)

This configuration, presented in Figure 9, is like the Lag-PLL, which adds a filter before the PI (MAF) to reject harmonics in the frequency measurement. The representation of the signal $x(t)$ is defined as follows [33]:

$$\bar{x}(t) = \frac{1}{T_\omega} \int_{t-T_\omega}^{t} x(\tau) d\tau. \tag{8}$$

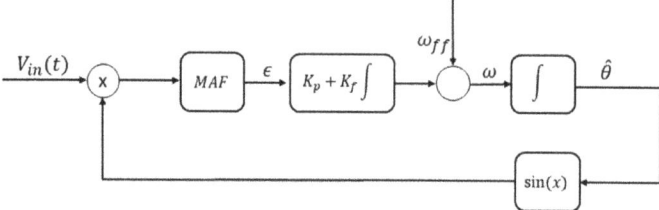

Figure 9. Diagram of the MAF-PLL.

Finally, Figure 10 shows the MAF-PLL configuration, which considers the transformation from $\Delta\omega$ to frequency (Hz).

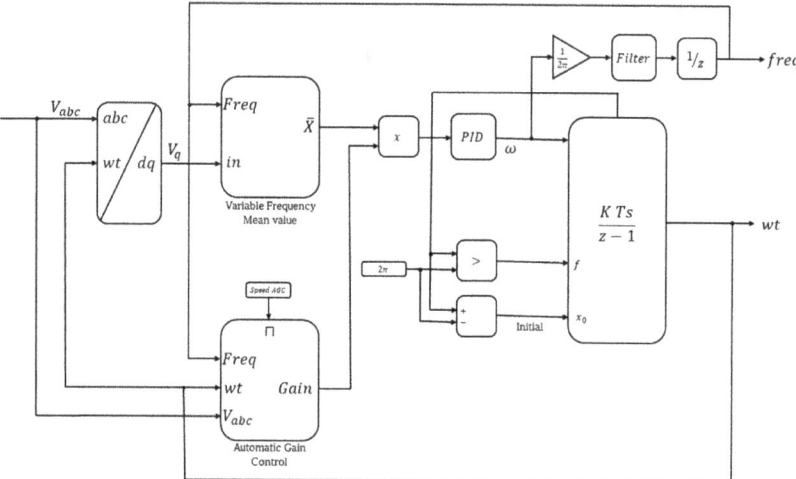

Figure 10. Diagram of the MAF-PLL VCO (voltage-controlled oscillator).

2.3. Test Power System

Figure 11 shows the power system test case used to compare the PLLs. This system considers a 50 MVA synchronous machine, a 10 MVA wind farm, and a three-phase parallel load with 40 MW and 2 MVAr (constant impedance load). The system inertia is provided by a steam turbine with a synchronous machine of 13.8 kV, and 3600 rpm. This turbine is controlled by a primary steam engine composed in complete tandem, including a speed control system, turbine steam with four stages, and a simple mass axis. The time constants and regulation parameters are obtained by considering the elements used in the research [34,35] and summarized in Table 1. A power system stabilizer (PSS) provides frequency and voltage stability control, which adds damping to the oscillations of the synchronous machine rotor by controlling its excitation, thus maintaining the system stability [36].

Five wind turbines of 2 MW are represented in the power system, considering the model proposed in [37]. Each type 4 wind turbine consists of a synchronous generator connected to a rectifier, a PWM boost converter based on a DC/DC IGBT, and a PWM converter based on a DC/AC IGBT with voltage sources. This type 4 technology achieves maximum wind energy for low wind speeds by optimizing turbine speed while minimizing mechanical stresses during wind gusts [37].

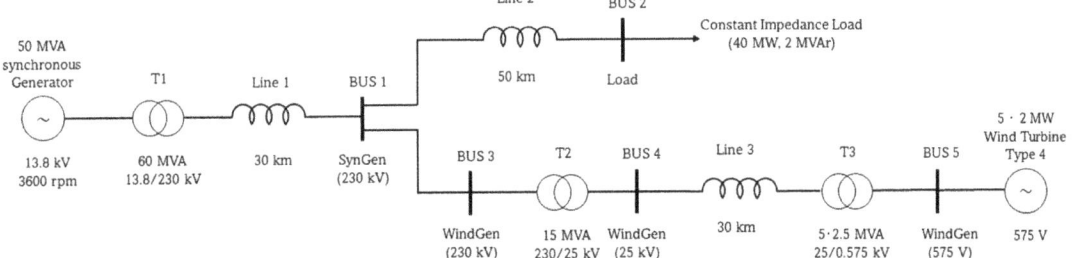

Figure 11. Power system test case used to compare the PLLs.

Table 1. Time constants and reactance parameters of the synchronous machine used in the study.

Parameter	Symbol	Value
d-axis subtransient short-circuit time constant	T_d''	0.023 s
d-axis transient short-circuit time constant	T_d'	1.32 s
d-axis transient open-circuit time constant	T_{do}'	4.5 s
Armature time constant	T_a	0.15 s
Subtransient d-axis reactance	X_d''	20%
Transient d-axis reactance	X_d'	25%
d-axis reactance	X_d	165%

Transmission lines are represented by a π model, following the recommendations of [38]. Two winding three-phase transformers are used to step up the voltage of the synchronous machine from 13.8 kV to 230 kV, and the wind turbine from 575 V to 25 kV and from 25 kV to 230 kV. The connections of the power transformers are carried out following the recommendations of [39].

2.4. Case Study

The different PLL configurations were evaluated on the basis of simulations of the test power system with MATLAB/Simulink. Just as an example of the implementation of the models in Simulink, Figure 12 shows a screenshot of the Simulink model 7 of the wind turbine used.

Simulations consider two different wind scenarios in the test power system under study:

- Scenario 1: Frequency measurement with a constant wind speed (15 m/s), constant load, and reactive power reference at 0 var.
- Scenario 2: Frequency measurement with variable wind speed data taken from [40] (day 055 of 1992), as presented in Figure 13. The speed data are expressed in m/s, sampled at 25 Hz (samples every 40 ms). A period of 430 s is considered for this study, with the wind speed kept constant for the first 130 s.

The frequency was measured with the PLLs located at the following buses presented in Figure 11:

(1) 230 kV bus in the synchronous generator zone (230 kV SynGen bus);
(2) 230 kV bus in the load zone (230 kV Load bus);
(3) 230 kV bus in the wind generator zone (230 kV WinGen bus);
(4) 25 kV bus in the wind generator zone (25 kV WinGen bus); and
(5) 575 V bus in the wind generator zone (575 V WinGen bus).

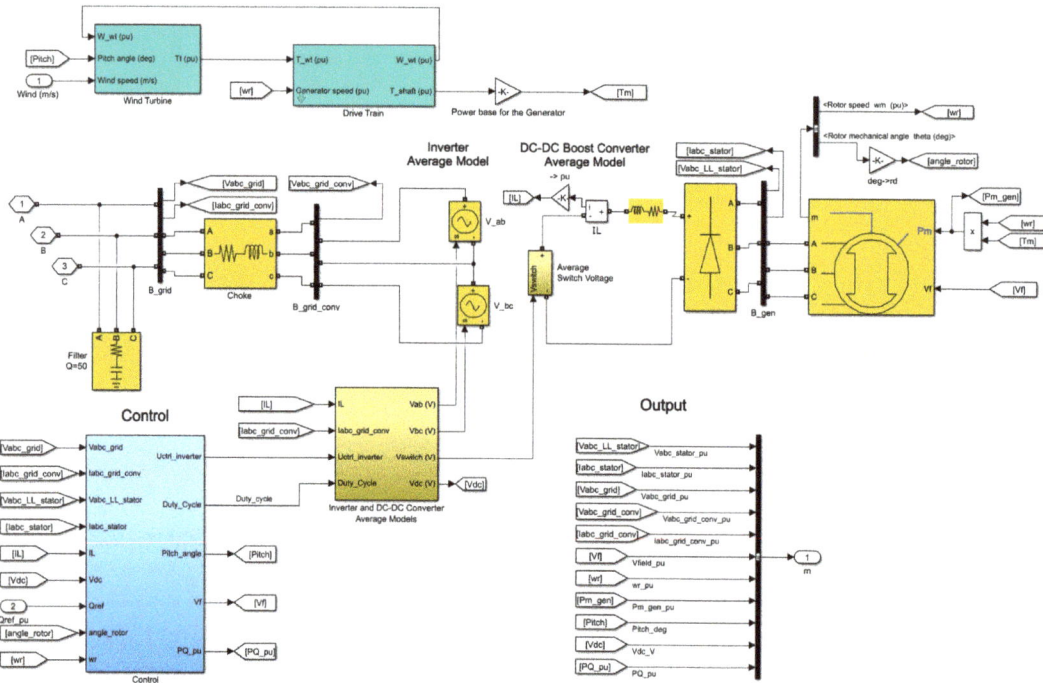

Figure 12. Simulink model of the wind generator and the control system.

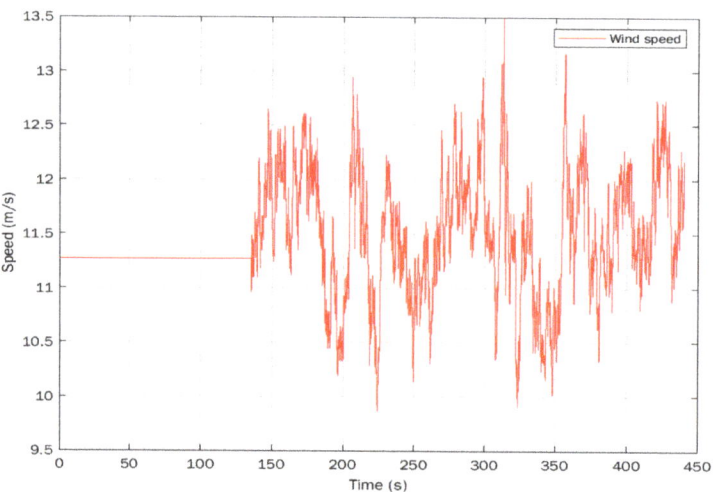

Figure 13. Variable wind speed data.

2.5. Measurement Deviation

The way to compare data is by calculating the measurement deviation. This value is compared to the reference speed of the synchronous machine. For this calculation, some comparison methodologies are used, related to indirect measurement, as described below.

2.5.1. Mean Absolute Error

The mean absolute error (MAE) is commonly used to compare predicted versus measured values. It can be used to compare different measurement techniques with an observable reference in several events. The mean absolute error (MAE) is the average value of the error e_i as presented in Equation (9), where n is the number of samples, y_i is the measured value, and x_i is the reference value [41].

$$MAE = \frac{\sum_{i=1}^{n} |e_i|}{n} = \frac{\sum_{i=1}^{n} |y_i - x_i|}{n}. \tag{9}$$

It can be expressed as a percentage of the reference values as:

$$MAE\% = \frac{\sum_{i=1}^{n} |y_i/x_i - 1|}{n} 100. \tag{10}$$

2.5.2. Root-Mean-Square Error

The root-mean-square error (RMSE) is a statistical metric commonly used for electrical magnitudes because of its usefulness in studying periodic waveforms. It gives the square root of the mean value of the squared function of the instantaneous deviations, as shown in Equation (11):

$$RMSE = \sqrt{\frac{\sum_{i=1}^{n}(y_i - x_i)^2}{n}}. \tag{11}$$

Or, as a percentage of the reference, as follows:

$$RMSE\% = \sqrt{\frac{\sum_{i=1}^{n}(y_i/x_i - 1)^2}{n}} 100. \tag{12}$$

2.5.3. Error of the Frequency Derivative

The analysis of the derivative of the frequency, also known as rate of change of frequency (RoCoF), is interesting for assessing the effectiveness of frequency control in power systems. For a given sample y_i at time t_i, it can be computed as in Equation (13):

$$RoCoF_i = \frac{y_i - y_{i-1}}{t_i - t_{i-1}}. \tag{13}$$

To assess the behavior of different PLLs in relation to their ability to track the RoCoF, in this work we use the absolute error of the frequency derivative (AEFD). For a given sample, it can be computed in terms of the reference signal x as:

$$AEFD_i = \left| RoCoF_i - \frac{x_i - x_{i-1}}{t_i - t_{i-1}} \right|. \tag{14}$$

As global metrics for a given period with n samples, in this work we use the cumulative relative AEFD (CAEFD%) and the cumulative relative root-mean-square error of the frequency derivative (CRMSEFD%), defined as:

$$CAEFD\% = \sum_{i=1}^{n} \left| \frac{RoCoF_i}{\frac{x_i - x_{i-1}}{t_i - t_{i-1}}} - 1 \right| 100. \tag{15}$$

$$CRMSEFD\% = \sqrt{\sum_{i=1}^{n} \left(\frac{RoCoF_i}{\frac{x_i - x_{i-1}}{t_i - t_{i-1}}} - 1 \right)^2} 100. \tag{16}$$

3. Results and Analysis

This section compares different PLLs in two scenarios (Scenario 1: constant wind speed and Scenario 2: variable wind speed). The error metrics (MAE%, RMSE% and AEFD%) are quantified and compared to identify the advantages and disadvantages of each PLL.

3.1. Scenario 1: Constant Wind Speed

This scenario is characterized by a constant wind speed of 15 m/s in the wind farm and an almost constant load, only disturbed by 1% step variations every 10 s. Figure 14 shows the frequency measurements with the PLLs located at the 230 kV WinGen bus during quasi-steady-state operation of the power system. Figure 14a presents the system frequency measured with the PLLs from seconds 15 to 35. This figure illustrates that all PLLs measure the frequency similarly in the 230 kV network, with values close to the reference. This frequency reference is computed as the product of the per unit rotational speed of the synchronous generator and the rated frequency (60 Hz). There are slight differences in the PLLs that are not easily perceived in this first figure because of the scale.

To better appreciate the differences, Figure 14b presents a zoomed-in image of the interval from seconds 22 to 22.2. As can be seen, different PLL implementations give rise to slight differences in comparison with the frequency reference, but most are close to representing the same behavior. In addition, the MAF averages the frequency signal more linearly than the other PLLs. The SRF-PLL, the simpler implementation, presents the most significant differences from the reference in the 230 kV network.

Figure 15 shows analogous frequency measurements but with the PLLs located at the 25 kV WinGen bus. Figure 15a presents the system frequency measured with the PLLs from seconds 15 to 35. As Figure 14a, it shows that all PLLs measured a frequency similar to that of the reference. However, compared to the slight differences presented in the 230 kV WinGen bus, the values obtained in the 25 kV WinGen bus present larger differences from the reference.

To appreciate the differences, Figure 15b shows a zoomed-in image of the interval from seconds 22 to 22.2. Again, the SRF-PLL presents significant measurement errors. Other PLLs present deviations from the reference, but they are relatively close. In this case, MAF-PLL and SOGI-PLL are closer to the reference during the different oscillations presented. However, the MAF-PLL cannot track the reference oscillations.

Finally, Figure 16 displays frequency measurements with the PLLs located at the low voltage level, 575 V WinGen bus. Figure 16a presents the system frequency measured with the PLLs from seconds 15 to 35, showing that all PLLs obtain a frequency measurement similar to the reference. However, compared to the measurements performed at the higher voltage levels, these measurements show representative and observable differences from the reference values. For a closer look, Figure 16b shows a zoomed-in image of the interval from seconds 22 to 22.2. The magnitude of the errors of SRF-PLL and LAG-PLL increase greatly.

Regarding the metrics of the measurement errors, as defined in Section 2.5, Table 2 shows the relative mean absolute error (MAE%) in quasi-steady-state operation for the PLLs located at the different system buses. The results show that the MAE% is low when measuring the frequency with the PLLs in the 230 kV buses, and those values increase at lower voltage levels. SOGI-PLL presents lower MAE than the other PLLs measuring in the 25 kV and 575 V buses. MAF-PLL is the best method to measure the frequency in the 230 kV buses. The MAE values for the SRF-PLL and LAG-PLL are similar for all cases except for the 575 V bus, where a slight difference can be observed.

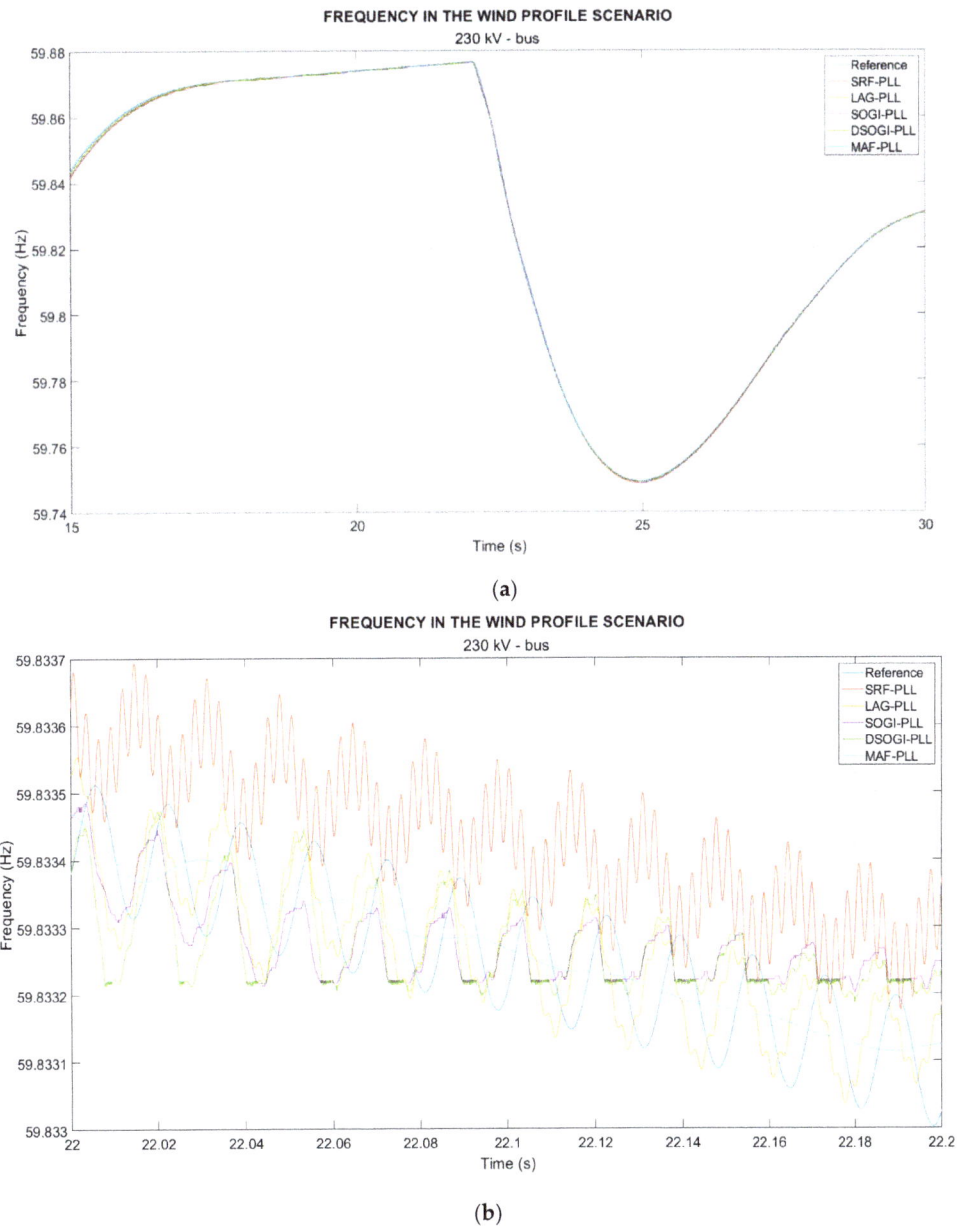

Figure 14. Frequency measurement with the PLLs located at the 230 kV bus: (**a**) PLLs measuring from seconds 15 to 35, and (**b**) detail of the measurements from seconds 22 to 22.2.

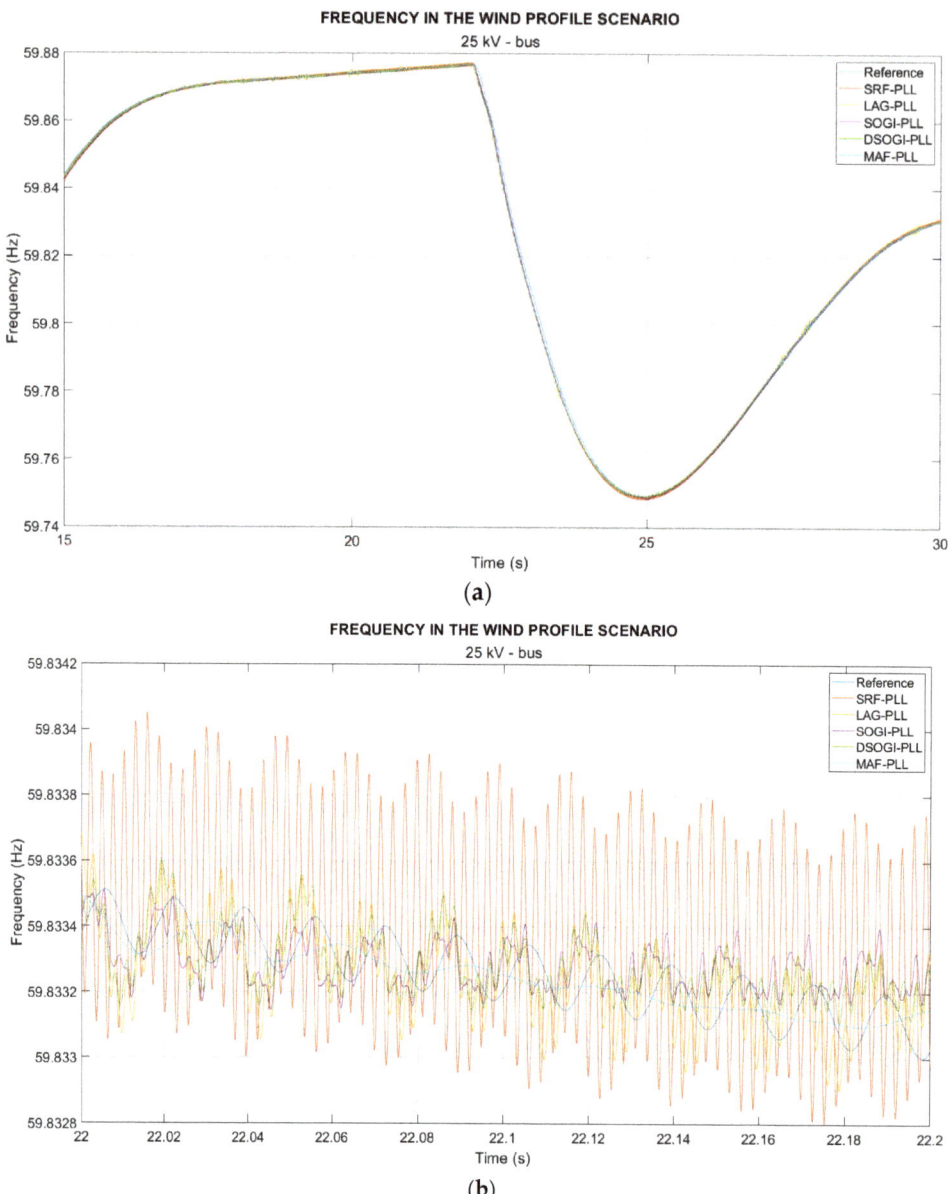

Figure 15. Frequency measurement with the PLLs located at the 25 kV WinGen bus: (**a**) PLLs measuring from seconds 15 to 35, and (**b**) detail of the measurements from seconds 22 to 22.2.

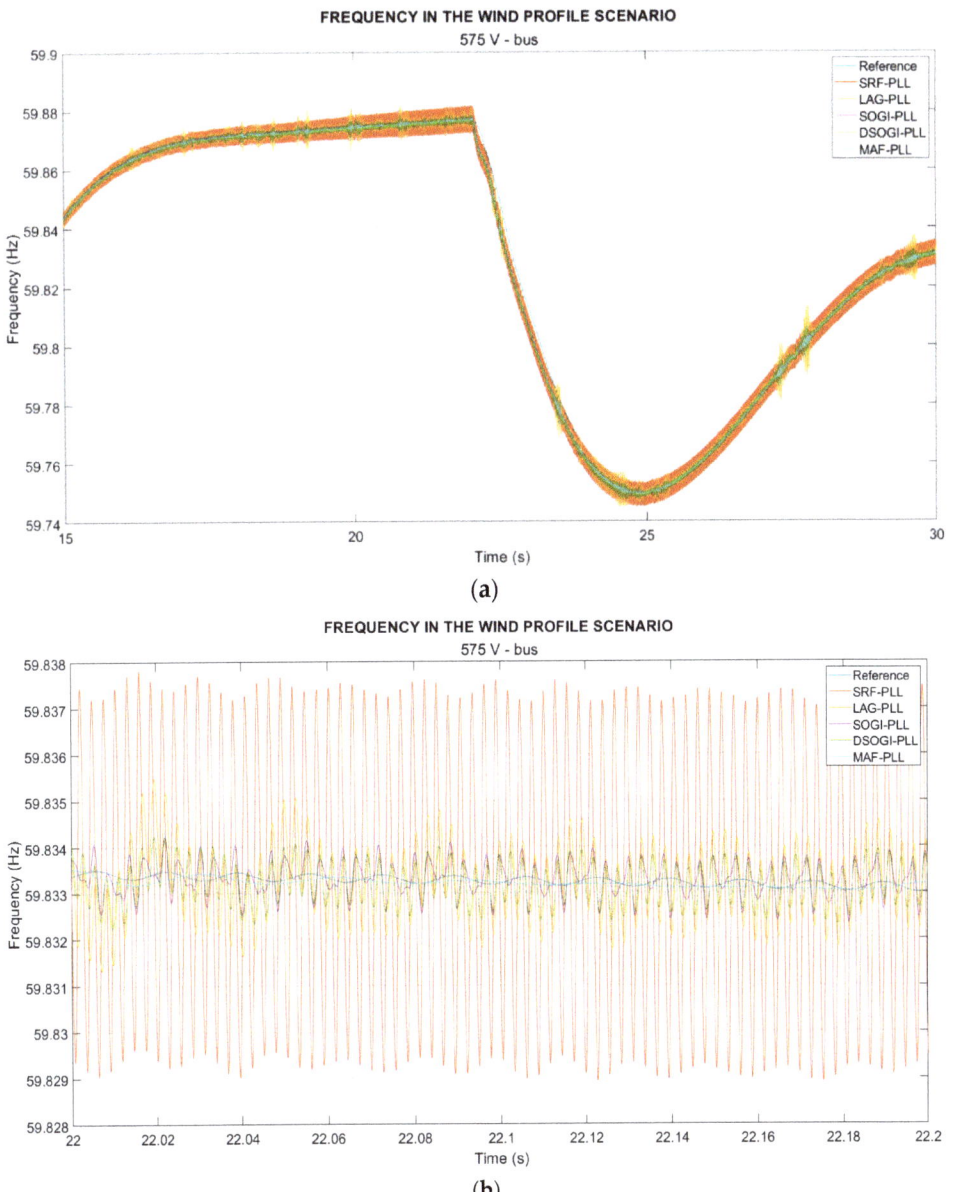

Figure 16. Frequency measurement with the PLLs located at the 575 V bus: (**a**) PLLs measuring from seconds 15 to 35, and (**b**) detail of the measurements from seconds 22 to 22.2.

Table 2. Relative mean absolute error for the PLLs located at the different buses in the constant wind speed scenario.

PLL	MAE% (Constant Wind Speed Scenario)				
	230 kV SynGen	230 kV WinGen	230 kV Load	25 kV WinGen	575 V WinGen
SRF-PLL	0.0385%	0.0385%	0.0380%	0.0628%	0.1728%
LAG-PLL	0.0377%	0.0377%	0.0371%	0.0667%	0.1437%
SOGI-PLL	0.0361%	0.0361%	0.0360%	0.0447%	0.1064%
DSOGI-PLL	0.0333%	0.0333%	0.0329%	0.0551%	0.1205%
MAF-PLL	0.0317%	0.0317%	0.0316%	0.0566%	0.1191%

Regarding the root-mean-square error (RMSE), all the PLLs give acceptable values for their measurements. In this case, the relative error (RMSE%) is close to 0.001%, which can be considered negligible in steady-state operation, and therefore inconclusive. Table 3 shows the RMSE% values obtained with the different PLLs located at the system buses in a constant wind speed scenario. All PLLs provide similar results, but lower values were obtained for the MAF-PLL at the different buses. In addition, the RMSE values for the SRF-PLL and the LAG-PLL were the same for all buses.

Table 3. Relative RMSE values for the PLLs located at the different buses in the constant wind speed scenario.

PLL	RMSE% (Constant Wind Speed Scenario)				
	230 kV SynGen	230 kV WinGen	230 kV Load	25 kV WinGen	575 V WinGen
SRF-PLL	0.000172%	0.000172%	0.000179%	0.000256%	0.000396%
LAG-PLL	0.000172%	0.000172%	0.000179%	0.000256%	0.000396%
SOGI-PLL	0.000542%	0.000542%	0.000548%	0.000369%	0.000403%
DSOGI-PLL	0.000333%	0.000333%	0.000326%	0.000301%	0.000319%
MAF-PLL	0.000020%	0.000020%	0.000020%	0.000102%	0.000267%

The AEFD also provides essential information for determining the performance of the PLLs. The cumulative relative AEFD (CAEFD%) was computed in all cases in the manner defined in Equation (15), and the results are compiled in Table 4. The results show that the SRF-PLL is the most affected at all voltage buses. The SRF-PLL, LAG-PLL, SOGI-PLL, and DSOGI-PLL produce a significant deviation in the 25 kV and 575 V buses; however, the MAF-PLL behaves better at these voltage levels compared to the other PLLs. In addition, MAF-PLL has a similar percentage at the 230 kV and 575 V buses, except for the 25 kV bus, where the percentage increases. DSOGI-PLL presents the best behavior of the PLLs in this indicator.

Table 4. Cumulative relative AEFD values for the PLLs located at the different buses in the constant wind speed scenario.

PLL	CAEFD% (Constant Wind Speed Scenario)				
	230 kV SynGen	230 kV WinGen	230 kV Load	25 kV WinGen	575 V WinGen
SRF-PLL	190.54%	190.54%	249.63%	1770.19%	9277.65%
LAG-PLL	25.50%	25.50%	12.97%	341.27%	1981.73%
SOGI-PLL	13.65%	13.65%	15.76%	115.26%	716.09%
DSOGI-PLL	9.38%	9.38%	3.90%	168.94%	1152.07%
MAF-PLL	43.10%	43.10%	42.91%	18.24%	48.21%

Similar results are obtained by using the cumulative relative RMSEFD, as shown in Table 5.

Table 5. Cumulative RMSEFD values for the PLLs located at the different buses in the constant wind speed scenario.

PLL	CRMSEFD% (Constant Wind Speed Scenario)				
	230 kV SynGen	230 kV WinGen	230 kV Load	25 kV WinGen	575 V WinGen
SRF-PLL	174.12%	174.12%	226.00%	1621.03%	8536.99%
LAG-PLL	30.63%	30.63%	18.89%	327.67%	1847.97%
SOGI-PLL	73.38%	73.38%	71.07%	193.20%	797.12%
DSOGI-PLL	93.39%	93.39%	88.71%	227.48%	1085.21%
MAF-PLL	28.52%	28.52%	28.35%	1.48%	79.38%

3.2. Scenario 2: Variable Wind Speed

Figure 17 displays the frequency measurement with the PLLs located at the 230 kV WinGen bus in the variable wind speed scenario. Figure 17a presents the frequency in a wide period from seconds 100 to 450. All PLLs present frequency measurements similar to the reference. However, as in previous figures, there are slight differences in the PLLs that are not easily perceived because of the scale.

To better appreciate the differences, Figure 17b,c show some details with different zoom levels. This shows that all PLLs introduce some differences from the reference, but most are close to representing the same behavior. In addition, the MAF averages the frequency signal more linearly than the other PLLs. The SRF-PLL shows the worst performance in the 230 kV network.

Figure 18 displays the frequency measurement with the PLLs located at the 25 kV WinGen bus in the variable wind speed scenario. Figure 18a presents the frequency in a wide period from 100 to 450 s. This result reveals that all PLLs present frequency measurements similar to the reference, and no difference is appreciable in this range. To better appreciate the differences, Figure 18b,c show some details with different zoom levels. Both figures show that all PLLs show significant differences regarding the reference, but some represent the form of the reference signal better. In addition, they are not in phase with the reference, and MAF-PLL has fewer variations in the frequency measurement. The noise of the frequency signal generated by the SRF-PLL and LAG-PLL increases slightly.

Figure 18 shows analogous frequency measurements, but with the PLLs located at the 25 kV WinGen bus. Figure 18a presents the system frequency measured with the PLLs from seconds 100 to 450; Figure 18b, from seconds 173.8 to 174.1; and Figure 18c, from 173.8 to 173.9. The last figures show that all of the PLLs show significant differences from the reference, but some represent the form of the reference signal. In addition, they are not in phase with the reference, and MAF-PLL has fewer variations. SRF-PLL and LAG-PLL behave the worst.

Finally, Figure 19 displays frequency measurements with the PLLs located at the low voltage level, the 575 V WinGen bus, with three different zoom levels. Compared to the measurements performed at the higher voltage levels, these measurements show greater differences from the reference values. SFT-PLL introduces a wider variation with respect to the frequency measurement. The frequency measurements performed with LAG-PLL, SOGI-PLL, DSOGI-PLL, and MAF-PLL are close to each other.

The metrics of measurement errors, as defined in Section 2.5, are compiled in Tables 6–9 for the variable wind speed scenario in the interval from second 130 to second 430. Table 6 shows the relative mean absolute error (MAE%). The results show that LAG-PLL presents the highest measurement error in the 230 kV network, followed by DSOGI-PLL. In addition, MAF-PLL produces a lower error. SOGI-PLL, DSOGIPLL, and MAF-PLL give lower measurement errors in the 25 kV and 575 V networks. Furthermore, SOGI-PLL gives the lowest error values in the 25 kV WinGen bus.

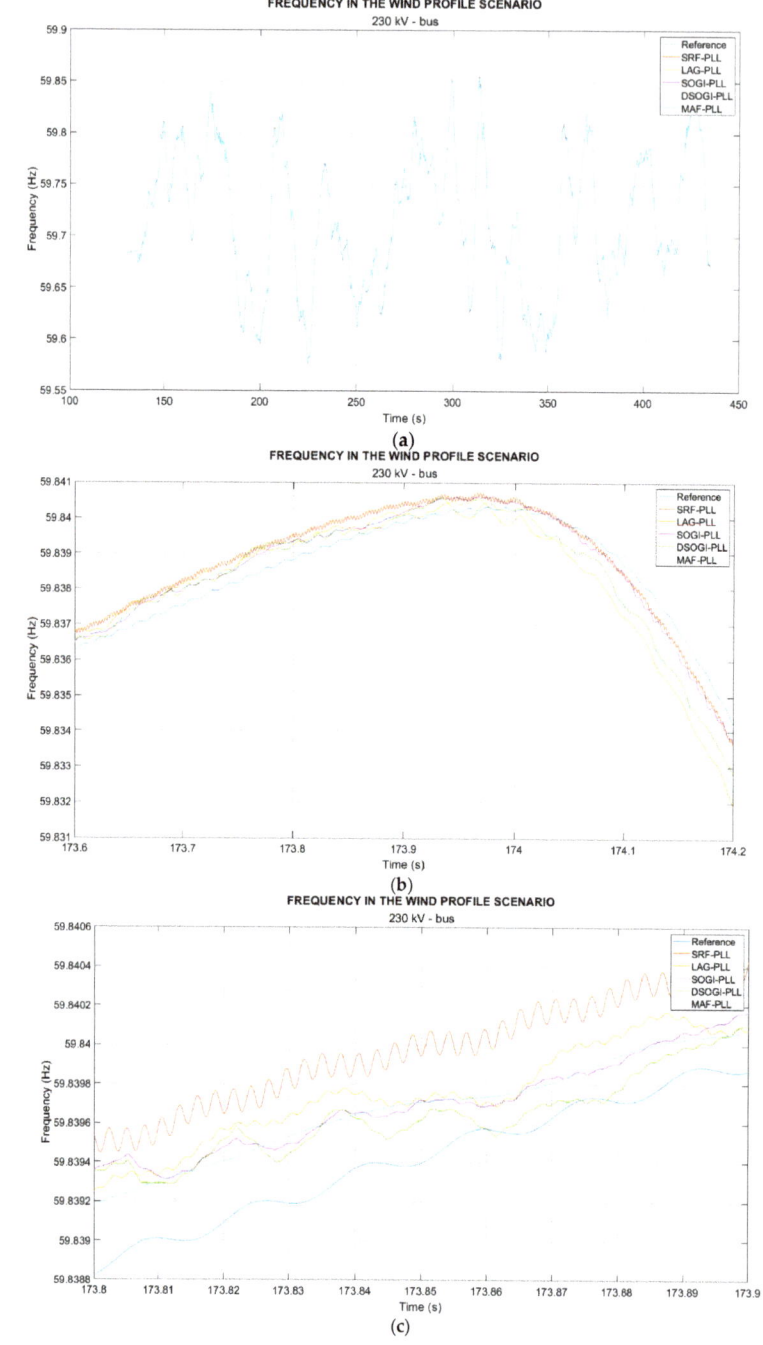

Figure 17. Frequency measurement with the PLLs located at the 230 kV WinGen bus in the variable wind speed scenario. The measurements are shown with different zoom levels: (**a**) from seconds 100 to 450, (**b**) from seconds 173.6 to 174.2, and (**c**) from seconds 173.8 to 173.9.

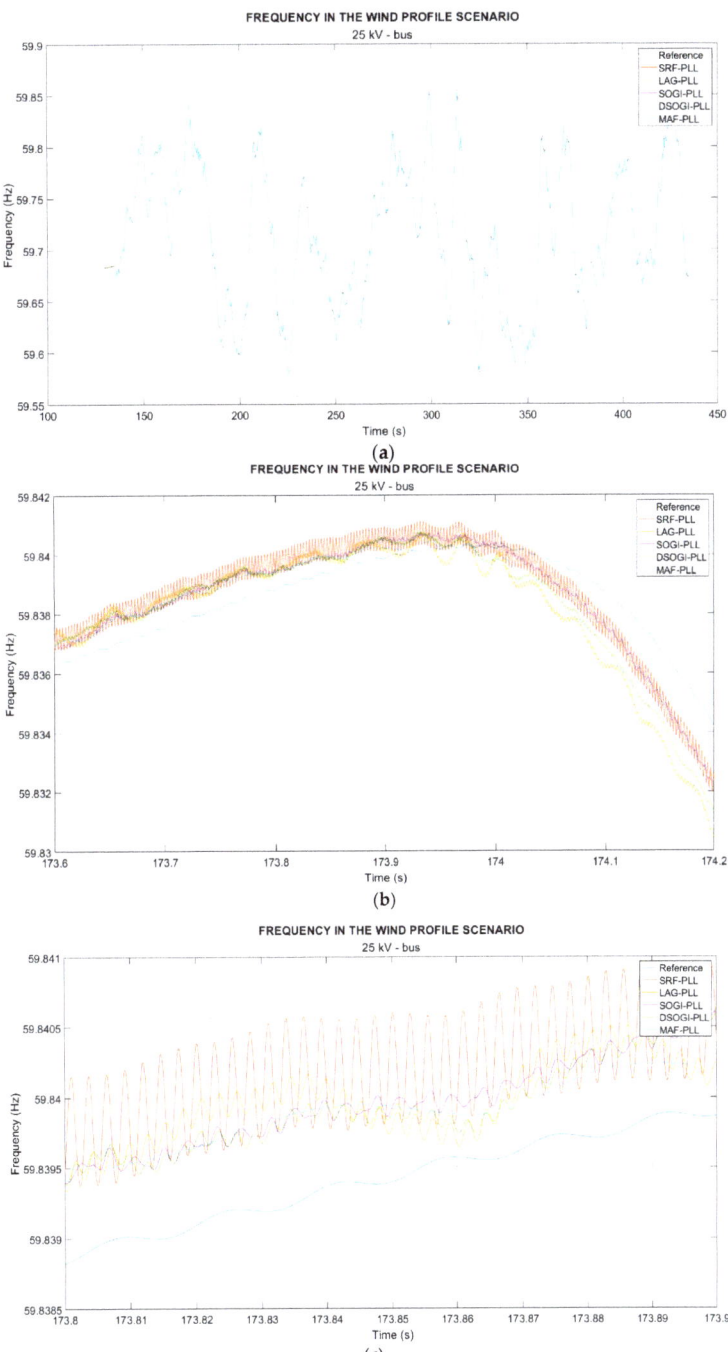

Figure 18. Frequency measurement with the PLLs located at the 25 kV WinGen bus in the variable wind speed scenario. The measurements are shown with different zoom levels: (**a**) from seconds 100 to 450, (**b**) from seconds 173.6 to 174.2, and (**c**) from seconds 173.8 to 173.9.

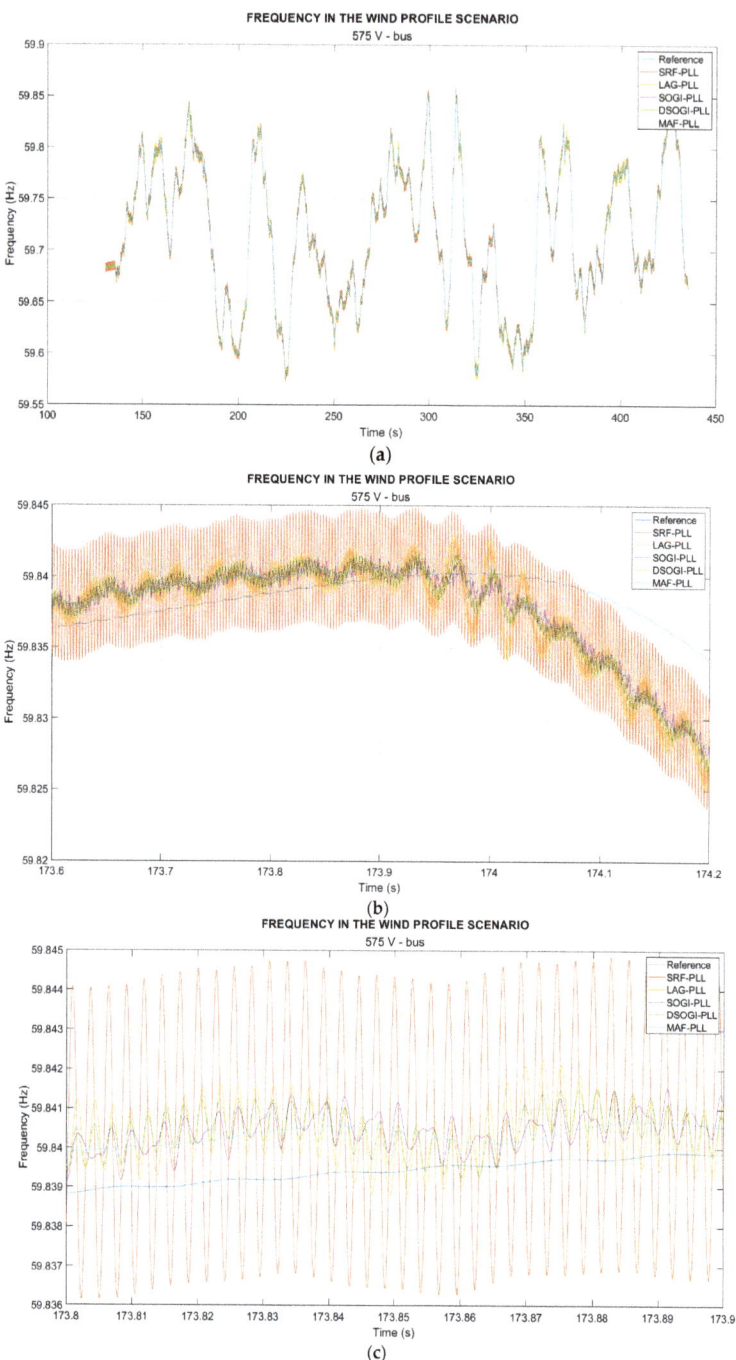

Figure 19. Frequency measurement with the PLLs located at the 575 kV WinGen bus in the variable wind speed scenario. The measurements are shown with different zoom levels: (**a**) from seconds 100 to 450, (**b**) from seconds 173.6 to 174.2, and (**c**) from seconds 173.8 to 173.9.

Table 6. Relative mean absolute error for the PLLs located at different buses in the variable wind speed scenario.

PLL	MAE% (Variable Wind Speed Scenario)				
	230 kV SynGen	230 kV WinGen	230 kV Load	25 kV WinGen	575 V WinGen
SRF-PLL	0.0221%	0.0221%	0.0222%	0.0477%	0.1614%
LAG-PLL	0.0259%	0.0259%	0.0258%	0.0506%	0.1187%
SOGI-PLL	0.0218%	0.0218%	0.0217%	0.0341%	0.0771%
DSOGI-PLL	0.0245%	0.0245%	0.0244%	0.0405%	0.0898%
MAF-PLL	0.0200%	0.0200%	0.0200%	0.0395%	0.0866%

Table 7. Relative RMSE values for the PLLs located at different buses in the variable wind speed scenario.

PLL	RMSE% (Variable Wind Speed Scenario)				
	230 kV SynGen	230 kV WinGen	230 kV Load	25 kV WinGen	575 V WinGen
SRF-PLL	0.000025%	0.000025%	0.000025%	0.000032%	0.000064%
LAG-PLL	0.000025%	0.000025%	0.000025%	0.000032%	0.000064%
SOGI-PLL	0.000043%	0.000043%	0.000043%	0.000050%	0.000075%
DSOGI-PLL	0.000043%	0.000043%	0.000043%	0.000050%	0.000064%
MAF-PLL	0.000018%	0.000018%	0.000018%	0.000032%	0.000057%

Table 8. Cumulative relative AEFD values for the PLLs located at different buses in the variable wind speed scenario.

PLL	CAEFD% (Variable Wind Speed Scenario)				
	230 kV SynGen	230 kV WinGen	230 kV Load	25 kV WinGen	575 V WinGen
SRF-PLL	658.37%	658.37%	823.96%	4807.51%	24742.68%
LAG-PLL	141.30%	141.30%	165.67%	1040.80%	5488.64%
SOGI-PLL	68.84%	68.84%	73.67%	419.08%	1993.61%
DSOGI-PLL	139.75%	139.75%	145.96%	583.90%	3263.35%
MAF-PLL	12.99%	12.99%	13.50%	86.07%	262.25%

Table 9. Cumulative RMSEFD values for the PLLs located at different buses in the variable wind speed scenario.

PLL	CRMSEFD% (Variable Wind Speed Scenario)				
	230 kV SynGen	230 kV WinGen	230 kV Load	25 kV WinGen	575 V WinGen
SRF-PLL	455.37%	455.37%	574.22%	3469.70%	17951.74%
LAG-PLL	103.61%	103.61%	118.63%	757.63%	4003.72%
SOGI-PLL	198.87%	198.87%	203.23%	461.29%	1731.32%
DSOGI-PLL	255.17%	255.17%	259.94%	544.70%	2390.31%
MAF-PLL	13.86%	13.86%	14.29%	83.03%	262.22%

Table 7 shows the RMSE% values obtained with the different PLLs located at the system buses. Although the RMS values were not conclusive in the 25 kV network, the results show that SRF-PLL, LAG-PLL, and MAF-PLL were able to obtain the values closest to the reference (i.e., low errors). However, after analyzing all errors, they were not very sensitive to small disturbances such as wind speed change, but were very sensitive to noise.

Table 8 shows the cumulative relative AEFD (CAEFD). In this case, SRF-PLL presented the highest differences of all PLLs, and the lowest was obtained with MAF-PLL. The errors increase at lower system voltages for all PLLs, and MAF-PLL presents the lowest values. Therefore, MAF-PLL gives a clear advantage with respect to the AEFD for all of the evaluated cases.

Similar results were obtained when using the cumulative relative RMSEFD, as shown in Table 9.

3.3. Summary of Results

After testing the PLLs located at different buses in a power system with generators and considering two scenarios, the following summary was extracted from the results:

- SRF-PLL: It is more sensitive to small frequency changes produced by wind speed variations. Therefore, the method is more suitable for frequency measurements in a constant wind speed scenario than in a variable wind speed scenario. However, it is more sensitive to voltage harmonics, generating more significant noise than other PLLs.
- LAG-PLL: In the constant wind speed scenario, the LAG-PLL behaves better than the SRF-PLL, making it suitable for applications where it is unnecessary to consider the dynamic behavior of the frequency. A filter of the voltage signal before the PI makes it unreliable for dynamic behavior, as demonstrated with the frequency measurement in the variable wind speed scenario.
- SOGI-PLL: Frequency measurements in the lower voltage levels are accurate in the two simulated scenarios. It provides low error and follows the sinusoidal behavior of the reference, showing a better filtering capacity for the voltage signal facing noise. It is sensitive to the changes produced by small wind speed variations. This PLL is used for single-phase systems and can give errors in the case of unbalanced systems.
- DSOGI-PLL: As the three-phase version of the SOGI-PLL, it offers a sensitivity similar to that of the single-phase version. Although the frequency measurement error is increased, this cannot be considered representative, knowing that this type may become more accurate in unbalanced networks. Because of the sensitivity, it generates noise in the frequency measurement, affecting the RMS value of the frequency derivative. However, the single-phase model and the MAF-PLL are the only ones better.
- MAF-PLL: It is a PLL that responds adequately to the constant wind speed scenario. Although it averages the signal and tries to flatten sine waves, it generates the lowest measurement errors in the constant and variable wind speed scenarios at the higher voltage levels. It can filter the signal to make it less sensitive to slight changes in the measurement or an increase in the noise level of the input signal. This latter behavior was also observed at the lower voltage levels in the constant and variable wind speed scenarios.

4. Conclusions

No particular PLL implementation can be recommended as the optimal solution for frequency measurement in a low-inertia power system. The best PLL version depends on the particular characteristics of the system and on the voltage level and location of the generator that is going to make use of the measurements. The optimal PLL for a given application should be selected according to a complete frequency measurement analysis.

Author Contributions: O.D.G.-B.: Conceptualization, data curation, investigation, methodology, software, validation, visualization, and writing—original draft; S.M.: Conceptualization, formal analysis, funding acquisition, investigation, methodology, project administration, resources, supervision, and writing—review and editing; J.E.C.-B. and E.M.: Formal analysis, writing—review and editing. All authors have read and agreed to the published version of the manuscript.

Funding: This research was funded by the Spanish national research agency Agencia Estatal de Investigación, grant number PID2019-108966RB-I00/AEI/10.13039/501100011033.

Institutional Review Board Statement: Not applicable.

Informed Consent Statement: Not applicable.

Data Availability Statement: Not applicable.

Acknowledgments: The authors thank to the Escuela Técnica Superior de Ingenieros Industriales, Universidad Politécnica de Madrid. The work of John E. Candelo-Becerra was supported by Universidad Nacional de Colombia, Sede Medellín.

Conflicts of Interest: The authors declare no conflict of interest.

References

1. Hernández-Callejo, L.; Gallardo-Saavedra, S.; Alonso-Gómez, V. A Review of Photovoltaic Systems: Design, Operation and Maintenance. *Sol. Energy* **2019**, *188*, 426–440. [CrossRef]
2. Tawalbeh, M.; Al-Othman, A.; Kafiah, F.; Abdelsalam, E.; Almomani, F.; Alkasrawi, M. Environmental Impacts of Solar Photovoltaic Systems: A Critical Review of Recent Progress and Future Outlook. *Sci. Total Environ.* **2021**, *759*, 143528. [CrossRef] [PubMed]
3. Peng, Q.; Jiang, Q.; Yang, Y.; Liu, T.; Wang, H.; Blaabjerg, F. On the Stability of Power Electronics-Dominated Systems: Challenges and Potential Solutions. *IEEE Trans. Ind. Appl.* **2019**, *55*, 7657–7670. [CrossRef]
4. Guerra, K.; Haro, P.; Gutiérrez, R.E.; Gómez-Barea, A. Facing the High Share of Variable Renewable Energy in the Power System: Flexibility and Stability Requirements. *Appl. Energy* **2022**, *310*, 118561. [CrossRef]
5. Bloom, A.; Helman, U.; Holttinen, H.; Summers, K.; Bakke, J.; Brinkman, G.; Lopez, A. It's Indisputable: Five Facts About Planning and Operating Modern Power Systems. *IEEE Power Energy Mag.* **2017**, *15*, 22–30. [CrossRef]
6. Liu, B.; An, M.; Wang, H.; Chen, Y.; Zhang, Z.; Xu, C.; Song, S.; Lv, Z. A Simple Approach to Reject DC Offset for Single-Phase Synchronous Reference Frame PLL in Grid-Tied Converters. *IEEE Access* **2020**, *8*, 112297–112308. [CrossRef]
7. Li, Y.; Fan, L.; Miao, Z. Wind in Weak Grids: Low-Frequency Oscillations, Subsynchronous Oscillations, and Torsional Interactions. *IEEE Trans. Power Syst.* **2020**, *35*, 109–118. [CrossRef]
8. Ortega, A.; Milano, F. Comparison of Different PLL Implementations for Frequency Estimation and Control. In Proceedings of the 2018 18th International Conference on Harmonics and Quality of Power (ICHQP), Ljubljana, Slovenia, 13–16 May 2018; pp. 1–6.
9. Karimi-Ghartemani, M.; Iravani, M.R. Robust and Frequency-Adaptive Measurement of Peak Value. *IEEE Trans. Power Deliv.* **2004**, *19*, 481–489. [CrossRef]
10. Liu, C.; Jiang, J.; Jiang, J.; Zhou, Z. Enhanced Grid-Connected Phase-Locked Loop Based on a Moving Average Filter. *IEEE Access* **2020**, *8*, 5308–5315. [CrossRef]
11. Golestan, S.; Guerrero, J.M.; Vasquez, J.C.; Abusorrah, A.M.; Al-Turki, Y. Standard SOGI-FLL and Its Close Variants: Precise Modeling in LTP Framework and Determining Stability Region/Robustness Metrics. *IEEE Trans. Power Electron.* **2021**, *36*, 409–422. [CrossRef]
12. Zhang, C.; Foyen, S.; Suul, J.A.; Molinas, M. Modeling and Analysis of SOGI-PLL/FLL-Based Synchronization Units: Stability Impacts of Different Frequency-Feedback Paths. *IEEE Trans. Energy Convers.* **2021**, *36*, 2047–2058. [CrossRef]
13. Ranjan, A.; Kewat, S.; Singh, B. DSOGI-PLL With In-Loop Filter Based Solar Grid Interfaced System for Alleviating Power Quality Problems. *IEEE Trans. Ind. Appl.* **2021**, *57*, 730–740. [CrossRef]
14. Nicastri, A.; Nagliero, A. Comparison and Evaluation of the PLL Techniques for the Design of the Grid-Connected Inverter Systems. In Proceedings of the 2010 IEEE International Symposium on Industrial Electronics, Bari, Italy, 4–7 July 2010; pp. 3865–3870.
15. Silva, S.M.; Lopes, B.M.; Cardoso Filho, B.J.; Campana, R.P.; Boaventura, W.C. Performance Evaluation of PLL Algorithms for Single-Phase Grid-Connected Systems. In Proceedings of the Conference Record of the 2004 IEEE Industry Applications Conference, 2004, 39th IAS Annual Meeting, Seattle, WA, USA, 3–7 October 2004; Volume 4, pp. 2259–2263.
16. Darambazar, G.; Moukadem, A.; Colicchio, B.; Wira, P. A Comparison of PLL for Online Frequency Tracking in Power Grids. In Proceedings of the 2021 IEEE 30th International Symposium on Industrial Electronics (ISIE), Kyoto, Japan, 20–23 June 2021; pp. 1–6.
17. Setiawan, I.; Facta, M.; Priyadi, A.; Purnomo, M.H. Comparison of Three Popular PLL Schemes under Balanced and Unbalanced Grid Voltage Conditions. In Proceedings of the 2016 8th International Conference on Information Technology and Electrical Engineering (ICITEE), Yogyakarta, Indonesia, 5–6 October 2016; pp. 1–6.
18. Royan; Andromeda, T.; Facta, M.; Hermawan; Setiawan, I. Comparison of SOGI-FLL with SOGI-PLL for Single-Phase Grid-Connected Inverters. In Proceedings of the 4th International Conference on Energy, Environment, Epidemiology and Information System (ICENIS 2019), Semarang, Indonesia, 7–8 August 2019.
19. Rueda-Escobedo, J.G.; Tang, S.; Schiffer, J. A Performance Comparison of PLL Implementations in Low-Inertia Power Systems Using an Observer-Based Framework. *IFAC-PapersOnLine* **2020**, *53*, 12244–12250. [CrossRef]
20. Jamaludin, N.F.; Saidina Omar, A.M.; Isa, S.S.M.; Ahmad, N.D.; Ramli, S.S. Comparison Techniques Using Phase—Loop Locked (PLL) and Synchronous References Frame (SRF) Controller to Mitigate Voltage Flicker. *J. Phys. Conf. Ser.* **2019**, *1349*, 012124. [CrossRef]
21. Prakash, S.; Singh, J.K.; Behera, R.K.; Mondal, A. Comprehensive Analysis of SOGI-PLL Based Algorithms for Single-Phase System. In Proceedings of the 2019 National Power Electronics Conference (NPEC), Tiruchirappalli, India, 13–15 December 2019; pp. 1–6.

22. Ullah, I.; Ashraf, M. Comparison of Synchronization Techniques Under Distorted Grid Conditions. *IEEE Access* **2019**, *7*, 101345–101354. [CrossRef]
23. Singh, U.K.; Basak, A. Performance Study of Different PLL Schemes Under Unbalanced Grid Voltage. In Proceedings of the 2019 IEEE Region 10 Symposium (TENSYMP), Kolkata, India, 7–9 June 2019; pp. 66–71.
24. Santos Filho, R.M.; Seixas, P.F.; Cortizo, P.C.; Torres, L.A.B.; Souza, A.F. Comparison of Three Single-Phase PLL Algorithms for UPS Applications. *IEEE Trans. Ind. Electron.* **2008**, *55*, 2923–2932. [CrossRef]
25. Bifaretti, S.; Zanchetta, P.; Lavopa, E. Comparison of Two Three-Phase PLL Systems for More Electric Aircraft Converters. *IEEE Trans. Power Electron.* **2014**, *29*, 6810–6820. [CrossRef]
26. Godave, A.; Choudhari, P.; Jadhav, A. Comparison and Simulation of Analog and Digital Phase Locked Loop. In Proceedings of the 2018 9th International Conference on Computing, Communication and Networking Technologies (ICCCNT), Bengaluru, India, 10–12 July 2018; pp. 1–4.
27. Aguilera, R.P.; Acuna, P.; Konstantinou, G.; Vazquez, S.; Leon, J.I. Basic Control Principles in Power Electronics. In *Control of Power Electronic Converters and Systems*; Elsevier: Amsterdam, The Netherlands, 2018; pp. 31–68.
28. Zhou, D.; Song, Y.; Blaabjerg, F. Modeling and Control of Three-Phase AC/DC Converter Including Phase-Locked Loop. In *Control of Power Electronic Converters and Systems*; Elsevier: Amsterdam, The Netherlands, 2018; pp. 117–151.
29. Ortega, A.; Milano, F. Impact of Frequency Estimation for VSC-Based Devices with Primary Frequency Control. In Proceedings of the 2017 IEEE PES Innovative Smart Grid Technologies Conference Europe (ISGT-Europe), Turin, Italy, 26–29 September 2017; pp. 1–6.
30. Yuan, X.; Merk, W.; Stemmler, H.; Allmeling, J. Stationary-Frame Generalized Integrators for Current Control of Active Power Filters with Zero Steady-State Error for Current Harmonics of Concern under Unbalanced and Distorted Operating Conditions. *IEEE Trans. Ind. Appl.* **2002**, *38*, 523–532. [CrossRef]
31. Rodriguez, P.; Luna, A.; Candela, I.; Mujal, R.; Teodorescu, R.; Blaabjerg, F. Multiresonant Frequency-Locked Loop for Grid Synchronization of Power Converters Under Distorted Grid Conditions. *IEEE Trans. Ind. Electron.* **2011**, *58*, 127–138. [CrossRef]
32. Rodriguez, P.; Teodorescu, R.; Candela, I.; Timbus, A.V.; Liserre, M.; Blaabjerg, F. New Positive-Sequence Voltage Detector for Grid Synchronization of Power Converters under Faulty Grid Conditions. In Proceedings of the 37th IEEE Power Electronics Specialists Conference, Jeju, Korea, 18–22 June 2006; pp. 1–7.
33. Robles, E.; Ceballos, S.; Pou, J.; Zaragoza, J.; Gabiola, I. Grid Synchronization Method Based on a Quasi-Ideal Low-Pass Filter Stage and a Phase-Locked Loop. In Proceedings of the 2008 IEEE Power Electronics Specialists Conference, Rhodes, Greece, 15–19 June 2008; pp. 4056–4061.
34. Report, I. Dynamic Models for Steam and Hydro Turbines in Power System Studies. *IEEE Trans. Power Appar. Syst.* **1973**, *PAS-92*, 1904–1915. [CrossRef]
35. IEEE Subsynchronous Resonance Working Group of the Dynamic System Performance Subcommittee and Power System Engineering Commitee. Second Benchmark Model for Computer Simulation of Subsynchronous Resonance. *IEEE Trans. Power Appar. Syst.* **1985**, *PAS-104*, 1057–1066. [CrossRef]
36. Kundur, P. *Power System Stability and Control*, 1st ed.; McGraw-Hill, Inc.: Palo Alto, CA, USA, 1994; ISBN 007035958X.
37. Gagnon, R.; Turmel, G.; Larose, C.; Brochu, J.; Sybille, G.; Fecteau, M. Large-Scale Real-Time Simulation of Wind Power Plants into Hydro-Quebec Power System. In Proceedings of the 9th International Workshop on Large-Scale Integration of Wind Power into Power Systems as well as on Transmission Networks for Offshore Wind Power Plants, Québec, QC, Canada, 18–19 October 2010; Betancourt, U., Ackermann, T., Eds.; energynautics gmbH: Québec, QC, Canada, 2010; pp. 73–80.
38. CIGRE Working Group 02 (Study Committee 33). *Guidelines for Representation of Network Elements When Calculating Transients*; Cigré: Paris, France, 1990.
39. IEC 60076-1:2011; Power Transformers—Part 1: General. International Electrotechnical Commission: Geneva, Switzerland, 2011.
40. Hansen, K.S.; Vasiljevic, N.; Sørensen, S.A. Wind Resource, SCADA Data and Time Series of Wind and Turbine Loads from Tjareborg, DK; Dataset; Technical University of Denmark: Kongens Lyngby, Denmark, 2021. [CrossRef]
41. Willmott, C.J.; Matsuura, K. Advantages of the Mean Absolute Error (MAE) over the Root Mean Square Error (RMSE) in Assessing Average Model Performance. *Clim. Res.* **2005**, *30*, 79–82. [CrossRef]

Article

More Enhanced Swing Colpitts Oscillators: A Circuit Analysis

Tatsuya Nomura and Toru Tanzawa *

Graduate School of Integrated Science and Technology, Shizuoka University, Hamamatsu 432-8561, Japan
* Correspondence: toru.tanzawa@shizuoka.ac.jp

Abstract: In this paper, we show that an additional inductor–capacitor–inductor filter can increase the oscillation amplitude of the enhanced swing Colpitts oscillator (ESCO), and call this topology the more enhanced swing Colpitts oscillator (mESCO). When it is connected with a rectifier, the DC–DC boost conversion ratio can be increased, especially for low-voltage sensor ICs or energy harvesting. This paper focuses on the electrical characteristics of mESCO. The oscillation frequency was modeled as a function of the circuit parameters of mESCO. The common gate voltage gain (A_{CG}), defined by the ratio of the drain voltage amplitude to the source voltage amplitude of the switching MOSFET of mESCO, was also modeled under the assumption that all the circuit elements are ideal. The model was validated with a SPICE simulation. For $A_{CG} < 1.5$, the model was in good agreement with the SPICE results within 10%. In addition, the drain voltage amplitude v_{da} was modeled by assuming that the average transconductance of the MOSFET in a half cycle is null when the long-channel Shockley model is used. v_{da} needs to be sufficiently high to have a large DC–DC boost conversion ratio. The model can predict the tendency that v_{da} increases as A_{CG} approaches unity. We found that the voltage difference of the drain voltage amplitude to the source voltage amplitude is a constant even when the circuit parameters, and thereby A_{CG} are varied.

Keywords: enhanced swing Colpitts oscillator; circuit analysis; circuit model

1. Introduction

Battery-free IoT sensor modules are required to eliminate battery replacement to reduce costs. Wireless power transfer (WPT) charges the modules with electromagnetic waves [1–4]. An energy transducer (ET) transforms environmental energy such as lights, heat flow, and vibration into electric power [5,6]. Those techniques can remove the batteries out of the modules. Circuit designs have improved the power efficiency of power converters even with low power received via WPT and ET. Multisine WPT can increase the peak power with the same average transmitter power, resulting in improvement in power efficiency [7–9]. Figure 1 graphically explains how it works. Each of the N multisine waves has power of 1/N to attain the same power as the conventional continuous wave. At the receiving antenna, the peak voltage amplitude can be theoretically increased by a factor of $\sqrt{N}$ with beating multisine waves when the input impedance is common for N multisine waves with different frequencies. Due to the nonlinearity of the rectifying diode, the multisine waves can output more averaged current than the continuous wave.

The Colpitts oscillator is one of the oscillator circuit topologies that provides a carrier frequency for wireless communication [10–13]. The phase noise of the oscillator is a critical factor limiting the sensitivity of wireless communication. It is important to increase the output voltage amplitude of the oscillator to reduce the phase noise. In order to increase the voltage amplitude, an enhanced swing Colpitts oscillator (ESCO) was proposed [14–18]. What about adding beating to the ESCO to further increase the output voltage amplitude in DC–DC boost converter applications for low-voltage sensor ICs or energy harvesting? In this paper, we show that an additional inductor–capacitor–inductor filter can increase the oscillation amplitude of the ESCO, and call this topology the more enhanced swing Colpitts oscillator (mESCO). Rectifiers were connected with the output terminals of ESCO and mESCO to output boosted voltages, called ER (ESCO followed by rectifier) and mER (mESCO followed by rectifier), respectively. A SPICE simulation was run to compare the performance of ER and mER. The result showed that mER output a higher open circuit voltage and higher output current at a certain voltage than ER.

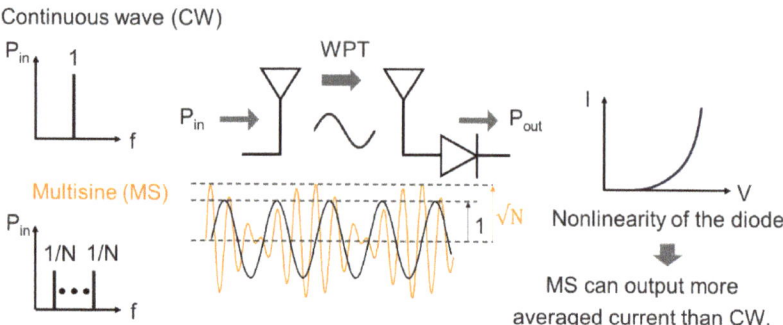

Figure 1. Efficiency improvement in wireless power transfer with multisine electromagnetic waves.

The rest of the paper discusses a circuit analysis of the mESCO. The oscillation frequency is shown as a function of the circuit parameters of mESCO. The common gate voltage gain A_{CG}, defined by the ratio of the drain voltage amplitude to the source voltage amplitude of the switching MOSFET of mESCO, was modeled under the assumption that all the circuit elements are ideal. The drain voltage amplitude v_{da} was also modeled by assuming that an averaged transconductance of the MOSFET in a half cycle is null when the long-channel Shockley model is used. v_{da} needs to be sufficiently high to have a large DC–DC boost conversion ratio. The model can predict the tendency that v_{da} increases as A_{CG} approaches unity. We also found that the voltage difference of the drain voltage amplitude to the source voltage amplitude is a constant even when the circuit parameters, and thereby A_{CG}, are varied. The paper is organized as follows: Section 2 proposes the mESCO and mER. The performance of mER is compared with that of ER. Section 3 analyzes the oscillation frequency, common gate voltage gain, and drain voltage amplitude of mESCO. The models are validated with SPICE simulation. The conclusion is given in Section 4.

2. More Enhanced Swing Colpitts Oscillator (mESCO), and DC–DC Converter with mESCO and Rectifier (mER)

Let us consider on-chip DC–DC boost converters composed of an oscillator whose peak output voltage is higher than the input DC voltage V_{IN} and a rectifier to supply power to building blocks in sensor/RF IC, as shown in Figure 2. When the decoupling capacitor C_{DEC} is too large to stabilize the input power rails, the oscillator runs with the DC supply voltage, as shown in Figure 2a. On the other hand, if C_{DEC} is set to a relatively small value, the AC component adds to the DC supply voltage to create beat tones into the oscillator, as shown in Figure 2b.

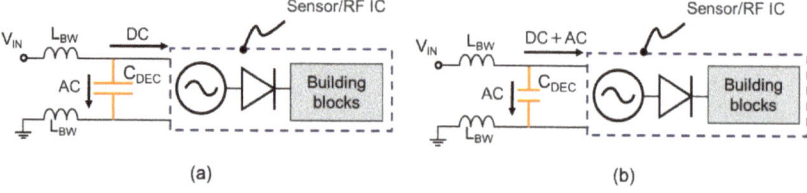

Figure 2. (a) Relatively large decoupling capacitor to filter out the AC component; (b) relatively small decoupling capacitor to create beat tones into the oscillator.

Figure 3a illustrates a boost converter (ER) with an enhanced swing Colpitts oscillator (ESCO) followed by a rectifier to drive the load R_L. The drain voltage of M1 exceeds V_{IN}. M2 transfers the current when the peak drain voltage of M1 is higher than the target voltage V_{OUT}. To increase the V_{SS} of the ESCO, a small decoupling capacitor is connected between the V_{IN} and V_{SS} through the parasitic inductance of bonding wires, as shown in Figure 3b. Additional oscillation at V_{SS} increases the drain voltage of M1, resulting in a higher output current at the same V_{OUT} as ER.

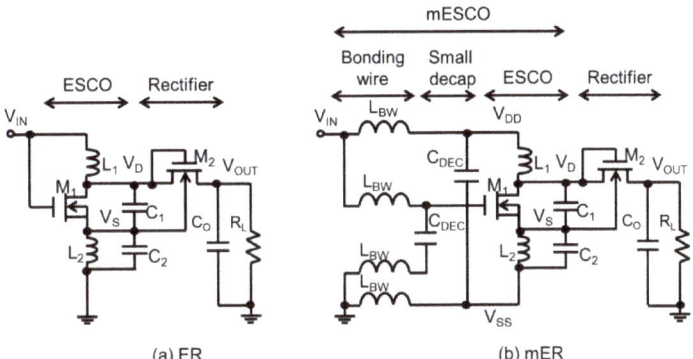

Figure 3. (a) Enhanced swing Colpitts oscillator (ESCO) followed by rectifier (ER); (b) ER with LC filter (more enhanced swing Colpitts oscillator followed by rectifier (mER).

A SPICE simulation was run with $V_{IN} = 0.3$ V, $L_{BW} = 2$ nH, $C_{DEC} = 25$ pF, $L_1 = 0.239$ nH, $L_2 = 2.93$ nH, $C_1 = 4$ pF, and $C_2 = 1.5$ pF. The parameters L_1, L_2, C_1, and C_2 are common to both circuits. The SPICE model in 65 nm CMOS was used in this study. Figure 4a shows the waveform of V_D and V_S of ER and mER when the outputs are open. The highest peak voltages of V_D were 1.08 V with ER and 2.01 V with mER. In mER, the peak voltages were alternately high and low. Figure 4b shows the V_{OUT} vs. I_{OUT} of ER and mER. In addition to an increase in the maximum attainable output voltage, mER can have a larger output current at any operating output voltage than ER. In Section 3, a circuit analysis for mESCO is conducted.

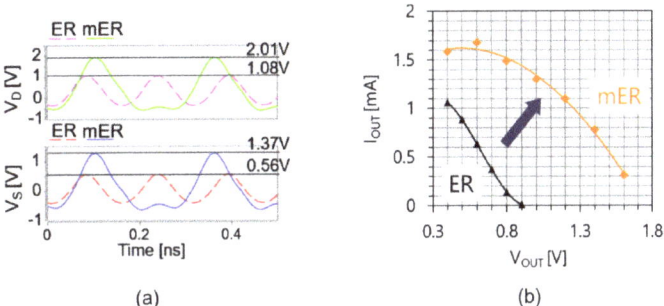

Figure 4. Comparison of mESCO with ESCO; (a) waveform of V_D and V_S when the outputs are open, (b) $V_{OUT} - I_{OUT}$.

3. Circuit Analysis of mESCO

Let us define the notation of voltages in this work, as shown in Figure 5. The DC offset and voltage amplitude are described by V_X and v_{xa}, respectively. The voltage differences from the ground and DC offset are described by V_x and v_x as a function of phase θ, respectively.

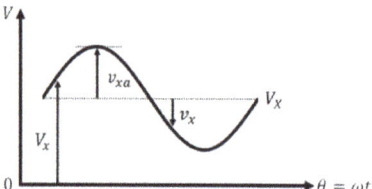

Figure 5. Notation of voltages in this work.

3.1. Oscillation Frequency

The oscillation frequency of ESCO was modeled in [16] by ignoring any real part of impedance and conductance, assuming the ESCO operates in steady state. We can similarly formulate the oscillation frequency of mESCO. Figure 6 shows the circuit reduction of mESCO from Figure 6a through Figure 6g. A small-signal equivalent circuit of Figure 6a is reduced to Figure 6b. Introducing L_{tb} for the series connection of L_t and L_b with $L_{tb} = L_t + L_b$, and eliminating M_1 results in Figure 6c under the assumption that any real part of impedance and conductance is omitted for a simple model. When the impedances of the parallel connections of L_{tb} and C_{IN} and of L_2 and C_2 are capacitive, they can be replaced with single capacitors C_{eq1} and C_{eq2}, respectively, by using the formula shown in Figure 6d, where ω is the angular velocity of a signal of interest. Likewise, when the impedance of the series connection of L_1 and C_1 is inductive, we can replace it with a single inductor L_{eq}, by using the formula shown in Figure 6e. Thus, the circuit shown in Figure 6c is reduced to Figure 6f using L_{eq}, C_{eq1} and C_{eq2}. Finally, we can obtain an LC circuit as shown in Figure 6g, where $C_{eq} = C_{eq1} + C_{eq2}$. Thus, (1)–(4) hold for mESCO.

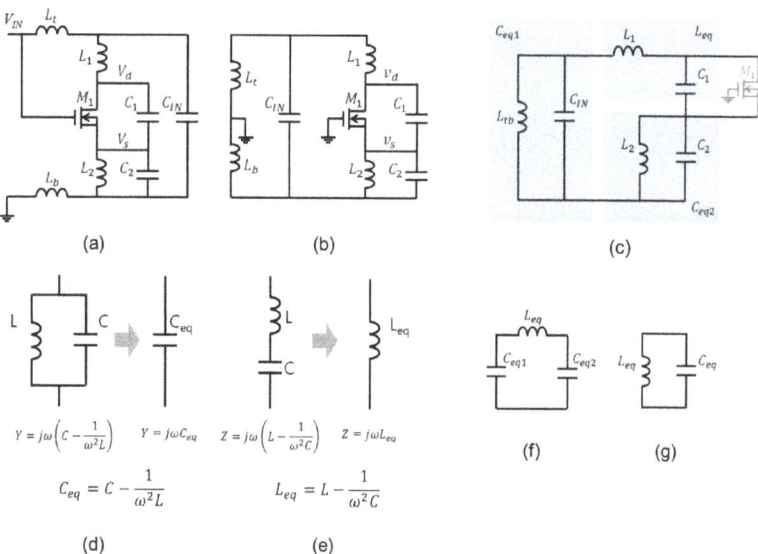

Figure 6. Circuit reduction of mESCO from (**a**) through (**g**); (**a**) original mESCO, (**b**) small-signal equivalent circuit of (**a**), (**c**) omitting M1, (**d**) equivalent capacitance of L and C connected in parallel, (**e**) equivalent inductance of L and C connected in series, (**f**) circuit reduced from (**c**) with (**d**) and (**e**), and (**g**) circuit reduced from (**f**).

$$C_{eq1} = C_{in} - \frac{1}{\omega^2 L_{tb}} \tag{1}$$

$$C_{eq2} = C_2 - \frac{1}{\omega^2 L_2} \qquad (2)$$

$$L_{eq} = L_1 - \frac{1}{\omega^2 C_1} \qquad (3)$$

$$C_{eq} = \frac{C_{eq1} C_{eq2}}{C_{eq1} + C_{eq2}} \qquad (4)$$

$$f = \omega/2\pi = 1/2\pi \sqrt{L_{eq} C_{eq}} \qquad (5)$$

A fundamental frequency is given by the solution in cubic Equation (5) in terms of f^2, and thereby can be resolved with three different values. To validate the models proposed in Section 3 with SPICE simulation, the nominal condition shown in Table 1 was used. The values of the inductors and capacitors were much larger than the ones fabricated in a single chip because the SPICE model in 180 nm CMOS was used for M_1. For parameter response on electrical characteristics, the remaining ones except for the sweeping parameter were set as shown in Table 1.

Table 1. Nominal condition to validate the models proposed in Section 3 with SPICE simulation.

Parameter	Default Value
L_1	5 µH
L_2	16 µH
L_t (=L_b)	5 µH
C_1	3 nF
C_2	8 nF
C_{IN}	1 nF
V_{IN}	0.8 V

The numerical solutions under wide ranges of circuit parameters were in good agreement with the SPICE results within 10% at most, as shown in Figure 7. Among the three solutions, the highest one was selected because the other two frequencies are too low to have L_{eq} and C_{eq} positive values.

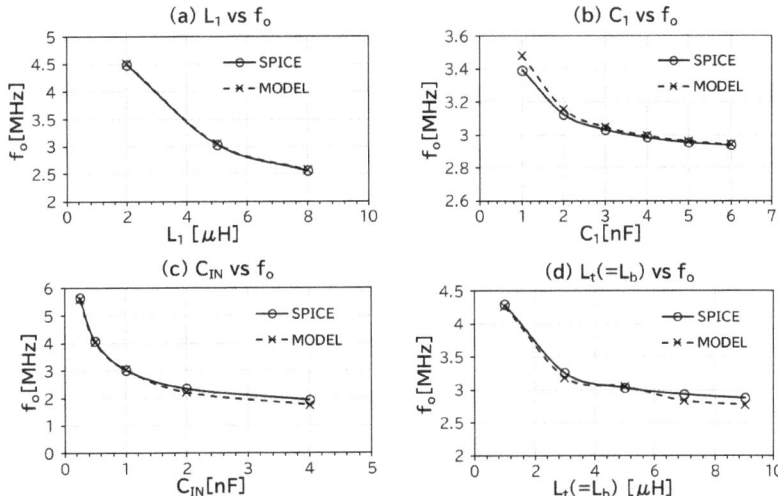

Figure 7. Operation frequency as a function of each circuit parameter. (a) L_1 vs. fo, (b) C_1 vs. fo, (c) C_{IN} vs. fo, (d) L_t(=L_b) vs. fo.

3.2. Common-Gate Voltage Gain

For DC–DC boost converters to have large boost ratios, a large voltage amplitude at the drain of M1 is required. Let us determine a common gate voltage gain A_{CG} as a function of the circuit parameters first. As performed for modeling the operation frequency of mESCO, a circuit transformation was produced from an original circuit diagram of mESCO as shown in Figure 8a to its small-signal equivalent circuit as shown in Figure 8b, and then a circuit model of mESCO as shown in Figure 8c.

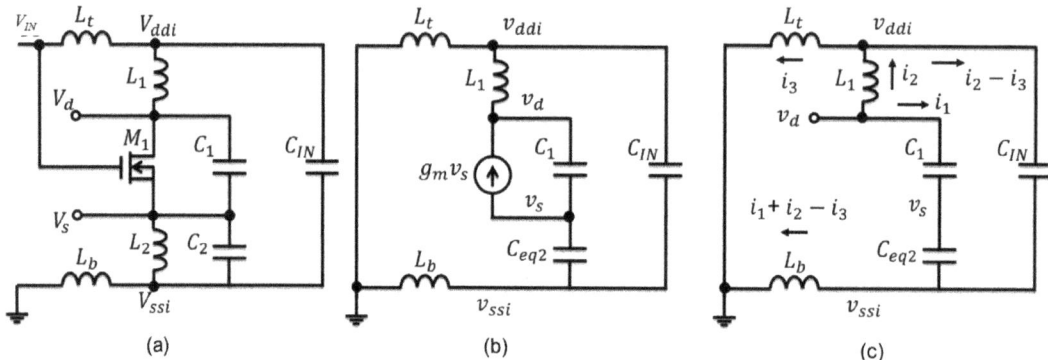

Figure 8. Circuit transformation: (**a**) an original circuit diagram of mESCO, (**b**) its small-signal equivalent circuit, and (**c**) a circuit model of mESCO to extract its common-gate voltage gain A_{CG}.

When v_d is forced, what voltage appears at v_s? Seven variables (four voltages and three currents) among six equations were applied, as shown by (6)–(11).

$$v_{ssi} = j\omega L_b(i_1 + i_2 - i_3) \tag{6}$$

$$v_s - v_{ssi} = i_1 / j\omega C_{eq2} \tag{7}$$

$$v_d - v_{ddi} = j\omega L_1 i_2 \tag{8}$$

$$v_{ddi} - v_{ssi} = (i_2 - i_3) / j\omega C_{IN} \tag{9}$$

$$v_{ddi} = j\omega L_t i_3 \tag{10}$$

$$v_d - v_s = i_1 / j\omega C_1 \tag{11}$$

Therefore, an equation can relate any two variables. After some calculations, (12) was derived for the common gate voltage gain A_{CG}. With (13)–(18), (12) provides a value for A_{CG} when the circuit parameters are given.

$$A_{CG} = v_d / v_s = T_{SQ1} / T_{SQ2} \tag{12}$$

$$T_{SQ1} = (1 + \beta)(T_{SQ3} - L_X C_X) + L_X C_{eq2} \tag{13}$$

$$T_{SQ2} = \beta(T_{SQ3} - L_X C_X) + L_t C_{IN} \tag{14}$$

$$T_{SQ3} = \omega^2 C_{IN}^2 L_1 L_t \tag{15}$$

$$\beta = C_1 / C_{eq2} \tag{16}$$

$$L_X = \omega^2 C_{IN} L_1 L_t - L_1 - L_t \tag{17}$$

$$C_X = C_{eq2} + C_{IN} - 1/\left(\omega^2 L_b\right) \tag{18}$$

where C_{eq2} is given by (2). β, L_X, and C_X, defined by (16), (17), and (18), respectively, were used to calculate T_{SQ1-3}. Figure 9 shows A_{CG} as a function of each design parameter. The tendencies of A_{CG} vs. L_1 (a) and C_1 (b) are matched with those for ESCO [16]. As expected, the smaller the C_{IN}, the closer to unity for A_{CG} in (c). (This tendency validated increasing the drain voltage amplitude with a smaller C_{IN} in the following sub-section, as expected in Section 1). There were substantial discrepancies in A_{CG} between the model and SPICE results for $C_{IN} > 2$ nF. A physical background is required here, but its investigation will be conducted in future work. Figure 9d suggests that Lt and Lb can be minor contributors to A_{CG}, resulting in no significant impact on the drain voltage amplitude, as discussed in the following subsection. In summary, the model calculation results were in good agreement with the SPICE results, except for $C_{IN} > 2$ nF.

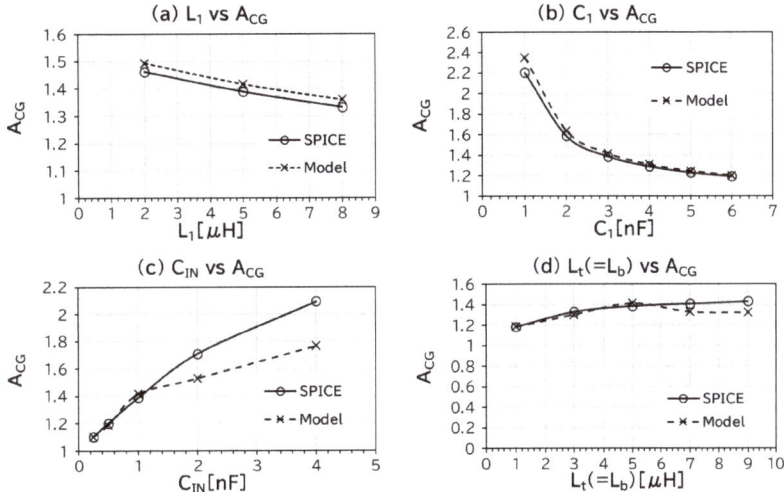

Figure 9. A_{CG} as a function of each design parameter. (**a**) L_1 vs. A_{CG}, (**b**) C_1 vs. A_{CG}, (**c**) C_{IN} vs. A_{CG}, (**d**) $L_t(=L_b)$ vs. A_{CG}.

3.3. Drain Voltage Amplitude v_{da}

In this subsection, the drain voltage amplitude v_{da} is modeled. In reality, there was a distortion in V_d and V_s due to the nonlinear behavior of the transconductance and drain conductance of M1, but it was assumed for simplicity in this study that the AC components of V_d and V_s are modeled with sinusoidal waveforms whose amplitudes are v_{da} and v_{sa}, respectively, as shown in Figure 10.

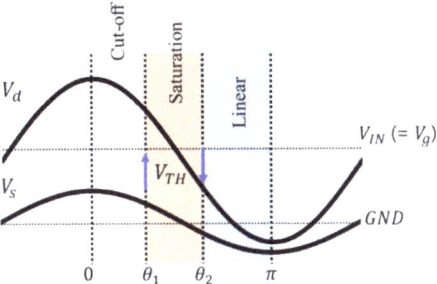

Figure 10. Waveform of V_d and V_s and operation modes in one cycle.

V_d has an offset voltage of V_{IN}. Thus, V_d and V_s can be written as (19) and (20), respectively.

$$V_d = V_{IN} + v_{da} \cos \theta \tag{19}$$

$$V_s = v_{sa} \cos \theta = \frac{v_{da}}{A_{CG}} \cos \theta \qquad (20)$$

When v_{sa} is large enough, M1 operates in three different modes, i.e., in cut-off, saturation, and linear operation modes. θ_1 is the boundary between cut-off and saturation, resulting in (21), where V_{TH} is the threshold voltage of M1. θ_2 is the boundary between saturation and linear, resulting in (22).

$$\theta_1 = \cos^{-1} \frac{V_{IN} - V_{TH}}{v_{sa}} \qquad (21)$$

$$\theta_2 = \cos^{-1} \frac{-V_{TH}}{v_{da}} \qquad (22)$$

Let us assume a simple Shockley model for M1, as described in (23) and (24), where Ids_sat and Ids_lin are the drain current in saturation and liner modes, respectively, and k is a proportional coefficient of the drain current.

$$I_{ds\_sat} = \frac{1}{2} k (V_{gs} - V_{th})^2 \qquad (23)$$

$$I_{ds\_lin} = k \left\{ (V_{gs} - V_{th}) V_{ds} - \frac{1}{2} V_{ds}^2 \right\} \qquad (24)$$

The transconductance is expressed by (25) and (26) in saturation and liner modes, respectively.

$$g_{m_{sat}} = \frac{\partial I_{ds_{sat}}}{\partial V_{gs}} = k (V_{gs} - V_{th}) \qquad (25)$$

$$g_{m\_lin} = \frac{\partial I_{ds\_lin}}{\partial V_{gs}} = k V_{ds} \qquad (26)$$

Let us assume (27) holds when mESCO runs in steady state, where the peak drain voltage does not change by cycle, because when the left side value of (27) is positive, the amplitude increases by a cycle; whereas when it is negative, the amplitude decreases by a cycle.

$$\int_0^\pi g_m(\theta) d\theta = 0 \qquad (27)$$

Using (21), (22), (25) and (26), (27) resulted in (28).

$$\begin{aligned} \int_0^\pi g_m(\theta) d\theta &= \int_{\theta_1}^{\theta_2} g_{m\_sat}(\theta) d\theta + \int_{\theta_2}^\pi g_{m\_lin}(\theta) d\theta \\ &= V_{IN}(\pi - \theta_1) - V_{th}(\theta_2 - \theta_1) + v_{sa} \sin \theta_1 - v_{da} \sin \theta_2 = 0 \end{aligned} \qquad (28)$$

Equation (28) shows that v_{da} is a function of A_{CG}, V_{IN} and V_{TH}. Therefore, the model was compared with the SPICE results in terms of v_{da} vs. A_{CG}, as shown in Figure 11a. Dots in colors show the SPICE results where the circuit parameters are varied as much as the ones in Figure 9. Because the SPICE model for NMOSFET used in this study has no breakdown at high drain voltages, all the simulated data were plotted. However, because there is a strict specification for the maximum voltages in reality, it can limit the design space for the circuit parameters. Even though the model result has an offset from the trend curve of the SPICE results, the model well-represents the tendency that v_{da} is determined by A_{CG} rather than individual circuit parameters. It is interesting to note that the data points of v_{da} and v_{sa} are plotted on a linear line with a slope of 1.00 for both the SPICE results and model calculated results with a slightly different offset of 1.05 and 1.25 V for the SPICE results and model calculated results, respectively, as shown in Figure 11b.

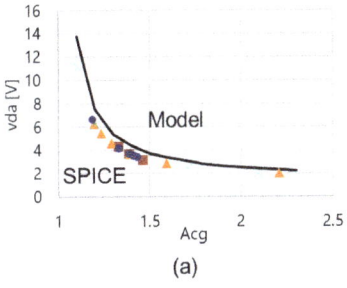
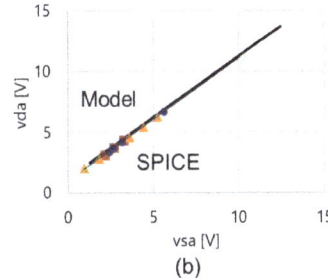

Figure 11. (**a**) A_{CG} vs. v_{da} and (**b**) v_{sa} vs. v_{da}.

Figure 12a,b show the waveforms for voltage, current, and *gm* in cases of A_{CG} = 1.2 and 1.8, respectively. The waveform for *gm* in Figure 12a suggests that *gm* in a linear operation can partially contribute to surplus for a very large voltage amplitude. For a relatively low voltage swing in Figure 12b, positive and negative *gm* appear in the saturation and linear regions, respectively.

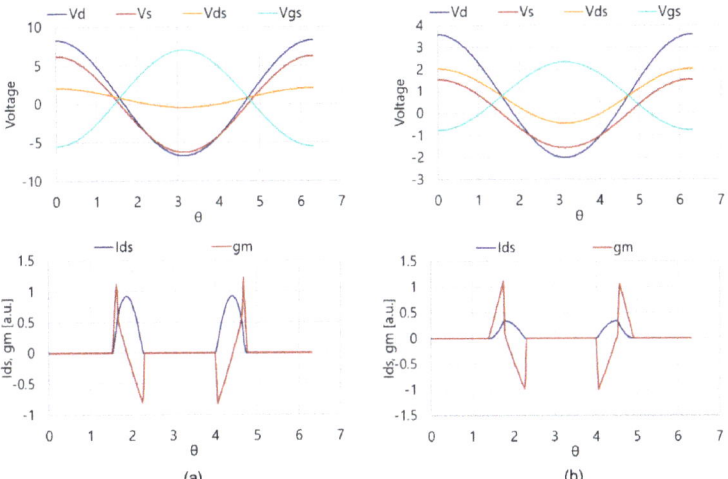

Figure 12. Waveform in cases of A_{CG} = 1.2 (**a**) and 1.8 (**b**).

To compare the v_{da} of mESCO with that of ESCO, SPICE simulations and model calculations based on [16] were made with the same parameter conditions for L_1, C_1, and V_{IN} as mESCO. Figure 13 shows the comparison results. Even though the model accuracy of (28) for mESCO is not as sufficient as that of [16] for ESCO, the trend over circuit parameters represents the SPICE results. With the same values for L_1, L_2, C_1, and C_2 as those of ESCO, mESCO has a 2× or larger v_{da} than ESCO.

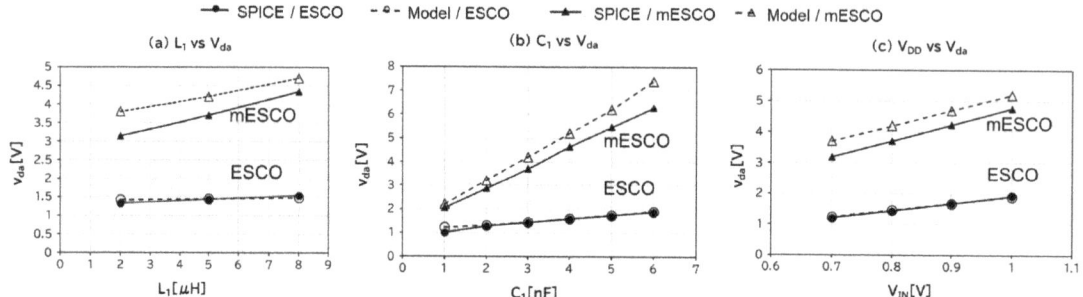

Figure 13. v_{da} of ESCO and mESCO as a function of L_1 (**a**), C_1 (**b**), and V_{IN} (**c**).

The data in Figure 13 are placed in a single $v_{da}-A_{CG}$ graph as shown in Figure 14. mESCO, as well as ESCO, has a unified characteristic curve. It is essential to design mESCO and ESCO with A_{CG} as close to unity as possible to have a large v_{da}.

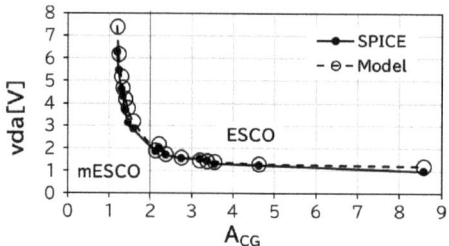

Figure 14. v_{da} of ESCO and mESCO as a function of A_{CG}.

4. Conclusions

We found that an additional L–C–L filter for ESCO, called mESCO, increased the peak drain voltage, which will contribute to increasing the boost ratio when it is used in DC–DC boost converter applications. In this study, the operation frequency, common gate voltage gain, and drain voltage amplitude were analyzed with simple proposed models for mESCO. Even though the frequency model potentially has three different frequencies as a solution, the lower two components were not allowed because an equivalent inductor and capacitor would have had negative inductance and capacitance, respectively. The highest frequency was matched with the SPICE results in wide circuit parameter ranges. The common gate voltage gain was also modeled with a simple circuit transformation. The model calculation results are in good agreement with the SPICE results within a 10% error, except for large C_{IN}. In addition, the drain voltage amplitude was modeled with an assumption that the average transconductance of the switching transistor over a half cycle is null. Even with a simple Shockley model, the drain voltage amplitude was successfully modeled so that it is a function of the common gate voltage gain rather than individual circuit parameters. This fact is valid for ESCO as well as mESCO. In wide ranges of L_1, C_1, and V_{IN}, the drain voltage amplitude of mESCO was 2× or larger than that of ESCO. ESCO and mESCO had the same trend in the drain voltage amplitude over the common gate voltage gain.

Further experiments to validate the model and SPICE results and an application of mESCO to DC–DC boost converters will be conducted in the future. When a rectifier is added to mESCO for the DC–DC boost converter, it would have another impedance at the drain of the switching transistor, potentially yielding a loss in the drain voltage amplitude and thereby a degradation of the output power of the DC–DC converter. One would need to analyze its impact to design a DC–DC converter with sufficient output power.

Author Contributions: Conceptualization, T.T.; methodology, T.N. and T.T.; software, T.N.; validation, T.N. and T.T.; formal analysis, T.N. and T.T.; investigation, T.N. and T.T.; writing—original draft preparation, T.N.; writing—review and editing, T.T.; funding acquisition, T.T. All authors have read and agreed to the published version of the manuscript.

Funding: This research was funded by JSPS KAKENHI grant number 22K04042.

Institutional Review Board Statement: Not applicable.

Informed Consent Statement: Not applicable.

Data Availability Statement: Not applicable.

Acknowledgments: This work was supported by JSPS KAKENHI grant number 22K04042.

Conflicts of Interest: The authors declare no conflict of interest.

Nomenclature

A_{CG}	Common gate voltage gain
C_{DEC}	Decoupling capacitor
ER	ESCO followed by rectifier
ESCO	Enhanced swing Colpitts oscillator
ET	Energy transducer
IoT	Internet of Things
L_{BW}	Inductance of bonding wires
mER	mESCO followed by Rectifier
mESCO	more Enhanced Swing Colpitts Oscillator
SPICE	Simulation Program with Integrated Circuit Emphasis
v_{da}	Drain voltage amplitude
V_{IN}	Input DC voltage
V_{OUT}	Output DC voltage
V_X	DC offset
V_x	Voltage difference from ground
v_x	Voltage difference from the DC offset
V_{xa}	Voltage amplitude
WPT	Wireless power transfer
θ	Phase

References

1. Shinohara, N. Power without wires. *IEEE Microw. Mag.* **2011**, *12*, S64–S73. [CrossRef]
2. Xie, L.; Shi, Y.; Hou, Y.T.; Lou, A. Wireless power transfer and applications to sensor networks. *IEEE Wirel. Commun.* **2013**, *20*, 140–145. [CrossRef]
3. Amar, A.B.; Kouki, A.B.; Cao, H. Power approaches for implantable medical devices. *Sensors* **2015**, *15*, 28889–28914. [CrossRef] [PubMed]
4. Qian, L.; Cui, K.; Xia, H.; Shao, H.; Wang, J.; Xia, Y. An Inductive Power Transfer System for Powering Wireless Sensor Nodes in Structural Health Monitoring Applications. *IEEE Trans. Microw. Theory Tech.* **2022**, *70*, 3732–3740. [CrossRef]
5. Mitcheson, P.D.; Yeatman, E.M.; Rao, G.K.; Holmes, A.S.; Green, T.C. Energy Harvesting From Human and Machine Motion for Wireless Electronic Devices. *Proc. IEEE* **2008**, *96*, 1457–1486. [CrossRef]
6. Kazmiersuki, T.; Beedy, S. *Energy Harvesting Systems: Principles, Modeling and Applications*; Springer: Berlin/Heidelberg, Germany, 2010; pp. 1–78.
7. Trotter, M.S.; Griffin, J.D.; Durgin, G.D. Power-optimized waveforms for improving the range and reliability of RFID systems. In Proceedings of the 2009 IEEE International Conference on RFID, Orlando, FL, USA, 27–28 April 2009; pp. 80–87. [CrossRef]
8. Boaventura, A.S.; Carvalho, N.B. Maximizing DC power in energy harvesting circuits using multisine excitation. In Proceedings of the 2011 IEEE MTT-S International Microwave Symposium, Baltimore, MD, USA, 5–10 June 2011; pp. 1–4. [CrossRef]
9. Collado, A.; Georgiadis, A. Optimal Waveforms for Efficient Wireless Power Transmission. *IEEE Microw. Wirel. Compon. Lett.* **2014**, *24*, 354–356. [CrossRef]
10. Clarke, K.K.; Hess, D.T. *Communication Circuits: Analysis and Desig*; Addison-Wesley Publishing Company: Boston, MA, USA, 1971; Chapter 6.
11. Zhang, M.; Du, L.; Fang, Z.; Zhao, Z. A sensitivity-enhanced film bulk acoustic resonator gas sensor with an oscillator circuit and its detection application. *Micromachines* **2017**, *8*, 25. [CrossRef]

12. Sharma, S.; Gao, H.; Hueber, G.; Mazzanti, A. A Magnetically Coupled Dual-Core 154-GHz Class-F Oscillator with -177.1 FoM and -87 dBc/Hz PN at 1-MHz Offset in a 22-nm FDSOI with Third-Harmonic Extraction. In Proceedings of the 2022 IEEE Symposium on VLSI Technology and Circuits (VLSI Technology and Circuits), Honolulu, HI, USA, 12–17 June 2022; pp. 12–13. [CrossRef]
13. Liu, S.-H.; Hung, C.-M.; Chuang, H.-R.; Huang, T.-H. A W-band Push-Push VCO with Gm-Boosted Colpitts Topology in 90-nm CMOS Technology. In Proceedings of the 2021 IEEE International Symposium on Radio-Frequency Integration Technology (RFIT), Hualien, Taiwan, 25–27 August 2021; pp. 1–3. [CrossRef]
14. Troedsson, N.; Sjoland, H. An ultra low voltage 2.4 GHz CMOS VCO. In Proceedings of the RAWCON 2002 IEEE Radio and Wireless Conference (Cat. No.02EX573), Boston, MA, USA, 11–14 August 2002; pp. 205–208. [CrossRef]
15. Hsieh, H.; Lu, L. A High-Performance CMOS Voltage-Controlled Oscillator for Ultra-Low-Voltage Operations. *IEEE Trans. Microw. Theory Tech.* **2007**, *55*, 467–473. [CrossRef]
16. Brown, T.W.; Farhabakhshian, F.; Roy, A.G.; Fiez, T.S.; Mayaram, K. A 475 mV, 4.9 GHz Enhanced Swing Differential Colpitts VCO With Phase Noise of -136 dBc/Hz at a 3 MHz Offset Frequency. *IEEE J. Solid-State Circuits* **2011**, *46*, 1782–1795. [CrossRef]
17. Machado, M.B.; Schneider, M.C.; Galup-Montoro, C. On the Minimum Supply Voltage for MOSFET Oscillators. *IEEE Trans. Circuits Syst. I Regul. Pap.* **2014**, *61*, 347–357. [CrossRef]
18. Lim, B.-M.; Seo, J.-I.; Lee, S.-G. A Colpitts Oscillator-Based Self-Starting Boost Converter for Thermoelectric Energy Harvesting With 40-mV Startup Voltage and 75% Maximum Efficiency. *IEEE J. Solid-State Circuits* **2018**, *53*, 3293–3302. [CrossRef]

Article

Design of Switched-Capacitor DC-DC Voltage-Down Converters Driven by Highly Resistive Energy Transducer

Yosuke Demura and Toru Tanzawa *

Faculty of Engineering, Shizuoka University, Hamamatsu 432-8561, Japan; demura.yosuke.18@shizuoka.ac.jp
* Correspondence: toru.tanzawa@shizuoka.ac.jp

Abstract: Electrostatic vibration energy transducers have a relatively high output impedance (R_{ET}) and open-circuit voltage (V_{IN}), so that voltage-down conversion is required for sensor/RF ICs. Switched-capacitor converters are the best candidate to create small-form-factor technology and are a low-cost solution because of their capability to fully integrate into sensor/RF ICs. To design switched-capacitor voltage-down converters (SC-VDCs) with a minimum circuit area for electrostatic vibration energy transducers, two steps are required. The first step requires an optimum design of DC-DC SC-VDCs driven by high R_{ET} with a minimum circuit area, and the second step requires an optimum design of AC-DC SC-VDCs based on the first step, to minimize the converter circuit area. This paper discusses circuit analysis and design optimization aimed at the first step. Switching frequency, the number of stages and the capacitance per stage were determined as a function of R_{ET}, V_{IN} and the output voltage (Vo) and current (Io) to the load, to achieve a minimum circuit area. The relationship between Io and the power conversion efficiency was studied as well. The performance was validated by SPICE simulation in 250 nm BCD technology. An optimum design flow was proposed to design DC-DC SC-VDCs driven by high R_{ET} with a minimum circuit area under conditions where R_{ET}, V_{IN}, Vo and Io were given. The second design step remains as future work.

Keywords: switched-capacitor converter; voltage-down converter; energy transducer; optimum design; electrostatic vibration energy harvesting; fully integrated; IoT

Citation: Demura, Y.; Tanzawa, T. Design of Switched-Capacitor DC-DC Voltage-Down Converters Driven by Highly Resistive Energy Transducer. *Electronics* **2022**, *11*, 1874. https://doi.org/10.3390/electronics11121874

Academic Editors: Shailendra Rajput, Moshe Averbukh and Noel Rodriguez

Received: 4 June 2022
Accepted: 13 June 2022
Published: 14 June 2022

Publisher's Note: MDPI stays neutral with regard to jurisdictional claims in published maps and institutional affiliations.

Copyright: © 2022 by the authors. Licensee MDPI, Basel, Switzerland. This article is an open access article distributed under the terms and conditions of the Creative Commons Attribution (CC BY) license (https://creativecommons.org/licenses/by/4.0/).

1. Introduction

Energy harvesting (EH) is technology for harvesting power for IoT edge devices from environmental energy using energy transducers (ETs) [1]. Electrostatic energy transducers (ES-ETs) can convert vibration energy into electronic power [2,3]. Due to high output impedance (R_{ET}), open-circuit voltages (V_{IN}) have to go beyond 10 V to generate power of 10 μW or larger. Switching regulators were proposed in [4,5] with a high-voltage full-bridge rectifier. An HV rectifier is composed of four diodes for converting the AC power of ES-ETs into DC power in the converter. As the DC voltage is much higher than the maximum voltage acceptable in sensor CMOS ICs, power management circuits in DC-DC converters need to be fabricated using a BCD process, which provides an HV CMOS operating even at high voltages of 10 V or higher. Buck converters require external components, such as inductors, capacitors and resistors (LCRs), to convert the DC-input voltage of an order of 10 V into an output voltage of an order of 1 V. DC-DC buck converters are used in applications of very high-power conversion. In [6], monolithic integrated high frequency GaN DC-DC buck converters were proposed to output 15 V at a power density of 1 W/mm². Another type of switching converter is a boost converter. In [7], a boost converter with a piezoelectric energy harvester could generate 1 V from a low-input voltage of 0.12 V with an output power of 4.2 mW for wearable biomedical applications.

An alternative design for ES-ETs is a shunt regulator, which enables the elimination of inductors [8]. The circuit can sufficiently reduce overstress, even with a standard 1 V CMOS, resulting in full integration, apart from the decoupling caps, and provides a low-cost solution. A drawback of the shunt regulator is low power efficiency. As the peak open-circuit voltage increases, the power conversion efficiency decreases. A third option is switched-capacitor converters, which can be fully integrated as well, and have moderate power efficiency [9]. In [10], the design of switched-capacitor voltage-up converters for a DC-energy transducer was discussed, where the operating clock frequency was assumed to be constant, regardless of the number of capacitors and the capacitance of each capacitor. To the best knowledge of the authors, there has been no formulation to design switched-capacitor voltage-down converters for highly resistive energy transducers. To optimally design switched-capacitor voltage-down converters (SC-VDCs) for ES-ETs, the first step requires an optimum design of DC-DC SC-VDCs driven by high R_{ET}, and the second step requires an optimum design of AC-DC SC-VDCs based on the first step.

This paper discusses circuit analysis and design optimization aimed at the first step. Switching frequency, the number of stages and the capacitance per stage were determined as a function of R_{ET}, V_{IN} and the output voltage (Vo) and current (Io) to the load, to achieve a minimum circuit area. The relationship between Io and the power conversion efficiency was studied as well. The performance was validated by SPICE simulation in 250 nm BCD technology. The second design step remains as future work. This paper is organized as follows: Section 2 develops circuit models with no R_{ET} case as ideal and a high R_{ET} condition. The sensitivity of Io on the design parameters are discussed. Optimum clock cycle time and the optimum number of capacitors are determined to maximize Io at Vo. Optimization design flow is proposed in Section 3. The results are also shown.

2. Circuit Model

2.1. Ideal Case with No R_{ET}

Figure 1 illustrates a block diagram of an energy transducer (ET) and a switched-capacitor voltage-down converter (SC-VDC). The electrical characteristics can be expressed by an open-circuit voltage V_{IN} and output resistance R_{ET}. In this paper, V_{IN} is assumed to be DC to propose design optimization of SC-VDC driven by a highly resistive ET, which will be able to apply to AC-DC SC-VDCs for electrostatic vibration energy transducers in future work. An SC-VDC is composed of multiple capacitors and switches to vary the configuration of capacitors between input and output terminals in two states per cycle of an input clock CLK.

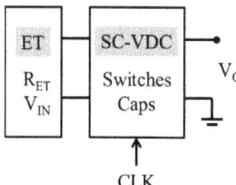

Figure 1. Block diagram of energy transducer (ET) and switched-capacitor voltage-down converter (SC-VDC).

Figure 2 shows those two configurations of DC-DC SC-VDC with CLK = H and L in (a) and (b), respectively, namely in a serial state and in a parallel state. An SC-VDC has N capacitors, each of which has the same capacitance C. The input current I_{IN} flows in the serial state. The output currents I_{OP} and I_{OS} flow in the serial and the parallel states, respectively. Figure 2c shows the waveform of V_P at the interface between ET and SC-VDC. The serial state required a longer period (Ts) than the parallel one required (Tp) because the capacitors were charged via a large resistor R_{ET} in Ts, whereas they were discharged via a small on-resistance of switches in Tp. Thus, the clock frequency was limited by Ts. When Ts increased, the amount of charge stored in the capacitors increased, and the cycle time also increased. Overly long Ts could reduce the average output current (I_O) because the amount of charge saturated for long Ts. On the other hand, when Ts decreased too much, the charge transferred into the capacitors decreased as well. Ts that was too short could also reduce I_O. As a result, there should be an optimum T_S to maximize Io between two extreme conditions. Firstly, we will look at the circuit behavior in the case where R_{ET} is sufficiently small, and then, we will investigate the case where R_{ET} is significantly large.

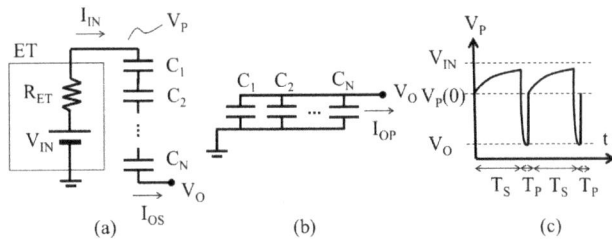

Figure 2. Two states of SC-VDC: (**a**) serial connection to extract power from ET; (**b**) parallel connection to output power to V_O; (**c**) waveform of V_P.

An ideal circuit model of SC voltage-up converters was discussed in [11,12] and the optimum number of capacitors to minimize the circuit area under the condition that the circuit outputs a target current at a given output voltage was also discussed. In this section, we will start with a similar set of equations to represent the circuit performance. All of the parasitic resistance of the power supply and switches was assumed to be adequately small. Therefore, the clock cycle T was considered to be long enough for the charge to be transferred to the capacitors or to the output. Under such conditions, the output charge in the serial state (Q_{OS}) and the average current over T (I_{OS}) were given by (1) and (2), respectively, as follows:

$$Q_{OS} = \frac{C}{N}(V_{IN} - (N+1)V_o) \tag{1}$$

$$I_{OS} = \frac{Q_{OS}}{T} = \frac{1}{N} \times \frac{CV_{IN}}{T}\left(1 - \frac{(N+1)V_o}{V_{IN}}\right) \tag{2}$$

Similarly, the output charge in the parallel state (Q_{OP}) and the average current over T (I_{OP}) were given by (3) and (4), respectively. The total average output current (I_O) was therefore given by (5).

$$Q_{OP} = N \times Q_{OS} = C(V_{IN} - (N+1)V_o) \tag{3}$$

$$I_{OP} = \frac{Q_{OP}}{T} = \frac{CV_{IN}}{T}\left(1 - \frac{(N+1)V_o}{V_{IN}}\right) \tag{4}$$

$$I_O = I_{OS} + I_{OP} = \frac{N+1}{N} \cdot \frac{CV_{IN}}{T}\left(1 - \frac{(N+1)V_o}{V_{IN}}\right) \tag{5}$$

The average input current (I_{IN}) was equal to I_{OP} (6). Thus, the input and output power were expressed by (7) and (8), respectively. The power conversion efficiency (η) defined by P_O/P_{IN} was calculated as (9).

$$I_{IN} = I_{OS} \tag{6}$$

$$P_{IN} = V_{IN}I_{IN} = \frac{CV_{IN}2}{NT}\left(1 - \frac{(N+1)V_o}{V_{IN}}\right) \tag{7}$$

$$P_O = V_O I_O = \frac{(N+1)CV_{IN}V_O}{NT}\left(1 - \frac{(N+1)V_o}{V_{IN}}\right) \tag{8}$$

$$\eta = \frac{P_O}{P_{IN}} = \frac{(N+1)\ V_O}{V_{IN}} \tag{9}$$

N needed to meet (10) to have finite I_O based on (5). From the point of view of high power-conversion efficiency, a larger N was recommended. The largest number of N to meet the equation of $N < V_{IN}/V_O - 1$ had the highest η. On the other hand, from the point of view of high I_O, a smaller N was recommended because I_O was a monotonic function of N, as shown by (11).

$$N < \frac{V_{IN}}{V_O} - 1 \tag{10}$$

$$\frac{\partial I_O}{\partial N} \propto -N\left(\frac{V_{IN}}{V_O} + 2\right) - 2\left(\frac{V_{IN}}{V_O} - 1\right) \tag{11}$$

2.2. Practical Case with Large R_{ET}

Like the previous model, where the switch resistance was low enough under the slow-switching limit, it was assumed that the parallel state did not require a long period to transfer all of the charges via the switches with low on-resistance. On the other hand, it was assumed that the charges transferred during the serial state were limited by T_S. The voltage at the top plate of the top capacitor (V_P) in the case where the bottom plate of the bottom capacitor was connected to the output terminal was determined by a differential Equation (12).

$$\frac{V_{IN} - V_p(t)}{R_{ET}} = \frac{C}{N}\frac{d}{dt}(V_p(t) - V_o) \tag{12}$$

With the initial condition as shown in (13), (12) was solved to be (14), where the time constant τ was given by (15).

$$V_p(0) = (N+1)V_O \tag{13}$$

$$V_p(t) = V_{IN}\left(1 - \left(1 - \frac{(N+1)V_o}{V_{IN}}\right) \cdot e^{-\frac{t}{\tau}}\right) \tag{14}$$

$$\tau = \frac{CR_{ET}}{N} \tag{15}$$

The average output current during the serial state over one period of $T = T_P + T_S$ (I_{OS}), which was equivalent to the average input current, could be estimated using (16).

$$I_{OS} = I_{IN} = \frac{C(V_P(T_S) - V_P(0))}{NT} = \frac{CV_{IN}}{NT}\left(1 - \frac{(N+1)V_o}{V_{IN}}\right)\left(1 - e^{-\frac{T_S}{\tau}}\right) \tag{16}$$

Because the total transferred charges from the energy transducer in the serial state appeared to be all N capacitors, the charges to the output terminal in the parallel state were given by (17).

$$I_{OP} = NI_{OS} \tag{17}$$

Therefore, an average output current in a period could be estimated by (18). The input and output power were simply given by (19) and (20), respectively.

$$I_O = I_{OS} + I_{OP} = \frac{N+1}{N} \cdot \frac{CV_{IN}}{T}\left(1 - \frac{(N+1)V_o}{V_{IN}}\right)\left(1 - e^{-\frac{T_S}{\tau}}\right) \tag{18}$$

$$P_{IN} = V_{IN}I_{IN} = \frac{CV_{IN}^2}{NT}\left(1 - \frac{(N+1)V_o}{V_{IN}}\right)\left(1 - e^{-\frac{T_S}{\tau}}\right) \tag{19}$$

$$P_O = V_O I_O = \frac{(N+1)CV_{IN}V_O}{NT}\left(1 - \frac{(N+1)V_o}{V_{IN}}\right)\left(1 - e^{-\frac{T_S}{\tau}}\right) \tag{20}$$

As a result, when all of the parasitic capacitance, such as bottom and top plate capacitance and junction capacitance of switches was negligibly small, the power conversion efficiency (η) became (21), which was equal to (9). Equations (16), (18)–(20) became identical to (2), (5), (7) and (8) when R_{ET} approached zero.

$$\eta = \frac{P_O}{P_{IN}} = \frac{(N+1)V_O}{V_{IN}} \tag{21}$$

One can find an optimum Ts to maximize Io based on (18). With $\frac{\partial I_O}{\partial T_S} = 0$, (22a) held in the case that $\sqrt{\tau T_P} \gg T_P$. Similarly, with $\frac{\partial I_O}{\partial N} = 0$ and (22a), (22b) held. As a result, I_O approached the maximum attainable current I_{O_ATT} given by (22c), which was I_O under impedance matching.

$$T_{S\_OPT} = \sqrt{\tau T_P} \tag{22a}$$

$$N_{OPT} = \frac{V_{IN}}{2V_O} - 1 \tag{22b}$$

$$I_{O\_ATT} = \frac{V_{IN}^2}{4R_{ET}V_O} \tag{22c}$$

2.3. Characteristics of SC-VDC for Highly Resistive ET

To see how Io varied as a function of N, C and Ts, a demonstration was performed with the default parameters shown in Table 1.

Table 1. Design parameters used as a demonstration.

Parameters	Default Value
V_{IN}	10 V
R_{ET}	100 kΩ (10 Ω for reference)
V_O	1.0 V
C	1.0 nF
N	4
T_S	10 µs
T_P	100 ns

When N, C or Ts was varied, the remaining parameters were set at the default values. R_{ET} of 100 kΩ and 10 Ω were used to verify the significance of a large R_{ET} value. In Figure 3a, the number of capacitors (N) was varied. As predicted, Io was maximized with N of one when R_{ET} was sufficiently small. Conversely, Io was maximized to three or four when R_{ET} was quite large, as predicted by (22b). N_{OPT} was estimated to be four when V_{IN} = 10 V and Vo = 1 V by (22b). Figure 3b shows that the response of C to Io was scaled by R_{ET}. The ratio of 100 kΩ to 10 Ω was 10^4. When one drew the curve of I_O − C for R_{ET} = 10 Ω by shifting four orders in the horizontal and the vertical axes, the two curves were matched well. Figure 3c shows that there was an optimum Ts depending on the value of R_{ET}. Ts that was too short did not allow charges to be transferred from ET, whereas Ts that was too long simply decreased Io~Qo/Ts, wherein Qo was saturated for long Ts. The estimate equation (22a) gave us T_{S_OPT} of 15 µs and 1.5 µs for R_{ET} of 100 kΩ and 10 Ω, respectively, which were in agreement with Figure 3c.

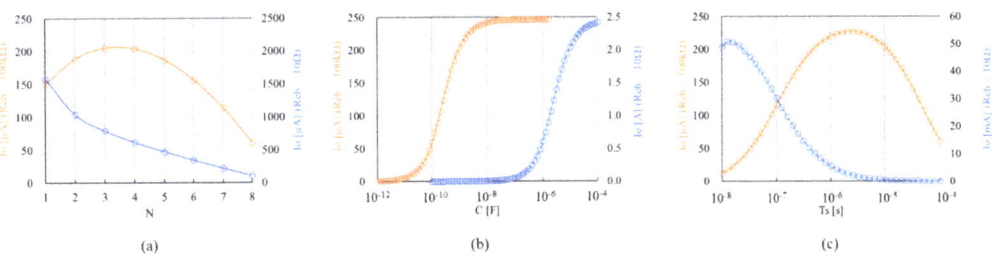

Figure 3. Io as a function of N (**a**); C (**b**); T_S (**c**).

How can circuit designers maximize Io when the total capacitance is given? I_O vs. T_S plots for various N can tell them the answer. Figure 4 is a demonstration assuming

$C_{TOT} = CN = 100$ pF and the other parameters are given by Table 1. The optimum Ts to maximize Io depended on N because τ varied as N^{-2} when CN was constant ($\tau = R_{ET} C/N = R_{ET} C_{TOT}/N^2$). One can find the maximum Io (I_{O_MAX}) for each N at T_{S_OPT} from Figure 4a. Figure 4b shows I_{O_MAX} vs. N when CN = 100 pF. In this demonstration, one can extract 160 μA at 1 V with N = 3 and Ts = 500 ns. The above procedure to determine the optimum N and Ts will be used in Section 3.

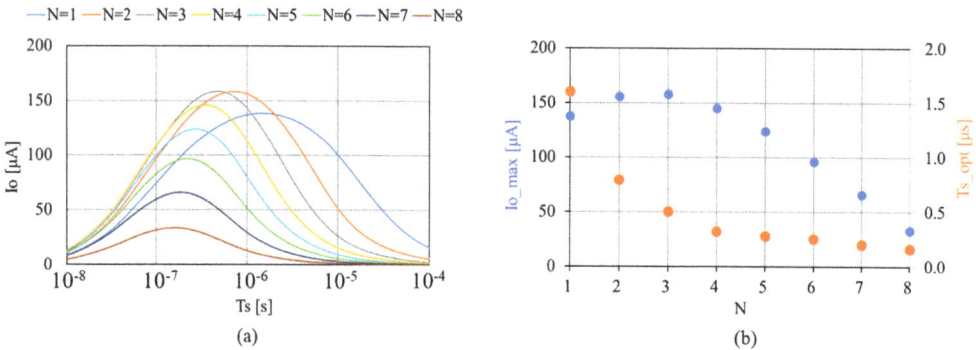

Figure 4. (a) Io as a function of Ts when $C_{TOT} = CN = 100$ pF; (b) I_{O_MAX} vs. N.

Figure 5 shows η vs. N based on (9) and (21). The two lines were identical. As N increased, the voltage ripple of each capacitor decreased, which contributed to a reduction in conduction loss, i.e., an increase in η [13]. Note that (9) and (21) did not take any parasitic capacitance into account for simplicity. When the parasitic capacitance, such as the top and bottom plate capacitance to the ground, and the junction capacitance of switches was considered, η was degraded especially for converters with many capacitors [14]. Improvement of the models discussed in this paper will be needed for more accurate initial design.

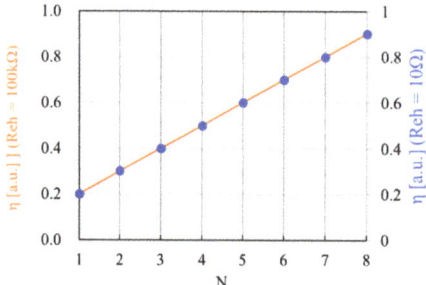

Figure 5. η as a function of N.

The above procedure could be performed for various C_{TOT} as shown in Figure 6a. The maximum attainable power from a given ET specified with V_{IN} and R_{ET} (P_{ATT}) was given by (22c) under a power match, when the input impedance of the converter was matched with R_{ET}. In case of the conditions given in Table 1, P_{ATT} was 250μW ($10 V^2/4 \times 100$ kΩ). As shown in Figure 6a, by increasing C_{TOT}, I_{O_MAX} approached P_{ATT}/V_O. The value of N_{OPT} that provided the largest I_{O_MAX} was the one with a small C_{TOT}, whereas the value given by (22b) was one with a sufficiently large C_{TOT}.

One can draw Figure 6b by combining Figure 6a with Figure 5, which suggests that there was no chance to design an SC-VDC for highly resistive ET to maximize both I_O and η. Which one should be prioritized for circuit designers? If a set of ET and SC-VDC was considered as a power source, which was a viewpoint from the load, Io must be a higher priority than η.

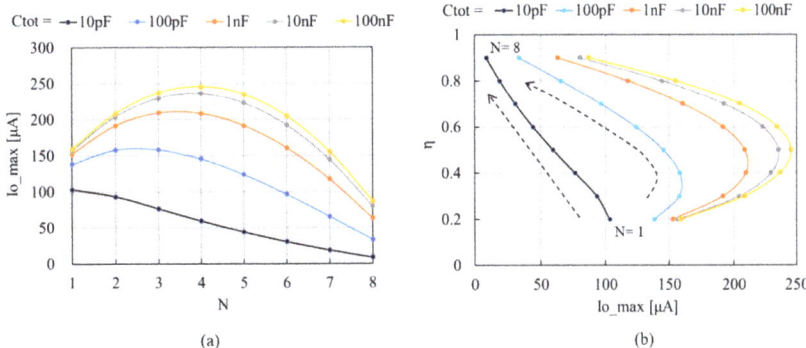

Figure 6. (a) I_{O_MAX} as a function of N for each value of C_{TOT}; (b) η as a function of I_{O_MAX} for each value of C_{TOT}.

Let us analyze Figure 6a in more detail. Figure 7a–c is N_{OPT} (a), T_{S_OPT} (b) and I_{O_MAX} (c) as a function of C_{TOT} based on Figure 6a. With C_{TOT} of 10 pF, N_{OPT} was one and T_{S_OPT} was 400 ns. This condition was close to a "no R_{ET} case", which had N_{OPT} of one. I_{O_MAX} was 100 μA at the most. Circuit designers may want to have a higher Io because the attainable output current was 250 μA. There was no other way to increase Io without a sacrifice of circuit area. Even though one could increase Io by increasing C_{TOT}, the rate of increase in Io was noticeably lower than the rate of increase in C_{TOT}. This was because Ts must also be increased for an increased τ, and N_{OPT} must be increased as well. The larger the value of N, the smaller the series capacitance C/N, and therefore the lower Io. For instance, one can have Io of 200 μA with C_{TOT} of 1 nF. With 100× C_{TOT}, Io barely increased by a factor of two.

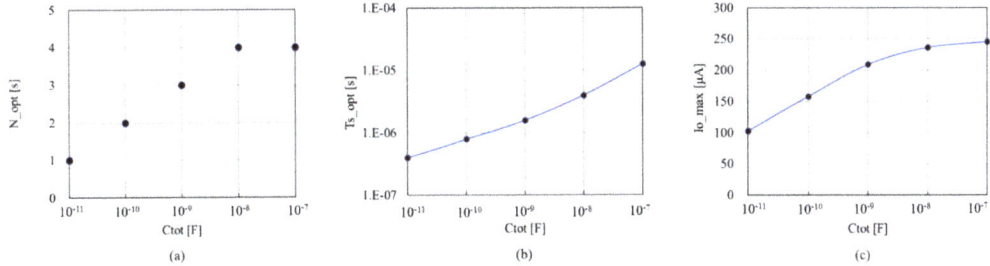

Figure 7. N_{OPT} (a); T_{S_OPT} (b); I_{O_MAX} (c), as a function of C_{TOT}.

2.4. Validation of the Model

To validate the model expressed by (18), a two-stage SC-VDC was designed in 250 nm BCD technology, as shown in Figure 8a. First, 12 V CMOS transistors were used to manage V_{IN} of 10 V in SPICE simulation. Transistors need to operate in a safe-operating region, i.e., the drain (source) voltage of N(P)MOSFETs must be equal to or greater than the source (drain) voltage. As a result, some switches were realized with two series transistors whose gates are driven by "ser1" and "ser2". The timings were slightly different, as shown in Figure 8b.

SPICE simulations were run with various Ts, resulting in Figure 9. The model still had a mismatch against SPICE, but if the model was requested to determine the optimum conditions for Ts (500 ns in this example), the model was considered to be in agreement with the SPICE result. To design SC-VDCs precisely, one could run SPICE multiple times, starting at the conditions which the model predicts.

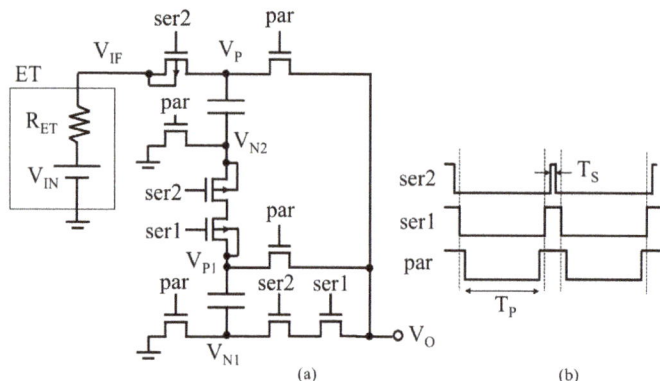

Figure 8. (**a**) Circuit diagram with N = 2 for model validation; (**b**) waveform of control signals.

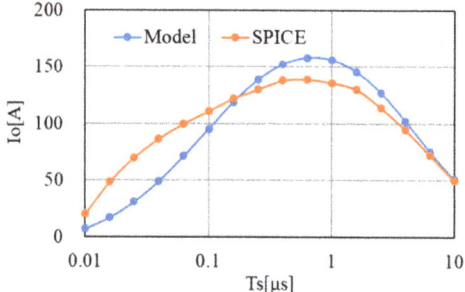

Figure 9. Comparison of Io vs. Ts between model calculation and SPICE simulation.

3. Optimum Design Flow

In this section, a design flow is proposed to design an SC-VDC for highly resistive ET so that the circuit area is minimized under the condition that a target Io (I_{O_TARGET}) is provided at a target Vo. The key idea is (1) one can design an SC-VDC to maximize Io when its circuit area or the total capacitance is given; (2) if the maximized Io provided in (1) is lower (higher) than I_{O_TARGET}, one can increase or decrease the circuit area gradually; and (3) finally one reaches SC-VDC with a minimum circuit area to barely output I_{O_TARGET}.

Figure 10 shows the design flow. The following are performed step by step.

(S1) V_{IN} and R_{ET} are assumed from the ET side, and Vo and I_{O_TARGET} are required from the load side. At this point, one can check whether there is any solution for SC-VDC based on (22c). If the estimated P_{ATT} is lower than Vo × I_{O_TARGET}, the circuit designers must request to increase the input power to the ET side, or to decrease the output power to the load side.

(S2) An initial value of the total capacitance CN is assumed, which is called Ao in this flow. One can start at any value for Ao because the feedback loop will reach the final solution as long as there is a value for Ao.

(S3) One can draw Io vs. Ts for each SC-VDC with a different N by using (18), as shown in Figure 4a.

(S4) One can find a maximum I_{O_MAX} at an optimum T_{S_OPT} among all of the possible designs, as shown in Figure 4b.

(S5) Then, a parameter α is calculated with Io/I_{O_TARGET}, which indicates how much Io deviates from the target.

(S6), (S8) If $1 < \alpha < 1.1$, the design determined in (S4) is the optimum design, which has a minimum circuit area with a design margin of 10% or less in Io. Therefore, the design flow is closed. If $\alpha < 1$, it is considered that Ao is not sufficient to output I_{O_TARGET} at Vo.

(S7) Then, Ao is increased by a factor of $1/\alpha$. The second trial starts at (S3) with Ao/α.

(S8) If $\alpha > 1.1$, Ao is more than enough to output the I_{O_TARGET} at Vo. Then, Ao is decreased by a factor of Ao/α at (S7) to feedback to (S3) for the next loop.

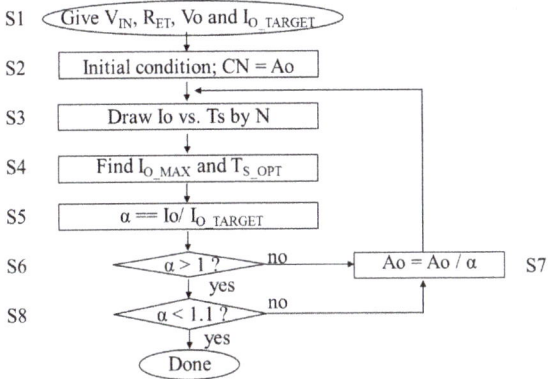

Figure 10. Optimum design flow to have a minimum circuit area.

A demonstration is made for I_{O_TARGET} of 100 µA at Vo of 1 V and A_O of 100 pF. By running the design flow as shown in Figure 10, C_{TOT}, T_{S_OPT}, N_{OPT} and thereby I_{O_MAX} were determined in each loop as shown in Figure 11. N_{OPT} varied from three in the first loop to one in the final tenth loop in this demonstration. T_{S_OPT} increased at the moment when N_{OPT} decreased, because τ decreased. In total, Ao gradually decreased from an initial condition of 100 pF to the final value of 7.5 pF where I_{O_MAX} reached 110 µA.

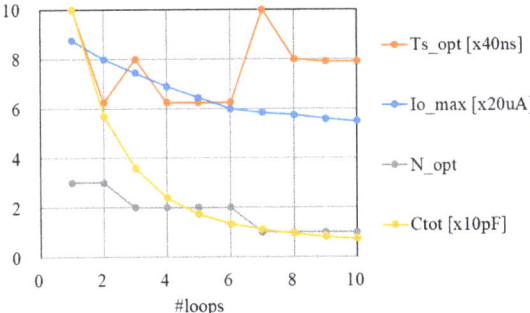

Figure 11. I_{O_MAX}, T_{S_OPT}, N_{OPT} and C_{TOT} vs. loop cycles under the condition of I_{O_TARGET} = 100 µA and Ao = 100 pF.

4. Conclusions

This paper developed a circuit model of DC-DC SC-VDC for highly resistive ET. Dependence on T_{S_OPT} and N_{OPT} to maximize I_O on R_{ET}, V_{IN} and V_O was demonstrated under the condition that a circuit area was given. Then, the optimum design flow was proposed to minimize the circuit area to meet the constraints of R_{ET}, V_{IN}, V_O and I_O. Its demonstration was presented. The results in this paper will be used to design AC-DC SC-VDC for highly resistive ET effectively.

Author Contributions: Conceptualization, T.T.; methodology, Y.D. and T.T.; software, Y.D.; validation, Y.D. and T.T.; formal analysis, Y.D. and T.T.; investigation, Y.D. and T.T.; writing—original draft preparation, Y.D.; writing—review and editing, T.T.; funding acquisition, T.T. All authors have read and agreed to the published version of the manuscript.

Funding: This research received no external funding.

Acknowledgments: This work was supported by d-lab.VDEC, Synopsys, Inc. (Mountain View, CA, USA) and Cadence Design Systems, Inc. (San Jose, CA, USA).

Conflicts of Interest: The authors declare no conflict of interest.

References

1. Kazmiersuki, T.; Beedy, S. *Energy Harvesting Systems: Principles, Modeling and Applications*; Springer: Berlin/Heidelberg, Germany, 2010; pp. 1–78.
2. Fu, Q.; Suzuki, Y.; Suzuki, Y. MEMS vibration electret energy harvester with combined electrodes. In Proceedings of the 2014 IEEE 27th International Conference on Micro Electro Mechanical Systems (MEMS), San Francisco, CA, USA, 26–30 January 2014; IEEE: Piscataway, NJ, USA, 2014; pp. 409–412. [CrossRef]
3. Hashiguchi, G. Electromechanical theory of microelectromechanical devices. *IEICE Electron. Express* **2014**, *11*, 20142007. [CrossRef]
4. Stanzione, S.; Van Liempd, C.; Van Schaijk, R.; Naito, Y.; Yazicioglu, R.F.; Van Hoof, C. A self-biased 5-to-60 V input voltage and 25-to-1600 μW integrated DC-DC buck converter with fully analog MPPT algorithm reaching up to 88% end-to-end efficiency. In Proceedings of the 2013 IEEE International Solid-State Circuits Conference Digest of Technical Papers, San Francisco, CA, USA, 17–21 February 2013; IEEE: Piscataway, NJ, USA, 2013; pp. 74–75.
5. Stanzione, S.; Van Liempd, C.; Nabeto, M.; Yazicioglu, F.R.; Van Hoof, C. 20.8 a 500 nW batteryless integrated electrostatic energy harvester interface based on a DC-DC converter with 60 V maximum input voltage and operating from 1 μW available power, including MPPT and cold start. In Proceedings of the 2015 IEEE International Solid-State Circuits Conference—(ISSCC) Digest of Technical Papers, San Francisco, CA, USA, 22–26 February 2015; IEEE: Piscataway, NJ, USA, 2015; pp. 1–3.
6. Wang, C.-C.; Tolentino, L.K.S.; Chen, P.-C.; Hizon, J.R.E.; Yen, C.-K.; Pan, C.-T.; Hsueh, Y.-H. A 40-nm CMOS Piezoelectric Energy Harvesting IC for Wearable Biomedical Applications. *Electronics* **2021**, *10*, 649. [CrossRef]
7. Lai, L.; Zhang, R.; Cheng, K.; Xia, Z.; Wei, C.; Wei, K.; Luo, W.; Liu, X. Monolithic integrated high frequency GaN DC-DC buck converters with high power density controlled by current mode logic level signal. *Electronics* **2020**, *9*, 1540. [CrossRef]
8. Ishida, Y.; Tanzawa, T. A Fully Integrated AC-DC Converter in 1 V CMOS for Electrostatic Vibration Energy Transducer with an Open Circuit Voltage of 10 V. *Electronics* **2021**, *10*, 1185. [CrossRef]
9. Meyvaert, H.; Pique, G.V.; Karadi, R.; Bergveld, H.J.; Steyaert, M.S.J. A Light-Load-Efficient 11/1 Switched-Capacitor DCDC Converter with 94.7% Efficiency While Delivering 100 mW at 3.3 V. *IEEE J. Solid State Circuits* **2015**, *50*, 2849–2860. [CrossRef]
10. Tanzawa, T. Design of DC-DC Switched-Capacitor Voltage Multiplier driven by DC Energy Transducer. In Proceedings of the IEEE International Conference on Electronics, Circuits and Systems (ICECS) 2014, Marseille, France, 7–10 December 2014; IEEE: Piscataway, NJ, USA, 2015; pp. 327–330. [CrossRef]
11. Tanzawa, T.; Atsumi, S. Optimization of word-line booster circuits for low-voltage Flash memories. *IEEE J. Solid State Circuits* **1999**, *34*, 1091–1098. [CrossRef]
12. Tanzawa, T. *On-Chip High-Voltage Generator Design: Design Methodology for Charge Pumps*, 2nd ed.; Springer: Cham, Switzerland, 2016. [CrossRef]
13. Le, H.-P.; Sanders, S.R.; Alon, E. Design techniques for fully integrated switched-capacitor DC-DC converters. *IEEE J. Solid State Circuits* **2011**, *46*, 2120–2131. [CrossRef]
14. Tanzawa, T. On two-phase switched-capacitor multipliers with minimum circuit area. *IEEE Trans. Circuits Syst. I Regul. Pap.* **2010**, *57*, 2602–2608. [CrossRef]

Article

Global Maximum Power Point Tracking of Photovoltaic Module Arrays Based on Improved Artificial Bee Colony Algorithm

Kuei-Hsiang Chao [1,*] and Jia-Yan Li [2]

1 Department of Electrical Engineering, National Chin-Yi University of Technology, Taichung 411, Taiwan
2 Ph.D. Program, Prospective Technology of Electrical Engineering and Computer Science, National Chin-Yi University of Technology, Taichung 411, Taiwan; as26393586@gmail.com
* Correspondence: chaokh@ncut.edu.tw; Tel.: +886-4-2392-4505 (ext. 7272); Fax: +886-4-2392-2156

Abstract: In this paper, an improved artificial bee colony (I-ABC) algorithm for the maximum power point tracking (MPPT) of a photovoltaic module array (PVMA) is presented. Even though the P-V output characteristic curve with multi-peak was generated due to any damages or shading discovered on the PVMA, the I-ABC algorithm could get rid of stuck on tracking the local maximum power point (LMPP), but quickly and stably track the global maximum power point (GMPP), thereby improving the power generation efficiency. This proposed I-ABC algorithm could search for the higher power point of a PVMA by a small bee colony, determine the next tracking direction through the perturb and observe (P&O) method, and keep tracking until the GMPP is obtained. This method could prevent tracking the GMPP for too long due to applying a small bee colony. First, in this study, the photovoltaic modules produced by Sunworld Co., Ltd. were used and were configured as a PVMA with four series and three parallel connections under different numbers of shaded modules and different shading ratios, so that corresponding P-V output characteristic curves with multi-peak values were generated. Then, the GMPP was tracked by the proposed MPPT method. The simulation and experimental results showed that the proposed method performed better both in dynamic response and steady-state performance than the traditional artificial bee colony (ABC) algorithm. According to the experimental results, it showed that the tracking accuracy for the GMPP based on the proposed MPPT with 100 iterations under 5 different shading ratios was about 100%; on the other hand, that of the traditional ABC algorithm was 70%, and that of the P&O method was lower at about 30%.

Keywords: improved artificial bee colony (I-ABC); maximum power point tracking (MPPT); photovoltaic module array; local maximum power point (LMPP); global maximum power point (GMPP)

Citation: Chao, K.-H.; Li, J.-Y. Global Maximum Power Point Tracking of Photovoltaic Module Arrays Based on Improved Artificial Bee Colony Algorithm. *Electronics* **2022**, *11*, 1572. https://doi.org/10.3390/electronics11101572

Academic Editors: Shailendra Rajput, Moshe Averbukh and Noel Rodriguez

Received: 10 April 2022
Accepted: 11 May 2022
Published: 14 May 2022

Publisher's Note: MDPI stays neutral with regard to jurisdictional claims in published maps and institutional affiliations.

Copyright: © 2022 by the authors. Licensee MDPI, Basel, Switzerland. This article is an open access article distributed under the terms and conditions of the Creative Commons Attribution (CC BY) license (https://creativecommons.org/licenses/by/4.0/).

1. Introduction

When the photovoltaic module array is shaded or failed, multi-peak values will be observed in the P-V output characteristic curve with different conditions. In order to maximize the output power of the photovoltaic module array, it shall be controlled by the maximum power point tracker of the power conditioner [1]. Due to the consideration of development costs, most current commercial power conditioners use traditional methods for MPPT, such as incremental conductance (INC) [2], perturb and observe (P&O) [3], power feedback, and the constant voltage method, etc. However, as the P-V output characteristic curve with multi-peak values is generated due to any shading or failures discovered on the module array, those above-mentioned traditional methods for MPPT will fail to track the GMPP, thereby reducing the output power.

In recent years, many scholars have focused on those methods for the MPPT in response to such a P-V output characteristic curve with multi-peak values, caused by some modules shaded in the photovoltaic module array. To solve the problem of being stuck on the local maximum power point tracking (LMPPT) based on traditional algorithms for

MPPT, these studies mainly apply algorithms for artificial MPPT. Most popular algorithms for artificial MPPT are ant colony optimization (ACO) [4], differential evolution (DE) [5], artificial bee colony (ABC) [6], and particle swarm optimization (PSO) [7], etc. The ACO algorithm is a probabilistic algorithm for optimizing routes, and its update formula is exponential as stated in reference [8], thereby making its path length and pheromone concentration as random values. Such random path length and pheromone concentration might get rid of stuck on tracking the LMPP, but it would make the tracking time too long. In addition, the differential evolution is similar to the genetic algorithm (GA), which applies real number coding for specific races and accomplishes searching for the global best value through differencing variance and one-to-one competitive survival strategy. However, it makes tracking time increased due to the multiple formulas that are required for operating while individuals carry out mutation. On the other hand, the ABC algorithm optimizes the group foraging process by sending employed bees to find food sources, wherein those employed bees will transfer information about the location and direction of the food sources to other bees by dancing. However, those employed bees search for food sources randomly, so as to make their search abilities less stable; moreover, the number of employed bees dispatched is proportional to the searching time during the food source search, so it takes much longer if more employed bees are dispatched for searching [8]. In addition, the PSO algorithm, proposed in 1995 by two scholars, Kennedy and Eberhart, who were inspired by the predation behavior of birds, is an artificial algorithm [9]. This algorithm has the advantages of fewer parameters and a simple iterative formula, but if the particle moving is too large, it may not be capable of tracking the GMPP but rather oscillate back and forth in its vicinity; on the contrary, if the particle moving is too small, it is easily stuck on tracking the LMPP, resulting in the tracking speed being slow.

Therefore, in this paper, an I-ABC algorithm for the MPPT of a photovoltaic module array with some modules shaded or failed is developed. It is characterized by less employed bees and a shorter searching time because it can combine with the P&O method to determine the moving direction of the bee colony according to the amount of food source; therefore, it can reduce the number of employed bees and shorten the search time. Compared with the traditional ABC algorithm, this method can quickly find the best food source through less employed bees. Therefore, it could get rid of stuck on tracking the LMPP, and address such time-consuming issues found in traditional artificial algorithms for the global maximum power point tracking (GMPPT), thereby improving the output power of a photovoltaic module array.

2. Traditional Artificial Bee Colony Algorithm

The traditional ABC algorithm is a swarm artificial algorithm, proposed by Karaboga in 2005 [10,11], based on the artificial foraging behavior of bee colonies. In order to find the best nectar during foraging, the bees are divided into employed bees, onlookers, and scouts, wherein the employed bees are responsible for collecting nectar and transferring information, the scouts are responsible for finding food sources, and the onlookers are responsible for optimizing the best flight routes. A scout will search for food sources either based on previous experience or just randomly and become an employed bee to collect nectar and memorize certain information about the food sources found. Later, when it brings the nectar back to the hive, it will pass that information about the food source to the onlooker. As such information has been passed, this employed bee may go back to the mentioned food source to continue nectar collection or return to be a scout to continue a new food source search again based on previous experience or randomly. On the other hand, the onlooker will determine the best route for nectar collection based on the information about food sources taken early or abandon those food sources with less nectar stock. Figure 1 is a schematic diagram of collecting the nectar of a bee colony. According to reference [12], in the traditional ABC algorithm, the tracking speed and steady-state performance will be affected by the number of scouts and there may be some errors of information about food sources memorized by the employed bees; therefore, there may be some errors of the best routes optimized by onlookers if the wrong information is received, which will slow down the tracking speed in the later stage. Therefore, it really needs to introduce other algorithms for improving the tracking speed.

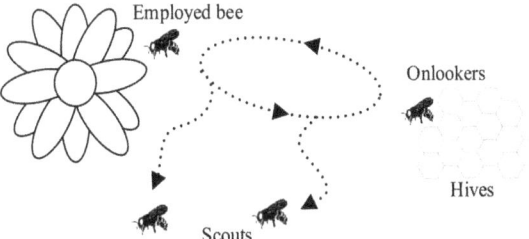

Figure 1. Schematic diagram of collecting nectar of bee colony.

Please refer to the steps of the traditional ABC algorithm as follows:

Step 1. Set initial parameters, including the maximum number of iterations (ME), the number of employed bees (SN), the initial number of food sources searched by each employed bee x_i^0, and the initial number of the best and worst food sources searched by all employed bees v_{best}^0 and v_{worst}^0, and the initial number of iterations $j = 0$.

Step 2. Substitute the food sources x_i^j randomly searched after the j-th iteration by each employed bee into the random search Equation (1) for searching new food sources.

$$x_i^{j+1} = x_i^j + rand[0,1](v_{best}^j - v_{worst}^j) \quad i = 1,2,\ldots,SN; j = 0,1,\ldots,ME \quad (1)$$

wherein, x_i^{j+1} is the value of the $(j+1)$-th iteration obtained by the i-th employed bee; x_i^j is the value of the j-th iteration obtained by the i-th employed bee; v_{best}^j is the best value of j-th iteration obtained by the SN employed bees; v_{worst}^j is the worst value of the j-th iteration obtained by SN employed bees; and rand [0, 1] is a random number between 0 and 1.

Step 3. Each employed bee moves according to Equation (2) to search for new food sources.

$$v_i^{j+1} = x_i^{j+1} + rand[-1,1](x_i^{j+1} - x_k^{j+1}) \quad i = 1,2,\ldots,SN; j = 0,1,\ldots,ME \quad (2)$$

wherein, v_i^{j+1} is the new food sources searched after the $(j+1)$-th iteration by the movement of the i-th employed bee; x_i^{j+1} is the value of the iteration of Equation (1); and x_k^{j+1} is the value of the $(j+1)$-th iteration obtained by employed bee k which is rounded to closest to x_i^{j+1}; and $rand[-1,1]$ is a random number between -1 and 1. Figure 2 is a schematic diagram of the movement of employed bees at two iterations of Equations (1) and (2).

Step 4. Calculate the fitness P_i of food sources searched after the $(j+1)$-th iteration by the SN employed bees through the Equation (3) with the roulette wheel method. Wherein, the maximum fitness P_i of the food source is expressed as v_{best}^{j+1}, and the minimum one is expressed as v_{worst}^{j+1}.

$$P_i = \frac{v_i^{j+1}}{\sum_{i=1}^{SN} v_i^{j+1}}, i = 1,2,\ldots,SN \quad (3)$$

Step 5. Stop to generate iterations until the maximum number of iterations (i.e., j = ME) is reached. Otherwise, set the maximum fitness P_i of food sources $v_{best}^j = v_{best}^{j+1}$, the minimum one $v_{worst}^j = v_{worst}^{j+1}$, and $x_i^j = x_i^{j+1}$, and let $j = j+1$, then skip to step 2 for the next iteration.

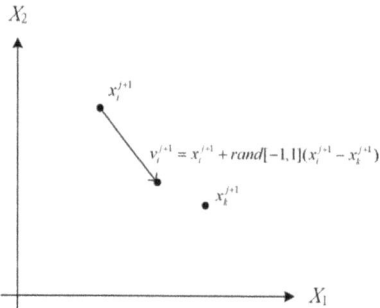

Figure 2. Two-dimensional schematic diagram of the movement of employed bees.

Figure 3 is the flowchart of the traditional ABC algorithm. If there are more bees, tracking accuracy will be higher accordingly. However, the searching time is proportional to the number of bees during the algorithm implemented with a microcontroller, i.e., the operation time is longer for a larger population; on the contrary, the operation time of the algorithm can be reduced if the number of bees is reduced, but it will be more difficult to obtain the optimal solution. Therefore, in order to address the issue that the optimal solution cannot be obtained within a limited number of iterations due to the reduction of the number of bees, an I-ABC algorithm with fewer bees combined with the P&O method is presented and applied for the MPPT of photovoltaic module array to fast track the GMPP.

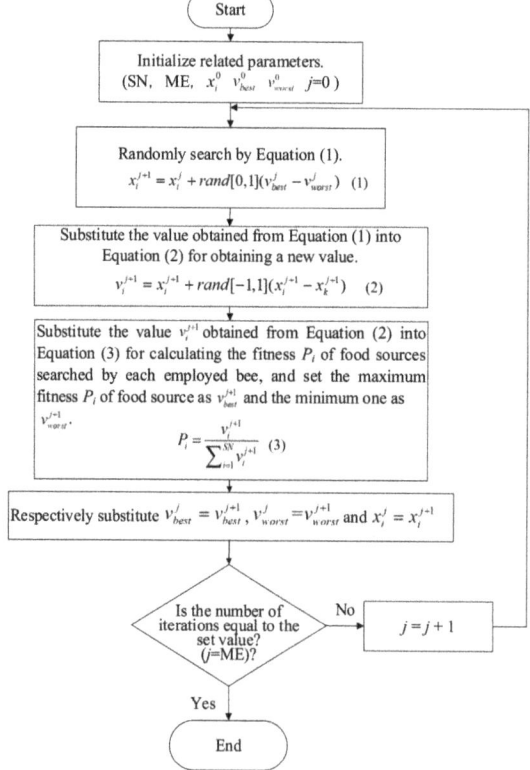

Figure 3. Flowchart of the traditional ABC algorithm.

3. Proposed Maximum Power Point Tracker for Photovoltaic Module Array

Figure 4 is the architecture of the maximum power point tracker for photovoltaic module array based on the I-ABC algorithm proposed in this paper, which includes the photovoltaic module arrays, the DC/DC boost converter [13], and the digital signal processor (DSP) [14] for implementing the I-ABC algorithm.

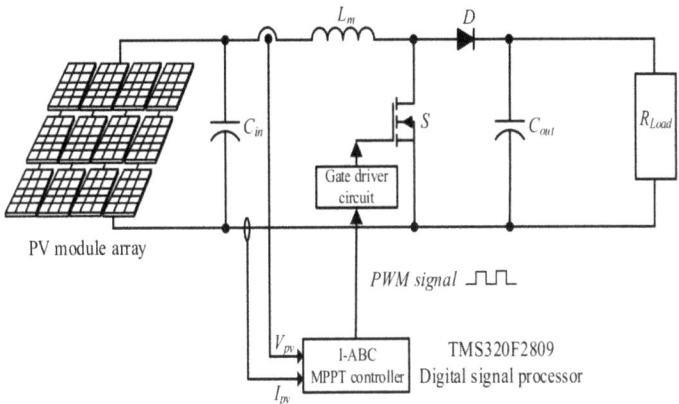

Figure 4. Architecture of the maximum power point tracker for photovoltaic module array based on the I-ABC algorithm.

3.1. Composition of Photovoltaic Module Array

In this paper, the SWM-20W modules produced by Sunworld [15] were used to be configured as an array with four series and three parallel connections, and some of those modules were set with different shading ratios and failures. Later, the EKO MP-170 I-V tracker [16] was used to measure output, which was input into the Matlab software to simulate corresponding P-V output characteristic curves. The simulation results of MPPT could be comparable with the test results of the actual photovoltaic module array later. For specifications of electrical parameters of photovoltaic modules SWM-20W under standard test conditions (STC) (i.e., air mass (AM) as 1.5, the intensity of insolation as 1000 W/m^2, and temperature of the photovoltaic module as 25°C), refer to Table 1.

Table 1. Specifications of electrical parameters of photovoltaic modules SWM-20W produced by Sunworld [15].

Parameters	Value
Rated maximum output power (P_{mp})	20 W
Current of maximum power point (I_{mp})	1.10 A
Voltage of maximum power point (V_{mp})	18.18 V
Short circuit current (I_{sc})	1.15 A
Open circuit voltage (V_{oc})	22.32 V
Length and width of module	395 mm × 345 mm

3.2. DC/DC Boost Converter

The designed parameter settings of components of the DC/DC boost converter used in this paper are listed in Table 2 [17].

Table 2. Parameter settings of components of the DC/DC boost converter [17].

Component Name	Models and Specifications
Inductor (L_m)	1.152 mH
Input capacitor (C_{in})	390 μF/450 V
Output capacitor (C_{out})	390 μF/450 V
Switching frequency (f_s)	25 kHz
Power switching transistor (S)	MOSFET IRF460 (500 V/20 A)
Diode (D)	IQBD60E60A1 (600 V/60 A)

3.3. Improved Artificial Bee Colony Algorithm

In this paper, the digital signal processor TMS320F2809 produced by Texas Instruments was used to implement the I-ABC algorithm with the boost converter for the GMPPT of a photovoltaic module array while the photovoltaic module shaded or failed partially. The I-ABC algorithm used was obtained from improving the traditional ABC algorithm described in step 4, Section 2, and applied for the MPPT of a photovoltaic module array, wherein v_{best}^{j+1} was the duty cycle of the boost converter at the optimal output power of the photovoltaic module array. The specific practice was as follows:

The practice substituted the optimal solution v_{best}^{j+1} (which was obtained in step 4, Section 2 about the traditional ABC algorithm) into the P&O method [3] to increase or decrease the terminal voltage of the photovoltaic module array with a fixed disturbance, and to determine the direction where the output power increased, thereby keeping perturbing in this direction for the optimal solution v_{best}^{j+1} of the next iteration. This method addressed such time-consuming issues of searching the local maximum values found in the traditional ABC algorithm, which only searched values randomly in the vicinity, so the I-ABC algorithm could determine the correct searching direction only through the P&O to quickly get rid of stuck on tracking the LMPP, thereby quickly tracking to the GMPP.

Therefore, in this paper, an algorithm that could quickly track the GMPP was proposed by combining with the P&O method and the ABC algorithm. First, the GMPP was tracked by the ABC algorithm. Then, the global peak value was tracked quickly by the P&O method. This method could address the time-consuming issue of searching the global maximum values when there is a small bee colony, and the failure to track the GMPP issue due to multi-peak values presented by the P&O method. For its detailed flowchart, refer to Figure 5.

In order to shorten the operation time of the I-ABC algorithm, small bee colonies were applied in this paper. For its parameter settings, refer to Table 3. In addition, in order to confirm its tracking performance, tests of the MPPT were performed on the photovoltaic module array with four series and three parallel connections under five different working conditions, as shown in Table 4.

Table 3. Parameter settings of the I-ABC algorithm.

Parameter Name	Settings
Number of bees (SN)	8
Number of iterations (ME)	50
Disturbance (Δd)	0.5% (duty cycle)

Table 4. Five different shading and failure conditions selected for testing.

Case	Parallel Series Configuration and Shading Ratio	The Number of Peaks in the P-V Curve
1	4 series and 3 parallel (shaded 0%)	Single-peak
2	4 series and 3 parallel (one module with shaded 30%)	Double-peak
3	4 series and 3 parallel (two modules with shaded 30% and 50%, respectively)	Triple-peak
4	4 series and 3 parallel (three modules with shaded 30%, 50%, and 70%, respectively)	Quadruple-peak
5	4 series and 3 parallel (one module with snail trails)	Double-peak

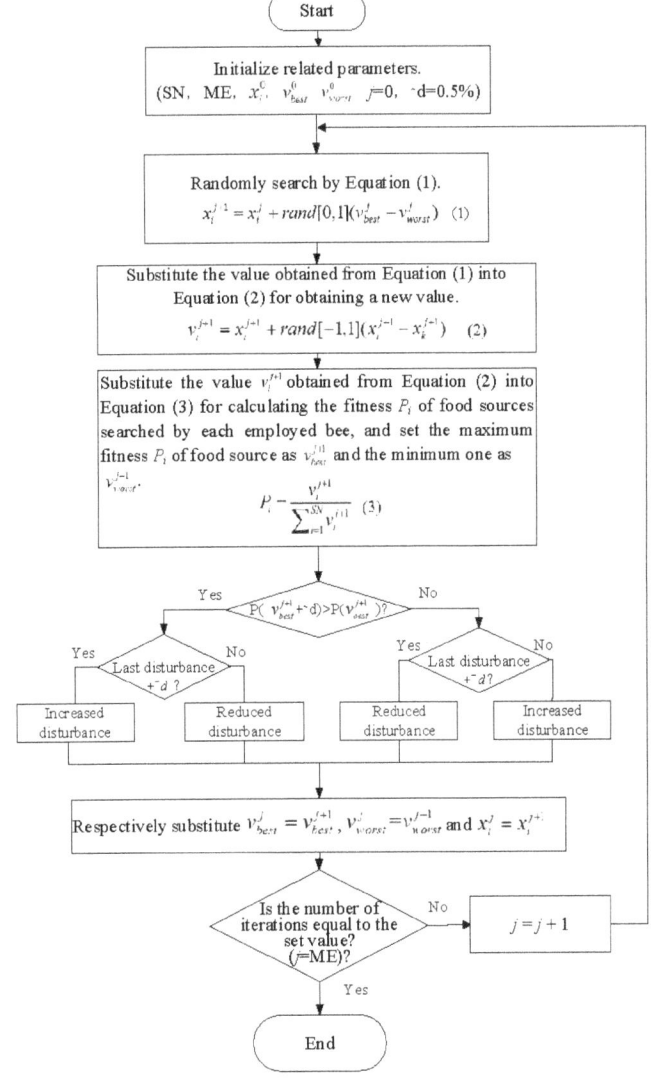

Figure 5. Flowchart of the I-ABC algorithm.

4. Simulation Results

In this paper, Matlab software was used to read the data measured by the MP-170 I-V checker under five different test conditions (as shown in Table 4), and to simulate MPPT based on the I-ABC algorithm, traditional ABC algorithm, and the P&O method, respectively, as well as to compare the tracking performance among different methods.

The initial voltage of the MPPT during simulation in this paper was set to 0.8 times of the voltage (about 58.176 V) of the maximum output power point (V_{mp}) of modules with four series connections under the standard test condition (STC), because according to reference [18], the voltage of the maximum power point of a photovoltaic module array under any conditions was about 0.8~1.1 times of V_{mp} under STC. Figure 6 shows the P-V characteristic curve of the photovoltaic module array under normal operating conditions and the intensity of insolation as 742 W/m^2 in Case 1, wherein the single-peak value was presented (P_{mp} = 183.29 W). According to the simulation results of the three tracking methods shown in Figure 7, it was observed that as the single-peak value presented, the GMPP could be tracked quickly either based on the I-ABC algorithm or the P&O method, but it could be tracked slowly based on the traditional ABC algorithm. In order to be fair in the tracking performance, the number of bees was set as eight both in the traditional ABC algorithm and the I-ABC algorithm; however, the required time for tracking the GMPP was longer based on the former algorithm due to the smaller bee colony.

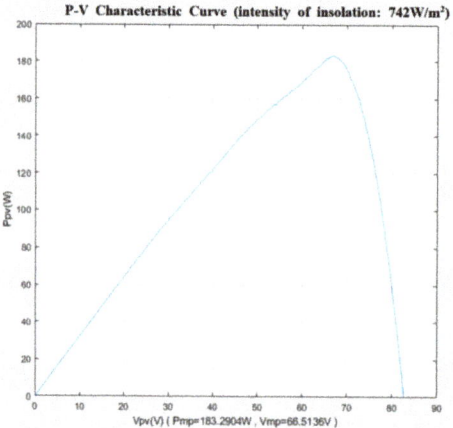

Figure 6. P-V characteristic curve of the photovoltaic module array in Case 1 (with single-peak value).

Figure 8 shows the P-V characteristic curve of the photovoltaic module array under the intensity of insolation as 712 W/m^2 and one module shaded 30% in Case 2, wherein double-peak values were presented and the real MPP P_{mp} was 147.28 W. If the shading position of modules changed, only the double-peak values of the P-V characteristic curve would be changed accordingly. In order to speed up the tracking speed, the initial tracking voltage in this case was still set as 0.8 times of the voltage V_{mp} of the maximum output power point of the module array under the STC condition, i.e., 58.176 V. According to the simulation results of the three tracking methods shown in Figure 9, it was observed that the P&O method failed to track the GMPP (P_{mp} = 147.2 W) due to being stuck on the LMPP (P_{pv} = 135 W), and that the traditional ABC algorithm could track the GMPP, but its tracking speed was slower than that of the I-ABC.

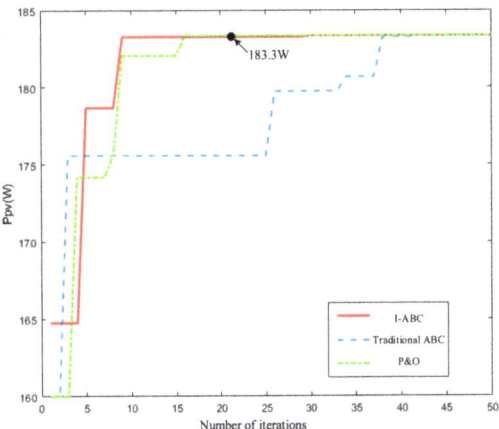

Figure 7. Comparison of simulation results for the MPPT in Case 1.

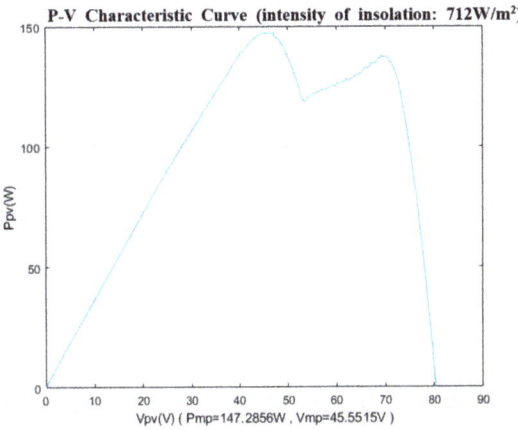

Figure 8. P-V characteristic curve of the photovoltaic module array in Case 2 (with double-peak values).

Figure 10 shows the P-V characteristic curve of the photovoltaic module array under insolation intensity as 525 W/m² and two modules shaded 30% and 50%, respectively, in Case 3, wherein triple-peak values were presented and the real MPP P_{mp} was 102.18 W. According to the tracking simulation results of the three tracking methods shown in Figure 11, it was observed that both the I-ABC algorithm and the traditional ABC algorithm could track the GMPP (P_{mp} = 102.1 W). Still, the later algorithm was easier to stop near the GMPP. The reason was that if a smaller bee colony was applied in the traditional ABC algorithm, it would slow down the speed of finding the nectar sources significantly, thereby causing difficulty for the bee colony to quickly track the GMPP. On the other hand, the I-ABC algorithm proposed in this paper could quickly track the GMPP (P_{mp} = 102.1 W) by combining it with the P&O method. However, if only the traditional P&O method was adopted, it would only track the LMPP (P_{pv} = 75 W).

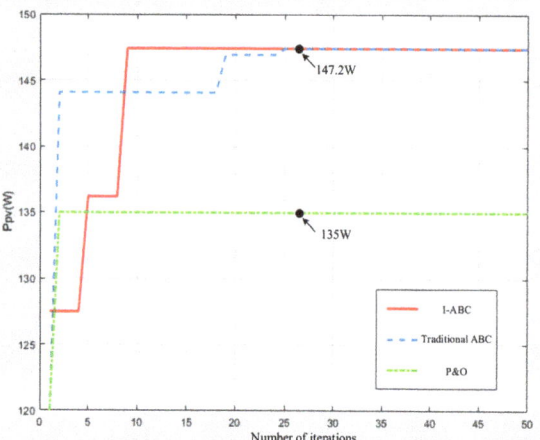

Figure 9. Comparison of simulation results for the MPPT in Case 2.

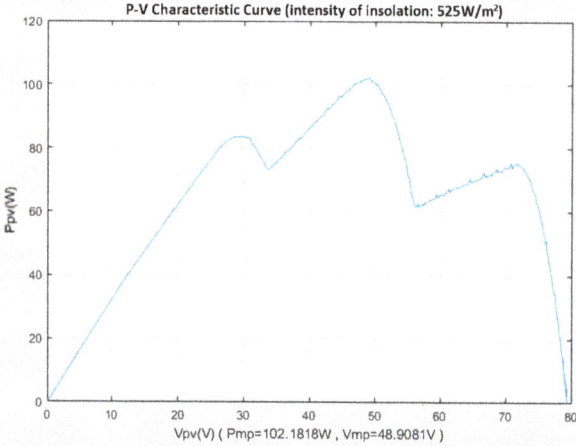

Figure 10. P-V characteristic curve of photovoltaic module array in Case 3 (with triple-peak values).

Figure 12 shows the P-V characteristic curve of the photovoltaic module array under insolation intensity as 534 W/m² and three modules shaded 30%, 50%, and 70%, respectively, in Case 4, wherein quadruple-peak values were presented and the real MPP P_{mp} was 83.84 W. According to the simulation results of the three tracking methods shown in Figure 13, it was observed that the I-ABC algorithm could track the GMPP (P_{mp} = 83.8 W) with only 5 iterations, but 25 for the traditional ABC algorithm. As per the P&O method, the initial tracking voltage was near the point at the valley area where the GMPP was located, so the GMPP could be tracked smoothly but more iterations are needed.

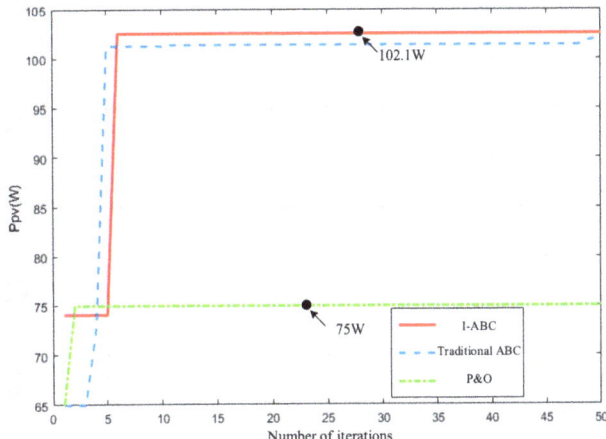

Figure 11. Comparison of simulation results for the MPPT in Case 3.

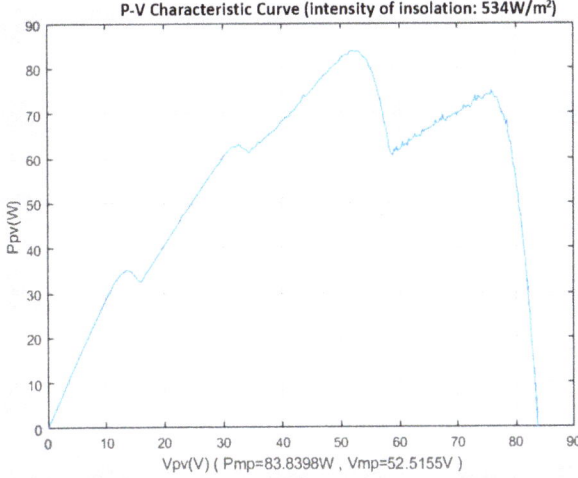

Figure 12. P-V characteristic curve of photovoltaic module array in Case 4 (with quadruple-peak values).

Figure 14 shows the P-V characteristic curve of the photovoltaic module array under the intensity of insolation as 639 W/m², wherein double-peak values were presented while one module with snail trails [19,20] and the real MPP P_{mp} was 133.59 W. From the simulation results of the three tracking methods in Figure 15, it was observed that both the improved and traditional ABC algorithms could track the GMPP (P_{mp} = 133.5 W), as could the P&O method with the initial tracking voltage as 58.176 V. However, the I-ABC algorithm still performed best in the tracking response among the three methods.

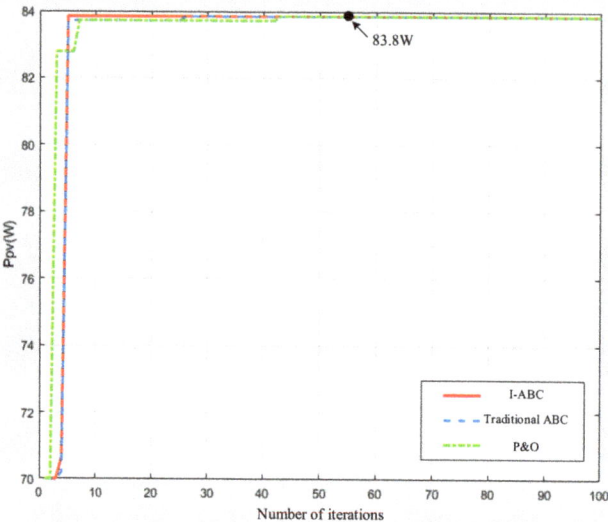

Figure 13. Comparison of simulation results for the MPPT in Case 4.

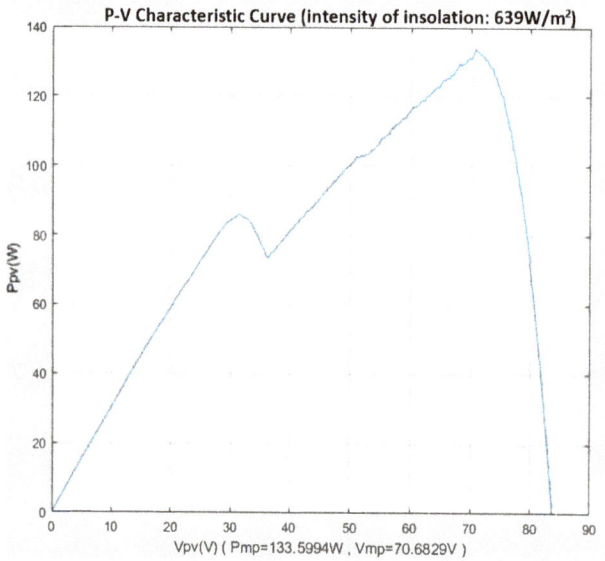

Figure 14. P-V characteristic curve of the photovoltaic module array in Case 5 (with double-peak values).

In this paper, the traditional ABC and the I-ABC were applied to perform 50 MPPT tests for the selected five cases, respectively. The numbers of iterations required for each GMPPT were summed up and averaged. For those results, refer to Table 5. Although both algorithms could track the GMPP, it was observed that the average number of iterations required by the I-ABC in the five cases was less than the one by the traditional ABC in Table 5. This showed a better tracking performance in the proposed I-ABC for the MPPT, especially because the greater the number of peaks in the P-V characteristic curves, the greater difference in tracking performance.

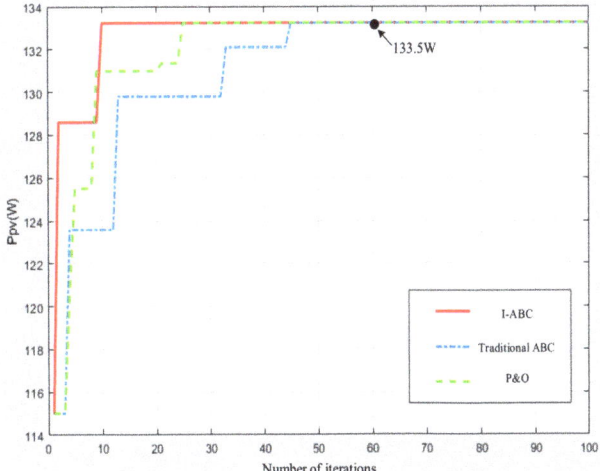

Figure 15. Comparison of simulation results for the MPPT in Case 5.

Table 5. Comparison of the average number of iterations of the GMPPT based on two algorithms in 5 cases.

Case	Number of Peaks in the P-V Characteristic Curves	Average Number of Iterations	
		Traditional ABC Algorithm	I-ABC Algorithm
1	Single-peak	10.64	4.56
2	Double-peak	15.23	6.45
3	Triple-peak	34.42	7.39
4	Quadruple-peak	38.86	10.18
5	Double-peak	27.13	10.57

In order to reduce the calculation time of the traditional ABC algorithms for speeding up the tracking response, this can only be achieved by means of the reduction of the number of bees, resulting in getting lost for GMPP and increasing the difficulty of finding the GMPP in traditional ABC algorithms. So, in this paper, we introduced the method of identifying and tracking moving directions by combining with the P&O method, and made those straying bees find their correct tracking direction after the reduction of the number of bees. By combining these two algorithms, not only could the calculation time be reduced, but also the correct tracking direction could be found during the tracking process. According to the simulation results, the proposed MPPT method of the I-ABC algorithm performed much better in tracking than the traditional ABC algorithms under the same number of bees.

5. Experimental Results

In order to verify the correctness of the simulation results in the previous section, in this paper, the 62050H-600S programmable DC power supply produced by Chroma CO., Ltd. (Taipei, Taiwan) [21] was applied to simulate the actual output P-V characteristic curves of the photovoltaic module array under STC in five cases. The MPP was tracked based on the improved and traditional ABC algorithms, respectively. The test curve was presented by the output voltage V_{PV} and current I_{PV} of the photovoltaic module array, and the tracked power P_{PV} was obtained by multiplying the mentioned V_{PV} by I_{PV} with the internal operation function of the oscilloscope. The initial voltage of the MPPT was still set to 0.8 times (about 58.176 V) of the voltage of the maximum output power point V_{mp} under the STC, and the pros and cons of the response speed of the MPPT based on the traditional ABC and the I-ABC were observed, respectively.

5.1. Case 1 (0% Shaded)

Figure 16a shows the P-V characteristic curve of the photovoltaic module array with four series and three parallel connections under STC in Case 1, which was simulated by the 62050H-600S programmable DC power supply produced by Chroma CO., Ltd., and the single-peak value (P_{mp} = 247.5 W) was presented. The simulated photovoltaic module arrays were tracked based on the traditional ABC and the I-ABC, respectively. From the test results shown in Figure 16b,c, it was observed that the traditional and improved ABC algorithms both could track the MPP. Still, the response speed of the MPPT based on the I-ABC algorithm was about 0.16 s faster than that of the traditional ABC.

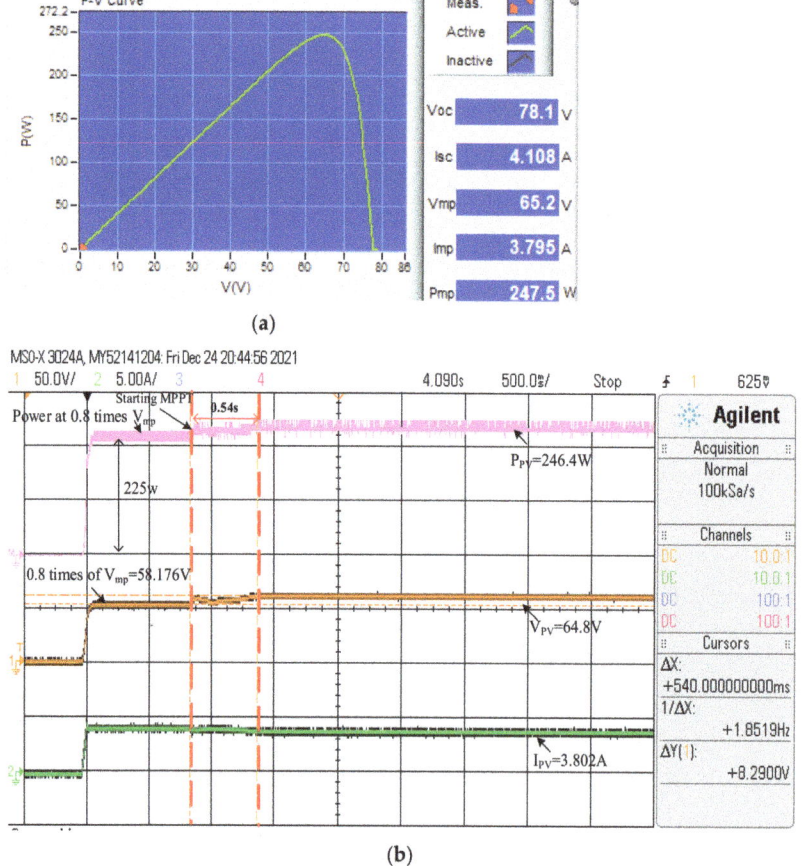

(a)

(b)

Figure 16. *Cont.*

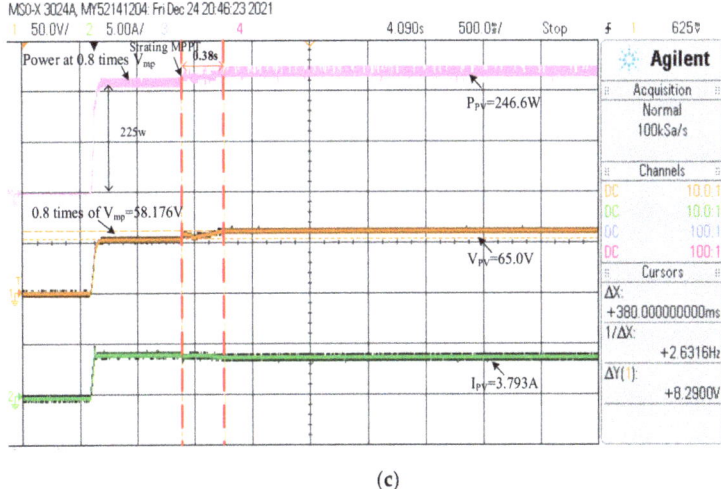

(c)

Figure 16. Test results of the MPPT of photovoltaic module array in Case 1: (**a**) P-V characteristic curve; (**b**) tracking curve of the traditional ABC algorithm (P_{mp} = 246.4 W); (**c**) tracking curve of the I-ABC algorithm (P_{mp} = 246.6 W).

5.2. Case 2 (One Module with 30% Shaded)

Figure 17a shows the P-V characteristic curve of the photovoltaic module array with four series and three parallel connections under STC in Case 2, and double-peak values were presented due to one module shaded and its GMPP P_{mp} was 200.3 W. From the test results shown in Figure 17b,c, it was observed that the response speed of the MPPT based on the I-ABC algorithm was about 0.84 s faster than that of the traditional ABC.

5.3. Case 3 (Two Modules with 30% and 50% Shaded, Respectively)

Figure 18a shows the P-V characteristic curve under STC in Case 3, and triple-peak values were presented due to two modules shaded with different ratios and its GMPP P_{mp} was 148.9 W. From the test results of the MPPT based on two algorithms shown in Figure 18b,c, it was observed that the response speed of the MPPT based on the I-ABC algorithm was about 0.26 s faster than that of the traditional ABC.

5.4. Case 4 (Three Modules with 30%, 50%, and 70% Shaded, Respectively)

Figure 19a shows the P-V characteristic curve of the photovoltaic module array with four series and three parallel connections under STC in Case 4, and quadruple-peak values were presented due to three modules shaded with different ratios and its GMPP P_{mp} was 107.7 W. From the test results of the MPPT based on two algorithms shown in Figure 19b,c, it was observed that the response speed of the MPPT based on the I-ABC algorithm was about 0.33 s faster than that of the traditional ABC.

5.5. Case 5 (Three Modules with 30%, 50%, and 70% Shaded, Respectively, in Each Series)

Figure 20a shows the P-V characteristic curve of the photovoltaic module array with four series and three parallel connections under STC. Multiple-peak values were presented due to three modules shaded with different ratios in each series and its GMPP P_{mp} was 77.27 W. From the test results of the MPPT based on two algorithms shown in Figure 20b,c, it was observed that the two algorithms both could track the MPP. Still, the response speed of the MPPT based on the I-ABC algorithm was about 0.96 s faster than that of the traditional ABC.

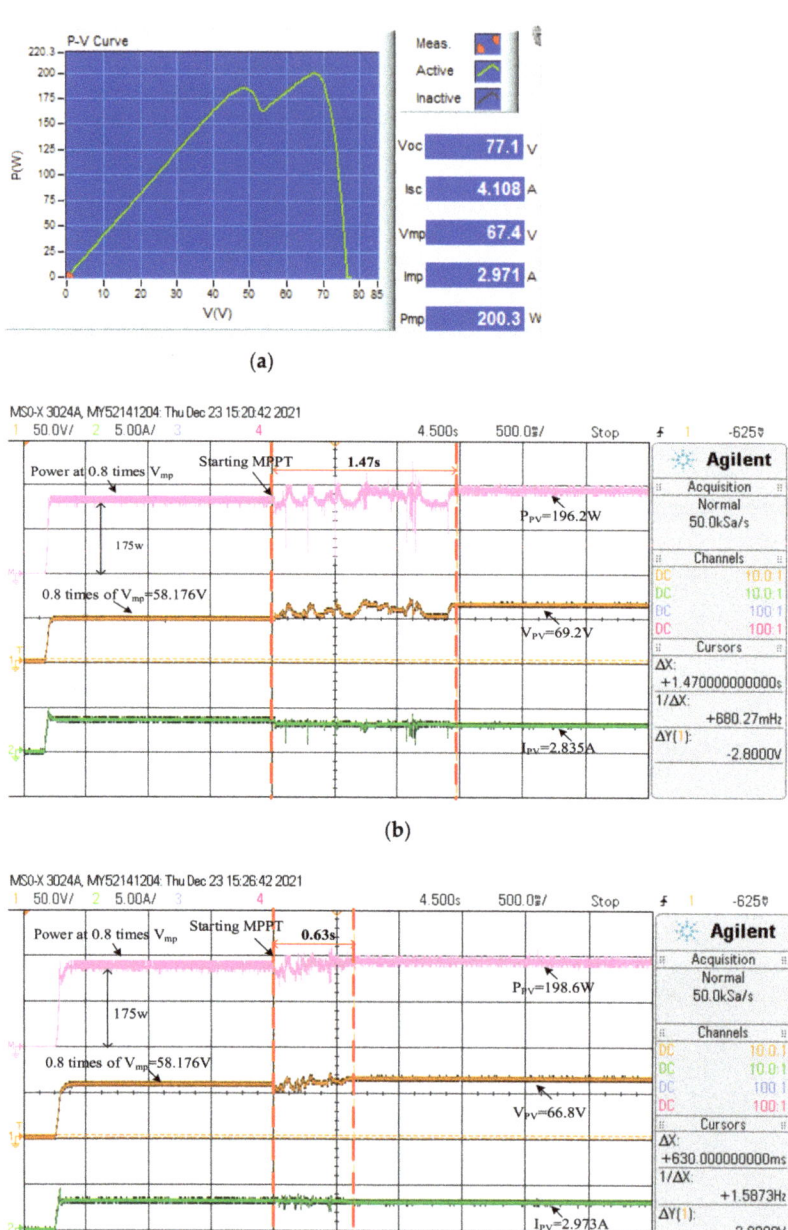

Figure 17. Test results of the MPPT of photovoltaic module array in Case 2: (**a**) P-V characteristic curve; (**b**) tracking curve of the traditional ABC algorithm (P_{mp} = 196.2 W); (**c**) tracking curve of the I-ABC algorithm (P_{mp} = 198.6 W).

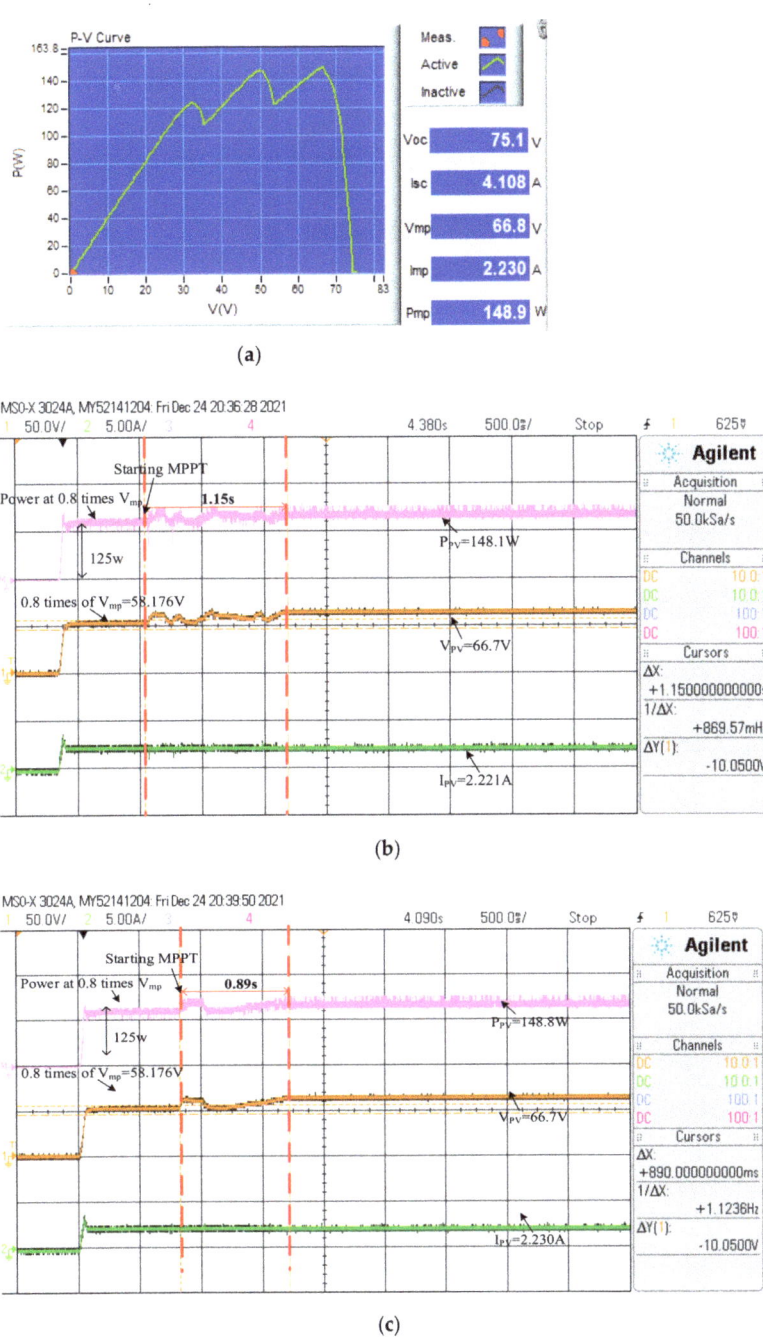

Figure 18. Test results of the MPPT of photovoltaic module array in Case 3: (**a**) P-V characteristic curve; (**b**) tracking curve of the traditional ABC algorithm (P_{mp} = 148.1 W); (**c**) tracking curve of the I-ABC algorithm (P_{mp} = 148.8 W).

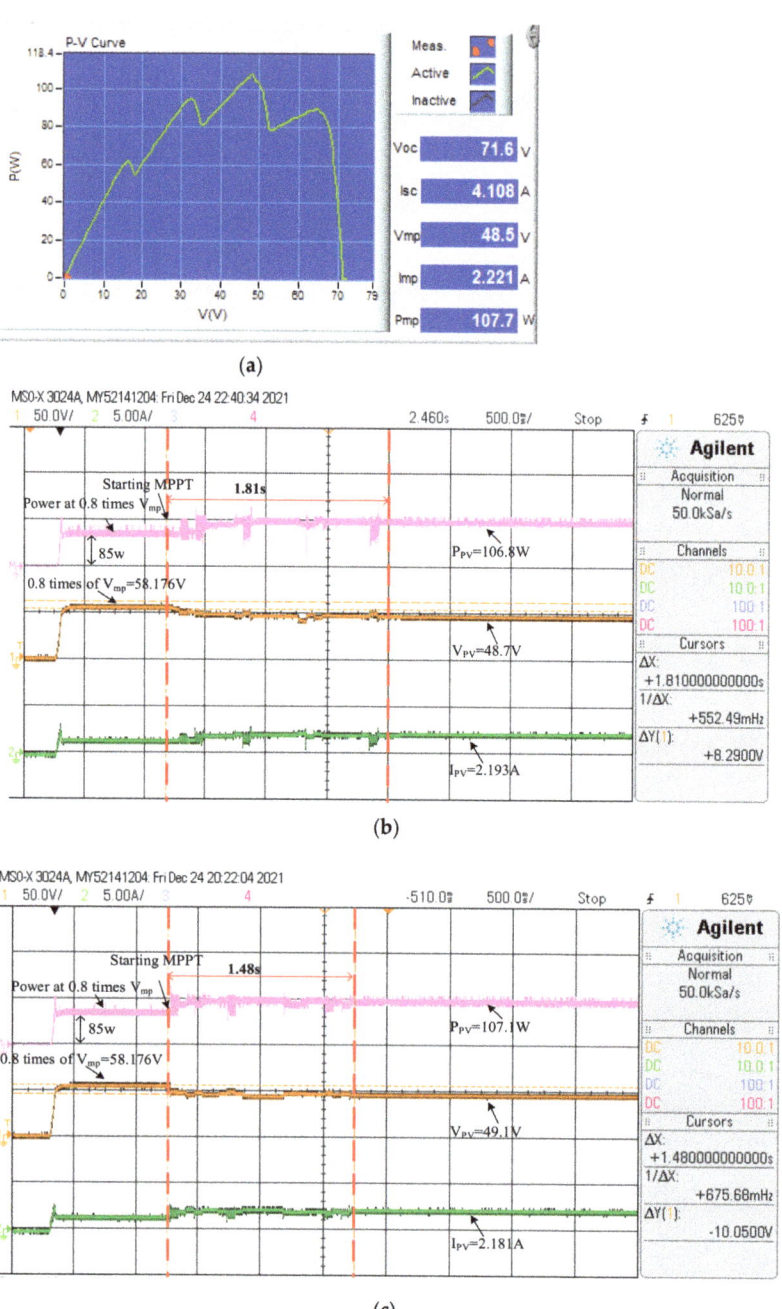

Figure 19. Test results of the MPPT of photovoltaic module array in Case 4: (**a**) P-V characteristic curve; (**b**) tracking curve of the traditional ABC algorithm (P_{mp} = 106.8 W); (**c**) tracking curve of the I-ABC algorithm (P_{mp} = 107.1 W).

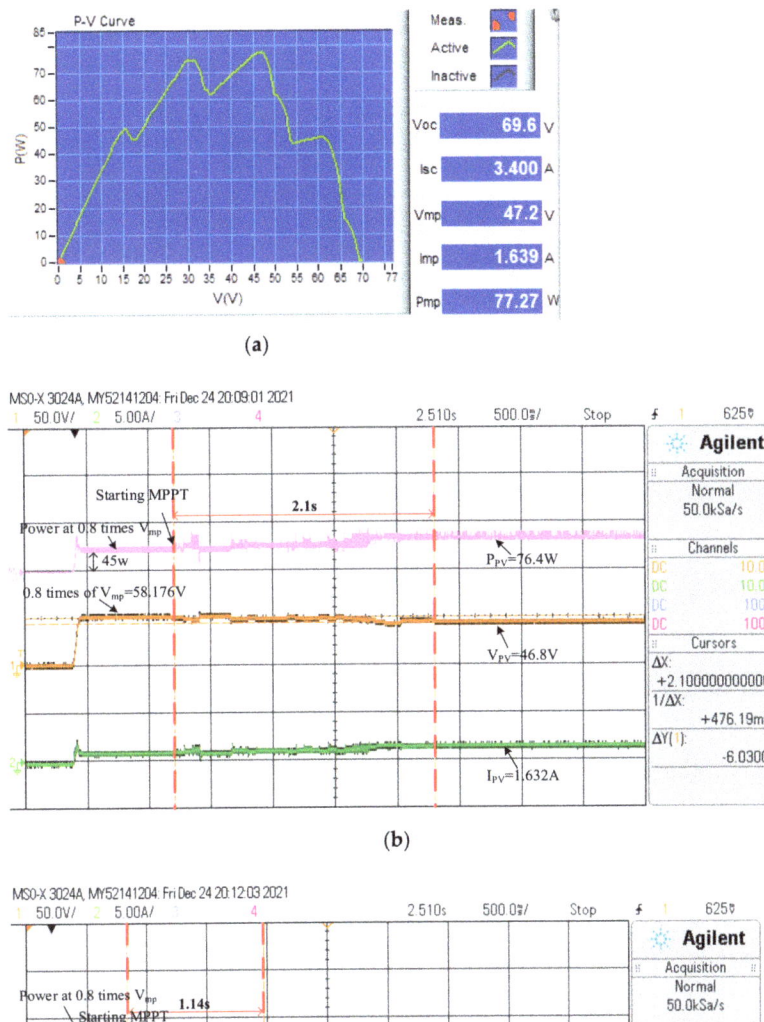

Figure 20. Test results of the MPPT of photovoltaic module array in Case 5: (**a**) P-V characteristic curve; (**b**) tracking curve of the traditional ABC algorithm (P_{mp} = 76.4 W); (**c**) tracking curve of the I-ABC (P_{mp} = 77.1 W).

By combining with the traditional P&O, the I-ABC algorithm can increase its accuracy when determining the direction of the MPPT. In addition, comparing with traditional ABC algorithms, it can reduce the possibility of losing direction and increase the tracking speed. Although the traditional P&O has a simple structure and fast-tracking response for normal operated PVMAs, it will only track the LMPP when some modules are shaded or failed. On the other hand, the I-ABC algorithm can get rid of stuck on tracking LMPP, so that the PVMAs will operate at the GMPP accordingly. The particle swarm optimization (PSO) proposed in [7] is an intelligent algorithm, commonly used in recent years. To improve the tracking accuracy, it needs to use a large number of particle swarms, thereby making a longer time for the global tracking; on the other hand, it may get lost during the global tracking based on the reduced number of particle swarms, which makes it difficult to track the GMPP eventually. For the I-ABC algorithm, it can confirm the tracking directions with the characteristics provided by the P&O method, which is not lost even with the reduction of the number of bees. Photovoltaic module arrays with four series and three parallels under five different shading ratios as shown in Table 4 were used to perform 100 times of the tracking based on different MPPT methods, respectively, and the average values of the two performance indicators, response time and the tracked GMPP are listed in Table 6 for comparison. According to the results of the different shading ratios seen in Table 6, the I-ABC algorithm proposed in this paper performed better in various tracking performances than those similar algorithms.

Table 6. Comparison of experimental results for the five selected cases.

Case	Number of Peak(s) of the P-V Curve	PSO Proposed in [7]		Traditional P&O		Traditional ABC		I-ABC Proposed in This Study	
		Average Tracking Time	Average Maximum Power	Average Tracking Time	Average Maximum Power	Average Tracking Time	Average Maximum Power	Average Tracking Time	Average Maximum Power
1	1	0.57 s	246.2 W	0.41 s	246.7 W	0.54 s	246.4 W	0.38 s	246.6 W
2	2	1.62 s	194.7 W	0.58 s	197.6 W	1.47 s	196.2 W	0.63 s	198.6 W
3	3	2.50 s	147.8 W	0.72 s	147.5 W	1.15 s	148.1 W	0.89 s	148.8 W
4	4	2.61 s	106.2 W	Trap in LMMP	91.2 W	1.81 s	106.8 W	1.48 s	107.1 W
5	Multiple	3.27 s	76.2 W	Trap in LMMP	46.2 W	2.10 s	76.4 W	1.14 s	77.1 W

6. Conclusions

In order to enhance the power generation efficiency of the photovoltaic power generation system, an artificial GMPPT based on an I-ABC algorithm was proposed in this paper. It combined with the P&O method to determine the direction for next tracking, so that it could accurately and quickly track the GMPP. From the multiple simulation results based on the proposed I-ABC in each case, it was observed that the average numbers of iterations of the GMPPT were all less than that of the traditional ABC, especially the worst ones shown in Case 3 (with triple-peak values) and Case 4 (with quadruple-peak values) based on the traditional ABC. For other cases with failures such as snail trails found, the corresponding tracking performance was not satisfied either, due to multiple-peak values and certain similar local solutions presented in the P-V characteristic curves, resulting in the fact that the traditional ABC would be stuck easily on tracking the LMPP and need more iterations for the GMPPT. In addition, from the test results, it was also observed that the tracking response speed would be much faster if the initial voltage of the MPPT was still set to 0.8 times of the voltage of the maximum output power point V_{mp} under STC, but not zero voltage. Moreover, those tracking speeds based on the I-ABC in different cases were all faster than those of the traditional ABC, because the proposed I-ABC algorithm would combine with the P&O method, which made it not be stuck easily on tracking the

LMPP, and the number of iterations reduced significantly. The time required for the GMPPT shortened, thereby dramatically improving the output power of the photovoltaic module array accordingly. It mainly focused on improving the power generation efficiency of PVMAs in this paper. To set PVMAs under the conditions for obtaining the best efficiency, the GMPP was tracked within the shortest time based on the I-ABC algorithm, thereby reducing the power generation lost during the tracking process. In addition, this algorithm was also suitable for the photovoltaic power generation system (PVPGS) connected with the grid. In the PV grid-connected system, the PV inverter generally controls its output voltage and current, which both are sine waves and the same phase, as no abnormal fluctuation is found in the system voltage and its output power factor (PF) is 1.0. Therefore, the PVPGS can output all as active power to the grid-connected system. On the other hand, if the insolation rises or falls sharply, the power of the large PV grid-connected system delivered into the grid system will also rise or drop sharply. If the load end cannot consume or make up for the sudden power rise or drop, the voltage at the grid connection point will also rise or drop sharply, which will cause the load end equipment to be damaged accordingly. To avoid such a situation, it is recommended to adjust the active and reactive power by a smart inverter for stabilizing the voltage at the grid connection point. Therefore, it is recommended to address the problem of unstable voltage of the power supply in the grid system caused by the fluctuation of load power consumption or the fluctuation of electricity supplied by smart inverter for controlling voltage-power or by establishing an energy storage system, which is irrelevant to the MPPT method proposed in this paper. The power-voltage regulation of a smart inverter will be the topic of future research.

Author Contributions: K.-H.C. planned the project and completed the writing, editing, and review. K.-H.C. completed the analysis and optimized the intelligent algorithm. J.-Y.L. was responsible for data curation, software, and experimental corroboration. K.-H.C. administered the project. All authors have read and agreed to the published version of the manuscript.

Funding: The authors gratefully acknowledge the support and funding of this study by Ministry of Science and Technology, Taiwan, under the Grant Number MOST 110-2221-E-167-007–MY2.

Conflicts of Interest: The authors of the manuscript declare no conflict of interest.

References

1. Sarah, L.; Tianqi, J. A study into the impact of the choice of maximum power point tracking technique on the reliablilty of the power electronics interface for photovoltaic systems. In Proceedings of the Australasian Universities Power Engineering Conference (AUPEC), Hobart, Australia, 29 November–2 December 2020; pp. 1–5.
2. Liu, F.; Duan, S.; Liu, F.; Liu, B.; Kang, Y. A Variable Step Size INC MPPT Method for PV Systems. *IEEE Trans. Ind. Electron.* **2008**, *55*, 2622–2628.
3. Femia, N.; Granozio, D.; Petrone, G.; Spagnuolo, G.; Vitelli, M. Predictive and Adaptive MPPT Perturb and Observe Method. *IEEE Trans. Aerosp. Electron. Syst.* **2007**, *43*, 934–950. [CrossRef]
4. Dorigo, M.; Birattari, M.; Stutzle, T. Ant Colony Optimization. *IEEE Comput. Intell. Mag.* **2006**, *1*, 28–39. [CrossRef]
5. Tajuddin, M.F.N.; Ayob, S.M.; Salam, Z. Tracking of maximum power point in partial shading condition using differential evolution (DE). In Proceedings of the IEEE International Conference on Power and Energy (PECon), Kota Kinabalu, Malaysia, 2–5 December 2012; pp. 384–389.
6. Gao, W.; Liu, S.; Huang, L. A Global Best Artificial Bee Colony Algorithm for Global Optimization. *J. Comput. Appl. Mathemat.* **2012**, *236*, 2741–2753. [CrossRef]
7. Qiang, Z.; Changwei, L. Two-Stage Multi-Swarm Particle Swarm Optimizer for Unconstrained and Constrained Global Optimization. *IEEE Access* **2020**, *8*, 124905–124927.
8. Sundareswaran, K.; Sankar, P.; Nayak, P.S.R.; Simon, S.P.; Palani, S. Enhanced Energy Output from a PV System under Partial Shaded Conditions through Artificial Bee Colony. *IEEE Trans. Energy Convers.* **2014**, *6*, 198–209. [CrossRef]
9. Iacca, G.; Mallipeddi, R.; Mininno, E.; Neri, F.; Suganthan, P.N. Global supervision for compact differential evolution. In Proceedings of the IEEE Symposium on Differential Evolution (SDE), Paris, France, 11–15 April 2011; pp. 1–8.
10. Xia, J.; Wang, Y.; Li, Y. A navigation satellite selection method based on Tabu search artificial bee colony algorithm. In Proceedings of the IEEE 3rd International Conference on Electronic Information and Communication Technology (ICEICT), Shenzhen, China, 13–15 November 2020; pp. 421–425.
11. Lee, W.P.; Chang, C.Y.; Hsieh, M.H. Novel Artificial Bee Colony Algorithm Using the Global Best Information and Activation Strategy. *Adv. Eng.* **2018**, *13*, 63–71.

12. Mehmet, C.; Asim, K. Optimum fuel cost in load flow analysis of smart grid by using artificial bee colony algorithm. In Proceedings of the International Artificial Intelligence and Data Processing Symposium (IDAP), Malatya, Turkey, 21–22 September 2019; pp. 1–5.
13. Hussain, I.S.; Jaafar, S. Linking knowledge and industry needs through problem-based learning in power electronics course. In Proceedings of the IEEE 8th International Conference on Engineering Education (ICEED), Kuala Lumpur, Malaysia, 7–8 December 2016; pp. 16–21.
14. Texas Instruments TMS320F2809 Datasheet. Available online: https://www.ti.com/lit/ds/symlink/tms320f2809.pdf?ts=1594465026502&ref_url=https%253A%252F%252Fwww.ti.com%252Fproduct%252FTMS320F2809.pdf (accessed on 12 November 2021).
15. SunWorld Datasheet. Available online: http://www.ecosolarpanel.com/ecosovhu/products/18569387_0_0_1.html (accessed on 21 July 2021).
16. MP-170 I-V Checker. Available online: http://www.ecosolarpanel.com/ecosovhu/products/14585574.html (accessed on 21 July 2021).
17. Shulin, L.; Yibo, M. Optimization design of the inductance of boost converters. In Proceedings of the International Conference on Electrical and Control Engineering, Wuhan, China, 25–27 June 2010; pp. 3949–3952.
18. Solar Power Generation Technology Using MPPT Algorithm—Active Power Optimizer or Micro Inverter. Available online: https://archive.eettaiwan.com/www.eettaiwan.com/ART_8800677750_675763_TA_9ed8e7b1.HTM (accessed on 21 June 2021).
19. Ziar, H.; Mansorpour, S.; Afjei, E. Detecting harmful overcurrents in PV arrays at shadow condition through binary coding method. In Proceedings of the 3rd Power Electronics and Drive System Technology (PEDSTC), Tehran, Iran, 15–16 February 2012; pp. 251–254.
20. Chang, J.; Yang, H.; Wang, H.; Cao, D. The investigation of snail trails in photovoltaic modules. In Proceedings of the 2015 IEEE 42nd Photovoltaic Specialist Conference (PVSC), New Orleans, LA, USA, 14–19 June 2015; pp. 1–5.
21. Chroma Model 62000H-S Series. Available online: https://www.chromaate.com/tw/product/solar_array_simulator (accessed on 5 October 2021).

Review

An Investigation on Hybrid Particle Swarm Optimization Algorithms for Parameter Optimization of PV Cells

Abha Singh [1], Abhishek Sharma [2,3,*], Shailendra Rajput [2,4], Amarnath Bose [5] and Xinghao Hu [6,*]

[1] Department of Basic Science, College of Science and Theoretical Study, Saudi Electronic University, Dammam-Female Branch, Dammam 32242, Saudi Arabia; asingh@seu.edu.sa
[2] Department of Electrical and Electronic Engineering, Ariel University, Ariel 40700, Israel; shailendra.phy@gmail.com
[3] Department of Research & Development, University of Petroleum and Energy Studies, Dehradun 248007, India
[4] Department of Physics, University Centre for Research & Development, Chandigarh University, Mohali 140431, India
[5] Sustainability Cluster, School of Engineering, University of Petroleum & Energy Studies, Dehradun 248007, India; abose@ddn.upes.ac.in
[6] Institute of Intelligent Flexible Mechatronics, Jiangsu University, Zhenjiang 212013, China
* Correspondence: abhishek_sharma@ddn.upes.ac.in (A.S.); huxh@ujs.edu.cn (X.H.)

Abstract: The demands for renewable energy generation are progressively expanding because of environmental safety concerns. Renewable energy is power generated from sources that are constantly replenished. Solar energy is an important renewable energy source and clean energy initiative. Photovoltaic (PV) cells or modules are employed to harvest solar energy, but the accurate modeling of PV cells is confounded by nonlinearity, the presence of huge obscure model parameters, and the nonattendance of a novel strategy. The efficient modeling of PV cells and accurate parameter estimation is becoming more significant for the scientific community. Metaheuristic algorithms are successfully applied for the parameter valuation of PV systems. Particle swarm optimization (PSO) is a metaheuristic algorithm inspired by animal behavior. PSO and derivative algorithms are efficient methods to tackle different optimization issues. Hybrid PSO algorithms were developed to improve the performance of basic ones. This review presents a comprehensive investigation of hybrid PSO algorithms for the parameter assessment of PV cells. This paper presents how much work is conducted in this field, and how much work can additionally be performed to improve this strategy and create more ideal arrangements of an issue. Algorithms are compared on the basis of the used objective function, type of diode model, irradiation conditions, and types of panels. More importantly, the qualitative analysis of algorithms is performed on the basis of computational time, computational complexity, convergence rate, search technique, merits, and demerits.

Keywords: energy harvesting; photovoltaic; metaheuristic; particle swarm optimization

1. Introduction

In the 26th United Nations Climate Change Conference (COP26), countries decided to move towards clean energy to limit the increase in average global temperature. It is very important to reduce dependency on the usage of fossil fuels, as these fuels are the main drivers of global warming. These circumstances direct us towards clean and renewable energy [1]. Scientific and industrial communities put substantial efforts in harvesting energy from surrounding energy sources (e.g., solar, wind, and hydropower) [2–4].

Among numerous clean energy sources, solar energy harvesting is an appropriate candidate, and the market share of solar energy systems is speedily rising [5,6]. Solar energy generation plants are designed by connecting several photovoltaic (PV) cells in serial or parallel arrangements. Electricity distribution grids and solar energy plants are connected and simultaneously operated [7,8]. Power output from solar energy plants is influenced by operational and environmental conditions [9,10]. Instabilities in power generation affect the economic prospect of solar energy plants [11,12]. Therefore, the efficiency of solar energy generation systems should be enhanced by the effective modeling and parameter assessment of PV cells or modules. The assessment of unknown parameter PV cells and the appropriate modeling of PV systems are of the utmost importance. Parameter assessment is a nontrivial task because of nonlinear, multivariable, and multimodal characteristics [13]. Throughout the past few decades, there have been noteworthy advancements to understand the characteristics of PV systems by means of mathematical modeling. PV cells could be successfully analyzed through single-(SDM), double- (DDM), and triple-diode (TDM) models [13–15].

Metaheuristic algorithms are widely discussed and have successfully been applied for the parameter estimation of PV systems and various other applications [16–31]. Metaheuristic algorithms are computational intelligence paradigms that are especially used for sophisticated solutions of optimization problems. The advantages and disadvantages of these algorithms are classified on the basis of good trade-offs regarding exploitation and exploration abilities. One essential circumstance is that various algorithms should be benchmarked and equated on a job that is similar to the design optimization problem at hand. Metaheuristic algorithms can be classified in a variety of ways due to their various characteristics [24]. Figure 1 demonstrates the classification of metaheuristic algorithms into four groups: evolution-based, human-related, nature-inspired, and bio-inspired algorithms. Another probable classification of some particular methods is represented in Figure 2.

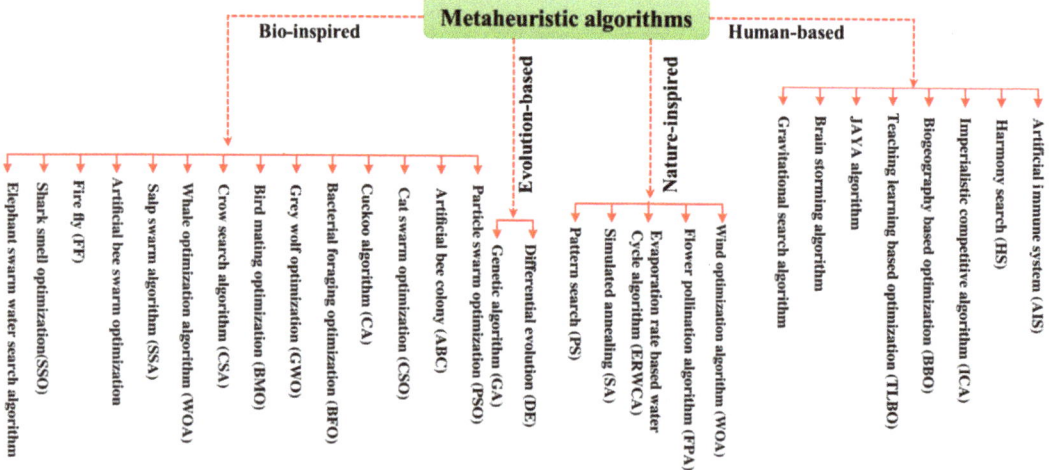

Figure 1. Different metaheuristic methods for assessment of unknown parameters of PV cells or modules (adapted with permission from Ref. [13]. Copyright 2022 John Wiley and Sons).

In a very recent work, Karambasti et al. employed a genetic (GE) algorithm for small-scale power-water production based on the integration of a Stirling engine and a multieffect evaporation desalination system [32]. For partially shaded conditions, an ant colony optimization (ACO)-based hybrid MPPT controller for photovoltaic systems was studied by Chao et al. [33]. Recently, we implemented arithmetic algorithm for the parameter extraction of fuel cells [34]. The grey wolf optimization (GWO) algorithm was employed to enhance the performance of a dual-energy gamma-ray-based three-phase flow meter [35]. Artificial neural network (ANN)-based methods were also used to solve optimization problems [36,37]. Orosz et al. summarized different nature-inspired multiobjective optimization techniques [24]. Different types of population-based optimization methods, e.g., genetic algorithm (GA), differential evolution (DE), cuckoo search (CS), firefly algorithm (FA), tunicate swarm algorithm (TSA), whale optimization algorithm (WOA), opposition-based TSA (OTSA), and particle swarm optimization (PSO), were successfully used for parameter optimization of solar cells [23–31].

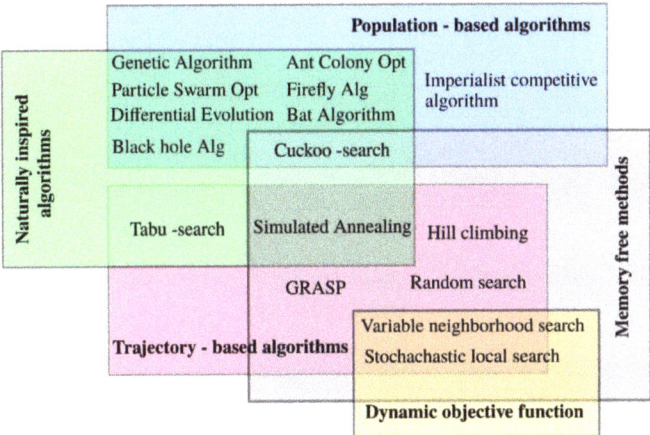

Figure 2. Metaheuristic methods and their categorization (reprinted from Ref. [24]).

Swarm-intelligence-based algorithms are stimulated by the social behavior of animals, insects, birds, and fish. A widespread method is particle swarm optimization (PSO), which is inspired by the actions of bird flocks. These birds fly to find their best location (position) through the search space. Though several PSO and other metaheuristic algorithms were developed, none provides an optimal explanation to all sets of problems, as per the 'no such thing as a free lunch' theorem [38,39]. This directs researchers and scientists to further develop new algorithms or modify previous algorithms to resolve optimization problems. PSO and modified PSO algorithms are studied for various engineering applications e.g., speech emotion recognition, railway controls, job shop scheduling problems, geotechnical engineering, load flow control, source seeking problems, elevator door systems, quad assignment problems, equipment possession quantity, optimal designs of PID controllers, parameter estimation of photovoltaic cells or modules, and the beam-slab layout design of rectangular floors [40–49]. Hajihassani et al. studied PSO algorithms for applications in geotechnical engineering [43]. In a very recent work, Huang et al. proposed a multilayer hybrid fuzzy classification-based PSO for speech emotion recognition [40].

This review article summarizes recent developments in hybrid PSO algorithms for the parameter assessment of PV cells or modules. This article is useful for researchers who are working on the parameter optimization of different issues. Although PSO algorithms are applicable for different types of applications, we limited this analysis to only the parameter optimization of PV cells or modules.

2. Estimating PV Cell/Module Parameters

Figure 3 illustrates the different processes involved in the parameter assessment of PV cells or modules. Generally, any PV cell or module is modeled using an electrical equivalent circuit, which preferably includes a current source, diode, and resistors. Equivalent circuits can be articulated employing three types of models, namely, SDM, DDM, and TDM, and each model has advantages and disadvantages. The number of diodes in the model decides the accuracy of I–V curve estimation. SDMs are usually employed for modeling PV cells or modules because of their reliability, accuracy, and simplicity [49]. Other models are also used for more accurate curve reproduction and the inclusion of recombination losses [13–15]. However, the complexity of the simulation process is significantly increased.

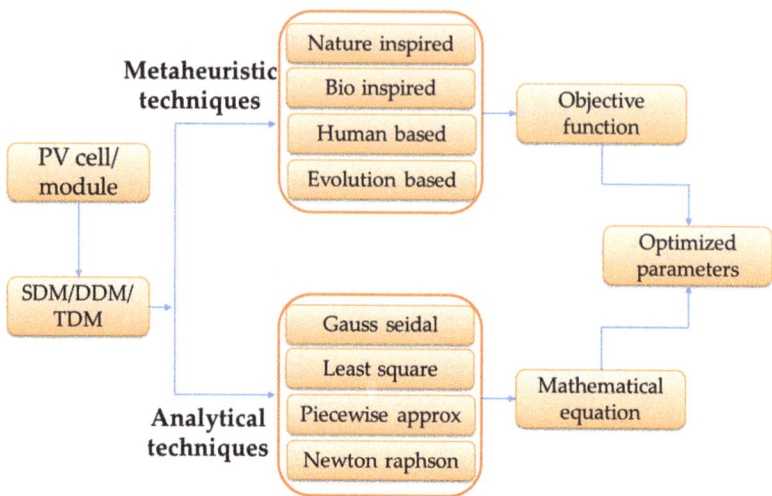

Figure 3. Different processes for modeling and parameter estimation of PV cells. PV: photovoltaic, SDM: single-diode model, DDM: double-diode model, and TDM: triple-diode model (adapted with permission from Ref. [13]. Copyright 2022 John Wiley and Sons).

Figure 4 illustrates the SDM equivalent circuit of a standard PV cell. The diode (D) is connected to the current source in parallel. Moreover, the shunt resistor (R_{sh}) and series resistance (R_s) are connected for the consideration of losses due to carrier recombination and metallic junction. According to Figure 4, the electrical behavior of PV cell is expressed as:

$$I = I_p - I_0 \left[exp\left(\frac{q_e V}{ak_B T}\right) - 1 \right] \qquad (1)$$

where I, I_p, I_0, V, a, and T are output current, photocurrent, reverse saturation current, output voltage, quality factor, and cell temperature, respectively. The Boltzmann constant (k_B) is 1.3806×10^{-23} m$^2 \cdot$kg/s^{2}K, and elementary charge (q_e) is 1.602×10^{-19} C.

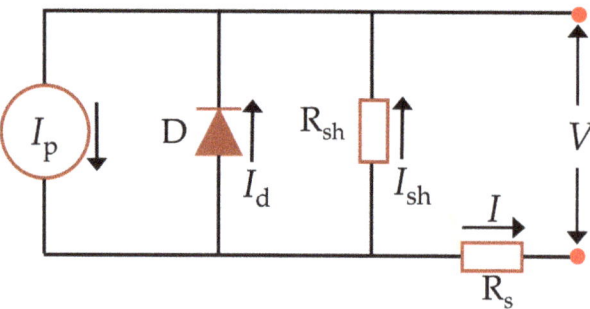

Figure 4. SDM equivalent circuit of standard PV cell.

The assessment of each unknown parameter and the process of PV modeling are of utmost importance. Besides model selection, another key step is to select a method for the estimation of unknown parameters. Generally, the two technique types that are employed for unknown-parameter determination are analytical and metaheuristic methods [50]. Analytical methods apply different operating conditions and available manufacturer datasheets to attain PV characteristics [50,51]. Metaheuristic methods employ the curve fitting technique to assess PV characteristics (I–V curve). Thus, the datasheet of a predicted I–V curve is matched with the manufacturer and/or measured datasheets [52]. Metaheuristic methods are more useful for enhanced performance and reduced computational load than analytical ones are. A combination of the two methods can also provide superior performance.

Table 1 displays the different error functions applicable for the evaluation of metaheuristic and other optimization algorithms. These functions are absolute error (AE), individual absolute error (IAE), relative error (RE), mean square error (MSE), mean bias error (MBE), root mean square error (RMSE), and the sum of squared error (SSE) [53–55]. Among them, the commonly used objective function to analyze efficiency is the RMSE metric. In the case of SDM, five parameters (I_p, I_{sd}, a, R_s and R_{sh}) should be assessed to obtain the minimal value of the RMSE.

Table 1. Various performance parameters.

Error Metrics	Function
Individual absolute error	$IAE = \|I_m - I_s\|$
Relative error	$RE = \frac{(I_m - I_s)}{I_s}$
Absolute error	$AE = \left\|\sum_{i=0}^{N} I_m - I_s\right\|$
Mean absolute error	$MAE = \sum_{i=0}^{N} \frac{(I_m - I_s)}{N}$
Normalized mean absolute error	$NMAE = \sum_{i=0}^{N} \frac{(I_m - I_s)/I_s}{N}$
Mean bias error	$MBE = \frac{(I_m - I_s)}{N}$
Root mean square error	$RMSE = \sqrt{\frac{\left(\sum_{i=0}^{N} I_m - I_s\right)^2}{N}}$

Note: I_m, actual (measured) current; I_s, calculated/estimated current; number of data points in I–V characteristics, N.

Different algorithms are mainly employed to optimize the unknown parameters of equivalent models (SDM, DDM, and TDM) of PV cells. Another objective is to diminish the error among measured and assessed datasets. The RMSE objective function is expressed as

$$RMSE = \sqrt{\frac{1}{k} \sum_{N=1}^{k} f(V_l, I_l, X)} \qquad (2)$$

where, I_l and V_l are the measured current and voltage parameters of the PV cell/module. The number of the experimental dataset is represented by parameter k. Vector X denotes the best solution. In the case of SDM [13,15]:

$$\begin{cases} f_{single}(V_l, I_l, X) = I_p - I_{sd}\left[exp\left(\frac{q(V_l+I_l R_s)}{a_1 k_B T}\right) - 1\right] - \frac{V_l + I_l R_s}{R_{sh}} - I_l \\ (X = I_p, I_{sd}, a, R_s, R_{sh}) \end{cases} \qquad (3)$$

For the DDM [14,15]:

$$\begin{cases} f_{double}(V_l, I_l, X) = I_p - I_{sd_1}\left[exp\left(\frac{q(V_l+I_l R_s)}{a_1 k_B T}\right) - 1\right] \\ -I_{sd_2}\left[exp\left(\frac{q(V_l+I_l R_s)}{a_2 k_B T}\right) - 1\right] - \frac{V_l + I_l R_s}{R_{sh}} - I_l \\ (X = I_p, I_{sd_1}, I_{sd_2}, a_1, a_2, R_s, R_{sh}) \end{cases} \qquad (4)$$

For the TDM [14,15]:

$$\begin{cases} f_{double}(V_l, I_l, X) = I_p - I_{sd_1}\left[exp\left(\frac{q(V_l+I_l R_s)}{a_1 k_B T}\right) - 1\right] \\ -I_{sd_2}\left[exp\left(\frac{q(V_l+I_l R_s)}{a_2 k_B T}\right) - 1\right] - I_{sd_3}\left[exp\left(\frac{q(V_l+I_l R_s)}{a_3 k_B T}\right) - 1\right] - \frac{V_l + I_l R_s}{R_{sh}} - I_l \\ (X = I_p, I_{sd_1}, I_{sd_2}, I_{sd_3}, a_1, a_2, a_3, R_s, R_{sh}) \end{cases} \qquad (5)$$

As stated previously, equivalent circuit models can be differentiated on the basis of number of diodes in the circuit. Therefore, the number of unknown parameters is different for different models. Thus five, seven, and nine parameters need to be estimated for SDM, DDM, and TDM, respectively. The characteristics (V–I and P–I) of PV cells are described on the basis of the best-optimized parameters. Distinctive V–I and P–I curves of PV cells in standard conditions are shown in Figure 5.

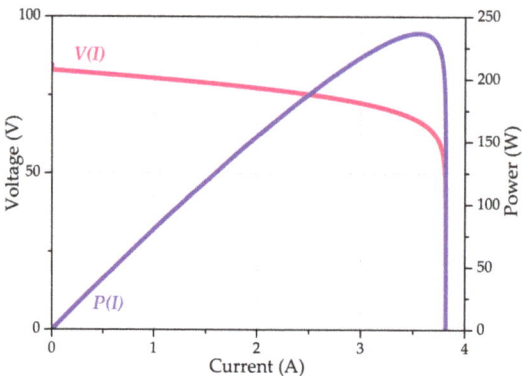

Figure 5. Characteristic curve of PV cells at standard conditions (reprinted from Ref. [10]).

3. Particle Swarm Optimization

The particle swarm optimization (PSO) method was introduced by J. Kennedy and R. C. Eberhard for solving nonlinear functions [56,57]. It is a population-based self-adaptive and nature-inspired stochastic optimization technique. The PSO algorithm works as follows. Initial particles are first created and assigned as initial velocities. The objective function is evaluated at every particle's location. The best function value and location are determined. In the next step, new velocities are selected on the basis of recent velocity, the best locations of individual particles, and the best locations of their adjacent particles. After that, the location, velocities, and neighbors of particles are iteratively updated. The new location is assessed by adding the velocity to the previous location. Locations are altered to retain particles within bounds. The process continues for several iterations till the algorithm arrives at a stopping criterion.

The PSO algorithm explores the space of an optimization problem by modifying the paths of individual members, called particles because these paths form partwise paths in a quasistochastic fashion. The motion of the swarming particle consists of two major parts, the stochastic and the deterministic parts. In this technique, each potential solution is considered to be a particle with its own random velocity and location in the search space. The search space is defined as the set of all probabilistic solutions for the problem to be optimized. Each particle achieves its best position and velocity according to the best solution (fitness) in the solution space. The i-th particle in the PSO algorithm updates its velocity and position at every t-th step according to the equations given below:

$$V_i^{t+1} = wV_i^t + r_1 C_1 \left(P_{best} - X_i^t\right) + r_2 C_2 \left(G_{best} - X_i^t\right) \tag{6}$$

In the above expression, the first, second, and third terms are previous velocity, cognitive learning, and social learning, respectively.

$$X_i^{t+1} = X_i^t + V_i^{t+1} \tag{7}$$

where X_i^t and V_i^t designate the position and velocity vector of the i-th particle in the swarm, w represents the inertial weight to maintain the balance between local and global search ability, and C_1 and C_2 denote the acceleration constant and are predefined by the user.

r_1 and r_2 are random numbers generated in the range of (0, 1). P_{best} is the personal best position of the i-th particle at time t, and G_{best} is the global best position of the i-th particle within the swarm. The term inertial weight (w) was not initially included in the ordinary PSO; it was included by Shi and Eberhart in 1998 [56].

The representation of the PSO model is shown in Figure 6, where bold lines depict the velocity and position of the particle after each iteration, dotted lines depict the components of Equation (6), P_{best} denotes the personal best position of the particle, G_{best} represents global best position of particular particle in a search space, and X and Y represent the horizontal and vertical direction of search in a solution space, respectively.

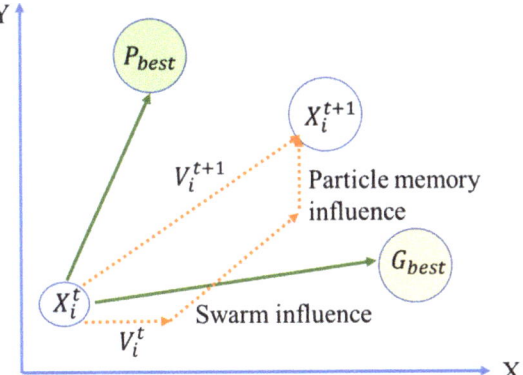

Figure 6. Representation of particle swarm optimization (PSO) model.

Pseudocode for implementation of PSO algorithm [Algorithm 1] is as follows:

Algorithm 1. Pseudocode of PSO

1. Objective function $f(x), x = (x_i, \ldots, x_p)^t$
2. Initialize locations X_i^t and velocity V_i^t of ith particles
3. Find G_{best} from min $[f(x_1), f(x_n)]$ (at $t = 0$)
4. while (max iteration)
5. $t = t + 1$ (iteration counter)
6. for loop over all ith particles and all p dimensions
7. Generate new velocity V_i^{t+1} using Equation (6)
8. Calculate new locations $X_i^{t+1} = X_i^t + V_i^{t+1}$
9. Evaluate objective functions at new locations X_i^{t+1}
10. Find best current for each particle P_{best}
11. end for
12. Find the current global best G_{best}
13. end while
14. Output results P_{best} and G_{best}

The PSO algorithm also has certain advantages compared with numerous other continuous optimization techniques.

✔ It does not produce assertions about the consistency and the convexity of the optimization problem to be optimized.
✔ It is not necessary to measure the coefficient of the optimal solution.
✔ There is no need for good initial points of reference or extensive a priori knowledge of its most interesting regions of the search domain.

Now, we discuss modified and hybrid PSO algorithms, which are the derivative of basic PSO. Several investigators have endeavored to hybridize PSO through different methods and guaranteed upgrades according to the exhibition perspective.

4. Hybrid PSO Algorithms

PSO algorithms are efficient methods to tackle different optimization issues. Nevertheless, the fundamental PSO regularly experiences untimely convergence, and demonstrates poor performance for many intricate and multimodal optimization problems [42,49,57]. Several studies were conducted to improve the performance of basic PSO [58–73]. These improvements were largely focused on the population structure and the estimation process of the next velocity of every other particle. This helped to upsurge the effectiveness and consistency of the initial hunt process, and avert the amount of miscellany. Detailed analysis is devoted to monitoring the expansion of velocity, consistency, and convergence, and parameter changes. The hybridization of PSO through additional algorithms could significantly improve the performance of basic PSO [49,57–62]. The convergence rate of PSO could be exceptionally expanded by changing the speed increase proportion to the best design utilizing auxiliary boundaries [42]. Table 2 summarizes various hybrid PSO algorithms for the parameter assessment of PV cells.

Table 2. Comparison of different hybrid PSO algorithms for parameter approximation of PV systems.

Hybrid PSO	Objective Function Used	Type of Diode Model	Irradiation Conditions	Types of Panel
FODPSO (Fractional Order Darwinian PSO) [60]	IAE SIAE RMSE	SDM DDM	1000 W/m² at 33 °C	RTC silicon solar cell
			1000 W/m² at 45 °C	Photowatt PWP201PV Module
			675 W/m² at 48.3 °C	Monocrystalline cell (TSM185M-72M)
			616.4 W/m² at 47.4 °C	Polycrystalline cell (SW 250–260 poly)
NPSOPC (niche PSO in parallel computing) [61]	RMSE	SDM DDM PMM	1000 W/m² at 33 °C	RTC silicon solar cell
			1000 W/m² at 45 °C	Photowatt-PWP201PV module
EPSO (enhanced PSO) [63]	MSE	SDM DDM TDM	1000 W/m² at 33 °C	RTC silicon solar cell
			1000 W/m² at 45 °C	DPL Photowatt-PWP201PV module
PSOGWO (grey wolf optimization combined with PSO) [63]	RMSE	SDM	1000 W/m² at 25 °C	KC200GT PV module
			800 W/m² at 20 °C	SQ85 PV module
WOAPSO (whale optimization combined with PSO) [49]	RMSE	SDM DDM	1000 W/m² at 30 °C	RTC France solar cell
			1000 W/m², 870 W/m², 720 W/m², and 630 W/m² at 25 °C	PV module (SS2018P)
CIWPSO (chaotic inertial weight PSO) [64]	RMSE IAE AE	SDM DDM	1000 W/m² at 33 °C	RTC France solar cell
			1000 W/m² at 45 °C	Photowatt PWP201PV module
			1000 W/m² at 47 °C, 800 W/m² at 44 °C, 600 W/m² at 42 °C, 400 W/m² at 36 °C, 200 W/m² at 27 °C	JKM330P-72 PV module

Table 2. *Cont.*

Hybrid PSO	Objective Function Used	Type of Diode Model	Irradiation Conditions	Types of Panel
CPMPSO (classified perturbation mutation-based PSO) [65]	RMSE IAE	SDM DDM	1000 W/m^2 at 45 °C	Photowatt-PWP201PV module
			1000 W/m^2 at 33 °C	RTC France solar cell
			51	STM6-40/36 PV module
			55	STP6-120/36 PV module
DEDIWPSO (double exponential function-based dynamic inertial weight PSO) [66]	RMSE IAE	SDM DDM	1000 W/m^2 at 33 °C	RTC France solar cell
			1000 W/m^2 at 45 °C	Photowatt PWP201PV module
SAIWPSO (simulated annealing inertia weight PSO) [67]	RMSE	SDM DDM	1000 W/m^2 at 33 °C	RTC France solar cell
PSOAG (autonomous groups PSO) [68,69]	CR RMSE MAE	SDM	1000 W/m^2 at 33 °C	RTC France solar cell
CPSO (chaos PSO) [70]	RMSE MAE RACF *	SDM DDM	1000 W/m^2 at 33 °C	RTC France solar cell
HPSOSA (hybrid PSO and simulated annealing) [70]	RMSE MAE RACF *	SDM DDM	1000 W/m^2 at 33 °C	RTC France solar cell

* RACF: residual autocorrelation function.

4.1. FODPSO

In a very recent work, Ahmed et al. proposed a fractional order Darwinian PSO (FODPSO) algorithm to find the parameters of PV cells [60]. In this research work, a modification was proposed for controlling the velocity of each particle by incorporating the concept of fractional order derivative.

The Grunwald–Letnikov definition is used to define the fractional derivatives as given below [60]:

$$D^\alpha[X(t)] = \frac{1}{T^\alpha} \sum_{k=0}^{r} \frac{(-1)^k \Gamma(\alpha+1) x(t-kh)}{\Gamma(\alpha+1)\Gamma(\alpha-k+1)} \quad (8)$$

where α is the derivative order, T is the period of sampling, and r is the truncation order. Other elements of Equation (8) were defined in [60]. The original velocity to implement fractional-order calculus on PSO (Equation (6)) is rewritten as:

$$V_{t+1} + V_t = C_1 \times rand(P - X_T) + C_2 \times rand(G - X_T) \quad (9)$$

The left-hand side of the above equation represents the discrete formula of the derivative of order number $\alpha = 1$. Let us assume that $T = 1$; we arrive at

$$D^\alpha[V_{t+1}] = C_1 \times rand(P - X_T) + C_2 \times rand(G - X_T) \quad (10)$$

Equation (11) denotes the application of the fraction order number (Equation (8)) on the speed of particles with a range from $\alpha = 0$ to $\alpha = 1$ ($\Delta \alpha = 0.1$) and $r = 4$:

$$V_{t+1} = \alpha V_t + \frac{1}{2}\alpha(1-\alpha)V_{t-1} + \frac{1}{6}\alpha(1-\alpha)(2-\alpha)V_{t-2} + \frac{1}{24}\alpha(1-\alpha)(2-\alpha)(3-\alpha)V_{t-3} + \\ C_1 \times rand(P - X_T) + C_2 \times rand(G - X_T) \quad (11)$$

The main benefit of the fractional calculus derivatives is the additional level of degree of freedom. Equation (11) shows the possibility to govern the speed of particles concerning the derivative order (α). This is the key benefit as compared to the basic PSO algorithm. The additional level of opportunity of fractional calculus derivation induction takes into consideration an exact depiction of the conduct of many cycles through the exact enhancement of framework display, planning, and control.

To show the effectiveness of FODPSO, eight metaheuristic algorithms (existing in the literature) are compared. Furthermore, two types of diode models (SDM and DDM) are exploited to show the efficiency of FODPSO. However, the authors considered only standard testing conditions for the measurement of current and voltage. Furthermore, there was no emphasis given on other objective functions such as MAE, NMAE, and MBE.

4.2. NPSOPC

The niche particle swarm optimization in parallel computing (NPSOPC)-based optimization algorithm was proposed by Lin and Wu in 2020 [61]. Niches in parallel architecture were set up with a PSO-based parameters extraction model to improve extraction performance. The process flow diagram of NPSOPC is provided in Figure 7.

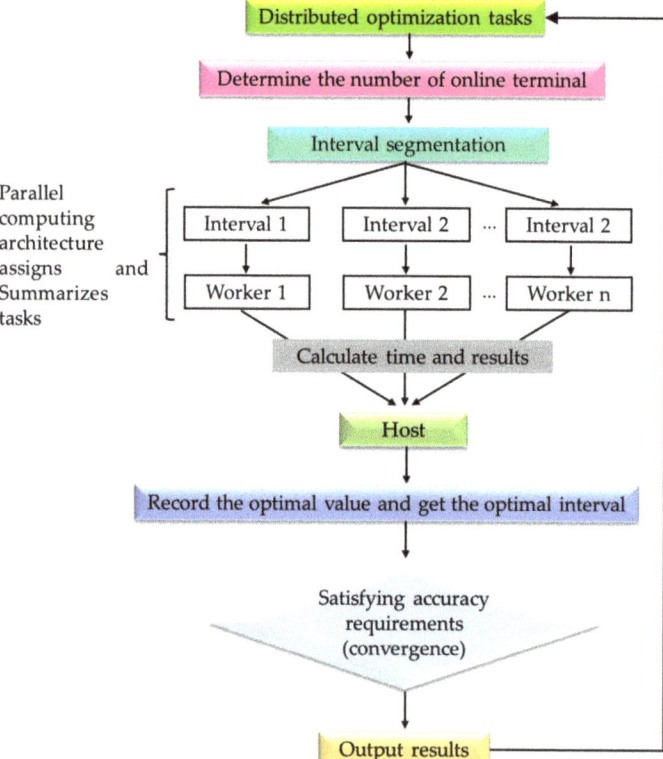

Figure 7. Process flow chart of parallel computing of NPSOPC (reprinted with permission from Ref. [61]. Copyright 2022 Elsevier).

Experimental validation was conducted by parameters identifying the cation of SDM and DDM for solar cells and monocrystalline PV modules. However, there is no experimental validation on other recent PV technologies such as thin-film and perovskite solar cells.

4.3. EPSO

In 2021, Wang R proposed an enhanced version of PSO termed as enhanced particle swarm optimization (EPSO). In this latest modification, the authors implemented an orthogonal opposition-based learning mechanism for initializing the position of the particles [62]. This method increased the PSO algorithm's convergence speed and improved global optimization quality. The swarm initiation employed in this investigation is shown in the following equation:

$$\begin{cases} \theta_{ld}(0) = \theta_{d,\min} + rand[\theta_{d,\max} - \theta_{d,\min}] \\ \quad l = 1, 2, L, N_p/2 \\ \theta_{ld}(0) = \theta_{d,\max} + \theta_{d,\min} - \theta_{l+N_p/2, d}(0) \\ \quad l = N_p/2 + 1, N_p/2 + 2, L, N_p \end{cases} \quad (12)$$

where $\theta_{ld}(0)$, $\theta_{d,\min}$, and $\theta_{d,\max}$ are the initial value, minimal, and maximal values of the candidate solution in the d-th dimension, respectively.

EPSO was tested for three diode models: SDM, DDM, and TDM. Experimental voltage and current were taken for the validation. The effectiveness of EPSO was verified on an RTC France solar cell and Photowatt PWP 201 PV module under standard temperature conditions. However, there was no validation for other types of PV modules such as monocrystalline and thin-film. Furthermore, there was no comparison provided by the authors for varying irradiance and temperature levels.

4.4. PSOGWO

In 2020, Premkumar et al. proposed a novel hybrid version of PSO known as particle swarm optimization and grey wolf optimization (PSOGWO) [63]. In this hybrid version, the GWO assists the PSO in decreasing the probability of escaping the local-optimum trap. To avoid the potential of a local-minimum trap, the GWO's exploration capabilities are employed to steer some particles towards partially improved positions rather than random locations. The mathematical model of PSOGWO is illustrated by the following equations.

$$V_{q+1}^{-i} = wV_q^{-i} + c_1 r_1 \left(X_1 - X_q^{-i} \right) + c_2 r_2 \left(X_2 - X_q^{-i} \right) + c_3 r_3 \left(X_3 - X_q^{-i} \right) \quad (13)$$

In addition to this, the efficacy of the hybrid PSOGWO was validated for the problem of parameter assessment, and its performance was compared with that of GWO and grey wolf optimizer–cuckoo search (GWOCS). However, PSOGWO and GWOCS algorithms have a great computing cost due to hybridization. Furthermore, the authors did not emphasize experimental validation under different climatic conditions.

4.5. WOAPSO

Recently, Sharma et al. proposed another hybrid version of whale optimization and PSO algorithms (WOAPSO) for the parameter optimization of PV cells [49]. The exploitation ability of PSO with adaptive weight function was used in pipeline mode with a WOA for its enhancement and to improve convergence speed of basic PSO. Figure 8 displays the process flowchart of WOAPSO algorithm implementation.

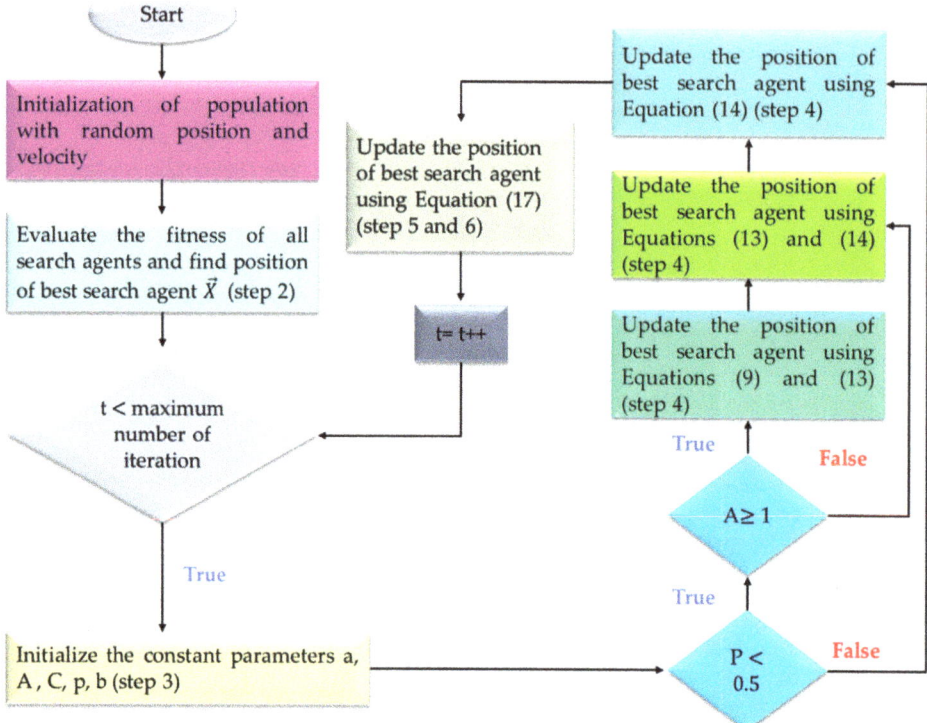

Figure 8. Flowchart of WOAPSO algorithm (reprinted from Ref. [49]).

4.6. CIWPSO

Recently, Kiani et al. developed an improved PSO employing chaotic inertial weight and acceleration coefficients [64]. In the CIWPSO algorithm, the performance of basic PSO is enhanced by employing two approaches: control inertial weight and acceleration coefficients. First, an appropriate balance between local and global search is accomplished by utilizing a sine chaotic inertial weight approach. Subsequently, an optimal solution is found by guiding acceleration coefficients with the tangent chaotic tactic (Figure 9).

The mathematical model of sine iterator based on chaotic search function is expressed as

$$X_{n+1} = \sin \pi x_n \tag{14}$$

Using Equation (14), the chaotic sequence (X_{n+1}) is engendered between 0 and 1. Factor w is exhibited as

$$w(it+1) = \varnothing \times \sin(\pi w_t) + \tau, \tag{15}$$

where $\varnothing$ and τ are constants [64]. The proposed CIWPSO method produced better outcomes to the DDM at the expense of greater computational weight than those of the SDM for the RTC France solar cell. For the Photowatt PWP201 PV module, SDM and DDM displayed similar outcomes as far as RMSE is concerned; however, DDM is computationally bulky in light of the number of included obscure parameters.

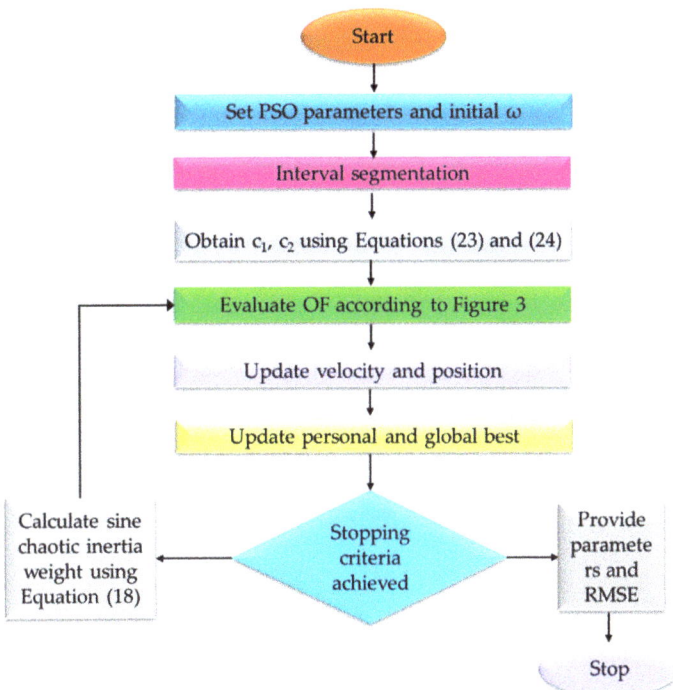

Figure 9. Flowchart of CIWPSO algorithm for parameter estimation of PV models (reprinted from Ref. [64]). Here, Figure 3 of Ref. [64] demonstrated the Newton Raphson method for the formulation of the objective function.

4.7. CPMPSO

A characterized perturbation mutation-based PSO algorithm was proposed by Liang et al. for the accurate parameter extraction of PV modules [65]. The two strategies of perturbation mutation and damping bound handling were employed in a conventional PSO to provide a good trade-off between exploration and exploitation steps. For improving exploration, a larger perturbation mutation strategy was employed for the low-quality personal best location, and to avoid falling into the local optimum, a damping bound handling method was used.

$$z_{i,d} = \begin{cases} pbest_{i,d} + rand(pbest_{k_1,d} - pbest_{k_2,d}) & \text{If } f(pbest) < mean(fitnesspbest) \\ pbest_{k_1,d} + rand(pbest_{k_2,d} - pbest_{k_3,d}) & \text{otherwise} \end{cases} \quad (16)$$

where $mean(fitnesspbest) = \left(\sum_{i=1}^{NP} f(pbest_i)\right)/NP$. NP represents the size of the population, and $z_{i,d}$ signifies the d-th dimension magnitude of the trail vector. The randomly generated integers within $[1, NP]$ were defined as k_1, k_2, and k_3, and they were mutually different. These integers were also dissimilar after i.

The variable value of trail vector that violates the boundary conditions is rearranged as follows:

$$z_{i,d} = \begin{cases} xmax_d, & \text{if } z_{i,d} > xmax_d \\ xmin_d, & \text{if } z_{i,d} < xmin_d \end{cases} \quad (17)$$

where $xmax_d$ and $xmin_d$ are the maximal and minimal boundary conditions of the d-th dimension of one inconstant.

$$z_{i,d} = \begin{cases} \text{If } x_{i,d} > xmax_d \\ x_{i,d} = xmax_d;\, v_{i,d} = -v_{i,d} \cdot rand \\ \text{elseif } x_{i,d} < xmin_d \\ x_{i,d} = xmin_d;\, v_{i,d} = -v_{i,d} \cdot rand \end{cases} \quad (18)$$

where $x_{i,d}$ is the d-th dimension of the position, and $v_{i,d}$ is d-th dimension of the velocity of the i-th particle. The range of the random numbers (*rand*) was from 0 to 1.

The authors validated the efficiency of CPMPSO on three types of solar panels: polycrystalline KC200GT, single-crystalline SM55, and thin-film ST40. However, there was no perfect match between experimental and simulated values.

4.8. DEDIWPSO

Kiani et al. proposed a double exponential function-based dynamic inertial weight (DEDIW) approach for the optimal parameter forecast of PV cells or modules. This method upholds a proper equilibrium between the exploitation and exploration processes to alleviate the early convergence issue of basic PSO [66].

The DEDIW method is propelled by the fast-developing nature of the exponential function, and consolidates the Gompertzian function, which is a vanishing double exponential function given below:

$$w(it+1) = y(exp - \exp(-R_i)) \quad (19)$$

$$R_i = \left(\frac{maxit - it}{maxit} \right) \quad (20)$$

where $y = 1$. The performance index (R_i) is assessed for individual particles at each iteration. The magnitude of w diminishes as the number of iterations increases.

Three case studies were performed for the assessment of the suggested technique: PV module (Photowatt PWP201), RTC France PV cell, and polycrystalline PV module JKM330P-72 (310 W) under actual climatic circumstances. However, computation time was longer than that of the conventional PSO because of the large number of tuning parameters in DEDIWPSO.

4.9. SAIWPSO

The SAIWPSO algorithm by Kiani et al. assessed the parameter of PV cells [67]. Inertial weight had a higher value at the initial stage (heating process) for global search. However, it progressively decreases (moderate cooling process) for local search. The mathematical formulation of the SAIWPSO search mechanism is given by the following equation:

$$w(iter) = w_{\min} + (w_{\max} - w_{\min}) \times temp^{(iter-1)} \quad (21)$$

SAIWPSO performed very well for the parameter extraction of RTC France solar cells. However, the computational complexity of SAIWPSO was greater than that of other metaheuristic algorithms. In addition to this, current and voltage are measured under standard temperature conditions.

4.10. PSOAG

In 2021, an improved version of PSO known as AGPSO was presented [68]. In AGPSO, all particles are first divided into different groups, and these groups then use the different types of functions for tuning social and cognitive parameters. This modification leads to fast convergence and avoids local minima.

Pseudocode for the implementation of the PSOAG algorithm [Algorithm 2] is as follows [68,69]:

Algorithm 2. Pseudocode of the PSOAG algorithm.

Create and initialize a D-dimensional PSO
Randomly divide particles into autonomous groups
Repeat
   Calculate particles fitness P_{best} and G_{best}
   For each particle:
     Extract the particle group
     Use its group strategy to update C_1 and C_2
     Use C_1 and C_2 to update velocities (6)
     Use new velocities to define new positions (7)
   End for
Until stopping condition is satisfied.

Experimental results in this study depict that there was 14% improvement in computation cost, and 20% improvement in terms of convergence rate compared to other metaheuristic algorithms. However, no comparison was provided with new metaheuristic techniques.

4.11. CPSO

The CPSO algorithm was proposed as a low-computational-complexity method for parameter estimation of PV cells/modules [70,71] where the chaotic search-based method is employed to overcome the tendency of PSO to become stuck in a local solution. Chaos is a well-known nonlinear event in physical systems. Randomicity, monotonicity, and nonrepeat ability are features of chaotic variables. The following equation illustrates the efficient search strategy of the chaos mechanism. Inertial weight in CPSO decreased linearly:

$$w = w_{\max} + itr_{\text{curr}}(w_{\max} - w_{\min})G \qquad (22)$$

where $w_{\max}$, $w_{\min}$, itr_{curr}, and G are the maximal inertial weight, minimal inertial weight, current number of iterations, and maximal number of iterations, respectively.

In that research study, the effectiveness of CPSO is shown by taking three indices: RMSE, MBE, and MAE. However, there was no proper validation provided by the authors for different environmental conditions.

4.12. Hybrid PSO and Simulated Annealing (HPSOSA)

Mughal et al. proposed another hybrid version of PSOSA for the parameter estimation of PV cells. In this hybrid version, premature convergence problem PSO was removed by including the simulated annealing (SA) algorithm in pipeline mode [70]. First, the best global solution is generated by PSO algorithm. Then, this best solution is taken as input by SA algorithm to further improve the solution (Figure 10).

Furthermore, the authors took RMSE and MAE as two objective functions for measuring the effectiveness of HPSOSA, and tested their algorithm on the RTC France solar cell. No experimental validation was provided by the authors for other solar panels under different climatic conditions.

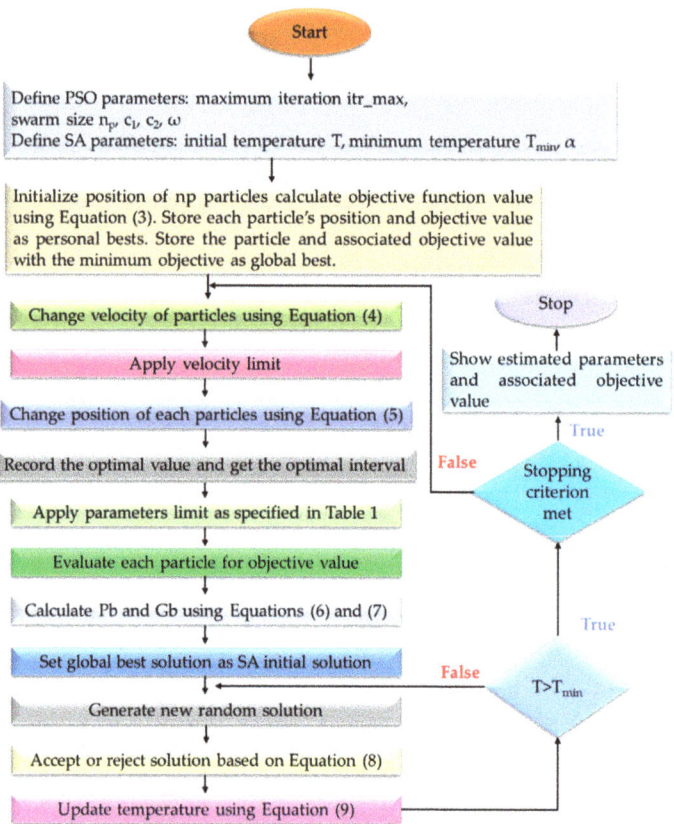

Figure 10. Process flowchart of parallel computing of HPSOSA (reprinted from Ref. [70]).

5. Qualitative Analysis

This segment compares the SI-based algorithms presented in Section 3 on the basis of key parameters for the parameter estimation of solar cells or modules. These key parameters are computational complexity, convergence speed, optimization function, computational time, and search technique. The comparison of the algorithms is shown in Table 3.

Table 3. Qualitative comparison of hybrid PSO for parameter estimation of PV cells or modules.

Name of Algorithm	Computational Time	Computational Complexity	Convergence Rate	Search Technique	Merits	Demerits
FODPSO [60]	Low	High	Low	Mutation	High scalability, good diversity	Poor accuracy
NPSOPC [61]	Medium	Medium	Low	Mutation and crossover	Good at exploration	Not good at exploitation
EPSO [62]	Low	Low	High	Selection	High adaptivity	Not good for high dimension problem
PSOGWO [63]	High	High	Low	Selection	Can easily escape from local minima	Poor accuracy

Table 3. *Cont.*

Name of Algorithm	Computational Time	Computational Complexity	Convergence Rate	Search Technique	Merits	Demerits
WOAPSO [49]	Low	Low	High	Mutation and Selection	Good convergence speed for high dimensional problem	Not suitable for high-dimension problems
CIWPSO [64]	Medium	Low	High	Selection	Suitable for solving distributed optimization problem	Low diversity
CPMPSO [65]	Medium	Low	Medium	Selection	High adaptivity	Low diversity
DEDIWPSO [66]	High	High	Medium	Mutation and crossover	High diversity	Large number of tuning parameters
SAIW-PSO [67]	High	High	Medium	Mutation	Low tuning parameters	Low diversity
PSOAG [68]	Medium	Low	High	Selection	High diversity	Not suitable for high-dimension problems
CPSO [70]	Low	Low	High	Selection	Low tuning parameters	Poor accuracy
HPSOSA [70]	High	High	Medium	Selection	Good diversity and adaptability	Uncertain convergence time

Computational complexity is the system's demand for computation resources as a function of the number of parameters to be optimized. Resources are specified by the expected calculation time and computational storage needed for generating the optimized solution. Algorithms employing partitioning techniques have relatively lower computational costs.

The pace at which the algorithm can find the optimal solution is referred to as the *convergence rate*. An effective algorithm should have a fast convergence rate and be capable of avoiding local optimal solutions. Premature convergence is described as the convergence of an SI-based algorithm before obtaining a globally optimal solution, and it is typically caused by a deficiency of diversity.

Computation time is the amount of time needed to complete a computational process. A computation is represented as a set of rule applications, with computation time being related to the quantity of the rule applications.

The search technique denotes the exact method by which the algorithm solves a problem. The majority of SI-based algorithms employ one of three kinds of search techniques: crossover, mutation, and selection. The process for global exploration is a mutation, whereas selection serves two functions: one is to accept the optimal available solution in the search space, and the other is to preserve a driving factor for convergence. Lastly, a crossover broadens the search space's diversity. For the RTC France solar cell, a comparison of hybrid PSO algorithms for the parameter estimation of SDM and DDM is shown in Tables 4 and 5, respectively.

Table 4. Comparison of hybrid PSO algorithms for parameter estimation of RTC France solar cell (single-diode model).

Algorithms	I_p (A)	R_s (Ω)	R_{sh} (Ω)	I_d (μA)	a	RMSE
FODPSO	0.7609	0.0364	51.9512	0.3187	1.4806	9.7486×10^{-4}
NPSOPC	0.7608	0.0363	53.7583	0.3325	1.4814	9.8856×10^{-4}
EPSO	NA	NA	NA	NA	NA	0.0010
PSOGWO	NA	NA	NA	NA	NA	NA
WOAPSO	0.7597	0.0342	83.0131	0.499	1.5483	7.1700×10^{-4}
CIWPSO	0.7607	0.0365	53.3394	0.0312	1.4762	7.7300×10^{-4}
CPMPSO	0.7607	0.0363	53.7185	0.3230	1.4811	9.8602×10^{-4}
DEDIWPSO	0.7607	0.0365	52.8898	0.3106	1.4755	7.7300×10^{-4}
SAIWPSO	0.7607	0.0365	52.8898	0.3106	1.47559	7.7300×10^{-4}
PSOAG	NA	NA	NA	NA	NA	NA
CPSO	0.7607	0.0354	59.012	0.4000	1.5033	NA
HPSOSA	0.7608	0.0365	52.8898	0.3107	1.4753	7.7301×10^{-4}

Table 5. Comparison of hybrid PSO algorithms for parameter estimation of RTC France solar cell (double diode model).

Algorithms	I_p (A)	R_s (Ω)	R_{sh} (Ω)	I_{d_1} (μA)	I_{d_2} (μA)	a_1	a_2	RMSE
FODPSO	0.7609	0.0365	52.7589	0.3857	0.2664	1.9999	1.4654	9.7334×10^{-4}
NPSOPC	0.7607	0.0366	55.1170	0.2509	0.5454	1.4598	1.9994	9.8208×10^{-4}
EPSO	NA	NA	NA	NA	NA	NA	NA	0.0010
PSOGWO	NA	NA	NA	NA	NA	NA	NA	NA
WOAPSO	0.7601	0.0311	100	0.5	0.5	1.5755	1.7314	9.8412×10^{-4}
CIWPSO	0.7608	0.0379	60.9400	0.1353	8.0314	1.4022	NA	7.1837×10^{-4}
CPMPSO	0.7607	0.0367	55.4854	0.7493	0.2259	2	1.4510	9.8248×10^{-4}
DEDIWPSO	0.7608	0.0379	60.9353	0.3523	8.0117	1.4027	2.4999	7.1823×10^{-4}
SAIWPSO	0.7608	0.0377	56.2704	0.0703	1.000	1.3627	1.7943	7.4193×10^{-4}
PSOAG	NA	NA	NA	NA	NA	NA	NA	NA
CPSO	NA	NA	NA	NA	NA	NA	NA	NA
HPSOSA	0.7608	0.0374	55.5392	0.1119	0.8559	1.3959	1.8201	7.7583×10^{-4}

6. Discussion

Here, we discussed the application of hybrid PSO algorithms for the parameter optimization of PV cells. Hybrid PSO algorithms are also applicable for various other applications: maritime transportation [74], space trusses [75], Internet of Things [76], managing deliveries of pharmaceuticals [77], load dispatching [78], power quality improvement [79], economic emission dispatch problems [80], pressurized water reactors [81], the partial shading of PV systems [82], the stability of security systems [83], the control of hybrid energy storage systems [84], the operation of integrated energy systems [85], the control optimization of an inverted pendulum [86], optimal chiller loading [87], and many more [73,88–93].

PSO algorithms are widely useful for microwave engineering [94], parameter optimization in electromagnetic shields [95,96], saving energy in antennas [97], saving energy in electromagnetic conductors [98] and many more [99]. Thus, scholars and researchers are encouraged to conduct further research on the theory and applications of PSO algorithms in forthcoming years. The following years will almost certainly see further refinement of the methodology and its incorporation with different procedures, such as applications moving out of the exploration lab into industry and trade. Further comprehension is required of the overall qualities of PSO and different methods, and of the difficulties in sending a PSO-based framework. PSO is a welcome expansion to advancement tool kits. The future exploration of planning mind-boggling issues in multilevel-headed (or many-objective) optimization issues and tackling them with appropriate parallelization procedure could be invaluable directions. Additionally, for issues with few factors or huge information issues, parallelization could adequately upgrade the proficiency and execution by utilizing equal adaptations of heuristics.

7. Conclusions

Hybridization is a developing area of intelligent framework research that means to consolidate the advantageous properties of various ways of relieving their singular shortcomings. This paper presents a bird's eye view of hybrid PSO algorithms applied for the parameter assessment of PV cells or modules. The algorithms were compared on the basis of the used objective function, type of diode model, irradiation conditions, and types of panels. The qualitative analysis of algorithms was performed on the basis of computation time, computational complexity, convergence rate, search technique, and merits and demerits. Several hybrid PSO algorithms were proposed and employed for various applications apart from the parameter assessment of PV cells. However, this review article studied hybrid PSO algorithms employed for the parameter assessment of PV cells during 2020–2022, namely, the FODPSO, NPSOPC, EPSO, CPMPSO, DEDIWPSO, PSOG-WO, WOAPSO, CIWPSO, HPSOSA, PSOAG, and SAIW-PSO algorithms. The hybridization of basic PSO with additional methods significantly enhances the efficiency of parameter assessment.

Author Contributions: Conceptualization, S.R. and A.S. (Abhishek Sharma); methodology, software, validation, A.S. (Abha Singh), A.B., X.H., S.R., and A.S. (Abhishek Sharma); formal analysis, investigation, resources, data curation, A.S. (Abha Singh), X.H., and A.S. (Abhishek Sharma); writing—original draft preparation, A.S. (Abha Singh) and A.S. (Abhishek Sharma); writing—review and editing, S.R. and X.H.; supervision, project administration, funding acquisition, S.R., X.H. and A.S. (Abhishek Sharma). All authors have read and agreed to the published version of the manuscript.

Funding: Financial support from the program of the Natural Science Foundation of China (grant no. 52105057), Natural Science Foundation of Jiangsu (grant no. BK20200916), China Postdoctoral Science Foundation (no. 2021M691307), and Research Foundation for Advanced Talents (grant no. 5501110013) is acknowledged.

Data Availability Statement: The data presented in this study are available on request from the corresponding author.

Conflicts of Interest: The authors declare no conflict of interest.

References

1. Lowitzsch, J.; Hoicka, C.E.; Van Tulder, F.J. Renewable energy communities under the 2019 European Clean Energy Package–Governance model for the energy clusters of the future? *Renew. Sust. Energy Rev.* **2020**, *122*, 109489. [CrossRef]
2. Rajput, S.; Averbukh, M.; Yahalom, A. Electric power generation using a parallel-plate capacitor. *Int. J. Energy Res.* **2019**, *43*, 3905–3913. [CrossRef]
3. Liu, H.; Fu, H.; Sun, L.; Lee, C.; Yeatman, E.M. Hybrid energy harvesting technology: From materials, structural design, system integration to applications. *Renew. Sust. Energy Rev.* **2021**, *137*, 110473. [CrossRef]
4. Sezer, N.; Koç, M. A comprehensive review on the state-of-the-art of piezoelectric energy harvesting. *Nano Energy* **2021**, *80*, 105567. [CrossRef]
5. REN21. *Renewables 2019 Global Status Report—REN21*; REN21: Paris, France, 2019.
6. Doshi, Y. Solar Photovoltaic (PV) Panels Market Overview. Available online: https://www.alliedmarketresearch.com/solar-photovoltaic-panel-market (accessed on 12 September 2019).
7. Amiel, I.; Rajput, S.; Averbukh, M. Capacitive reactive power compensation to prevent voltage instabilities in distribution lines. *Int. J. Electr. Power Energy Syst.* **2021**, *131*, 107043. [CrossRef]
8. Rajput, S.; Amiel, I.; Sitbon, M.; Aharon, I.; Averbukh, M. Control the Voltage Instabilities of Distribution Lines using Capacitive Reactive Power. *Energies* **2020**, *13*, 875. [CrossRef]
9. Zsiborács, H.; Hegedűsné Baranyai, N.; Csányi, S.; Vincze, A.; Pintér, G. Economic Analysis of Grid-Connected PV System Regulations: A Hungarian Case Study. *Electronics* **2019**, *8*, 149. [CrossRef]
10. Rajput, S.; Averbukh, M.; Yahalom, A.; Minav, T. An Approval of MPPT Based on PV Cell's Simplified Equivalent Circuit During Fast-Shading Conditions. *Electronics* **2019**, *8*, 1060. [CrossRef]
11. Yao, X.; Yi, B.; Yu, Y.; Fan, Y.; Zhu, L. Economic analysis of grid integration of variable solar and wind power with conventional power system. *Appl. Energy* **2020**, *264*, 114706. [CrossRef]

12. Mousavi, S.B.; Ahmadi, P.; Pourahmadiyan, A.; Hanafizadeh, P. A comprehensive techno-economic assessment of a novel compressed air energy storage (CAES) integrated with geothermal and solar energy. *Sustain. Energy Technol. Assess.* **2021**, *47*, 101418. [CrossRef]
13. Venkateswari, R.; Rajasekar, N. Review on parameter estimation techniques of solar photovoltaic systems. *Int. Trans. Electr. Energy Syst.* **2021**, *31*, e13113. [CrossRef]
14. Bayoumi, A.S.; El-Sehiemy, R.A.; Mahmoud, K.; Lehtonen, M.; Darwish, M.M.F. Assessment of an Improved Three-Diode against Modified Two-Diode Patterns of MCS Solar Cells Associated with Soft Parameter Estimation Paradigms. *Appl. Sci.* **2021**, *11*, 1055. [CrossRef]
15. Ramadan, A.; Kamel, S.; Hassan, M.H.; Khurshaid, T.; Rahmann, C. An Improved Bald Eagle Search Algorithm for Parameter Estimation of Different Photovoltaic Models. *Processes* **2021**, *9*, 1127. [CrossRef]
16. Agrawal, P.; Abutarboush, H.F.; Ganesh, T.; Mohamed, A.W. Metaheuristic Algorithms on Feature Selection: A Survey of One Decade of Research (2009–2019). *IEEE Access* **2021**, *9*, 26766–26791. [CrossRef]
17. Dokeroglu, T.; Sevinc, E.; Kucukyilmaz, T.; Cosar, A. A survey on new generation metaheuristic algorithms. *Comput. Ind. Eng.* **2019**, *137*, 106040. [CrossRef]
18. Morales-Castañeda, B.; Zaldivar, D.; Cuevas, E.; Fausto, F.; Rodríguez, A. A better balance in metaheuristic algorithms: Does it exist? *Swarm Evol. Comput.* **2020**, *54*, 100671. [CrossRef]
19. Ting, T.O.; Yang, X.S.; Cheng, S.; Huang, K. Hybrid metaheuristic algorithms: Past, present, and future. In *Recent Advances in Swarm Intelligence and Evolutionary Computation*; Springer: Cham, Switzerland, 2015; pp. 71–83.
20. Li, S.; Gong, W.; Gu, Q. A comprehensive survey on metaheuristic algorithms for parameter extraction of photovoltaic models. *Renew. Sust. Energy Rev.* **2021**, *141*, 110828. [CrossRef]
21. Abdel-Basset, M.; Mohamed, R.; Abouhawwash, M.; Nam, Y.; El-Fergany, A. Recent Meta-Heuristic Algorithms with a Novel Premature Covergence Method for Determining the Parameters of PV Cells and Modules. *Electronics* **2021**, *10*, 1846. [CrossRef]
22. Yang, B.; Wang, J.; Zhang, X.; Yu, T.; Yao, W.; Shu, H.; Zeng, F.; Sun, L. Comprehensive overview of metaheuristic algorithm applications on PV cell parameter identification. *Energy Convers. Manag.* **2020**, *208*, 112595. [CrossRef]
23. Gao, S.; Wang, K.; Tao, S.; Jin, T.; Dai, H.; Cheng, J. A state-of-the-art differential evolution algorithm for parameter estimation of solar photovoltaic models. *Energy Convers. Manag.* **2021**, *230*, 113784. [CrossRef]
24. Orosz, T.; Rassõlkin, A.; Kallaste, A.; Arsénio, P.; Pánek, D.; Kaska, J.; Karban, P. Robust Design Optimization and Emerging Technologies for Electrical Machines: Challenges and Open Problems. *Appl. Sci.* **2020**, *10*, 6653. [CrossRef]
25. Sharma, A.; Sharma, A.; Dasgotra, A.; Jately, V.; Ram, M.; Rajput, S.; Averbukh, M.; Azzopardi, B. Opposition-Based Tunicate Swarm Algorithm for Parameter Optimization of Solar Cells. *IEEE Access* **2021**, *9*, 125590–125602. [CrossRef]
26. Farayola, A.M.; Sun, Y.; Ali, A. 8-Parameter Extraction in Photovoltaic Cell Using Firefly Optimization Technique. In Proceedings of the IEEE Electrical Power and Energy Conference (EPEC), Toronto, ON, Canada, 22–31 October 2021; pp. 184–189.
27. Yousri, D.; Abd Elaziz, M.; Oliva, D.; Abualigah, L.; Al-qaness, M.A.; Ewees, A.A. Reliable applied objective for identifying simple and detailed photovoltaic models using modern metaheuristics: Comparative study. *Energy Convers. Manag.* **2020**, *223*, 113279. [CrossRef]
28. Sharma, A.; Dasgotra, A.; Tiwari, S.K.; Sharma, A.; Jately, V.; Azzopardi, B. Parameter Extraction of Photovoltaic Module Using Tunicate Swarm Algorithm. *Electronics* **2021**, *10*, 878. [CrossRef]
29. Nunes, H.G.G.; Silva, P.N.C.; Pombo, J.A.N.; Mariano, S.J.P.S.; Calado, M.R.A. Multiswarm spiral leader particle swarm optimisation algorithm for PV parameter identification. *Energy Convers. Manag.* **2020**, *225*, 113388. [CrossRef]
30. Malik, H. *Metaheuristic and Evolutionary Computation: Algorithms and Applications*; Springer Nature: Singapore, 2020; Volume 916.
31. Singla, M.K.; Nijhawan, P. Triple diode parameter estimation of solar PV cell using hybrid algorithm. *Int. J. Environ. Sci. Technol.* **2021**, 1–24. [CrossRef]
32. Karambasti, B.M.; Ghodrat, M.; Ghorbani, G.; Lalbakhsh, A.; Behnia, M. Design methodology and multi-objective optimization of small-scale power-water production based on integration of Stirling engine and multi-effect evaporation desalination system. *Desalination* **2022**, *526*, 115542. [CrossRef]
33. Chao, K.-H.; Rizal, M.N. A Hybrid MPPT Controller Based on the Genetic Algorithm and Ant Colony Optimization for Photovoltaic Systems under Partially Shaded Conditions. *Energies* **2021**, *14*, 2902. [CrossRef]
34. Sharma, A.; Khan, R.A.; Sharma, A.; Kashyap, D.; Rajput, S. A Novel Opposition-Based Arithmetic Optimization Algorithm for Parameter Extraction of PEM Fuel Cell. *Electronics* **2021**, *10*, 2834. [CrossRef]
35. Karami, A.; Roshani, G.H.; Nazemi, E.; Roshani, S. Enhancing the performance of a dual-energy gamma ray based three-phase flow meter with the help of grey wolf optimization algorithm. *Flow Meas. Instrum.* **2018**, *64*, 164–172. [CrossRef]
36. Jamshidi, M.B.; Lalbakhsh, A.; Alibeigi, N.; Soheyli, M.R.; Oryani, B.; Rabbani, N. Socialization of Industrial Robots: An Innovative Solution to improve Productivity. In Proceedings of the IEEE 9th Annual Information Technology, Electronics and Mobile Communication Conference (IEMCON), Vancouver, BC, Canada, 1–3 November 2018; pp. 832–837.
37. Sattari, M.A.; Roshani, G.H.; Hanus, R.; Nazemi, E. Applicability of time-domain feature extraction methods and artificial intelligence in two-phase flow meters based on gamma-ray absorption technique. *Measurement* **2021**, *168*, 108474. [CrossRef]
38. Wolpert, D.H.; Macready, W.G. No free lunch theorems for optimization. *IEEE Trans. Evol. Comput.* **1997**, *1*, 67–82. [CrossRef]

39. Joyce, T.; Herrmann, J.M. A review of no free lunch theorems, and their implications for metaheuristic optimisation. In *Nature-Inspired Algorithms and Applied Optimization*; Studies in Computational Intelligence; Yang, X.S., Ed.; Springer: Cham, Switzerland, 2018; Volume 744, pp. 27–51.
40. Huang, S.; Dang, H.; Jiang, R.; Hao, Y.; Xue, C.; Gu, W. Multi-Layer Hybrid Fuzzy Classification Based on SVM and Improved PSO for Speech Emotion Recognition. *Electronics* **2021**, *10*, 2891. [CrossRef]
41. Gong, T.; Tuson, A.L. Particle swarm optimization for quadratic assignment problems-a forma analysis approach. *Int. J. Comput. Intell. Res.* **2007**, *2*, 1–9. [CrossRef]
42. Babor, M.; Senge, J.; Rosell, C.M.; Rodrigo, D.; Hitzmann, B. Optimization of No-Wait Flowshop Scheduling Problem in Bakery Production with Modified PSO, NEH, and SA. *Processes* **2021**, *9*, 2044. [CrossRef]
43. Hajihassani, M.; Armaghani, D.J.; Kalatehjari, R. Applications of Particle Swarm Optimization in Geotechnical Engineering: A Comprehensive Review. *Geotech. Geol. Eng.* **2018**, *36*, 705–722. [CrossRef]
44. Balicki, J. Many-Objective Quantum-Inspired Particle Swarm Optimization Algorithm for Placement of Virtual Machines in Smart Computing Cloud. *Entropy* **2022**, *24*, 58. [CrossRef]
45. Mesquita, R.; Gaspar, P.D. A Novel Path Planning Optimization Algorithm Based on Particle Swarm Optimization for UAVs for Bird Monitoring and Repelling. *Processes* **2022**, *10*, 62. [CrossRef]
46. Liu, J.; Fang, H.; Xu, J. Online Adaptive PID Control for a Multi-Joint Lower Extremity Exoskeleton System Using Improved Particle Swarm Optimization. *Machines* **2022**, *10*, 21. [CrossRef]
47. Yang, C.; Zhu, T.; Zhang, Y.; Ning, H.; Chen, L.; Liu, Z. Parallel Particle Swarm Optimization Based on Spark for Academic Paper Co-Authorship Prediction. *Information* **2021**, *12*, 530. [CrossRef]
48. Długosz, Z.; Rajewski, M.; Długosz, R.; Talaśka, T. A Novel, Low Computational Complexity, Parallel Swarm Algorithm for Application in Low-Energy Devices. *Sensors* **2021**, *21*, 8449. [CrossRef] [PubMed]
49. Sharma, A.; Sharma, A.; Averbukh, M.; Jately, V.; Azzopardi, B. An Effective Method for Parameter Estimation of a Solar Cell. *Electronics* **2021**, *10*, 312. [CrossRef]
50. Cotfas, D.T.; Cotfas, P.A.; Oproiu, M.P.; Ostafe, P.A. Analytical versus Metaheuristic Methods to Extract the Photovoltaic Cells and Panel Parameters. *Int. J. Photoenergy* **2021**, *2021*, 3608138. [CrossRef]
51. Kota, V.R.; Bhukya, M.N. A novel linear tangents based P&O scheme for MPPT of a PV system. *Renew. Sustain. Energy Rev.* **2017**, *71*, 257–267.
52. Singh, A.; Sharma, A.; Rajput, S.; Mondal, A.K.; Bose, A.; Ram, M. Parameter Extraction of Solar Module Using the Sooty Tern Optimization Algorithm. *Electronics* **2022**, *11*, 564. [CrossRef]
53. Beiranvand, V.; Hare, W.; Lucet, Y. Best practices for comparing optimization algorithms. *Optim. Eng.* **2017**, *18*, 815–848. [CrossRef]
54. Monsef, H.; Naghashzadegan, M.; Jamali, A.; Farmani, R. Comparison of evolutionary multi objective optimization algorithms in optimum design of water distribution network. *Ain Shams Eng. J.* **2019**, *10*, 103–111. [CrossRef]
55. Abderazek, H.; Yildiz, A.R.; Mirjalili, S. Comparison of recent optimization algorithms for design optimization of a cam-follower mechanism. *Knowl. Based Syst.* **2020**, *191*, 105237. [CrossRef]
56. Kennedy, J.; Eberhart, R. Particle swarm optimization. In Proceedings of the ICNN'95-International Conference on Neural Networks, Perth, Australia, 27 November–1 December 1995; Volume 4, pp. 1942–1948.
57. Sharma, A.; Sharma, A.; Pandey, J.K.; Ram, M. *Swarm Intelligence: Foundation, Principles, and Engineering Applications*, 1st ed.; CRC Press: Boca Raton, FL, USA, 2022.
58. Lalwani, S.; Sharma, H.; Satapathy, S.C.; Deep, K.; Bansal, J.C. A survey on parallel particle swarm optimization algorithms. *Arab. J. Sci. Eng.* **2019**, *44*, 2899–2923. [CrossRef]
59. Elsheikh, A.H.; Abd Elaziz, M. Review on applications of particle swarm optimization in solar energy systems. *Int. J. Environ. Sci. Technol.* **2019**, *16*, 1159–1170. [CrossRef]
60. Ahmed, W.A.E.M.; Mageed, H.M.A.; Mohamed, S.A.; Saleh, A.A. Fractional order Darwinian particle swarm optimization for parameters identification of solar PV cells and modules. *Alex. Eng. J.* **2022**, *61*, 1249–1263. [CrossRef]
61. Lin, X.; Wu, Y. Parameters identification of photovoltaic models using niche-based particle swarm optimization in parallel computing architecture. *Energy* **2020**, *196*, 117054. [CrossRef]
62. Wang, R. Parameter Identification of Photovoltaic Cell Model Based on Enhanced Particle Swarm Optimization. *Sustainability* **2021**, *13*, 840. [CrossRef]
63. Premkumar, M.; Sowmya, R.; Umashankar, S.; Jangir, P. Extraction of uncertain parameters of single-diode photovoltaic module using hybrid particle swarm optimization and grey wolf optimization algorithm. *Mater. Today Proc.* **2021**, *46*, 5315–5321. [CrossRef]
64. Kiani, A.T.; Nadeem, M.F.; Ahmed, A.; Khan, I.A.; Alkhammash, H.I.; Sajjad, I.A.; Hussain, B. An Improved Particle Swarm Optimization with Chaotic Inertia Weight and Acceleration Coefficients for Optimal Extraction of PV Models Parameters. *Energies* **2021**, *14*, 2980. [CrossRef]
65. Liang, J.; Ge, S.; Qu, B.; Yu, K.; Liu, F.; Yang, H.; Wei, P.; Li, Z. Classified perturbation mutation based particle swarm optimization algorithm for parameters extraction of photovoltaic models. *Energy Conver. Manag.* **2020**, *203*, 112138. [CrossRef]
66. Kiani, A.T.; Nadeem, M.F.; Ahmed, A.; Khan, I.; Elavarasan, R.M.; Das, N. Optimal PV Parameter Estimation via Double Exponential Function-Based Dynamic Inertia Weight Particle Swarm Optimization. *Energies* **2020**, *13*, 4037. [CrossRef]

67. Kiani, A.T.; Nadeem, M.F.; Ahmed, A.; Sajjad, I.A.; Haris, M.S.; Martirano, L. Optimal Parameter Estimation of Solar Cell using Simulated Annealing Inertia Weight Particle Swarm Optimization (SAIW-PSO). In Proceedings of the 2020 IEEE International Conference on Environment and Electrical Engineering and 2020 IEEE Industrial and Commercial Power Systems Europe (EEEIC/I&CPS Europe), Madrid, Spain, 9–12 June 2020; pp. 1–6.
68. Alshabi, M.; Ghenai, C.; Bettayeb, M.; Ahmad, F.F. Estimating one-diode-PV model using autonomous groups particle swarm optimization. *IAES Int. J. Artif. Intell.* **2021**, *10*, 166. [CrossRef]
69. Mirjalili, S.; Lewis, A.; Sadiq, A.S. Autonomous particles groups for particle swarm optimization. *Arab. J. Sci. Eng.* **2014**, *39*, 4683–4697. [CrossRef]
70. Mughal, M.A.; Ma, Q.; Xiao, C. Photovoltaic Cell Parameter Estimation Using Hybrid Particle Swarm Optimization and Simulated Annealing. *Energies* **2017**, *10*, 1213. [CrossRef]
71. Wei, H.; Cong, J.; Lingyun, X.; Deyun, S. Extracting solar cell model parameters based on chaos particle swarm algorithm. In Proceedings of the 2011 International Conference on Electric Information and Control Engineering, Wuhan, China, 15–17 April 2011; pp. 398–402.
72. Ding, J.; Schulz, S.; Shen, L.; Buscher, U.; Lü, Z. Energy aware scheduling in flexible flow shops with hybrid particle swarm optimization. *Comput. Oper. Res.* **2021**, *125*, 105088. [CrossRef]
73. Bhatia, N.; Chauhan, P.; Yadav, H. Applications of Hybrid Particle Swarm Optimization Algorithm: A Survey. In *Proceedings of the Second International Conference on Information Management and Machine Intelligence*; Lecture Notes in Networks and Systems; Goyal, D., Gupta, A.K., Piuri, V., Ganzha, M., Paprzycki, M., Eds.; Springer: Singapore, 2021; Volume 166.
74. Zhao, W.; Wang, H.; Geng, J.; Hu, W.; Zhang, Z.; Zhang, G. Multi-Objective Weather Routing Algorithm for Ships Based on Hybrid Particle Swarm Optimization. *J. Ocean Univ. China* **2022**, *21*, 28–38. [CrossRef]
75. Goodarzimehr, V.; Omidinasab, F.; Taghizadieh, N. Optimum design of space structures using hybrid particle swarm optimization and genetic algorithm. *World J. Eng.* **2022**. [CrossRef]
76. Loganathan, G.; Kannan, M. Optimized Production of Biodiesel Using Internet of Things Sensed Temperature with Hybrid Particle Swarm Optimization. *J. Chem.* **2022**, *2022*, 3793739. [CrossRef]
77. Wu, X.; Li, R.; Chu, C.H.; Amoasi, R.; Liu, S. Managing pharmaceuticals delivery service using a hybrid particle swarm intelligence approach. *Ann. Oper. Res.* **2022**, *308*, 653–684. [CrossRef]
78. Zhang, X.; Wang, Z.; Lu, Z. Multi-objective load dispatch for microgrid with electric vehicles using modified gravitational search and particle swarm optimization algorithm. *Appl. Energy* **2022**, *306*, 118018. [CrossRef]
79. Kumar, R. Fuzzy particle swarm optimization control algorithm implementation in photovoltaic integrated shunt active power filter for power quality improvement using hardware-in-the-loop. *Sustain. Energy Technol. Assess.* **2022**, *50*, 101820. [CrossRef]
80. Xiong, G.; Shuai, M.; Hu, X. Combined heat and power economic emission dispatch using improved bare-bone multi-objective particle swarm optimization. *Energy* **2022**, *244*, 123108. [CrossRef]
81. Ejigu, D.A.; Liu, X. Gradient descent-particle swarm optimization based deep neural network predictive control of pressurized water reactor power. *Prog. Nucl. Energy* **2022**, *145*, 104108. [CrossRef]
82. Ibrahim, A.W.; Shafik, M.B.; Ding, M.; Sarhan, M.A.; Fang, Z.; Alareqi, A.G.; Almoqri, T.; Al-Rassas, A.M. PV maximum power-point tracking using modified particle swarm optimization under partial shading conditions. *Chin. J. Electr. Eng.* **2020**, *6*, 106–121. [CrossRef]
83. Awad, H.; Hafez, A. Optimal operation of under-frequency load shedding relays by hybrid optimization of particle swarm and bacterial foraging algorithms. *Alex. Eng. J.* **2022**, *61*, 763–774. [CrossRef]
84. Zhang, S. Optimal Control of Hybrid Energy Storage System of New Energy Power Generation System Based on Improved Particle Swarm Algorithm. *J. Interconnect. Netw.* **2022**, 2145004. [CrossRef]
85. Chen, J.; Ning, K.; Xin, X.; Shi, F.; Zhang, Q.; Li, C. Day-Ahead Optimal Scheduling of an Integrated Energy System Based on a Piecewise Self-Adaptive Particle Swarm Optimization Algorithm. *Energies* **2022**, *15*, 690. [CrossRef]
86. Jusof, M.F.M.; Mohammad, S.; Razak, A.A.A.; Rizal, N.A.M.; Nasir, A.N.K.; Ahmad, M.A. Hybrid Manta ray foraging—Particle swarm algorithm for PD control optimization of an inverted pendulum. In *Recent Trends in Mechatronics Towards Industry 4.0*; Springer: Singapore, 2022; pp. 1–13.
87. Gao, Z.; Yu, J.; Zhao, A.; Hu, Q.; Yang, S. Optimal chiller loading by improved parallel particle swarm optimization algorithm for reducing energy consumption. *Int. J. Refrig.* **2022**. [CrossRef]
88. Xin-gang, Z.; Ze-qi, Z.; Yi-min, X.; Jin, M. Economic-environmental dispatch of microgrid based on improved quantum particle swarm optimization. *Energy* **2020**, *195*, 117014. [CrossRef]
89. Adnan, R.M.; Mostafa, R.R.; Kisi, O.; Yaseen, Z.M.; Shahid, S.; Zounemat-Kermani, M. Improving streamflow prediction using a new hybrid ELM model combined with hybrid particle swarm optimization and grey wolf optimization. *Knowl. Based Syst.* **2021**, *230*, 107379. [CrossRef]
90. Islam, M.A.; Gajpal, Y.; ElMekkawy, T.Y. Hybrid particle swarm optimization algorithm for solving the clustered vehicle routing problem. *Appl. Soft Comput.* **2021**, *110*, 107655. [CrossRef]
91. Kilinc, H.C. Daily Streamflow Forecasting Based on the Hybrid Particle Swarm Optimization and Long Short-Term Memory Model in the Orontes Basin. *Water* **2022**, *14*, 490. [CrossRef]
92. Wang, R.; Hao, K.; Chen, L.; Wang, T.; Jiang, C. A novel hybrid particle swarm optimization using adaptive strategy. *Inf. Sci.* **2021**, *579*, 231–250. [CrossRef]

93. Zomorodi-moghadam, M.; Abdar, M.; Davarzani, Z.; Zhou, X.; Pławiak, P.; Acharya, U.R. Hybrid particle swarm optimization for rule discovery in the diagnosis of coronary artery disease. *Expert Syst.* **2021**, *38*, e12485. [CrossRef]
94. Wang, Y.; Zhang, Z.; Yi, Y.; Zhang, Y. Accurate microwave filter design based on particle swarm optimization and one-dimensional convolution autoencoders. *Int. J. RF Microw. Comput. Aided Eng.* **2021**, *32*, e23034. [CrossRef]
95. Mouna, H.; Mekaladevi, V.; Devi, N.M. Design of Microwave Absorbers using Improvised Particle Swarm Optimization Algorithm. *J. Microw. Optoelectron. Electromagn. Appl.* **2018**, *17*, 188–200.
96. Robinson, J.; Rahmat-Samii, Y. Particle swarm optimization in electromagnetics. *IEEE T Antenn. Propag.* **2004**, *52*, 397–407. [CrossRef]
97. Pantoja, M.F.; Bretones, A.R.; Ruiz, F.G.; Garcia, S.G.; Martin, R.G. Particle-Swarm optimization in antenna design: Optimization of log-periodic dipole arrays. *IEEE T Antenn. Propag. M* **2007**, *49*, 34–47. [CrossRef]
98. Cao, Y.; Liu, J.; Xu, Z. A hybrid particle swarm optimization algorithm for RFID network planning. *Soft Comput.* **2021**, *25*, 5747–5761. [CrossRef]
99. Houssein, E.H.; Gad, A.G.; Hussain, K.; Suganthan, P.N. Major advances in particle swarm optimization: Theory, analysis, and application. *Swarm Evol. Comput.* **2021**, *63*, 100868. [CrossRef]

MDPI AG
Grosspeteranlage 5
4052 Basel
Switzerland
Tel.: +41 61 683 77 34

Electronics Editorial Office
E-mail: electronics@mdpi.com
www.mdpi.com/journal/electronics

Disclaimer/Publisher's Note: The statements, opinions and data contained in all publications are solely those of the individual author(s) and contributor(s) and not of MDPI and/or the editor(s). MDPI and/or the editor(s) disclaim responsibility for any injury to people or property resulting from any ideas, methods, instructions or products referred to in the content.

www.ingramcontent.com/pod-product-compliance
Lightning Source LLC
LaVergne TN
LVHW070211100526
838202LV00015B/2032